Frommer's®

W9-AXZ-054

European Cruises
& Ports of Call

5th Edition

by Matt Hannafin & Heidi Sarna

Here's what the critics say about Frommer's:

"Amazingly easy to use. Very portable, very complete."
—*Booklist*

"Detailed, accurate, and easy-to-read information for all price ranges."
—*Glamour Magazine*

"Hotel information is close to encyclopedic."
—*Des Moines Sunday Register*

"Frommer's Guides have a way of giving you a real feel for a place."
—*Knight Ridder Newspapers*

WILEY

Wiley Publishing, Inc.

Published by:

Wiley Publishing, Inc.

111 River St.
Hoboken, NJ 07030-5774

ISBN: 978-0-470-18562-9
Editor: Naomi P. Kraus
Production Editor: Lindsay Conner
Cartographer: Guy Ruggiero
Photo Editor: Richard Fox
Production by Wiley Indianapolis Composition Services

For information on our other products and services or to obtain technical support, please contact our Customer Care Department within the U.S. at 800/762-2974, outside the U.S. at 317/572-3993 or fax 317/572-4002.

Wiley also publishes its books in a variety of electronic formats. Some content that appears in print may not be available in electronic formats.

Manufactured in the United States of America

5   4   3   2   1

Contents

Part 1: Planning, Booking & Preparing for Your Cruise

12 Ports of Call in Northern Europe & the British Isles   381

List of Maps

About the Authors

Matt Hannafin is a freelance writer, editor, and musician based in Portland, Oregon. Author of *Frommer's Vancouver Day by Day* and coauthor of *Frommer's Cruises & Ports of Call*, he also writes a biweekly column for Frommers.com; freelances for numerous newspapers, magazines, and websites; and was a major contributor to the recent bestseller *1,000 Places to See in the USA and Canada Before You Die*. His editing clients include U.N. agencies, major consultancy firms, and book publishers, and his musical activities range from teaching Persian classical percussion to performing concerts of contemporary free improvisation. He still pines for his hometown of New York, NY, but is getting used to the Pacific Northwest now that he's bought a good raincoat.

Heidi Sarna is a freelance writer who has sailed the oceans blue for more than a decade, often with her young twin sons and lucky husband in tow. Coauthor of *Frommer's Cruises & Ports of Call* and a contributor to several other guidebooks, she also writes regular travel columns for Frommers.com and *Porthole* magazine. She's written for many magazines, newspapers, and websites, including CNN.com, *Forbes Traveler*, the *International Herald Tribune*, *Condé Nast Traveler*, *Gourmet*, *Parenting*, *Brides*, *Modern Bride*, the *Boston Herald*, and *Travel Weekly*.

Acknowledgments

A select group of travel writers and travel experts contributed to this book. **Mike Driscoll,** editor of the probing industry newsletter *Cruise Week*, provided insights into current booking trends. Our editor, **Naomi Kraus,** kept her cool when we were how late with that manuscript? Merchant Marine officer and travel writer **Ben Lyons** provided insight into several lines, and freelance writer **Marilyn Green** updated our Costa chapter. Many thanks to them all, and also to the Frommer's Europe authors who helped us out with our ports chapters.

Lastly, Matt would like to thank his wife, **Rebecca,** who thinks writing about cruise ships is a really strange way to make a living, or at least part of one. Ain't that the truth. Heidi thanks her best shipmates, twin sons **Kavi** and **Tejas,** for being such good sailors at the ripe old age of five (16 cruises and counting), and salutes hubby **Arun** for going along with the crazy cruising life all these years.

—Matt Hannafin & Heidi Sarna

Other Great Guides for Your Trip:

Frommer's Europe

Frommer's Cruises & Ports of Call

Frommer's France

Frommer's England

Frommer's Italy

Frommer's Greece

An Invitation to the Reader

In researching this book, we discovered many wonderful places—hotels, restaurants, shops, and more. We're sure you'll find others. Please tell us about them, so we can share the information with your fellow travelers in upcoming editions. If you were disappointed with a recommendation, we'd love to know that, too. Please write to:

Frommer's European Cruises & Ports of Call, 5th Edition
Wiley Publishing, Inc. • 111 River St. • Hoboken, NJ 07030-5774

An Additional Note

Please be advised that travel information is subject to change at any time—and this is especially true of prices. We therefore suggest that you write or call ahead for confirmation when making your travel plans. The authors, editors, and publisher cannot be held responsible for the experiences of readers while traveling. Your safety is important to us, however, so we encourage you to stay alert and be aware of your surroundings. Keep a close eye on cameras, purses, and wallets, all favorite targets of thieves and pickpockets.

Frommer's Icons & Abbreviations

We use **two feature icons** that point you to the great deals, in-the-know advice, and unique experiences that separate travelers from tourists. Throughout the book, look for:

Tips   Insider tips—great ways to save time and money

Value   Great values—where to get the best deals

The following **abbreviations** are used for credit cards:

AE American Express	DISC Discover	V Visa
DC Diners Club	MC MasterCard	

Frommers.com

Now that you have this guidebook to help you plan a great trip, visit our website at **www.frommers.com** for additional travel information on more than 3,600 destinations. We update features regularly to give you instant access to the most current trip-planning information available. At Frommers.com, you'll find scoops on the best airfares, lodging rates, and car rental bargains. You can even book your travel online through our reliable travel booking partners. Other popular features include:

- Online updates of our most popular guidebooks
- Vacation sweepstakes and contest giveaways
- Newsletters highlighting the hottest travel trends
- Online travel message boards with featured travel discussions

Introduction

Of all the places we've cruised, Europe has left us with the most lingering memories. There was that lunch at the cliff-top town of Fira in Santorini, enjoying a plate of grilled calamari and a local wine while ogling the harbor views below. Or renting a motorscooter in Corfu and touring the island's lush interior by the seat of our pants, no schedule in mind. Heidi loved taking her young sons to the Coliseum in Rome for the first time and watching their eyes grow wide as they saw where gladiators actually battled lions. Matt loved walking the streets of Venice long past midnight, with his steps echoing off the centuries-old walls. Renting a sports car and zipping around the French Riviera for a few hours also ranks, as does spending a day at Malta's Blue Grotto, checking out the rock formations from a local fishing boat. Did we mention doing a wine tasting at a gorgeous Majorcan *finca,* or taking in the breathtaking views from Dubrovnik's old fortress walls? How about running a mock race in Olympia, Greece, or kayaking in the shadows of St. Peter's Castle in Bodrum, Turkey?

From your ship, depending on the route you choose, you will have easy access to Europe's historic and cultural capitals (including London, Paris, and Rome), ancient cities such as Pompeii and Ephesus, modern port cities, charming small towns, gorgeous islands and scenic fjords, rugged coastlines, and glamorous resorts. You can visit museums, cathedrals, palaces, and monuments and learn about the region's history. Or you can concentrate on the Europe of today, checking out the newest trends in art, food, and fashion.

WHY A CRUISE?

Europe is a popular cruising region and growing, second only to the Caribbean and followed by Alaska in third place. It's a no-brainer to see why. The region truly offers something for everyone: great sights, shopping, beaches, museums, and a diverse range of cultures and landscapes. The **ports** are also close together, meaning ships can visit several in a limited period of time; the seas are relatively calm; and the climate is pleasant, even in the shoulder seasons. In recent years, the European cruising season has expanded to March through December, and there are even winter cruises, mostly in the warmer Mediterranean, but also in frozen Norway.

A cruise is also one of the most practical and comfortable ways to see Europe: You unpack only once, and you don't have to deal with the hassle of getting around by plane or train. It's also an extremely **economical** choice, especially for Americans in the age of the fluctuating dollar: Because your transport, accommodations, and meals were prepaid back home, you don't have to worry about sucky exchange rates.

On a cruise you are fed, pampered, and taken care of in a stress-free environment. In port, you can be as daring or as lazy as you wish: walking around to get the local

Europe

perspective, taking a train and exploring nearby cities such as Rome and Pisa on your own, or signing up for one of the ship's organized tours and letting your guide do all the thinking.

Sure, on a cruise, you get only 1 day in port (or occasionally 2 or 3 in places such as Venice and St. Petersburg), so you can't see it all, but it's still a great way to check out the highlights. You can always go back.

EUROPEAN CRUISING 2008

After some rocky post-9/11 years, by 2007 the European cruise biz was downright booming, with lines pulling ships from the Caribbean to handle the increased demand. Royal Caribbean will have seven ships in Europe in 2008–2009, including the brand-new *Independence of the Seas*, the largest cruise ship ever based in Europe. Holland America will have six ships there. Carnival Cruise Line, king of the Caribbean, will have its two newest ships, Carnival *Splendor* and *Freedom,* based in Europe in the summer of 2008. You get the picture. Of course, no one has a crystal ball, but depending on what's happening in the world, 2008 and 2009 are likely to be superhot years for European cruising.

Travelers can choose from all sorts of itineraries—from the French Riviera to the Norwegian fjords, and from short 3- and 4-night cruises to 7-nighters and longer 10-, 12-, or even 20-night options—and there's a variety of ships to suit everyone's tastes.

Royal Caribbean's offerings are a good example of the wide range of **itinerary options.** The line has Europe cruises as short as 4 nights and as long as 2 weeks. Several sailings include 2-day visits to marquee ports such as Venice, Istanbul, and Livorno (for Florence/Pisa). Beginning in May 2008, *Brilliance of the Seas* will be homeported in Barcelona year-round, doing 10- and 12-night sailings to

Italy and the Greek Isles or Dalmatian Coast. The brand-new, action-packed, 3,634-guest *Independence of the Seas* will be Royal Caribbean's newest ship in the Mediterranean when she debuts in May 2008 to do 6 months' worth of 10- to 14-night sailings from Southampton, England. For great short takes, *Jewel of the Seas* offers 3- and 4-night North Sea cruises that depart from Amsterdam, Oslo, and Hamburg, visiting either Copenhagen or Brussels. You also have a lot of options as far as vessel type is concerned: You can cruise in Europe on a giant floating **American-style resort ship** with Las Vegas–style entertainment, a glitzy casino, a lavish spa, and a mostly American clientele. Or you can choose a ship that's more like a **floating European hotel,** where multiple languages are spoken, Americans are the minority, and meals are a form of entertainment. You can choose to see the Continent in **luxury** with the very best in service and cuisine, or you can pick a small, **casual ship** where you can sometimes leap off the stern for a swim.

A European cruise is a big-ticket item, but you can save money by booking early. And while Europe has traditionally drawn a senior crowd, the cruise lines, through shorter itineraries and a greater diversity of product, have lately done a good job of attracting families, younger couples, singles, and honeymooners.

BON VOYAGE!

Just the fact that you've bought this book means you've got a hankering to cruise. Now it's our job to find the cruise that's right for you from among the huge selection of ships and cruise experiences in the market. In the following chapters, we'll detail the diverse itineraries in Europe, the types of ships that can take you there, and the options available on ship and in port. Ready? Go.

The Best of European Cruising

People are always asking us which are the best ships, and we always say, "Well, what do you like to do when you're *not* on a ship?" In this section we've broken out different kinds of cruises, interests, and destinations to help you find one that best matches what you're looking for. You'll find complete information on each pick in part 2, "The Cruise Lines & Their Ships," and part 3, "The Ports of Call."

1 Our Favorite Mainstream Ships

Mainstream ships are the big boys of the cruise biz, carrying the most passengers and providing the most diverse cruise experiences.

- **Celebrity's Millennium class:** *Summit* and *Constellation* offer elegant decor, incredible spas, great service, edgy art collections, and the best alternative restaurants at sea. Class, charm, personality—what's not to like? See p. 104.
- **NCL's** *Jewel, Gem,* **and** *Jade:* NCL's best ships yet, this nearly identical trio combines an incredible number of dining choices, great entertainment, an always-casual vibe, and decor that's just plain fun. They have the best beer-and-whiskey bars at sea,

too, with a selection that's light-years ahead of the competition. See p. 161.
- **Royal Caribbean's** *Brilliance* **and** *Jewel of the Seas:* The most elegant vessels Royal Caribbean has produced to date, *Brilliance* and *Jewel* combine a sleek, seagoing exterior; some great, nautically themed public rooms; and acres of windows. See p. 196.
- **Princess's** *Crown* **and** *Emerald Princess:* These huge, well-accoutered vessels are very easy to navigate, never feel as crowded as you'd expect, and are amazingly intimate for their size. Their onboard ambience is restrained yet fun, tailored to a modern, "Pottery Barn" kind of adult demographic. See p. 176.

2 Best Luxury Cruises

Here's the very best for the cruiser who's used to traveling deluxe and who doesn't mind paying for the privilege. These ships have the best cuisine, accommodations, and service at sea.

- **Silversea** *Cloud, Whisper,* **and** *Wind:* Silversea is the best of the highbrow small-ship luxury lines, offering exquisite cuisine, roomy suites, over-the-top service, and niceties that include complimentary free-flowing champagne. See p. 250.

- **SeaDream Yacht Club** *SeaDream I* **and** *II:* What's not to love? These cool 110-passenger yachts are elegant but casual, and carry along jet skis, mountain bikes, and kayaks for jaunts around ports such as St. Tropez and Monte Carlo. See p. 248.
- **Peter Deilmann** *Deutschland:* An idyllic ocean-goer with old-world ambience, the 513-passenger *Deutschland* offers English-speakers a chance to immerse themselves in a truly

European experience, from the European boutique-hotel interiors to the fine service, onboard classical concerts, and German-speaking fellow passengers. See p. 226.

- **Sea Cloud Cruises *Sea Cloud:*** You wanna talk luxury? *Sea Cloud* was built in 1931 by Wall Street tycoon E. F. Hutton as a gift for his wife, Marjorie Merriweather Post—and those folks knew luxury. Today the ship offers cabins for 64 passengers, the luckiest (and richest) of whom can stay in Post's own suite, with its Louis XIV–style bed and nightstands, marble fireplace and bathroom, chandeliers, and intricate moldings. See p. 275.

- **Crystal *Symphony* and *Serenity:*** Carrying 940 to 1,080 passengers, these are the best midsize ships out there, big enough to offer lots of dining, entertainment, and fitness options, and small enough to bathe passengers in luxury. The range and number of expert lecturers is the best in the biz, and so is the Internet center and its roster of computer classes. See p. 204.

3 The Most Romantic Cruises

Of course, all cruises are pretty romantic when you consider the props they have to work with: the sparkling sea all around, moonlit nights on deck, cozy dining and cocktailing, and cozier cabins. Here are the best lines for getting you in the mood.

- **SeaDream Yacht Club *SeaDream I and II:*** With comfy Balinese daybeds lining the teak decks, champagne flowing freely, and the option of dining at your own private table out on deck, these 110-passenger playboy yachts spell romance for the spoiled sailing set. See p. 243.

- **Sea Cloud Cruises:** Really, when it comes right down to it, what setting is more movie-star romantic than a zillionaire's sailing yacht? That's what you get with *Sea Cloud,* once owned by Edward F. Hutton and Marjorie Merriweather Post. Some cabins retain their original grandeur. See p. 275.

- **Star Clippers:** With the wind in your hair and sails fluttering overhead, the tall-masted *Royal Clipper* and *Star Clipper* provide one of the most romantic settings at sea. Below decks, the comfy cabins, lounge, and dining room make these ships one of the most comfortable adventures in the cruise biz. See p. 276.

- **Cunard:** Like real royalty, *Queen Mary 2* was born with certain duties attendant to her station, and one of the biggest of those duties is to embody the romance of transatlantic travel and bring it into the new century. Take a stroll around that promenade deck, dine in that fabulous dining room, or spin around that old-world ballroom dance floor like they did in the golden age of passenger liners. See p. 214.

- **Windstar Cruises:** Windstar's tall-masted *Wind Surf, Wind Star,* and *Wind Spirit* offer a truly unique cruise experience, giving passengers the delicious illusion of adventure and the ever-pleasant reality of great cuisine, service, and itineraries. See p. 286.

4 Best Cruises for Families with Kids

All the lines included here offer supervised activities for three to five age groups between ages 2 or 3 and 17, plus well-stocked playrooms, group and/or private babysitting, wading pools, kids' menus, and cabins that can accommodate three to five. See "Cruises for Families," in chapter 1 and the cruise line reviews in chapters 6 through 8 for more info.

- **Royal Caribbean:** The huge Voyager-class ships are truly theme parks at sea, with features such as onboard rock-climbing walls, ice-skating rinks, in-line skate rinks, miniature golf, burger-joint diners, and Disneyesque Main Streets running down their centers, with parades and other entertainment throughout the day. The Radiance-class ships are also a great family choice, and even the line's older ships have impressively roomy kids' facilities. See p. 184.

- **Carnival Cruise Lines:** While Carnival's let-the-good-times-roll attitude appeals to adults, the line also does a particularly fine job with kids. Several hundred per cruise is pretty normal. *Freedom* and *Splendor* offer some of the biggest and brightest playrooms in the fleet, with computer stations, a climbing maze, a video wall showing movies and cartoons, arts and crafts, and oodles of toys and games, plus great water slides out on the main pool deck. See p. 86.

- **Princess Cruises:** The Grand-class ships each have a spacious children's playroom, a sizable piece of fenced-in outside deck for toddlers, and another for older kids, with a wading pool. Teen centers have computers, video games, a sound system, and private sunbathing decks with hot tubs. See p. 171.

- **Cunard:** Though you'd hardly expect it from such a serious line, the *QM2* has a great program and facilities for kids, starting at age 1. Aside from Disney (which isn't currently sailing in Europe), no other line offers such extensive care for children so young. There's even a special daily children's teatime that's perfect as an early dinner, and the children's programming is free of charge until midnight daily. See p. 214.

5 Best Cruises for Pure Relaxation

Sometimes it's all about doing absolutely nothing, but some ships are better at letting you do nothing (in style and comfort) than others.

- **SeaDream Yacht Club:** SeaDream's two intimate 110-passenger yachts deliver an upscale yet very casual experience without regimentation. Cabin beds are fitted with fine linens, but the best snooze on board is to be had in one of the 18 queen-size, Bali-style sun beds that line each vessel's top deck. Reading lights are provided at night, and some guests end up sleeping out there. See p. 243.

- **Oceania Cruises:** Aboard Oceania's midsize, classically styled ships, the dress code is "country club casual" at all times; you can show up for dinner whenever you like; activities and entertainment are small-scale and personal; itineraries visit many quiet, refined ports; and the cabin beds are some of the best at sea. For the ultimate, you can rent a private on-deck cabana with retractable shade roof, a plush daybed built for two, and a dedicated attendant to bring you food and drink, spritz you with cold water, and order up massages. Step aboard, take a deep breath, and *relax*. See p. 164.

- **Celebrity Cruises:** If your idea of relaxation involves regular massages; lolling around in ornate steam rooms, mud baths, and hydrotherapy pools; and then letting your limbs tingle in gorgeous solariums, Celebrity's Millennium-class ships are tops. Afterward, have a long, relaxed dinner at the ships' amazing alternative restaurants, then decide what kind of pillow you want: The line's Concierge Class suites feature a whole menu of different varieties, plus tension-absorbing mattresses and comfy duvets. See p. 97.

- **Star Clippers:** Here's the drill on Star Clippers' tall-masted modern clipper ships: Find a deck chair beneath the acres of sails shining in the sun and watch the sailors work the winches as you head for the next small yachting port. No megaship bustle here. See p. 276.

- **Windstar:** Beyond "don't wear shorts in the dining rooms," there's no real dress code here, and most men don't even bother with sport jackets at dinner. There are also zero rah-rah activities, keeping days loose and languid: Explore ashore (the itineraries visit a port almost every day) or kick back and relax aboard ship without a lot of distraction. See p. 286.

6 Best Cuisine

Here's where you'll find the finest restaurants afloat, with food rivaling what you'd find in the world's major cities.

- **Silversea Cruises:** Hit it on a sunset departure from port and the windowed, candlelit La Terrazza restaurant becomes a window to the passing scenery and a home for some of the best Italian cuisine at sea, created by chef Marco Betti. Excellent wines accompany dinner and are included in the cruise rates. A second alternative venue offers a new twist on cruise dining, offering menus that pair food with wine rather than the other way 'round. (Though those wines'll cost ya.) See p. 250.

- **Crystal Cruises:** While all the food you'll get on these ships is first class, their reservations-only Asian specialty restaurants are the best at sea, especially *Serenity*'s Silk Road restaurant, overseen by Master Chef Nobuyuki "Nobu" Matsuhisa. The accouterments help set the tone, too—chopsticks, sake served in tiny sake cups and decanters, and sushi served on thick, square-glass platters. An Asian-themed buffet lunch, offered at least once per cruise, gives passengers an awesome spread, from jumbo shrimp to chicken and beef satays, to stir-fry dishes. See p. 204.

- **Regent Seven Seas Cruises:** The award-winning chefs aboard all of this line's ships produce artful culinary presentations that compare favorably to world-class shore-based restaurants, and the waiters are some of the industry's best. See p. 227.

- **Seabourn Cruise Lines:** There's nothing quite like dining at the outdoor restaurant called 2, which serves five- to six-course tasting menus for only about 50 guests a night. With the ship's wakes shushing just below, it's a rare opportunity to dine with the sea breezes and starry night sky surrounding you. See p. 235.

- **Celebrity Cruise Line:** It doesn't get much better than the alternative restaurants on *Summit* and *Constellation,* designed to mimic dining experiences aboard the golden-age ocean liners of yesteryear—*Normandie* on *Summit* and *Ile de France* on *Constellation*. A highly trained staff dotes on diners with table-side cooking while musicians play elegant period pieces—the entire decadent experience takes about 3 hours. See p. 104.

- **Oceania Cruises:** Oceania's dining experience is near the top in the mainstream category, with menus created by renowned chef Jacques Pepin. Passengers are able to choose among four different restaurants, all of them excellent. Service is doting and fine-tuned, even at the casual semibuffet dinner option offered on an outdoor terrace that's elegant and totally romantic at sunset. See p. 164.

- **Norwegian Cruise Lines:** NCL gets onto this list by sheer weight of numbers. Get this: The line's Europe-based ships offer 10 different restaurants, including multiple main dining rooms, multiple specialty restaurants, teppanyaki rooms, and casual options. While the fare in the main dining rooms is totally average, it's quite good in some of the alternative venues, including the sushi bar and the elegant French/Continental Le Bistro. See p. 157.

- **The French river barges:** This is the closest many of us will ever come to having a private chef. The French-trained chefs aboard these barges work to incorporate great local ingredients in their menus. See chapter 9.

7 Best Ports

- **Overall:** There are so many great ports in Europe it's hard to choose, but our personal favorite is **Venice,** a city where every view is perfection. See p. 375. **London,** one of the world's great cities, makes a good runner-up. See p. 399. **Paris** would have made the list easily if it was a port, but to reach it you have to drive 3 hours from Le Havre—doable via shore excursions, but hardly convenient. See p. 415.

- **For Ancient History:** You can't top Athens or Rome; the ancient cities of Ephesus in Turkey (accessible via Kusadasi); and Pompeii in Italy (accessible via Naples and Sorrento). See chapter 11.

- **For Shopping:** Head to the French Riviera (Nice, Villefranche, Cannes, and Monaco) or to ports in Italy (including Venice and Rome) for your retail therapy. See chapter 11.

- **For Fun:** The French Riviera offers great art museums, shopping, and people-watching, especially on the beaches. The Greek Isles offer beaches and stunning beauty. Fun times can be had in Copenhagen, home of the famous Tivoli Gardens amusement park. And fun of a different kind can be had in Amsterdam, a youthful city where marijuana and hashish are perfectly legal. See chapters 11 and 12.

- **For Quaintness:** It's hard to beat Portofino, Italy. See p. 338.

- **Other Faves:** Barcelona is a fun, bustling port with some wonderful attractions; Lisbon is a perpetual favorite for its old-world character; and Istanbul's exotic (yet crowded) ambience always impresses. Bergen, Norway, is a surprise, with its excellent museums and historic waterfront; and Edinburgh and Dublin offer the best of the British Isles (along with London, of course). See chapters 11 and 12.

Part 1

Planning, Booking
& Preparing for Your Cruise

With advice on choosing and booking your ideal cruise and tips on getting ready for the cruise experience.

1 Choosing Your Ideal Cruise

2 Booking Your Cruise & Getting the Best Price

3 Things to Know Before You Go

4 The Cruise Experience

Choosing Your Ideal Cruise

Forget the "overfed, newlywed, nearly dead" stereotype. Today's cruises are tailored for your tastes, whether you're a traveling family, a swinging single, a granddad, a wheelchair user, or a swinging, wheelchair-using granddad. You can sail on a floating country club around the Riviera, take a sailing ship among the Greek Isles, do the grand Mediterranean tour aboard a huge megaship, sail the Balkans on a midsize boutique vessel, or go expeditionary on a cruise to the Scandinavian Arctic. Which is for you? That's

one question we address in this chapter, along with explaining the types of itineraries, types of ships, and types of onboard experiences from which you can choose. When do you want to go? What size ship will make you most comfortable? Do you want to sail with mostly English-speakers or with a more international mix? What special things should you know if you are a family traveler, a honeymooner, or a person with disabilities? In this chapter, we'll deal with all these nuts-and-bolts questions to get your planning in gear.

1 The European Cruise Season

The European cruise season is generally considered to be **April to November,** although some lines operate into December, and a few (notably Italian lines Costa and MSC Cruises) even sail the Mediterranean year-round. April, early May, and November/December are considered **shoulder season,** when lower fares are usually available. **High season** is the summer months.

If you are considering travel in the shoulder season, keep in mind that some visitor facilities will operate on more limited hours, and some may not be open at all. The least expensive cruises are typically the first and last runs of the season, though these have their own charm: Specifically, you'll avoid the big tourist crush, which can really make a difference in some port towns. During the high season in Venice, for instance, you can't swing a cat without hitting five families from Duluth.

WEATHER

Europe is a continent of distinct seasons, but, just as in North America, there can be great variations in temperature from one part to another. The warmest months are July and August. August is the month when many Europeans go on vacation, and when beaches and other resort facilities will be particularly packed.

Here's the typical summer weather you can expect to encounter by region:

- **Britain & Ireland:** Average temperatures in the low- to mid-60s Fahrenheit (high teens Celsius), although weather may be warmer in Ireland. August, September, and October tend to be the sunniest months.
- **Scandinavia:** Average temperatures in the south tend to stay in the 70s (low 20s Celsius), with Denmark tending to be the mildest. You may see some rain in the

What Time Is It?

Want to know what time it is at home? Based on U.S. Eastern Standard Time, Britain, Ireland, and Portugal are 5 hours ahead; Greece, Estonia, and Ukraine are 7 hours ahead; and western Russia is 8 hours ahead. The rest of the countries in this book are 6 hours ahead. The European countries observe daylight saving time, but it does not necessarily start or end on the same day or in the same month as in the U.S.

fjords, and if you venture above the Arctic Circle you'll feel temperatures in the mid-50s (13°C).

- **Holland & Belgium:** Average temperatures in the high 60s (about 20°C) in Holland and Germany, with possible rain in May; in the low 70s (low 20s Celsius) in Belgium, with the sunniest weather in July and August.
- **France:** In Paris, temperatures average in the mid-70s (mid-20s Celsius), while temperatures in the Riviera can be in the high 80s or above (30s Celsius).
- **The Baltics:** Average temperatures in the 70s (20s Celsius), with the best weather in late summer.
- **Italy, Greece, Spain, Portugal & Turkey:** Temperatures in the high 80s or higher (30s Celsius), but there may be nice breezes along the coast. Portugal tends to be cooler, more like the mid-70s (20s Celsius), but also rainier. Greece and Turkey are the hottest, and if you're not a hot-weather lover, you're better off visiting these countries mid-April to June or mid-September to the end of October.

2 European Cruise Itineraries

There's really no such thing as a standard European itinerary. Instead, cruises focus on specific regions (and sometimes more than one region), mixing and matching among scores of ports in a part of the world that's been defined by sea travel for well over 2,000 years. Each region offers dozens of different variations, following different routes and taking in different ports.

The range of **home ports** is also more diverse than in other popular cruising regions such as the Caribbean and Alaska. In Europe, cruises can begin and end in dozens of port cities, though Barcelona, Rome, Athens, and Venice are the clear favorites in the Mediterranean, and Copenhagen, Stockholm, and London stand out in northern Europe.

TYPICAL CRUISE ITINERARIES

- **The Grand Tour:** A typically 2-week version of the old Victorian Grand Tour concentrates on the Continent's major cities, providing a great overview for people who've never been to Europe before. Some cruises concentrate on the Mediterranean, Adriatic, and Aegean seas, visiting such cities as Rome, Venice, Naples, and Florence (Italy); Barcelona (Spain); Athens and Mykonos (Greece); Dubrovnik (Croatia); Marseille (France); and Istanbul and Kusadasi (Turkey). Others mix the Mediterranean with ports in the Baltic and along Europe's Atlantic coast—for example, sailing from Rotterdam (Netherlands) to Athens (Greece) by way of Le Havre (France, for access to Paris), Cadiz and Barcelona (Spain), Monte Carlo (Monaco), Rome (Italy), and Kusadasi (Turkey).

- **The Greek Isles/Eastern Mediterranean:** These cruises sail in the Aegean and Mediterranean seas and often the Adriatic as well, with port calls in Athens and the Greek islands (Rhodes, Santorini, Mykonos, and others), Kusadasi and sometimes Istanbul (Turkey), and Dubrovnik or other ports in Croatia.
- **Western Mediterranean:** The area from Barcelona (or Lisbon, on the Atlantic side of the Iberian Peninsula) to Rome. Ships may call at any of the dozens of ports in Spain, France, and Italy.
- **Spain & France:** A more Iberian version of the western Mediterranean cruise may concentrate on ports in Spain (such as Barcelona, Malaga, Cadiz, and the island ports of Ibiza and Palma de Mallorca) and France (typically Marseille), and may also dip down to Morocco, visit Gibraltar, or scoot into the Atlantic for a call in Lisbon (Portugal).
- **The Riviera:** Riviera cruises typically call in St-Tropez, Nice, Cannes, and Villefranche (French Riviera); Monte Carlo (Monaco); and small Italian Riviera ports such as Portofino. Some cruises also include Rome.
- **Scandinavia, the Baltics & Russia:** Cruises in northern Europe sail principally in the Baltic Sea, visiting ports such as Copenhagen (Denmark), Stockholm (Sweden), Helsinki (Finland), Tallinn (Estonia), and St. Petersburg (Russia). Less common stops include Oslo (Norway), Gdansk (Poland), and Hamburg, Warnemunde, or Rostock (Germany). The German ports all offer excursions to Berlin.
- **The British Isles:** Cruises here visit such ports as London, Portsmouth, and the Channel Islands (England); Dublin, Cork/Waterford, and Belfast (Ireland); Edinburgh, Glasgow, and Inverness/Loch Ness (Scotland); and Holyhead (Wales). Some also hop across the English Channel to the French port of Le Havre, for access to Paris and Normandy.
- **The Norwegian Fjords:** Cruises here follow the Norwegian coast from Bergen up to Honningsvag and the North Cape, sometimes penetrating high into the Arctic.
- **The Black Sea/Middle East:** The area from Athens or Istanbul to Yalta, with port calls in Bulgaria, Romania, and the Ukraine. Some cruises on these routes also visit ports in Egypt and Israel.

RIVER CRUISES

Europe's inland waterways offer a wealth of cruise opportunities on smaller vessels specifically designed for river and canal travel, including luxurious **barges** that ply the waterways of inland France, Holland, Ireland, Belgium, and England, offering close-up views of the local culture.

There are also larger **river ships** in France, Holland, Belgium, Germany, Austria, and the former Soviet countries, as well as in Italy and Portugal. (See chapter 9.)

COMPARING ITINERARIES

LENGTH OF CRUISE   In choosing a region or regions to visit, you will obviously have to consider the length of the cruise you want to take. Itineraries in Europe range from a few days to several weeks. The shortest cruises, lasting **3 and 4 nights,** can be found mostly in the Greek Isles and on inland waterways. Hurtigruten also does 5- and 6-day cruises along the Norwegian coast. **One-week** cruises are regularly offered throughout Europe: in the Greek Isles/eastern Mediterranean, the western Mediterranean, the British Isles, the Baltics, Scandinavia, and the Riviera, and on Europe's inland waterways. Even more common are **10- and 12-night** cruises. Cruises of 2 weeks or more are also available.

DAYS IN PORT VS. DAYS AT SEA   It's important when comparing itineraries to note the number of days a ship is actually in port. Almost every cruise contains at least 1 or 2 **days at sea,** sometimes for practical reasons (the ship needs time to get to its next destination) and sometimes for relaxation. The ratio of sea days to port days should suit your temperament. If you're looking to pack in as much sightseeing as possible, be sure to book a cruise that emphasizes port days over sea days. If you're looking to relax (or if you think you'll need downtime between ports), opt for one that balances the two.

Some ships **overnight in key ports** such as Venice, Monte Carlo, and Istanbul, giving you time to explore the area by day and enjoy the local nightlife, too. Some small ships may spend most evenings in port.

PRE- & POST-CRUISE ADD-ONS   Cruise lines offer a variety of options for extending your vacation on land, either before or after your cruise. These range from simple 1- and 2-night add-on **hotel packages** to longer resort stays and full-blown **land tours** of a week or longer. The latter, known as **cruisetours,** add an escorted land package of 4 to 6 nights or more onto your cruise, with the price of hotels, transportation, tours, and some meals bundled together.

3 Choosing Your Ship

Different cruise lines offer different kinds of experiences, but physical factors such as the size and age of a ship also figure into the kind of trip you'll have. What kind of ship floats your boat?

MEGASHIPS (1,800–3,600 PASSENGERS)

For the past dozen years, the so-called "megaships" have dominated the cruise market, carrying upward of 1,800 passengers and offering an onboard experience any city dweller will recognize: food and drink available at any hour, entertainment districts filled with neon and twinkling lights, monumental architecture, big crowds, and a definite buzz. You often won't see the same faces twice from day to day, and, in fact, if you don't plan specific times and places to meet up with your spouse, lover, or friend, you may roam the decks for hours looking for them. (Some passengers even bring a set of walkie-talkies to stay in touch—annoying to the rest of us, maybe, but it keeps them happy.) The megas have as many as 15 passenger decks full of shops, restaurants, bars, and lounges, plus a huge range of cabins, from windowless insides to palatial suites. Most have a grand multistory atrium lobby; three or four swimming pools and hot tubs; a large theater and several small nightclubs; a huge spa and gym; an Internet center; a pizzeria and specialty coffee shop; one or more reservations-only restaurants in addition to their main dining rooms; and vast children's areas that often include splash pools, playrooms, computer rooms, and video arcades. Countless activities are offered all day long, including wine tastings, fashion shows, dance lessons, art auctions, aerobics classes, bingo, bridge, lectures, cooking demonstrations, pool games, computer classes, and trivia contests. And at night you have a choice of piano bars, discos, martini and champagne bars, sports bars, casinos, theaters, and big glitzy showrooms.

But even the megas aren't all alike. **Carnival**'s ships (along with **Costa**'s newer megaships) are the most theme-park-like, with their over-the-top decor and ambience. **Royal Caribbean**'s and **NCL**'s megas are more like Times Square hotels, blending a lot of flash with some elegant areas. **Princess** goes for a sort of Pottery Barn design sense and fun but not-too-daring activities and shows; **Holland America** blends tradition with some bright, modern spaces; **MSC's** new megaships are bright and modern but not too over-the-top; and **Celebrity** is all about chic modernity.

These ships are so large that they're sometimes limited as to where they can go, as some ports lack large enough docking facilities and some waterways are just too shallow or narrow.

MIDSIZE SHIPS (500–1,800 PASSENGERS)

For a while it looked as if midsize vessels were going the way of the dodo, but the past few years have seen a small resurgence in their fortunes. A number of older but still not *old*-old midsize ships continue to soldier on, and a few new midsize vessels are even on the drawing board.

The term *midsize* is, of course, relative. Measuring in at between 20,000 and 60,000 gross tons, most of these ships are still larger than some of the great old ocean liners. *Titanic,* for instance, was only 46,000 tons. They're plenty big and spacious enough to provide a diverse cruise experience, though you won't find the range of activities and attractions you do on the megaships. Consider that a good thing: For some people, a more toned-down, lower-key cruise is just what the doctor ordered. Most of **Holland America**'s fleet fits the midsize description, aside from its megasize Vista-class ships. Ditto for the fleets of **Oceania Cruises** and Celebrity subbrand **Azamara Cruises,** plus two of the ships **Princess** has positioned in Europe this year, all of which carry only about 700 passengers apiece, with a country-club-type ambience. Oceania is currently building a new, larger class of vessels, but they're still on the small size, measuring in at 65,000 gross tons and carrying 1,260 passengers. In Europe, the **Costa** and **MSC Cruises** fleets are split between big new megaships and several midsize vessels that carry between 560 and 1,500 passengers. The newest vessels of **Hurtigruten** are in the 670-passenger range, offering more public rooms and better accommodations than the line's older, smaller vessels.

Among the true ultraluxury lines, midsize is about as big as it gets, excluding Cunard's megaliners. **Crystal** and **Regent Seven Seas** both operate ships in the 50,000-ton range, carrying 700 to 940 passengers—a telling figure when you consider that MSC's and NCL's similarly sized ships pack in twice as many passengers. Along with high-toned service, cuisine, and amenities, personal space is a major difference between the mainstream and luxe lines. **Peter Deilmann Cruises'** 22,400-ton, 513-passenger *Deutschland* is not quite as superspacious but is superbeautiful, with an old-world decor that harkens back to the grand liners of the early 20th century.

SMALL SHIPS (100–500 PASSENGERS)

If the thought of sailing with thousands of other people makes you want to jump overboard, a smaller ship may be more up your alley. Small ships are ideal for those who crave a calm, intimate experience where conversation is king. As in a small town, you'll quickly get to know your neighbors, as you'll see the same faces at meals and on deck throughout the week.

The small ships in this book can be broken down into four main groups: small luxury ships, sailing ships, expedition ships, and river ships.

The **small luxury ships** of high-end lines such as **Seabourn, Silversea,** and **SeaDream** offer a refined, ultraelegant ambience. Cabins are spacious, service is gracious, gourmet meals are served on fine china, and guests dress to impress. These ships offer few activities besides watersports, putting more emphasis on quiet relaxation. Itineraries

Onboard Medical Care

The vast majority of ships have a nurse and sometimes a doctor aboard to provide medical services for a fee. Most of their cases involve seasickness, sunburn, and the like, but they may also be required to stabilize a patient with a more serious ailment until he or she can be brought to a hospital at the next port of call (or, in extreme cases, be evacuated by helicopter). If they're very unlucky, the medical staff may also have to deal with an outbreak of **norovirus,** the flulike gastrointestinal bug that's been striking ships for the past several years. More common than the common cold, the virus causes vomiting, stomach cramps, diarrhea, and general nausea for a few days, and is brought on by simple contagion: One infected passenger comes aboard, leaves his germs on a handrail, and all of a sudden everyone's sick—just like kindergarten. Outbreaks are relatively rare but make for really bad media, so cruise lines have stepped up their already vigilant sanitation routines to further reduce the chance of transmission.

All large ships have **staffed infirmaries,** but if you have special needs, check with the line to see exactly what medical services are provided. The quality of ships' staffs and facilities can definitely vary. Generally, big ships have the best-equipped facilities and largest staff since they're dealing with such a huge number of passengers and crew. In 2003, the author of an extensive *New York Times* article concluded that **Holland America** and **Princess** had the best onboard medical facilities, as well as the most generous pay packages for their doctors. Princess's Grand-class ships, for instance, carry at least one and sometimes two doctors, as well as two to five nurses, and are linked via a live video and camera system with U.S.-based medical centers. All Holland America ships can consult 24 hours a day (via phone or e-mail) with the University of Texas Medical Branch at Galveston, and their Vista-class ships have a teleradiology system that allows X-rays to be transmitted to a shore-side medical facility. (Princess's *Sea Princess* and Carnival's Spirit- and Conquest-class ships also have this system.) HAL's *Amsterdam* has the capability to do live television telemedicine conferencing and transmit X-rays to shore-side medical facilities. Note that shipboard doctors are not necessarily certified in the United States and aren't always experts in important areas such as cardiology.

tend to be split between Europe's great cities and smaller ports that aren't congested with passengers from the big megaships.

Sailing ships, obviously, have sails, but (sorry to spoil the romance) the ones in this book also have engines, which are a necessity if they're going to keep to their scheduled itineraries—not to mention keep the lights on. **Star Clippers** and **Sea Cloud Cruises** both operate truly extraordinary vessels based on classic sailing ship designs (except for Sea Cloud's namesake *Sea Cloud,* which actually is a classic sailing ship, built in the early 1930s). The three **Windstar Cruises** ships are much more of a hybrid: huge by sailing ship standards (though tiny compared to megaships), with sails that are furled and unfurled by computer control.

Expedition ships are represented in this book by Lindblad and Hurtigruten. **Lindblad Expeditions'** *National Geographic Endeavour* is one of the most expeditionary vessels in the world, with itineraries that range from pole to pole, taking in Scandinavia and western Europe along the way. Lindblad also operates the tiny river ship *Lord of the Glens* in Scotland and sometimes charters Sea Cloud's *Sea Cloud II* for the Mediterranean. **Hurtigruten** is mostly about exploring Norway's long, fjord-pocked coast, all the way up to the Arctic. The bulk of its fleet is made up of ships carrying fewer than 500 passengers. Its newest vessel, the 12,700-ton, 318-passenger *Fram*, is the only ship ever designed specifically to sail Arctic Greenland.

Two small and smallish ships in Europe fit none of these categories—no surprise, as they're operated by **easyCruise,** a newish company that offers ultraflexible and casual itineraries in the Riviera and Greek Isles, aboard vessels that carry about 232 and 500 passengers apiece.

OLD SHIP OR NEW?

Ship age is a funny thing. For some people, the older the better: Age implies classic nautical lines, old-time luxury, and a smaller, more human-scaled feel. On the other hand, it's a fact that ships age about as fast as dogs: Get up around age 15 and they start to look a little long in the tooth, not to mention being increasingly expensive for cruise lines to maintain.

Of the world's five major cruise regions (the Caribbean, Europe, Alaska, the Mexican Riviera, and Hawaii, in that order), Europe is the place where you're most likely to find older ships still chugging happily along. And doesn't that make sense? After all, when you're visiting cities that have stood for millennia or more, it seems pretty silly to quibble about a few years of ship age.

Among the ships reviewed in these pages, only **Costa** and **MSC Cruises** maintain older ships as significant chunks of their fleets, all left over from the days before both lines began building their new megaship fleets. Today these ships are mostly marketed to European passengers.

4 Cruises for Families

European cruises have become increasingly popular with families, for a variety of reasons: They're easy (or at least as easy as traveling with kids ever is), safe, fun, and educational for the kids, and relaxing for mom and dad. Cruise lines have been going to great lengths to please parents and kids alike, as families become an ever larger and more influential segment of the cruising public.

The megaships cater most to families and attract the largest numbers of them, offering playrooms, video arcades, and complimentary **supervised activities** for children ages 2 or 3 to 17, broken down into several age categories. Some lines set a minimum age for children to sail aboard (usually 6–12 months), and young children must usually be potty trained to participate in group activities.

Royal Caribbean, Carnival, Norwegian, Princess, and **Celebrity** offer the most family-friendly ships in the European market for 2008–2009, but even lines traditionally geared to older folks are getting in on the kid craze. Holland America has renovated all of its ships' kids' facilities over the past few years, and the kids' facilities and programs on Cunard's *QM2* are one of the best-kept kid secrets at sea.

See the section "Best Cruises for Families with Kids," on p. 7, for more info.

Family Cruising Tips

Here are some suggestions for better sailing and smoother seas on your family cruise.

- **Reserve a crib.** If you'd like a crib brought into your cabin, request one when booking your cruise.
- **Bring baby food and diapers.** If your infant is still on jar food, you'll have to bring your own. You can store milk and snacks in your cabin's minifridges/minibar, which comes standard on most new ships. (Ships more than 5 or 10 years old may offer them only in suites.) If yours is pre-stocked with beer and peanuts, you can ask your steward to clear it out.
- **Keep a tote with you on embarkation day.** Fill it with diapers, baby food, a change of clothes, bathing suits, and anything you'll need for the afternoon. After boarding a big ship, it may take a few hours for your luggage to be delivered to your cabin.
- **Pack some basic first-aid supplies, and even a thermometer.** Cruise lines have limited supplies of these items and charge for them, too. If an accident should happen on board, virtually every ship (except the smallest ones) has its own infirmary staffed by doctors or nurses. Keep in mind that first aid can usually be summoned more readily aboard ship than in port.
- **Warn younger children about the danger of falling overboard,** and make sure they know not to play on the railings.
- **Make sure your kids know their cabin number** and what deck it's on. The endless corridors and doors on the megaships often look exactly alike, though some are color-coded.
- **Prepare kids for TV letdown.** Though many ships today receive satellite TV programming, you won't get the range of options you have at home.

BABYSITTING   After the complimentary daylong roster of supervised activities wraps up somewhere between about 7 and 10pm, most mainstream lines offer slumber-party-style **group babysitting** in the playroom. Services are usually from about 10pm until about 1 to 3am and are for ages 3 to 12, costing about $4 to $6 per hour per child. Some lines do accommodate younger kids, with toys, cribs, and nap areas geared to infants and toddlers: Carnival, for instance, includes kids as young as 4 months. The counselors will even change diapers. **Private in-cabin babysitting** by a crewmember is also offered by Celebrity, MSC, Royal Caribbean, and most high-end lines at a steeper $8 to $10 per hour (and sometimes a few bucks more for additional siblings). Using a private babysitter every night isn't cheap, but Heidi's gone this route when her boys were babies, and she swears by it—how else to dine and have a cocktail or two in peace after a long kid-centric day? Try to get them tucked in and asleep before the sitter arrives so they won't have to deal with a new face just before bedtime.

FAMILY-FRIENDLY CABINS   Worried about spending a whole week with the family in a cramped little box? Depending on your budget, you may not have to.

On the low end, a family of four can share a cabin that has bunk-style third and fourth berths, which fold out of the walls just above the regular beds. A few lines, such as Carnival and NCL, will even accommodate a fifth person on a rollaway bed on certain ships, if space permits, and a **baby crib** can be brought in if requested in advance. There's no two ways about it, though: A standard cabin with four people in it will be cramped, and with one bathroom . . . well, you can imagine. However, when you consider how little time you'll spend in the cabin, it's doable, and many families take this option. The incentive is price: Whether children or adults, the rates for third and fourth persons sharing a cabin with two full-fare (or even heavily discounted) passengers are usually about half of the lowest regular rates. Norwegian Cruise Line allows children under 2 to sail free with two full-fare passengers (though you must pay port charges and government taxes for the kids, which run about $100–$200 per person). *Note:* Because prices are based on double adult occupancy of cabins, single parents sailing with children usually have to pay adult prices for their kids, though deals for single parents are offered every once in a while.

Families who can afford it should **consider booking a suite or junior suite.** Many have a pullout couch in the living room (or, better yet, two separate bedrooms) and can accommodate up to three or four children.

If you have older kids, it may be cheaper to book **connecting cabins**—two separate standard cabins with interconnecting doors. Almost every ship reviewed in this book offers connecting cabins, with the exception of most small ships and a small handful of midsize and megaships.

The handful of **sailing ships** and small **expedition ships** covered in this book tend not to cater to kids.

5 Cruises for Solo Travelers

Cruising solo has its upsides and its downsides. On the up, you needn't worry about dining alone (as you'll be seated with other guests), touring alone (you can take group shore excursions), and having people to talk to aboard ship (as things are pretty congenial, with onboard activities to encourage mixing). Your ship may even host a party to give singles a chance to get to know one another and/or offer social hosts as dance partners.

The downside is that singles may have to pay more for the cruise experience than those sharing a room. Because cruise line rates are based on two people per cabin, some lines charge a **single supplement,** which means solo travelers pay from 110% to an outrageous 200% of the per-person, double-occupancy fare. As cruise lines sometimes reduce their single supplements to help fill up underselling cruises, ask your travel agent to keep an eye out for deals as they come up. If you're sociable, you could also sail with Holland America, which is currently the only line still offering a **cabin-share service,** in which they pair you with another single so you can pay the usual double-occupancy fare. You may not be able to get much information about your roommate before the sailing, although all lines match gender and most also try to match age.

To increase your chances of meeting other singles, you can book an escorted group tour for singles through **Vacations To Go** (© **800/419-5179;** www.singlecruise.com), which offers a cabin-share program as well as onboard singles cocktail parties and mixers, games, group excursions, and "single-mingle" dining. Pre-cruise, you can even log on to their singles chat site to get to know the people you'll be cruising with. Singles in these groups tend to be in their 30s to 50s.

6 Cruises for Honeymooners & Anniversary Couples

Practically all cruises have what it takes to make your honeymoon or anniversary memorable: moonlight and stars, the undulating sea all around, dimly lit restaurants, and the pure romance of travel. Of course, different ships are romantic to different kinds of people. The megaships offer a big, flashy experience, like a trip to Vegas without the dry heat. The ultraluxury lines are more like a trip to Paris, with gourmet cuisine, fine wine, perfect service, and the finest bed linens. The sailing ships are like . . . sailing ships—and what's more romantic than that? Beyond the ships themselves are the ports of call, offering experiences that are variously exotic, charming, exciting, and sybaritic.

HONEYMOON & ANNIVERSARY PACKAGES

"Honeymoon" and "cruises" go together like "weddings" and "Vegas," and cruise lines offer a variety of incentives to help keep it that way. Some lines offer **honeymooner freebies** such as a special cake in the dining room one night, or an invitation to a private cocktail party to which couples celebrating anniversaries are also invited. To get your share of freebies, be sure to tell your travel agent or the cruise line reservation agent that you'll be celebrating on the cruise. Beyond the freebies, the mainstream cruise lines aren't shy about selling a variety of **honeymoon/anniversary packages.** You'll get a pamphlet describing the available packages when you receive your cruise tickets in the mail. NCL's $79 Honeymoon Package is about average for its price range and includes champagne and strawberries at embarkation, a dinner for two with complimentary wine at the ship's specialty restaurant, an invitation to a cocktail party, a keepsake photo, and canapés in your cabin one evening. Their $229 Deluxe Package adds breakfast in bed one day and two 25-minute massages at the spa. All the mainstream lines offer similar deals, with packages in the $300 to $500 range generally piling on more spa treatments, champagne, shore excursions, canapés, chocolate-covered strawberries, and the like. These packages must be ordered before the cruise.

The ultraluxe lines (Silversea, Seabourn, Regent Seven Seas, SeaDream, and Crystal) are less involved in these kinds of promotions, but that's because free champagne and canapés, en suite whirlpool tubs, and five-course dinners served in your cabin are all a matter of course on these lines.

VOW-RENEWAL & "ROMANCE" PACKAGES

Some lines offer vow-renewal packages for couples who'd like to celebrate their marriage all over again, or packages that simply add romance to a vacation. On Holland America, for example, couples can renew their vows at a special group ceremony at sea, catered with drinks and cold hors d'oeuvres; the $149 package includes a floral arrangement in your cabin, a photo and photo album, a certificate presented by the captain, and dinner for two at the Pinnacle alternative restaurant. Princess offers souped-up vow-renewal packages for $205 and $485 per couple. The former includes the ceremony, an orchid bouquet and boutonniere, a bottle of champagne and souvenir champagne glasses, a framed formal portrait of the ceremony, a commemorative

Getting Married On Board or in Port

Shipboard and destination weddings are more difficult to arrange in Europe than they are in the Caribbean and other Western Hemisphere areas, due to typically long residency requirements. Italy, Greece, and Malta have less stringent requirements, and therefore tend to be the most popular sites for legal destination weddings. Many lines also offer symbolic ceremonies in countries such as Spain, France, and the UK, meaning you get all the hoopla of a wedding but no actual legal certificate. For that, you have to pay a visit to your justice of the peace when you get home. Packages tend to start around $2,500 for onboard ceremonies and around $3,500 for destination weddings, plus a license fee of around $500.

Practically all the mainstream lines offer wedding packages, but **Princess Cruises** has the edge in Europe because it's currently the only line where the captain himself does the onboard honors. Ceremonies take place in the wedding chapels on many of the line's megaships, with assistant pursers in dress-blue uniforms available to escort the bride down a short aisle. Three different ceremony packages are offered, starting at $1,800 per couple (plus $450 for licensing fees). Depending on which you choose, they can include photography, video, music, and salon treatments for the bride. You can also arrange onboard receptions that can be custom tailored with a variety of options—hors d'oeuvres, champagne, wedding cake, and so on. Friends and relatives who aren't sailing can even monitor the wedding courtesy of the ships' chapel Web cams, which broadcast an updated photo every minute or so. There's often a waiting list for Princess's onboard weddings, so don't wait till the last minute if you're considering this option.

certificate signed by the captain, and a framed photo of the ceremony; the latter adds a champagne breakfast in bed, two terry-cloth robes, a visit to the spa for half-hour massages or facials, canapés or petits fours in your stateroom every evening, and a personalized invitation from the captain to visit the bridge while in port. These are fairly representative of what's offered by the other mainstream lines.

7 Cruises for Gays & Lesbians

A number of specialized travel agencies offer cruises for gays and/or lesbians, either chartering a full ship outright or reserving blocks of cabins with cruise lines that are known to be particularly gay friendly. Full-charter cruises typically bring aboard their own entertainers (as well as the ship's usual entertainment staff) and program many of their own activities. Hosted group trips typically have cocktail parties for group members and special programmed activities on board and in port.

- **Atlantis Events Inc.,** 9200 Sunset Blvd., Suite 500, West Hollywood, CA 90069 (© **800/628-5268** or 310/859-8800; www.atlantisevents.com), offers all-gay charters with lines such as Celebrity, Royal Caribbean, and NCL. In addition to the lines' own entertainment, Atlantis brings aboard its own featured performers. Past guests have included Patti LuPone, Cybill Shepherd, and Chaka Khan.

- **Friends of Dorothy Travel,** 1177 California St., Suite B, San Francisco, CA 94108-2231 (℃ **800/640-4918** or 415/864-1600; www.fodtravel.com), offers many full-gay charters and hosted tours with lines such as Celebrity, NCL, Cunard, and the ultraluxe SeaDream Yachts, as well as small European river ships.
- **Olivia Cruises and Resorts,** 434 Brannan St., San Francisco, CA 94107 (℃ **800/631-6277** or 415/962-5700; www.olivia.com), offers full-ship charters targeted specifically at the lesbian community; guest performers in recent years have included k. d. lang, the Indigo Girls, Wynonna Judd, Shawn Colvin, and Melissa Etheridge. In Europe, the company also offers cruises on small river vessels.
- **Pied Piper Travel,** 330 W. 42nd St., Suite 1804, New York, NY 10036 (℃ **800/874-7312** or 212/239-2412; www.piedpipertravel.com), offers hosted gay cruises that include various onboard parties and activities, and arranged visits with the gay community at the various ports of call.
- **RSVP Vacations,** 2535 25th Ave. S., Minneapolis, MN 55406 (℃ **800/328-7787** or 612/729-1113; www.rsvpvacations.com), offers full-ship charters on lines such as Holland America, Star Clippers, and river cruise line Uniworld. All sailings are targeted to both gays and lesbians, and bring aboard their own guest performers. RSVP works through more than 10,000 different travel agencies; locate one by calling the 800 number or checking the website above.

8 Cruises for People with Health Issues & Disabilities

Most cruise ships built in the past 15 years were designed with accessibility in mind, and some older ships have been retrofitted to offer access. Most ships that can accommodate wheelchair-bound passengers require that they be accompanied by a fully mobile companion. The ship reviews in chapters 6 through 8 include information about access and facilities in the "Cabins" sections, but be sure to discuss your needs fully with your travel agent prior to booking.

See the "Onboard Medical Care" box above for information on medical facilities aboard ship.

ACCESSIBLE CABINS & PUBLIC ROOMS   Most ships have a handful of cabins specifically designed for travelers with disabilities, with extrawide doorways, large bathrooms with grab bars and roll-in showers, closets with pull-down racks, and furniture built to a lower height. The "Ships at a Glance" chart on p. 64 identifies ships with accessible cabins, and the "Cabins" section in each of the ship reviews in chapters 6 through 8 indicates how many. The vast majority of the ships reviewed in the **mainstream** and **luxury** categories (chapters 6 and 7) have accessible cabins, but of the small ships, sailing ships, and river ships reviewed in chapters 8 and 9, only easyCruise's *easyCruiseOne* is even moderately wheelchair friendly.

Most newer vessels have ramps to allow access to all levels of the public rooms, and some also have lifts to help passengers with disabilities into the pools. A few older ships still have small sills or lips in cabin and bathroom doorways that may rise as high as 6 to 8 inches (and were originally created to contain water). Those that do may be able to install temporary ramps to accommodate wheelchair users. This must be arranged in advance.

ELEVATORS   Most shipboard elevators (particularly aboard today's megaships) are wide enough to accommodate wheelchairs, but make sure before booking. Due to the size of the megaships (where it can sometimes be a long way from place to place), cabins designed for wheelchair users are intentionally located near elevators. If you don't use a wheelchair but have trouble walking, you'll want to choose a cabin close to an elevator to avoid a long hike. The vast majority of small vessels and sailing ships do not have elevators.

TENDERING INTO PORT   If your ship is too large for a particular port's dock, or if a port's docks are reserved for other vessels, your ship may anchor offshore and shuttle passengers to land via small boats known as **tenders.** Some tenders are large and stable and others are not, but the choppiness of the water can be a factor when boarding either way. If you use a wheelchair or have trouble walking, it may be difficult or impossible to get aboard. For liability reasons, many lines forbid wheelchairs to be carried onto tenders, meaning you may have to forgo a trip ashore and stay on board when visiting these ports. An exception to this is **Holland America,** which has a wheelchair-to-tender transport system aboard all of its ships except *Prinsendam.* The system works by locking a wheelchair on a lift, which transports it safely between the gangway and the tender.

Check with your travel agent to find out if itineraries you're interested in allow your ship to dock at a pier. Note that weather conditions and heavy traffic may occasionally affect the way your ship reaches a port.

TRAVEL-AGENT SPECIALISTS   A handful of experienced travel agencies specialize in booking cruises and tours for travelers with disabilities. **Accessible Journeys,** 35 W. Sellers Ave., Ridley Park, PA 19078 (© **800/846-4537** or 610/521-0339; www.disabilitytravel.com), organizes both group and individual cruises on accessible ships, with accessible airport transfers and shore excursions, as well as an escort on group tours. **Flying Wheels Travel,** 143 W. Bridge St., Owatonna, MN 55060 (© **507/451-5005;** www.flyingwheelstravel.com), is another option.

2

Booking Your Cruise & Getting the Best Price

Bottom line: The only thing consistent about cruise pricing is its unpredictability. When the overall economy and conditions within the industry and the travel agent community shift, it all affects cruise rates. Though there's no magic secret to getting the best price on your cruise, we can help you hedge your bets and map out the best savings strategy. In this chapter, we've laid out the best booking strategies for 2008, along with other money-saving suggestions and booking tips.

1 Europe: The Hottest Place on Earth

It's classic Econ 101: Supply and demand determine cruise rates. When the lines have more ships than they can fill, prices are low. They're higher when people are clamoring to cruise. Right now, Europe is second in popularity only to the Caribbean. Expect to pay at least $1,800 a person for a 10-night Europe cruise, and much more for balcony cabins or suites. The cruise lines are deploying a record number of ships in Europe for 2008, and at press time the ships were filling up fast. Sure, there may be the odd last-minute deal, but you've gotta be ultraflexible about when you can travel and which ship you take. Even then, you just can't count on the kind of discounting that's done in the Caribbean.

"Europe is hot these days; it's safe to say it's the no. 1 cruise destination in the world," says Mike Driscoll, editor of industry bible *Cruise Week*. Especially for cruise-tour packages, cruises longer than 10 nights, and more unique itineraries, it's advisable to book at least 6 months ahead. If you wait till the last minute, you'll likely be out of luck (Driscoll says in summer 2007, the 7-night itineraries more likely had last-minute space). And then there's airfare to consider: Flights to major embarkation ports such as Barcelona, Venice, and Rome can be tough to get if you don't reserve way ahead of time; you can almost forget snagging seats at the last minute.

As for the actual booking process, cruise lines still tend to do what they've been doing for years, relying on traditional **travel agents** and **websites** to sell their product rather than retaining huge in-house reservations departments.

Generally, travel agents have less leeway in discounting than they used to, as the cruise lines have taken more control of their pricing. This means you're less likely than in the past to find rates being dramatically different from travel agent to travel agent.

For tips on using both online and brick-and-mortar agencies to the best advantage, see "Agents & the Web: Finding the Best Deals," later in this chapter.

2 The Prices in This Guide

Just like the airbrushed models dancing and lounging all over the cruise lines' brochures, the prices printed in those brochures aren't real, varying from just a little more than people really pay to wildly inflated. Apparently, even the cruise lines are ignoring them these days: We've heard from a reliable industry insider that many lines are planning to phase them out altogether. In any case, remember that **you'll always pay less,** except aboard some of the specialized small-ship lines.

Many cruise guides and magazines print these brochure rates despite knowing how useless they are in the real world, but we've come up with a new approach, working with Nashville, Tennessee–based **Just Cruisin' Plus** (© **800/888-0922;** www.just cruisinplus.com) to present a sample of the **actual prices** people are paying for cruises aboard all the ships in this book. The brochure rate for a 7-night eastern Mediterranean cruise aboard Costa Cruises *Costa Serena* is $2,039 for a low-end outside cabin. In reality, however, during our sampling period (Sept 2008 cruises, priced in mid-Jan 2008), customers were able to get that same cabin for $749. In the ship-review chapters, we've listed these realistic prices for every ship. The ship reviews give prices for the lowest-priced **inside cabins** (ones without windows) and lowest-priced **outside cabins** (with windows) aboard each ship, and also provide sample discount prices for the cheapest **suites.** Remember that cruise ships generally have many different categories of cabins within the basic divisions of inside, outside, and suite, all priced differently. The rates we've listed represent the *lowest priced* (which usually equates to smallest) in each division. If you're interested in booking a roomier, fancier cabin or suite, the price will be higher, with rates for high-end inside cabins being close to those for low-end outsides, and rates for high-end outsides being close to those for low-end suites.

Remember that rates are always subject to the basic principles of supply and demand, so those listed here are meant as a guide only and are in no way etched in stone—the price you pay may be higher or lower, depending on when you book, when you choose to travel, whether any special discounts are being offered by the lines, and a slew of other factors. All rates are cruise only, per person, based on double occupancy, and, unless otherwise noted, include **port charges** (the per-passenger fee each island charges the cruise line for entry). Government fees and taxes are additional.

3 The Cost: What's Included & What's Not

Overall, a cruise is superconvenient and adds up to a pretty good deal when you consider that your main vacation ingredients—accommodations; meals and most snacks; stops at ports of call; a packed schedule of activities; use of gyms, pools, and other facilities; and shows, cabaret, jazz performances, and more—are covered in the cruise price. Just don't think it's *all* free. In Europe, the big extras are shore excursions. They can be darn pricey considering the skyrocketing euro—expect to pay $200 to $400 per person for most tours. To beef up their bottom lines as much as possible, cruise lines push other **added-cost onboard extras** as well. You can always just say no, but if you're like most of us, you'll have an "oh, what the heck" attitude once you step across that gangway. So, when figuring out your budget, add on a bare minimum of another $500 per person, if not double or triple that, for tours, drinks, fancy coffees, Internet access, tips, spa treatments, and other hard-to-resist stuff (see list below). **Gratuities** are typically charged to guests' accounts at the end of the cruise; the cruise lines pay their service staff minimal salaries on the assumption that they'll make most of their pay in tips. Generally, you can expect to tip about $100 per person during a 10-night cruise. (For more on tipping, see chapter 3, "Things to Know Before You Go.") If you're the gambling type, you're a prime candidate for increasing your ship's revenue stream, whether your game is craps or bingo, or the one-arm bandits. And of course, don't forget to factor in airfare to the ship.

4 Money-Saving Strategies

From early-booking discounts and last-minute deals to shared cabins and senior and frequent-cruiser discounts, there are a lot of ways to save money on your cruise.

As they have for years, cruise lines continue to offer **early-booking discounts,** and some are better than others (generally, they're better for Europe cruises than Caribbean, for example). "Generally speaking, when it comes to the major cruise lines, the farther away your cruise goes from North America, the farther out (that is, the earlier) you should book it," says travel guru Driscoll. Price aside, when booking early, you naturally have much more assurance of getting exactly what you want in terms of cruise line, ship, and everything else.

If you're in the habit of traveling at the last minute, your best chance for snagging a good deal in Europe is cruising during the shoulder season, which some lines have stretched to as early as April and as late as November (June, July, and Aug are the prime expensive months). When booking late, be prepared to take the ship, itinerary, and cabin category that's available, whether it's the one that you wanted or not. As

Average Cost of Onboard Extras

Just so you're not shocked when your shipboard account is settled at the end of your trip, here are some average prices for onboard extras.

Laundry	$1–$6 per item
Self-service laundry	$1–$2 per load
Pressing	$1–$4 per item
5×7-inch photo from ship photographer	$7–$10
Scotch and soda at an onboard bar	$4–$6.50
Bottle of beer (domestic/imported)	$3.95/$6
Bottle of wine to accompany dinner	$20–$300+
Glass of wine	$6–$12
Bottle of Evian water (.5 liter/1.5 liters)	$1.50/$3.50
Can of Coca-Cola	$1.50–$2
Ship-to-shore phone call or fax	$4–$15 per minute
Cellphone calls at sea	$1.70 per minute
Sending e-mails	50¢–$1 per minute
50-minute massage	$109–$139
Sunscreen, 6-ounce bottle	$10
Disposable camera	$15–$20

we've said before, getting airfare at the last minute might be impossible. Plus, most last-minute deals are completely nonrefundable; if you book a week before the cruise, for example, the full fare is due upfront and you get zip back if you change your mind a few days later.

You'll find **last-minute deals** advertised online and in the travel section of a handful of Sunday newspapers, namely the *Miami Herald, Los Angeles Times, Chicago Tribune,* and *New York Times.* But the best route is checking with a travel agent who specializes in cruises and getting on his or her e-mail blast list to be alerted about special promotions and discounts. See "Agents & the Web: Finding the Best Deals," later in this chapter.

From time to time, some cruise lines offers discounts to **seniors** (usually defined as anyone 55 years or older), so don't keep your age a secret, and always ask your travel agent about these discounts when you're booking. For discounts in general, the best organization to belong to is **AARP,** 601 E St. NW, Washington, DC 20049 (© **888/ 687-2277;** www.aarp.org), the biggest outfit in the United States for people 50 and over.

If you've cruised with a particular cruise line before, you're considered a valued **repeat passenger** and will usually be rewarded with 5% to 10% discounts (sometimes higher) on future cruises. Depending on how many times you've sailed, you may also get cabin upgrades, invitations to private cocktail parties, priority check-in at the terminal, casino vouchers, logo souvenirs, a special newsletter, and a bottle of wine or a fruit basket in your cabin on embarkation days. The catch to all of this is that repeat-passenger discounts often cannot be combined with other pricing deals, particularly in the case of the mainstream lines.

If you're a serious repeater, though, the generous booty you get on the small upscale ships can add up to something substantial. After you sail a total of 140 days with Seabourn, for instance, you're entitled to a free 14-day cruise, while Silversea passengers get a free 7-night cruise after sailing 350 days and a free 14-night cruise after 500 days. Some of the small adventure-oriented lines offer similar deals. ACCL, for instance, gives passengers an 11th cruise free after their 10th paid cruise of at least 12 nights.

Some cruise lines offer reduced **group rates** to folks booking at least eight or more cabins, but this is really based on supply and demand. If a ship is selling well, group deals may not be available, but if it isn't, lines have a lot more incentive to wheel and deal. Groups may be family reunions and the like, but travel agents may also create their own "groups" whose members don't even know they're part of one. *Quick explanation:* The travel agents reserve a block of cabins on a given ship and the cruise line, in turn, gives a discounted group rate that agents can pass on to their clients. The cruise line benefits because they're potentially selling a lot of cabins through agency X, and the agents benefit because they can offer their clients a good price. So always ask your travel agent if you can be piggybacked onto some group space.

Very small groups—three or four people max, in most cases—can share one cabin if it's equipped with **third or fourth berths** (sofa beds or bunk-style berths that pull down from the ceiling or wall). This route isn't recommended for anyone who suffers from claustrophobia, although Heidi has survived many a cruise with her two kids and husband (or friend) in a standard cabin without too much psychological damage. Carnival and NCL go one better by offering standard cabins geared to families that can accommodate five people. The rates for third, fourth, and fifth passengers in a cabin, whether adults or children, are typically 30% to 60% or more off the normal adult fare. You can also look into **sharing a suite.** Many can accommodate five to seven people, and some are almost outlandishly roomy.

If cruising solo, you'll be charged something called the **single supplement,** which entails a charge that adds 50% to 100% to the standard per-person cruise fare—a consequence of cruise lines basing their revenue expectations on two people sharing every cabin. Some lines quietly forego or reduce this kind of supplemental charge if a ship isn't filling up as a particular departure date approaches, but there's no way to predict this kind of thing. A few lines (HAL, for instance) offer a **cabin-share service** that matches you with a same-gender roommate. If the cruise line can't find a roommate for you, you'll probably get the cabin at the regular double occupancy rate anyway. Very few ships offer cabins specifically designed for solo passengers anymore.

5 Agents & the Web: Finding the Best Deals

Today practically everybody has a website, and the difference between so-called **Web-based cruise sellers** and more **traditional travel agencies** is that the former rely on their sites for actual bookings, while the latter use theirs as glorified advertising space to promote their offerings, doing all actual business in person or over the phone. With a few exceptions, the cruise lines also have **direct-booking engines** on their own sites, but we don't recommend using them. Why? Because agents and Web-based sellers may have negotiated group rates with the lines, be part of a consortium with which a line is doing an upgrade promotion, or have other deals going that enable them to offer you lower rates. Though it may sound peculiar, the cruise lines actually prefer that you book through third parties because having agents and websites do the grunt work allows the lines to maintain small reservations staffs and, simultaneously, maintain goodwill in a system that works—something they have to consider because the vast majority of cruises are booked through agencies of one type or another. Typically, mainstream cruise lines report that about 75% to 85% of their bookings come from more traditional travel agencies (for the luxury lines, about 98% use travel agents). "The more you pay, the more likely you are to need or want a travel agent," says Driscoll.

WHICH OFFERS BETTER PRICES?

As far as cruise prices go, there's no absolutely quantifiable difference between the real, live travel agents (whether your hometown brick-and-mortar mom-and-pop agency or a big anonymous mega-agency) and Internet-based cruise sellers. For some years now, the major lines have been doing something they had talked about for years, offering all agencies—large or small—the same rates, a major coup for small agencies struggling to keep up with the Expedias of the world. Norwegian, Royal Caribbean, Crystal, and Celebrity, for example, have declared in one way or another that they offer all agencies the same rates and, further, that they will have no dealings with any agency that publicly (via print or website advertising) doles out rebates to clients—that is, gives their customers additional discounts by sacrificing some of their own commissions. The lines believe rebating and cutthroat discounting among agencies cheapens the cruise product; lines want travel agents to emphasize the benefits of cruise vacations, not just the fact that one agent is offering a cheaper price than another. Don't think there aren't any loopholes—there are. Customers and agents can privately wheel and deal, plus it's not uncommon for some agencies to now offer customers gift cards, bottles of wine, spa treatments, or other incentives in lieu of reduced rates.

Be Savvy & Beware of Scams

With the number of offers a potential cruise buyer sees, it can be difficult to know if an agency is or isn't reliable, legit, or, for that matter, stable. It pays to be on your guard against fly-by-night operators and agents who may lead you astray.

- **Get a referral.** A recommendation from a trusted friend or colleague (or from this guidebook) is one of the best ways to hook up with a reputable agent.
- **Use the cruise lines' agent lists.** Many cruise line websites include agency locator lists, naming agencies around the country with whom they do business. These are by no means comprehensive lists of all good or bad agencies, but an agent's presence on these lists is usually another good sign of experience.
- **Beware of snap recommendations.** If an agent suggests a cruise line without asking you a single question first about your tastes, beware. Because agents work on commissions from the lines, some may try to shanghai you into cruising with a company that pays them the highest rates, even though that line may not be right for you.
- **Always use a credit card to pay for your cruise.** It gives you more protection in the event the agency or cruise line fails. When your credit card statement arrives, make sure the payment was made to the cruise line, not the travel agency. If you find that payment was actually made to the agency, it's a big red flag that something's wrong. If you insist on paying by check, you'll be making it out to the agency, so it may be wise to ask if the agency has default protection. Many do. (*Note:* The only exception to this is when an agency is running a charter cruise—for example, a music cruise with special entertainment.)
- **Always follow the cruise line's payment schedule.** Never agree to a different schedule the travel agency comes up with. The lines' terms are always clearly printed in their brochures and usually require an initial deposit, with the balance due no later than 75 to 45 days before departure. If you're booking 2 months or less before departure, full payment is usually required at the time of booking.
- **Keep on top of your booking.** If you ever fail to receive a document or ticket on the date it's been promised, inquire about it immediately. If you're told that your cruise reservation was canceled because of overbooking and that you must pay extra for a confirmed and rescheduled sailing, demand a full refund and/or contact your credit card company to stop payment.

WHICH PROVIDES BETTER SERVICE?

Because pricing is closer to being equitable across all types of cruise agencies than ever before, it's really service that distinguishes one agency from another. Most websites give you only a menu of ships and itineraries to select from, plus a basic search capability that takes into account only destination, price, length of trip, and date, without consideration of the type of cruise experience each line offers. That's fine if you know exactly what you want and are comfortable on the computer. If, on the other hand, you have limited experience with cruising and with booking on the Web, it may be better to see a traditional agent, who can help you wade through the choices and answer your questions. For instance, a good agent can tell you which cabins have their views obstructed by lifeboats; which are near loud areas such as discos and the engine room; which ships and itineraries you should avoid if you're not looking for a party vibe; and, in general, what the major differences are between cabin categories. A lot of this kind of detailed information won't be found on the Web—you need to hear it from a person. To be better prepared before you call an agent, it's a good idea to do some research on the Web first.

Keep in mind, though, that you need to find an agent who really knows the business—and this applies to every type of agent: those who work out of their home or an agency office, those who work for large conglomerates and deal mostly over the phone, and those who staff toll-free numbers associated with Web-based sellers. Some are little more than order-takers: They may not know much more than pricing and may never even have been on a cruise themselves. This system works okay for selling air travel, where the big question is coach or first class, case closed, but a lot more variables are associated with booking a cruise. An experienced cruise agent—someone who's sailed on or inspected a variety of ships and booked many customers aboard in the past—will be able to tell you about special promotions (such as cabin upgrades), act as an intermediary should any problems arise with your booking, order special extras such as a bottle of champagne in your cabin when you arrive, and, in general, make your planning easy.

So how do you know if an agent is any good? The best way, of course, is to use one who has been referred to you by a reliable friend or acquaintance. This is particularly valuable these days, when agents are being pressed to squeeze more profit from every sale, making them less likely to take the time to discuss options. When searching for a good agent, it's an added bonus if an agent is an **Accredited Cruise Counselor (ACC), Master Cruise Counselor (MCC),** or **Elite Cruise Counselor (ECC),** designations doled out by the Cruise Lines International Association (CLIA), an industry trade organization, after agents take classes and inspect a number of ships. Many of the cruise lines' websites list **preferred agencies** (generally broken down or searchable by city or state), as does the CLIA site (**www.cruising.org**). Many of the most reliable agencies are also members of **agent groups,** such as Virtuoso, Signature Travel Network, and Vacation.com. In the sections below, we list some of the best agencies and also evaluate the major cruise-selling websites.

6 Recommended Agencies & Websites

Of the approximately 20,000 U.S. travel agencies (including home based, the largest-growing segment), 15% (or about 3,000 agencies) sell 90% of all cruise travel in North America; about 10% to 15% of those are considered cruise only. Agencies come in all shapes and sizes, from small neighborhood stores to huge chain operations. Like banking, telecommunications, and media, the travel industry has been rife with consolidation over the past decade, so even that mom-and-pop travel agency on Main Street may turn out to be an affiliate of a larger agency. When it comes to home-based agents, they may or may not be affiliated with a national group such as CruiseOne or

SeaMaster Cruises. It's better if they are so they have access to more resources and competitive rates. Use a home-based agent only if she's been doing this for a long time.

Even though you'll get similarly low rates from both traditional and Web-based agencies these days, we can't stress enough that service counts for something, too. There's value in using a travel agent you've worked with in the past or one who comes highly recommended by someone you trust. A good agent will be there for you if problems arise.

TRADITIONAL AGENCIES SPECIALIZING IN MAINSTREAM CRUISES

To give you an idea of where to begin, here's a sampling (by no means comprehensive) of both cruise-only and full-service agencies that have solid reputations selling cruises with mainstream lines such as Princess, Carnival, Royal Caribbean, Celebrity, Holland America, and Norwegian. A few are affiliated with the big chains; most are not. While all have websites to promote current deals, the agencies listed primarily operate from a combination of walk-in business and toll-free telephone-based business.

- **America's Vacation Center,** 520 West Valley Park Way, Suite A, Escondito, CA 92025 (*(C)* **800/788-0970;** www.americasvacationcenter.com)
- **The Cruise Company,** 10760 Q St., Omaha, NE 68127 (*(C)* **800/289-5505** or 402/339-6800; www.thecruisecompany.com)
- **Cruise Holidays,** 7000 NW Prairie View Rd., Kansas City, MO 64151 (*(C)* **800/ 869-6806** or 816/741-7417; www.cruiseholidayskc.com)
- **Cruises Only,** 10 Harbor Park Dr., Port Washington, NY 11050 (*(C)* **800/278- 4737;** www.cruisesonly.com), is part of World Travel Holdings, the largest cruise retailer in the world.
- **Cruise Value Center,** 6 Edgeboro Rd., Suite 400, East Brunswick, NJ 08816 (*(C)* **800/231-7447** or 732/257-4545; www.cruisevalue.com)
- **Just Cruisin' Plus,** 5640 Nolensville Rd., Nashville, TN 37211 (*(C)* **800/888- 0922** or 615/833-0922; www.justcruisinplus.com)
- **Vacations To Go,** 1502 Augusta Dr., Suite 415, Houston, TX 77057 (*(C)* **800/ 419-5104** or 713/974-2121; www.vacationstogo.com)

Another way to find a reputable travel agency in your town is by contacting one of a handful of **agency groups** or **consortiums,** which screen their members. The following groups, whose members specialize in mainstream cruises, all maintain websites that allow you to search for local agencies with your zip code or city: **TravelSavers** (*(C)* **800/366-9895;** www.travelsavers.com) is a group of more than 1,000 agencies; **Cruise Ship Centers** (*(C)* **800/707-7327;** www.cruiseshipcenters.com) has about 80 locations in Canada; and **Vacation.com** (*(C)* **800/843-0733;** www.vacation.com) is the largest group in the U.S., with some 6,000 members. **Carlson Wagonlit Travel** (www.carlsontravel.com) and **Cruise Holidays** (www.cruiseholidays.com) are both large, reputable chains, and their websites allow you to find a local branch near you.

TRADITIONAL AGENCIES SPECIALIZING IN LUXURY CRUISES

This sampling of reputable agencies, both cruise only and full service, specializes in selling ultraluxury cruises such as Cunard, Seabourn, Silversea, Crystal, Radisson Seven Seas, and SeaDream Yacht Club.

- **All Cruise Travel,** 1213 Lincoln Ave., Suite 205, San Jose, CA 95125 (*(C)* **800/ 227-8473** or 408/295-1200; www.allcruisetravel.com)

- **All-Travel,** 2001 S. Barrington Ave., Suite 315, Los Angeles, CA 90025 (© **800/ 300-4567**or 310/312-3368; www.all-travel.com)
- **Cruise Professionals,** 130 Dundas St. E., Suite 103, Mississauga, Ontario L5A 3V8, Canada (© **800/265-3838** or 905/275-3030; www.cruiseprofessionals.com)
- **Landmark Travel,** 12 SE 8th St., Ft. Lauderdale, FL 33316 (© **800/547-0727** or 954/523-0727; www.landmark-travel.com)
- **Strictly Vacations,** 108 W. Mission St., Santa Barbara, CA 93101 (© **800/447- 2364;** www.strictlyvacations.com; expert on Windstar)

If you're looking for a top-of-the-line cruise, definitely use an agency that's a member of one of the following agency groups whose members specialize in luxury cruises. Agency members can pass on lots of great extras to clients, from cabin upgrades to private cocktail parties. Members are ultraknowledgeable, and it's not unusual for someone from the agency to sail on board the cruise to assist clients. All maintain websites that allow you to search for local agencies with your zip code or city. **Virtuoso** (© **866/401-7974;** www.virtuoso.com) is a consortium of more than 300 member agencies nationwide, including some on the list above. To find an agency in your area, call their toll-free number or e-mail **travel@virtuoso.com.** Another group is **Signature Travel Network** (© **800/339-0868;** www.signaturetravelnetwork.com), with about 200 member agencies across the country. Call to find an agency in your area, or e-mail **info@signaturetravelnetwork.com.**

WEB-BASED AGENCIES SPECIALIZING IN MAINSTREAM CRUISES

The following sites are reputable Web-based cruise specialists (though, again, not a comprehensive list). All allow searches by destination, date of travel, length of cruise, and price range, as well as cruise line or ship if you know exactly what you want. All allow you to book online for at least some, if not most, lines. In many cases, though, this does not involve a live connection with the cruise line's reservations database, so you'll have to wait up to 24 hours for a confirmation via e-mail, fax, or a phone call. Sometimes you can research your cruise online, but you have to call a toll-free number when you're ready to get down to business. Keep in mind that these websites are constant works in progress, adding new features all the time.

- **Cruise411.com** (www.cruise411.com; © **800/553-7090**)
- **Expedia** (www.expedia.com; © **888/249-3978**)
- **Icruise.com** (www.icruise.com; © **888/427-8473**)
- **Travelocity** (www.travelocity.com; © **877/815-5446**)

7 Choosing Your Cabin

When it comes right down to it, choosing a cabin is really a question of money. From a windowless lower-deck cabin with upper and lower bunks to a 1,400-square-foot suite with a butler and mile-long private veranda, cruise ships can offer a dozen or more stateroom categories that differ by size, location in the ship, amenities, and, of course, price. To see what we mean, go to the Cruises Only website (**www.cruisesonly. com**) for 360-degree tours and photos of most ships.

It's traditionally been a rule of thumb that the higher up you are and the more light that gets into your cabin, the more you pay; the lower you go into the bowels of the ship, the cheaper the fare. On some of the more modern ships, however, that old rule doesn't always ring true. On ships launched recently by Carnival, for instance, designers

Smoking at Sea . . . or Not

Once upon a time, all the cool kids smoked—Sinatra, JFK, even Joe DiMaggio. It was an era when life was seen through a swirling bluish haze, and, at least in the movies, nobody ever coughed. Today? Not so much. Even in usually smoke-friendly Europe, countries like **England, Ireland,** and **Norway** have banned smoking in most public places nationwide, including pubs. It's enough to make a smoker want to run away to sea . . . except that won't necessarily work anymore either.

As goes public opinion, so go the cruise lines, which generally prohibit smoking now in all restaurants, theaters, corridors, elevators, and many other public areas, too. If you want to light up, most lines still let you do so in the smoking sections of bars and lounges, out on the open decks, and in your cabin and private balcony, but some are even clamping down on those retreats. On the other side of the smoker/non-smoker debate, anti-puffers face the fact that no cruise line that permits in-cabin smoking has designated smoking or non-smoking cabins—you just get what you get, though the cruise lines do scrub their cabins well between cruises, if necessary by shampooing the rug and using air purifiers. In our hundreds of cruises, we've never found a cabin that reeked from last week's Marlborough Man.

Different lines have different levels of anti-smoking regulations. Among the mainstream lines, the best for non-smokers are **Azamara Cruises** and **Oceania Cruises,** each of which bans smoking in all cabins and all but two small public areas aboard each ship. **Royal Caribbean** bans smoking from all cabins in its fleet, though it's still allowed in designated areas of the ships' bars and lounges, on cabin balconies, and in some areas of the outside decks. Honorable mention goes to **Norwegian Cruise Line,** which allows smoking in cabins but prohibits it in most public areas—including most of its ships' bars.

Among the small luxury lines, **SeaDream Yacht Club** and German Line **Peter Deilmann Cruises** have the most stringent smoking rules, prohibiting smoking everywhere except certain outdoor decks. **Regent Seven Seas** also bans smoking from cabins on its mid-size luxe ships, while **Crystal** allows smoking in staterooms but not on stateroom verandas. Sailing-ship lines **Windstar** and **Star Clippers** allow smoking only in designated areas of one or two public lounges and bars, and outdoors. Small-ship line **Lindblad Expeditions** bans smoking everywhere except in designated areas of the outside decks.

have scattered their most desirable suites on midlevel decks as well as top decks, thereby diminishing the prestige of an upper-deck cabin. For the most part, though, and especially on small ships, where most cabins are virtually identical, cabins on higher decks are still generally more expensive, and outside cabins (with windows or balconies) are more expensive than inside cabins (those without). Outside cabins whose windows are obstructed by lifeboats will be cheaper than ones with good views.

EVALUATING CABIN SIZE

Inch for inch, cruise ship cabins are smaller than hotel rooms. Of course, having a private balcony attached to your cabin, as many do, makes your living space that much bigger.

A roomy **standard cabin** is about 170 to 190 square feet, although some of the smallest are about 85 to 100 square feet. Celebrity's standards are spacious enough, at around 170 to 175 square feet, with those on its Millennium-class ships sometimes as big as 191 square feet. Carnival and Holland America's are about 185 square feet or more. By way of comparison, equivalent standard cabins on a good number of ships in the Norwegian and Royal Caribbean lines are quite a bit smaller—try 120 to 160 square feet—and can be cramped. Cabins on the small-ship lines such as Star Clippers can be as snug as 100 square feet.

All the standard cabins on the high-end lines are roomy—in fact, many of the high-end ships are "suite only." For example, on Silversea's *Silver Shadow* and *Silver Whisper*, cabins are 287 square feet, plus a 58-square-foot balcony. Across the board, from mainstream to luxe, **suites and penthouses** are obviously the most spacious, measuring from about 250 square feet to more than 1,400 square feet, plus private verandas.

Most cruise lines publish schematic drawings in their brochures, with square footage and, in some cases, measurements of length and width, which should give you some idea of what to expect. (We also include square footage ranges for inside cabins, outside cabins, and suites in the cruise ship descriptions in chapters 6–8.) Consider measuring off the dimensions on your bedroom floor and imagining your temporary oceangoing home, being sure to block out part of that space for the bathroom and closet. As a rough guideline, within a cabin of around 100 square feet, about a third of the floor space is gobbled up by those functional necessities.

Now, while you may be thinking, "Gee, that's really not a lot of space," remember that, like a bedroom in a vacation home, your cabin will, in all likelihood, be a place you use only for sleeping, showering, and changing clothes.

THE SCOOP ON INSIDE CABINS VS. OUTSIDE CABINS

Whether you really plan to spend time in your cabin is a question that should be taken into account when deciding whether to book an inside cabin or an outside cabin (that is, one without windows or one with windows or a balcony). If you plan to get up bright and early, and tour all day, you can probably get away with booking an inside cabin and save yourself a bundle. Inside cabins are generally neither as bad nor as claustrophobic as they sound. Many, in fact—such as those aboard most of the Holland America and Celebrity fleets—are the same size as the outside cabins, and most cruise lines design and decorate them to provide an illusion of light and space.

If, on the other hand, you want to lounge around and take it easy in your cabin, maybe ordering breakfast from room service and eating while the sun streams in and the ship rolls into Naples, Valletta, Villefranche, or some other incredibly picturesque port—or, better yet, eating out *in* the sun, on your private veranda—then an outside cabin is definitely a worthwhile investment. Remember, though, that if it's a view of the sea you want, be sure when booking that your window or balcony doesn't just give you a good view of a lifeboat or some other obstruction (and remember, there are likely to be balconies on the deck right above your balcony, so they're more like porches than actual verandas). Some cruise line brochures tell you which cabins are obstructed, and a good travel agent or a cruise line's reservation agent can tell you which cabins on a particular ship might have this problem.

OTHER CABIN MATTERS TO CONSIDER

Unless you're booking at the last minute (a few weeks or less before sailing), as part of a group, or in a cabin-share or cabin-guarantee program (which means you agree to a price, and find out your exact cabin at the last minute), you can work with your agent to pick an exact cabin. If possible, try to go into your talks with some idea of what kind of cabin category you'd like, or at least with a list of must-haves or must-avoids. Need a **bathtub** rather than just a shower? That narrows your choices on most ships. Want **connecting cabins** so you and your kids, friends, or relatives can share space? Most ships have 'em, but they sometimes book up early, as do cabins with **third or fourth berths** (usually pull-down bunks or a sofa bed). Almost all ships have cabin TVs these days, but a few don't. Want an **elevator** close by to make it easy to get between decks? Is the view out the cabin's windows obstructed by lifeboats or other ship equipment? Most important, **keep cabin position in mind if you suffer from seasickness.** A midship location on a middle deck is best because it's a kind of fulcrum point, the area least affected by the vessel's rocking and rolling in rough seas.

8 Booking Your Air Travel

Airfare is sometimes included in the price of Europe cruises, especially on the luxury lines, but generally it's not. You'll have to either purchase airfare on your own through an agent or online, or buy it as a package with your cruise. The latter is often referred to as an **air add-on** or **air/sea package.** You can usually find information on these programs in the back of cruise line brochures and on their websites, along with prices on flights from more than 100 U.S. and Canadian cities to the port of embarkation. Here are the pros and cons to booking your airfare through the cruise line.

- **Pros:** When you book through the cruise line, they'll know your airline schedule and, in the event of delayed flights and other unavoidable snafus, will do what they can to make sure you get to the ship. People who book their air transportation and transfers separately are on their own.
- **Cons:** Odds are, it will be more expensive to book through the cruise line than on your own. In the past, cruise lines offered more competitive fares, but the airlines aren't giving them the bulk discounts they used to, meaning prices have gone up. Consequently, fewer passengers are now booking the lines' air packages. Also, if you book through the lines, you probably won't be able to use any frequent-flier miles you've accumulated, and the air add-on could require a circuitous routing—with indirect legs and layovers—before you finally arrive at your port of embarkation. Sources tell us only about 10% of passengers book airfare through the cruise lines.

If you choose to arrange your own air transportation, make sure that airfare is not included as part of your cruise contract. If it is, you're often granted a deduction off the cruise fare. If you purchase your own airfare, you can buy **bus transfers from the airport to the ship** through the cruise line (if you buy the cruise line airfare, transfers are often included in the price), or hop in a taxi (keep in mind that taxis in Italy, for example, are extremely expensive).

9 Prebooking Your Dinner Table & Arranging Special Diets

In addition to choosing your cabin when booking your cruise, on most ships you can choose an **early or late seating** for dinner in the main restaurant (the buffet restaurants on most ships are always open seating), and sometimes even put in a request for the size table you're interested in (tables for 2, 4, 8, 10, and so on). Assignments for breakfast and lunch are rarely required, as dining rooms operate with open seating during these meals. At night, though, early seatings allow you to get first dibs on shipboard nightlife (or, conversely, promptly hit the sack), while late seatings allow you to linger a little longer over your meal. In the past few years, more lines—especially Norwegian and, to a slightly lesser extent, Princess and Holland America—have junked this traditional early-late paradigm (in at least some of their restaurants) in favor of **open-seating dining,** in which you simply show up when hunger pangs strike. For a more detailed discussion, see "Onboard Dining Options," on p. 58.

If you follow a **special diet**—whether vegetarian, low salt, low fat, heart healthy, kosher, halal, or any other, or if you have certain food allergies—make this known to your travel agent when you book, or at least 30 or more days before the cruise, and make sure your diet can be accommodated at all three meals (sometimes special meal plans will cover only breakfast and dinner). The vast majority of ships offer vegetarian meals and health-conscious choices as part of their daily menus these days (Crystal even offers kosher food as part of its daily offerings), but it can't hurt to arrange things ahead of time. A cruise is not the place to go on an involuntary starvation diet.

10 Booking Pre- & Post-Cruise Hotel Stays

Cruise lines often offer hotel stays in the cities of embarkation and debarkation, and because most of these cities are tourist attractions in their own right, you may want to spend some time in Barcelona, Rome, or Venice. The cruise lines' package deals usually include hotel stays and transportation from the hotel to the ship (before the cruise) or from the docks to the hotel (after the cruise). Inquire with your travel agent, and compare what the line is offering with what you may be able to arrange independently. Nowadays, you may be able to get a hotel stay much cheaper on your own.

11 Cancellations & Insurance

Sure, stuff happens. Given today's unpredictable geopolitical situation and instances of extreme weather conditions, you just never know. A cruise could be canceled, for example, because of shipyard delays (if you've booked an inaugural cruise), the outbreak of an infectious disease, mechanical breakdowns (such as nonfunctioning air-conditioning or an engine fire), the cruise line going out of business, an act of war, or a major flood. Some people feel more comfortable buying cancellation protection and insurance just in case.

That said, in today's competitive market, cruise lines have been making extraordinary efforts to appease disappointed passengers, whether they bought insurance or not. Typically, a line will reschedule the canceled cruise and offer passengers big discounts on future cruises—after all, they don't want the bad press they'd get if they cheated hundreds or thousands of people. There are, however, no set rules on how a line will compensate you over and above a refund, in the event of a cancellation.

Now, if the shoe's on the other foot and you need to cancel your own cruise, you'll generally get a refund—most lines give you every cent back if you cancel at least 2 to 3 months before your departure date, although details vary from line to line. If you cancel closer to departure, you'll usually get a partial refund up until about 15 to 30 days before the cruise; cancel closer in than that, and you'll forfeit 100% of what you paid.

Still, if you have worries about cruise lines going belly up, sudden illness, or other emergencies before your cruise or once on board, or even if you just change your mind, you may want to think about purchasing **travel insurance.** On the other hand, if you're *just* worried about missing the ship, go a day early and spend your money on a hotel and nice dinner instead. Because most flights to Europe are overnight, it's nice to land in city like Barcelona or Venice and have at least a day and a night to recuperate and explore before hopping right on the ship.

"Unless you're elderly, have medical issues, or have an unpredictable job that may require you to cancel your trip at the last minute, don't bother with insurance," says *Cruise Week* editor Mike Driscoll. It's a personal decision.

Except for the small coastal cruisers described in chapter 8, most cruise ships have an infirmary staffed by a doctor and a nurse or two, but in the event of a dire illness, the ship's medical staff can do only so much. Therefore, if you are going to buy insurance, you may want a policy that covers **emergency medical evacuation** and, if your regular insurance doesn't cover it, the potential cost of major medical treatment while away from home.

There are policies sold through the cruise lines (with details varying from line to line) and others sold independently. Both sources have pros and cons.

CRUISE LINE POLICIES VS. THIRD-PARTY INSURERS

A good travel agent can tell you about policies sold through the cruise lines and ones sold independently of the lines. No matter which you choose, it's absolutely crucial to read the fine print because terms vary from policy to policy.

Both kinds typically reimburse you in some way when your trip is affected by unexpected events (such as canceled flights, plane crashes, dockworkers' strikes, or the illness or death of a loved one, as late as the day before or day of departure), but not by "acts of God," such as hurricanes and earthquakes (the exception being if your home is made uninhabitable, putting you in no mood to continue with your cruise plans). Both also typically cover **cancellation of the cruise** for medical reasons (yours or a family member's); **medical emergencies** during the cruise, including evacuation from the ship; lost or damaged luggage; and a cruise missed due to airline delays (though some cover only delays over 3 hours). Neither kind of policy will reimburse you if your travel agent goes bankrupt, so using a travel agent you're very familiar with or who has been recommended to you is the safest precaution you can take. (And, of course, *always use a credit card,* never a check. If a corrupt travel agent cashes it or a decent one just goes out of business, then you could get screwed.) Note that most cancellation policies do not cover cancellations due to work requirements.

THIRD-PARTY COVERAGE   Even though agents get a commission for selling both cruise line policies and independent policies, most agents and industry insiders believe that non-cruise-line policies are the best bet because some, such as Access America (see below), will issue insurance to those with **preexisting medical conditions** if the condition is stable when purchasing the insurance (a doctor would have to verify this if you ever made a claim) and if you purchase the policy within 14 days of your initial deposit on the cruise. They also offer **supplier-default coverage** that kicks in if a cruise line goes bankrupt, which a handful did between 2000 and 2003.

Still, you shouldn't be afraid to book a cruise. A well-connected travel agent should see the writing on the wall months before a cruise line fails—commissions will slow or stop being paid, phone calls won't be returned, and industry trade publications will report on any problems. The less customer-service-driven cruise sellers may not stop pushing a troubled cruise line, however, and may continue selling these lines up to the very last minute.

According to the Fair Credit Billing Act, if you paid by credit card (and, again, you should *always* pay with a credit card), you'll generally get your money back if you dispute the charge within 60 days of the date the charge first appears. If you paid in full 4 months before the cruise, you'll likely be out of luck going the credit-reimbursement route and may have to resort to litigation. Also, while many lines post a multimillion-dollar bond with the Federal Maritime Commission, creating a fund from which they can reimburse creditors should they fail financially, it's no guarantee you'll get all or any of your money back. Technically, the bond covers cruise payments for all passengers embarking from U.S. ports, but because the line would have banks or other vendors to pay off first, you'd likely get only pennies on the dollar, if that. Still, it's better that a cruise line have a bond than not—and if you learn that a line is having trouble making bond payments, it may be a sign of serious financial woes.

Policies are available from reputable insurers such as **Access America,** Box 71533, Richmond, VA 23286 (© **866/807-3982;** www.accessamerica.com), and **Travel Guard International,** 1145 Clark St., Stevens Point, WI 54481 (© **800/826-4919;** www. travelguard.com), whose websites maintain lists of the lines they cover (or no longer cover); these are helpful in figuring out which lines may be considered financially shaky.

CRUISE LINE COVERAGE   Cruise lines offer their own policies, many of them administered by New York–based **BerkelyCare** (© **800/797-4514**). If you opt for this type of policy out of sheer convenience (the cost is added right onto your cruise fare), keep in mind they do not cover you in the event of a cruise line bankruptcy (though using a credit card can save you here; see above) or for cancellation of your cruise due to preexisting medical conditions, which is usually defined as an unstable condition existing within 60 days of your buying the insurance. Some lines' policies will issue a cruise credit for the penalty amount if a medical claim is deemed preexisting and will issue you cash if you cancel for a covered reason. Generally, the cancellation penalty imposed by the cruise line will be 100% of the cruise fare, for example, if you cancel a few days before the cruise (assuming you've paid in full), or it could be just $300 if you cancel right after making the initial cruise deposit. Be sure the coverage offered is truly an insurance policy. In some cases, the coverage is really a cancellation waiver that provides a credit for a future cruise under limited conditions.

Sounds like the third-party policies win hands down, right? Well, to make it just a little more complicated, a handful of cruise line policies are actually better in some areas than outside policies. For example, **Princess Cruises** has an insurance policy that allows you to cancel for all the reasons that an outside policy would (illness, injury) and get cash reimbursement, or they will let you cancel for any reason whatsoever (from fear of flying to a bad hair day) up until the day of departure and have 75% to 90% of the normal penalty for canceling your cruise applied toward a future trip. **Norwegian, Celebrity,** and **Royal Caribbean** offer similar "any reason" policies, which provide a cruise credit for up to 75%. For an extra $100 above their standard insurance fee (or $250 if purchased alone), high-end **Silversea** allows you to cancel cruises for any reason 1 to 14 days before sailing and get a credit for 100% of the penalty amount (including airfare, if booked through Silversea), applicable toward any cruise within the following 12 months. Many other lines offer similar cancellation plans. The cruise lines using the BerkelyCare policies (see above) also reimburse passengers for days missed on a cruise—say, if you missed your flight and had to join up with the cruise 2 days later—covering hotel costs during the missed days and transportation to the ship (though typically only to a max of $500). Keep in mind that cruise line policies do change, so before purchasing insurance, be sure you understand exactly what you're getting.

12 Putting Down a Deposit & Reviewing Tickets

If you're booking several months or more ahead of time, then you have to leave a deposit to secure the booking; if you're booking at the last minute, the full fare will be due when you make the reservation. Depending on the policy of the line you selected, the amount will either be fixed at a predetermined amount or represent a percentage of the ticket's total cost. The length of time cruise lines will hold a cabin without a deposit is getting shorter by the minute. It seems pretty clear, in this age of near-obsessive "shopping around," that the cruise lines are doing their part to discourage it. It used to be a cruise could be held for a week before you had to plunk down cash; most lines have now shortened this window to 1 to 3 days (exceptions include exotic itineraries that aren't ultracompetitive).

The balance of the cruise price is due anywhere from about 60 to 90 days before you depart; holiday cruises may require final payments earlier, perhaps 90 days before departure; and for some long cruises, it may be 120 days or more before you depart. The payment schedule for deposits on groups is often more liberal. Booking at the last minute usually requires payment in full at the time of booking.

Credit card payments are made directly to the cruise line, but payments by check are made out to the agency, which then passes payment on to the cruise line. As we've said repeatedly, it's preferable to pay by credit card, for the added protection it offers.

"Except in certain circumstances, if the travel agency asks, prefers, or insists on running your credit card through the agency processing terminal, it is a *major* red flag that most often should send you running from the building," says Charlie Funk, co-owner of Just Cruisin' Plus in Nashville. The only exception to this is when an agency is doing a charter or group with special entertainment or features, and the cruise is offered only through the agency.

Carefully review your ticket, invoice, itinerary, and/or vouchers to confirm that they accurately reflect the departure date, ship, and cabin category you booked. The printout usually lists a specific cabin number; if it doesn't, it designates a cabin category. Your exact cabin location may sometimes not be assigned to you until you board ship.

If you need to cancel your cruise after putting down a deposit, you'll get all or most of your money back, depending on how close you are to departure. With Royal Caribbean, for instance, customers get a 100% refund if they cancel more than 70 days ahead. Less than 30 days from the cruise, the refund drops to 50%, and within the last week, it's your loss. Note that some travel agencies charge an administrative fee for cancellation regardless of whether the cruise line does. More service-oriented agencies tend not to charge these fees in most cases. Always ask *before* handing over your credit card number.

3

Things to Know Before You Go

You've bought your ticket and you're getting ready to cruise. Here are nuts and bolts, odds and ends, FYIs, and helpful hints to consider before you go.

1 Passports & Visas

Citizens of non-E.U. countries need a **passport** to enter any European country. As you would before any trip abroad, make two photocopies of your passport's information pages before leaving home. Take one set with you as a backup (keeping it in a different piece of luggage from the one holding your originals) and keep one at home.

APPLYING FOR A NEW PASSPORT

U.S. RESIDENTS If you don't currently have a passport or you need to replace an expired one, the **U.S. State Department website** (http://travel.state.gov) provides information. You can also inquire at your local passport acceptance facility, or call the **National Passport Information Center** (© 877/487-2778). Fees for new passports are $97 adults, $82 children under 16. Renewals cost $67. Allow plenty of time before your trip to apply for a passport. In the U.S., processing normally takes about a month, but at press time new regulations mandating passports for all border crossings had created a logjam, stretching processing times to 3 months or more. That should be cleared up by the time you read this, but the point is, don't dilly-dally. If you're leaving within a few weeks, you can pay an additional $60 fee to have your passport expedited.

CANADA RESIDENTS Passport applications are available at travel agencies throughout Canada or from **Passport Canada** (© 800/567-6868; www.ppt.gc.ca).

U.K. RESIDENTS You can pick up an application for a standard 10-year passport (5-year passport for children under 16) at passport offices, major post offices, or WorldChoice travel agencies. Residents of the U.K. can also download an application from the website of the **Home Office's Identity & Passport Service** (© 0870/521-0410; www.ukpa.gov.uk).

IRELAND RESIDENTS The Passport Express service is available from most offices of An Post and guarantees that passports will be issued within 10 working days. If you're in no rush, you can also apply through the regular mail. For more information, contact the **Department of Foreign Affairs** (© 353/1-4780822; http://foreign affairs.gov.ie).

AUSTRALIA RESIDENTS Australians residing in Australia can download an application form from the website of the **Australian Passport Information Service** (© 131-232; www.passports.gov.au) or pick up an application from your local post office or any branch of Passports Australia. Applications should be personally lodged at an Australia Post outlet, and an appointment may be necessary.

What to Do If You Lose Your Passport

If you lose your passport, notify the ship's purser. He or she will help you arrange a visit to the nearest consulate of your home country as soon as possible to have the passport replaced.

NEW ZEALAND RESIDENTS   You can pick up a passport application at any **New Zealand Passports Office** (© **0800/225-050;** www.passports.govt.nz) or download one from their website. Applications can be completed by mail.

TURNING OVER PASSPORTS TO THE CRUISE LINES

Your cruise line will check your passport before allowing you to board ship at the beginning of your cruise and may well hang on to it for the duration of your trip. This allows the line to facilitate clearance procedures quickly at each port. Your documents will be returned to you after the ship has departed the last foreign port of call, en route back to your home port.

VISAS

Your cruise line will advise you if any visas are needed for the countries you will visit (if in doubt, call the line or ask your travel agent). In most cases, a visa is not required if you are visiting a country for a limited amount of time (less than 24 hr.). If you are visiting **Russia,** you need a visa if you're planning to tour on your own, but usually not if you'll be touring exclusively by organized shore excursion.

If you do need a visa, be sure to apply well in advance of your trip. The easiest way to do so is through a **visa service;** your travel agent can guide you to one in your area and advise you regarding the service's fees. You can also apply by contacting the embassy of the country you'll be visiting.

2 Money Matters

Know how they say cruises are all-inclusive vacations? They're lying. True, the bulk of your vacation expense is covered in your fare, but there are plenty of extras. See "The Cost: What's Included & What's Not," in chapter 2, for a rundown on what will cost you extra. In this section, we'll examine the way monetary transactions are handled on board and in port.

ONBOARD CHARGE CARDS

Cruise ships operate on a cashless basis. Basically, this means you have a running tab and simply sign for what you buy on board during your cruise—bar drinks, meals at specialty restaurants, spa treatments, shore excursions, gift-shop purchases, and so on—then pay up at the end. Very convenient, yes—and also very, very easy to forget your limits and spend more than you intended to.

Shortly before or after embarkation, a purser or check-in clerk will take an imprint of your credit card and issue you an **onboard charge card,** which, on most ships, also serves as your room key and as your cruise ID, which you swipe through a scanner every time you leave or return to the ship. Some ships issue separate cards for these functions, or a card and an old-fashioned room key. Some ships that carry 100 or fewer passengers just ask for your cabin number for onboard purchases.

On some **European ships,** prices for onboard purchases and services will be listed in euros, or in pounds sterling for British ships. Be sure you know the conversion rates. We've included a chart in chapter 10 showing relative values of the major European currencies at press time. For more current conversions, see **www.xe.com.**

On the last night of your cruise, an **itemized account** of all you've charged will be slipped beneath your cabin door. If you agree with the charges, they'll automatically be billed to your credit card. If you'd rather pay in cash or if you dispute any charge, you'll need to stop by the office of the ship's cashier or purser. There may be a long line, so don't go if you don't have to.

At the end of your cruise, you'll probably be **tipping** your cabin steward, waiter, and several other people on the staff. Many lines these days are either automatically adding a suggested gratuity to your end-of-cruise bill or offering passengers the option of charging gratuities. Where this is not the case, you should reserve some cash so that you won't feel like Scrooge at the end of your cruise. See "Tipping, Customs & Other End-of-Cruise Concerns," later in this chapter, for more on this subject. The "Service" section of each cruise line review in chapters 6 through 8 details how the individual lines handle gratuities.

BRINGING CASH ASHORE

The cashless system works just fine on board, but remember, you'll need cash in port. Many people get so used to not carrying their wallets aboard ship that they get off in port and find themselves without any money in their pockets—a minor annoyance if your ship is docked and it just means trudging back aboard for cash, but a major annoyance if it's anchored offshore and you have to spend an hour ferrying back and forth by tender.

Most restaurants, shops, and hotels in Europe accept major **credit cards** such as MasterCard and Visa, American Express, and Diners Club (but not Discover). However, we recommend also keeping some cash on hand, ideally in small denominations, to cover the cost of taxi rides, tips for tour leaders, or purchases you make from small shops, markets, and street vendors. Information on local currency is included in chapters 10 through 12.

ATMS & CURRENCY EXCHANGE

These days, even the term *exchange* has been rendered a bit meaningless by the advent of **ATMs** hooked into international networks. ATMs are easy to find in all the ports covered in this guide and are by far the easiest way to secure local currency. They're also generally the cheapest way to get cash. Currency exchange booths take a huge commission or give an unfavorable rate, or both, so even if your bank charges a higher rate for international withdrawals, you'll probably still save.

⌐Tips Dear Visa: I'm Off to Europe . . .

Some credit card companies recommend that you notify them when you're going abroad so they won't become suspicious of unusual charges and block you from making more. Even if you don't call in advance, you can always call the card's emergency number (noted on the back of your card) if a charge is refused. In general, it's wise to carry more than one card with you on your trip; a card might not work for any number of reasons, so having a backup is the smart way to go.

Vaccinations & Travel Advisories

You're unlikely to come into contact with any bizarre diseases in Europe, but if you're the supercautious type you might want to check the website of the U.S. **Centers for Disease Control and Prevention (www.cdc.gov)** for vaccination advisories. If you need other things to worry about, skip over to the **U.S. State Department** website **(http://travel.state.gov)** and click on "Travel Warnings."

Check the back of your bank card to see which ATM network you belong to. The **Cirrus** (© 800/424-7787; www.mastercard.com) and **PLUS** (© 800/843-7587; www.visa.com) networks span the globe. If your card is part of another network, call or check online for ATM locations at your destinations. Be sure you know your **personal identification number (PIN)** before you leave home, and be sure to find out your daily withdrawal limit before you depart. *Note:* You may need a **four-digit PIN**—many European ATMs don't recognize six-digit numbers.

You can also often get a **cash advance** through your Visa or MasterCard, either from a bank or through an ATM, provided you know your PIN. If you've forgotten yours, or didn't know you had one, call the number on the back of your credit card well before your trip and ask the bank to send it to you. Some will provide the number over the phone if you tell them your mother's maiden name or other personal information.

TRAVELER'S CHECKS

Traveler's checks used to be the best alternative to traveling with large amounts of cash, but these days they've been all but outmoded by 24-hour ATMs, and some vendors are no longer accepting them, especially in small towns. If you have a nostalgic streak, you can still get traveler's checks at almost any bank, most commonly through American Express, Visa, and MasterCard. All charge service fees of between 1% and 4%. Many cruise lines will cash traveler's checks at the purser's desk. Some will also cash **personal checks** of up to about $200 or $250.

IF YOUR CREDIT CARDS ARE LOST OR STOLEN

If your credit cards are lost or stolen, immediately call your credit card issuers' **emergency numbers** to cancel the cards and request emergency services such as a cash advance or rush delivery of a replacement card. Before you travel, write down the emergency numbers listed on the back of each of your credit cards, then store the list (along with the matching card numbers) in a separate place from your cards. You can also make a collect (reverse charges) call to the following emergency numbers: **Visa** (© 1-410/581-9994), **MasterCard** (© 1-636/722-7111), **American Express** (© 1-336/393-1111), and **Diners Club** (© 1-303/799-1504).

VALUE-ADDED TAX (VAT)

All European countries charge a value-added tax (VAT) of 15% to 25% on goods and services, which is already included in the price you see. Rates vary from country to country. Citizens of non-E.U. countries can get back most of the tax on purchases (but not on services) if you spend a designated amount in a single store (usually $50–$200).

Regulations vary by country (you should check when you get there or with your ship's purser), but generally you can collect your refund for goods purchased in any

E.U. country at the airport as you leave Europe, or have it mailed to you. To do this, you will be required to have forms and receipts from the store where your purchases were made (make sure to ask for the forms), and you may be required to show the items purchased to a VAT official at the airport. Allow an extra 30 minutes at the airport to get through the process.

3 Keeping in Touch While at Sea

Some people take a cruise to get away from it all, but others are communication addicts. For them, today's mainstream and luxury vessels (and some small ships) offer a spectrum of ways to keep in touch.

CELLPHONES & SAT PHONES

Over the past 3 years, more and more cruise ships have been wired with technology that enables cellphone users to make and receive calls aboard ship, even when far out at sea. **Costa Cruises** was the first to introduce it, in late 2003 (with service going fleetwide in 2006), and now **Royal Caribbean, NCL, Celebrity, Carnival, Holland America,** and **Oceania** offer service aboard all of their Europe-based ships. **MSC Cruises** offers service aboard *Lirica, Opera, Musica,* and *Orchestra.* Among the luxury lines, cell service is available aboard **Silversea, Seabourn, Crystal,** and **Regent Seven Seas.** Among the small/sailing-ship lines, only **Windstar** offers any cellular connectivity, aboard its 308-passenger *Wind Surf* only.

Holdouts against the cellphone tide include Cunard, Princess, SeaDream, and almost all the small-ship lines.

The service is turned on once a ship sails beyond the range of shore-side towers, typically at about 12 miles. Calls are billed through your regular carrier according to its usual roaming rates, which can vary depending on your provider and sometimes on where in the world you're calling from. Rates can range from a few dollars a minute up to an outrageous $8—not so far off the average $8 or $9 per minute (and sometimes up to $15 a minute) cruise lines typically charge for **in-cabin satellite-phone service.** Text messages from cellphones and e-mails sent from PDAs are more affordable, sometimes costing only a few cents, making them a great idea for couples and families trying to find each other aboard very large megaships.

Be aware that not all cellphones are supported by the ships' technology. Check with your service provider to find out if yours is. Also note that you should keep your phone turned off while on board unless you're expecting an important call; otherwise, you'll be charged for an incoming call even if you don't answer it.

In addition to cell service and in-cabin SAT phones, each ship has a **central phone number,** fax number, and e-mail address, which you'll sometimes find in the cruise line's brochure and usually in the documents you'll get with your tickets. Distribute these to family members or friends in case they have to contact you in an emergency. It also can't hurt to leave behind the numbers of the cruise line's headquarters and/or reservations department, both of whom will be able to put people in touch with you.

INTERNET & E-MAIL AT SEA

Aside from some of the small ships in chapters 8 and 9, pretty much every cruise ship has computers from which passengers can send and receive e-mail and browse the Internet. In many cases, their computer centers are decked out with state-of-the-art flatscreen monitors, plush chairs, coffee bars, and Web cams. They're usually open 'round the clock, and many offer basic classes for computer novices.

E-mail access is usually available through the Web via your Earthlink, AOL, Hotmail, Yahoo!, or other personal account, with charges calculated on a per-minute basis (usually 50¢–$1) or in prepurchased blocks (say, $40 for a 3- or 4-night cruise or $90 for a 7-night cruise).

Over the past several years, many ships have been set up with **Wireless Internet (Wi-Fi)** service, allowing passengers who travel with laptops to log on in several public areas and sometimes in cabins. Wi-Fi is available aboard Azamara, Carnival, Celebrity, Crystal, Cunard (*QM2* only), Holland America, Lindblad Expeditions, MSC, NCL, Oceania, Princess, Regent, Royal Caribbean, Seabourn, Silversea, and Windstar. A few ships—the small luxury ships of Seabourn and Silversea and the huge *Carnival Valor*—offer wireless access everywhere on board. To take advantage of this service, you must have a wireless card for your laptop, rent a card, or rent a laptop, then purchase minutes either on an as-used basis or in packages. Some ships also have cabins wired with **dataports,** allowing laptop users to log on in privacy.

KEEPING ON TOP OF THE NEWS

Most ships have CNN and sometimes other news stations as part of their regular TV lineup. Some ships also maintain the old tradition of reprinting headline news stories pulled off the wire and slipping them under passengers' doors each morning.

4 Packing

One of the great things about cruising is that even though you'll be visiting several countries (or at least several ports) on a typical weeklong itinerary, you won't be living out of your suitcase: You just check into your cabin on day one, put your clothes in the closet, and settle in. The destinations come to you. But what exactly do you need to pack? This section will get you started.

SHIPBOARD DRESS CODES (OR LACK THEREOF)

Ever since Norwegian Cruise Line started the casual trend back at the turn of the century, cruise lines have been toning down or turning off their dress codes. During the day, no matter what the itinerary, you'll find T-shirts, polo shirts, and shorts or khakis predominating, plus casual dresses for women and sweat shirts or light sweaters to compensate for the air-conditioning. The vibe is about the same on the luxury lines, though those polos and khakis probably sport better labels. On the megaships, retractable glass roofs mean the pool scene keeps going strong no matter what the weather outside. So pack that **bathing suit,** as well as a cover-up and sandals if you want to go right from your deck chair to one of the restaurants or public rooms. If you plan on hitting the gym, don't forget sneakers and your **workout clothes.**

Evenings aboard ship used to be a lot more complicated, requiring passengers to pack for more situations than today's cruises demand. On most lines these days, **formal nights** have either melted away entirely or slid closer to what used to be considered semiformal. When Oceania Cruises started up in 2003, its dress code was set as "country club casual" every single night, on every voyage. NCL has also pretty much ditched formal nights completely, though its "optional formal" captain's cocktail night accommodates those who choose to dress up. Most other mainstream lines still have two traditional formal nights during any 7-night itinerary—usually the second and second-to-last nights of the cruise, the former for the captain's cocktail party. For these, men are encouraged to wear tuxedos or dark suits; women dress in cocktail dresses, sequined jackets, gowns, or other fancy attire. If you just hate dressing up,

Tuxedo Rentals

Despite the casual trend, there's usually a contingent of folks on board who like to get all decked out. If you don't own a tux or don't want to bother lugging one along, you can often arrange a rental through the cruise line or your travel agent for about $75 to $120 (the higher prices for packages with shirts and both black tux jacket and white dinner jacket). Shoes can be rented for an additional $10 to $12. In some cases, a rental offer arrives with your cruise tickets; if not, a call to your travel agent or the cruise line can facilitate a rental. If you choose this option, your suit will be waiting in your cabin when you arrive.

women can get away with a blouse and skirt or pants—and, of course, jewelry, scarves, and other accessories can dress up an otherwise nondescript outfit. (Most cabins have personal safes where you can keep your good jewelry when you're not wearing it.) Men can get away with a blue blazer and tie if they choose to. **Casual nights** (sometimes called "smart casual" or something similar) make up the rest of the week, though some lines still cling to an old distinction between full casual (decent pants, collared shirts, and maybe a sports jacket for men; dresses, skirts, or pantsuits for women) and semiformal (suits or sports jackets; stylish dresses or pantsuits). Suggested dress for the evening is usually printed in the ship's daily schedule. Cruise lines also describe their dress codes in their brochures and on their websites.

Most of the **ultraluxury lines** maintain the same ratio of formal, semiformal, and casual nights, with passengers tending to dress on the high end of all those categories. Tuxedos are very common. That said, even the luxe lines are relaxing their dress standards. Seabourn doesn't request ties for men anymore except on formal nights, and Windstar and SeaDream have a casual "no jackets required" policy every day, though dinners usually see some men in sports jackets and women in nice dresses.

Aboard all the **small-ship and sailing-ship lines** in chapter 8, it's very rare to see anything dressier than a sports jacket at any time, and those usually appear only for the captain's dinner. Most of these lines are 100% casual 100% of the time, with passengers sometimes changing into clean shirts, trousers, and dresses at dinner. Ditto for most of the **river-cruise ships** discussed in chapter 9, though some (such as Peter Deilmann Cruises) have a mix of smart-casual and formal evenings, with a jacket and tie suggested for men and a cocktail dress suggested for women.

DRESSING FOR YOUR DESTINATION

Obviously, what you pack will be determined by when you plan to travel and where (northern Europe and Scandinavia are cooler than the Mediterranean). Consult chapter 1 for average temperatures in the different European cruise destinations.

As a general rule, you are best off packing loose and comfortable cotton or other **lightweight fabrics.** Especially in the Mediterranean, pack a **swimsuit,** a sun hat, sunglasses, and plenty of sunscreen. If you're traveling in northern Europe, bring clothing you can layer. Comfortable **walking shoes** are a must, as many tours involve walking on cobblestones and other uneven surfaces. If you plan on hitting the gym, don't forget sneakers and your workout clothes. You might also want to consider a **light sweater** (for protecting against overactive air-conditioning on board, if nothing else) and a folding umbrella.

SUNDRIES

Like hotels, most ships' cabins come equipped with hair dryers and bathroom amenities such as soap, shampoo, conditioner, and lotion. If you bring your hair dryer, electric razor, curling iron, or laptop, you might want to bring a **plug adapter/voltage converter kit** because not all ships in Europe run on 110 volts. (The cruise line will let you know about the power situation on your ship.)

No need to pack a **beach towel,** as they're almost always supplied on board.

If you wear **glasses or contact lenses,** bring an extra pair. And remember to pack whatever **toiletries** you require, as you probably won't be able to find your preferred brands in Europe. If you forget to pack a personal effect or two, almost all ships offer items such as razor blades, toothbrushes, sunscreen, and film on board, though you'll pay a premium price.

Most ships have **laundry service** and some offer **dry-cleaning** service as well. A price list will be somewhere in your cabin. Some ships also offer **self-service laundry rooms** (see the "Service" sections of the cruise line reviews) so you can wash, dry, and iron your own clothes.

If you like reading but don't want to lug three or four hefty novels on board, there are options. Most ships of all sizes have **libraries** stocked with books and magazines, though the quality of the selection varies. Also, most ships stock **paperback bestsellers** in their shops.

LUGGAGE RESTRICTIONS & ADVICE

Keep in mind that most airlines restrict passenger luggage to two checked bags and one or two small carry-ons per person. Any more than that and you'll pay an extra fee. Ditto if your checked bags are above a certain weight (usually over 50 pounds apiece). Note that the rules in Europe are not always the same as in the U.S., so check ahead before you go.

Plan to bring a piece of **carry-on luggage** in which you should pack all valuables, prescription and over-the-counter medications, your passport, cruise documents and air tickets, your house and car keys, claim checks for airport parking, and any reading material you want. Here's some sage advice, too: Pack a **change of clothing.** If your luggage gets delayed in transit, you'll be happy you have it.

5 Sundry Shipboard Services & Facilities

RELIGIOUS SERVICES

Some ships, including those in the Costa fleet, have priests on board who lead Catholic Mass. Most ships have a nondenominational service on Sunday and a Friday-night Jewish Sabbath service, usually run by a passenger. On holidays, whether Jewish or Christian, clergy is typically aboard large ships to lead services in libraries or conference rooms, although some ships have chapels, and the *QE2* has its own synagogue.

MEDICAL CARE

Unless you're on a very small ship, your vessel will have a medical facility staffed by a doctor and a nurse, ready to handle medical emergencies that may arise at sea. Some facilities are quite elaborate. The *Grand Princess* and *Star Princess,* for instance, have high-tech medical equipment that, using cameras and a live video system, links the ships' medical team to doctors at Cedars-Sinai Medical Center in Los Angeles. (We've met doctors on ships as passengers, and even they were wowed by such facilities.) The

Tips Pitch & Roll: Dealing with Seasickness

Unless you're prone to seasickness, you don't need to worry if you're on a big ship (small ships can be bumpier). But if you get seasick, helpful medications include Dramamine, Bonine, and Marezine (although it's recommended that if you use these medications you not drink alcohol, as they can make you drowsy). All can be bought over the counter, and most ships have supplies available on board—the purser's office or medical center staff may even give them out free. Another option is the Transderm patch for seasickness, available by prescription only, which goes behind your ear and time-releases medication. The patch can be worn for up to 3 days but comes with a slew of side-effect warnings. Some people have had success curbing seasickness by using ginger capsules available at health-food stores or by wearing the acupressure wristbands available at most pharmacies.

medical center will typically be open during set office hours, with the medical team available on a 24-hour basis to deal with emergencies. (On some ships, the doctor can handle everything up to and including an appendectomy, but more typically, he or she dispenses seasickness shots and antibiotics, and treats sprained muscles.) If there is a major medical emergency, the passenger will be taken off the ship either at the nearest port or by helicopter.

If you have a chronic health problem, it's best to check with your doctor before booking your cruise; and if you have any specific needs, notify the cruise line in advance. This will ensure that the ship's medical team is properly prepared to meet your needs.

GETTING THE NEWS

Most newer ships offer **CNN International** on their in-room TVs, and nearly every ship will post the latest news from the wire services outside the purser's office. Some lines even excerpt information from leading newspapers and deliver daily printouts to your cabin.

STAYING IN TOUCH

In addition to the telephone in your cabin (which will cost you big bucks if you use it to call home), you may be able to send **faxes** home via your ship's business center. And most ships offer **e-mail.** In some cases, the ship has a real Internet cafe setup where you can go online. On the newest ships, there may even be wireless access in certain areas of the ship (usually a lounge area near the purser's office, for one). In other cases, however, you can set up a shipboard account, and while you are able to send and receive e-mail from that account, you can't actually get on the Internet. Standard fees for e-mail are 50¢ to $1.50 per minute. If you can find an Internet cafe at your ports of call, you'll definitely get a much cheaper rate, and a faster connection, too.

If the ship does offer e-mail, you can send your friends back home nifty **e-post-cards.** For those into more traditional modes of communication, the purser's office on your ship should have **postcards,** local stamps (U.S. stamps don't work in Europe), and a mailbox that is emptied at each port of call.

6 Tipping, Customs & Other End-of-Cruise Concerns

We know you don't want to hear about the end of your cruise before you've even gone, but it's best to be prepared. Here's a discussion of a few matters you'll have to take care of before heading home.

THE DEBARKATION TALK

On the last full day of your cruise, the cruise director will offer a debarkation talk covering areas such as tipping, settling your onboard account, packing, dealing with Customs and Immigration, and how the debarkation procedure will work. If you're a first-time cruiser or have specific questions, you may want to attend the talk. Otherwise, you might be able to catch a broadcast of the session on your in-room TV or find printed instructions in your daily bulletin. Some lines offer prize drawings to encourage your attendance at the session.

TIPPING

Most cruise lines pay their service staff low base wages with the understanding that the bulk of their income will come from tips. Each line has clear guidelines for gratuities, which are usually printed in their brochures and on their website, in your cruise documents, and in the daily schedule toward the end of your trip. The traditional way of tipping was to simply hand your waiter, assistant waiter, and cabin steward little envelopes full of cash, but these days most lines (Azamara, Carnival, Costa, Cunard, Holland America, MSC, NCL, Oceania, and Princess, to be exact) add an **automatic gratuity** (sometimes called a "service charge") to a passenger's onboard account—generally between $8.50 and $12 per person, per day, with the amount adjustable up or down if you request it at the purser's desk before the end of the cruise. Some other lines, such as Celebrity and Royal Caribbean, give you the option of paying cash directly to staff or adding the gratuities onto your account. Some small-ship lines pool the tips and divide them equitably among all crew. Ultraluxury lines Silversea, Seabourn, Sea-Dream, and Regent include tips in the cruise rates. Windstar promotes its "tipping not required" policy, but *required* is the operative word: Tipping really is expected.

Among lines that don't add an automatic charge, **suggested tipping amounts** vary slightly with the line and its degree of luxury, from about $8 to $14 total per passenger, per day, and half that for children. As a rule of thumb, each passenger (not each couple) should expect to tip at least $3.50 per day for his cabin steward, $3.50 for his dining room waiter, and about $2 for his assistant waiter, and sometimes 75¢ for his headwaiter. Some lines suggest you tip the maître d' about $5 per person for the week and slip another couple bucks to the chief housekeeper, but it's your choice. If you've never even met these people, don't bother. Guests staying in suites with butler service should also send $3.50 per day his way. A 15% gratuity is usually included on every **bar bill** to cover gratuities to bartenders and wine stewards. The captain and other professional officers definitely do not get tips. That'd be like tipping your doctor.

On lines that follow traditional person-to-person gratuity policies, tip your waiter and assistant waiter during the cruise's final dinner, and leave your cabin steward his or her tip on the final night or morning, just before you disembark. Tip **spa personnel** immediately after they work on you, but note that on some ships the spa will automatically add a tip to your account unless you indicate otherwise, so inquire before adding one yourself.

SETTLING UP

See "Money Matters" earlier in this chapter for information on settling your onboard bill.

DEBARKATION

It's a good idea to begin packing before dinner on your final night aboard. Be sure to fill out the **luggage tags** given to you and attach them securely to each piece. Most ships ask that you leave your luggage outside your cabin door by midnight or so, after which service staff will pick it up and spirit it away. Two points here: (1) First-time cruisers always worry about leaving their bags out in public, but we've never heard an instance of anything being stolen; (2) because ship's personnel have to get thousands of pieces of luggage into bins and off the ship, don't expect your luggage to be treated gently. Rather than packing bottles of duty-free liquor and other breakables, carry them off the ship yourself.

Once you debark, you'll find your bags waiting for you in the terminal, organized by the colored or numbered tags you attached. Attendants are standing by to help you, should your bag not be where it's supposed to be.

Ships normally arrive in port on the final day between 6 and 8am, and need at least 90 minutes to unload baggage and complete docking formalities. Debarkation rarely begins much before 9am, and sometimes it may be 10am before you're allowed to leave the ship, usually via debarkation numbers assigned based on flight times. (Not surprisingly, suite passengers get expedited debarkation.) Have breakfast. Have coffee. Have patience.

If you booked your air through the cruise line and are heading right home, you will collect your bags and proceed to the bus to the airport. Porters will be on hand if you need help with your luggage. If you booked air passage yourself, you're on your own to retrieve your bags and catch a cab to the airport or your next destination.

If you're on a post-cruise tour, you'll receive special instructions from the cruise line.

CLEARING CUSTOMS & IMMIGRATION

Make sure you allow enough time at your European airport to check in, collect any value-added-tax refunds owed you on the purchases you made (see "Money Matters" earlier in this chapter for more on the VAT), and clear Immigration.

When you return to your home country, you'll again have to show your passport at Immigration, collect your bags, and then clear Customs. At embarkation or while aboard the plane, you'll be handed a Customs form to fill out.

U.S. RESIDENTS   Returning U.S. citizens who have been away for at least 48 hours are allowed to bring back $800 worth of merchandise duty-free, with a flat rate charged for the next $1,000 worth of purchases. Any dollar amount beyond that is dutiable at whatever rates apply. There are also limits on the amount of alcoholic beverages (usually 1 liter), cigarettes (1 carton), cigars (100 total, and no Cubans), and other tobacco products you may include in your personal duty-free exemption. Be

---

Is the Earth Moving, or Is It Me?

When you get off the ship, and especially when you close your eyes, you might experience a rocking sensation, as if you're still on the water. Don't worry: It's perfectly normal and should go away within a day or so.

sure to have your receipts or purchases handy to expedite the declaration process. *Note:* If you owe duty, you are required to pay it upon your arrival in the United States, by either cash, personal check, government or traveler's check, money order or, in some locations, Visa or MasterCard.

Family members traveling together can fill out one **joint Customs declaration.** For instance, for a husband and wife with two children, the total duty-free exemption from most destinations would be $3,200.

With some exceptions, you cannot bring **fruits and vegetables** into the United States. For specifics on what you can bring back, download the invaluable free pamphlet *Know Before You Go* online at **www.cbp.gov/xp/cgov/travel/vacation/kbyg/**.

CANADA RESIDENTS   Canadians returning to the country after an absence of at least 1 week can bring back C$750 worth of goods duty-free. Alcohol and tobacco carry certain restrictions: You are allowed to import only 1.5 liters of wine *or* 1.14 liters of hard liquor, and you can bring back 200 cigarettes, 50 cigars or cigarillos, and 200 grams of manufactured tobacco. For a full summary of Canadian rules, download the booklet *I Declare* from the website of the **Canada Border Services Agency** (© **800/461-9999;** www.cbsa-asfc.gc.ca/publications/pub/bsf5056-eng.html).

U.K. RESIDENTS   Citizens of the U.K. returning from a European Union (E.U.) country go through a separate Customs exit for E.U. travelers. In essence, there is no limit on what you can bring back through this channel, as long as the items are for personal use and you have already paid the necessary duty and tax. If you bring back more than 3,200 cigarettes, 200 cigars, 400 cigarillos, 3 kilograms of smoking tobacco, 10 liters of spirits, 90 liters of wine, 20 liters of fortified wine (such as port or sherry), or 110 liters of beer, however, you may be asked to prove that the goods are for your own use. How would you prove that? We're not sure. In any case, you can get more details from **HM Customs & Excise** (© **0845/010-9000;** www.hmrc.gov.uk). U.K. citizens returning from non-E.U. countries may bring back £145 worth of goods and face lower duty-free allowances.

IRELAND RESIDENTS   No additional duty or tax is charged on goods purchased in another E.U. country, provided the goods are for your personal use and you've already paid duty and tax. "Personal use" is considered less than the following: 800 cigarettes, 400 cigarillos, 200 cigars, 1kg of tobacco, 10 liters of hard liquor, 90 liters of wine, 20 liters of fortified wine, and 110 liters of beer. More information can be obtained through the **Irish Tax and Customs** website (**www.revenue.ie**).

AUSTRALIA RESIDENTS   The duty-free allowance in **Australia** is A$900. Citizens can bring in 250 cigarettes or 250 grams of cigars or loose tobacco, and 2.25 liters of alcohol. For more information, check the *Know Before You Go* brochure available on the **Australian Customs Service** website at **www.customs.gov.au/webdata/ resources/files/GuideForTravellers.pdf**.

NEW ZEALAND RESIDENTS   The duty-free allowance for **New Zealand** is NZ$700. Citizens over 17 can bring in 200 cigarettes, 50 cigars, or 250 grams of tobacco, plus 4.5 liters of wine and beer, or 1.125 liters of liquor. For more information, contact **New Zealand Customs** (© **0800/428-786;** www.customs.govt.nz/ travellers/default.htm).

4

The Cruise Experience

Cruise ships evolved from ocean liners, which were once the only way of getting from point A to point B, assuming there was an ocean in between. This was often no easy matter, entailing a real journey, sometimes of several weeks and often in harsh weather. Competition quickly came down to two elements over which the shipping lines had some control: speed ("Get me off this damn ship as fast as possible") and comfort ("Don't rush on my account, I'm having a great time"). While the former was great for businessmen in a rush, the latter had more intriguing possibilities, and it wasn't long before ship owners began offering pleasure cruises around scenic parts of the world, lavishing their passengers with shipboard comforts between ports of call. And thus the cruise industry was born.

Today, though the cruise experience varies from ship to ship, the common denominator is choice, with nonstop entertainment and activities, multiple dining options, and opportunities to be as sociable or private and as active or lazy as you want to be. In the pages that follow, we'll give you a taste of the modern cruise life.

1 Airport Rigamarole, Flight Delays & Lost Luggage

If you're flying to Europe, be sure to confirm your flight before the trip, and make sure that you get to the airport 2 to 3 hours before your scheduled flight time. This will give you time to check in, make your way through security, and pick up anything you need for the long flight.

Make sure your bags are tagged properly with your name and contact information, and also with the **luggage tags** the cruise line sent.

You'll probably be arriving in Europe at least a day early, so **flight delays** shouldn't be a problem. If you're overnighting it, though, and it looks like a delay might affect your ability to get to your ship on time, inform an airline representative. He or she may be able to get you onto another flight. Also call the cruise line to advise the ship of your delay (there should be an emergency number in your cruise documents). Keep in mind that you may not be the only passenger delayed, and the line just might hold the ship until you arrive. If your ship does leave without you, you'll be flown or driven to the next port. If you booked your flights through the cruise line, you won't be charged for this service, but if you booked your flight on your own, you may have to pay.

If your luggage is lost or delayed, what happens depends on how soon your ship is leaving. If you're staying at a hotel overnight, the airline might drop your luggage off there. If your ship is departing sooner, they may be able to deliver it before departure, or they may have to send it on to your first port of call. Be sure to go to the ship's reception desk as soon as you board and inform them of the situation so their passenger-service staff can work with the airline for you.

If you have to do without for several days, cruise lines will generally help out, usually by providing overnight kits and sometimes with onboard credits to buy new clothing, plus free laundry service. Most travel insurance policies, whether bought through a cruise line or through a third party, will also cover the cost of gearing up in the event of lost luggage. If your cruise line does not provide a credit, seriously consider putting off any clothing purchases until you reach your first port of call, where items will likely cost much less than in the onboard shops.

2 Checking In, Boarding & Settling into Your Cabin

When you arrive at your destination airport, **uniformed attendants** will be waiting at baggage claim, holding signs bearing your cruise line's or ship's name and ready to direct you to buses bound for the terminal (or your hotel if you've booked a pre-cruise hotel stay). You probably already paid for these **transfers** when you bought your ticket. If not, you can arrange them now or take a taxi. If it's morning or early afternoon and your ship is leaving that day, don't feel rushed. Remember, another shipload of passengers is just getting off, and cabins still need to be cleaned, supplies loaded, and paperwork and Customs documents completed before you can board. Even if your ship has been berthed since 6am, new passengers are often not allowed on board until about 1pm, though lines are increasingly offering **preboarding**—which means you can get on at 11am or noon, have lunch, and start checking out the ship, though your cabin probably won't be ready until early afternoon.

When you arrive at the port, you'll find an army of **porters** to help transport your luggage into the terminal (at a cost of at least 1€ or US$2 per bag) and another army of cruise line employees waiting to direct you to the check-in desks. Once you're inside, your tagged luggage will be taken from you, scanned, and delivered to your cabin, sometimes arriving not long after you check in but more often showing up a few hours later. For this reason, it's a good idea to pack a small **essentials bag** you can carry on board with you, containing a change of clothes and maybe a swimsuit, plus sunglasses and any toiletries, medications, or other essentials you may need immediately.

Once in the terminal, you'll hand over your cruise tickets, show your **passport** (see "Passports & Visas," in chapter 3, for information), and give an imprint of your credit card to establish your **onboard account** (see "Money Matters," in chapter 3, for more on this). Depending on when you arrive and how large the crowd is, you may find yourself waiting in line for an hour or more, but usually it's less.

After you clear the check-in area, you will likely be corralled into posing for the **ship's photographer.** The prints sell for about $7 to $9 a pop and will be displayed later for your perusal at the ship's photography shop. You are under no obligation to buy them, and for that matter, you're under no obligation to pose. If you want to skip it, you can. As you actually step onto ship, though, there's another photo you can't avoid: the one for **shipboard security.** Once your photo is in their system, it'll come up on their monitors every time you swipe your cruise card to leave or reboard the ship, letting them make sure you are who you say you are.

Once on board, you may be guided to your **cabin** (you don't need to tip the person who leads you, though we usually give a couple bucks if he's carried our bags), but in many cases you'll have to find it on your own. Your **cabin steward** will probably stop by shortly to introduce him- or herself, inquire if the configuration of beds is appropriate (that is, whether you want separate twin beds or a pushed-together double), and give you his or her extension so you can call if you need anything. If your

Hey, Where's My Luggage?

If you've been aboard for a while but your bags still haven't been delivered to your cabin, don't panic. On big ships, where stewards must deliver some 4,000 or 5,000 bags, it can sometimes take a while. If you're hours into the sailing and getting concerned, though, don't hesitate to ask your cabin steward or call the guest-relations desk, as it's possible that your bag was delivered to the wrong place or the tag with your cabin number on it was lost.

steward doesn't put in an appearance, feel free to call housekeeping to request anything you need. The brochures and **daily programs** in your cabin will answer many questions you may have about the day's activities, the recommended dress for dinner that night, and the ship's safety procedures. There may also be a **deck plan** that will help you find your way around. If not, you can pick one up at the guest services desk—signs near the staircases and elevators should be able to guide you there.

Ships vary in terms of their in-cabin **electrical outlets,** with some using the North American style (twin flat prongs, 110 AC current), some the European (multiprong, 220 AC), and some both. Cruise line brochures and websites often give details on the situation aboard their ships, but if you're planning to bring a hair dryer, electric razor, curling iron, or other appliance, you should plan to bring a **plug adapter/voltage converter kit.** Some lines will also provide adapters on request.

Most ships have **in-cabin safes** for storing your valuables, usually operated via a self-set combination. On ships that don't offer them, you can usually check valuable items at the purser's desk.

A **lifeboat safety drill** will be held either just before or sometime soon after sailing, as required by maritime law. Attendance is mandatory, lifejackets are required, and the crew often takes roll. A notice on the back of your cabin door lists the procedures and indicates how to get to your assigned **lifeboat muster station.** You will be alerted as to the time of the drill in the daily program, in repeated public announcements, and probably by your steward as well. Your cabin should have been pre-stocked with enough life preservers for everyone in your party. If you are traveling with kids, there should be special jackets for them too. If not (or if anything else is amiss with your cabin), alert your cabin steward.

3 A Typical Day at Sea: Onboard Activities

In Europe, you'll probably want to spend most of your time exploring the ports (see chapter 10 for a discussion of joining shore excursions vs. going it on your own), but what are you going to do when you're aboard ship in the evenings and on days at sea? The answer: as much or as little as you like. The mainstream lines and the larger luxury ships offer an extensive schedule of activities throughout each day, listing them all in a **daily program** that's delivered to your cabin each evening, usually while you're at dinner. A cruise director and his or her staff are in charge of the festivities and do their best to make sure passengers are having a good time. As a general rule, the smaller the ship, the fewer the activities: The ultraluxury ships of Silversea, Seabourn, and SeaDream, and the midsize mainstream ships of lines such as Oceania and Azamara are intentionally low-key, while most of the small adventure and sailing-ship lines shun organized activities unless they involve the nature, culture, and history of their destinations.

ONBOARD LEARNING OPPORTUNITIES

For years, lists of shipboard classes read as if they'd been lifted straight out of the Eisenhower-era home-entertainment playbook: napkin folding, vegetable carving, scarf tying, and the like. Old habits die hard, so you'll still find these kinds of things aboard many ships, but in recent years the cruise lines have finally started catching up to the modern world. Today most mega- and midsize ships also offer **informal lectures** on topics from basic computer literacy to the arts. Many lines also feature cooking demonstrations, **wine-tasting seminars,** dance classes, and various health, fitness, and beauty clinics. Wine seminars usually cost $5 to $15, but the others are mostly free. In general, the ultraluxury lines have more refined and interesting enrichment programs, with **Crystal** and **Cunard** leading the pack.

ONBOARD GAMES

Vacations promote mental health by allowing people to do things they would never do at home—for instance, participate in **wacky poolside contests** on days at sea. Almost all the mainstream lines continue this tradition, in which passengers compete to see who can do the best belly-flop, who has the hairiest back, and so on. Often, volunteers are arranged into teams, as in the **team water-bottle relay,** where one person chugs a bottle of water, and (as Holland America's printed instructions for the sport advise) "puts it in their swimsuit." The other team members then use sponges to fill that bottle with ice water, which they have to get from a bucket on the other side of the deck. You get the idea.

Game shows, such as the classic **Newlywed/Not-So-Newlywed Game,** are also popular, as are trivia quizzes, passenger talent shows, and chess, checkers, bridge, and backgammon tournaments.

CASINOS & GAMES OF CHANCE

Almost every cruise ship has a **casino,** with the megaships offering scores of slot machines plus roulette, blackjack, poker, and craps tables. Luxury lines such as Regent and Seabourn have scaled-down versions. Stakes aboard most ships are relatively low, with maximum bets rarely exceeding $200. Average minimum bets at blackjack and poker tables are generally $5 or $10; the minimum at roulette is typically 50¢ or $1. Ships are free to offer gambling in international waters, but local laws almost always require onboard casinos to close down whenever a ship is in port. Most ships also have a **card room,** and many hold bridge tournaments. Another time-honored shipboard tradition is **horse racing,** a very goofy activity in which toy horses mounted on poles are moved around a track by hand, based on rolls of the dice.

ART AUCTIONS

You'll find shipboard art auctions either a fun way to buy pictures for your living room or an incredibly annoying and blatantly tacky way for the cruise lines to make more money by selling fantastically overpriced prints and animation cels to unsuspecting passengers—not that we're taking sides, of course. They're big business on mainstream and luxury lines, held a few times a week for an hour or two at a time. The one big plus about these auctions? **Free champagne,** and they'll keep bringing it to you whether you bid or not. Just look interested.

QUIET DIVERSIONS

For those seeking quieter times, there is always the option of planting yourself in a deck chair with a good book. Many ships have **libraries** stocked with classics, new titles, and books about the places you're visiting. Some ships (particularly the luxury lines) also have **DVD/video libraries** from which you can borrow for use in your cabin, and almost every ship offers both standard TV movies and **pay-per-view movies** on in-cabin TVs. Many ships also show recent-release films in the theater or in a dedicated cinema.

4 Keeping Fit: Gyms, Spas & Sports

Since the early 1990s, cruise lines have been making their spa and fitness areas bigger and more high-tech, moving them out of windowless corners of bottom decks and into prime top-deck positions with great views from floor-to-ceiling windows. The megaships pack the most punch, with well-equipped gyms; jogging tracks; outdoor volleyball, basketball, and paddle-tennis courts; and several pools in which you might even be able to swim some laps or do aqua-aerobics, if the kids will just stay out of your way. The most mega of the megas—Royal Caribbean's enormous Freedom- and Voyager-class ships—pack a bona fide ice-skating rink, an outdoor rock-climbing wall, an in-line skating track (on the Voyager ships), a surfing simulator (on the Freedoms), a full-size basketball court, miniature golf, and lots more.

In port, just about every line offers **golf excursions,** which bundle early debarkation, transportation, priority tee times, golf pro escort, cart rental, and greens fees into one excursion cost, with clubs and golf shoes available for demo, rental, or purchase if you don't want to lug your own.

ONBOARD GYMS

The well-equipped **fitness centers** on the megaships may feature 20 or more treadmills and just as many stationary bikes (many with virtual reality screens), step machines, upper- and lower-body machines, free weights, large aerobics rooms, and spinning and Pilates classes. Expect great gym facilities on Royal Caribbean's Freedom-, Radiance- and Voyager-class ships; Carnival's Conquest, Spirit, and Destiny classes; Princess's Grand and Coral class; all of NCL's modern megaships; Holland America's Vista-class ships; and Celebrity's Millennium-class ships. Working out on your own is free, as are many basic aerobics and stretching classes, but if you want to take a trendier class such as boxing, spinning, Pilates, yoga, or tai chi, it'll usually cost you $10 or more per class. **Personal training sessions** are usually also available for around $75 a pop.

Gyms on the few older ships remaining in the cruise market are generally smaller and more spartan, but you'll usually find at least a couple of treadmills, a stationary bike or step machine, and some free weights. On ships with limited or no gym facilities, aerobics and stretching classes may be held out on deck or in a lounge.

ONBOARD SPAS

For the past 15 years, spas have been big business on cruise ships, and have gotten progressively more amazing as the years have gone by. Most are perched on top decks and boast views from as many as 20 or so treatment rooms, where you can choose from dozens of massages, mud packs, facials, and even teeth whitening, acupuncture, and other esoteric treatments.

If you've taken a few cruises and noticed that the spas on different lines look suspiciously alike, that's because almost all of them (as well as the ships' hair salons) are staffed and operated by the London-based firm **Steiner Leisure.** The young, mostly female Steiner employees are professional and charming for the most part, but we've found that some are definitely more talented than others. Overall, **massages** are a pretty safe bet, whether you choose a standard full-body massage, a deep-tissue sports massage, or a hot-stone massage (in which the therapist rubs you down with heated river rocks and oil). Other treatments range from the pleasantly frivolous (mud wraps, electrode facials, and the like) to the suspiciously esoteric (such as Ionithermie slimming/detox treatments, which we suspect—and this is just our opinion, mind you—are just a load of hooey).

Here's a sampling of treatments and their standard Steiner rates:

- 25-minute Swedish massage: $60 to $75
- 50-minute full-body massage: $90 to $130
- 75-minute hot stone massage: $140 to $190
- 50-minute facial: $90 to $130
- Manicure: $25 to $45
- Pedicure: $40 to $65
- 40-minute teeth-whitening session: about $200

Note that rates for identical treatments can vary by as much as $20 or $30 from ship to ship, and even on a single ship, rates will vary depending on whether you get the treatment on a day at sea (more expensive) or a day in port (less). Treatments are charged to your onboard account. Usually they do not include a **gratuity,** but on a few lines Steiner does add them directly to your bill. Before you sign, ask your therapist or the desk attendant whether a tip is included, and write one in if it's not. Of course, if you were unhappy with your treatment, you're under no obligation to tip at all.

It's almost guaranteed that at the end of your session, just as you're coming out of a semiconscious trance, your Steiner therapist will give you an itemized list of expensive **creams, exfoliants, moisturizers, toners,** and **masks** that will help you get the spa effect at home—all for just a couple of hundred bucks. The products are often very good, but the sales pitch is just a little too shameless. So remember our mantra: *Just say no*—unless, of course, you're in a spending mood.

Tip: Make your spa appointments on the first day out to snag the best times.

5 Programs for Kids & Teens

It's a kid's world out there. Just take a look at the effort cruise lines put into creating children's amenities and services. They're on par with what's offered for adults. Cruise execs know that if the kiddos are happy, mom and dad will be, too (and will hopefully want to book more cruises). Dedicated playrooms, camplike counselors, computers, state-of-the-art video arcades, pools, and new teen centers have most kids so gaga for cruising, you'll have to drag them away kicking and screaming at the end of the week. Even if your kids are too young to join the programming (which typically starts at age 2 or 3), there are more options than ever. In this age of play dates, it's no surprise that a line, Royal Caribbean, has introduced daily 45-minute **playgroups** for infants, toddlers, and parents.

The youngest kids frolic in toy- and game-stocked **playrooms,** listen to stories, go on treasure hunts, and do arts and crafts; older kids keep busy with **computer games,** lip-sync competitions, pool games, volleyball, and even some educational activities focused on art, science, music, and exercise (though don't get the wrong idea—mostly it's all about meaningless fun). Video screens and TVs show movies or cartoons off and on the day, and, for the younger ones, there might be ball bins and plastic jungle gyms to crawl around in. Many megaships have shallow kiddie pools for diaper-trained tots; the best are sequestered on an isolated patch of deck.

The newest ships of the mainstream lines invite hard-to-please **teens** to hang out in their very own space, complete with a dance floor, bar (nonalcoholic, of course), video wall for movie watching, video arcade, and sometimes private Internet area. The best facilities are on the *Carnival Freedom* and *Splendour;* Royal Caribbean's Freedom, Voyager, and Radiance classes; *Norwegian Jade, Jewel,* and *Gem;* and the *Grand, Crown,* and *Emerald Princess.*

See "Cruises for Families" in chapter 1 for more details, including information on **babysitting.**

6 Onboard Dining Options

Perhaps nothing has changed the cruise experience as much as the evolution of dining. When we started covering ships more than a decade ago, pretty much every ship offered traditional five-course, assigned-seating dinners in formal dining rooms, plus an optional buffet for breakfast and lunch. Now it's a free-for-all, with numerous **casual dining options** that allow passengers not only to dress down, but also to dine with complete flexibility, choosing when, with whom, and where they want to eat, with several different restaurant options. In mid-2000, **Norwegian Cruise Line** got the ball rolling with its Freestyle Cruising arrangement, which allows passengers to dine anytime between 5:30pm and midnight in any of several venues, with the last seating at 10pm. **Oceania Cruises**'s much smaller ships operate on essentially the same system, as do most of the high-end lines, and both **Princess** and **Holland America** offer passengers the option of choosing flexible or traditional dining.

Formal or casual aside, the point is that cruise lines are willing to feed you till you pop, and these days are offering more and more cuisine options, too. On the megaships, you can get fairly elegant **multicourse meals** served in grand two- and three-story dining rooms; make reservations at an intimate specialty restaurant for Asian, Italian, French, Tex-Mex, Pacific Northwest, or Creole cuisine; drop in at the ship's buffet restaurant or cafe for an ultracasual meal; take in some **24-hour** pizza or other late-night option; and maybe have some **sushi** to top it all off. Carnival offers pizza, Caesar salad, and garlic rolls 24 hours a day, and many lines now deliver pizza to your cabin; and Royal Caribbean's Freedom- and Voyager-class ships have entire 1950s-style diners out on deck. The midsize and smaller ships generally have fewer choices. All but the most cost-conscious cruise lines will attempt to satisfy reasonable culinary requests, so if you follow a **special diet,** inform your line as early as possible, preferably when booking your cruise, and make sure they'll be able to satisfy your request at all three meals. **Vegetarian dishes** and a selection of **healthier, lighter meals** are available as a matter of course on just about every ship, but some of the small-ship lines need advance notice for any special requests. Most large ships will provide kosher and halal meals if requested in advance, but expect them to be prepackaged.

Traditional dinners are generally served from about 6:30 to 10pm. Some ships operate on an open-seating basis (come in, sit where there's room, eat) and others offer **assigned seatings,** usually with early and late dining hours. Elderly passengers and families with children tend to choose the **early seating** (served at around 6 or 6:30pm). If you choose **late seating** (served around 8 or 8:30pm), you won't have to rush through pre-dinner showering and dressing after an active day in port, and the meal tends to be more leisurely.

If you get assigned to the first seating and you want the second, or vice versa (or you get no assignment at all), see the maître d' staff, which will probably have a table set up in the dining room during embarkation for this purpose. Most can accommodate your wishes, if not on the first night of sailing, then on the second. Ditto if you find that you don't get along with your assigned tablemates. Most of the time you'll be seated at a table with 4 to 10 people. If you want privacy, you can request a table for two, but unless you're sailing aboard one of the smaller, more upscale ships, don't get your hopes up, as couples' tables are usually few and far between.

Seven-night cruises offering traditional dining generally have 2 **formal nights** per week, when the dress code in the main dining room may call for dark suits or tuxedos for men and cocktail dresses or fancy pantsuits for women. Other nights in the main dining rooms will probably be designated informal and/or casual. Ten- to 14-night cruises usually have 3 formal nights. (See "Packing," in chapter 3, for more information.) If you want to skip formality altogether, most ships offer casual dining in the buffet restaurant every evening and/or other casual alternative options (see below).

Though a few ships still offer early and late seatings for breakfast and lunch (served around 7 and 8:30am and noon and 1:30pm, respectively), most ships are now offering open-seating setups within certain hours.

Smoking is prohibited in virtually all ships' dining rooms.

SPECIALTY DINING

Variety + intimacy = specialty dining. Over the past several years, all the mainstream lines and most of the luxe lines have retooled their ships' layouts to make room for a greater number of small, alternative dining venues, where 100 or so guests can sample various international cuisines with sometimes elaborate presentations. Of course, you often have to pay for the treat, with most specialty restaurants charging between $10 and $30 per person, per meal (except on the luxury lines, where it's all included). Holland America and Celebrity, for instance, ask for $30 per person, while NCL's fees are $10 to $20 a head, and Princess is $15 or $20 a pop. Frankly, sometimes the food isn't any better than in the main dining rooms, but the venues are at least quieter and more intimate. The best, without a doubt, are on the Celebrity, Crystal, Silversea, and Regent ships. NCL also gets special mention for having so many of them—six on the line's newest ships, plus casual choices.

CASUAL DINING

If you'd rather skip the formality and hubbub of the main dining room, all but the tiniest ships serve breakfast, lunch, and dinner in a **casual, buffet-style restaurant.** Usually located on the Lido Deck, with indoor and outdoor poolside seating, these restaurants serve a spread of both hot and cold items. On the megaships, a grill may be nearby where, at lunchtime, you can get burgers, hot dogs, and often chicken and veggie burgers; sometimes you can find specialty stations offering taco fixings, deli sandwiches, or Chinese food, too. On most ships, breakfast and lunch buffets are generally served for a 3- to 4-hour period, so guests can stroll in and out whenever they want, but many of the mainstream lines also keep portions of their Lido cafes open almost 'round the clock. Most lines serve nightly buffet-style dinners here as well, with some offering a combination of sit-down service and buffet—dinner here is especially popular on European itineraries when people are often too tired after a long day of touring to bother with the regimented seating and dining times of the main restaurants.

BETWEEN-MEAL SNACKING

"Between-meal snacking" is the cruise industry's middle name. If you don't have a lot of self-control, consider yourself screwed. Options you'll find on the megaships include pizza, soft-serve ice cream, burgers and dogs from the poolside grill, afternoon tea, cookies and pastries from the buffet, and sometimes gourmet coffee and brand-name ice cream (the latter two at extra cost). The daily **midnight buffet,** a staple of old-time cruising, is now a rarity, though many ships still offer it once a week.

If you'd rather not leave your cabin, most ships offer **24-hour room service** from menus that vary from limited to lush. Passengers on luxury ships (and suite guests on all ships) can usually have the same meals being served in the dining room delivered to their rooms course by course.

7 Shopping Opportunities on Ship & Shore

Even the smallest ships have at least a small shop on board selling T-shirts, sweatshirts, and baseball caps bearing the cruise line logo. The big new megaships, though, are like minimalls, offering as many as 10 different stores selling items from toiletries and sundries to high-end china. All merchandise sold on board while a ship is at sea is **tax-free** (though you must declare them at Customs when returning to the U.S.); to maintain that tax-free status, the shops are closed whenever a ship is in port.

Part 2

The Cruise Lines & Their Ships

Detailed, in-depth reviews of all the cruise lines sailing in Europe, with discussions of the type of experiences they offer and the lowdown on all their ships.

5

The Ratings & How to Read Them

The following five chapters are the heart and soul of this book, our expert reviews and ratings of the cruise lines operating in the European market. This chapter is your instruction manual on how to use the reviews to compare the lines and find the one that's right for you.

1 Cruise Line Categories

To make your selection easier (and to make sure you're not comparing apples and oranges), we've divided the cruise lines into five categories, given each category a chapter of its own, and rated each line only in comparison with the other lines in its category (see more about this in "How to Read the Ratings," below). The categories are as follows:

THE MAINSTREAM LINES (chapter 6)   This category includes the most prominent players in the industry, the jack-of-all-trades lines with the biggest ships, carrying the most passengers, and providing the most diverse cruise experiences to suit many different tastes. While most of these lines cater primarily to Americans, a few (including megalines Costa and MSC, and smaller lines such as Swan Hellenic) cater primarily to Europeans and so offer a more international flavor.

THE ULTRALUXURY LINES (chapter 7)   These are the Dom Perignon of cruises, offering elegance and refinement, doting service, extraordinary dining, spacious cabins, and high-toned entertainment, all aboard intimate, finely appointed small and midsize vessels—and at a high price.

SMALL SHIPS, SAILING SHIPS & ADVENTURE CRUISES (chapter 8)   If the usual cruise experience just doesn't seem right for you, look here for sailing ships that recapture an earlier era; small, casual vessels that turn the cruise paradigm on its head; and tough expedition ships that take you off the beaten path, often up in Europe's northernmost reaches.

RIVER CRUISES (chapter 9)   These intimate barges and small river ships get you inland on Europe's rivers and canals, emphasizing the continent's culture, history, landscapes, and people.

2 Reading the Reviews & Ratings

Each cruise line's review begins with **The Line in a Nutshell** (a quick word about the line in general) and **The Experience,** which is just what it says: a short summation of the kind of cruise experience you can expect to have aboard that line, followed by a few major **pros and cons.** The **Ratings Table** judges the individual elements of the line's cruise experience compared with the other lines in the same category (see below for ratings details). The text that follows fleshes out these summations, providing all the details you need to get a feel for what kind of vacation the cruise line will give you.

The individual **ship reviews** give you details on each vessel's accommodations, facilities, amenities, comfort level, upkeep, and vital statistics—size, passenger capacity, year launched and most recently refurbished, number of cabins, number of crew, and so on—to help you compare. Size is described in terms of **gross register tons (GRT),** which is a measure not of actual weight, but of the interior space (or volume) used to produce revenue on a ship: 1 GRT equals 100 cubic feet of enclosed, revenue-generating space. By dividing the GRTs by the number of passengers aboard, we arrive at the **passenger/space ratio,** which gives you some idea of how much elbowroom you'll have on each ship. To compare the amount of personalized service you can expect, we've listed the **passenger/crew ratio,** which tells you approximately how many passengers each crewmember is expected to serve—though this doesn't literally mean a waiter for every two or three passengers, since "crew" includes everyone from officers to deckhands to shop clerks.

Note that when several vessels are members of a class—built on the same design, with usually only minor variations in decor and attractions—we've grouped them together into one **class review.**

HOW TO READ THE RATINGS

To make things easier on everyone, we've developed a simple ratings system based on the classic customer-satisfaction survey, rating both the cruise line as a whole and the individual ships as poor, fair, good, excellent, or outstanding on a number of important qualities. The **cruise line ratings** cover all the elements that are usually consistent from ship to ship within the line (overall enjoyability of the experience, dining, activities, children's program, entertainment, service, and value), while the **individual ship ratings** cover those things that vary from vessel to vessel—quality and size of the cabins and public spaces, comfort, appearance and upkeep, decor, number and quality of dining options, gyms/spas, and children's facilities—plus a rating for the overall enjoyment of the onboard experience. To provide an **overall score,** we've given each ship a star rating (for example, ★★★ ½) based on the combined total of our poor-to-outstanding ratings, translated into a 1-to-5 scale:

1	=	Poor	4	=	Excellent
2	=	Fair	5	=	Outstanding
3	=	Good			

In instances where a category doesn't apply to a particular ship (for example, some of the small-ship, expedition, and sailing-ship lines lack children's facilities), we've simply noted "not applicable" (N/A) and absented the category from the total combined score, as these unavailable amenities would be considered a deficiency only if you plan to travel with kids.

Now for a bit of philosophy: The cruise biz today offers a profusion of experiences so different that comparing all lines and ships by the same set of criteria would be like comparing an Irish cottage to a palace on Venice's Grand Canal. That's why we've used a **sliding scale,** rating lines and ships on a curve that compares them only with others in their category—mainstream with mainstream, luxe with luxe, and alternative

continued on p. 76

Ships at a Glance

Cruise Line	Ship	Frommer's Star Rating	Year Built
Azamara (mainstream): Offbeat itineraries aboard comfy, midsize vessels.	Azamara Journey	★★★★	2000
	Azamara Quest	★★★★	2000
Carnival (mainstream): Colorful, jumbo-size resort ships full of flamboyant fun.	Carnival Freedom	★★★★ ½	2007
	Carnival Liberty	★★★★ ½	2005
	Carnival Splendor	Not yet in service	2008
Celebrity (mainstream): Celebrity offers an elegant and refined cruise experience, yet one that's fun and active, and doesn't cost a bundle. Each ship is spacious, glamorous, and comfortable, mixing sleekly modern and Art Deco styles, and throwing in cutting-edge art collections, to boot.	Century	★★★★ ½	1995
	Constellation	★★★★★	2002
	Galaxy	★★★★ ½	1996
	Summit	★★★★★	2001
Costa (mainstream): Imagine a Carnival-style megaship hijacked by an Italian circus troupe: That's Costa. The words of the day are fun, festive, and international.	Costa Atlantica	★★★ ½	2000
	Costa Classica	★★★ ½	1991
	Costa Concordia	★★★★	2006
	Costa Europa	★★★ ½	1986
	Costa Fortuna	★★★★	2003
	Costa Magica	★★★★	2004
	Costa Marina	★★★ ½	1990
	Costa Mediterranea	★★★ ½	2003
	Costa Romantica	★★★ ½	1993
	Costa Serena	★★★★	2007
	Costa Victoria	★★★★	1996

Gross Tonnage	Passenger Capacity (Double Occupancy)	Passenger/Space Ratio	Passenger/Crew Ratio	Wheelchair Access	Sailing Regions	Full Review on Page
30,277	710	42.6	1.8 to 1	Yes	Mediterranean/Adriatic, Atlantic Europe, British Isles, Scandinavia/Russia, Norwegian Fjords, Egypt/Israel	83
30,277	710	42.6	1.8 to 1	Yes	Mediterranean/Adriatic, Greece/Turkey, Black Sea	83
110,000	2,974	37	2.5 to 1	Yes	Mediterranean/Greek Isles	94
110,000	2,974	37	2.5 to 1	Yes	Northern Europe, Mediterranean/Greek Isles (2009 only)	94
112,000	3,006	37.3	2.6 to 1	Yes	Northern Europe, Mediterranean/Greek Isles (2008 only)	94
70,606	1,750	40.3	2 to 1	Yes	Northern Europe/Russia, Scotland & Ireland, Arctic Norway, the Norwegian Fjords, Atlantic Europe, and the Mediterranean	107
91,000	1,950	46.7	2 to 1	Yes	Scotland & Ireland, Northern Europe/Russia	104
77,713	1,896	41	2 to 1	Yes	Mediterranean	107
91,000	1,950	46.7	2 to 1	Yes	Atlantic Europe, Mediterranean	104
85,000	2,112	40.2	2.3 to 1	Yes	Mediterranean, Northern Europe	120
52,926	1,302	40.6	2 to 1	Yes	Mediterranean	125
112,000	3,000	37.3	2.8 to 1	Yes	Mediterranean	115
53,872	1,494	36.1	2.4 to 1	Partial	Mediterranean	128
105,000	2,720	38.6	2.5 to 1	Yes	Mediterranean	118
105,000	2,720	38.6	2.5 to 1	Yes	Mediterranean	118
25,500	776	32.9	2 to 1	No	Mediterranean, Northern Europe/Russia, the Norwegian Fjords, Svalbard Archipelago, Atlantic Europe	127
85,000	2,112	40.2	2.3 to 1	Yes	Mediterranean, Northern Europe	120
54,000	1,350	40	2.1 to 1	Yes	Mediterranean	125
112,000	3,000	37.3	2.8 to 1	Yes	Mediterranean	115
75,000	1,928	39	2.4 to 1	Yes	Mediterranean, Northern Europe	123

continued

Ships at a Glance (continued)

Cruise Line	Ship	Frommer's Star Rating	Year Built
Crystal (luxury): Fine-tuned and fashionable, Crystal gives passengers pampering service and scrumptious cuisine aboard ships large enough to offer generous fitness, dining, and entertainment facilities.	Crystal Serenity	★★★★ ½	2003
	Crystal Symphony	★★★★ ½	1995
Cunard (luxury): A legendary line with a nearly legendary new vessel—the largest ocean liner in the world.	Queen Mary 2	★★★★★	2004
	Queen Victoria	Not yet in service	2007
easyCruise (small ship): Ultracasual, ultracheap.	easyCruise Life	Not yet in service	1981
	easyCruiseOne	★★★	1990
Holland America (mainstream): In business since 1873, Holland America has hung on to more of its seafaring history and tradition than any line today except Cunard. It offers a moderately priced and casual yet classic and refined cruise experience.	Eurodam	Not yet in service	2008
	Maasdam	★★★★	1993
	Noordam	★★★★	2006
	Prinsendam	★★★★ ½	1988
	Rotterdam	★★★★ ½	1997
	Zuiderdam	★★★★	2002
Hurtigruten (adventure): Hurtigruten is unlike any other cruise line in the world, in that it's not really a cruise line at all. Instead, its ships function as a mix of cruise vessel, ferry, and cargo carrier, sailing the entire gorgeous coast of Norway and calling at 35 villages, towns, and cities along the way.	Finnmarken	★★★ ½	2002
	Fram	★★★★	2007
	Kong Harald	★★★	1993
	Lofoten	Not rated	1964
	Midnatsol	★★★ ½	2003
	Nordkapp	★★★	1994
	Nordlys	★★★	1994
	Nordstjernen	Not rated	1960

Gross Tonnage	Passenger Capacity (Double Occupancy)	Passenger/Space Ratio	Passenger/Crew Ratio	Wheelchair Access	Sailing Regions	Full Review on Page
68,000	1,080	63	1.7 to 1	Yes	Mediterranean/Adriatic/ Greek Isles, Black Sea, Northern Europe, Turkey/ Egypt	210
51,044	940	54.3	1.7 to 1	Yes	Mediterranean, Northern Europe/Russia, British Isles	212
150,000	2,620	57.2	2.1 to 1	Yes	Transatlantic, Mediterranean	222
90,000	2,014	44.7	1.6 to 1	Yes	Mediterranean/Aegean/ Greek Isles, Northern Europe/Russia, Norwegian Fjords/North Cape, Black Sea, Egypt/Turkey	220
12,600	500	25.2	6.3 to 1	Yes	Greek Isles/Aegean	261
4,077	170	24	3.1 to 1	Partial	Greek Isles/Ionian Sea	261
86,000	1,850	46.5	2.3 to 1	Yes	Northern Europe/Russia, Norwegian Fjords/Scotland	135
55,451	1,266	44	2.1 to 1	Yes	Norway/Iceland/ Newfoundland	142
85,000	1,848	46	2.3 to 1	Yes	Mediterranean	136
37,845	790	47.9	1.7 to 1	Yes	Atlantic Europe, Northern Europe/Russia, British Isles, the Norwegian Fjords, Norway/Iceland/Greenland, Black Sea, Egypt/Israel	145
56,652	1,316	43	2.2 to 1	Yes	Mediterranean, Black Sea/ Egypt/Israel, Norwegian Fjords/North Cape/Scotland, Northern Europe/Russia	140
85,000	1,848	46	2.3 to 1	Yes	Mediterranean/Greek Isles	136
15,000	643	23.4	4.3 to 1	Yes	Norwegian fjords	267
12,700	318	38.7	4.2 to 1	Yes	Greenland	266
11,200	490	22.9	7 to 1	Yes	Norwegian fjords	268
2,661	171	15.6	4.3 to 1	No	Norwegian fjords	265
15,000	674	22.6	4.5 to 1	Yes	Norwegian fjords	267
11,386	490	23.2	7 to 1	Yes	Norwegian fjords	268
11,200	482	23.2	6.9 to 1	Yes	Norwegian fjords	268
2,568	164	15.7	4.1 to 1	No	Norwegian fjords	265

continued

Ships at a Glance (continued)

Cruise Line	Ship	Frommer's Star Rating	Year Built
Hurtigruten (continued)	**Polarlys**	★★★	1996
	Polar Star	Not rated	1969
	Richard With	★★★	1997
	Trollfjord	★★★ ½	2002
Lindblad Expeditions (sm. ship): One of the most adventure-oriented small-ship lines, with a serious nature focus.	**National Geographic Endeavour**	★★★ ½	1966
	National Geographic Explorer	Not yet in service	1982
MSC Cruises (mainstream): Based in Italy, MSC's all about "Italian style": Italian menus, lots of Italians (and other Europeans) on board, European-style enter-tainment, and a laid-back, nearly laissez-faire attitude.	**Armonia**	★★★ ½	2001
	Fantasia	Not yet in service	2008
	Lirica	★★★ ½	2003
	Melody	Not rated	1982
	Musica	★★★★	2006
	Opera	★★★ ½	2004
	Orchestra	★★★★	2007
	Poesia	★★★★	2008
	Rhapsody	Not rated	1977
	Sinfonia	★★★ ½	2002
	Splendida	Not yet in service	2009
Norwegian (mainstream): NCL is king of the mainstream center, with always-casual dining (and lots of it); bright, cheerful decor; and fun innovations like gourmet beer bars and onboard bowling alleys.	**Norwegian Gem**	★★★★★	2007
	Norwegian Jade	★★★★★	2006
	Norwegian Jewel	★★★★★	2005

Gross Tonnage	Passenger Capacity (Double Occupancy)	Passenger/Space Ratio	Passenger/Crew Ratio	Wheelchair Access	Sailing Regions	Full Review on Page
12,000	482	24.9	6.9 to 1	Yes	Norwegian fjords	268
3,500	100	35	Not available	No	Spitzbergen	264
11,205	490	22.9	7 to 1	Yes	Norwegian fjords	268
15,000	674	22.6	4.5 to 1	Yes	Norwegian fjords	267
3,312	110	30.1	2.9 to 1	No	Northern Europe/Russia, Atlantic Europe, British Isles	273
6,257	148	42.3	Not yet available	Partial	Not yet available	270
58,600	1,586	36.9	2.1 to 1	Yes	Mediterranean (plus Black Sea or Egypt), Northern Europe/Russia, Norwegian Fjords/North Cape	154
133,500	3,300	40.5	2.5 to 1	Yes	Mediterranean	151
58,600	1,586	36.9	2.1 to 1	Yes	Mediterranean, Northern Europe/Russia, Norwegian Fjords	154
35,143	1,064	33	2 to 1	No	Mediterranean	150
89,600	2,550	35.1	2.6 to 1	Yes	Mediterranean/Greek Isles	152
58,600	1,756	33.5	2.1 to 1	Yes	Mediterranean, Northern Europe/Russia, Norwegian Fjords	154
89,600	2,550	35.1	2.6 to 1	Yes	Mediterranean	152
89,600	2,550	35.1	2.6 to 1	Yes	Mediterranean	152
16,852	780	21.6	2.1 to 1	No	Mediterranean	150
58,600	1,586	36.9	2.1 to 1	Yes	Mediterranean	154
133,500	3,300	40.5	2.5 to 1	Yes	Not yet available	151
93,000	2,380	339	2 to 1	Yes	Mediterranean	161
92,100	2,466	37.3	2.4 to 1	Yes	Northern Europe	161
93,502	2,376	39.3	2 to 1	Yes	Mediterranean, Egypt/Greek Isles, Norwegian Fjords/North Cape, Northern Europe/British Isles	161

continued

Ships at a Glance (continued)

Cruise Line	Ship	Frommer's Star Rating	Year Built
Oceania (mainstream): Casual premium line, with great itineraries, service, and cuisine.	Insignia	★★★★	1998
	Nautica	★★★★	2000
	Regatta	★★★★	1998
Peter Deilmann Cruises (luxury): Sumptuous German ship, re-creating the old liner experience.	Deutschland	★★★★★	1998
Princess (mainstream): Princess offers a quality mainstream cruise experience with a nice balance of tradition and innovation, relaxation and excitement, casualness and glamour, all aboard a mostly megaship fleet.	Crown Princess	★★★★ ½	2006
	Emerald Princess	★★★★ ½	2007
	Grand Princess	★★★★ ½	1998
	Pacific Princess	★★★★	2002
	Royal Princess	★★★★	2001
	Sea Princess	★★★★	1998
Regent Seven Seas (luxury): Casually elegant and subtle line offering style, extreme comfort, and excellent cuisine.	Seven Seas Navigator	★★★★	1999
	Seven Seas Voyager	★★★★ ½	2003

Gross Tonnage	Passenger Capacity (Double Occupancy)	Passenger/Space Ratio	Passenger/Crew Ratio	Wheelchair Access	Sailing Regions	Full Review on Page
30,200	684	44	1.8 to 1	Yes	Mediterranean/Aegean, Greek Isles/Adriatic, Egypt/Israel	168
30,200	684	44	1.8 to 1	Yes	Mediterranean/Greek Isles/ Aegean, Black Sea, Egypt/ Israel	168
30,200	684	44	1.8 to 1	Yes	Mediterranean/Aegean/ Greek Isles, Northern Europe/Russia, Atlantic Europe	168
22,400	487	46	1.8 to 1	Yes	Mediterranean, Atlantic Europe, British Isles, North-ern Europe/Russia, Norwe-gian Fjords, Black Sea	226
113,000	3,080	36.7	2.6 to 1	Yes	Northern Europe/Russia	176
113,000	3,080	36.7	2.6 to 1	Yes	Mediterranean/Greek Isles	176
109,000	2,600	41.9	2.4 to 1	Yes	Mediterranean/Greek Isles, Atlantic Europe, British Isles, Norwegian Fjords/ North Cape, Iceland/ Norway/British Isles, Egypt/Aegean	176
30,277	670	45.2	1.8 to 1	Yes	Mediterranean, Holy Land, Crimean/Aegean	180
30,277	670	45.2	1.8 to 1	Yes	Northern Europe/Russia/ Atlantic Europe	180
77,000	1,950	39.5	2.2 to 1	Yes	Mediterranean, Northern Europe	182
33,000	490	67.3	1.5 to 1	Yes	Mediterranean/Adriatic/ Greek Isles, Atlantic Europe	233
46,000	700	65.7	1.6 to 1	Yes	Mediterranean/Adriatic/ Greek Isles/Egypt, Atlantic Europe, British Isles, North-ern Europe/Russia, Norwe-gian Fjords/North Cape	231

continued

Ships at a Glance (continued)

Cruise Line	Ship	Frommer's Star Rating	Year Built
Royal Caribbean (mainstream): Royal Caribbean offers some of the best-looking, best-designed, most activity-packed, and just plain fun megaships in the biz. Along with NCL, they're also out in the fore-front of innovation, always challeng-ing the status quo regarding what can and can't be done aboard ships.	Brilliance of the Seas	★★★★ ½	2002
	Independence of the Seas	★★★★ ½	2008
	Jewel of the Seas	★★★★ ½	2004
	Legend of the Seas	★★★ ½	1995
	Navigator of the Seas	★★★★ ½	2003
	Splendour of the Seas	★★★ ½	1996
	Voyager of the Seas	★★★★ ½	1999
Seabourn (luxury): Seabourn's ships are floating pleasure palaces, giving passengers doting service and some of the finest cuisine at sea.	Seabourn Legend	★★★★	1992
	Seabourn Odyssey	Not yet in service	2009
	Seabourn Pride	★★★★	1988
	Seabourn Spirit	★★★★	1989
Sea Cloud Cruises (sailing ships): Classic luxe.	Sea Cloud	★★★★★	1931
	Sea Cloud II	★★★★★	2001
SeaDream (luxury): An upscale yet casual line without the traditional regimentation.	SeaDream I	★★★★ ½	1984
	SeaDream II	★★★★ ½	1985
Silversea (luxury): Silversea caters to guests who won't settle for anything but the best, with free-flowing champagne and exceptional service.	Silver Cloud	★★★★★	1994
	Silver Whisper	★★★★★	2001

Gross Tonnage	Passenger Capacity (Double Occupancy)	Passenger/Space Ratio	Passenger/Crew Ratio	Wheelchair Access	Sailing Regions	Full Review on Page
90,090	2,100	42.9	2.5 to 1	Yes	Atlantic Europe, Mediterranean, Morocco/Canary Islands	196
160,000	3,634	44	2.7 to 1	Yes	Ireland, Canary Islands, Mediterranean	189
90,090	2,100	42.9	2.5 to 1	Yes	Northern Europe/Russia	196
74,137	1,804	41.1	2.5 to 1	Yes	Italy/Croatia, Mediterranean/Greek Isles	199
142,000	3,114	45.6	2.7 to 1	Yes	Mediterranean	192
69,130	1,804	38.3	2.5 to 1	Yes	Mediterranean, Greek Isles, Croatia/Greece, Greece/Turkey	199
142,000	3,114	45.6	2.7 to 1	Yes	Mediterranean	192
10,000	208	48	1.5 to 1	Yes	Mediterranean	241
32,000	450	71.1	Not yet available	Yes	Mediterranean/Black Sea (2009 only)	240
10,000	208	48	1.5 to 1	Yes	Mediterranean, Atlantic Europe, Northern Europe/Russia	241
10,000	208	48	1.5 to 1	Yes	Mediterranean/Black Sea	241
2,532	64	39.6	1 to 1	No	Mediterranean/Greek Isles/Aegean	275
3,849	94	40.9	1.6 to 1	No	English Channel, Northern Europe/Russia, Germany, Atlantic Europe, Mediterranean/Adriatic, Iberian Peninsula	275
4,260	110	38.7	1.2 to 1	No	Mediterranean/Adriatic/Greek Isles/Black Sea, Atlantic Europe	248
4,260	110	38.7	1.2 to 1	No	Mediterranean/Adriatic/Greek Isles, Atlantic Europe	248
16,800	296	56.8	1.4 to 1	Yes	Mediterranean/Greek Isles/Adriatic/Black Sea, Atlantic Europe, Northern Europe/Russia, Norwegian Fjords, British Isles, Atlantic Europe	257
28,258	382	74	1.3 to 1	Yes	Mediterranean/Greek Isles/Adriatic	255

continued

Ships at a Glance (continued)

Cruise Line	Ship	Frommer's Star Rating	Year Built
Silversea (continued)	**Silver Wind**	★★★★★	1994
Star Clippers (sailing ships): Classic clipper ships with all the amenities.	**Royal Clipper**	★★★★	2000
	Star Clipper	★★★ ½	1992
Swan Hellenic (mainstream): Classic British line.	**Minerva**	not rated	1996
Windstar (sailing ships): The no-jackets-required policy aboard Windstar sums up the line's casually elegant attitude. The ships feel like private yachts—they're down-to-earth, yet service and cuisine are first class.	**Wind Spirit**	★★★ ½	1988
	Wind Star	★★★ ½	1986
	Wind Surf	★★★★	1990

Gross Tonnage	Passenger Capacity (Double Occupancy)	Passenger/Space Ratio	Passenger/Crew Ratio	Wheelchair Access	Sailing Regions	Full Review on Page
16,927	296	57.2	1.4 to 1	Yes	Northern Europe/Russia, Norwegian Fjords/North Cape, British Isles, Atlantic Europe, Iberian Peninsula, Mediterranean/Greek Isles/Adriatic, Black Sea	257
5,000	227	22	2.2 to 1	No	Mediterranean	282
2,298	170	13.5	2.4 to 1	No	Mediterranean/Greek Isles/Adriatic	284
12,500	384	32.6	2.4 to 1	Yes	Norwegian Fjords/North Cape, Northern Europe/Russia, British Isles, Mediterranean, Sicily/Adriatic/Aegean/Black Sea	201
5,350	148	36	1.6 to 1	No	Mediterranean/Greek Isles	293
5,350	148	36	1.6 to 1	No	Mediterranean/Greek Isles/Adriatic	293
14,745	308	48	1.9 to 1	No	Mediterranean/Greek Isles	290

lines with alternative lines. Once you've determined what kind of experience is right for you, you can look for the best ships in that category based on your particular needs. For example, if you see in the "Small Ships, Sailing Ships & Adventure Cruises" chapter that Windstar achieves an "outstanding" rating for dining, that means that among the lines in that category/chapter, Windstar has the best cuisine. It may not be up to the level of, say, the ultraluxurious Silversea (it's not), but if you're looking for a sailing-ship cruise that also has terrific food, this line would be a great bet.

3 Evaluating & Comparing the Listed Cruise Prices

As we explain in detail in chapter 2, the cruise lines' brochure prices are almost always wildly inflated—they're the "sticker prices" cruise line execs would love to get in an ideal world. In reality, passengers typically pay anywhere from 10% to 50% less. Instead of publishing these inflated brochure rates, then, we've worked with Nashville's **Just Cruisin' Plus** (📞 **800/888-0922;** www.justcruisinplus.com) to provide you with samples of the **actual prices** customers were paying at press time. Other travel agencies and online sites will generally offer similar rates. Each ship review includes **per diem prices** (the total cruise price divided by the number of days) for the following three basic types of accommodations:

- Lowest-priced inside (without windows) cabin
- Lowest-priced outside (with windows) cabin
- Lowest-priced suite

Remember that cruise ships generally have several categories of cabins within each of these three basic divisions, all priced differently, and that the prices we've listed represent the *lowest* categories for inside and outside cabins and suites. Remember, too, that the prices we've listed are not applicable to all sailings and are meant as a guide only—the price you pay may be higher or even lower, depending on when you choose to travel, when you book, what specials the lines are offering, and a slew of other factors. Prices listed include **port charges** (the per-passenger fee ports charge for ships to dock) but do not include taxes.

See chapter 2, "Booking Your Cruise & Getting the Best Price," for more details on pricing.

4 Itineraries & Cruising Season

The "Ships at a Glance" chart in this chapter notes where each ship will be sailing during its 2008 season. At press time, exact itineraries were not yet available for 2009, but many ships are likely to repeat the same (or nearly the same) routes that we've listed. In chapters 6 though 8, the "Fleet Itineraries" tables go into more depth, listing the embarkation/debarkation ports frequented by each vessel. See the cruise lines' websites or a travel agent for full port listings and other details for each itinerary. Note that we have not listed itineraries outside the geographical range of this book.

As noted in chapter 1, nearly every ship in this book sails Europe during the same general season: roughly **April to November,** though some lines operate into December and a few (notably Costa and MSC Cruises in the Mediterranean and Hurtigruten in Norway) sail in Europe year-round.

6

The Mainstream Lines

These are the cruise lines you know—the ones that get on TV, jump up and down, and say, "*This* will be the vacation you've been looking for!" Maybe yes, maybe no. That depends on you.

Today's mainstream ships are part theme park, part shopping mall, part gym, and part faux downtown entertainment and dining district, all packaged in a sleek hull with an oceanview resort perched on top. The biggest are *really* big: 14 stories tall, 1,000 feet long, with cabin space for between 2,000 and 4,000 passengers plus a couple thousand crew. Most of the mainstream lines (but particularly the "Big Four": Carnival, Royal Caribbean, Princess, and Norwegian) have spent the past 10 years pumping billions into ever-newer, bigger, and fancier ships, and the intense competition means they're constantly trying to outdo each other with entertainment and activities. The newer the ship, the more whoopee you can expect: ice-skating rinks, bowling alleys, water parks, on-deck movie theaters, pottery studios, surfing machines, giant spas, rock-climbing walls, full-size basketball courts, and virtual-reality golf, plus classics like hot tubs, theaters, water slides, and bars, bars, bars. The action is just outside your cabin door, though if you crave some downtime, there's

Frommer's Ratings at a Glance: The Mainstream Lines

1 = poor   2 = fair   3 = good   4 = excellent   5 = outstanding

Cruise Line	Enjoyment Factor	Dining	Activities	Children's Program	Entertainment	Service	Worth the Money
Azamara	5	4	4	N/A	4	5	5
Carnival	4	3	3	4	3	3	4
Celebrity	5	4	4	3	3	5	5
Costa	3	2	4	2	3	2	3
Holland America	4	4	3	2	4	5	5
MSC Cruises	3	3	2	3	3	2	4
Norwegian	5	4	4	4	4	4	5
Oceania	4	4	2	N/A	3	4	4
Princess	4	4	4	4	4	4	4
Royal Caribbean	5	4	5	4	4	4	5

Note: Cruise lines have been graded on a curve that compares them only with the other mainstream lines. See "How to Read the Ratings," in chapter 5, for a detailed explanation of the ratings methodology.

always your private balcony or some quiet lounge that's deserted while everybody else is at the pool.

The more elegant and refined of the lines are sometimes referred to as **premium,** a notch up in the sophistication department from others that are described as **mass-market.** Quality-wise, they're all more similar than they are different, especially in regard to dining and entertainment. Ditto for lines such as Oceania and Azamara, whose midsize ships are almost throwbacks to the days before supersizing, but still offer well-rounded cruises for a fairly diverse mix of passengers.

DRESS CODES   For the most part, just about anything goes. Norwegian Cruise Line was the first to completely do away with "mandatory" formal nights earlier this decade, and many of the other mainstream lines have followed. Aside from Azamara and Oceania (which are all casual, all the time), the rest of the lines in this chapter still have one or two formal (or "formal optional") nights a week, with the remaining nights designated as semiformal and casual. Most ships also have at least one casual dining venue open every night, in case you just can't face dressing up. (See chapter 3 for more on dress codes.)

1 Azamara Cruises

1050 Caribbean Way, Miami, FL 33132. ℂ 877/999-9553. www.azamaracruises.com.

THE LINE IN A NUTSHELL   Launched in mid-2007, Azamara Cruises is a more high-end, adult-oriented, and exploratory sub-brand of Celebrity Cruises, offering more out-of-the-way itineraries, better service and cuisine, more enrichment opportunities, and lots of little extras that make the experience superspecial. The line's two ships are midsize gems that were originally built for now-defunct Renaissance Cruises.

THE EXPERIENCE   The idea behind Azamara is pretty much the same idea that animates all the other former Renaissance vessels, whoever they sail for: smaller, more intimate ships sailing longer itineraries, visiting out-of-the-ordinary ports, and offering a casual yet country-clubbish experience, with great service. That's not to call Azamara a copycat, though. Fact is, there are only so many different kinds of cruise experiences you can offer, and this is the kind that these ships were made for. In an age dominated by bigger and bigger megaships, we welcome the return of midsize vessels with open arms and are happy that another mainstream line is putting the resources into keeping this kind of cruise option alive.

Overall (and like Oceania), Azamara offers an experience that straddles the mainstream and luxe segments of the cruise biz—somewhere between Celebrity and Crystal or Regent. On the pool deck, a quiet jazz trio replaces the usual, loud pop/reggae band found on most mainstream ships, and in the cafe you'll often find a harpist plucking out traditional and classical tunes, spiced with pop standards. Service is exceptional, from the butlers who attend to all cabins to little touches such as the cold towels offered at the gangway after a hot day in port. At dinner, things are entirely flexible—just show up when you like, either at the main restaurant, at two reservations-only alternatives, or at a casual but still waiter-serviced option in the buffet restaurant. Onboard activities run from the usual (bingo, napkin folding, team trivia) to the unusual, including poetry reading/writing get-togethers and seminars on the Afrikaans language. At night you can take in a floor show at the theater, catch a performance by a guest magician or comedian, do the karaoke thing, catch a late-night movie, or take in music in several of the public rooms.

Pros

- **Perfect-size ships:** *Azamara Journey* and *Azamara Quest* are the perfect-size ships—large enough to keep things interesting over a long itinerary, but small enough to be cozy, comfortable, and easy to get around.
- **Long, interesting itineraries:** On their 10- to 16-night European itineraries, Azamara's ships mix visits to popular ports with stops at less-visited spots such as Bilbao (Spain), Bordeaux (France), Bari (Italy), and St. Peter Port (Channel Islands, U.K.).
- **Interesting & unusual grace notes:** At breakfast, passengers can get fresh fruit or vegetable juice or a smoothie at a bar in the buffet. At the pool grill, there are hot pretzels available all day. Public areas are dotted with ornate fresh flower displays. In the public bathrooms, real rolled towels replace the cheesy paper kind. And when was the last time you went to a shipboard workshop on performing Shakespearean monologues?
- **Nonsmoking policy:** Smoking is permitted only in one corner of the pool deck and one corner of the nightclub. (Of course, this is a "con" for smokers.)

Cons

- **Crowded pool deck on sunny days:** On warm sea days, the smallish pool deck can get packed to the gills. Compensating factor? The wonderful, thickly cushioned wooden deck chairs.
- **No children's program:** The lack of any kind of kids' programs or playrooms discourages families from bringing kids on board—which may be the point, actually.

AZAMARA: MICRO CHIC

When Renaissance Cruises folded in 2001, its beautiful fleet of eight identical and almost brand-new midsize ships was disbursed to the four winds. Oceania got two (and later three), Princess got two (and later three), and two ended up being operated by Spain's Pullmantur S.A., that country's largest cruise line. In late 2006, **Celebrity Cruises'** parent company, Royal Caribbean, purchased Pullmantur and soon pulled the old switcheroo, sending Celebrity's elderly *Zenith* to Spain and claiming the two ex-Renaissance ships in her place. Celebrity initially announced plans to fold the ships into its regular fleet but then opted instead to create an entirely new cruise line around them, dedicated to longer, more exotic itineraries, taking in ports not frequented by the vast majority of mainstream ships. And thus was born Azamara Cruises.

When we sailed, during *Azamara Journey*'s inaugural season, it was clear that the "Azamara experience" was still in a bit of a puppy stage—on the path to looking like its adult self, but still a tiny bit awkward. As one company executive told us, "We put

Compared with the other mainstream lines, here's how Azamara rates:

	Poor	Fair	Good	Excellent	Outstanding
Enjoyment Factor					✓
Dining				✓	
Activities				✓	
Children's Program	N/A				
Entertainment				✓	
Service					✓
Worth the Money					✓

the line together in about two months . . . . You don't even introduce a new candy bar in that short a time." All in all, they did a great job, but we'd bet money that things change for the better as things progress and that many of the very Celebrity-esque elements of the onboard experience take on their own distinct Azamara flavor.

As **Azamara Quest** had not yet debuted at press time, this review describes sister-ship *Journey* only, unless otherwise stated.

PASSENGER PROFILE
Though we have only Azamara's first few months of business on which to base an assessment of its typical passengers, we can project the following: The line will likely draw from the typical cruise demographic, roughly **ages 45 and up.** The relatively long and unusual itineraries and the quiet onboard experience will probably appeal to a more cultured, accomplished crowd, while the higher-than-mass-market prices and the length of the itineraries will probably draw a large proportion of retirees. Based on Celebrity's typical sales patterns, we can predict about 60% to 80% of the line's passengers on European sailings will be American, with the remaining numbers hailing from Europe and elsewhere.

The lack of children's programming will limit the number of families with kids who book this line, while the **stringent smoking regulations** (the strictest in the mainstream and luxe categories, along with Oceania's) mean few smokers will book—and those who do will be *very* unhappy.

DINING
Dining on Azamara is a step up from Celebrity in both cuisine and presentation. Dining service—which is excellent on Celebrity—is at least as good here, and probably better. At mealtimes, passengers have full flexibility in terms of where, when, and with whom they dine. Dinner is available in four restaurants: one traditional, two specialty, and one casual.

TRADITIONAL   The main dining room aboard each ship is a one-level space with tables for 2, 4, 6, 8, and 10, serving breakfast, lunch, and dinner, the latter within a 3½-hour window. Menus run to five courses, with passengers able to choose from among five appetizers, three soups, two salads, and five main courses. Appetizer selections may include dishes such as marinated and cured salmon in cucumber dill cream; beef, Gruyere, and caramelized onion turnover; wild mushroom and chicken quiche; and scallops with Thai curry sauce and coconut rice cake. Soups might include oven-roasted tomato and garlic soup with goat cheese crostini; Louisiana gumbo with andouille sausage and okra; and rustic cannellini bean soup with beef, basil, roasted tomato, and olive oil. For main courses, expect the likes of herb-crusted South African white fish with toasted quinoa; sesame seared yellow-fin tuna steak with tamarind stir-fried Asian vegetables; New York strip steak with roasted potatoes, green beans, and blue cheese butter; penne pasta tossed with four cheeses; and beef short ribs braised in red Burgundy wine with creamy polenta, carrots, and turnips. In addition, you can always choose from an assortment of classic favorites (grilled filet of salmon with herb butter, lemon-marinated roasted chicken, etc.). Unlike Celebrity, Azamara does not offer a dedicated **vegetarian** menu, though options are always available or can be made by request. (We had some wonderful vegetarian curries while aboard *Journey*.)

SPECIALTY   Each ship has two specialty, reservations-only restaurants. Passengers can dine here without charge once per cruise (twice per cruise for suite passengers) and are free to make as many additional reservations as they like, paying the regular per-person cost.

Prime C is a classic steakhouse with a hardwood floor and dark wall paneling, a chunky bar, a mix of modern art and classic Hollywood photos, and wraparound windows. The per-person cost is $25. Appetizers here include chilled jumbo shrimp cocktail, beef carpaccio, crispy popcorn rock shrimp, and lump crab cake. There's also a selection of soups and salads. Main courses run just like you'd figure, with a choice of steaks (16-oz. cowboy bone-in rib-eye, 12-oz. New York strip, 8-oz. filet mignon, or 8-oz. Kobe-style flat-iron), chops (double-cut Colorado lamb chop, 14-oz. veal chop, or 12-oz. Berkshire pork chop), and "other" (including oven-roasted sea bass, sesame grilled tuna, roasted organic chicken, surf 'n' turf, or seafood pappardelle). At the entrance to the restaurant, a raised table for 14 is set up in front of a glass-fronted wine locker and is used for **wine-appreciation seminars.**

Right next door, in the stern on Deck 10, **Aqualina** is a Mediterranean/American restaurant adorned with white faux pillars, a rich sea-blue carpet, and a bright, sunny vibe that contrasts sharply with Prime C's manly woodiness. Appetizers include pan-seared diver scallops and brie in crisp phyllo dough with candied pecans and cranberry compote. There's also a selection of soups and salads. Main courses include sautéed Chilean sea bass, rock lobster thermidor and lobster pot pie, and veal osso bucco with a butternut squash ragout. Passengers can choose to dine off the regular menu (at $20 per person) or choose the $50 **tasting menu,** which includes wine but does not include a gratuity for your servers.

CASUAL   Each ship offers a traditional buffet restaurant with seating inside or on a nice stern-facing outdoor deck. In the morning, the restaurant has all the standards (eggs, bacon and sausage, made-to-order omelets, Virginia ham, cheese blintzes, a fruit selection, breads, a cold cereal bar, etc.), plus two nice extra touches: a separate window for waffles and pancakes, and a **juice bar** where attendants will whip you up a fresh carrot-apple, tomato, or carrot-ginger juice (or whatever combination you like), or a fresh smoothie. This is a true rarity in the cruise market and a wonderful, healthful touch. At lunch, the buffet serves an adventurous spread of salads, meats, pastas, and other dishes.

At night, the buffet is transformed, with one section given over to **Breeza,** a casual restaurant where passengers can order from a fixed menu or, if they choose, wander over to the buffet for sushi, made-to-order pasta, and other options. Though technically entrance is by reservation, you can usually do walk-ins here. Guests sitting elsewhere in the restaurant are free to graze the buffet.

Out on deck, the **poolside grill** offers the usual burgers, hot dogs, veggie burgers, and pizza, plus fun oddities such as seafood-and-veggie shish kabobs, gyros, hot pretzels, and nachos. Toppings such as grilled onions and mushrooms are available for the burgers.

SNACKS & EXTRAS   On each ship, an **Italian-style coffee shop** offers specialized coffee drinks and fine teas at extra cost, plus a cart of free tea sandwiches, cookies, and desserts that's kept stocked from about 7am to 1am. A similar traditional **teatime** spread is put out daily between 4 and 5pm at the Michael's Club lounge/library/piano club. **Room service** is available 24 hours a day.

ACTIVITIES

A full roster of onboard activities identifies Azamara's roots in the mainstream, though the way it's spiced with truly unusual touches shows that the line is trying for more depth. At press time, though, they had a ways to go to catch up with lines such as Crystal and Cunard.

For those who like to stick to cruise ship tradition, there are pool games, team trivia contests, quizzes, darts and Ping-Pong tournaments, golf putting, shuffleboard, chess, bridge, bingo, spelling bees, pet lovers' get-togethers, and cheesy art auctions. There are also computer classes, digital photography seminars, golf clinics, and wine-appreciation seminars (some at extra cost), as well as culinary demonstrations, mixology clinics, and beauty and fitness clinics offered by the spa staff. For more unusual ways to spend a spare hour, check out the improvisational acting and Shakespearean monologue workshops, the poetry writing/reading get-togethers, and the introductions to the Afrikaans language. Both ships also offer relatively large **casinos.**

The ship's spa offers the usual array of massages, facials, manicures, pedicures, body-cleansing treatments, and wraps, as well as several expensive **spa packages** that bundle a number of treatments into a themed package. The "His Journey" package, for instance (which we assume will be called "His Quest" on *Quest*), combines a 55-minute deep-tissue sports massage with a 25-minute "Frangipani Hair & Scalp Conditioning Ritual" and a 55-minute "Pro-Collagen Grooming with Shave," the latter a mind-bogglingly wonderful succession of latherings, shaves, mild facial massages, and applications of fragrant goo. The individual elements of the package can be booked separately, and there appears to be no real savings in booking them by the package.

CHILDREN'S PROGRAM
None. These ships have no children's facilities or programs.

ENTERTAINMENT
Azamara offers a mixed bag of entertainment, with evenings in the show lounges rotating between musical production shows and guest comedians, magicians, and musical acts, and lounges offering quality musical acts.

During *Journey's* first season, **production shows** featured five singers/dancers backed up by a live band, with the musical selections tilted toward American standards. While production shows aren't necessarily our cup of tea, these get extra points for their intimacy (the ships' show lounges have no stage, so the performers are down at floor level, just steps from the audience), for the energy of their featured performers, and for their 100% live-ness, with no pre-recorded backing tracks or lip-synching involved. Other shows on our trip included an improv comedian, a Bermudian steel-pan player, a cabaret entertainer, and the very talented magician Carl Andrews, who's performed aboard Crystal, NCL, HAL, Princess, Regent, and Celebrity Cruises.

Azamara Fleet Itineraries

Ship	Sailing Regions	Home Ports
Azamara Journey	10- to 16-night voyages in the Mediterranean/Adriatic, Northern Europe/Russia, Atlantic Europe, the British Isles, the Norwegian Fjords, and Egypt/Israel	Barcelona, Venice, Copenhagen, Athens, Lisbon
Azamara Quest	14-night voyages in the Mediterranean/Adriatic/Greek Isles/Black Sea (various combinations)	Civitavecchia/Rome, Athens

Musicians perform daily in various parts of the ship. In the cafe, our cruise featured harpist/vocalist Jacqueline Dolan, who dazzled during 3 hour-long sets per day, mixing classical, traditional, and popular melodies. A pianist performed after hours, while one evening a five-piece jazz ensemble performed a set of standards and classic jazz tunes. On the pool deck, Azamara replaces the usual thumping dance band with a quiet, subtle guitar/bass/drums jazz trio. Around the ship, even the piped-in background music is of a higher quality than you hear aboard most ships, mixing jazz, standards, New Agey selections, a few pop songs, and the occasional novelty number to get your attention.

For those who like to entertain themselves, there's also **karaoke** some evenings, as well as dancing in the disco "till late."

SERVICE

Service is one of the high points at Azamara, as it is aboard parent line Celebrity. In cabins, butlers do the usual cabin steward job but also help with packing/unpacking, making restaurant and spa reservations, serving full en suite breakfasts, delivering daily canapes, shining shoes, etc. Service is unobtrusive but very personal when it does obtrude: butlers know your name from day one and will go out of their way to greet you in the corridors. Dining service is good in the main restaurant and excellent in the specialty restaurants.

Like Celebrity, Azamara handles **tipping** automatically, with each passenger billed $12.25 per day. As at other lines, a 15% tip is automatically added to all bar transactions.

There are no self-serve laundries, just regular send-out **laundry and dry cleaning.** Captain's Club members (those who have sailed with Celebrity before) get a booklet that, among other things, has a **coupon for bulk laundry service:** Fill up the large bag provided, and a wash/dry/fold will cost you only $15. (Available all but the last day of the cruise.)

Azamara Journey •
Azamara Quest

The Verdict

We wish more ships were like *Journey* and *Quest:* large enough to be interesting during long itineraries, but small enough to keep things cozy, comfortable, and convenient. These are some of our favorite mainstream cruise ships.

Azamara Journey *(photo: Azamara Cruises)*

Specifications

Size (in Tons)	30,277	Crew	390
Passengers (Double Occ.)	710	Passenger/Crew Ratio	1.8 to 1
Passenger/Space Ratio	42.6	Year Launched	2000
Total Cabins/Veranda Cabins	355/241	Last Refurbishment/Upgrade	2007

Frommer's Ratings (Scale of 1–5)

★★★★

Cabin Comfort & Amenities	4	Dining Options	4
Appearance & Upkeep	4	Gym, Spa & Sports Facilities	4
Public Comfort/Space	4.5	Children's Facilities	N/A
Decor	4	Enjoyment Factor	4

Journey and *Quest* are exactly the kind of cruise ships we love: small-scale, cozy, and traditionally decorated, with an onboard vibe that's all about passengers' personal interaction rather than eye-catching gimmicks. Like all the former Renaissance vessels, they're more boutique hotel than Vegas resort, with a decor that harkens back to the golden age of ocean liners, all warm, dark woods; rich fabrics; and clubby, intimate public areas. When they took over the ships, Celebrity put nearly $40 million into major refurbishments, moving the walls around on some cabin decks to create 32 new suites on each vessel; designing new specialty restaurants; expanding the spa; adding a cafe; and installing a new art collection, decking, carpets, paint schemes, bedding, cushions, drapes, table linens, and other soft goods. The result is a pair of lovely, practically new-looking ships, with only a few dents in cabins corridors (courtesy of luggage carts) betraying the fact that these ships have already been in service for the better part of a decade, under several owners.

As *Quest* hadn't yet joined the Azamara fleet as press time, this review describes *Journey* only, unless stated otherwise.

Cabins & Rates

Cabins	Per Diem From	Sq. Ft.	Fridge	Hair Dryer	Sitting Area	TV
Inside	$175	158	Yes	Yes	Yes	Yes
Outside	$210	170–175	Yes	Yes	Yes	Yes
Suite	$370	266–560	Yes	Yes	Yes	Yes

CABINS   Cabins on *Journey* and *Quest* are divided into just seven configurations: standard inside and oceanview cabins, deluxe oceanview (with veranda), "Sunset" veranda cabins (all facing the bow or stern), Sky Suites, Royal Suites, and Penthouse Suites.

Standard inside, oceanview, and oceanview balcony cabins are all almost identical in size and amenities. Each has a sitting area with a sofa bed and small table, a flatscreen TV that's awkwardly mounted flush to the wall (meaning you can watch only straight-on from the couch), a minifridge, and a writing desk. Closet space is only just adequate for the long itineraries these vessels sail, though an abundance of drawers and storage space under the bed help matters some. Bathrooms are on the small side, with a small shower stall and awkwardly angled toilet, and are stocked with Elemis bath products. Cabin decor is nicely understated, with off-white walls, wood-tone furnishings and headboard, and upholstery and carpeting done in easy-on-the-eyes blues and golds. More than half the accommodations on board are oceanview veranda cabins, which include a smallish 40-square-foot balcony.

Sky Suites add considerably to your elbow room with such amenities as a 60-square-foot balcony, bathroom tub, and DVD/CD player. Royal Suites and Penthouse Suites have separate bedrooms and living rooms, balconies that run between 105 and

233 square feet, master baths with a whirlpool tub and shower, a guest bathroom, and (Penthouses only) a dressing room with vanity.

Four cabins on each ship are wheelchair accessible.

PUBLIC AREAS   Public rooms on these ships are clustered on decks 5, 9, and 10. On Deck 5 forward, the Cabaret has space to seat about half the passengers on board. It has no raised stage so productions are, by definition, floor shows. Aside from the semicircular banquettes that divide the room's slightly elevated perimeter from the main floor, all seating is in comfortable chairs interspersed with cocktail tables. The best seat in the house is a high table at the center of the rear bar area, between and slightly behind the two spotlights. In addition to production shows, the room is used for late-night movies, bingo, and other activities. Moving toward midships, there's a relatively large casino with a big-screen TV in one corner for sports events; the ship's two understated retail shops; and the cafe, a warm, inviting space that offers snacks 18 hours a day, along with fancy, extra-charge coffee drinks and teas. A harpist and pianist perform here regularly throughout the day.

Deck 9 is primarily given over to the buffet restaurant, pool, and spa (see below), but tucked inside one corner are an Internet center and a small conference room.

On Deck 10 forward, the Looking Glass disco/observation lounge has wraparound floor-to-ceiling windows, a dance floor, and cocktail tables for two and four set in a large but still comfortably intimate space. Toward midships, Michael's Club is a combination library and piano lounge that maintains a generally quiet, gentlemen's club feel, with dark-wood bookcases and wall paneling, velvety couches, leather armchairs, oriental-patterned rugs, a chessboard, and a couple of globes showing the world that was. A faux fireplace, racing-dog ceramics, and a trompe l'oeil conservatory ceiling complete the picture. Afternoon tea is served here daily.

Note: Some public rooms on *Journey* (specifically, Michael's Club and the Cova Cafe) mimic those on Celebrity's ships, as the vessel was originally intended to join the Celebrity fleet. Word is, though, that *Quest* will have completely different, Azamara-specific public rooms when she debuts, and that *Journey* may be retrofitted later to match.

DINING OPTIONS   Dining in *Journey*'s and *Quest*'s main dining room is ideally a two-step process. First, you set a time to meet your friends at the clubby, wood-paneled Martini Bar, located just outside the maître d's station. Set below Sistine Chapel–esque ceiling murals there's a chunky semicircular bar, couches, and comfy armchairs, with a faux fireplace and curio cabinets separating it from the dining room itself. Next, get a table for dinner, preferably in the central portion of the room, where they seem to be more widely spaced than those along the periphery. Decor-wise, the room continues the ship's overall country-club feel, with Romanesque paintings, dark-wood paneling, decorative pillars, and understated upholstery. Tables are available for 2, 4, 6, 8, and 10 people.

At the stern on Deck 10, each ship's two specialty restaurants sit side by side, each with a stern view from its rearmost tables. Aqualina is decorated with a Mediterranean sensibility to match its menu, with a polished black tile floor and a color scheme that favors white and blue. Next door, Prime C is a thoroughgoing steakhouse. At the entrance, a wood-floored bar area is dominated by a high table for 14 at which wine-tasting seminars are given. On the walls, a modern painting of a Paris cafe scene mingles with black-and-white publicity shots of old-time Hollywood stars. Tables for four dominate the rest of the C-shaped restaurant, with fine views from practically every one.

On Deck 9, Windows Cafe is a standard buffet restaurant with a few nonstandard features. At breakfast, you can get freshly made carrot, apple, celery, or tomato juice, or a complicated smoothie from the "Health Nut" juice bar, and fresh pancakes and waffles from a dedicated window to the side of the buffet lines. At dinner, the space serves sushi and custom-made pasta dishes, along with a spread of favorites. Seating is available inside and out. On the pool deck, the grill spices up the usual burger-and-dogs menu with seafood shish kabobs, gyros, hot pretzels, and nachos.

POOL, FITNESS, SPA & SPORTS FACILITIES   The pool decks on these ships offer one smallish pool, two hot tubs, a small performance stage, and a bar, along with some of the best deck chairs we've ever seen—heavy, wooden, and dressed in thick navy-blue cushions with flip-back pillows. On the rear port side, a covered seating area offers double-width deck lounges for couples. On warm days at sea, the pool deck can get very crowded, but a little walking (not much—these are small ships) will net you much less crowded lounging spots on the Sun Deck, two levels up. There's also a lovely little half-moon of sunning space and a hot tub just forward of the gym and spa. Shade worshippers can head to the Promenade Deck, which is filled with those same great deck chairs but gets little traffic.

The gym, located just forward of the pool deck, offers treadmills, stationary bikes, elliptical trainers, dumbbells, weight machines, and a large aerobics floor. Though the space is not huge, it's adequate for the relatively small number of passengers on board. It got crowded only once during out last cruise. Pilates, spinning, stretch, abs, and yoga classes are offered throughout the cruise at no extra charge. Next door there's a beauty salon; a spa offering treatments in several pleasant rooms; and a separate suite offering acupuncture, laser hair removal, and microdermabrasion.

A corner of the pool deck has Ping-Pong tables, and shuffleboard and a small golf-putting green are available on the Sun Deck.

2 Carnival Cruise Lines

3655 NW 87th Ave., Miami, FL 33178-2428. ℂ **800/227-6482** or 305/599-2200. Fax 305/405-4855. www.carnival.com.

THE LINE IN A NUTSHELL   When you're hankering for an utterly unpretentious and totally laid-back cruise, Carnival's colorful, jumbo-size resort ships deliver plenty of bang for the buck. If you like the flash of Vegas and a party vibe, you'll love Carnival's brand of flamboyant fun.

THE EXPERIENCE   The everyman cruise, Carnival's got the most recognized name in the biz and serves up a very casual, down-to-earth, middle-American vacation, whether cruising the Med or the Caribbean. Food and service are pretty decent, considering the huge numbers served, and Carnival gets points for trying to offer a higher-quality vacation than in years past. Enhancements include partnering with Michelin three-star chef Georges Blanc to create a series of signature dishes for the dining rooms, switching from plastic to china in the buffet restaurants, and stocking cabins with thicker towels, duvet blankets, and more TV channels. The fleet has even gone wireless, offering Wi-Fi access throughout each ship.

On many ships in the fleet you'll find a sushi bar, supper club, wine bar, coffee bar, and great amenities for children. Like the frat boy who's graduated to a button-down shirt and an office job, Carnival has definitely moved up and on, to some extent. But like that reformed frat boy who stills like to meet his old pals for happy hour every week, Carnival hasn't lost touch with its past. Sure, the line's decor, like its clientele, has mellowed, to some degree, since its riotous, party-hearty beginnings, but each ship is still an exciting, bordering-on-nutty collage of textures, shapes, and images. Where else but on these floating play lands would you find a giant octopus-like chandelier with lights that change color, bar stools designed to look like baseball bats, or real oyster-shell wallpaper? The outrageousness of the decor is part of the fun. Evolved yes, dull no.

Pros

- **Fun, theme-park ambience:** The fanciful, sometimes wacko decor on these vessels is unmatched.
- **Large standard cabins:** At 185 square feet or larger, Carnival's standard inside and outside cabins are among the roomiest in the mainstream category.
- **Melting pot at sea:** You name 'em, they'll be on a Carnival cruise, from rowdy, pierced 20-something singles and honeymooners to *Leave It to Beaver* families with young kids, to grandparents along for the show.
- **An insomniac's delight:** When passengers on most ships are calling it a night, Carnival's guests are just getting busy with diversions such as midnight adult comedy shows, raging discos, and 24-hour pizza parlors.

Cons

- **You're never alone:** Not in the hot tubs, on shore excursions, in the pool, while sunbathing, at the gym, at the frozen-yogurt machine . . . unless, of course, you stay aboard in port when everyone else is off exploring.
- **No enrichment stuff:** Activities are pretty much confined to fun and games on the pool deck; no guest speakers lecturing on ports like most other mainstream lines offer.

CARNIVAL: BIG LINE, BIG FUN

Carnival has enjoyed an extended run as big cheese of the cruise world. The assets of its parent company, Carnival Corporation, are enormous and growing: In addition to its own fleet of 22 ships for its Carnival brand, Carnival Corp. holds full ownership of Cunard, Seabourn, Costa, and Holland America Line—all told, the company has a stake in 10 cruise brands in North America, Europe, and Australia. And in April 2003, Carnival beat out Royal Caribbean to acquire P&O Princess, adding yet another major cruise brand to its cruise dynasty. When all is said and done, Carnival Corp. operates a combined fleet of 82 ships, with another 17 scheduled for delivery through June 2011.

Compared with other mainstream lines, here's how Carnival rates:

	Poor	Fair	Good	Excellent	Outstanding
Enjoyment Factor				✓	
Dining			✓		
Activities			✓		
Children's Program				✓	
Entertainment			✓		
Service			✓		
Worth the Money				✓	

The origins of the Miami-based company were as precarious as they were accidental. Company patriarch Ted Arison, a somewhat reclusive billionaire who died in 1999, had sold an airfreight business in New York in 1966 and intended to retire to his native Israel to enjoy the fruits of his labor—after a few more little ventures. After he negotiated terms for chartering a ship, he assembled a group of paying passengers, then discovered that the ship's owner could no longer guarantee the vessel's availability. According to latter-day legend, a deal was hastily struck whereby Arison's passengers would be carried aboard a laid-up ship owned by Knut Kloster, a prominent Norwegian shipping magnate. The ship was brought to Miami from Europe, and the combination of Arison's marketing skill and Kloster's hardware created an all-new entity that, in 1966, became the corporate forerunner of Norwegian Cruise Line.

After a bitter parting of ways with Kloster, Carnival got its start in 1972 when Arison bought *Empress of Canada,* known for its formal and somewhat stuffy administration, and reconfigured it into Carnival's first ship, the anything-but-stuffy *Mardi Gras.* The brightly painted ship, carrying hundreds of travel agents, ran aground just off the coast of Miami on its first cruise. After a shaky start, Arison managed to pick up the pieces and create a company that, under the guidance of astute and tough-as-nails recently retired company president Bob Dickinson and chairman Micky Arison (Ted's son), eventually evolved into the most influential trendsetter in the cruise ship industry. The rest, as they say, is history.

Today Carnival's fleet includes two ships deployed in the Mediterranean; the rest stick mostly to the Caribbean and The Bahamas year-round. In spring 2008, a new class of ship will debut. Based on the Conquest ships, the 112,000-ton, 3,006-passenger *Carnival Splendor* will sport some new features, including a water park and the line's largest and most elaborate spa and kids' facilities to date. In fall 2009 and summer 2011, a pair of 130,000-ton ships named the *Carnival Dream* and *Carnival Magic,* respectively, will be introduced as Carnival's largest vessels so far.

PASSENGER PROFILE

A Carnival cruise is a huge melting pot—couples, singles, and families of all ages—though since the Europe cruises happen during the summer, the passenger mix automatically skews to more families. In July and August in Europe, there's a slightly more diverse nationality mix as well (the rest of the year, it's pretty much 95% North American). No matter what the itinerary, you'll be just as likely to meet a doctor on a Carnival ship as a truck driver. And no matter what their profession, you'll see people wearing everything from Ralph Lauren shirts and Gucci sunglasses to Harley-Davidson tank tops and eyebrow studs. At least half of all passengers are first-time cruisers. Although it's one of the best lines to choose if you're single, Carnival's ships certainly aren't overrun by singles—families and couples are definitely in the majority.

Regardless of their age, passengers tend to be young at heart, ready to party, and keyed up for nonstop fun and games. Many have visited the casinos of Las Vegas and Atlantic City, and the resorts of Cancún and Jamaica, and are no strangers to soaking in sardine-can hot tubs, sunbathing, hitting the piña coladas and beer before lunch, and dancing late into the night.

The typical Carnival passenger likes to dress casual, even at dinner, with sweat suits, jeans, and T-shirts just as prevalent as Dockers, sundresses, and Hush Puppies on all but formal nights—and even on formal nights, it's not uncommon for some passengers to run back to their cabins to change out of their dressier duds and put on shorts or jeans before heading out to the discos and bars. Tuxedos are in the minority here.

Carnival's Vacation Guarantee

Unhappy with your Carnival cruise? Dissatisfied guests may disembark at their first non-U.S. port of call and, subject to some restrictions, get a refund for the unused portion of their cruise and reimbursement for coach-class airfare back to their ship's home port. To qualify, passengers must inform the ship's purser before their first port of call.

A few don't even bother with dressing up at all, even on formal nights. As a Carnival hotel director told Heidi about the restaurant dress codes, "We're very flexible on this," adding that they draw the line only at bathing suits and T-shirts or hats with "bad words." Otherwise, just about anything goes.

DINING

Like most lines these days, Carnival offers a raft of dining options. Though not to the degree of flexibility that NCL—and, to a lesser extent, Princess and Holland America—offers, Carnival's Conquest-class ships offer about as many dining venues as you'll really need.

TRADITIONAL   In its two-story "formal" dining rooms (and take *formal* with a grain of salt—some Carnival passengers don't seem to know anything but T-shirts and jeans), Carnival's food quality and presentation, plus its wine selection, are much improved from its early days, and for the most part on par with Royal Caribbean, Princess, and NCL. You'll find more exotic options such as chicken satay with peanut sauce and Indian-themed meals that include lamb chops, basmati rice, lentils (*dal*), and potatoes (*aloo*), as well as all-American favorites such as lobster and prime rib, plus pasta dishes, grilled salmon, and Thanksgiving-style turkey served with all the trimmings. Some dishes and certain wines are tied to the region, so cruising Europe, expect more Spanish and Italian wines, for example. Unfortunately, the preparation is uneven (as is true on many of the mainstream lines); one night your entree is great, the other it's blah. A couple of years back, Carnival entered a partnership with French master chef Georges Blanc, whose six restaurants in France have earned the coveted three stars from Michelin; his dishes tend to be the better ones on the menu. There are some 50 healthier **"Spa Carnival"** dishes (which include calorie, fat, sodium, and cholesterol stats), and **vegetarian** options are also on each menu.

Despite the hectic pace and ambience, dining service is usually friendly and somewhat classier than in earlier years, if not always the most efficient. The staff still presents dessert-time song-and-dance routines, at times quite elaborate, and passengers seem to love it. Sophistication goes only so far, however: Carnival still has its waiters handle all wine service rather than employing sommeliers; and on a *Liberty* cruise, Heidi was unpleasantly surprised to find the lights turned up abruptly at 9:30pm each evening in the dining room, just 1 to 1½ hours after the late dinner seatings started. It was clearly a very inelegant way to encourage any stragglers to finish their coffee and dessert ASAP and hit the road so the staff could clean up and close the dining room for the night.

In a nod to a more flexible system in its formal restaurants, Carnival offers **four different seatings** on most ships rather than the traditional two. However, because you can choose to dine only early (5:45 and 6:15pm) or late (8 or 8:30pm), with the line selecting your exact time, it's hardly more flexible (though it's better for the galley staff, who have a more spaced window to prepare meals).

SPECIALTY   In the two-level, reservations-only supper club restaurant, service is more gracious, and dedicated sommeliers are on hand to take your wine order. The cover charge is $30 per person. Menus are leather bound, and elegant table settings feature beautiful Versace show plates and Rosenthal, Fortessa, and Revol china. Tables for two and four are available, and a musician or two serenades diners with soft ballads. There's even a dance floor. Like a traditional steakhouse, the menu includes starters, salads, and side dishes such as creamed spinach and mashed potatoes. The steaks range from New York strip to porterhouse and filet mignon, and other options include grilled lamb chops and a fish and chicken dish. The experience is intentionally designed to be slow and lingering, so don't go if you're looking for a fast meal. The food and service are the most doting you'll find on Carnival.

CASUAL   At the opposite end of the alternative-dining spectrum, guests can opt to have any meal in the buffet-style Lido restaurants at no extra charge. For an unstructured and casual dinner, walk in any time between about 6 and 9:30pm for serve-your-self entrees such as chicken, pasta, stir-fry, and carved meats. At lunch, buffets in the Lido feature the usual suspects—salads, meats, cheeses, pastas, grilled burgers, and chicken filets, and several hot choices such as fish and chips, roast turkey, and stir-fry. The lunchtime buffets also feature specialty stations, serving up things such as pasta or Chinese food or a Cajun fish dish. All ships have a deli station for sandwiches; a pizza station open 24 hours, where you can also get a Caesar salad; and an outlet for grilled chicken sandwiches, burgers, hot dogs, and fries—just be prepared for a looooooooong line at lunchtime on sea days, as the Carnival crowd loves burgers and fries. In general, the various buffet sections can get backed up at times as passengers wait for bins to be restocked and servers scramble to fill them. Though the food is unmemorable, upgrades to tableware are not: Kudos to Carnival for bringing in colorful ceramic sugar bowls, salt and pepper shakers, and dinnerware in place of the old white plastic stuff.

SNACKS & EXTRAS   But wait, there's 24-hour pizza (500 to 800 pies are flipped a day!), calzones that are surprisingly tasty, Caesar salad with or without chicken, and self-serve soft ice cream, as well as a complimentary **sushi bar** in the promenade and a deli. There are nightly **midnight buffets** in the Lido restaurant, with a gala, pull-out-all-the-stops buffet once per cruise. You'll also find specialty (read: not free) coffee and pastry bars, some with milkshakes and banana splits, too.

All ships offer **24-hour room service,** with a menu including such items as a focaccia sandwich with grilled zucchini, fresh mozzarella, and portobello mushrooms, plus the standard tuna salad, cookies, fruit, and so on. Kids can select from **children's menus.** Kids and adults can buy the Funship Fountain Card for unlimited fountain sodas throughout the cruise; you'll see the ubiquitous plastic cups that are part of the deal all over the ship.

ACTIVITIES

Carnival is all about lounging by the pool, drink in hand (or bucket of beers at foot), and soaking up the sun and some loud music or whatever **goofy contests** may be taking place. On sea days, you can get a hoot out of watching (or joining, if you're not the wallflower type) the men's hairy chest contest or similar tomfoolery, participate in a trivia contest, or sign up for some group dancing lessons. A blaring band will play a few sets by the pool, and on the line's newest ships (including both *Freedom* and *Splendor*), a **giant video screen** smack dab in the center of the pool area broadcasts movies, concerts, and various shipboard activities at eardrum-shattering decibels (and we do

Handy Hot Line

Carnival offers a 24-hour hot line for help with unexpected snafus or emergencies. Call 𝄐 **877/885-4856** toll-free, or 305/406-4779.

---

mean loud—don't expect to have a conversation without shouting). It's a little quieter up on the second tier of the Sun Deck, and each ship has a quieter pool and sunbathing area at the stern, sans loudspeakers. One of the four pools on the Conquest-class ships is quieter and covered by a retractable glass roof.

Slot machines begin clanging by 8 or 9 in the morning in the **casino** when the ship is at sea (tables open at 11am), and servers start tempting passengers with trays of fruity cocktails long before the lunch hour. Expect to hear the cheesy art auctioneer shouting into a microphone about some Peter Max masterpiece. There are **line-dancing and ballroom classes,** trivia contests, facial and hairdo demonstrations (intended to entice passengers to sign up for expensive treatments), singles and newlywed parties, game shows, shuffleboard, bingo, art auctions, and movies. Overall, though, there's not as much variety of activities as aboard lines such as Norwegian, Holland America, and Celebrity (read: even in Europe, you get absolutely no enrichment lectures on history or other cerebral topics).

You can spend some time in the roomy gyms (and take the handful of **free aerobics classes** or the ones they charge $10 for, such as Pilates, yoga, and spinning) or play volleyball on the top deck, or treat yourself to one of dozens of relaxing (and expensive) treatments in the Steiner-managed **spas.** There's a covered and lighted golf driving net, with **golf pros** sailing on board to give lessons with video analysis starting at $25 for a 15-minute session and $80 for an hour. Pros also accompany guests on golf excursions on shore, and clubs, golf shoes, balls, gloves, and other paraphernalia are available for rent.

If you want to escape it all and find a truly quiet nook for a while, retire to the subdued library/card/game room and 24-hour **Internet center;** you'll find Wi-Fi service fleetwide as well. You can also use your cellphone while at sea or in port.

CHILDREN'S PROGRAM

Carnival is right up there with the best ships for families—during the summer months, expect in the neighborhood of 1,000 kids and teens per cruise. Forget about finding a kid-free hot tub. The **child facilities** are fairly extensive on the newer ships, including the *Freedom* and *Splendor,* offering big, bright playrooms with arts and crafts, oodles of toys and games, video screens and televisions showing movies and cartoons, and computer stations loaded with the latest educational and entertainment software.

The **Camp Carnival program** offers complimentary supervised kids' activities on sea days nearly nonstop from 9am to 10pm, and on port days, from 8am or earlier, if there are shore excursions departing earlier for ages 2 through 14 in four age groups: toddlers 2 to 5, juniors 6 to 8, intermediates 9 to 11, and teens 12 to 14. Ten to 16 counselors (all of whom are trained in CPR and first aid) organize the fun and games on each ship, which include face painting, computer games, puzzles, fun with Play-Doh, picture bingo, pirate hat making, and pizza parties for toddlers. For juniors, there's PlayStation 2, computer games, ice cream parties, story time and library visits, T-shirt coloring, and swimming. For intermediates, there are scavenger hunts, trivia, bingo, Ping-Pong, video-game competitions, arts and crafts (some tied into the European ports of call), computer games, dance classes, and talent shows. Across all age groups, activities with a somewhat educational bent may include art projects with papier-mâché, oil paintings, and watercolors; music appreciation, which gets kids acquainted with different musical instruments; science projects for kids to make their own ice cream and create minihelicopters; and a fitness program that encourages today's couch-potato, computer-head kids to actually get up and run around. Club 02 teen centers are geared to 12- to 14-year-olds (the cruise director's department schedules activities for the 16 to 18 set) and are quite elaborate on the newest ships. Besides karaoke parties, computer games, scavenger hunts, talent shows, card and trivia games, and Ping-Pong, teens can watch movies there and go to dance parties. Most ships are also equipped with iMacs, but there is no Internet center specifically for teens, as some ships offer. Of course, teens can also hang out in the video arcades—the newest ships have virtual-reality games and air hockey tables. For something more refined, Carnival now offers a collection of spa treatments geared to teens. If you're between the ages of 12 and 17, you can also sign up for "just for teens" shore excursions in European ports that are supervised by Camp Carnival teen counselors (read: no parents!).

The entire fleet has children's wading pools, though they're very basic compared to what you'll find on some of the Royal Caribbean, Celebrity, NCL, and Princess ships, and for bigger kids there's a great signature snaking slide at the main pool of each ship. A new activity is the "Water Wars" water balloon attraction that's based on a diversion offered in amusement parks around the world. It basically boils down to teams flinging water balloons at each other with catapults.

Parents wanting a kid-free evening can make use of the supervised children's activities, offered from 7 to 10pm nightly free of charge, after which time group **slumber-party-style babysitting** kicks in for ages 4 months through age 11 till 3am in the playroom at $6 per hour for the first child, $4 per hour for each additional child. No private babysitting is available. Infants between 4 and 23 months can also be cared for on port days between 8am and noon, but it's considered babysitting and the hourly fee mentioned above will apply. On sea days between noon and 2pm, you can also drop off children under 2 at the rate above, or parents may use the playroom with their babies for these 2 hours at no charge. And yes, counselors will change diapers (though parents are asked to provide them along with wipes). Parents with kids age 8 and under checked into the children's program get free use of beepers on most ships, in case their kids need to contact them. A handful of strollers are available for rent fleetwide for $25 for 7- and 8-night cruises (less for shorter cruises), as well as a limited number of bouncy seats, travel swings, and Game Boys for rent.

Mom and Dad can get an earlier start on their kid-free evening when the counselors supervise **kids' mealtime** in the Lido restaurant between about 6 and 7pm in a special section reserved for kids; it's offered nightly except the first night of the cruise, and on cruises 5 nights or longer, it's also not offered on the last night. The children's dining room menu, printed on the back of a fun coloring/activity book (crayons are provided), features the usual favorites—hot dogs, hamburgers, french fries, chicken nuggets, pepperoni pizza, peanut-butter-and-jelly sandwiches, banana splits, Jell-O, and a daily special.

Cribs are available if requested when making your reservations. When you first board, head for the kids' playroom to get a schedule for the week and to sign up your child for the program. Children must be at least 4 months old to sail on board.

ENTERTAINMENT

You know what they say, "When in Rome . . . ." Acts geared to the Mediterranean ports visited include a Venetian mask party, Italian opera night on deck, and Greek music night in the lobby. Otherwise, hit the casino—they're so large you'll think you've died and gone to Vegas—or check out the line's **Broadway-inspired musicals.** Carnival megaships each carry about 8 to 16 flamboyantly costumed dancers for twice- or thrice-weekly shows. One or two live soloists carry the musical part of the show, while dancers lip-sync the chorus. An 8- to 10-piece orchestra of traditional and digital instruments deftly accompanies the acts each night, sometimes enhanced by synchronized recorded music. You'll also find comedians, jugglers, acrobats, rock 'n' roll bands, country-and-western bands, classical string trios, pianists, and Dorsey- or Glenn Miller–style big bands, all performing during the same cruise, and sometimes on the same night.

Besides the main theater, most entertainment happens somewhere along the indoor Main Street–like promenade (except on the Spirit-class ships, which are more spread out). Many are called the "Something-or-other Boulevard" or "Something-or-other Way"; it stretches along one entire side of each ship and is lined with just about the entire repertoire of the ships' nightclubs, bars, lounges, patisseries, disco, and casino. One bar welcomes cigar smoking, and fleetwide, cigars are sold at the pool bar and during midnight buffets.

By day, entertainment includes an ultraloud Caribbean-style calypso or steel-drum band performing Bob Marley tunes and other pop songs on a deck poolside, and a pianist, guitarist, or string trio playing in the atria of the line's newest ships. The newest ships, including the *Freedom* and *Splendor,* have a giant video screen up on the pool deck that tends to monopolize much of the day by loudly (and I mean loudly) broadcasting concerts, movies (sometimes tied into the cruising region), and ship-board activities. Personally, we don't like 'em. Sure, a couple of movies in the late after-noon and evening are nice, but who needs the thing screeching away all day long?

SERVICE

All in all, a Carnival ship is a well-oiled machine, and you'll certainly get what you need—but not much more. When you board, for instance, you're welcomed by polite and well-meaning staff at the gangway, given a diagram of the ship's layout, and then pointed in the right direction to find your cabin on your own, carry-on luggage in tow. Chalk it all up to the size of the line's ships. It's a fact of life that service aboard all megaliners is simply not as attentive as that aboard smaller vessels—with thousands of guests to help, your dining-room waiter and cabin steward have a lot of work ahead of them and have little time for chitchat. Lines can get long at the breakfast and lunch buffets and, at certain times, at the pizza counter, though there always seem to be plenty of drink servers roaming the pool decks, looking to score drink orders.

Carnival Fleet Itineraries

Ship	Sailing Regions	Home Ports
Carnival Freedom	12-night voyages in the Mediterranean/Greek Isles	Civitavecchia/Rome
Carnival Liberty	12-night voyages in Northern Europe and the Mediterranean/Greek Isles (2009 only)	Dover/London, Civitavecchia/Rome
Carnival Splendor	12-night voyages in Northern Europe and the Mediterranean/Greek Isles (2008 only)	Dover/London, Civitavecchia/Rome

Preview: *Carnival Splendor*

Based on the Conquest ships, the 113,000-ton, 3,006-passenger *Carnival Splendor* is slated to debut in June 2008. It'll be a tiny bit larger and will sport some new stuff, including a water park and the line's largest and most elaborate spa and kids' facilities to date. It will have the line's first thalassotherapy pool covered by a glass dome, and a thermal suite. Adjacent to the spa will be 68 spa staterooms. Other developments include a giant video screen on deck and cabins with flatscreen TVs.

As for the decor, ship architect Joe Farcus summed it up like this: "The central idea that ties the rooms together is the concept of fine, luxurious, sumptuous elegance. So we used elements like pearls, gold leaf, and wood grains to give the ship a feeling of richness."

Of course, one man's sumptuous elegance is another man's Peter Max painting. At press time, design details included an Atrium decked out in stainless steel and stylized wood laminates, and a nightclub called the Red Carpet Dance Club with mannequin groupies posing behind a velvet rope "greeting" the VIPs (er, passengers) as they enter. The ship will spend its inaugural months of July and August doing 12-nighters round-trip out of Dover/London, calling on Copenhagen, Warnemunde/Berlin, Helsinki, St. Petersburg, Tallinn, and Amsterdam.

Like most of the major lines these days, gratuities for the crew are **automatically added to your account** at the end of your cruise to the tune of $10 per person, per day fleetwide, and they're divvied up among the staff automatically. You can adjust the amount—or eliminate it completely and hand out cash in envelopes—by visiting the purser's desk. On Carnival and the other lines with automatic tipping policies, we've found waiters and cabin stewards don't seem as eager to please as they did when the tip carrot was hanging directly over them.

There is a **laundry service** aboard each ship for washing and pressing only (with per-piece charges), as well as a handful of **self-service laundry rooms** with irons and coin-operated washers and dryers. There's a pleasant-smelling liquid soap and shampoo dispenser in cabin bathrooms fleetwide, plus a small basket of trial-size toiletries (refilled only upon request).

Carnival Freedom • Carnival Liberty

The Verdict

Freedom and *Liberty* offer Carnival's largest children's and teen's facilities, a giant video screen on the pool deck, and plenty of bars and lounges—all packaged in a pastiche of both pleasing and jarring colors and design themes.

Carnival Freedom *(photo: Carnival Cruise Lines)*

Specifications

Size (in Tons)	110,000	Passenger/Crew Ratio	2.5 to 1
Passengers (Double Occ.)	2,974	Year Launched	
Passenger/Space Ratio	37	*Liberty*	2005
Total Cabins/Veranda Cabins	1,487/556	*Freedom*	2007
Crew	1,160	Last Refurbishment/Upgrade	N/A

Frommer's Ratings (Scale of 1–5)   ★★★★ ½

Cabin Comfort & Amenities	4.5	Dining Options	4
Appearance & Upkeep	5	Gym, Spa & Sports Facilities	5
Public Comfort/Space	4.5	Children's Facilities	4.5
Decor	4	Enjoyment Factor	4

The 110,000-ton, 2,974-passenger *Freedom* and *Liberty* are two of five nearly identical $500-million Conquest-class ships—Carnival's largest vessels until the slightly bigger 113,000-ton *Splendor* debuts in July 2008. If all berths are occupied, each of these vessels can carry an eyebrow-raising 3,700-plus passengers (and that's not counting the more than 1,000 crew), and keep them well lubricated and entertained via more than 20 bars and lounges, giant children's facilities, and an entire separate zone dedicated to teens.

Cabins & Rates

Cabins	Per Diem From	Sq. Ft.	Fridge	Hair Dryer	Sitting Area	TV
Inside	$83	185	Yes	Yes	No	Yes
Outside	$117	185–220	Yes	Yes	Yes	Yes
Suite	$287	275–345	Yes	Yes	Yes	Yes

CABINS   Standard outside cabins measure a roomy 220 square feet. These categories (6A and 6B) take up most of the Riviera and Main decks. The standard balcony cabins (categories 8A–8E) measure a still-ample 185 square feet plus a 35-square-foot balcony. For those who simply must have a bigger balcony, a little extra dough buys an "extended balcony" (60 sq. ft.) or "wraparound large balcony." There are only a handful of these category-9A accommodations, and they're tucked all the way aft on the Upper, Empress, and Verandah decks. The 42 suites are a full 275 square feet plus a 65-square-foot balcony, and bigger still are the 10 Penthouse Suites, at 345 square feet plus an 85-square-foot balcony. Most of the suites are sandwiched in the middle of the ship on Deck 7 and between two other accommodations decks, eliminating the danger of noisy public rooms above or below. Specially designed family staterooms, at a comfortable but not roomy 230 square feet, are located one deck below the children's facilities, and a couple of them can be connected to the room next door. In lieu of a private veranda, these family staterooms feature floor-to-ceiling windows for ocean views.

All categories of cabins come with a TV, safe, hand-held hair dryer (not the wall-mounted, wimpy variety), stocked minifridge (items consumed are charged to your onboard account), desk/dresser, chair and stool, and bathroom with shower and a handy makeup/shaving mirror. But the best part about Carnival's cabins these days is the beds. Called the Carnival Comfort Bed sleep system, they're darn comfortable.

Mattresses, duvets, linens, and pillows are superthick and ultracomfy. The towels and bathrobes in each cabin are pretty luxurious, too.

There are 28 cabins for passengers with disabilities.

PUBLIC AREAS   *Freedom* and *Liberty,* like the rest of the Conquest ships, are bright and playful, with soaring, nine-deck-high atriums and a full 22 bars and lounges clustered on the Atlantic and Promenade decks. The 1,400-seat Show Lounge stages Carnival's big production shows. There's also a secondary entertainment venue for dance bands and late-night comedians, as well as a piano bar, wine bar (the best place for people-watching, as it's open to the main promenade), and another live-music venue where combos belt out oldies, country, and requests.

For *Freedom,* architect Joe Farcus was inspired by world history from ancient Babylonia to 19th-century Victorian era and the disco days of the 1970s. The Victoriana show lounge is named after the queen, and the circa-1880s decor features ornate moldings, fancy marble, and gold leaf. The focal point is a mural-decorated dome with a crystal chandelier. The Habana Cigar Bar has barstools and tabletops shaped like cigars, and the poolside Freedom Restaurant has Statue of Liberty replicas worked into practically every square inch.

On *Liberty,* "artisans and their crafts" is the motif, for better or worse. The Paparazzi wine bar is a cool place that's all about photography, with a huge 3-D collage of celebrity photographs covering the walls and images of cameras covering the ceiling and bar front. *Liberty*'s atrium, stair landings, and elevators are covered with floral laminate walls overlaid with arabesque curlicues.

Nobody does disco better than Carnival. On *Freedom,* it's a 1970s disco theme with pulsating lights, spinning disco balls, and funky seating in a giant seven and zero shape. On *Liberty,* the theme is tattoos. Downstairs is the ship's most elegant lounge, done in dark woods, and the Internet cafe is tucked away off a back corner of the room; it's a real quiet retreat, if you can find it.

The casino has a Hanging Gardens of Babylon theme and sprawls across 8,500 square feet, packing in almost 300 slot machines and a couple dozen gaming tables. To one side is the sports bar, which on *Freedom* pays tribute to the 1950s with lots of chrome, sports medallions, and memorabilia of famous teams from the mid–20th century. On *Liberty,* a boxing theme is worked into the furniture and decor.

The Conquest class boasts by far the biggest children's facilities in the fleet: At 4,200 square feet, Children's World and the separate teen center offer more than triple the space for kids and teens available on Destiny-class ships. Children's World sits atop the spa and holds an arts-and-crafts station, 16-monitor video wall, computer lab, PlayStation 2 consoles, and lots of fun toys for younger children, from play kitchens to push toys, mini sliding boards, farm sets, and more. The enclosed adjacent deck offers a dipping pool that's oddly industrial looking when compared to the kids' pools on many NCL, Celebrity, and Royal Caribbean ships. The ships' nod to teenagers, Club 02, is so large (at 1,800 square feet) that it forms its own secondary promenade, branching off the main one. On one end is a soda bar, separate dance floor, and sound and lighting system; on the other is a huge video game area with air hockey tables that is open to all passengers. Club 02 plays into a new millennium motif, with plasma screens everywhere showing continuously changing posters, paintings, and landscapes.

DINING OPTIONS   Each ship has a pair of two-story main restaurants, styled in keeping with the ship's theme. On *Freedom,* the dining rooms are called Chic and

Posh, and walls are covered with polished marble and a special wood veneer laminated in a python skin pattern. Zillions of tiny light bulbs make the place sparkle. Hmmm. . . . As Heidi's husband is fond of saying, "You can't eat ambience." Well, then, bring out the lobster. You'll see broiled tail on the menu once a cruise, and there are six desserts nightly. Low-fat, low-carb, low-salt Spa Carnival Fare, vegetarian dishes, and children's selections are also available.

Atop the 9-deck atrium, reservation supper clubs serve USDA prime-aged steaks, fish, and other deluxe items for a $30-per-person cover charge. The best food and most refined service on board are here, where dinner is meant to stretch over several hours and several bottles of wine (for which there's an extra charge).

Breakfast, lunch, and dinner are served in the two-story restaurant on the Lido Deck, where you'll also find a 24-hour pizza counter (the mushroom and goat cheese pies are scrumptious). Separate buffet lines (to alleviate crowding) are devoted to Asian and American dishes, deli sandwiches, salads, and desserts. On the upper level is Sur Mer, a fish-and-chips shop whose choices also include such goodies as calamari, lobster salad, and bouillabaisse. There's no charge here or for the stand-up sushi bar down on the main promenade, but the pastries, cakes, and specialty coffees at the patisserie cost a couple of bucks each.

There's also 24-hour room service with new menus that include items such as a chicken fajita with greens and guacamole in a jalapeño and tomato wrap, plus the standard tuna salad, cookies, fruit, and so on.

POOL, FITNESS, SPA & SPORTS FACILITIES   The ships' four swimming pools include the main pool, with its two huge hot tubs and a stage for live (and reallly loud) music. If you don't love reggae and calypso, don't go here. This space is where all the action (and noise) of pool games plus the occasional outbreak of line dancing occurs (though on port days in Europe, the place will be relatively dead). Carnival's trademark 214-foot-long twisty slide shoots into a pool one deck up. The aft pool, covered by a retractable glass dome, usually provides a more restful setting, although the pizzeria and burger grill are here (along with two more oversize hot tubs). The fourth pool is a really basic one for kiddies outside the playroom.

The ships' 12,000-square-foot health clubs and salons, with neat his-and-hers oceanview steam and sauna rooms, perch high on Deck 11. Though the decor is a real yawner, you'll find today's latest treatments available, from hot stone massages to hair and scalp massages. The spa is run by Steiner, the company that controls most cruise ship spas, so expect a hard sell for products right after your treatment. One more pet peeve: You won't find a hair dryer, Q-tips, cotton balls, or any other amenities in the locker room—it's unabashedly no frills. On the fitness side, you'll find the nontrendy aerobics classes offered for free (such as stretching and step), and the cool stuff everyone wants to do, such as Pilates and spinning, going for $10 a class. There's a hot tub that sits in a glass-enclosed space jutting into the fitness room.

3 Celebrity Cruises

1050 Caribbean Way, Miami, FL 33132. Ⓒ **800/437-3111** or 305/539-6000. Fax 800/722-5329. www.celebrity.com.

THE LINE IN A NUTSHELL   You can have it all with Celebrity: If you like elegance without stuffiness, fun without bad taste, and pampering without a high price, Celebrity delivers.

THE EXPERIENCE   Celebrity juices up the mainstream cruise experience with a touch of refinement and a dash of class, and the most original decor at sea, all while keeping things fun, active, and within the price range of Joe and Sally Cruiser. Each ship is spacious, glamorous, and comfortable, mixing sleekly modern and Art Deco styles, and throwing in cutting-edge art collections, to boot. An exceedingly polite and professional staff contributes greatly to the elegant mood. Dining-wise, the dashing alternative restaurants on *Summit, Constellation,* and their sister ships outclass all other mainstream ship restaurants for both quality of food and gorgeous decor.

Like all the big-ship lines, Celebrity offers lots for its passengers to do, though its focus stays mainly on mellower pursuits such as bridge, spelling bees, darts challenges, and expert-led seminars on such topics as wildlife, astronomy, photography, personal investing, and history. The line's AquaSpas are among the most attractive at sea.

Pros

- **Best mainstream alternative restaurants at sea:** *Summit* and *Constellation* offer remarkable service, food, and wine in their classy alternative venues, whose elegant decor incorporates artifacts from cherished old ocean liners such as the *Normandie* and SS *United States.*
- **Spectacular spas:** Beautiful and well equipped, Celebrity's spas are some of the best at sea.
- **Contemporary art:** *Century* and *Galaxy* feature outstanding collections of contemporary art, thanks to the line's art-savvy original owners.

Cons

- **Mechanical problems on Millennium-class ships:** When Celebrity introduced *Summit, Constellation,* and its other two Millennium-class ships between 2000 and 2002, little did they know that their much-vaunted Mermaid Pod propulsion system—in which propellers are mounted on swiveling pods attached to the ship's hull—would turn into the headache they have, with worn bearings requiring the line to cancel a few sailings pretty much every year. Affected passengers are compensated very well, receiving full refunds, a certificate applicable toward a future cruise, and/or onboard credit, depending on the extent to which their trip is affected.
- **Nickel-and-diming:** Though almost all cruise lines now supplement their income by offering extra-charge alternative restaurants, fancy coffee drinks, specialty ice creams, and the like, Celebrity's high-toned image means the line's passengers get more ticked off by this kind of nickel-and-diming. For instance, passengers we polled on one recent cruise were uniformly outraged by the $30 bingo charge.

Compared with the other mainstream lines, here's how Celebrity rates:

	Poor	Fair	Good	Excellent	Outstanding
Enjoyment Factor					✓
Dining				✓	
Activities				✓	
Children's Program			✓		
Entertainment			✓		
Service					✓
Worth the Money					✓

CELEBRITY: MEGA CHIC

Celebrity's roots go back to the powerful Greek shipping family Chandris, whose patriarch, John D. Chandris, founded a cargo shipping company in 1915. The family expanded into the cruise business in the late 1960s, and by 1976 had the largest passenger-cruise fleet in the world. In the late 1970s, they introduced the down-market Chandris-Fantasy Cruises, which served a mostly European clientele. In 1989, the Chandris family dissolved Fantasy and created Celebrity Cruises, building beautiful, innovative ships that were immediately recognizable by their crisp navy-blue-and-white hulls and their rakishly angled funnels decorated with a giant X—which was really the Greek letter *chi,* for Chandris.

The company's rise to prominence was so rapid and so successful that in 1997 it was courted and acquired by the larger and wealthier Royal Caribbean Cruises Ltd., which now operates Celebrity as a sister line to Royal Caribbean International. With their distinctive profiles and striking contemporary decor, Celebrity's ships are some of the most distinctive and stylish out there, but Celebrity nevertheless has been having a hard time distinguishing itself in the marketplace since it became part of RCCL. Perhaps some new developments, though, will help garner the attention it deserves. In 2006, Celebrity announced construction of four new 118,000-ton, 2,850-passenger ships, the *Celebrity Solstice* (slated to debut in fall 2008), *Celebrity Equinox* (due in summer 2009), *Celebrity Eclipse* (due in 2010), and an as-yet-unnamed sister for 2011. It also acquired two smaller, 30,277-ton, 710-passenger vessels originally built for defunct Renaissance cruises, and used them to create its new deluxe, destination-intensive sub-brand **Azamara Cruises** (see page 78).

PASSENGER PROFILE

While Celebrity pitches itself as a megaship experience for tasteful middle- to upper-middle-income cruisers and even wealthy patrons, the fact is that its generally low prices (more or less comparable to those of Carnival and Royal Caribbean) ensure that its demographic stays democratically wider. Clients who choose their cruise based on more than just price like Celebrity because it offers a well-balanced cruise with lots of activities and a glamorous, exciting atmosphere that's both refined and fun.

Most passengers are couples in their 40s and up, with passengers in Europe tending to skew toward the older end of the scale. Geographically, about 60% to 80% of the line's passengers are North American, with the remaining 20% to 30% hailing from Europe and elsewhere. On any given cruise you'll find a decent number of families on board.

DINING

When Celebrity got its start, truly exceptional cuisine was one of the hallmarks of its experience, but over the years it's edged down closer to that of mainstream peers Princess, Royal Caribbean, NCL, and Holland America. **Dining service,** however, remains excellent, and the experience in *Summit*'s and *Constellation*'s specialty restaurants is still superb. In mid-2007, the line brought in a new culinary head-man with an instinct to shake things up, so our money is on Celebrity announcing upgrades to its dining program soon.

TRADITIONAL In the main dining rooms, dinner menus have recently featured entrees such as veal shank cooked in an aromatic tomato velouté with orange zest, served with risotto; broiled sliced tenderloin with béarnaise and madeira sauces; and boneless chicken breast with bananas and ham, coated with coconut flakes and served with curry peanut sauce. At every meal, Celebrity also offers lighter "spa" fare whose calorie, fat, cholesterol, and sodium breakdowns are listed on the back of the menu. Vegetarians, meanwhile, can enjoy one of the few **dedicated vegetarian menus** offered in the cruise biz. It's available upon request and changes every night, with multiple appetizer and entree options. Celebrity offers a good wine list that includes a line of proprietary wines called the Cellarmaster Selection. Guests who wish to get a deep wine experience can participate in **wine-appreciation seminars** hosted by sommeliers trained by the folks at Austria's Riedel Crystal. Lasting 1 hour, each workshop will give guests a chance to sample and compare multiple fine wines served in Riedel's Vinum glass collection, then depart with a set of four glasses. The hour-long workshops are offered once per sailing for a fee.

SPECIALTY   Cuisine, service, and ambience really shine at *Summit*'s and *Constellation*'s intimate alternative restaurants, each of which carries a $30-per-person cover charge and seats 140 passengers. Presentation is paramount: Decor is centered around artifacts from the historic passenger vessels that give the restaurants their names, there often seems to be more waitstaff than diners, Caesar salads and zabaglione are prepared tableside, maître d's carve passengers' meat dishes with the finesse of a concert pianist, and a selection of excellent French cheeses arrives at the end of the meal.

Menus feature at least one menu item inspired by a dish served aboard the venue's namesake. Appetizers include such items as creamy lobster broth, tartare of salmon garnished with quail eggs, and goat cheese soufflé with tomato coulis, followed by entrees such as sea bass brushed with tapenade, scampi flambéed in Armagnac, and rack of lamb coated with mushroom duxelles and wrapped in a puff pastry. For dessert, you can't go wrong with a chocolate soufflé or a plate of bite-size desserts. You can order a la carte or opt for a set multicourse tasting menu, with an optional $28 slate of wine pairings. Wines are also available by the glass or bottle.

Century offers a dinner alternative at Murano, a European-themed restaurant whose elaborate, multicourse meals follow the style of Celebrity's Millennium-class specialty restaurants, featuring tableside cooking, carving, and flambé. *Galaxy* is the only Celebrity ship in Europe this year that lacks a dedicated alternative dinner venue.

CASUAL   Breakfast and lunch in the buffet restaurants are on par with those of lines such as Royal Caribbean and Princess, and include such features as a **made-to-order pasta bar** and a **pizza station** serving very tasty pies. On most nights, the buffet space is transformed into the **Casual Dining Boulevard,** with waiters serving entrees such as pasta, gourmet pizzas, and chicken between about 6 and 10pm. Reservations are recommended, though if there's space, walk-ins are accepted, too. During dinnertime, Celebrity also offers a **sushi bar** in one section of the buffet restaurant, serving both appetizer-size portions and full meals.

Light breakfast eaters or those looking for a pre- or post-breakfast snack will want to grab an incredibly good croissant from **Cova Café.** They're free, but you'll have to pony up a few bucks for an accompanying latte or cappuccino. *Summit* and *Constellation* also have an **Aqua Spa Cafe** in a corner of the thalassotherapy pool area where you can get low-cal treats for lunch or dinner from noon to 10pm, including raw veggie platters, poached salmon with asparagus tips, vegetarian sushi, and pretty salads with tuna or chicken. Spa breakfasts offer items such as bagels and lox, fresh fruit, cereal, and boiled eggs. For the opposite of spa cuisine, **outdoor grills** on all ships offer burgers and the like.

SNACKS & EXTRAS The line offers **afternoon tea** at least once per cruise fleetwide, with white-gloved waiters serving tea, finger sandwiches, scones, and desserts from rolling carts. Several nights per cruise, roving waiters present a late-night culinary soiree known as **Gourmet Bites,** serving upscale canapés and hors d'oeuvres in the ship's public lounges between midnight and 1am. There's also a traditional **midnight buffet** on one night, and occasional themed lunches (Asian, Italian, Tex-Mex, tropical smorgasbord) in the buffet restaurant.

The line's room service allows passengers to order off a limited menu 24 hours a day and also from the lunch and dinner menus during set meal hours. You can even get tasty **pizza** delivered right to your cabin between 3 and 7pm and 10pm and 1am daily, in a box and pouch just like the ones used by your local pizzeria.

ACTIVITIES

Celebrity offers lots of options for those who want to stay active, but it also caters to those who want to veg.

Celebrity's **spas** are some of the best in the business, beautifully appointed and offering a nice raft of treatments, from the exotic to the everyday-but-it-still-feels-good. If you're looking for the latter, make it a point to ask: Often (as on its website) Celebrity tends to list its fancy, high-priced treatments but not its standard massages, facials, and pedicures. If you're the "try something new type," the line offers its **Acupuncture at Sea program** on all cruises, with professionals offering acupuncture and medicinal herbal treatments for pain management, smoking cessation, weight loss, stress management, and other ailments. Free talks on acupuncture and other holistic health treatments are offered at various times throughout the cruise. In the gyms, various aerobic-type classes are available throughout the day. Basic classes are free, while the cool ones, such as **Pilates and yoga,** cost extra. Passengers can attend at a per-class fee or book at a package price at the start of the cruise.

Other activities include wine tastings (for a fee), horse racing, bingo, bridge, art auctions, trivia games, game shows, arts and crafts, cooking demos, computer classes (from Web page design to the basics of Excel), and ballroom and line-dancing lessons. Up to four featured speakers/performers also sail on every cruise, offering **complimentary enrichment lectures.** Speakers may include chefs from well-regarded restaurants and wine experts who offer onboard seminars and pre-dinner tastings. From

---

Preview: *Celebrity Solstice*

Celebrity hasn't launched a new vessel in 6 years, but that'll change in fall 2008 when the line introduces the 118,000-ton, 2,850-passenger *Celebrity Solstice,* its largest vessel ever. Though few details of the ship's amenities had yet been announced at press time, we do know that she'll boast ten restaurants (including an Asian fusion room and a steakhouse) and a tremendous number of outside cabins (more than 90% of the total, with more than 85% of those having balconies) and that the average standard cabin will be quite roomy, at some 215 square feet.

The vessel is currently under construction at Germany's Meyer Werft shipyard, which was responsible for Celebrity's first five newbuilds—*Horizon, Zenith, Century, Galaxy,* and *Mercury.* A sister ship to *Solstice* named **Celebrity Equinox** is slated to debut in summer 2009, followed by *Celebrity Eclipse* in 2010 and an as-yet-unnamed sister in 2011.

Celebrity Fleet Itineraries

Ship	Sailing Regions	Home Ports
Century	5- to 12-night voyages in Northern Europe/ Russia, British Isles, the Norwegian Fjords/ Arctic Norway, Atlantic Europe, and the Mediterranean	Amsterdam, Barcelona
Constellation	9- to 14-night British Isles, Northern Europe/Russia	Dover/London, Harwich/London, Stockholm
Galaxy	11-night Mediterranean	Civitavecchia/Rome
Summit	12-night voyages in Atlantic Europe and the Mediterranean	Southampton/London, Barcelona, Venice

time to time, actors, politicians, and journalists also sail aboard and hold talks. Recent speakers included former NBC News chief economics correspondent Irving R. Levine, maritime historian and author John Maxtone Graham, and actors Dick Van Patten and Rita Moreno.

During the day, a live pop band plays on the pool deck for a couple of hours, and you can expect a pool game or two, such as a pillow fight, volleyball match, or "King of the Ship" contest.

CHILDREN'S PROGRAM

Celebrity pampers kids as well as adults, especially during the summer months. Each ship has a dedicated youth team of 12 trained staff who supervise playroom activities practically all day long and offer group babysitting in the evenings. *Summit*'s and *Constellation*'s indoor/outdoor kids' facilities are much better than those aboard *Century* and *Galaxy,* with features like ball bins, slides, jungle gyms, and wading pools (the latter also available on *Galaxy*). Teen centers feature computers with Internet access, digital jukeboxes, video game consoles, and more.

Supervised activities are geared toward four age groups for ages 3 to 17. Kids ages 3 to 6 (dubbed "Ship Mates") and ages 7 to 9 (called "Cadets") can participate in "edutainment"-style programs that teach about European culture, arts, sports, sea life, and more. Other activities include treasure hunts, themed parties, T-shirt painting, dancing, movies, ship tours, and pizza- and ice-cream-sundae-making parties. Ten- to 12-year-olds ("Ensigns") get activities such as karaoke, computer games, board games, trivia contests, arts and crafts, movies, sushi demonstrations, game shows, and pizza parties. There are also masquerade parties where Ship Mates and Cadets make their own masks and outfits and then parade around the ship (the "pirates" parade was a big hit with kids on our last cruise), and Junior Olympics where kids compete in relay races, diving, and basketball free throws while their families cheer. Various activities and tours give kids a behind-the-scenes look at the ship's entertainment, food and beverage, and hotel departments.

Toddlers under age 3 can participate in activities and use the playroom if accompanied by a parent.

For **teens** ages 13 to 17 (subdivided into two groups, 13–15 and 16–17), Celebrity's ships have attractive teen discos/hangout rooms with fancy lighting and "teen-appropriate" pop art, plus Xboxes, Nintendo Wii, and PlayStation PS3s, and activities such as talent shows, game shows, karaoke, and pool games.

Group babysitting in the playroom ($6 per child, per hour) is available for ages 3 to 12 between noon and 2pm on port days, and every evening from 10pm to 1am for children ages 3 to 12. Kids can dine with the counselors most nights between 5 and 7pm (free on sea days; $6 per child, per hour, on port days). A new **V.I.P. Party Pass** covers all group babysitting for your cruise at a 40% discount, and kids get to attend one big-screen movie, with free popcorn and refreshments, behind-the-scenes tours, and souvenirs. Prices vary by itinerary. On the last night of the cruise, a complimentary **Parents' Night Out party** is offered between 5pm and 1am, and includes pizza and fun activities for kids while their parents step out. Female crewmembers offer evening **private in-cabin babysitting** on a limited basis, for $8 per hour for up to two children. Kids must be at least 6 months old, and the service must be requested 24 hours in advance.

There is no **minimum age** for sailing.

ENTERTAINMENT

Celebrity offers all the popular cruise favorites, such as magicians, comedians, cabaret acts, **passenger talent shows,** and Vegas-style musical revues. The overall quality of music and comedy acts is good, but on our last sailing the musical revues were pretty stinkeroo. For something a little different, the line offers some nice, understated entertainment touches such as **harpists** and **string quartets** performing in various lounges.

All the ships also have cozy lounges and bars where you can retreat for a romantic nightcap and some music, from laid-back jazz to interpretations of contemporary hits. There are also the elegant and plush **Michael's Club** piano lounges for cordials and quiet conversation. Each ship has a large **casino,** as well as late-night disco dancing, usually until about 3am. You'll also find recent-release movies in the ships' theaters and cinemas, and **karaoke** in one or another of the bars.

SERVICE

Service is Celebrity's strongest suit, with staff uniformly polite, attentive, cheerful, knowledgeable, and professional. Stewards wear white gloves at embarkation as they escort passengers to their cabins. Waiters have a poised, upscale-hotel air about them, and their manner does much to create an elegant mood. There are very professional sommeliers in the dining room, and waiters are on hand in the buffet restaurants at breakfast and lunch to carry passengers' trays to a table of their choice. If you occupy a suite, you'll get a **tuxedo-clad personal butler** who serves afternoon tea, complimentary cappuccino and espresso, and complimentary pre-dinner hors d'oeuvres. If you ask, he'll also handle your laundry, shine your shoes, make sewing repairs, deliver messages, and even serve a full five-course dinner en suite or help you organize a cocktail party. (You foot the bill for food and drinks, of course.) Other hedonistic treats bestowed upon suite guests include a bottle of champagne on arrival, personalized stationery, terry robes, oversize bath towels, priority check-in and debarkation, express luggage delivery at embarkation, and so on. **ConciergeClass staterooms**—a middle zone between regular cabins and suites—offer some of the same perks but without the high price of actual suites (and no butler, sorry).

When it comes to **tipping,** Celebrity passengers can dispense gratuities personally, in cash, at the end of the cruise, or choose to add them to their onboard accounts at a rate of $10.25 per person, per day for passengers in regular staterooms, $13.75 per person for passengers in suites.

Laundry and dry-cleaning services are available fleetwide for a nominal fee, but there are no self-service laundry facilities.

Summit • Constellation

The Verdict

Among the classiest big ships at sea, these ships offer all the leisure, sports, and entertainment options of a megaship and an atmosphere that combines old-world elegance and modern casual style.

Summit *(photo: Celebrity Cruises)*

Specifications

Size (in Tons)	91,000	Passenger/Crew Ratio	2 to 1
Passengers (Double Occ.)	1,950	Year Launched	
Passenger/Space Ratio	46	*Summit*	2001
Total Cabins/Veranda Cabins	975/590	*Constellation*	2002
Crew	999	Last Refurbishment/Upgrade	N/A

Frommer's Ratings (Scale of 1–5)   ★★★★★

Cabin Comfort & Amenities	5	Dining Options	5
Appearance & Upkeep	5	Gym, Spa & Sports Facilities	5
Public Comfort/Space	5	Children's Facilities	4
Decor	5	Enjoyment Factor	5

In creating its third generation of newbuilds, Celebrity took the best ideas from its older ships and ratcheted them up in terms of both scale and number: bigger ships, bigger spas and theaters, more veranda cabins, more dining options, more lounges, and more sports and exercise facilities, plus more of the same great service, decor, and high-style onboard art for which the company was already known.

If there's one downside to these beautiful vessels, it's their Mermaid Pod propulsion systems, whose propellers are mounted on swiveling pods attached to the ship's hull, offering greater maneuverability. Great idea, but apparently not without glitches: In the past few years, Celebrity has had to cancel several cruises and send one or another of the ships to dry dock to replace worn bearings, a circumstance that's cost the line in both revenue and passenger goodwill. There's nothing unsafe about them, mind you; it's just annoying and expensive. Passengers on cancelled sailings generally receive refunds and vouchers that can be applied to a future cruise.

The other two ships in the Millennium class, *Millennium* and *Infinity*, do not sail in Europe this year.

Cabins & Rates

Cabins	Per Diem From	Sq. Ft.	Fridge	Hair Dryer	Sitting Area	TV
Inside	$132	170	Yes	Yes	Yes	Yes
Outside	$164	170–191	Yes	Yes	Yes	Yes
Suite	$357	251–1,432	Yes	Yes	Yes	Yes

CABINS Improving upon Celebrity's already respectable cabins, *Summit* and *Constellation* push the bar up yet another notch, with their elegant striped, floral, or patterned fabrics in shades such as butterscotch and pinkish terra cotta, along with Art Deco–style lighting fixtures and marble desktops. Standard inside and outside cabins are a roomy 170 square feet and come with a small sitting area, stocked minifridge, TV, safe, ample storage space, cotton robes, and shampoo dispensers built right into the shower. Only thing missing? Individual reading lights above the beds, though there are table lamps on the nightstands.

Premium and Deluxe staterooms have slightly larger sitting areas and approximately 40-square-foot verandas. The 12 simply titled "Large" oceanview staterooms in the stern measure in at a very large 271 square feet and have two entertainment centers with TVs/VCRs, a partitioned sitting area with two convertible sofa beds, and very, very, very large 242-square-foot verandas facing the ships' wake.

Passengers booking the Concierge Class staterooms on Sky Deck get a bunch of cushy extras, including a bottle of champagne, custom pillow menu, upgraded bedding, oversize towels, double-thick Frette bathrobes, priority for just about everything (dining, shore excursions, luggage delivery, embarkation, and disembarkation), and cushioned chairs and high-powered binoculars on their 41-square-foot balconies. Unfortunately, many of those balconies (as well as those attached to several Deluxe Ocean View cabins at Sky Deck midships) catch a little shadow from the overhanging deck above. *Hint:* Several Concierge Class cabins on Sky Deck (9038 and 9043) and Panorama Deck (8045 and 8046) offer extralarge verandas at no extra cost. Ask your travel agent.

Suites on *Summit* and *Constellation* offer 24-hour butler service and come in four levels, from the 251-square-foot Sky Suites with balconies to the eight 467-square-foot Celebrity Suites (with dining area, separate bedroom, two TV/VCR combos, and whirlpool bathtub, but no verandas) and the 538-square-foot Royal Suites (also with a separate living/dining room, two TV/VCR combos, a standing shower and whirlpool bathtub, and a huge 195-sq.-ft. veranda with whirlpool tub). At the top of the food chain, the massive Penthouse Suites measure 1,432 square feet and offer herringbone wood floors, a marble foyer, a computer station, a Yamaha piano, and a simply amazing bathroom with ocean views and a full-size hot tub. And did we mention a 1,098-square-foot veranda that wraps around the stern of the ship and features a whirlpool tub and full bar? The only downside is you sometimes feel the vibrations of the engines a few decks below. If these suites have a Park Avenue feel, it's no wonder— the designer, Birch Coffey, also does apartments for New York's super-rich.

Passengers requiring use of a wheelchair have a choice of 26 cabins, from Sky Suites to balcony cabins, to inside staterooms.

PUBLIC AREAS There's simply nothing else at sea like the Grand Foyer Atrium, the stunning hub of each vessel. Each rectangular, three-deck area features a translucent, inner-illuminated onyx staircase that glows beneath your feet, plus giant silk flower arrangements and topiaries, oceanview elevators, and an attractive Internet center.

In each ship's bow is an elegant three-deck theater whose warm glow is provided by faux torches spaced all around. Seating on all three levels is unobstructed except on the far reaches of the balconies. You'll also find elegant martini, champagne, and caviar bars, as well as brighter, busier lounges for live music. For the real dancing, head up to the stunning observation lounge/disco on Sunrise Deck. Other rooms include a two-deck library, a large casino, an oceanview florist/conservatory (created with the help of Paris-based floral designer Emilio Robba and filled mostly with silk flowers and trees, some of which are for sale), and the huge high-tech conference center and cinema. Michael's Club is a quiet, dignified piano bar, replete with fake fireplace and comfy leather club chairs. Little-used during the day, it's a great place to snuggle up with a good book, while at night it's an excellent place for an after-dinner drink.

The ships' Emporium Shops have a nice variety of high-end name brands, as well as cheaper souvenirs.

For kids, the Shipmates Fun Factory has both indoor and outdoor soft-surface jungle gyms, a wading pool, a ball bin, a computer room, a movie room, an arts-and-crafts area, a video arcade, a teen center, and more.

DINING OPTIONS   The main dining rooms are beautiful two-level spaces with huge stern-facing windows, oversize round windows to port and starboard, and a dramatic central double staircase. *Summit's* dining room boasts a 7-foot Art Deco bronze of the goddess Athena that once overlooked the grand staircase on the legendary French liner *Normandie.* (She'd resided for years near the pool at Miami's Fontainebleau Hotel before Celebrity bought her and returned her to sea.)

The real *pièce de résistance* on these ships, however, is their alternative, reservations-only restaurants, which offer dining experiences unmatched on any other ship today. *Summit's* Normandie restaurant features original gold-lacquered panels from *Normandie's* smoking room, while *Constellation's* Ocean Liners restaurant has artifacts from a variety of luxury liners, including sets of original red-and-black lacquered panels from the 1920s' *Ile de France,* which add a whimsical Parisian air. Dining here is a 2- to 3-hour commitment, with a maximum of 140 guests served by a gracious staff of more than 20, including 8 dedicated chefs, 6 waiters, 5 maître d's, and 4 sommeliers. Cuisine is a combination of Continental specialties mixed with original recipes from the ships the restaurants are named after, and includes tableside flambé cooking. Waiters remove domed silver dish covers with a flourish, exceptional cheeses are offered post-meal, and a pianist or a piano/violin duo performs period music. Diners can order a la carte or choose a multicourse tasting menu for $30 per person. A menu of suggested wine pairings is available for $28.

The huge buffet restaurant on each ship is open for breakfast, lunch, and dinner, offering regular buffet selections plus pizza, pasta, and ice cream specialty stations. Depending on how busy the restaurant is, waiters may carry passengers' trays to their tables and fetch coffee. For snacks, visit the appealing Cova Café, a bustling, Italian-style joint with rich fabrics, cozy banquettes, and wood-frame chairs, serving exceptionally good freshly baked pastries (complimentary) and specialty coffees (for an extra charge).

POOL, FITNESS, SPA & SPORTS FACILITIES   The spas on *Summit* and *Constellation* are gorgeous and sprawling, their 25,000 square feet taken up with hydrotherapy treatment rooms, New Agey "Persian Garden" steam suites (whose nooks offer showers that simulate a tropical rainforest, heated tiled couches, and steam scented with chamomile, eucalyptus, and mint), and large, bubbling thalassotherapy pools with soothing pressure jets in a solarium-like setting under a glass roof. The pool is free to all adult guests, and you can stretch out the experience by grabbing a casual breakfast or lunch at the AquaSpa Cafe, set back by the oceanview windows.

The spa itself offers all the usual treatments, plus a series of special multihour spa packages that combine several Eastern-influenced treatments to induce bliss—at about $200 to $400 per package. Next door to the spa there's a very large gym with dozens of machines, free weights, and a large aerobics floor.

Up top, the Sports Deck has facilities for basketball, volleyball, quoits, and paddle tennis. Just below, on the Sunrise Deck, are a jogging track and a golf simulator. Below that is the well-laid-out pool deck, where you'll find two pools, four hot tubs, a couple of bars, and a sunning area. Head up to the balcony level—above the pool, at both the bow and the stern—for quieter sunbathing spots.

Century • Galaxy

The Verdict

Though now a decade old, *Century* and *Galaxy* remain some of the most attractive and appealing megaships at sea: modern and elegant, yet casual and friendly.

Galaxy *(photo: Celebrity Cruises)*

Specifications

Size (in Tons)		Crew	
Century	70,606	*Century*	843
Galaxy	77,713	*Galaxy*	900
Passengers (Double Occ.)		Passenger/Crew Ratio	2 to 1
Century	1,750	Year Launched	
Galaxy	1,896	*Century*	1995
Passenger/Space Ratio	41	*Galaxy*	1996
Total Cabins/Veranda Cabins		Last Refurbishment/Upgrade	
Century	875/61	*Century*	2006
Galaxy	948/220		

Frommer's Ratings (Scale of 1–5)   ★★★★ ½

Cabin Comfort & Amenities	5	Dining Options	4
Appearance & Upkeep	4	Gym, Spa & Sports Facilities	5
Public Comfort/Space	5	Children's Facilities	4
Decor	5	Enjoyment Factor	5

These are the ships that ushered Celebrity into the megaship world and also sealed the line's rep for offering elegant, gorgeously designed vessels with a truly modern flair. It's difficult to say what's most striking: The elegant spas and their 15,000-gallon thalassotherapy pools? The distinguished Michael's Club piano lounges with their leather wingbacks and velvet couches? The two-story, old-world dining rooms set back in the stern, with grand floor-to-ceiling windows allowing diners to spy the ship's wake glowing under moonlight? Collections of world-class modern art that are unmatched in the industry? Take your pick—you won't go wrong.

In 2006, *Century* underwent a $55-million refurbishment that spruced up dated interiors and added many of the features associated with the line's more modern Millennium-class vessels (*Summit, Constellation,* and their sister ships). For instance, you'll now find a 76-seat sushi bar, a Cova Café, a "Persian Garden" steam suite, a

54-seat Spa Cafe, an outdoor Sunset Bar, 314 verandas added to existing staterooms, 14 new suites, an expanded number of Concierge Class staterooms, and a new 66-seat specialty restaurant called Murano. No word yet on whether *Galaxy* will undergo a similar treatment anytime soon.

Cabins & Rates

Cabins	Per Diem From	Sq. Ft.	Fridge	Hair Dryer	Sitting Area	TV
Inside	$98	170–175	Yes	Yes	No	Yes
Outside	$130	170–175	Yes	Yes	Some	Yes
Suite	$260	246–1,433	Yes	Yes	Yes	Yes

CABINS   The simple yet pleasing decor is cheerful and based on light-colored furniture and muted color themes. Standard inside and outside cabins are larger than the norm (although not as large as Carnival's 185-footers), and suites, which come in four categories, are particularly spacious, with marble vanity/desk tops, Art Deco–style sconces, and rich inlaid wood floors. Some, such as the Penthouse Suite, offer a huge amount of space (1,219 sq. ft., expandable to 1,433 sq. ft. on special request), plus such wonderful touches as a private whirlpool bath on the veranda. Royal Suites run about half that size (plus 100-ft. balconies) but offer touches such as French doors between the bedroom and seating area, both bathtub and shower in the bathroom, and TVs in each room. *Galaxy*'s 246-square-foot Sky Suites have verandas that, at 179 square feet, are among the biggest aboard any ship—bigger, in fact, than those in the more expensive Penthouse and Royal suites on these ships (you may want to keep your robe on, though, as people on the deck above can see down onto part of the Sky Suite verandas). All suite bathrooms have bathtubs with whirlpools and magnified makeup mirrors. Like *Summit* and *Constellation, Century* and *Galaxy* offer Concierge Class staterooms, giving some suite-life extras without the full-suite price. They're mostly located on the Sky and Penthouse decks.

All cabins have built-in vanities/desks, minifridges, hair dryers, cotton robes, and safes. Closets and drawer space are roomy and well designed, as are the bathrooms. Cabin TVs are wired with an interactive system that allows guests to order room service from on-screen menus, select wine for dinner, play casino-style games, or go shopping.

Eight cabins aboard each ship (one inside and seven outside) were specifically designed for passengers with disabilities.

PUBLIC AREAS   *Century* and *Galaxy* are designed so well that it's never hard to find a quiet retreat when you want to feel secluded but don't want to be confined in your cabin. Both vessels boast a cozy, wood-paneled Michael's Club piano bar, decorated like the parlor of a London men's club. They're great spots for a fine cognac or a good single-malt Scotch while enjoying soft music. For those who don't find that clubby ambience appealing, the Rendezvous Lounge and the Cova Café offer alternatives, the former an elegant nightclub, the latter serving specialized upscale java at an extra cost. *Galaxy* also offers a champagne bar. Various other bars, both indoor and outdoor, are tucked into nooks and crannies throughout both ships.

The spacious, multistoried, glass-walled nightclubs/discos are cleanly and modernly elegant, designed with lots of cozy nooks for romantic conversation over champagne. Both ships have double-decker theaters with unobstructed views from almost every seat (though avoid those at the cocktail tables at the back of the rear balcony boxes, unless you have a really long neck).

DINING OPTIONS   The two-story formal dining rooms on *Century* and *Galaxy* are truly stunning spaces reminiscent of the grand liners of yesteryear, with wide, dramatic staircases joining the two levels and floor-to-ceiling walls of glass facing astern to a view of the ship's wake. If you lean toward the dramatic, don a gown or tux and slink down the stairs nice and slow like a 1930s Hollywood starlet. There aren't many places you can do that these days.

Century, which got a major renovation in 2006, now offers a dinner alternative at the Murano restaurant, decorated with chandeliers from its namesake Venetian island, which is famous for ornate blown glass. The restaurant's decor also includes a floor designed to resemble medieval European paving stones; a hand-painted mural themed on travel and adventure; and glass-fronted, polished nickel wine armoires displaying backlit bottles. Elaborate, multicourse meals follow the style of *Summit*'s and *Constellation*'s specialty restaurants, with their tableside cooking, carving, and flambé.

Each ship also has an indoor/outdoor buffet restaurant open for breakfast, lunch, and dinner, as well as pizza and ice cream stations.

POOL, FITNESS, SPA & SPORTS FACILITIES   Pool decks aboard these vessels feature a pair of good-size swimming areas rimmed with teak benches for sunning and relaxation. Even when the ships are full, these areas don't seem particularly crowded. Aboard *Galaxy*, a retractable dome covers one of the swimming pools during inclement weather.

The ships' excellent 10,000-square-foot AquaSpa and fitness facilities are as aesthetically pleasing as they are functional. The gym wraps around the starboard side of an upper forward deck like a hook, the large spa straddles the middle, and a very modern and elegant beauty salon faces the ocean on the port side. On *Galaxy*, the focal point of the spa is a 115,000-gallon thalassotherapy pool, a bubbling cauldron of warm, soothing seawater. A day pass is $20, a weeklong pass is $99, and you get use of the pool free if you book any spa package. Unfortunately, *Century*'s thalassotherapy pool was removed during her 2006 renovation. Spas on both ships offer massages, facials, and exotic treatments such as the Rasul, a mud and steam experience for couples.

The gyms are generously sized, with aerobics classes in a separate room. Standard classes are free, but trendy ones, such as Pilates and spinning, are $10 a pop. Each ship also has an outdoor jogging track on an upper deck, a golf simulator, and one deck that's specifically designed for sports.

4 Costa Cruises

200 S. Park Rd., Suite 200, Hollywood, FL 33021-8541. ✆ **800/462-6782** or 954/266-5600. Fax 954/266-2100. www.costacruises.com.

THE LINE IN A NUTSHELL   Imagine a Carnival megaship hijacked by an Italian circus troupe: That's Costa. The words of the day are fun, festive, and international aboard both the line's big, bright new megaships and its older, cozier vessels. Expect a really good time and a European flavor throughout, from the ubiquitous espressos and delicious crusty bread being consumed to the exchange of *buon giornos* from the many Italian officers.

THE EXPERIENCE   For years, Costa has played up its Italian heritage as the main factor that distinguishes it from Carnival, Royal Caribbean, and the rest—even though the line is part of the Carnival Corporation empire, and many members of the service staff are as Italian as Chico Marx. Still, sailing in Europe with Costa is a very

European experience: The dining portions are smaller, the hours are later, the entertainment edgier, and the noise level louder. Expect not only lots more pasta dishes on the menu than on other lines, but more classical Italian music among the entertainment offerings; Italian-flavored activities facilitated by a young, mostly Italian, and ridiculously attractive "animation staff"; and quite a number of Italian Americans among the passengers. The interiors of the line's newest ships are by Carnival's designer-in-chief Joe Farcus, who took inspiration from Italy's traditions of painting and architecture but still stuck close to his signature "more is more" style—think Venice a la Vegas, although European feedback has had a muting impact on the most recent design. The art on board, for instance, is usually chosen by the Italian head of Costa and is extremely individual and appealing, anything but generic. This is one of the few cruise lines in which passengers drag one another into their bathrooms to see the art. The Murano glass on Costa ships is so beautiful that the line is considering a way to allow passengers to order the bedside lamps after dozens of requests.

Note: Americans should remember that onboard pricing in Europe on all Costa ships is in euros—that's the shops, the bars, babysitting, casino, etc.

Pros
- **Italian flavor:** Entertainment, activities, and cuisine are presented with an Italian carnival flair.
- **Very active, very fun:** There are a lot of activities, and Costa passengers love to participate, creating a festive and social environment morning to night.

Cons
- **Very few cabins on older ships with private verandas.** The newer ships have them, but the other ships have just a few.
- **Lots of languages.** Activities and entertainment are geared to a five-language audience, so be prepared to wait till they get around to yours.

COSTA: INTERNATIONAL FLAVOR IN EUROPE

Costa's origins are as Italian as could be. In 1860, Giacomo Costa established an olive-oil refinery and packaging plant in Genoa. After his death, his sons bought a ship called *Ravenna* to transport raw materials and finished products from Sardinia through Genoa to the rest of Europe, thereby marking the founding of Costa Line in 1924. Between 1997 and 2000, Carnival Corporation bought up shares in Costa until it became whole owner. Today Costa's Italianness is as much a marketing tool as anything else, but it must be working: The line's presence in Europe is huge—and it's even

Compared with the other mainstream lines, here's how Costa rates:

	Poor	Fair	Good	Excellent	Outstanding
Enjoyment Factor			✓		
Dining		✓			
Activities				✓	
Children's Program		✓			
Entertainment			✓		
Service		✓			
Worth the Money			✓		

got a foothold in the Far East, too—and in the past 4 years it's introduced five new megaships: *Costa Mediterranea* and *Costa Fortuna* in 2003, *Costa Magica* in 2004, *Costa Concordia* in 2006, and *Costa Serena* in 2007. *Luminosa* will debut in summer 2009. In other regions, Costa is bringing mass-market pricing to exotic locations with ships in Dubai, Singapore, India, and China.

PASSENGER PROFILE

Most of Costa's ships sail in Europe, where they sail with 80% to 85% Europeans and the rest North Americans (in the Caribbean, it's the opposite). In general, Costa passengers are big on participation, the goofier the better: And we've never seen as many guests crowding the dance floor, participating in contests, or having a go at mask painting as aboard Costa's ships. There's also spontaneity on both sides; don't be surprised if while waiting in line for dinner a ship's musician, accordion or violin in tow, comes along and gets everyone dancing.

Typically you won't see more than 40 or 50 kids on any one cruise except during summer and major holidays, when there may be as many as 500 children on board. Because of the international mix, public announcements, lifeboat drills, and some entertainment options are given in English, Italian, French, German, and Spanish. The multilingual staff impressively moves between many languages, so don't worry about not being understood.

Because Costa's passengers are mostly European, they have a different view of personal space. Whereas a group of North Americans getting on a bus will typically take seats alone, Europeans fill each row before moving to the next one; the same is true in lounge and bar seating on the ships. In the dining room, too, there are fewer "private" tables for two and four diners.

DINING

Though it varies from ship to ship, Costa's cuisine has definitely improved over the years. Pastas are totally authentic and are often very good, and the Sicilian-style pizza is fantastic. On a recent cruise, the crusty Italian rolls baked from scratch were addictive, and it was difficult to sample the Parmigiano cheese wheel and prosciutto ham at the lunch buffet in moderation. The *millefoglie,* a flaky puff pastry cake layered with cream or chocolate, was one of the best cruise ship desserts Heidi has ever eaten. The waitstaff generally handles their international charges with finesse, checking, for example, if diners prefer their salad before dinner (the American way), with dinner (like the Italians prefer), or after (as the English do).

TRADITIONAL   Each dinner menu features five courses from a different region of Italy—Liguria one night, Sicily the next, and so on—plus several alternatives for each course, including the traditional pasta course. Most of the pasta, from fettuccini to spaghetti and ravioli, is shipped in direct from Italy. Many of these dishes are heavy on the cream and are richer than some Americans are used to, but they're definitely the dining highlight. If you feel like a change from the pasta course, try one of the interesting risottos—the crabmeat-and-champagne selection on our last cruise was fantastic. Otherwise, expect cruise staples such as poached salmon, lobster tail, grilled lamb chops, roast duck, and beef tenderloin, plus always-available classic selections such as Caesar salad and baked or grilled fish or chicken. **Vegetarian options** are available at each meal, and **Health and Wellness menu** selections are listed with their calorie, fat, and carbohydrate breakdowns. On the second formal night, flaming baked Alaska is paraded through the dining room and complimentary champagne is poured.

Other desserts include tiramisu, gelato, zabaglione (meringue pie), and a tasty chocolate soufflé. In keeping with the European style of eating, early seating is offered at 7pm and late at 9:15pm.

SPECIALTY   Each ship features a reservations-only alternative restaurant ($23 per person) offering Mediterranean dishes, such as rigatoni served with lobster and tomatoes, or grilled lamb chops. A Tuscan steakhouse menu is also available. The ambience is considerably quieter and more romantic than in the main dining room, with pleasant piano music and a small dance floor if you feel like a waltz between courses. *Magica*'s Vincenza Club Restaurant is worthwhile and very romantic—all Versace china, dark woods, and Italy-inspired art. If you order wine, you're in for a show, with a steward decanting your bottle using a steady hand and a candle.

Aboard the *Concordia* and *Serena* (and in spring 2009, the *Atlantica* and *Mediterranea*), the dedicated spa restaurant serves breakfast, lunch, and dinner, and also features the cuisine of Michelin-starred Ettore Bocchia. His signature "molecular cuisine" is rich in flavor but light in fat. Bocchia now oversees the menus for all Costa ships' specialty restaurants as well.

CASUAL   Each ship offers a large buffet restaurant with multiple serving areas. Breakfast is a standard mix of eggs, meats, fruits, cereals, and cheeses. At lunch, several of the stations will serve standard dishes while others will be given over to a different national or regional cuisine (Spanish, Greek, Asian, and so forth). Casual dining is also available nightly till 9:30pm. The line's **fresh-baked pizza** (offered in one section of the buffet noon–2am) looks a little weird, but trust us, it's fantastic—one of the highlights of the food on board. On our last *Mediterranea* cruise, a Costa staffer quipped that because it was real Italian pizza (very thin, without excess cheese and sauce), you can eat as much as you like and not get fat. We *believe* him. Out on deck there's a **grill** serving burgers and hot dogs, as well as a **taco bar** at lunch. If you're looking for another afternoon snack, head over to the ice cream station in the buffet area, which offers daily specials such as fresh banana or coconut, along with traditional flavors.

SNACKS & EXTRAS   Most cruise lines have scrapped their **midnight buffets,** but Costa still offers them nightly, often focusing on a theme taken from that evening's activity. On Mediterranean Night, the buffet offers pastry, fruits, desserts, pastas, and savories from Spain, Greece, France, and Turkey. On another night, the guests head below to the ship's massive galley for the buffet. Look for the polenta with mushroom sauce there—on our last cruise, it was excellent. **Room service** is available 24 hours a day. Suite guests can order full meals delivered; all others can choose from various sandwiches, appetizers, and a full bar menu.

ACTIVITIES

More than anything else, Costa is known for its lineup of exuberant activities, and passengers on these ships love to participate. From beach parties to costume balls to '70s themes, passengers in Europe play along, though they always seem to somehow retain style and elegance while doing it.

The young superfriendly international social hosts are pros at figuring out how to engage passengers of all nationalities. Expect lively dancing lessons, ranging from mambo to the meringue, to be very popular and offered by the pool. On sea days, arts and craft classes are popular, ranging from batik T-shirt making to creating get-ups for a costume party. The occasional cooking demo, Italian language classes, and port talks are sprinkled throughout the schedule, along with cruise staples such as bingo, art auctions, horse racing, bridge, Ping-Pong, and goofy poolside competitions. Each ship also has a combo library and Internet center, as well as a card room.

Enrichment lectures focus on topics such as personal finance, romance, and health. Many Europeans tend to be content just sunbathing and sipping espresso for much of the day. On a recent cruise, the pool area was a mini Riviera, with suntanned bodies of all ages and sizes outfitted in skimpy bathing suits.

A **Catholic Mass** is held almost every day in each ship's small chapel.

CHILDREN'S PROGRAM

Costa's kids' programs aren't nearly as extensive as those on Royal Caribbean (or Carnival's Conquest-class and Spirit-class ships), but then, there are usually far fewer children on board. At least two full-time youth counselors sail aboard each ship, with additional staff whenever more than a dozen or so kids are on the passenger list. **Supervised activities** are offered for kids 3 to 18, divided into two age groups unless enough children are aboard to divide them into three (3–6, 7–12, and 13–18 years) or four (3–6, 7–10, 11–14, and 15–18). The **Costa Kids Club,** for ages 3 to 12, includes such activities as Nintendo, galley tours, arts and crafts, scavenger hunts, Italian-language lessons, bingo, board games, face painting, movies, kids' karaoke, and pizza and ice cream sundae parties. The ships each have a children's playroom; it's bigger and brighter on the newer ships, which also have teen discos. If there are enough teens on board, the **Costa Teens Club** for ages 13 to 18 offers foosball and darts competitions, karaoke, and other activities. An added benefit of exposing your kids to such an international setting is that even the smaller kids wind up speaking a few words in three or four languages they picked up from other kids.

When ships are at sea, supervised Kids Club hours are typically from 9am to noon, 3 to 6pm, and 9 to 11:30pm. The program also operates during port days at no extra charge, but on a more limited basis.

Costa Fleet Itineraries

Ship	Sailing Regions	Home Ports
Costa Atlantica	10- to 13-night voyages in the Mediterranean and Northern Europe	Savona (Italy), Amsterdam
Costa Classica	7- to 11-night Mediterranean	Savona, Trieste (Italy)
Costa Concorida	7- and 11-night Mediterranean	Civitavecchia/Rome
Costa Europa	8- to 11-night Mediterranean	Savona (Italy)
Costa Fortuna	5- and 7-night Mediterranean	Venice, Savona (Italy)
Costa Magica	7-night Mediterranean	Savona (Italy)
Costa Marina	5- to 14-night Mediterranean, Norwegian Fjords, Northern Europe/Russia, and Atlantic Europe	Savona (Italy), Amsterdam
Costa Mediterranea	7- and 8-night voyages in the Mediterranean and Northern Europe	Savona (Italy), Copenhagen
Costa Romantica	7-night Mediterranean	Civitavecchia/Rome
Costa Serena	7- and 11-night Mediterranean	Venice, Savona (Italy)
Costa Victoria	6- to 14-night voyages in the Mediterranean and Northern Europe	Savona (Italy), Kiel and Hamburg (Germany)

On Gala nights there's a great complimentary **Parents' Night Out program** from 6 to 11:30pm during which kids 3 and older (they must be out of diapers) are entertained and given a special buffet or pizza party while Mom and Dad get a night out alone. All other times, **group babysitting** for ages 3 and up is available every night from 9 to 11:30pm at no cost, and from 11:30pm to 1:30am if you make arrangements in advance. No private, in-cabin babysitting is available.

Children must be at least 3 months old to sail with Costa; kids under 2 sail free.

ENTERTAINMENT

Expect most entertainment to be Italian, with concerts, operatic soloists, puppet or marionette shows, magicians, mimes, acrobats, crew talent shows, and cabaret—no language skills required. On a recent cruise, one of the shows had a unicycle-riding, ball-balancing, flame-juggling, plate-spinning entertainer—the kind you used to see on *The Ed Sullivan Show*. Other featured performers included an operatic tenor singing a program of high-note crowd pleasers and a classical pianist performing Beethoven and Gershwin. The line's production shows mostly follow the typical song-and-dance revue formula; on recent sailings, creative costumes and choreography got big points, and so did the enthusiasm and versatility of the dance troupe on the *Marina*. Participatory shows are much more fun overall and more in tune with what Costa passengers seem to want. Versions of the "Election of the Ideal Couple" and a *Newlywed Game* takeoff, for instance, both clip along at a frantic pace, with the cruise staff helping and hindering as appropriate to get the most laughs. Who knew the criterion for being an ideal couple was the ability to burst a balloon with your butt?

Casinos are glitzy on the newer, bigger ships. Fleetwide, expect the discos to be hopping, though things often get going only after 1am. Unlike many ships where you'll find a solitary couple in the disco late at night, Costa's tend to be jammed in the wee hours with very stylish Europeans who keep the special effects and music going until breakfast.

One very pleasant aspect of cruising on Costa in Europe is that guests can and do embark and disembark in several ports (unfortunately, due to the Passenger Shipping Act, U.S. citizens can't participate), so there is no "last night" drop in the ship's energy and disembarkation is easy, perhaps the smoothest and quickest we've seen compared to similar-sized megaships.

SERVICE

In past years, our main complaint about Costa was its service, which on particularly bad nights resembled a *Three Stooges* skit. But things seem to have gotten better. While it's still not the Four Seasons, our last cruises have showed marked improvement, with waiters better trained and more polished, cabin stewards more attentive and helpful, and everyone more accommodating and friendly. On Heidi's most recent cruise aboard the *Costa Marina*, the dining staff was excellent; on the other hand, on a recent *Fortuna* sailing, the service was disappointing.

There are no self-service laundry facilities on any of the Costa ships.

Costa Concordia •
Costa Serena

The Verdict

These very sleek ships that introduced dedicated spa staterooms to cruising have the
same fundamental layout but are very different in theme and mood, with an elaborate
tour of Europe theme on *Concordia* and a
mysterious feel to the Greek and Roman
mythology of *Serena*.

Costa Serena *(photo: Costa Cruises)*

Specifications

Size (in Tons)	112,000	Passenger/Crew Ratio	2.8 to 1
Passengers (Double Occ.)	3,000	Year Launched	
Passenger/Space Ratio	39.5	*Concordia*	2006
Total Cabins/Veranda Cabins	1,500/571	*Serena*	2007
Crew	1,068	Last Refurbishment/Upgrade	N/A

Frommer's Ratings (Scale of 1–5)   ★★★★

Cabin Comfort & Amenities	4	Dining Options	4
Appearance & Upkeep	4	Gym, Spa & Sports Facilities	5
Public Comfort/Space	4	Children's Facilities	3
Decor	4	Enjoyment Factor	4

Costa Concordia and *Costa Serena,* now Italy's largest ships, take the *Carnival Conquest*
design in directions that are purely Costa, both filled with playful and highly individual art and sharing the slightly surreal touches that set a cruise aside from everyday
life. When *Concordia's* new 67 Samsara spa staterooms and suites were snapped up
immediately, the line quickly adapted the *Serena* to carry 99 spa accommodations; *Costa
Atlantica* and *Costa Magica* will be retrofitted next spring with 44 spa staterooms each.

Cabins & Rates

Cabins	Per Diem From	Sq. Ft.	Fridge	Hair Dryer	Sitting Area	TV
Inside	$107	160–184	Yes	Yes	No	Yes
Outside	$150	160–184	Yes	Yes	Yes	Yes
Suite	$250	279–456	Yes	Yes	Yes	Yes

CABINS   Cabin colors tend toward very soft, restful colors, generally with neutral
walls. Charm and distinction are added by the unusual lithographs on the walls and
the glow of Murano glass lamps. The ships' Samsara spa cabins comprise several categories of rooms, and everything about them is the same as all the other cabins on
board except for their having private elevator access right into the spa. The spa cabins
also have Elemis bathroom amenities; otherwise, these cabins and all others have minibars, safes, hair dryers, and TVs with music stations and pay-per-view movies. The
beds can be arranged in twin or queen configuration, and the pillows are so unusually

comfortable that they became dinner conversation. Cabins are well organized and well lit, and have plenty of drawer and closet space. Suites and minisuites have bolder colors and decor, and private whirlpool baths.

Twenty-nine staterooms are wheelchair accessible.

PUBLIC AREAS   *Concordia's* interior is like a trip through Europe itself, with public areas named after cities ranging from Paris and London to Lisbon and Budapest. Colors and materials reflect the names, with the Tatra Library, for instance, showing off the light woods from a famous ski resort in the Tatra Mountains and the Barcelona Casino paying tribute to Gaudi with walls and ceilings covered with asymmetrical ceramic tiles. Some of the slot machines have some very amusing animation. The three-level, 1,287-seat Athens Theater has a chandelier made up of a hundred Greek masks; entertainment varies from Broadway-style shows to magic and comedy, and the special effects and sound are top-notch.

Serena, themed mostly around Greek and Roman mythology, is far more mysterious and harkens back to the *Atlantica* with some delightful, surreal furniture. The decks are named for heavenly constellations, so instead of arranging to meet in Prague, passengers rendezvous on Orion or Andromeda. Gods and goddesses dressed in magnificent brocades are suspended in clouds above the Pantheon Atrium, seen at their best from within the shadowy interior rather than up close from different levels of the ship. One of the most intriguing spaces is the library—dedicated to Clio, the muse of history and epic poetry—where the elegant striped-silk banquettes are usually occupied by people enjoying the multilingual collection of popular and coffee-table books. You really can't mistake the Cupid Lounge; not only is the winged god pictured prominently, but everything in sight is shaped like a heart. And in the Victorian sports bar, space is set off with rows of soccer balls that guests can't resist kicking—a bad idea; they are firmly anchored. The casino strikes a rather jarring note against the ship's mythological ambience, with hard geometric shapes and bright colors. The disco follows the Costa pattern of a multilevel high-tech tube that spontaneously comes to life sometime after midnight; on *Serena* it's placed under the auspices of Pan, the god of music and sensuality.

A huge digital movie screen on the pool deck has a multilingual audio system with movie packages including drinks (alcoholic or nonalcoholic for around 11€/$15 and 8.75€/$12, respectively).

DINING OPTIONS   On *Serena* and *Concordia,* Costa has taken another giant step up in providing far more consistent quality in dining. The a la carte Concordia Club (Club Bacco on *Serena*) underlines its Netherlands decor with geometric Mondrian patterns on the chairs. Candlelit dining, an extensive wine list, and fine service support the menu created by Ettore Bocchia, executive chef at the Michelin-starred Grand Hotel in Bellagio. Bocchia's molecular cuisine is famous for bringing out the extraordinary flavor of each ingredient, and the presentation is as good as the food.

The main dining rooms have huge windows and are filled to capacity at breakfast and dinner, though lighter at lunchtime. The cuisine consists of a very impressive choice of seafood, pasta dishes and traditional meats and poultry, with desserts tempting enough to inspire strategic planning to save room. On most nights, there is no buffet service at dinner, as Europeans strongly prefer a leisurely meal in the dining room, although the children's program sometimes has evening meals in the buffet. Room service provides a 24-hour menu of sandwiches, salads, desserts, and cheeses for those who want lighter fare.

On each ship, Samsara guests have tables permanently reserved in their own restaurant, although they can choose the regular dining rooms if they prefer. However, the menu created by Bocchia and the very personal service in the private room—decorated with gorgeous kimonos—is hard to beat. Although low in fat and high in flavor, the meals are by no means for ascetics, and the breadbasket and dessert list are designed to madden the low-carb crowd. After discovering on *Concordia* that Samsara guests are typically couples, the restaurant on *Serena* is set up with tables for two.

In the casual dining department, the Helsinki buffet showed perhaps the biggest upgrade in Costa's cuisine: very crisp vegetables and salads, hot and cold seafood dishes, at least four pasta selections, and fresh desserts.

For snacking, the chocolate fountain sends out a siren aroma from the Coffee and Chocolate Bar, and with a formidable teatime at 4:30pm and signature pizza from 11am to 1:30am, it takes real dedication to attend the crowded late-night buffets.

POOL, FITNESS, SPA & SPORTS FACILITIES   Costa's major innovation on *Concordia,* expanded on *Serena,* is the creation of Samsara spa accommodations with their own private elevator up a waterfall directly into the spa. Samsara guests can just put on a robe and slippers and have their treatments without emerging into public view; they receive a package of services and classes, special spa bathroom amenities, and a private restaurant that would be worth the 20% extra cost alone. Since *Concordia* debuted the concept in 2006, several other cruise lines and hotel chains have announced similar plans.

The Samsara wellness centers are exactly the same on both ships, and their theme is taken from various Asian cultures. *Concordia*'s 20,500-square-foot spa has 67 staterooms and suites located inside the spa center, increased to 99 on *Serena.* Guests booking these staterooms receive two free spa treatments, plus unlimited access to the magnificent thalassotherapy pool with its seawater jets and huge Foo Dog sculptures; the relaxation area with its solarium; and fitness and meditation classes.

The spa also has a full menu of standard treatments, along with Rasul; an aromatic Turkish bath scented with lavender, rosemary, and eucalyptus; body treatments using steam and three kinds of clay; and Ayurvedic treatments, plus special barbering services with shaves and skincare for men. The treatment rooms have gated little backyards with seats facing enormous windows that look out onto the sea; two couples' rooms have private Jacuzzis. The peaceful recovery area has curtained and canopied beds.

The fitness area has a huge array of techno-gym equipment, weights, cycles, and full-body aerobics machines. A glass-walled separate section of the gym is set aside for formal classes; the space is curtained for meditation classes. Complimentary stretch and aerobic classes are offered, and yoga, spinning, Pilates, and music therapy classes start at 11€ ($15)

In addition to the gym, there is a jogging track and a multisports court used for tennis, basketball, and volleyball. Each ship has four swimming pools, two with retractable glass roofs and a splash pool for children. The five Jacuzzis were in use day and night on our cruise. The Grand Prix driving simulator uses the same technology that trains championship drivers and is available for passengers 16 and over with height and weight limits; depending on the chosen course, the cost runs 5€ to 38€ ($7–$53).

Costa Magica •
Costa Fortuna

The Verdict

This pair of fun ships trends toward heavily decorated, Carnival-like interiors, but with a lighter, almost feminine feel.

Costa Fortuna *(photo: Costa Cruises)*

Specifications

Size (in Tons)	105,000	Crew	1,068
Passengers (Double Occ.)	2,720	Passenger/Crew Ratio	2.5 to 1
Passenger/Space Ratio	38.6	Year Launched	2003
Total Cabins/Veranda Cabins	1,358/522	Last Refurbishment/Upgrade	N/A

Frommer's Ratings (Scale of 1–5)   ★★★★

Cabin Comfort & Amenities	4	Dining Options	4
Appearance & Upkeep	4	Gym, Spa & Sports Facilities	5
Public Comfort/Space	4	Children's Facilities	3
Decor	4	Enjoyment Factor	4

Costa Fortuna and sister ship *Costa Magica* were both Costa's and Italy's largest ships before the debut of the Europe-based *Costa Concordia* in summer 2006. Elegant with an old-world touch, *Fortuna*'s public rooms and restaurants are rich with detail, including memorabilia from legendary and historic Italian liners, including vintage posters and ship models. On the *Magica,* the design theme is Italian palaces. As on most Costa ships, the discos are very lively, and many public rooms stay crowded long after the last show has finished.

Cabins & Rates

Cabins	Per Diem From	Sq. Ft.	Fridge	Hair Dryer	Sitting Area	TV
Inside	$83	160	Yes	Yes	No	Yes
Outside	$114	160	Yes	Yes	Yes	Yes
Suite	$243	275–345	Yes	Yes	Yes	Yes

CABINS   Standard cabins trend toward elegant, with soft, warm colors and magic-themed prints by Augusto Vignali. Some of the cabin furnishings, especially the lamps, are unusual and charming. Of the 1,358 cabins, 456 have balconies, as do the 64 suites. Inside cabins are very well designed, with two closet areas, a fairly generous amount of drawer space, twin or queen bed configuration, and showers. Outside staterooms with verandas are the same size, with an additional 65 square feet of private balcony; the latter holds lounge chairs and a small table. Suites range from 275 square feet with 65-square-foot balconies to 345 square feet with 85 square feet of private veranda. All staterooms have minibars, hair dryers, and safes; suites also have whirlpool baths.

Twenty-seven staterooms are wheelchair accessible.

PUBLIC AREAS   On *Magica,* dance and theater imagery dominate the Spoleto Ballroom, reflecting the Spoleto "Two Worlds" art festival. The smallish Sicily Casino has an uncanny atmosphere taken from the region's folklore and traditional puppetry. Sixty-five large puppets of medieval knights, court jesters, and musicians are scattered among the tables and slot machines. From the casinos on both ships (where the slots take euros), you can keep an eye out on the action in the disco, which seems to fill in response to an invisible summons. The decor on the *Fortuna* was inspired by grand Italian ocean liners of a bygone era; there's a wonderful display featuring 26 models of past and present Costa ships showcased from the ceiling of the main atrium. The restaurants and public lounge are named after famed liners, such as *Rex* and *Cristoforo Colombo*. Old map replicas, as well as murals of 1930s and 1940s ship scenes, are found throughout the ship along with copies of vintage ship posters and ads. Our favorite spaces on the *Fortuna:* the Conte Rossi 1921 Piano Bar, with its red color scheme, and the downright elegant Conte di Savoia 1932 Grand Bar. Likewise, one of the most enchanting areas on board the *Magica* is the Grand Bar Salento, with its fat gold columns; the ceiling above the dance floor is covered with images from the baroque churches of Lecce.

The ships' libraries double as card rooms and have very few books. On the *Magica,* where the Bressanome Library has an ecclesiastical theme, the big attractions are the tall blue, phone-booth-sized enclosed chairs modeled on ecclesiastical thrones—you'll see adults and children alike waiting to sit in them.

The ships' theaters are striking three-level venues. The nine-deck atriums are excellent people-watching spots. *Magica's* is lined with a photographic collage of Italy's most loved regions—a sort of summary of the ship. A bronze sculpture there has one of several haunting titles found among the ship's art: "There were four of us and now there are three of you."

DINING OPTIONS   Although Costa's food has been uneven, the choices show great improvement, and the Tavernetta Club Conte Grande restaurant is outstanding. Besides some more exotic choices, conservative tastes have plenty of steaks, seafood, fowl, and vegetables to choose from, along with outrageously good desserts and wines. The ambience is romantic, with Versace china and gold napkins standing out against rich, dark woods and shining gold ware, with friezes from Palladio's villas reproduced around a giant skylight. There are two main restaurants aboard each ship; on the *Fortuna,* Costa Michelangelo and Raffaello feature striking memorabilia from the great Italian ocean liners of the past. At the entrance to the Michelangelo restaurant, for example, is a 19-foot scale model of the famed transatlantic liner of the same name. Copies of vintage ship posters and ads from the 1920s and 1930s are also displayed in the two restaurants. Rounding out the dining options is a buffet restaurant. The Bellagio Lido restaurant on *Magica* (Restaurant Buffet Colombo 1954 on *Fortuna*) is unusually elegant for an informal buffet, with domes and columns. Burgers are available from an outdoor grill at lunch, and a portion of the Lido is turned into a casual pizza cafe at dinner (no additional charge). In addition to its more consistent food quality, Costa now offers more choices for vegetarians and passengers looking for sugar-free and other diet choices.

POOL, FITNESS, SPA & SPORTS FACILITIES   The 4,600-square-foot Saturnia Spas are spacious, and a huge wall of glass extends the space even more. The multilevel gym is similarly beautiful and well equipped with Pilates balls, free weights, and yoga mats. The Technogym equipment can be programmed to parameters set for you by one of the ship's personal trainers, with a digital key that will repeat the program every time you use it. Spinning bikes, treadmills, yoga classes, and health seminars supplement the range of skincare treatments, facials, wraps, and massages at the spa. A Turkish bath and sauna are also available.

The main pool area is built like an amphitheater and is clearly a place to see and be seen. The aft lido pool is covered by a removable glass roof, and on our cruise the pool and hot tubs were in use in the evenings as well as daytime. A third pool area is dedicated to children and their families.

Costa Atlantica •
Costa Mediterranea

The Verdict

Is it a carnival or is it Carnivale? Decorated in a Europe-meets-Vegas style, these ships are eye candy for the ADD set.

Costa Mediterranea *(photo: Costa Cruises)*

Specifications

Size (in Tons)	85,000	Crew	920
Passengers (Double Occ.)		Passenger/Crew Ratio	2.3 to 1
Atlantica	2,114	Year Launched	
Mediterranea	2,112	*Atlantica*	2000
Passenger/Space Ratio	40	*Mediterranea*	2003
Total Cabins/Veranda Cabins	1,056/678	Last Refurbishment/Upgrade	2008

Frommer's Ratings (Scale of 1–5)   ★★★ ½

Cabin Comfort & Amenities	4	Dining Options	3
Apperance & Upkeep	4	Gym, Spa & Sports Facilities	4
Public Comfort/Space	4	Children's Facilities	3
Decor	4	Enjoyment Factor	4

These sisters ushered in the future for Costa, being a kind of European version of the "Fun Ships" operated by sister company Carnival. *Atlantica* was the first of the Farcus-designed/Costa-designed ships and remains one of the most successful style combinations, going to the top, but not over it. True, there are flashing lights along the elevators, but there are also mosaics and frescoes throughout and enough Carrera marble to have driven a Renaissance sculptor crazy. The Fellini theme works particularly well to combine Italian flavor and Farcus's fantasy, and the art on board is spectacular. You could spend a whole cruise examining the elaborate doors and ceilings and the amusing and comfortable furniture. Cruising on the *Atlantica* is like being in an Escher painting: fantastic detail and endless illusion.

The two ships are almost identical, built along the same lines as Carnival's Spirit-class ships. At nearly 1,000 feet long, the ships cut a sleek profile, and their bright yellow, barrel-like smokestacks, emblazoned with a big blue COSTA C, distinguish them from their Carnival cousins.

Despite the obvious success of the Spirit-class design (six Carnival and Costa ships are based on it, and Holland America has adapted it for its Vista-class vessels), we're not completely in love with it. The main public decks have a zigzagging layout that lacks the easy flow of some competitors, and some areas in the bow are downright bizarre: For instance, the wide outdoor promenade on Deck 3 ducks indoors as it goes forward, becoming a long, strange, marble-floored lounge. Is it a place to sit? Is it a place to walk? No one seems to know, so it gets hardly any use. But maybe that's a plus, making its little marble tables, wicker chairs, and small couches decent places to escape the crowds.

Cabins & Rates

Cabins	Per Diem From	Sq. Ft.	Fridge	Hair Dryer	Sitting Area	TV
Inside	$112	160	Yes	Yes	No	Yes
Outside	$162	210	Yes	Yes	Yes	Yes
Suite	$314	360–650	Yes	Yes	Yes	Yes

CABINS   *Atlantica* runs to cherry woods and jewel-tone fabrics in its cabins, while *Mediterranea* features caramel-color wood tones and warm autumn-hued fabrics that create a pleasant environment; well over half of the cabins on both ships have private balconies. Each has a stocked, pay-as-you-go minifridge, hair dryer, personal safe, and more than adequate storage space, and all outside cabins have sitting areas with couches. The views from all category-4 cabins on Deck 4 are completely obstructed by lifeboats, and the category-6 balcony cabins directly above, on Deck 5, are partially obstructed as well. Bathrooms have good storage space.

The 32 Panorama suites on decks 5 and 6 measure 272 square feet and have a 90-square-foot balcony with attractive granite coffee tables, wooden chairs, and desks. Suites have large couches that can double as a bed, two separate floor-to-ceiling closets, lots of drawer space, and large bathrooms with whirlpool bathtubs, marble counters, and double sinks. Adjacent is a dressing room with a vanity table, drawers, and a closet. The Grand Suites are the largest accommodations aboard. Six are located amidships on Deck 7 and measure 372 square feet, plus 118-square-foot balconies; the other eight are aft on decks 4, 6, 7, and 8, and measure 367 square feet, plus 282-square-foot balconies.

Eight cabins are wheelchair accessible.

PUBLIC AREAS   Interiors on the *Mediterranea* are inspired by noble 17th- and 18th-century Italian *palazzi,* and are heavy on dance and theater imagery—in fact, they're heavy on just about everything. From her carpets to her decorated ceilings, hardly any surface aboard *isn't* decorated somehow. When you first lay eyes on her *Alice in Wonderland*–like fantasyland atrium, for instance, it's a bit jarring, all bright colors, glowing light panels, textured and sculpted metal surfaces, Roman-style ceiling murals, and fiber-optic squid swarming up eight decks. Soon, though, you'll grow attached to the buttery-soft, red-leather chairs (including several pairs of pleasantly absurd ones with towering tall backs) and huge framed black-and-white photographs of dancers that fill the space, with its dramatic central bar and more intimate wings spreading out to port and starboard. Just astern, another bar/lounge leads to the two-story dining room.

Atlantica's theme is taken from Fellini's movies and displays huge stills from his classics and blown-up paparazzi photos of stars. Each deck is named for a Fellini film—*La Dolce Vita, La Strada,* etc.—and the eighth deck is dubbed 8½. Fantasy permeates the ship, from the lipstick-red leather chairs to the suspended glass staircase connecting the two levels of Club Atlantica, the alternative restaurant/nightclub. The staircase was designed by the same Venetian sculptor who did the glass dancers by the Fred and Ginger pools (okay, it's not all Fellini). The details are beyond rich; even the elevator interiors deserve notice. People on board with us spent an incredible amount of time arguing the relative merits of the chairs with springs and tassels and those with little black boots.

On each ship the disco is a darkish, two-story, cavelike space with a staircase leading down into what is appropriately called Dante's on the *Atlantica*. Video-screen walls, fog machines, and translucent dance floors entertain the very stylish crowd that keeps the disco going into the wee hours of the morning. The three-level theater on each ship has velvety high-backed seating and very high-tech and elaborate stages. Downstairs, on the lowest passenger deck, a smaller show lounge used for late-night comedy acts, karaoke, and cocktail parties is decorated on *Mediterranea* with an underwater motif—don't worry, you're still above the waterline. There's also a big glitzy casino with a festive Vegas-style mood, several large lounges that feature musical entertainment in the evenings, a smallish but pleasant library/Internet center, and a roomy, elegant card room. A kids' playroom, teen center, large video arcade, and Catholic chapel (one of these things is not like the others . . .) are all squireled away in the bow on decks 4 and 5.

DINING OPTIONS On each ship, aside from an elegant two-story dining room, there's a two-story alternative, reservations-only restaurant high up on Deck 10, charging guests $23 per person for the privilege of dining (suite guests can go free of charge once per cruise). The alternative restaurants feature the molecular cuisine (low-fat, but rich in flavor) of Ettore Bocchia, executive chef at the Michelin-starred Grand Hotel in Bellagio. Its atmosphere is its best feature, with dim lights, candlelight, fresh flowers, soft live music, and lots of space between tables. For a quieter and more romantic mood, the alternative restaurant is a nice change of pace, but don't linger past 10pm if you don't want cigar smoke to spoil your elegant dinner: That's when the restaurant's second story becomes a cigar lounge.

For casual breakfast, lunch, and (6 nights a week) dinner, head to the sprawling indoor/outdoor buffet restaurant. Soft ice cream and pizza made with herbs and fresh mozzarella are served from stations here. Look up when you get to the very end of the restaurant, before heading out to the stern pool area: There's a huge, amazing Murano glass chandelier up there that you'd never notice unless you craned your head on purpose.

One of *Atlantica*'s most delightful spaces is a faithful copy of Venice's Caffe Florian, a great choice for a glass of wine or a specialty coffee.

POOL, FITNESS, SPA & SPORTS FACILITIES The gyms on both ships are pleasant two-tiered affairs with machines on many different levels and a large hot tub in the center. On the Technogym equipment, you set up your workout and it is saved on an electronic key, which you can also take with you to use on the same equipment in landside gyms.

The spa offers your typical menu of treatments, including 50-minute massages, facials, and reflexology treatments. There are three pools on each ship, two of them in the loud, active main pool area and another in the stern. Above the latter is a neat water slide for all ages. Other sports and relaxation amenities include four hot tubs, a golf driving net, and a combo volleyball, basketball, and tennis court. If you explore, you'll find lots of deck space for sunbathing and hiding away on a deck chair with a page-turner.

Costa Victoria

The Verdict

A sleek megaship, this all-around beauty boasts a European ambience and stunning decor.

Costa Victoria *(photo: Costa Cruises)*

Specifications

Size (GRT)	75,000	Crew	800
Passengers (Double Occ.)	1,928	Passenger/Crew Ratio	2.4 to 1
Passenger/Space Ratio	38	Year Launched	1996
Total Cabins/Veranda Cabins	964/246	Last Major Refurbishment	N/A

Frommer's Ratings (Scale of 1–5)

★★★★

Cabin Comfort & Amenities	4	Dining Options	3.5
Ship Cleanliness & Maintenance	4	Gym, Spa & Sports Facilities	3
Public Comfort/Space	4	Children's Facilities	3
Decor	5	Enjoyment Factor	4

The ship that launched Costa Cruises into the megaship era was built in Bremerhaven, Germany, and inaugurated in summer 1996. With an impressive cruising speed of 21 to 23 knots, *Costa Victoria* has a streamlined, futuristic-looking design with four tiers of glass-fronted observation decks facing the prow. Its size allows for more spacious and dramatic interior features, and more options for dining and after-dark diversions than the earlier Costa ships. When it was built, it was the largest and most technologically sophisticated ship ever launched by Costa.

Signature design elements include an abundant use of stainless steel, teak, suede, leather, tile mosaics, and Italian marble in swirled patterns of blues and greens—for instance, brilliant royal blue suede covers the tops of card tables, and deep salmon-colored suede is used on the walls of the Concorde Plaza lounge. The Bolero Buffet features teak floors, and a wraparound tile mosaic creates eye-catching walls in the Capriccio Lounge.

The sleek, seven-story Planetarium Atrium—a first for Costa at the time the ship was built—features four glass elevator banks and is punctuated by a thin string of ice-blue neon subtly spiraling toward the glass ceiling dome.

Cabins & Rates

Cabins	Per Diem From	Sq. Ft.	Fridge	Hair Dryer	Sitting Area	TV
Inside	$86	120	Yes	Yes	No	Yes
Outside	$124	150	Yes	Yes	No	Yes
Suite	$236	390	Yes	Yes	Yes	Yes

CABINS   Ironically, the cabins on this big ship are smaller than those on the *Romantica* and *Classica*. At 120 to 150 square feet, standard inside and outside cabins certainly won't win any awards for their size (the smallest are little more than walk-in closets), but the ship's sleek, minimalist design and decor bring a delicious European touch to the cruise experience. Decorative fabric panels hang on the wall above headboards, matching the bedspreads. Bedside tables and dressers have sleek styling. Stainless steel is used for all bathroom sinks and for dressers and mirrors in the minisuites. All cabins have TVs, music channels, hair dryers, minibars, and safes. During a 2004 refurbishment, 246 balconies were added to what had been outside cabins with portholes.

Especially desirable are 14 minisuites, which have separate living rooms, reading areas, and tubs with hydromassage equipment. Each is outfitted with one queen-size bed and two Pullman-style beds. What makes them a bargain is that they contain many of the same amenities and interior design features as the more expensive suites, and their space is very generous, at 301 square feet. For those with imperial taste, six full-size suites raise the beam on luxury, with one queen and two Pullman-style beds, and generous 430-square-foot proportions that make them feel roomy even if they're bunking four passengers. Furnishings in these suites are made of pear wood, with fabrics by Laura Ashley—who is not even remotely Italian, and whose particular patterns in this case are relatively bold and not particularly frilly looking. Some of the suites have floor-to-ceiling windows.

Four of the ship's cabins are specifically outfitted for passengers with disabilities. Cabins on Deck 6A don't benefit from direct elevator access and require that guests climb a half-flight of stairs from the nearest elevator bank.

PUBLIC AREAS   Public areas throb with color and energy, especially the big and brassy Monte Carlo Casino, which is linked to the Grand Bar Orpheus one floor below by a curving stairway whose glass stair treads are illuminated in almost psychedelic patterns. This bar is the preferred spot aboard for sampling an espresso or cappuccino, or, if it's late enough, a selection of grappas. (For the uninitiated, grappa is a particularly potent Italian liquor that is definitely not to be messed with!)

Designed to re-create an Italian piazza, the four-story Concorde Plaza is one of the *Victoria*'s signature public areas. Seating over 300, it boasts a four-story-high waterfall on one end and a wall of windows facing the sea on the other. It makes a great venue for evening dancing and music or for a relaxing drink by day.

Other public rooms include a play area for children, a club for teens, three conference rooms, an array of boutiques, a card room, a library, a disco, and an observation lounge that serves as a grand arena for socializing and special shipboard events, as well as a theater for evening entertainment.

DINING OPTIONS   Choices include two main dining rooms; a specialty restaurant called the Tavernetta Lounge with a cover charge of 23€ ($32) per person; a pizzeria; and a casual buffet restaurant open for breakfast, lunch, and dinner.

POOL, FITNESS & SPA FACILITIES   The *Victoria*'s Pompeii Spa includes its own indoor pool, decorated with richly colored mosaic tiles and Roman columns. You can release your tension in a steam bath, a sauna, or a Turkish bath, or sit and soak in the spa's Jacuzzi, which is perched artfully within the larger waters of the heated swimming pool. The attractive but smallish workout room shares a glass wall with the spa and pool area, and features over a dozen exercise machines. A beauty salon is also available on board.

Out on deck, there's a pair of swimming pools as well as a "misting pool" that cools off overheated sunbathers with fine jets of water. More decks wrap the pools and their sunbathing area, providing plenty of space for passengers to stretch out and soak up the rays, even when the ship is fully booked. The area looks like a resort on the Italian Riviera, with its bright yellow and blue deck chairs and its nautical blue-and-white-striped lounges. There are four Jacuzzis; a tennis court that doubles as a half-size basketball court; and a jogging track, four circuits of which equal 1 mile.

Costa Romantica •
Costa Classica

The Verdict

Italophiles will adore these midsize ships, which deliver an authentic slice of *la dolce vita,* but think Milan, not Rome.

Costa Romantica *(photo: Costa Cruises)*

Specifications

Size (GRT)		Crew	
Costa Romantica	54,000	*Costa Romantica*	640
Costa Classica	116,000	*Costa Classica*	640
Passengers (Double Occ.)		Passenger/Crew Ratio	
Costa Romantica	1,350	*Costa Romantica*	2.1 to 1
Costa Classica	3,100	*Costa Classica*	2.3 to 1
Passenger/Space Ratio		Year Launched	
Costa Romantica	40	*Costa Romantica*	1993
Costa Classica	32	*Costa Classica*	1991
Total Cabins/Veranda Cabins		Last Major Refurbishment	
Costa Romantica	678/10	*Costa Romantica*	2003
Costa Classica	654/10	*Costa Classica*	2001

Frommer's Ratings (Scale of 1–5)   ★★★ ½

Cabin Comfort & Amenities	4	Dining Options	2
Ship Cleanliness & Maintenance	4	Pool, Fitness & Spa Facilities	4
Public Comfort/Space	4	Children's Facilities	3
Decor	4	Enjoyment Factor	3

These ultramodern-style sister ships have a cool, European interior design that some people find almost clinical and that contrasts sharply with the lively shipboard atmosphere. The *Classica* is so knock-you-in-the-head modern with its white marble, hip art, metal accents, and glass walls that Costa mellowed its act when building sister ship *Romantica,* adding wood paneling and warmer colors. Both have fabulous art displays.

The vessels were the largest and most stylish ships in the Costa armada until 1996, when they were supplanted by *Costa Victoria.* Today they are distinctive for their simplicity (one-level dining, for example) and the purity of the Italian ambience rather than the more glitzy combined style of later Costa ships. Many passengers are repeat customers, drawn to these vessels for their emphasis on comfort and contemporary Italian design accented with the best of Italy's traditions. The ships' relatively small size means you'll begin to recognize your fellow passengers after a few days at sea. And with the public rooms located on the upper four decks, it's hard to get lost.

Cabins & Rates

Cabins	Per Diem From*	Sq. Ft.	Fridge	Hair Dryer	Sitting Area	TV
Inside	$78	175	No	Yes	No	Yes
Outside	$131	200	No	Yes	No	Yes
Suite	$221	340	Yes	Yes	Yes	Yes

Per diem rates based on lowest daily average for 4- to 11-night cruises on both ships.

CABINS   In a word, big. At 200 square feet, standard outside cabins are among the largest available on any mainstream cruise line and much bigger than those on most European lines. The well-designed modern cabins are attractively paneled with polished cherry wood and done up in warm colors. All are furnished with twin beds (some convert to queens), armchairs, small tables, desks, good-size closets, safes, hair dryers, TVs, and music channels.

Lower-end inside cabins are still large, at 175 square feet. Ten suites on each ship have verandas. The *Costa Romantica* has 6 (veranda-less) suites with panoramic, forward-facing windows, and 18 minisuites that measure 340 square feet. Each suite can accommodate up to six passengers (although they had better be pretty good friends!) and is furnished with a queen bed, single sofa bed, and Murphy bed, along with a sitting area, minibar, double vanity, and whirlpool bath.

Six inside cabins on the *Romantica* and five on the *Classica* are wheelchair accessible.

PUBLIC AREAS   Public areas take their names from the heritage of Italy and sometimes sport decors to match—for instance, in the *Costa Romantica's* Botticelli Restaurant, murals and window shades evoke themes from the Renaissance. Classic Italian touches in different areas include chandeliers from Murano, intricate mosaics, pearwood inlays, and lots and lots of brilliant white Carrara marble. Meanwhile, its modern Italian design shows in an abundance of steel, mirrors, and sharp, efficient edges.

One of the most stunning public spaces is the *Costa Romantica's* L'Opera Showroom, which resembles a Renaissance amphitheater complete with tiered seating. Rising two decks high, it contains 6 miles of fiber optics and mosaics inspired by 14th-century models.

The top-of-the-ship glass-walled circular observation lounge becomes the discotheque at night, one of several dance venues where guests try out ballroom, Latin, or disco. During the day, the space is often used by the children's program.

DINING OPTIONS   Each ship has a main dining room and an indoor/outdoor buffet that sometimes get a bit overcrowded—as do other public areas. The Romantica also has a specialty restaurant called Sirens, and the cover is 23€ ($32) per person.

FITNESS, POOL & SPA FACILITIES   These are definitely not ships for fitness fanatics, as facilities consist of a small, albeit pleasant gym with a wall of windows; a handful of Stairmasters and treadmills; and sauna, steam, and massage rooms. Because of a lack of exercise space, it's often necessary to conduct aerobics classes in the disco. It's obvious that working out is not a top priority for most passengers, whose only trips to the fitness area, it seems, are to weigh themselves on the scale. One good thing about the gyms, though, is that they operate Technogym equipment that allows you to computerize your workout regiment, print it out, and take it home with you so you can continue the good work.

On both ships, the Caracalla Spa has a Turkish bath, as well as treatment rooms offering a wide range of massages, wraps, facials, and hydrotherapy baths, but it pales in comparison to the *Costa Victoria's* Roman-style spa. There are two outdoor pools (one with a fountain and one adults-only) and four hot tubs (two on the *Costa Classica*), as well as a jogging track on Deck 11.

Costa Marina

The Verdict

This ship, small enough so you won't get lost, is comfortable and cozy, and really grows on you after a few days. Its quirkiness is a plus in this age of homogenous megaships.

Costa Marina *(photo: Costa Cruises)*

Specifications

Size (GRT)	25,000	Crew	385
Passengers (Double Occ.)	776	Passenger/Crew Ratio	2 to 1
Passenger/Space Ratio	32	Year Launched	1992
Total Cabins/Veranda Cabins	378/0	Last Major Refurbishment	2002

Frommer's Ratings (Scale of 1–5)

★★★ ½

Cabin Comfort & Amenities	3.5	Dining Options	3
Ship Cleanliness & Maintenance	4	Gym, Spa & Sports Facilities	3
Public Comfort/Space	4	Children's Facilities	2.5
Decor	4	Enjoyment Factor	4

There's no denying the midsized, 1992-built *Marina* (the hull and engines actually date back to 1969) has personality, and the peaks and valleys that go with it. High points include retro-style cabins with real wood furnishings and a classically elegant dining room with oversized portholes. Disappointing areas include limited spa, fitness, and salon offerings (there were no manicure and pedicure treatments available on a recent cruise) and a small, low-tech show lounge stage.

At full capacity, the ship can carry nearly 900 passengers, though anything more than about 700 feels cramped. Unlike today's city-sized megas that require a map to figure out where things are, the *Costa Marina* is more like a small town where it's easy to find your way around. The *Marina's* three main entertainment venues are on one deck, and there are only two restaurants to choose from. It's a cozy environment, though that doesn't mean there's a lot of co-mingling. One North American passenger who didn't seem to mind said on a recent cruise, "I love this ship because I don't have to talk to anyone. I don't understand them."

Cabins & Rates

Cabins	Per Diem From	Sq. Ft.	Fridge	Hair Dryer	Sitting Area	TV
Inside	$118	140	No	Yes	No	Yes
Outside	$154	158	No	Yes	No	Yes
Suite	$229	360	Yes	Yes	Yes	Yes

CABINS Unlike newer ships, staterooms have real wood cabinetry and bathroom floors are teak. The 170-square-foot standard cabins have generous storage, a neat little round vanity table, and quirky nautical wall prints—all a refreshing contrast to the generic hotel look of most new ships. Still, don't get us wrong: Some may find the cabins a tad old-fashioned and a bit rough around the edges. Few cabins have balconies (the eight suites do, but they're open to the deck above), and most twin beds cannot be pushed together. A good number of cabins can accommodate a third passenger with an extra Murphy bed–style option. All have televisions, but with limited channels.

PUBLIC AREAS This is not a cookie-cutter ship, by any means. The *Marina's* decor includes the typical upholstered cruise ship lounge furniture plus more eclectic touches such as leather chairs with chrome frames, ship models in display cases in the Marina Lounge, cream-colored leather banquettes and oversized portholes in the Cristallo restaurant, and an abstract green glass atrium sculpture Heidi's young son, Tejas, aptly named "the lettuce." Aside from the low-tech show lounge, there are two other entertainment lounge/bars that are appealing in a low-key way. The cluttered children's playroom is fine if there aren't many kids using it (usually not a problem on this ship), though on a recent cruise the sweet and enthusiastic counselors more than made up for the lack of hardware. The selection of books in the small library-cum-Internet-center is very disappointing and Heidi found the amazingly slow Internet connections at the four computer terminals to be a source of frustration.

DINING OPTIONS Restaurants include Cristallo (for breakfast, lunch, and dinner; at the latter there is candlelight) and the casual indoor/outdoor buffet restaurant up top, which serves breakfast and lunch (and occasionally dinner). There is no upscale, reservations-only restaurant on the *Costa Marina*. The setup of the buffet restaurant is quite basic compared to what's offered on newer ships, but the food, for the most part, was very decent on a recent sailing. An international corner offers the cuisine of a different nationality every day, with the Asian day, for example, featuring sweet-and-sour pork, papaya salad with crushed peanuts, and spring rolls.

POOL, FITNESS, SPA & SPORTS FACILITIES As might be expected on a ship this size, facilities are not terribly extensive. There's a swimming pool amidships adjacent to a pleasant outdoor bar, and also an odd-looking oversized shallow pool at the stern where Heidi's boys spent a lot of time. There's nothing aesthetically appealing about the uninspired little spa and beauty salon; they seem like afterthoughts.

Costa Europa

The Verdict

Costa Europa's old-world Mediterranean style is cozy and reminiscent of cruise ships of yesteryear.

Costa Europa *(photo: Costa Cruises)*

Specifications

Size (GRT)	53,872	Crew	612
Passengers (Double Occ.)	1,494	Passenger/Crew Ratio	2.4 to 1
Passenger/Space Ratio	36	Year Launched	1986
Total Cabins/Veranda Cabins	747/0	Last Major Refurbishment	2002

Frommer's Ratings (Scale of 1–5)

★★★ ½

Cabin Comfort & Amenities	3	Dining Options	2.5
Ship Cleanliness & Maintenance	4	Gym, Spa & Sports Facilities	3
Public Comfort/Space	4	Children's Facilities	3
Decor	4	Enjoyment Factor	4

Originally built in 1986, *Costa Europa* formerly sailed as Holland America's *Wester-dam* until being transferred to Costa's fleet (and then being refurbished) in 2002. The ship hearkens to the past with an elegant look—the use of marble and softly colored wood paneling runs throughout—but its refurbishment since coming to Costa means there's a lot of fresh color and verve. Decks are named after Greek constellations.

Cabins & Rates

Cabins	Per Diem From*	Sq. Ft.	Fridge	Hair Dryer	Sitting Area	TV
Inside	$130	155	No	Yes	No	Yes
Outside	$175	189	No	Yes	No	Yes
Suite	$334	440	Yes	Yes	Yes	Yes

* Rates represent average per diem for 10- to 11-night cruise.

CABINS   Cabins are relatively roomy—insides run from 153 square feet, ocean views from 189 square feet. Even the inside cabins have seating areas. Decor is warm, with fabrics in Laura Ashley–esque florals. There's plenty of storage space. Bathrooms are roomy, though they are shower only, except for suites. The suites are comparatively huge, at 414 square feet, and have combination seating/sleeping areas. All staterooms are air-conditioned and equipped with phones, televisions, safe-deposit boxes, and hair dryers.

PUBLIC AREAS   The Medusa Ballroom—you basically have to pass through it to get anywhere on the main public area deck—is the place to meet 'n' greet, whether for pre-dinner cocktails or after the evening show. Other favorites are the Orfeo Cinema (with its big comfy chairs that recline) and the cozy Delo Bar.

DINING OPTIONS   There are no specialty alternative restaurants; the two dining choices are the main Orion dining room and the Sirens Buffet, which has a casual atmosphere.

POOL, FITNESS & SPA FACILITIES   There are two pools on *Costa Europa:* one with a magrodome that closes during inclement weather, and a smaller version, located aft. Nereidi Fitness Center incorporates the spa and workout area; like on other Costa ships, the computerized Technogym equipment allows you to keep track of your workout program. Space is available for aerobics.

5 Holland America Line

300 Elliott Ave. W., Seattle, WA 98119. © **877/724-5425** or 206/281-3535. Fax 800/628-4855. www.holland america.com.

THE LINE IN A NUTSHELL   Because of its Dutch origins dating back to 1873, Holland America is a line that seems to belong in Europe. It's managed to hang on to more of its seafaring history and tradition than any line today except Cunard. It offers a moderately priced, classic, and casual yet refined cruise experience.

THE EXPERIENCE   Holland America is a classy operation, offering all-around appealing cruises with a touch of old-world elegance and such cushy amenities as plush bedding and flat-panel TVs with DVD players in all cabins. Though the line has been retooling itself to attract younger passengers and families, it still attracts a huge number of older folks, and so generally offers a more sedate and stately experience than other mainstream lines, plus excellent service for the money. Its fleet, which until a few years ago consisted of midsize, classically styled ships, is in the process of being supersized, and the new Vista- and Signature-class megaships are a mite bolder in their color palette, that's for sure. New or old, the vessels are all well maintained and have excellent (and remarkably similar) layouts that ease passenger movement. Throughout the public areas of the fleet (especially on the pre-Vista ships), you'll see flowers that testify to Holland's place in the floral trade, Indonesian touches that evoke the country's relationship with its former colony, and seafaring memorabilia that often harkens back to Holland America's own history.

Pros

- **Great service:** HAL's primarily Indonesian and Filipino staff is exceptionally gracious and friendly.
- **Traditional classic ambience:** The Vista- and Signature-class ships are pushing the HAL envelope, but overall the line's ships are classy, with impressive art collections and a touch of traditional ocean-liner ambience.
- **Beds:** They're the most comfortable Heidi's ever slept on.

Cons

- **Sleepy nightlife:** While there are always a few stalwarts and a couple of busyish nights, these aren't party ships. If you're big on late-night dancing and barhopping, you may find yourself partying mostly with the entertainment staff.
- **Fairly homogenous passenger profile:** Although younger faces are starting to pepper the mix (especially on 7-night cruises to warm-weather destinations), most HAL passengers still tend to be low-key, fairly sedentary 55-plus North American couples.

HOLLAND AMERICA: GOING DUTCH

One of the most famous shipping companies in the world, Holland America Line was founded in 1873 as the Nederlandsch-Amerikaansche StoomvAart Maatschappij (Netherlands-American Steamship Company). Its first ocean liner, the original *Rotterdam*, took her maiden, 15-day voyage from the Netherlands to New York City in 1872. By the early 1900s, the company had been renamed Holland America and was

Compared with the other mainstream lines, here's how HAL rates:

	Poor	Fair	Good	Excellent	Outstanding
Enjoyment Factor				✓	
Dining				✓	
Activities			✓		
Children's Program		✓			
Entertainment				✓	
Service					✓
Worth the Money					✓

one of the major lines transporting immigrants from Europe to the United States, as well as providing passenger/cargo service between Holland and the Dutch East Indies via the Suez Canal. During World War II, the company's headquarters moved from Nazi-occupied Holland to Dutch-owned Curaçao, then the site of a strategic oil refinery, and after the war the company forged strong links with North American interests. The line continued regular transatlantic crossings up until 1971, and then turned to offering cruises full time. In 1989, it was acquired by Carnival Corporation, which improved the line's entertainment and cuisine while maintaining its overall character and sense of history. Today most of HAL's vessels are named for other classic vessels in the line's history—*Rotterdam,* for example, is the sixth HAL ship to bear that name—and striking paintings of classic HAL ships by maritime artist Stephen Card appear in the stairways on every ship.

In addition to introducing its first three megaships in the past few years, by late 2006 HAL had completed a fleetwide $225-million upgrade program it calls "Signature of Excellence." All staterooms now have flat-panel plasma TVs and DVD players, extrafluffy towels, and terry-cloth bathrobes, plus new massage shower heads, lighted magnifying makeup mirrors, and salon-quality hair dryers. You'll now find plush triple-sheeted mattresses and 100% Egyptian cotton bed linens in all cabins. Suites have duvets, fully stocked minibars, and personalized stationery, and all suite guests have access to a one-touch 24-hour concierge service and exclusive concierge lounge. In addition to an expanded lecture series, each ship now sports a really cool demonstration kitchen where a Culinary Arts program offers interactive programs about food and wine. Fleetwide, there's a combination lounge, library, coffee shop, and Internet cafe called the Explorations Café that's the nerve center of the ship, plus there are pretty dramatically upgraded facilities for kids. Spa facilities have been enhanced to match the Greenhouse Spas introduced on the line's Vista-class megaships, with new treatments, expanded fitness and treatment facilities, a thermal suite (a kind of New Age steam room), and a hydrotherapy pool (a souped-up hot tub).

At press time, Holland America was in the midst of building a new pair of 2,044-passenger, 86,000-ton ships, called the Signature class, that are due in summer 2008 and spring 2010. Both ships are being built by Italy's Fincantieri shipyards.

PASSENGER PROFILE

For years, HAL was known for catering to an almost exclusively older crowd, with most passengers in their 70s on up. Today, following intense efforts to attract younger passengers, about 25% of the line's guests are under age 55 (with the average age being around 57), with a few young families peppering the mix, especially in summers and during holiday weeks. While the average age skews a bit lower on the newer Vista- and Signature-class ships, HAL just isn't Carnival or Royal Caribbean, and its older ships especially were designed with older folks in mind. On cruises longer than a week, there's no shortage of canes, walkers, and wheelchairs.

Passengers tend to be amiable, low key, better educated than their equivalents aboard sister line Carnival, and much more amenable to dressing up—you'll see lots of tuxedos and evening gowns on formal nights. Though you'll see some people walking laps on the Promenade Deck, others taking advantage of the ships' gyms, and some taking athletic or semiadventurous shore excursions, these aren't terribly active cruises, and passengers overall tend to be sedentary. HAL has a very high repeat-passenger rate, so many of the people you'll see aboard will have sailed with the line before.

Parties for solo travelers (only 30–40 of whom tend to be on any particular cruise) encourage mixing, and you can ask to be seated with other solo passengers at dinner. On cruises of 14 nights or longer, gentlemen hosts sail aboard to provide company for single women, joining them at dinner as well as serving as dance partners.

DINING

Much improved over the years, Holland America's cuisine is fine but hardly memorable. On a recent cruise, meals in the main restaurant were hit and miss, ranging from so-so to pretty good.

TRADITIONAL   In the line's lovely formal restaurants, appetizers may include prawns in spicy wasabi cocktail sauce, duck pâté, deep-fried hazelnut brie, and escargot; the soup-and-salad course always includes several options, from a plain house salad and minestrone to a chilled raspberry bisque and spicy two-bean soup; and main courses are heavy on **traditional favorites** such as broiled lobster tail, grilled salmon, beef tenderloin, roast turkey, seared tuna steak, grilled pork chop, and filet mignon. Those wanting something less substantial can opt for lighter dishes such as grilled fish or chicken, and a fresh fruit medley. A few entrees on most dinner menus are marked as signature dishes recommended by Master Chef Rudi Solamin, and include the likes of a salmon tartare with avocado appetizer and, as a main course, chicken cordon bleu. Some vegetarian entrees are available on the main menu, but you can also ask for a **full vegetarian menu,** with half a dozen entrees and an equal number of appetizers, soups, and salads. (Don't miss the tofu stroganoff and celery-and-stilton soup if they're offered—yum.) Children can enjoy tried-and-true staples such as pizza, hot dogs, burgers with fries, chicken fingers, and tacos, plus chef's specials such as pasta, and fish and chips.

During the first half of 2008, Holland America will introduce a new **As You Wish Dining** program similar to Princess's Personal Choice program. At booking, passengers will be asked to choose either traditional early or late seating dining (at the same table nightly, served on one level of the ship's main restaurant) or a completely flexible schedule (offered 5:15–9pm nightly on the restaurant's other level). Guests opting for flexible dining can make reservations during the day or just show up whenever they like. By late January, the program will be in place aboard *Noordam, Ryndam, Volendam, Statendam, Oosterdam,* and *Rotterdam,* followed by *Zaandam* and *Westerdam* (Feb), *Zuiderdam* (Mar), *Veendam* and *Maasdam* (Apr), and *Amsterdam* and *Prinsendam* (May).

In the spirit of having a little fun while you eat, a fresh take on the ol' dining room song-and-dance routine happens once per cruise. The special Signature Master Chef's Dinner, which is more circus than strict gourmet, features dancing waiters, a "napkin ballet," a salad dance, and flying pepper grinders. Guests are greeted by more than 75 service staff, including dining room stewards, cruise activities staff, and the ship's singers and dancers, and each guest is given a paper toque (chef's hat) to wear for the meal. It's a ball!

SPECIALTY   Aboard every vessel, the intimate Pinnacle Grill restaurant offers a menu of mostly steaks, chops, and fish. Options may include such dishes as Dungeness crab cakes, pan-seared rosemary chicken with cranberry chutney, wild mushroom ravioli with pesto cream sauce, or lamb rack chops with drizzled mint sauce, plus premium beef cuts. All entrees are complemented with regional wines from Chateau Ste. Michelle, Canoe Ridge, Willamette Valley Vineyards, and others. The cover charge is $30 per person for dinner and $20 for lunch. On a recent cruise, the service was top rate and the food exceeded our expectations. Don't miss the opportunity to dine here at least once per cruise. Make reservations as early as possible when you come aboard. In addition to dinner, the alternative restaurant may be open for lunch on sea days.

CASUAL   As has become the industry standard, **casual dining** is available each night in the ships' buffet-style Lido restaurants, which also serve breakfast and lunch. They're some of the best-laid-out buffets at sea, with separate stations for salads, desserts, drinks, and so on, keeping lines and crowding to a minimum. Diners here are offered open seating from about 6 to 8pm. Tables are set with linens and a pianist may provide background music, but service is buffet style, with waiters on hand to serve beverages. The set menu features the basics: Caesar salad, shrimp cocktail, or fresh-fruit-cup appetizer; French onion soup; freshly baked dinner rolls; and entree choices, which may include salmon, sirloin steak, roast chicken, or lasagna, served with a vegetable of the day and a baked potato or rice pilaf. Most main dishes are similar to what you'll find in the main restaurant that evening. At lunch, the buffet restaurants offer pasta, salads, stir-fry, burgers, and, usually an ethnic option, such as an Indian shrimp curry, sushi, or Dutch crepes. Pizza and ice cream stations are open till late afternoon. Out on the Lido Deck, by the pool, a **grill** serves hamburgers, hot dogs, veggie and turkey burgers, and a special of the day, such as knockwurst or spicy Italian sausage, between about 11:30am and 6pm. A **taco bar** nearby offers all the fixings for tacos or nachos, and it's generally open about the same hours. Once a week, the Lido also hosts a **barbecue buffet dinner.**

SNACKS & EXTRAS   Once per cruise, a special Royal Dutch High Tea features teatime snacks and music provided by the ships' string trio, making it one of the most truly "high" among the generally disappointing high teas offered on mainstream lines. On other days, a more standard **afternoon tea** has white-gloved waiters passing around teeny sandwiches, scones, and cookies in the dining room or one of the main lounges. We're told a new Indonesian Tea and Coffee Ceremony will also be offered once a cruise and feature such goodies as spring rolls, sweet rice balls, and coconut. Pizza and soft ice cream round out the afternoon offerings.

Free hot canapés are served in some of the bars/lounges during the cocktail hour, and free iced tea and lemonade are served on deck, one of many thoughtful touches provided at frequent intervals by the well-trained staff. The new **Explorations Café** has a coffee bar that serves a premium Starbucks blend, for a charge.

Each evening around midnight, a spread of snacks is available in the Lido restaurant, and at least once during each cruise the dessert chefs get to go wild in a midnight **Dessert Extravaganza.** Cakes are decorated with humorous themes, marzipan animals guard towering chocolate castles, and trays are heavy with chocolate-covered strawberries, truffles, cream puffs, and other sinful things.

Room service is available 24 hours a day and is typically efficient and gracious. As a plus, the breakfast options include eggs and meats, not just pastries and cereals like most mainstream ships offer. You can also order room service on the final morning of the cruise, another rarity.

ACTIVITIES

HAL get points for offering an impressive variety of things to do. You can take ballroom dance lessons; take an informal class in photography; play bingo or bridge; sit in on a trivia game or Pictionary tournament; participate in Ping-Pong, golf putting, basketball free-throw, or volleyball tournaments; take a gaming lesson in the casino or an aerobics class at the gym; take a self-guided iPod tour of the ship's art collection or

Holland America Fleet Itineraries

Ship	Sailing Regions	Home Ports
Eurodam	10- and 20-night voyages in Northern Europe/ Russia and the Norwegian Fjords/Scotland	Rotterdam, Copenhagen
Maasdam	15-night Norway/Iceland/Newfoundland	Rotterdam, Boston
Noordam	10- and 20-night Mediterranean	Civitavecchia/Rome
Prinsendam	11- to 38-night voyages in Atlantic Europe, Northern Europe/Russia, the British Isles, Norway/Iceland/Greenland, the Norwegian Fjords, the Black Sea, and Egypt/Israel	Lisbon, Amsterdam, Dover/ London, Greenwich/London, Civitavecchia./Rome, Piraeus/Athens
Rotterdam	10- to 15-night voyages in the Mediterranean, Black Sea/Egypt/Israel, Norwegian Fjords/North Cape/Scotland, and Northern Europe/Russia	Lisbon, Piraeus/Athens, Harwich/London, Copenhagen, Rotterdam
Zuiderdam	12- and 24-night Mediterranean/Greek Isles	Venice, Barcelona

a backstage theater tour; go high-toned at a wine tasting; or go low-toned at the goofy games poolside or in a lounge. During one frisky relay-race-like team game called Seaquest on a recent 14-night cruise, a group of mostly senior passengers enthusiastically slipped off their bras and dropped their drawers in the name of friendly competition—the team that deposited more undergarments on the show lounge stage won. The place was a sea of geriatric goofs tottering around in their boxer shorts or (yikes!) briefs, crumbled trousers in hand. It was a riot. Talk about young at heart.

Some cruises also feature model shipbuilding contests in which you can use only junk you can find around the ship, with seaworthiness tested in one of the ship's hot tubs. Each ship has a great **Explorations Café,** which is a combo Internet center, coffee bar, and library set in a well-traveled part of each ship. Comfy lounge chairs come equipped with music stations and headphones. Generous shelves of books, DVDs, and games line the walls, and a magazine stand holds current issues of popular magazines plus the latest edition of various newspapers, when the ship can get them. If you're a crossword buff, you can tackle the *New York Times'* crossword puzzles embedded under glass in the room's cafe tables (wax pencils are provided). Explorations also functions as the Internet cafe, but passengers toting their Wi-Fi-enabled laptops can take advantage of wireless hot spots here and throughout the ship. Another of the fleet's newer offerings is the **Culinary Arts** center, which includes free cooking demos, usually twice per 7-day cruise (go early to get a front-row seat, or sit in the back and watch the food preparation on the flat-panel TVs around the room), and more intimate, hands-on cooking classes (available for a charge). The center is also used for other demos, such as flower arranging.

If the ship is staying late in port, local dancers or musicians are brought on board to perform.

CHILDREN'S PROGRAM
Holland America will never be a kid-friendly line on the order of Royal Caribbean, but they're trying harder to cater to families with children. The biggest change to the Club HAL program a few years back was the lowering of the age minimum from 5 years down to 3. If there are more than about 30 kids aboard, activities are programmed for three age brackets (3–7, 8–12, and 13–17), and there's always at least

Preview: HAL's *Eurodam*

Inching up the size scale, at press time Holland America was in the midst of building a new pair of 2,104-passenger, 86,000-ton "Signature-class" ships in Italy's Fincantieri shipyards. The first, named *Eurodam,* is set to debut in June 2008 to do Baltic cruises; a sister will be introduced in spring 2010.

The ships will be a bit larger than the 85,000-ton, 1,848-passenger Vista-class vessels, adding one more deck and offering three alternative dining venues, including a new pan-Asian restaurant on Deck 10 with panoramic views, and an Italian venue. There will be an Explorations Café, the line's supersuccessful library/Internet Center/coffee bar, but this time located high up on Deck 11. A new atrium bar area; more shops, including a high-end jewelry boutique; and a high-tech photo center are also part of the fresh offerings. The *Eurodam* will have a culinary arts center like the rest of the fleet and a kids center that includes a teens-only loft.

one counselor on board every sailing, and more when demand warrants. You'll find the most children on cruises during summers and holiday weeks. At these times, there may be as many as 300 to 400 kids aboard the Vista- and Signature-class ships, though around 100 to 200 is typical overall. When there are fewer than 20 or 30 kids, a two-tiered Club HAL program is offered—children 3 to 12 in one group, teens in another—on a limited basis, generally about 6 hours on sea days and even fewer hours on port days. Typically, each evening kids receive a program detailing the next day's activities, which may include arts and crafts, youth sports tournaments, movies and videos, scavenger hunts, PlayStations, disco for teens, storytelling for younger kids, miniature golf, charades, bingo, Ping-Pong, and pizza, ice-cream, and pajama parties. The playrooms typically operate on a limited schedule on port days (and you often must book the time you'll be coming or risk the playroom being closed if no other kids are signed up). All the ships have dedicated playrooms with separate teen centers with video screens and a dance floor; the Statendam-class ships even have a totally cool outdoor space sequestered away on a top deck for teens called the Oasis, a beachlike setting complete with a waterfall, hammocks, and chaise lounges. Otherwise, the playrooms are bright and cheerful, though they lack the ball-jumps, padded climbing and crawling areas, and fanciful decor that make kids' facilities aboard Royal Caribbean, Princess, NCL, and Celebrity so compelling.

Group babysitting in the playroom is offered between 10pm and midnight for $5 per hour for ages 3 to 12. In-cabin babysitting is also offered, assuming a crewmember is available. The cost is $8 an hour for the first child (minimum age 12 weeks), and $5 per hour for additional kids. Inquire at the guest services desk.

Children must be 12 weeks or older to sail aboard.

ENTERTAINMENT

Don't expect HAL's shows to knock your socks off, but hey, at least they're trying. Each ship features small-scale **Vegas-style shows,** with live music (except on the Vista-class ships, where, we're told, there isn't enough space for a live orchestra in the main show lounges—ain't that the pits?), laser lights, and lots of glimmer and shimmer. Overall, though, you'll find better-quality entertainment from the soloists, trios, and quartets playing jazz, pop, and light-classical standards.

Recent-release movies are shown an average of twice a day in an onboard cinema, with free popcorn available for the full movie effect. There's also a **crew talent show** once a week, in which crewmembers (Indonesians one week, Filipinos the next) present songs and dances from their home countries. **Passenger-participation shows** are a different animal, with the crowd-pleasing *American Idol*–style contest called Superstar featuring passenger crooners being critiqued by a staff of judges (who are definitely nicer than Simon).

Aboard each ship, one of the lounges becomes a disco in the evening, with a small live band generally playing before dinner and a DJ taking over for after-dinner dancing. The new Vista- and Signature-class ships have the line's first dedicated discos, and on the other ships, the Crow's Nest lounges have been redecorated for a more disco-y feel.

SERVICE

Holland America is one of the few cruise lines that maintains a real training school (a land-based school in Indonesia known in HAL circles as "ms Nieuw Jakarta") for the selection and training of staffers, resulting in service that's efficient, attentive, and genteel. The soft-spoken, primarily Indonesian and Filipino staffers smile more often than not and will frequently remember your name after only one introduction, though they struggle occasionally with their English. (Be cool about it: Remember, you probably can't speak even a word of Bahasa Indonesia or Tagalog.) During lunch, a uniformed employee may hold open the door of a buffet, and at dinnertime, stewards who look like vintage hotel pages walk through the public rooms ringing a chime to formally announce the dinner seatings.

Like many other lines these days, HAL now automatically adds **gratuities** to passengers' shipboard accounts, at the rate of $10 per day, adjustable up or down at your discretion. A 15% service charge is automatically added to bar bills and dining room wine accounts.

Only the Vista- and Signature-class ships (and the *Prinsendam*) come with minifridges standard in cabins. On the other vessels, they can be rented for $2 a day (inquire before your cruise if you're interested). All cabins have complimentary fruit baskets on embarkation day. A new early-boarding program allows guests to get aboard in the port of embarkation as early as 11:30am, when some lounges and facilities will be open for their use, although cabins generally won't be ready until 1pm.

Onboard services on every ship in the fleet include **laundry** and **dry cleaning.** Each ship—except the new Vista- and Signature-class ships, oddly enough—also maintains several **self-service laundry rooms** with irons.

The Vista Class:
Zuiderdam • Noordam

The Verdict

Holland America's first foray into megasize ships marries traditional HAL style with a few funky, modern touches in a nod to staying fresh.

Zuiderdam *(photo: Holland America Line)*

Specifications

Size (in Tons)	85,000	Last Refurbishment/Upgrade	
Passengers (Double Occ.)	1,848	*Zuiderdam*	2005
Passenger/Space Ratio	46	*Noordam*	2006
Crew	800	Year Launched	
Passenger/Crew Ratio	2.3 to 1	*Zuiderdam*	2002
		Noordam	2006

Frommer's Ratings (Scale of 1–5)   ★★★★

Cabin Comfort & Amenities	4.5	Dining Options	4
Appearance & Upkeep	4	Gym, Spa & Sports Facilities	4.5
Public Comfort/Space	4	Children's Facilities	3
Decor	3.5	Enjoyment Factor	4

Built on a similar design as Carnival's Spirit-class ships, *Zuiderdam* (named for the southern point of the Dutch compass, and with a first syllable that rhymes with "eye"), *Oosterdam* (eastern, and with a first syllable like the letter *O*), *Westerdam,* and *Noordam* (northern compass point) are Holland America's biggest ships to date (until the slightly larger Signature class comes on line), though their 85,000-ton, 1,848-passenger size doesn't put them anywhere in the running among today's true behemoths—relatively speaking, they're downright cozy. Still, it's an attempt for HAL to finally shed its image as your grandmother's cruise line and compete better for the all-important baby-boomer and family cruise dollars. Can't fault them for that, but let's just say hipness isn't something you can grow overnight. *Zuiderdam* originally had giant red lips (yikes!) and an ice block sculpture in the disco, which have since been replaced with more toned-down pieces. By the time the fourth and final sister, *Noordam,* came on the scene (it replaced the previous *Noordam,* which left the fleet in Nov 2004), HAL seemed to get it right, mixing classic wine reds, dark blues, and earth tones, with just a hint of zany, seen in the silver-framed benches in the elevator landings and in the Pinnacle Grill and Pinnacle Bar. Overall, this class is a winner, especially the *Westerdam* and *Noordam.* All four sisters are extraordinarily spacious, with large standard cabins, truly glamorous two-level dining rooms, and distinctive specialty restaurants.

Cabins & Rates

Cabins	Per Diem From	Sq. Ft.	Fridge	Hair Dryer	Sitting Area	TV
Inside	$158	185	Yes	Yes	No	Yes
Outside	$183	194–200	Yes	Yes	Yes	Yes
Suite	$292	298–1,000	Yes	Yes	Yes	Yes

CABINS Cabins in all categories are comfortable and, as aboard every HAL ship, are among the industry's largest, with a simple decor of light woods, clean lines, and subtly floral bedding. Overall, more than two-thirds of them have verandas, with the deluxe veranda suites and staterooms in the stern notable for their deep balconies, nearly twice the size of those to port and starboard. You get a romantic view of the ship's wake, too, but because the decks are tiered back here, residents of the cabins above you can see right down. Keep your clothes on.

Standard outside and veranda cabins all have a small sitting area and a tub in the bathroom—a relatively rare thing in standard cabins these days. Closet space in all categories is good, with nicely designed fold-down shelves and tie rack. Each has a flatscreen TV and DVD player, makeup mirror, real hair dryer, massage shower head, bathrobes, and extra-thick supercomfortable bedding. Dataports allow passengers to access e-mail and the Internet from every cabin via their own laptops.

Suites run from the comfortably spacious Superior Veranda Suites (with wide verandas, large sofa bed, walk-in closet, separate shower and bathroom, and extra windows) to the Penthouse Veranda Suites—extremely large multiroom apartments with a flowing layout, pantry, palatial bathrooms with oversize whirlpool baths, and ridiculously large private verandas with a second, outdoor whirlpool. Their decor is reminiscent of 1930s moderne style. Guests in every suite category have use of a concierge lounge whose staff will take care of shore excursion reservations and any matters about which you'd normally have to wait in line at the front desk. The lounge is stocked with reading material, coffee, and juice, and a continental breakfast is served daily.

Twenty-eight cabins are wheelchair accessible.

PUBLIC AREAS   Public rooms on the Vista-class ships run the gamut from the traditional to the modern, and from the lovely to the weird (again, we're talking mostly the *Zuiderdam* and *Oosterdam*) when wacky color schemes go the way of blinding oranges, red, and purples. The more traditional spaces, done mostly in blues, teals, burgundy, and deep metallics, include the signature Explorer's Lounge, a venue for quiet musical performances and high tea. The top-of-the-ship Crow's Nest lounge, an observation lounge during the day and nightclub/disco at night, offers wide-open views, comfortable leather recliners toward the bow (a perfect reading perch during days at sea), and even a few rococo thrones on the starboard side, good for "wish you were here" cruise photos. The rear port corner of the Crow's Nest is the most truly elegant lounge area aboard, with high-style, striking, and comfortable furniture; it's also one of the ships' Wi-Fi hot zones.

Lower Promenade Deck is the hub of indoor activity on these ships. In the bow, the three-deck Vista Lounge is the venue for large-scale production shows, while the Queen's Lounge/Culinary Arts Center at midships hosts chef demos by day and comedians and other cabaret-style acts in the evening. Between the two there's a casino and a piano bar (that's really flashy on all but the *Noordam*). You'll also find HAL's first-ever dedicated discos, but they're uninspired, at best (and, on *Zuiderdam,* just butt-ugly). Our favorite room, the Sports Bar, looks as little like the standard rah-rah sports-hero-and-pennants sports bar as you can imagine, with comfortable free-form leather seating and table lamps. *Très* chic. Only the multiple TVs give away the place's true identity.

One deck up, the traditional Ocean Bar wraps around the understated three-deck atrium—whose focal point on all ships is a Waterford crystal chandelier—with bay windows to port and starboard looking out onto the promenade and the room's namesake. Moving forward, you pass through the drab shopping arcade, whose displays spill right into the central corridor courtesy of retractable walls, forcing you to browse as you walk from stem to stern. A lot of lines are doing this, and it's a pretty crass sales pitch; it gets a big thumbs-down from us. Once you get through, you come to Explorations Café, the ships' hub, and a combination specialty coffee shop, Internet center, and library, with HAL's signature in-laid marble tables.

Other public rooms include the Main Deck's Atrium Bar, a very comfortable small-scale nook vaguely reminiscent of a 1930s nightclub; the wicker-furnitured outdoor

Lido Bar on the Lido Deck (which, unfortunately, lacks the charm of similar spaces on the line's older ships); and the KidZone and WaveRunner children/teen centers, which are a bit bare, though roomy and sunny. Art in the public areas of the ships includes maritime artwork by Stephen Card, replica 18th-century Dutch engravings, ship models, and, on the *Zuiderdam*, some nice humorous paintings by Hans Leijerzapf, commedia dell'arte statues, and jazz sketches and paintings by Wil van der Laar.

Oceanview elevators at port and starboard midships are a little boxy, closing off some of the intended inspiring views. Much better views are to be had from outdoor areas forward on decks 5, 6, and 7, and from an area just forward of the gym, above the bridge. You can even check a ship's compass here.

DINING OPTIONS   The main Vista Dining Room is a two-deck affair, decorated traditionally but with nice touches of modernism, for instance in the *Zuiderdam*'s black high-backed wooden chairs, which are very sharp. On the *Noordam*, the elegant space is a throwback with wine-red fabrics, darkish woods, and a cozy living-room-like feeling. It's a lovely dining room. The ship's alternative Pacific Northwest restaurant, the 130-seat Pinnacle Grill, wraps partially around the three-deck atrium—ask for a table by the windows or in the aft corner for the coziest experience. The design is appealing, with marble floors, bright white linens, gorgeous Bulgari place settings, and ornate, organically sculpted chairs by Gilbert Libirge, who also created the ships' beautiful batik-patterned elevator doors.

Diners wanting something more casual can opt for the well-laid-out and attractive Lido buffet restaurant; the outdoor Grill for burgers, dogs, and the like; or, on all but the *Noordam*, the Windstar Café, serving specialty coffees (for a price), snacks, and light meals in a tall-ship atmosphere.

POOL, FITNESS, SPA & SPORTS FACILITIES   Gyms are well equipped with a full complement of cardio equipment and weight machines arranged in tiers around the cardio floor; the space is attached to another room where you'll find chaise longues and a large dipping pool. There's also a basketball/volleyball court on the Sports Deck. The Greenhouse Spa is fully 50% larger than any other in the HAL fleet, and besides offering the usual massage, mud, and exotic treatments, it has a couple of HAL firsts: a thermal suite (a series of saunas and other heat-therapy rooms) and a hydrotherapy pool, which uses heated seawater and high-pressure jets to alleviate muscle tension. Oddly, there's no compelling design motif like you'd find in other signature spas. Around the pool, extraheavy wooden lounge chairs are thickly padded and nap-worthy. The pool area doesn't quite work on *Zuiderdam*, where the colors are jarring and the materials cheap looking, but as in many other areas, *Oosterdam*'s, *Westerdam*'s, and *Noordam*'s are a vast improvement, very pleasant all around.

Outdoors, the wraparound Promenade Deck is lined with classy wooden deck chairs—a nice touch of classic ocean liner style—and is popular with walkers and joggers. The main pool deck is the hub of outdoor activity on sea days, with hot tubs, music, and pool games, and can be covered with a sliding roof in inclement weather. The hallmarks of the pool area on both ships are giant bronze animal statues—from a polar bear to a penguin and dolphin. Another pool, in the stern on Lido Deck, is a lovely spot for sunbathing and open views of the sea.

Rotterdam

The Verdict

A modern throwback to the glory days of transatlantic travel, without the stuffiness or class separation, this attractive, gloriously midsize ship offers great features, from classic art to rich mahogany woodwork, and elegant yet understated public rooms.

Rotterdam *(photo: Holland America Line)*

Specifications

Size (in Tons)	56,652	Crew	593
Passengers (Double Occ.)	1,316	Passenger/Crew Ratio	2.2 to 1
Passenger/Space Ratio	43	Year Launched	1997
Total Cabins/Veranda Cabins	658/161	Last Refurbishment/Upgrade	2005

Frommer's Ratings (Scale of 1–5)   ★★★★ ½

Cabin Comfort & Amenities	4.5	Dining Options	4
Appearance & Upkeep	4	Gym, Spa & Sports Facilities	4.5
Public Comfort/Space	5	Children's Facilities	3
Decor	5	Enjoyment Factor	4.5

The *Rotterdam* combines classic elegance with contemporary amenities and provides a very comfortable cruise, especially on the longer itineraries offered in Europe. Carrying just over 1,300 passengers double occupancy, the ship is a breath of fresh air in the sea of supermega ships that ply the oceans these days. *Rotterdam,* the sixth HAL ship to bear that name, is popular with passengers who previously sailed aboard the legendary *Rotterdam V,* which was sold in 1997.

Like the rest of the fleet, the *Rotterdam* was upgraded to feature HAL's Signature of Excellence enhancements, including the Explorations Café Internet center and coffee shop, beefed-up kids' facilities, a culinary arts demonstration kitchen, and upgraded cabin amenities.

Cabins & Rates

Cabins	Per Diem From	Sq. Ft.	Fridge	Hair Dryer	Sitting Area	TV
Inside	$185	182	No	Yes	Yes	Yes
Outside	$215	197	No	Yes	Yes	Yes
Suite	$335	225–937	Yes	Yes	Yes	Yes

CABINS   The decor here is lively, with corals, mangoes, blues, and whites brightening things up. The standard cabins are among the most spacious at sea and offer enough hanging and drawer space for 10-night-plus cruises. Bathrooms are generous as well, with bathtubs in all but the standard inside cabins. Each cabin has a sitting area, a desk, a safe, two lower beds convertible to a queen, and great reading lights above each bed, in addition to the line's new amenities: flat-panel plasma TVs and DVD players, terry-cloth bathrobes, massage shower heads, lighted magnifying makeup mirrors, and salon-quality hair dryers. Beds now have plush, amazingly comfy triple-sheeted mattresses and 100% Egyptian cotton bed linens.

Veranda Suites are 225 square feet and have a 59-square-foot private veranda; Deluxe Veranda Suites measure 374 square feet and have a 189-square-foot veranda and a dressing room. Both have sitting areas, whirlpool tubs, and stocked minibars, and are kept stocked with fresh fruit. Penthouse Suites measure 937 square feet and have a 189-square-foot veranda, living room, dining room, guest bathroom, and over-size whirlpool tub. All suite guests have use of a concierge lounge whose staff will take care of shore excursion reservations and any matters about which you'd normally have to wait in line at the front desk. The lounge is stocked with reading material, and a continental breakfast is served daily.

Twenty-one cabins are wheelchair accessible.

PUBLIC AREAS   The ship has a great easy-to-navigate layout that allows passengers to move easily among public rooms. Most of the inside public areas are concentrated on two decks; ditto for the pools, sunning areas, spa, sports facilities, and buffet restaurant, which are all on the Lido and Sports decks.

Overall, the Rotterdam gives you the feeling of an elegant old hotel, with dark red and blue upholstery and leathers, damask fabrics, mahogany tones, and gold accents. Artwork is everywhere, from the stairwells to the walkways on the Promenade and Upper Promenade decks. Aboard *Rotterdam,* the theme is Continental and Asian. In *Rotterdam's* atrium, passengers are greeted by a large reproduction Flemish clock.

The new Explorations Café is a main hub and the place to check your email or surf the Web while enjoying a cappuccino.

The Ocean Bar serves complimentary hot hors d'oeuvres before dinner nightly, and passengers pack into the bar to listen and dance to a lively trio. More elegant is the Explorer's Lounge, whose string ensemble performs a classical repertoire. Nearby is the open-sided piano bar.

The Crow's Nest observation lounge/disco gets fairly little use during the day unless there's a special event being held (such as line-dance classes), but it's a popular spot for pre-dinner cocktails and after-dinner dancing. On *Rotterdam,* a highlight of the Crow's Nest is the life-size terra-cotta human and horse figures, copies of ancient statues discovered in Xian, China.

The main showroom is more a nightclub than a theater. Sit on the banquettes for the best sightlines, as alternating rows of individual chairs sit lower and don't permit most passengers to see over the heads of those in front of them. The balcony offers decent sightlines.

Other public rooms include a large casino, a card room, and the Wajang Theater for movie viewing (it's also the spot where HAL's Culinary Arts demonstration kitchen resides).

DINING OPTIONS   The attractive two-level formal dining room has floor-to-ceiling windows and an elegant, nostalgic feel, and never seems crowded. The Pinnacle Grill seats fewer than 100 diners and offers romantic, intimate Pacific Northwest cuisine in an elegant setting. The only downside here: no windows. And be careful of those funky chairs; they tip forward if you lean too far toward your soup.

As in the rest of the fleet, a casual buffet-style breakfast, lunch, and dinner are offered in the Lido restaurant, a bright, cheerful place done in corals and blues. It's a well-laid-out space, with separate salad, drink, deli, dessert, and stir-fry stations. There's a taco bar poolside at lunchtime, and pizza is available in the afternoon.

POOL, FITNESS, SPA & SPORTS FACILITIES   The ship has a spacious, well-equipped gym with a large separate aerobics area, floor-to-ceiling ocean views, plenty of elbowroom, and a nice spa. There's a pair of swimming pools: one amidships on the Lido Deck, with a retractable glass roof and a pair of hot tubs, and another smaller, less trafficked, and thus more relaxing one in the stern, letting onto open views of the ships wake. There's a great wraparound Promenade Deck lined with wooden deck chairs, a quiet and nostalgic spot for reading, snoozing, or scoping the scenery or Europe.

There's a combo volleyball and tennis court on the Sports Deck, and Ping-Pong tables on the Lower Promenade in the sheltered bow.

Maasdam

The Verdict

This ship is well made and designed, and certainly holds its own in this age of gigantic circuslike megas. Public areas are functional and appealing, with just a dash of glitz and plenty of classic European and Indonesian art.

Maasdam *(photo: Holland America Line)*

Specifications

Size (in Tons)	55,451	Crew	602
Passengers (Double Occ.)	1,266	Passenger/Crew Ratio	2.1 to 1
Passenger/Space Ratio	44	Year Launched	1993
Total Cabins/Veranda Cabins	633/149	Last Refurbishment/Upgrade	2006

Frommer's Ratings (Scale of 1–5)   ★★★★

Cabin Comfort & Amenities	4	Dining Options	4
Appearance & Upkeep	4	Gym, Spa & Sports Facilities	4
Public Comfort/Space	5	Children's Facilities	3
Decor	4	Enjoyment Factor	4.5

Refreshingly intimate, agile, and handsome looking, the *Maasdam* (and her three Statendam-class sisters, *Statendam, Rydam,* and *Veendam*), like all the HAL ships, is extremely well laid out and easy to navigate. The Statendam class ships are cozy, at one-third the size of the today's biggest megas, and, relatively speaking, are classics at ages running from 13 to 16. Decor is a subdued scheme of earthy tones and traditional art works. Touches of marble, teak, polished brass, and multimillion-dollar collections of art and maritime artifacts lend a classic ambience, and many decorative themes emphasize the Netherlands' seafaring traditions. The onboard mood is low key (though things get dressy at night), the cabins are large and comfortable, and there are dozens of comfortable nooks all over the ships in which you can curl up and relax. And there's hardly anything more appealing about a ship than a sleek hull with a dark paint job, tiered aft decks, and a long sweeping foredeck—these are covered in teak, offering passengers a great place to view the passing scenery. All and all, these ships are among our favorites.

The *Maasdam* was recently upgraded and now features HAL's Signature of Excellence enhancements, most notably an Explorations Café Internet center, improved kids' facilities, a Culinary Arts demonstration kitchen, and upgraded cabin amenities.

Cabins & Rates

Cabins	Per Diem From	Sq. Ft.	Fridge	Hair Dryer	Sitting Area	TV
Inside	$185	186	No	Yes	Yes	Yes
Outside	$215	197	No	Yes	Yes	Yes
Suite	$335	284–1,126	Yes	Yes	Yes	Yes

CABINS   Cabins are roomy, unfussy, and comfortable, with light-grained furniture and fabrics in safe shades of blue, beige, and burgundy. Curtains separate the sleeping area from the sitting area. White-gloved stewards add a hospitable touch. All cabins have twin beds that can be converted to a queen and, in some cases, a king, all with plush triple-sheeted mattresses and 100% Egyptian cotton bed linens—the most comfortable cruise ship beds Heidi has ever slept on. About 200 cabins can accommodate a third and fourth passenger on a foldaway sofa bed and/or an upper berth. Closets and storage space are larger than the norm, and bathrooms are well designed and well lit, with bathtubs in all but the lowest category. All cabins have personal safes and music channels, plus flatscreen TVs and DVD players (great if you have kids—bring those cartoons from home!), terry-cloth bathrobes, massage shower heads, lighted magnifying makeup mirrors, and salon-quality hair dryers.

Outside cabins have picture windows and views of the sea, though those on the Lower Promenade Deck have pedestrian walkways (and, occasionally, pedestrians) between you and the ocean. Special reflective glass prevents outsiders from spying in during daylight hours. To guarantee privacy at nighttime, you have to close the curtains. No cabin views are blocked by dangling lifeboats or other equipment.

Minisuites are larger than those aboard some of the most expensive lines, such as SeaDream. Full suites are 563 square feet, and the Penthouse Suite sprawls across a full 1,126 square feet. Suite passengers have the choice of three pillow types.

Six cabins are outfitted for passengers with disabilities, and public areas are also wheelchair friendly, with spacious corridors, wide elevators, and wheelchair-accessible public toilets.

PUBLIC AREAS   For the most part, public areas are subdued, consciously tasteful, and soothing. The Sky Deck offers an almost 360-degree panorama where the only drawback is the roaring wind. One deck below, almost equivalent views are available from the ever-popular Crow's Nest nightclub, which has been redesigned in a fresh, new way. Highlights include a subtly glowing bar, banquettes in bright modern colors, and translucent white floor-to-ceiling curtains that function as both decor and moveable enclosures for private events. Cocktail mixology classes and other events are offered here during the day; after dinner, it becomes the ships' disco and nightclub where theme parties and dancing takes place. The ships' small three-story atria are pleasant enough and refreshingly unglitzy, housing the passenger-services and shore-excursions desks, as well as officers' offices.

The ships' two-story showrooms are modern and stylish, but not overdone. Unlike aboard most ships, which have rows of theaterlike seats or couches, the lower levels are configured with cozy groupings of cushy banquettes and chairs that can be moved.

The balcony, however, has bench seating, with low backs that make it impossible to lean back without slouching.

The trendiest spot is the Explorations Café, a well-stocked library and Internet center with a coffee bar and ocean views. A buzzing hub of activity, it has 12 computer stations and several plug points for those going wireless with laptops. Five leather chaise longues partnered with CD players and headphone stations face the sea through floor-to-ceiling windows, while other clusters of couches and chairs are set among the generous shelves of periodicals and books, which include everything from travel to fiction, science, history, gardening, and reference titles. A magazine rack holds current issues of popular magazines and newspapers, when the ship can get them. If you're a crossword buff, you can tackle the *Times'* puzzles embedded under glass in the room's cafe tables (wax pencils are provided).

There's a dark and cozy piano bar, where requests are taken, or head to the elegant Explorer's Lounge, a popular venue for high tea in the afternoon and for light classical and parlor music after dinner. A live band plays for dancers before dinner in the very popular Ocean Bar, and the nice-size casino is spacious though not as pleasingly designed as aboard the line's newer ships. A small movie theater shows films a few times a day, and this space also houses the new Culinary Arts demonstration kitchen—the movie screen descends in front of the kitchen during show times.

Young children get to play in a bright but smallish room decorated like a giant paint box, and preteens have a karaoke machine and video games. Lucky teens, however, get the Oasis, a top-deck sun deck with a wading pool with waterfall, teak deck chairs, hammocks, colorful Astroturf, and lamps designed as metal palm trees, all enclosed by a bamboo fence.

DINING OPTIONS   This ship has an elegant, two-story main dining room at the stern, with dual staircases swooping down to the lower level for grand entrances and a music balcony at the top where a duo or trio serenades diners. Ceilings are glamorous with their lotus-flower glass fixtures, and two smaller attached dining rooms are available for groups. HAL's specialty restaurant, the Pinnacle Grill (see "Dining," on p. 132), has a classy more modern feel to it.

The casual indoor/outdoor buffet restaurant is well laid out, with separate stations for desserts and drinks, which helps keep lines to a minimum. The restaurant serves breakfast, lunch, and dinner daily, and its pizza and ice cream stations are open until just before dinner. An outdoor grill on the Lido Deck serves burgers and other sandwich items throughout the afternoon, and a nearby station allows you to make your own tacos or nachos at lunch.

POOL, FITNESS, SPA & SPORTS FACILITIES   There's a sprawling expanse of teak-covered aft deck surrounding a swimming pool, a perfect place to plant yourself for great views watching the ship approach or depart a port. One deck above and centrally located is a second swimming pool, plus a wading pool, hot tubs, and a spacious deck—all under a sliding glass roof to allow use in inclement (or cool) weather. Imaginative, colorful tile designs and a dolphin sculpture add spice to the otherwise low-key decor, and the attractive Dolphin Bar here, with umbrellas and wicker chairs, is the perfect spot for a drink and snack in the late afternoon after a long day of touring.

The Sports Deck of each ship has combo basketball/tennis/volleyball courts, and the lovely Lower Promenade Deck offers an unobstructed circuit of the ship for walking, jogging, or just lounging in the snazzy, traditional-looking wooden deck chairs. The ships' windowed Ocean Spa gyms offer dozens of exercise machines, a large aerobics area, steam rooms, and saunas. The redesigned Greenhouse Spa is an improvement; the thermal suite has a hydrotherapy whirlpool and heated tile loungers.

The Forward Observation Deck, a huge expanse of open teak deck, is accessible only via two stairways hidden away in the forward (covered) portion of the Promenade Deck and so gets little use. But don't miss going there. There's no deck furniture here, but standing in the very bow as the ship plows through the ocean is a wonderful experience, and an amazing perch from which you can watch the ship enter or leave port.

Prinsendam

The Verdict

The *Prinsendam* is a small ship, but it feels spacious and has pleasing remnants of its luxurious past. It's great for those who shun the megavessel vibe.

Prinsendam *(photo: HAL)*

Specifications

Size (GRT)	38,000	Crew	443
Passengers (Double Occ.)	793	Passenger/Crew Ratio	1.9 to 1
Passenger/Space Ratio	47.8	Year Launched	1988
Total Cabins/Veranda Cabins	398/151	Last Major Refurbishment	2008

Frommer's Ratings (Scale of 1–5)   ★★★★ ½

Cabin Comfort & Amenities	4	Dining Options	3
Ship Cleanliness & Maintenance	5	Gym, Spa & Sports Facilities	3.5
Public Comfort/Space	4.5	Children's Facilities	2
Decor	4	Enjoyment Factor	4.5

The 38,000-ton *Prinsendam,* carrying just 793 passengers, is cozy and appealing, especially for those looking for a traditional cruise experience. Built in 1988 (as the *Royal Viking Sun*), the vessel was briefly part of the fleet of luxury brand Seabourn (sailing as the *Seabourn Sun*) and underwent an extensive renovation in spring 2002 when it joined the HAL fleet. Additions to the ship included an alternative dining venue, balconies on a good number of cabins, and an Internet cafe. Teak decks, quiet corners, and many public rooms furnished with antiques and Dutch art create a traditional ambience despite the ship's modern amenities.

Cabins & Rates

Cabins	Per Diem From	Sq. Ft.	Fridge	Hair Dryer	Sitting Area	TV
Inside	$164	138	Yes	Yes	No	Yes
Outside	$189	181–238	Yes	Yes	Some	Yes
Suite	$503	362–724	Yes	Yes	Yes	Yes

CABINS About 40% of the cabins have private verandas. Most cabins are of good size (the smallest outside cabins are 181 sq. ft.; the largest suite is 725 sq. ft.) and tastefully decorated. All of the outside cabins have both a tub and a shower. Eight of the cabins are wheelchair accessible. Mirrors make the spaces seem larger than they are, storage space is more than adequate, and bathrooms are compact and well designed.

PUBLIC AREAS The ship has 8 decks and some 22 public rooms, including the sophisticated Explorer's Lounge and the more intimate Ocean Bar (set in the center of the vessel, an excellent place for people-watching), as well as a coffee bar located near the casino. To sample the bustle of shipboard life—music, dancing, and lively conversation—the Crow's Nest Bar, topside, is the place to hang out. The intimate Oak Room offers a haven for smokers, complete with faux fireplace.

Unlike the rest of the fleet, the *Prinsendam*'s dining room, La Fontaine Room, is built on only one level. Occupying the entire rear portion of the Promenade Deck and much of the port side as well, it offers wonderful views. Casual meals are available in the redesigned Lido Deck restaurant, with indoor and outdoor (under an awning) seating.

Although the *Prinsendam* has no dedicated children's facilities, it does offer Club HAL programs for kids and teens using public rooms.

ALTERNATIVE DINING The Pinnacle Grill is a an appealing alternative dining venue with ocean views and an intimate feel. The menu includes most seafood, steaks, and chops. There is a $30 cover charge.

GYM, SPA & SPORTS FACILITIES The *Prisendam* has a classic ship feel, and the aft tiered decks are wonderful throwbacks. So is the wraparound promenade, where walkers will enjoy the view, especially on approaches to such picturesque ports as Valetta, Istanbul, Drubovnik, and any of the Greek Isles. There are two outside pools: The bigger one is designed for laps (an unusual offering), and the smaller has a swim-up bar. The elegantly decorated Greenhouse Spa, with its appropriately moody lighting, has saunas in addition to massage rooms and a beauty salon. Passengers can get active in the small fitness center or on the tennis practice courts.

6 MSC Cruises

6750 N. Andrews Ave., Fort Lauderdale, FL 33309. ℂ **800/666-9333**. www.msccruises.com.

THE LINE IN A NUTSHELL MSC is attempting the kind of change NCL has accomplished over the past 5 years, transforming itself from a catch-as-catch-can company offering cheap cruises on older ships into (it hopes) a true player. With six new mid- and megasize vessels built in the past decade and more on the way, they sure have the hardware, but they can still use a little work in the finesse department. In Europe, the majority of passengers tend to be European, with a growing number of Americans and other English-speakers mixed in. On board, announcements and other communications are in English, Italian, and whatever other languages are appropriate for the passengers aboard that week.

THE EXPERIENCE Based in Italy, where it was born as an adjunct of Mediterranean Shipping Company (the world's second-largest container-shipping operation), MSC's all about "Italian style": Italian menus, lots of Italians (and other Europeans) on board, European-style entertainment, and a laid-back, nearly laissez-faire attitude. This is not a line that holds its passengers' hands. In fact, how good a time you have is mostly up to you. By design, it mimics what cruising was like 30 years ago: more a venue for socializing and low-key activities than a something-for-everyone theme park. For some passengers, that lack of novelty has its own appeal, running totally counter to what you get from most American mainstream lines today. On the upside, there are few announcements to disturb the serenity of a drink or conversation in any number of cozy bars, or to intrude on the sanctity of passenger cabins. On the downside, the line has a way to go to compete with its mainstream rivals, particularly in its dining and menu options, presentation, and service.

The line operates a fleet of generally newer ships, including midsize sister ships *Armonia, Sinfonia, Lirica,* and *Opera,* and megaships *Musica* and *Orchestra.* The midsize vessels were all launched in the early half of this decade and are almost a throwback to an earlier era of cruising, carrying "only" 1,586 to 1,756 passengers, and with almost none of the pop-culture themes and flashiness of most modern ships. The newer megaships put a bit more muscle into the flash department, but the onboard ambience still conveys a time when cruising relied less on gadgets and gimmicks, and more on old-fashioned entertainment and socializing. Let's just say you won't be overwhelmed by the ships' printed program of daily activities.

Pros

- **Fun (if limited) activities:** As on Costa, the European entertainment staff knows how to get people in the mood for fun.
- **Italian cuisine:** MSC's distinctive regional dishes and pastas may be among the best at sea. Their pizza, in particular, wins high praise.
- **Unusual entertainment touches:** While production shows can lapse into the usual song-and-dance, the circus-style contortionists, acrobats, stilt performers, and even operatic singers add a nice touch.
- **Low prices:** Despite some negatives, this is still a line on which you can get good bang for your buck. If price is a big concern and your expectations aren't super-high, you won't be disappointed.

Cons

- **Lackadaisical service:** Staff can be surprisingly inattentive, provoking one passenger we met to comment, "You get the feeling that everyone has something more important to do than focus on you." In the dining room, waiters may be reluctant to accommodate off-the-menu requests, undermining the "sophisticated" atmosphere the line's promotions promise.
- **Small cabins & showers on midsize ships:** Standard inside and outside cabins aboard *Armonia, Sinfonia, Lirica,* and *Musica* are only 140 square feet, and the 247-square-foot suites would pass for junior suites aboard most vessels. Showers in these ships' cabin bathrooms are among the smallest in the cruise business.
- **No alternative dining on midsize ships:** In the evening, the only alternative to the two dining rooms is the late-night (11:30pm) buffet on the pool deck or pizza served until 8pm.

MSC: ITALIAN LINE GOES INTERNATIONAL

MSC Cruises came into being in 1990 as the cruise wing of Mediterranean Shipping Company, one of the world's largest container-shipping operations. Originally concentrating on the European market, the line began making overtures to U.S. passengers after buying the Big Red Boat *Atlantic* from defunct Premier Cruises in 1998 and

Compared with the other mainstream lines, here's how MSC rates:

	Poor	Fair	Good	Excellent	Outstanding
Enjoyment Factor			✓		
Dining			✓		
Activities			✓		
Children's Program			✓		
Entertainment			✓		
Service		✓			
Worth the Money				✓	

setting it off on 11-night Caribbean cruises. It was in 2003, 2004, and 2005, however, that the line really began its hard sell to the English-speaking world, first building its first-ever new ships (*Lirica* and *Opera*), then hiring former Celebrity Cruises exec Richard Sasso to head its North America division, then buying sister ships *Armonia* and *Sinfonia* from defunct Festival Cruises, then announcing construction of its first megaships. The twin 89,000-ton *Musica* and *Orchestra* launched in 2006 and 2007, and at press time the line is expecting three new ships for delivery in 2008 and 2009: the 89,000-ton *Poesia* (March 2008) and two 133,500-ton, 3,300-passenger superme-gas, *Fantasia* (June 2008) and *Splendida* (March 2009).

In addition to its modern ships, MSC continues to operate two much older vessels, the 1982-vintage *Melody* and 1977's *Rhapsody*. As their onboard offerings are so much different from the majority of the fleet, and since they carry such a small percentage of passengers overall (and even fewer English-speaking passengers), we have elected not to deal with them in the body of this review. See the sidebar on p. 150 for some details on these vessels.

PASSENGER PROFILE

MSC's Mediterranean itineraries tend to carry 85% European and 15% "other" passengers, including North Americans. The typical age range is mid-40s and up, and many passengers on European sailings (particularly in summer) are parents traveling with their kids. Public announcements are made in **English** and **Italian,** plus French, German, and/or Spanish, depending on the composition of the week's passenger list. English-speaking passenger must be prepared for an international onboard experience and be aware that you may have to repeat questions to the staff on occasion. And why shouldn't you? You're in Europe, after all, sailing on a European ship. The ball is in your court.

Evening shows are introduced in Italian and English, but because they're mostly music and dance extravaganzas rather than spoken performances, proficiency with language doesn't much matter.

DINING

In keeping with the line's intention of offering an old-fashioned cruise experience, dining service is generally traditional, with a touch of European sensibility. Dining service needs some work if it's going to try competing with the American mainstream lines (see "Service," below).

The tug of war between Italian, American, and "other" traditions plays itself out in both positive and negative ways. On the positive (and surprising) side, MSC is the

MSC Fleet Itineraries

Ship	Sailing Regions	Home Ports
Armonia	10- and 11-night voyages in the Mediterranean/Black Sea/Egypt (various combinations), Northern Europe/Russia, and the Norwegian Fjords/North Cape	Genoa, Dover/London
Fantasia	8- and 11-night Mediterranean	Genoa
Lirica	7-night voyages in the Mediterranean, Northern Europe/Russia, and the Norwegian Fjords	Civitavecchia/Rome, Copenhagen
Melody	7-night Mediterranean	Barcelona
Musica	7- and 11-night Mediterranean/Greek Isles/Egypt (various combinations)	Venice, Genoa
Opera	7-night voyages in the Mediterranean, Northern Europe/Russia, and the Norwegian Fjords	Trieste (Italy), Copenhagen
Orchestra	7- and 11-night voyages in the Mediterranean/Canary Islands/Egypt (various combinations)	Barcelona, Genoa
Poesia	7- and 11-night Mediterranean	Venice, Genoa
Rhapsody	7-night Mediterranean	Genoa
Sinfonia	7-night Mediterranean	Civitavecchia/Rome

only line on which we've noticed a kosher category on the wine list—and the only line we've been on where poppy-seed bagels are a staple at the buffet. (On every other line, it's plain bagels, period.) On the annoying side, you have to specially request coffee in the dining room after meals (only Americans do this, several Italian staff members told us), and you'll probably be asked to order your dessert selection at the same time you make your full meal request.

TRADITIONAL All of the line's modern midsize and megasize ships have two formal dining rooms apiece, serving traditional breakfast, lunch, and dinner in two fixed seatings, with an emphasis on Italian cuisine. Six-course lunches include appetizers such as smoked salmon tartare, tomatoes stuffed with tuna mousse, and barbecued chicken wings; a soup of the day; a choice of salads; pasta selections such as ravioli, risotto with pears and Bel Paese cheese, and traditional spaghetti; and main courses that might include pan-roasted chicken breast in a Riesling wine sauce, sliced sirloin, Caribbean red snapper filet, frittata with zucchini and Swiss cheese, or a plain old turkey sandwich. A selection of vegetables, cheeses, and desserts rounds out the offerings, along with a special **vegetarian menu,** burgers from the grill, and **healthy-choice options.**

Expect about the same for dinner, with appetizers such as lamb-and-mushroom quiche, avocado boat with seafood salad, and crispy fried spring rolls; a salad of the day; three soup selections, such as Trieste-style red bean soup, oxtail broth with sherry, and chilled orange and tomato cream soup; pasta selections such as risotto with artichokes and fresh mint leaves, and pappardelle pasta with white veal ragout; and main courses such as rock Cornish hen with mushrooms and crispy bacon, prime rib, grilled mahimahi filet, and vegetable couscous with raisins and cashews. As at lunch, dinner offers a vegetarian menu, a healthy menu, and a selection of cheeses and desserts (including sugar-free desserts), plus a bread of the day. The daily **Italian regional specialties** tend to be the highlight of the menu, winning nearly unqualified approval from every passenger nationality on board. An **always available** list rounds out the offerings with steak, chicken, salmon fillets, Caesar salad, baked potato, and corn on the cob.

SPECIALTY   Specialty restaurants are available only on the line's megaships, not aboard its four midsize vessels. Aboard the twin 2,550-passenger *Musica* and *Orchestra* (and soon-to-be-launched *Poesia*), part of the buffet restaurant is partitioned off at night and serves a more refined version of Italian cuisine than the main restaurants, with waiter service. Aboard *Musica,* the **Kaito Sushi Bar** is an a la carte specialty restaurant serving sushi, tempura, and other Japanese favorites. On *Orchestra* there's a stylish **Chinese Restaurant** in its place.

CASUAL   A **buffet restaurant** serves all three meals, with dinner available from 6 to 8pm. Pizza, burgers, and other items are available from the pool deck **grill** during the day.

SNACKS & EXTRAS   In true Italian style, every bar on these ships is also a **coffee bar,** so passengers can enjoy an espresso or macchiato anytime, anywhere. From late afternoon until around 8pm, the pool deck grill serves really excellent **pizza** and Italian specialty snacks. Inside, the ship offers one of the few daily **midnight buffets** left in the industry. At the other end of the spectrum, waiters on Captain's Night proffer an assortment of pleasant **free drinks**—not just punch and cheap champagne, but the kind of mixed drinks once ubiquitous aboard gracious ocean liners, such as Manhattans, whiskey sours, and martinis.

Room service is available 24 hours a day from a limited menu. In-room continental breakfast is served free from 7:30 to 10am, but using room service at other times will cost you a few euros per item.

ACTIVITIES

Activities on MSC tend toward cruise traditions, many of them with a European sense of fun. Outside, expect a round of **goofy pool games,** including water polo, treasure hunts, and various team games, plus darts and **golf tournaments,** the latter on a putting green that wraps around the top deck. Goofiness continues in the evenings, with the kind of participatory games for which Italian ships are known. Leave your self-consciousness at home. Flamenco and tango **dance lessons** might be held in one of

---

MSC's Classic Fleet

In addition to its recently built megaships and midsize vessels, MSC operates a small "classic fleet" of vessels that have been around for a while and are mostly marketed to Europeans. Though they lack the amenities of the line's modern ship, they hold definite appeal to fans of old-style ships.

The 35,143-ton, 1,064-passenger, 1982-built *Melody* may be familiar to Americans through her former service as the *Star/Ship Atlantic* (aka "The Big Red Boat") of now-defunct Premier Cruises. Built as the *Atlantic* of long-defunct Home Lines, she retains the look of her time, with a high white superstructure (read: no balconies) and distinctly '70s/'80s interiors. Her layout is fairly spacious, with most public rooms clustered on or just below the pool deck. Standard cabins are very simply done, with little style. Overall, the 16,852-ton, 780-passenger *Rhapsody* is a much prettier old ship. Launched in 1977 as *Cunard Princess,* she has a lovely low-slung exterior profile and relatively understated interiors. As aboard *Melody,* standard stateroom decor is nothing to write home about.

Preview: MSC's *Fantasia* & *Splendida*

The supermegaships *Fantasia* and *Splendida* represent MSC's step into the big leagues, and are the largest ships ever built by a European cruise company, measuring 133,500 gross register tons and carrying 3,900 passengers apiece. Though few details have yet been released about the vessels, we can tell you that they will feature 3-D cinemas, huge 16,146-square-foot spas, 24-hour Tex Mex restaurants, sports bars, and virtual "first class" sections with a dedicated concierge, butler service, a panoramic lounge, a swimming pool and solarium, and direct access to the spa—all for the exclusive use of guests booking the ships' 90 suites. *Fantasia* and *Splendida* are set to debut in June 2008 and March 2009, respectively.

the lounges. Other classes may include Italian language, basic computer use, and cooking, and the spa and salon staffs put on the usual raft of **beauty demonstrations.** The gyms offer stretching and standard aerobics classes, plus Pilates and yoga at an added charge ($14 per class, or five for $55). Other activities include cards and bingo, gambling in the **casinos,** arts and crafts, and various meet-and-greet events such as singles and honeymooners cocktail parties.

CHILDREN'S PROGRAM

Lirica, Opera, Sinfonia, and *Armonia* each have cute, if smallish, **Mini Clubs** for kids, while *Musica, Orchestra,* and the upcoming *Poesia* have larger, themed centers, plus outdoor play decks with wading pools and slides and a video game room, located nearby. Counselors, known as "animators," are on hand to organize activities such as arts and crafts, puppet shows, games, treasure hunts, mini-Olympics, painting classes, pizza parties, etc. Just remember (as one memorable sign said when we were aboard *Opera*), "It's not possible entry in the Mini-Club if is not present one animator!" Other kid-centric activities around the ship might include "baby disco" and balloon-tying shows.

Activities are tailored for several age groups, from ages 3 to 8, 9 to 13, and teens. Kids under 3 must be accompanied by an adult at all times. On days in port, parents can leave their kids at the Mini Club while they go on shore excursions—just be sure to make arrangements with the Mini Club supervisor a day in advance.

Armonia, Sinfonia, Musica, Orchestra, and *Poesia* also offer **teen clubs** with activities that include sports tournaments (minigolf, table tennis, etc.), theme quizzes, line dances, sail-away parties, pool parties, and disco nights.

ENTERTAINMENT

Evening entertainment is centered around each ship's main theater. On our most recent cruise, the usual Vegas song-and-dance routines caused yawns, but several shows drew on European circus traditions, featuring contortionists, acrobats, and stilt performers. It's that European influence—also evident at **audience-participation shows,** the lively disco, and the **karaoke** sessions—that distinguishes MSC's entertainment from the American cruise lines. Other shows in the lineup may include a Spanish show with flamenco and modern dancers, an Italian-style show featuring an operatic tenor, a classic concert, or a magic show. Quieter options around the ships include **daytime films** in the main theater and music in various bars and lounges.

SERVICE

Service is the number one downside that MSC must address if it wants to reach a wider audience. While the line touts its Italian officers and crew—a distinction that appeals to passengers who fondly recall the Golden Age of ocean travel—MSC has, in fact, blurred its Italianness by recruiting service staff from Indonesia and other Asian nations. As on other lines, the Asian crew distinguishes itself with its attention and eagerness, but in many instances the international crew mix has resulted in a Tower of Babel language barrier, even among the crew.

Real problems seem to stem more from the line's Italian staff, whose surprising inattentiveness—especially in the dining rooms—is a major deviation from the sophisticated ambience the line's advertising promises. On our most recent cruise (aboard *Lirica*), a request for egg whites at lunch in the main restaurant was received by the waiter with an insistent, "Only what's on the menu."

Tipping is handled on an automatic basis; 6€ ($8.40) per person, per day is added to your onboard account. The amount can be adjusted up or down by contacting the Reception Desk.

Laundry service is also available, though there are no self-serve laundries.

Musica • Orchestra • Poesia (Preview)

The Verdict

MSC's first modern megaships offer exceptional styling and a full range of activities and amenities, all in the line's typically international social setting.

Orchestra *(photo: MSC)*

Specifications

Size (in Tons)	89,600	Year Launched	
Passengers (Double Occ.)	2,550	*Musica*	2006
Passenger/Space Ratio	35.1	*Orchestra*	2007
Total Cabins/Veranda Cabins	1,275/827	*Poesia*	2008
Crew	987	Last Refurbishment/Upgrade	N/A
Passenger/Crew Ratio	2.6 to 1		

Frommer's Ratings (Scale of 1–5)   ★★★★

Cabin Comfort & Amenities	4	Dining Options	4
Appearance & Upkeep	4.5	Gym, Spa & Sports Facilities	4
Public Comfort/Space	4	Children's Facilities	4
Decor	4.5	Enjoyment Factor	4

Musica, Orchestra, and their not-yet-launched sister ship *Poesia* represent an evolutionary leap for MSC Cruises, which until now has concentrated on midsize vessels that get the job done but are a little short on pizzazz. These three, on the other hand, are truly modern megaships, offering high-style decor, multiple dining options, elaborate spas, wine-tasting bars, outdoor movies, a juice bar, a multistory theater, and many appealing lounges.

Because *Poesia* hadn't yet launched as of this writing, this review deals with *Musica* and *Orchestra* only.

Cabins & Rates

Cabins	Per Diem From	Sq. Ft.	Fridge	Hair Dryer	Sitting Area	TV
Inside	$150	152	Yes	Yes	No	Yes
Outside	$171	166	Yes	Yes	Yes	Yes
Suite	$286	269*	Yes	Yes	Yes	Yes

Including veranda

CABINS The majority of accommodations on these ships (some 63% of them) are outside cabins with balconies. Each is done up in a clean, pleasingly modern style, with lovely jewel-toned upholstery patterns and light-wood accents, though they're sized a bit smaller than cabins on many competing megaships. Standard inside and outside cabins offer a TV, minifridge, private safe, vanity/writing desk, a bathroom with shower, and Wi-Fi access. Outsides also have a small sitting area. Closet and storage space are adequate, and the bathrooms are efficiently designed, with good amounts of shelf space, though for toiletries you get only the basics. Suites add a larger sitting area, a larger balcony, a king-size bed, a tub in the bathroom, upgraded toiletries, and more closet space.

Seventeen cabins are wheelchair accessible—12 of them insides, 2 outsides with windows, and 3 outsides with balcony.

PUBLIC AREAS Public areas on *Musica* and *Orchestra* are done in an eclectic style that mixes the clean lines of Princess, the modernism of Celebrity, the flashy ornateness of Costa and Carnival, and the fun of NCL, yet manages to pull them all together into a unified whole.

In the bow, the three-deck theater is an explosion of lights and color, looking like fireworks caught in midburst. At midships, the three-deck atrium offers a curvaceous, aquiline feel, with a backlit central waterfall and illuminated ceiling, a transparent baby grand on a glass platform above the water, stairways sweeping between the decks, and amphora-shaped "streetlights" mixing it up with large potted greenery to create a resortlike feel. Lounges, bars, shops, an Internet center, a card room, a small library (don't expect much in English), and an art gallery radiate out from the atrium on its various levels.

Most public rooms are clustered on the two upper atrium decks. The showroom (Il Tucano on *Musica,* The Savannah Bar on *Orchestra,* each with a fanciful Art Deco motif to match each name) is a lively spot both during the day, when it's used for activities and demonstrations, and in the evening. Several shops and bars are located sternward. On the next deck up there's a large casino; a cigar lounge with comfy leather armchairs; a bright wine bar lit by faux skylights and serving vintages from all over Italy, with cheeses and meats to match; and a lounge done in 1930s martini-drinker style on *Orchestra* and in bright oranges and greens on *Musica,* like a pile of ripe fruit. At the top of the ship, the disco mixes touches of Deco styling with a futuristic dance-floor vibe.

For kids, there's a themed indoor play area (space travel on *Musica,* jungle adventure on *Orchestra*) with PlayStations, games, arts and crafts supplies, and more. Outdoors, there's an enclosed play area with a tube slide, wading pool, and other amenities.

DINING OPTIONS   *Musica* and *Orchestra* offer two main dining rooms, a buffet restaurant, and one specialty dining option. The main dining rooms are both single-level spaces, one decorated in traditional woody fashion, the other going for a more high-style Deco look, especially at *Musica*'s Le Maxim. Ceilings in these restaurants are a bit too low, making for loud meals. Breakfast and lunch are served in the spacious buffet restaurant, with multiple lines serving different specialties, and dishes labeled in both Italian and English. At night, part of the buffet restaurant is partitioned off and serves a more refined version of Italian cuisine than the main restaurants, with waiter service. Aboard *Musica*, the specialty **Kaito Sushi Bar** serves sushi, tempura, and other Japanese favorites. On *Orchestra*, a stylish **Chinese Restaurant** takes its place. A standard pool grill on deck serves burgers and the like during the day.

POOL, FITNESS, SPA & SPORTS FACILITIES   The main pool deck on *Musica* and *Orchestra* is an expansive space with an appropriately Mediterranean vibe and two separate pool areas linked by a pair of deck bars. There are two pools and four Jacuzzis in all, plus a movie screen above the forward pool area. A separate small sun deck immediately under the screen offers an escape from the busier main deck below. Like those aboard all MSC ships, lounge chairs on *Musica* and *Orchestra* have their own attached sun canopies—a neat feature we haven't seen on other lines. Nearby, a jogging track wraps around one deck above the pool, while a miniature golf course and sports court are located to port, on their own small patches of deck.

Indoors, the ships' Balinese-themed spas offer the usual range of massage, wellness, and beauty treatments, all in a lovely, relaxing atmosphere with hints of exotica, including two Turkish baths (one for women, one for men) with beautiful decorative tilework. A pre- or post-treatment relaxation room offers views, lounge chairs, and hydromassage pools (plus a thalassotherapy pool in an adjacent room), while a juice bar offers a menu of energy drinks and fresh fruit cocktails, usually from noon to 8pm. Nearby, the ship's gym is pretty small for vessels this size, with a limited number of aerobics machine and weights. Exercise classes are offered on the attached aerobics floor.

Armonia • Sinfonia • Opera • Lirica

The Verdict

Straightforward midsize vessels. Rather than hitting guests over the head with self-consciously "fun" decor, they just present a venue in which passengers and staff can create their own good times.

Opera *(photo: MSC)*

Specifications

Size (in Tons)	58,600	*Armonia/Sinfonia/Lirica*	760
Passengers (Double Occ.)		*Opera*	800
Armonia/Sinfonia/Lirica	1,586	Passenger/Crew Ratio	
Opera	1,756	*Armonia/Sinfonia/Lirica*	2.1 to 1
Passenger/Space Ratio		*Opera*	2.2 to 1
Armonia/Sinfonia/Lirica	37	Year Launched	
Opera	33.4	*Armonia*	2001
Total Cabins/Veranda Cabins		*Sinfonia*	2002
Armonia/Sinfonia/Lirica	795/132	*Lirica*	2003
Opera	878/200	*Opera*	2004
Crew		Last Refurbishment/Upgrade	N/A

Frommer's Ratings (Scale of 1–5)

★ ★ ★ ½

Cabin Comfort & Amenities	3.5	Dining Options	3
Appearance & Upkeep	4	Gym, Spa & Sports Facilities	3.5
Public Comfort/Space	4	Children's Facilities	3
Decor	3	Enjoyment Factor	4

Opera, Lirica, Sinfonia, and *Armonia* almost seem like a different species from today's brand of enormo-ships, lacking any kind of overt gimmicks—no planetariums, no rock-climbing walls, no "decorate every surface" design schemes. They are ships on which people can get together to talk, loll in the pool, throw away their inhibitions, and relax—all without having their senses overwhelmed. Whether that's a good thing depends on your point of view.

Another aspect of these ships' old-fashionedness? Their moderate size, which is on a par with Holland America's well-loved Statendam-class ships. Long and low, these vessels seem a lot larger than they really are, with a surprising amount of space both in their public rooms and out on the pool deck. For this, credit their small cabins.

Trivia: *Opera, Lirica, Sinfonia,* and *Armonia* were designed and built as nearly identical sister ships by the same French shipyard, but they didn't all begin life as MSC vessels. *Armonia* and *Sinfonia* were built for now-defunct Festival Cruises (aka First European Cruises), where they sailed as *European Vision* and *European Stars.* MSC acquired both ships following Festival's 2004 bankruptcy.

Cabins & Rates

Cabins	Per Diem From	Sq. Ft.	Fridge	Hair Dryer	Sitting Area	TV
Inside	$136	140	Yes	Yes	No	Yes
Outside	$171	140	Yes	Yes	No	Yes
Suite	$257	236–247	Yes	Yes	Yes	Yes

CABINS Aboard *Armonia* and *Sinfonia,* cabins come in only three varieties: standard 140-square-foot inside cabins, 140-square-foot oceanview, and suites that would pass for junior suites aboard most vessels. *Opera* and *Lirica* add 140-square-foot balcony cabins.

Though not palatial, staterooms are pleasantly and unfussily decorated, with simple light wood trim and upholstery patterns, good lighting and storage, and niceties such as a writing/makeup desk and minibar. Balcony cabins seem roomier than they are, thanks to strategically placed mirrors and extremely wide balcony doors. Bathrooms, on the other hand, are stuck with some of the smallest shower stalls in the industry—the only serious design flaw noted on board, and one they probably can't do much about. Suites have larger tub/shower combos.

Four cabins on *Lirica, Armonia,* and *Sinfonia,* and five on *Opera* are wheelchair accessible.

PUBLIC AREAS   Decor on these ships is as far a cry from Carnival's over-the-top themes as it is from the more chic decor of Celebrity. Somewhere between plain and restrained, their public areas are done up in blond woods, floral and geometric carpets, functional solid-colored chairs and banquettes, and a smattering of marble and brass. Fully mirrored walls—and lots of them—dominate most public spaces, brightening the areas, creating a soothing quality, and making the ships seem twice their size.

The ships' layout is simple and easy to navigate. Most public rooms are on two adjoining decks, starting with the main forward theater. Avoid seats in the back corners, which offer lousy sightlines even when other passengers don't stand at the rail in front of them, completely blocking the view. Heading aft there's a coffee bar wrapped around the small, comfortable atrium; a lounge for music, karaoke, and other entertainment; several shops; a casino; an intimate piano bar; several nook lounges and seating areas; and an Internet cafe. (Wi-Fi access is also available in several hot spots.) One deck down, just below the theater, is a pub/lounge that's your best bet for a quiet evening drink, as it's off the main evening traffic routes. Atop the ship is a disco/observation lounge with several dance floors and a generally hopping vibe.

Kids get a playroom tucked weirdly into the same complex as the spa, gym, and beauty salon, in the bow on the pool deck. On *Opera* the room has a Buffalo Bill Wild West theme, on *Lirica* it's done in a tropical pirate theme, *Armonia* has a Seven Dwarfs theme, and *Sinfonia* has a Pinocchio theme. *Armonia* and *Sinfonia* also have teen lounges on their top decks, right next to the adult disco and near the video game room.

DINING OPTIONS   Each ship's two restaurants are downright old-fashioned, eschewing the multiple levels, grand staircases, columns, and chandeliers common aboard most megaships, and favoring instead a simple one-story approach. Decor is restrained to the point of being irrelevant—just warmly colored walls and carpets, a smattering of ceiling and fixture lights, and lots of people dining at tables that are maybe just a little too close together.

A standard buffet restaurant occupies the stern of the pool deck, with an additional outdoor seating area separated off from the main pool. An outdoor grill serves pizza, burgers, pork cutlets, and the like. Pizza and Italian specialty snacks are also served indoors from late afternoon until around 8pm.

POOL, FITNESS, SPA & SPORTS FACILITIES   The main recreation deck has two pools and two hot tubs that are central to the vitality of the vessel during the day, with row upon row of sunbathers napping or reading. Like many other spaces on board, it's almost a throwback to early 1990s ship design—just a plain-vanilla pool deck without showy frills—but it does offer those great MSC lounge chairs, each with its own sun canopy. A jogging track wraps around the deck above.

Gyms are tiny and inadequately equipped for the number of people on board. On our last cruise, three treadmills were in such constant demand that passengers were asked to reserve time on them—a frequent point of contention when other passengers inadvertently cut the line. A bike machine, about a dozen weight machines, free weights, and a small aerobics floor complete the picture. Spa treatment rooms encircle the space, with a pre- or post-treatment "relaxation room" off to one side. Up on the top deck, a golf putting green encircles the stern.

7 Norwegian Cruise Line

7665 Corporate Center Dr., Miami, FL 33126. ℂ **866/234-0292** or 305/436-4000. Fax 305/436-4126. www.ncl.com.

THE LINE IN A NUTSHELL   NCL may be the most mainstream of the mainstream lines these days—and we mean that in a good way. At a time when even Carnival is pushing the "luxury" elements of its onboard program, NCL hews to the center, with always-casual dining (and lots of it); bright, cheerful decor; fun innovations such as gourmet beer bars and onboard bowling alleys; and some of the best new megaships in the business. Nutshell? NCL's the kind of cruise line you want to sit down and have a beer with.

THE EXPERIENCE   Back in the mid- to late '90s, NCL operated a mixed-bag fleet of older ships whose onboard vibe was only a couple steps above budget. What a difference a few years makes. Today it's one of the top players in the industry, with innovative itineraries, a fleet composed almost entirely of new megaships, a casual onboard atmosphere, top-drawer entertainment, and a staggering number of dining choices. The line was the first to dump the old system of formal/informal/casual nights, going totally casual in 2000 and starting a trend across the industry. The new program also did away with fixed dining times and seating assignments, leaving passengers free to choose when and where they want to dine among a variety of venues. Traditional tipping also went away, replaced by a system where gratuities are added directly to passenger accounts. Busy, busy, busy they've been, and it shows. This is one fun cruise line.

Pros

- **Flexible dining:** NCL's "Freestyle Cruising" policy lets you dine when and where you want, dressed "however."
- **Restaurants galore:** With between 8 and 10 places to have dinner, you won't know where to turn.
- **Above-average entertainment:** In addition to above-average Vegas-style shows and musical groups, NCL offers comedy shows by the Second City comedy troupe aboard *Norwegian Jewel, Gem,* and *Jade.*

Cons

- **Small cabins:** At about 142 and 158 square feet, respectively, standard inside and outside cabins are a tighter squeeze than those on most competitor lines.

NCL: SAY ALOHA TO INNOVATION

Talk about pulling yourself up by your bootstraps. Norwegian was one of the pioneers of the North American cruise market, beginning in 1966 as an alliance between Norwegian ship owner Knut Kloster and Israeli marketing genius Ted Arison, who later started Carnival Cruises. After these auspicious beginnings, it spent many years relegated to the industry's back seat as Carnival and Royal Caribbean gained ascendancy. Beginning in 1997, though (and especially since its purchase by Asian line Star

Compared with the other mainstream lines, here's how NCL rates:

	Poor	Fair	Good	Excellent	Outstanding
Enjoyment Factor					✓
Dining				✓	
Activities				✓	
Children's Program				✓	
Entertainment				✓	
Service				✓	
Worth the Money					✓

Cruises in 2000), NCL began a sequence of moves that transformed it into a true leader and innovator. In 2000 it led the industry in the "casual cruising" trend, and in 2004 it started the first U.S.-flagged cruise operation in decades, concentrating on the Hawaii market. It's also engaged in a veritable explosion of construction and upgrades, gradually replacing all its older vessels with wonderful new megaships. At this writing, only two ships from the old NCL fleet remain, and those will be gone in a year, too. Then we can watch for the *really* new tonnage: two huge, 150,000-ton, 4,200-passenger supermegaships are on order with French shipbuilder Aker Yards S.A. and will debut in 2009 and 2010.

For its European deployment this year, NCL has chosen three of its very newest and best vessels: *Norwegian Jade, Norwegian Jewel,* and *Norwegian Gem.*

PASSENGER PROFILE
The atmosphere aboard all NCL vessels is informal and well suited to casual types, party makers, first-time cruisers, families, and honeymooners. In Europe, NCL attracts mostly an older crowd, with an average age of around 60. About 90% are from North America, many are experienced cruisers, and they tend to have more cash in the bank than passengers who book NCL in the Caribbean.

DINING
All the restaurants on all NCL ships follow an **open-seating policy** each and every evening, allowing you to dine whenever you like within the 5:30 to 10pm window, sit with whomever you want (rather than having a table preassigned), and dress however you like: Anything goes except jeans, shorts, and tank tops. This flexible setup really works for families, groups, and anyone else who doesn't want to be tied down to fixed times and tables, and who wants to have a lot of different dinner companions instead of chatting up the same bunch all week. If you end up sitting with people you particularly like, you can always make plans to dine with them again.

The night of the captain's cocktail party is officially an **"optional formal" night,** meaning you can wear a suit, tie, or fancy dress if you like, but no one will complain if you don't. That said, we've been surprised at just how many people do dress up.

TRADITIONAL   The main dining rooms, like the rest of the ships' eating venues, operate with open seating and casual dress codes, so the only really "traditional" thing about them is their size and a touch of traditional ocean-liner elegance. Menus include dishes such as grilled swordfish with lemon-caper sauce, salmon or poached sea bass, beef Wellington, broiled lobster tail, chicken Parmesan, fettuccine Alfredo, Jamaican

NCL Fleet Itineraries

Ship	Itineraries	Home Ports
Norwegian Gem	7-night Mediterranean	Barcelona
Norwegian Jade	12-night Northern Europe	Dover/London
Norwegian Jewel	12- to 14-night voyages in the Mediterranean/Egypt/Greek Isles (various combinations), the Norwegian Fjords/North Cape, and Northern Europe/British Isles	Barcelona, Istanbul, Piraeus/Athens, Southampton/London

jerk pork roast, Wiener schnitzel, and roast prime rib. The wine lists appeal to standard mid-American tastes, and prices aren't offensively high.

A **light choice** (prepared with recipes from NCL partner *Cooking Light* magazine) and a **vegetarian entree** are available at lunch and dinner. **Children's menus** feature the popular standards (burgers, hot dogs, grilled cheese sandwiches and french fries, spaghetti and meatballs, ice cream sundaes, and so on) plus unexpected dishes such as vegetable crudités and cheese dip.

SPECIALTY   In addition to one or two main dining rooms, the three ships NCL has in Europe for 2008 have eight alternative specialty restaurants serving food that's on a par with all but the very best on the other mainstream lines. Each ship has a French/Continental restaurant called **Le Bistro**, a **pan-Asian restaurant,** a Japanese **teppanyaki room** where dishes are prepared theatrically at your table, a **sushi/ sashimi bar,** a family-style **Italian restaurant,** a traditional woody **steakhouse** called Cagney's, a casual **Latin restaurant** serving Tex Mex and tapas, and a 24-hour **diner/cafe** serving comfort food. The food in Le Bistro is better than that in the main dining rooms, and includes items such as a yummy Caesar salad made right at your table and a marvelously decadent chocolate fondue served with fresh fruit (both by request only). Tables are sometimes available for walk-ins, but make your reservations as early as possible, to be on the safe side.

Most of the specialty restaurants carry a cover charge, which ranges from $10 to $20 per person. Even with a reservations system, it inevitably happens that you'll sometimes have to wait for a table, but the large **computerized billboard screens** placed outside restaurants and in various public areas around the ship help you avoid that. Each displays a listing of every restaurant on board (with photos and a description of the cuisine), along with the restaurant's open/closed status, how busy it is at that moment, how close it is to filling up, and how long a wait there will be if it *is* filled up. For those who don't like to plan too far ahead, it's a great boon: You can head out for the evening and just decide where to dine on the fly. Maître d's at every restaurant can take reservations at any of the other restaurants, too, so if one looks like it's filling up, you won't have to sprint to catch that last table—just amble to the nearest restaurant and have them call ahead for you.

CASUAL   In addition to the numerous sit-down venues highlighted above (all of them casual in their own way), all NCL ships have a well-designed buffet restaurant with indoor/outdoor seating, open for breakfast, lunch, and dinner. In addition to standard fare such as carved meats, salads, and pastas, the buffets occasionally offer welcome oddities such as an all-vegetarian Indian buffet. There's also a **pool grill** out on deck, and comfort food is available 24 hours a day at the **Blue Lagoon** restaurant.

SNACKS & EXTRAS   Snacking ops include pizza and ice cream offered throughout the day from the buffet restaurant, a coffee bar serving specialty java and other beverages, and 24-hour room service for pizza, sandwiches, and other munchies. One night a week, you can also drool over the popular **Chocoholic Extravaganza** buffet.

ACTIVITIES

Aboard NCL's ships, you can take cha-cha lessons; watch a cooking demo; play bingo, shuffleboard, or basketball; attend an art auction or spa or beauty demonstration; and, on some cruises, sit in on enrichment lectures about classic ocean liners, nutrition, personal investing, or other topics. There are snorkeling demonstrations in the pool, makeovers, talent shows, wine tastings (for $15 per person), and trivia contests, plus your classic cruise ship "silly poolside games." *Norwegian Gem* also has one of the modern cruise world's only full-size, four-lane, 10-pin onboard **bowling alleys.**

Gyms fleetwide are open 24 hours and offer stretching, step, aerobics, and other standard classes at no extra charge. Spinning, kickboxing, Pilates, yoga, and other trendy choices cost an extra $10 per class. All three ships have golf driving cages where guests can practice their putting and swinging at their leisure.

CHILDREN'S PROGRAM

NCL's Kids Crew program offers **supervised activities** for children ages 2 to 17, divided into four age groups: Junior Sailors, ages 2 to 5; First Mates, ages 6 to 9; Navigators, ages 10 to 12; and teens, ages 13 to 17. Activities include sports competitions, dances, face painting, treasure hunts, magic shows, arts and crafts, cooking classes, T-shirt painting, and the Officer Snook Water Pollution Program, which uses games, crafts, storytelling, coloring books, a simulated beach cleanup, and other activities to educate young people about marine pollution and ways to prevent it. Kids get their own daily program detailing the day's events, which also include **family events** such as pizza-making parties and scavenger hunts.

All of NCL's Europe ships offer huge kids' facilities that include a separate teen center and a wading pool, as well as a large, well-stocked playroom. On sea days, youth programs are offered 9am to noon, 2 to 5pm, and then 7 to 10pm; on port days the complimentary hours are from 7 to 10pm. Port program times can also be adjusted to accommodate parents on shore excursions.

Once per cruise, the ships offer a **Mom and Dad's Night Out,** when kids dine with counselors. Otherwise, **group babysitting** for kids age 2 to 12 is offered nightly between 10pm and 1am (and 9am–5pm on port days) for $5 per child per hour, plus $3 an hour for each additional sibling. Counselors do not do diapers; parents are given beepers so they can be alerted when it's time for the dirty work. Private babysitting is not available.

Unlimited soda packages are $16 for kids under age 17 on 7-night cruises, and a "Teen Passport" coupon book is available for teens—for $30 they get up to 20 nonalcoholic drinks such as Virgin Daiquiris.

ENTERTAINMENT

NCL offers some of the best entertainment of all the mainstream lines, including sketch comedy shows by members of the famed **Second City comedy troupe,** which launched the careers of such legends as Bill Murray, John Belushi, and Gilda Radner.

Production shows are way above average, too, with talented performers and good choreography, costumes, and set design. Bollywood- and South Beach–inspired shows in recent years have been standouts. The musicians and comedians who play the ships' lounge circuit are also a cut above.

For closet entertainers, the line puts on **Star Seeker,** its version of the *American Idol* talent program, giving adults and kids the chance to prove themselves onstage. Videos of the winners are sent to NCL's shore-side entertainment department for consideration as one-time entertainers aboard a future free NCL cruise.

SERVICE

Fleetwide, cabin service, room service, and bar service tend to be speedy and efficient. Dining service is a mixed bag: On recent cruises, service in the main dining room and Pan-Asian restaurants was accommodating but less than stellar, while service in the Le Bistro and Cagney's Steakhouse alternative restaurants was very sharp and attentive.

Tipping is handled automatically, with a $10-per-day service charge added to each passenger's onboard account ($5 for kids 3–12). Though officially nonrefundable, the charge can be adjusted if you've experienced serious problems that the customer-service staff was unable to remedy.

NCL ships offer **laundry** and **dry-cleaning service,** as well as self-service launderettes and ironing facilities for guests.

Norwegian Jewel •
Norwegian Jade •
Norwegian Gem

The Verdict

Really original megaships don't come along too often these days, but these babies are it, with a mix of classy and fun spaces, a lively atmosphere, awesome kids' facilities, and more restaurant options than you'll likely have time to sample.

Norwegian Jewel *(photo: NCL)*

Specifications

Size (in Tons)			Jade	1,233/540
Jewel/Gem	93,502		Crew	
Jade	92,100		Jewel/Gem	1,150
Passengers (Double Occ.)			Jade	1,025
Jewel/Gem	2,376		Passenger/Crew Ratio	2 to 1
Jade	2,466		Year Launched	
Passenger/Space Ratio			Jewel	2005
Jewel/Gem	39.3		Jade	2006
Jade	37.3		Gem	2007
Total Cabins/Veranda Cabins			Last Refurbishment/Upgrade	N/A
Jewel/Gem	1,188/510			

Frommer's Ratings (Scale of 1–5)   ★★★★★

Cabin Comfort & Amenities	4	Dining Options	5
Appearance & Upkeep	5	Gym, Spa & Sports Facilities	4.5
Public Comfort/Space	5	Children's Facilities	5
Decor	4.5	Enjoyment Factor	5

Talk about innovation: These ships get straight A's. Want dining choice? You get 10 different restaurants apiece, from fancy steakhouses and teppanyaki restaurants to casual Tex-Mex and burger joints. Want something other than the generic Caribbean theme so prevalent on many ships? The ships mix it up with touches of Miami, Indonesia, and urban lounge. Want high style? Check out the "Bar Central" on Deck 6. Want fun? Try *Gem's* four-lane, 10-pin bowling alley. Want the biggest suites aboard any ship, anywhere? The ships' Garden Villas spread out up to a mind-blowing 5,350 square feet and feature private gardens, multiple bedrooms with extravagant bathrooms, separate living rooms, full kitchens, and private butler service. Zowie! Zowie, too, on their price: about $13,750 per person, per week, for the first two guests, and $499 for each additional (up to a maximum of six people). Normal cabins, on the other hand, come at normal prices. The ships' children's centers are a knockout, so large and completely kid-centric that we wished we were 5 again. Ditto for our reaction to the buffet restaurant's Kids' Café, a miniaturized version of the adult cafe, accurate down to tiny chairs and a miniature buffet counter. It's the cutest thing going.

Norwegian Jade began her life as NCL America's U.S.-flagged *Pride of Hawai'i,* but was pulled from the Hawaii market in 2008 and sent to sail in Europe, with an international crew. As for *Norwegian Gem,* she's due to debut after this book goes to press, so all details about her in this review are based on her near-identical twin sister, *Norwegian Pearl.*

Cabins & Rates

Cabins	Per Diem From	Sq. Ft.	Fridge	Hair Dryer	Sitting Area	TV
Inside	$88	142	Yes	Yes	Yes	Yes
Outside	$111	158–205	Yes	Yes	Yes	Yes
Suite	$193	229–5,350	Yes	Yes	Yes	Yes

CABINS   Standard cabins, though not overly large compared to some in the industry (particularly those of Carnival's and Holland America's ships), are larger than elsewhere in the NCL fleet. Decor is a mix, with stylish elements (such as cherrywood wall paneling and snazzy rounded lights), kitschy elements (such as bright island-colored carpeting), and cheap touches (such as some spindly chairs and end tables, and wall-mounted soap dispensers in the bathrooms). Each comes with a small TV and minifridge, a tea/coffeemaker, a private safe, and cool, retro-looking hair dryers. Closet and drawer space is more than ample for weeklong sailings, and bathrooms in all categories are well designed, with large sinks whose faucets swing out of the way, a magnifying mirror inset in the regular mirror, adequate though not exceptional counter/shelf space, and (in all but inside cabins) separate shower and toilet compartments. Balconies in standard cabins accommodate two metal pool chairs and a small table, but aren't terribly roomy.

Minisuites provide about 60 more feet of floor space than standard cabins, with a large foldout couch, a curtain between the bed and the sitting area, and a bathtub, while the so-called "Romance Suites" really are, with 288 square feet of space, stereo with CD/DVD library, bathroom with separate shower and tub, and nice wooden deck chairs on the balcony. Penthouse Suites offer the same, plus gorgeous bathrooms with a whirlpool tub and tiled, oceanview shower stall; a larger balcony; and a walk-in closet. Some suites offer a separate kids' bedroom and bathroom. Those facing the bow on decks 9 and 10 have large windows and deep balconies, but safety requirements mandate that instead of a nice glass door, these balconies are accessed via an honest-to-god steel bulkhead that's marked, "For your own safety, open only when the vessel is in port."

The ships' Owner's Suites are huge, with two balconies, living and dining areas, powder room, guest bathroom, and 750 square feet of space. Compared to the two Garden Villas up on Deck 14, however, these suites are shacks. The Garden Villas are, in a word, *huge,* the biggest at sea today, with three bedrooms, enormous living rooms, private courtyards with hot tubs and comfy deck chairs, panoramic views all around, private butler service, grand pianos, and totally extravagant seaview bathrooms with whirlpool tubs. They're priced beyond the range of . . . well, pretty much everybody.

Norwegian Jewel and *Gem* have an intermediate level of smaller Courtyard Villas on the same top-of-the-ship deck as the Garden Villa. They offer spacious suite accommodations coupled with access to a villa-guests-only courtyard, a private sun deck, and a staffed concierge lounge. The courtyard is a stunner, with a small private swimming pool, hot tub, and several plush, shaded sun beds. Suites (which, due to safety regulations, open to a hallway around the courtyard rather than right into it) are also knock-outs, with a separate bedroom and living/dining room; a huge, gorgeously appointed bathroom with oceanview whirlpool tub and shower; a large private balcony; and floor space that ranges from 440 to 572 square feet. The larger Courtyard Penthouses also offer a separate children's room with a foldout couch bed and second bathroom. Prices tend to hover in the $5,500 range for weeklong itineraries.

Jewel, Gem, and *Jade* each offer 27 wheelchair-accessible cabins.

PUBLIC AREAS   You'll be in a party mood from the moment you step aboard into the ships' large, broad, skylit atrium lobbies. Public areas throughout are fanciful and extremely spacious, done in a mix of bright storybook colors and high-style Art Deco, with lots of nooks and some downright wonderful lounges and bars mixed in among all the restaurant choices.

On the main entertainment deck, a multideck theater has a thousand seats sloping down to a large stage. There's also a nightclub for smaller-scale cabaret entertainment and dancing. Deck 12 features a complex of "sit-down" rooms, including a comfortable cinema with traditional theater seats, a library, a card room, a reading room, a "lifestyles" room (used for classes, private functions, and so on), several meeting rooms, and a small wedding chapel. Forward of these is an observation lounge/disco with some fanciful *Alice in Wonderland* seating. Up top, on Deck 13, there's a nice bar/lounge with piano entertainment in the evening. On Deck 6, three bars themed by beverage (beer/whiskey, martini/cocktail, and champagne/wine) are clustered together in a "Bar Central" arrangement. The beer and whiskey bars are the best at sea, with 46 beers and 63 whiskies to choose from. For a more swingin' evening, head to *Gem*'s Bliss nightclub. By day, the room is a high-style sports bar with video arcade games, multiple TVs showing sporting events, and four bowling lanes with computerized scoring. (Games are $5 per person, including shoe rental—and in normal weather the ship's motion doesn't seem to affect your ball's trajectory.) By night, the room becomes a superhip nightclub, with the alleys done up in mood lighting and the rest of the decor done in bordello-meets-Vampire-Lestat style—all red and purple velvet drapes and upholstery, classical paintings of reclining nudes, DJ entertainment, plasma screens showing music videos, and a series of plush king-size beds scattered among the couches and overstuffed chairs, putting the *night* in *nightlife.*

Other rooms include a spacious casino, an Internet center, several shops, and a coffee bar.

For kids, these ships have some of the better facilities at sea, with a huge, brightly colored crafts/play area, a big-screen TV room stuffed full of beanbag chairs, a huge ball jump/crawling maze play-gym, a computer room, and a small outdoor play area. There are video arcades and teen centers on all three ships, with computers, a dance floor equipped with a sound/video system, and a soda bar.

DINING OPTIONS   These ships are all about their restaurants, with 10 options on each—2 main formal restaurants plus a buffet, a 24-hour diner/cafe, a casual Tex Mex/tapas restaurant, a family-style Italian restaurant, a manly steakhouse, three Asian options, and a French/Continental option. The Asian restaurants offer a main pan-Asian restaurant as well as a separate sushi and sake bar and an intimate Japanese teppanyaki room where meals are prepared from the center of the table as guests look on. The high-end French/Continental restaurant, Le Bistro, serves classic and nouvelle cuisine in an atmosphere of floral tapestry upholstery and fine place settings.

Specialty restaurants cost between $10 and $20 per person.

Out on deck, each ship also has a casual grill serving up burgers, dogs, and fries during the day.

POOL, FITNESS, SPA & SPORTS FACILITIES   Main pool areas have the feel of a resort, ringed by flower-shaped "streetlamps," terraces of deck chairs leading down to the central pool and hot tubs, and (on *Jewel* and *Gem*) a large corkscrew water slide. A huge bar, running almost the width of the ship, serves ice cream on one side, drinks on the other. Spas are generally stylish, fronted by a large relaxation room with heated, tiled lounge chairs facing a wonderful bow view, plus a whirlpool bath with massage jets and built-in underwater loungers. All three ships offer some of the better onboard gyms of recent years—large and extremely well appointed, with dozens of fitness machines and a large aerobics/spinning room.

Outside there's an extralong jogging track, a sports court for basketball and volleyball, golf-driving nets, and facilities for shuffleboard and deck chess, plus acres of open deck space for sunning.

8 Oceania Cruises

8300 NW 33rd St., Suite 308, Miami, FL 33122. ✆ **800/531-5619** or 305/514-2300. www.oceaniacruises.com.

THE LINE IN A NUTSHELL   Oceania is the phoenix that rose from the ashes after Renaissance Cruises went belly-up in September 2001. Headed by former Renaissance executives, it operates the former *R1, R2,* and *R5* as *Regatta, Insignia,* and *Nautica,* and mimics some attributes of much pricier lines, with excellent service and cuisine, and a quiet, refined onboard feel.

THE EXPERIENCE   Oceania is positioned as an "upper premium" line intended to fill the gap—in terms of both ship size and level of luxury—between big-ship premium

Compared with the other mainstream lines, here's how Oceania rates:

	Poor	Fair	Good	Excellent	Outstanding
Enjoyment Factor				✓	
Dining				✓	
Activities		✓			
Children's Program	N/A*				
Entertainment			✓		
Service				✓	
Worth the Money				✓	

Oceania offers no children's program.

lines such as Celebrity and real luxe lines such as Radisson. It goes for a kind of floating country club feel, with an understated ambience, few organized activities, low-key entertainment, a casually sporty dress code, an emphasis on cabin comfort, and long itineraries that favor smaller, less-visited ports like St. Peter Port (Guernsey Islands) and Bordeaux. Despite such luxe-travel touches, the line's prices are competitive with—and often even lower than—those of the other premium lines.

Pros
- **Excellent cuisine:** In both the main dining room and specialty restaurants, Oceania is near the top among mainstream lines.
- **Excellent, personal service:** The ships' international crews are extremely friendly and eager to please.
- **Intimate size:** Oceania's ships carry only 684 passengers apiece, making for a much more human-scale feel than you get aboard a megaship.
- **Nonsmoking policy:** On these ships, smoking is permitted only in one corner of the pool deck and one corner of the nightclub. (Of course, this is a "con" for smokers.)

Cons
- **Few activities:** By design, Oceania generally leaves passengers to their own devices. This is a "con" only if you need constant stimulation.

OCEANIA: CLASS ACT, COZY SHIPS
Remember Renaissance Cruises? Founded in 1988, it made news in the '90s by building a large fleet of identical medium-size ships and going direct to consumers rather than working with travel agents. Both of these were fairly revolutionary moves back then, and, as often happens with revolutions, this one didn't work out too well. Already in bad financial shape on 9/11, the line was forced into bankruptcy when the resultant travel downturn came. Left high and dry, its eight ships were put up for auction to the highest bidder. Oceania, founded by former Renaissance CEO Frank Del Rio, started up in 2003 with two of the ships (the former *R1* and *R2*, renamed *Regatta* and *Insignia*) and added a third, *Nautica*, in late 2005. The remaining Renaissance vessels are now owned by Princess (*Pacific Princess, Tahitian Princess,* and *Royal Princess*) and Azamara Cruises (*Azamara Journey* and *Azamara Quest*).

Oceania Fleet Itineraries

Ship	Sailing Regions	Home Ports
Insignia	10- to 14-night voyages in the Mediterranean/Aegean/Greek Isles/Adriatic/Egypt/Israel (various combinations)	Piraeus/Athens, Barcelona, Civitavecchia/Rome, Lisbon, Istanbul, Venice
Nautica	10- to 14-night voyages in the Mediterranean/Greek Isles/Aegean/Black Sea/Egypt/Israel (various combinations)	Civitavecchia/Rome, Barcelona, Piraeus/Athens, Istanbul, Venice
Regatta	10- to 16-night voyages in the Mediterranean/Aegean/Greek Isles (various combinations), Northern Europe/Russia, and Atlantic Europe	Piraeus/Athens, Barcelona, Civitavecchia/Rome, Venice, Dover/London, Stockholm

PASSENGER PROFILE

Due partially to the length of these cruises (mostly 10, 12, and 14 days, going up to 26) and partially to the low-key onboard atmosphere, Oceania tends to attract older passengers who prefer to entertain themselves, reading in the library and enjoying the destination-heavy itineraries. Most are Americans, with many from the West Coast and many "returning," having sailed previously with Oceania or with Renaissance back in the old days. A sprinkling of younger couples is usually found on board as well, though children are rare enough to be surprising. Whatever their age, passengers tend to be drawn by the line's 100% casual dress code and ambience, and its off-the-beaten-path itineraries.

Because of Oceania's stringent **no-smoking rules,** most passengers are nonsmokers. Aside from one corner of the pool deck and one corner of the nightclub, smoking is not permitted anywhere on board—even in your cabin or private balcony.

DINING

Oceania's dining experience is one of its strongest suits, with menus created by renowned chef Jacques Pepin (one-time personal chef to Charles de Gaulle and, more recently, one of America's best-known chefs and food writers). Passengers are able to choose among four different restaurants for dinner: the main Grand Dining Room, the Mediterranean-style Toscana restaurant, the Polo Grill steakhouse, and the Tapas on the Terrace casual outdoor option. All four venues work on an open-seating basis (dine when you want, with whom you want), with meals usually served in a 3-hour window from 6:30 to 9:30pm.

TRADITIONAL   The **Grand Dining Room,** the main restaurant aboard each ship, features French-inspired Continental cuisine in five courses, with a string quartet providing music at dinner. Appetizers might include grilled marinated prawns, frog-leg mousse, and crushed new potatoes with chives and Malossol caviar, while soups might be as traditional as beef oxtail consommé or as unusual as Moroccan harira chicken soup. There are always several salads and a pasta of the day, and entrees are elaborate, well-presented versions of the big faves (lobster tail butterfly, beef Wellington, steamed Alaskan king crab legs), plus some uncommon dishes, such as sautéed sea bream filet and pheasant breast ballotine stuffed with morel mushrooms. There's always a tasty **vegetarian option,** plus an alternative selection of basics: grilled sirloin, broiled chicken, salmon filet, and the like.

SPECIALTY   As an alternative, passengers can make a reservation at the ships' specialty restaurants, the Italian **Toscana** or the **Polo Grill** steakhouse.

Toscana is sinfully overwhelming, serving half a dozen antipasti and an equal number of pasta dishes, soups, salads, and main courses such as medallions of filet mignon topped with sautéed artichoke and smoked mozzarella; swordfish steak sautéed in garlic, parsley, Tuscan olives, capers, and orvieto wine; and braised double-cut lamb chops in a sun-dried tomato, olive, and roasted garlic sauce. Desserts include the remarkable, if weird-sounding, chocolate lasagna.

Polo Grill serves chops, seafood, and cuts of slow-aged beef, with all the substantial trimmings: seafood appetizers, soups such as New England clam chowder and lobster bisque, straight-up salads such as Caesar and iceberg wedge with blue cheese and crumbled bacon, and side dishes such as a baked potato, wild mushroom ragout, and creamed spinach.

Passengers can make reservations for either restaurant during breakfast or lunch hours at the Terrace Cafe. There's no extra charge, but there's an initial two-reservation limit to ensure that all guests get a chance. If you'd like to dine here more than twice, add your name to the waiting list and you'll be contacted if there's space (which there usually is).

CASUAL   On the casual side, the **Terrace Cafe** is a standard cruise ship buffet serving a range of mains, sides, salads, and desserts. An attached **pizzeria** serves very tasty thin-crust pies. At lunch the pool deck's **grill** is also fired up, serving burgers, hot dogs, and specialty sandwiches. In the evening, the outdoor portion of the Terrace is transformed into **Tapas on the Terrace,** a romantic option with regional Spanish and Mediterranean specialties, other ethnic dishes, and home-style favorites served from a buffet. Waiters are on hand to serve drinks and be generally charming.

SNACKS & EXTRAS   **High tea** is served daily at 4pm in the Horizons Lounge, with a good spread of pastries, tea sandwiches, and scones. **Room service** is available 24 hours. Guests in Owners, Vista, and Penthouse suites can have full meals served course by course in their rooms.

ACTIVITIES

By design, activities are not a high priority for Oceania. Expect **enrichment lectures** themed around the region being visited, fitness and computer classes, informal health and beauty talks by the spa and salon staff, and a handful of old cruise standards: bingo, shuffleboard, and the like. For people who are self-motivated and/or prefer to spend their time aboard reading on deck or in one of the library's overstuffed leather armchairs, this is ideal. If you like a lot of organized activities, though, this is not the line for you.

All of Oceania's ships have smallish **casinos** that see a fair amount of action. Internet access is available in Deck 9's Oceania@Sea Internet center and at two terminals in the library. The ships' full-service **spas** are run by Mandara, a subsidiary of Steiner Leisure, which operates almost every spa at sea.

CHILDREN'S PROGRAM

There are no special facilities on these ships, and the line typically carries very few children.

ENTERTAINMENT

The good news: You won't be assailed by steel-drum bands doing bad Bob Marley covers. Instead, you'll get a 12-piece jazz band on deck in the afternoon and in the club at night; pianists performing Cole Porter, Hoagy Carmichael, and other standards at the martini bar before dinner; and an occasional string quartet.

The bad news: That's the high point of the onboard entertainment. Each night, the main show lounge presents a comedian, solo musician, folkloric act, or other headliner, but the shows don't have the breadth you'll find on larger vessels. Of course, there also aren't any big, bad Vegas-style song-and-dance revues, for which we whisper a prayer of thanks.

Other entertainment options include the occasional karaoke session or a movie presented out on deck.

SERVICE

The staff in the restaurants are crack troops, delivering each course promptly but without any sense that they're hurrying passengers through their meals. Service balances precision with friendliness, skewing close to the kind of understated professionalism you see on the real luxury lines. The relatively small number of passengers aboard also means service is more personal than you find aboard the megaships. In the bars, staff tend to remember your drink order by the second day, and cabin stewardesses greet their passengers by name in the corridors. Like many other lines, Oceania adds an **automatic gratuity** to your shipboard account ($11.50 per person, per day), which may be adjusted up or down at your discretion. For guests occupying Owner's, Vista, and Penthouse suites, an additional $3.50-per-day gratuity is added for butler service.

There's a **self-service laundry** and ironing room on Deck 7, in addition to standard laundry, dry cleaning, and pressing service offered by the ship's laundry.

Regatta • Insignia • Nautica

The Verdict

With their smallish size, understated decor, and serene atmosphere, these mostly non-smoking ships are more like quiet boutique hotels than cruise vessels, providing a comfortable, laid-back, yet stylish way to sail.

Regatta *(photo: Oceania)*

Specifications

Size (in Tons)	30,200	Year Launched	
Passengers (Double Occ.)	684	*Regatta/Insignia*	1998
Passenger/Space Ratio	44	*Nautica*	2000
Total Cabins/Veranda Cabins	343/232	Last Refurbishment/Upgrade	
Crew	400	*Regatta/Nautica*	2007
Passenger/Crew Ratio	1.7 to 1	*Insignia*	2008

Frommer's Ratings (Scale of 1–5)   ★★★★

Cabin Comfort & Amenities	4	Dining Options	4
Appearance & Upkeep	4	Gym, Spa & Sports Facilities	4
Public Comfort/Space	4.5	Children's Facilities	N/A
Decor	4	Enjoyment Factor	4

Imagine an old-style Ritz-Carlton hotel in the shape of a cruise ship, and you've pretty much got the idea. Like all of the former Renaissance vessels, *Regatta, Insignia,* and *Nautica* are comfortable and spacious, decorated mostly in warm, dark woods and rich fabrics. They're traditional and sedate, with an emphasis on intimate spaces rather than the kind of grand, splashy ones you'll find on most megaships. Of course, their small size means there'd be no *room* for grand spaces, even if they'd been wanted: Carrying only 684 passengers, the intimacy of these ships is one of their main selling points. The atmosphere is relaxed and clubby, with no formal nights that demand tuxedos and gowns.

Cabins & Rates

Cabins	Per Diem From	Sq. Ft.	Fridge	Hair Dryer	Sitting Area	TV
Inside	$233	160	No	Yes	Yes	Yes
Outside	$258	160–216*	No	Yes	Yes	Yes
Suite	$425	322–962*	Yes	Yes	Yes	Yes

* Including veranda

CABINS   Staterooms are straightforward, no-nonsense spaces with a hint of modern European city hotel: plain off-white walls, dark-wood trim and furniture, and rich carpeting. The highlight of each, though, is its Tranquility Bed, an oasis of 350-thread-count Egyptian cotton sheets and duvet covers, down duvets and pillows, custom-designed extra-thick mattresses, and a mound of throw pillows to prop you up during the late-late show. Spacious balconies have teak decking for a classic nautical look, and all cabins have televisions, safes, vanities with mirrors, hair dryers, phones, full-length mirrors, and French-milled toiletries. Closet space is a little skimpy, considering the lengthy itineraries these ships sail, but drawer space scattered around the cabin, and space under the beds help balance things out. Overall cabin size is in the 165-square-foot range—not tiny, but not exceptionally large, either. There are also some bizarre little quirks. Light switches, for instance, can be mystifying: There doesn't seem to be any way to turn off the bedside lights until you discover the tiny, almost hidden buttons up near their shades. There are also switches for the overheads right in the headboard, which makes it very easy to switch them on accidentally in your sleep.

Suites include minibars, bathtubs, and a small area with a cocktail table for intimate in-room dining. Ten Owner's Suites measure 786 to 982 square feet and are located at the ship's bow and stern, featuring wraparound balconies, queen-size beds, whirlpool bathtubs, minibars, living rooms, and guest bathrooms. Owner's Suites, Vista Suites, and Penthouse Suites feature butler service. Concierge-class staterooms (in between regular cabins and suites) add some warm-and-fuzzy to the amenities: a welcome bottle of champagne, DVD player, personalized stationary, cashmere throw blanket, complimentary tote bag, priority embarkation, dedicated check-in desk and priority luggage delivery, priority restaurant reservations, complimentary shoeshine service, and such additional bathroom amenities as massaging shower heads, luxury toiletries, and a hand-held hair dryer.

Lifeboats obstruct the view from 18 cabins on Deck 6. Three cabins on each ship are wheelchair accessible.

PUBLIC AREAS   Overall, *Regatta, Insignia,* and *Nautica* are elegant yet homey ships, with classic styling that includes dark-wood paneling, fluted columns, ornate faux-iron railings, gilt-framed classical paintings, Oriental-style carpets, frilly moldings, marble and brass accents, and deep-hued upholstery. More than almost any other ships at sea today, they mimic the look of the great old Edwardian liners. In the bow, the spacious, woody Horizons lounge has floor-to-ceiling windows and brass telescopes on three sides, and is used for dancing in the evenings and for various activities during the day. The 345-seat show lounge offers cabaret and variety acts, musical recitals, magic shows, and comedy; and the smallish but comfortable casino offers blackjack, poker tables, roulette, and slots. The attached Martini Bar has a ridiculously long martini list (some 30 recipes and an equal number of vodka choices) and is a very relaxing space in the pre-dinner hours, when a pianist plays standards. A jazz band performs here in the evenings.

Another notable space is the comfortable library, decorated in a traditional English style with warm red upholstery, mahogany paneling, trompe l'oeil garden skylight, and marble faux fireplace.

DINING OPTIONS   The main dining room is an elegant single-level space surrounded on three sides by windows. It's spacious and understated, with simple wood-veneer wall panels, wall sconces, and teal carpeting. Tables seating between two and eight are available, though the smaller arrangements go fast. Just outside the maître d' station is a cozy bar area where you can have a pre-dinner cocktail while waiting for your dinner companions. Each ship has two specialty restaurants, the Polo Grill and Toscana, both located in the stern on Deck 10 and decorated to match their cuisine: woody, old-Hollywood decor in Polo, and a bright white Mediterranean feel with Roman urns and reliefs in Toscana. The restaurants serve 96 and 90 guests, respectively. On Deck 9, the Terrace serves buffet breakfast, lunch, and dinner; the latter is served out under the stars, with drink service, Spanish cuisine, and candles flickering in lovely hurricane lamps. It's a very romantic spot if you can time your meal to sunset.

POOL, FITNESS, SPA & SPORTS FACILITIES   Each ship's attractive teak pool deck, dotted with canvas umbrellas, offers a pair of hot tubs plus a slew of deck chairs and large daybeds for sunbathing. The Patio, a shaded outdoor lounge located in the aft port corner of the pool deck, is furnished with thickly cushioned sofas, chairs, and daybeds. Drapes and general ambience add a hint of partition from the pool goings-on (not to mention shade), but you still feel like you're in the action. For more privacy, passengers can rent one of eight private cabanas on Deck 11, each with privacy partitions and white drapes that can be drawn or left open, plus great sea views, a retractable shade roof, and a plush daybed built for two. They're available for rent either daily ($50 on port days, $100 on sea days) or for the entirety of your cruise, and come with the services of a dedicated attendant who provides food and beverage service, chilled towels, and water spritzes. Guests can even arrange to get massages and other spa treatments in their cabana.

A small jogging track encircles the deck above the pool area, while the spa on Deck 9 offers a variety of treatments, including aromatherapy massages, hot-stone treatments, and various wraps and facials. Just forward of the spa there's an outdoor hydrotherapy whirlpool overlooking the bow. A decent-size oceanview gym and beauty salon are attached.

9 Princess Cruises

24305 Town Center Dr., Santa Clarita, CA 91355. *©* **800/PRINCESS** or 661/753-0000. Fax 661/259-3108. www. princess.com.

THE LINE IN A NUTSHELL   With a fleet of mostly large and extralarge megaships, Princess offers a quality mainstream cruise experience with a nice balance of tradition and innovation, relaxation and excitement, casualness and glamour.

THE EXPERIENCE   If you were to put Royal Caribbean, NCL, and Holland America in a blender and mix them together, then add a pinch of British maritime tradition and a dash of California style, you'd come up with Princess. Dining, entertainment, and activities are geared to a wide cross section of cruisers: The more traditional minded can spend some time in the library, join a bridge tournament, enjoy a traditional dinner in a grand dining room, and then take in a show. Those seeking something different can spin a pottery wheel or take a cooking class, then dine in an intimate Italian or steakhouse restaurant and take in a set of small-group jazz afterward. The line's largest vessels are some of the biggest at sea, yet still manage to offer intimate spaces for quiet time.

Pros

- **Beautiful, well-designed megaships:** Princess's Diamond-, Coral-, and Grand-class ships are some of the most appealing megaships at sea, with intimate, classically designed spaces that belie the ships' enormous size.
- **Lots of dining choices and flexibility:** Each ship offers two or three main dining rooms, plus an intimate alternative restaurant or two and a 24-hour buffet. The line's "Personal Choice" program allows you to dine at a fixed time and place or wing it as you go along.
- **Excellent lounge entertainment:** Princess books top-quality entertainers for its piano lounges and smaller showrooms.

Cons

- **Pottery Barn decor:** More of a qualifier than a con: Princess's ships are very pleasant, yes, but the sea of beiges and blues is so safe that it can be a bit of a yawn. Artwork in public areas and cabins tends toward bland.
- **Small gyms:** For such large vessels, the gyms are surprisingly small and can even feel cramped.

Compared with the other mainstream lines, here's how Princess rates:

	Poor	Fair	Good	Excellent	Outstanding
Enjoyment Factor				✓	
Dining				✓	
Activities				✓	
Children's Program				✓	
Entertainment				✓	
Service				✓	
Worth the Money				✓	

PRINCESS: SMART CASUAL

The Princess story goes back to 1962, when company founder Stanley McDonald chartered a vessel called the *Yarmouth* for use as a floating hotel at the Seattle World's Fair. In 1965, he officially started Princess Cruises, naming the company after another chartered vessel, the *Princess Patricia,* which offered cruises between Los Angeles, Alaska, and Mexico's Pacific coast. In 1974, Princess was snapped up by British shipping giant P&O, and later that decade got a big boost by having its ships featured in the TV series *The Love Boat.* To this day, Gavin "Captain Stubing" MacLeod acts as occasional pitchman for the line, though the original *Pacific Princess* and *Island Princess,* the twin 640-passenger vessels used in the series, finally left the fleet in 1999 and 2002. Their names have since been assigned to new vessels. In April 2003, P&O/Princess was purchased by Carnival Corporation, the 500-pound gorilla of the cruise world, but aside from some back-office changes, you'd never know it.

New in 2008 are the 3,070-passenger **Emerald Princess** (sister ship to 2006's *Crown Princess*) and the intimate, 710-passenger **Royal Princess.** *Royal Princess* was built for Renaissance Cruises before its 2001 collapse and brings the number of ex-Renaissance vessels now in the Princess fleet to three, along with *Pacific Princess* and *Tahitian Princess. Emerald, Crown, Royal,* and *Pacific* are all sailing in Europe for 2008, along with the older *Grand Princess* and *Sea Princess.*

PASSENGER PROFILE

The majority of Princess's passengers are in their 50s, 60s, and older, though more and more 30- and 40-somethings (and their families) are sailing these days, particularly during summer school holidays. Overall, Princess passengers are less boisterous than those aboard Carnival and not quite as staid as those aboard Holland America. Its ships all have extensive kids' facilities and activities, making them suitable for families, while their balance of formal and informal makes them a good bet for a romantic vacation, too, with opportunities for doing your own thing mixed in among more traditional cruise experiences.

DINING

All Princess ships sailing in Europe offer roughly the same variety of dining options, despite the fact that some are 3,100-passenger megaships and some are 700-passenger midsizers. Cuisine generally doesn't quite live up to the number and attractiveness of their restaurants, sitting squarely in the "average to tasty" range—approximately on par with what's served aboard Royal Caribbean and NCL.

TRADITIONAL   Available on all of Princess's Europe ships except *Royal* and *Pacific Princess* (which do traditional fixed seatings), the line's Personal Choice Dining program allows passengers two options: dining each night at a set time with the same companions in one of the ship's main restaurants, or just showing up anytime during a 4½-hour window and being seated by the maître d'. If you're not sure which option you'll prefer once you're on board, sign up for traditional, as it's easier to switch to anytime dining than it is to go the other way around. Passengers choosing the flexible option but wishing to be served by the same waiter nightly can usually be seated in his or her section if they make a special request.

Whether you choose traditional or flexible dining, your menu in the main dining room will be the same, offering several appetizers, soup and salad, and a choice of five to eight dinner entrees that may include prime rib, lobster, king crab legs, turkey and trimmings, mahimahi filet with dill butter sauce, rack of lamb with Dijon sauce,

Cornish hen, sautéed frogs' legs, duck a l'orange, or dozens of other options. There are always **healthy choices** and **vegetarian options,** too, plus staples such as broiled Atlantic salmon, grilled chicken, and grilled sirloin steak.

Unlike the no-dress-code plan that's part of NCL's "Freestyle" dining, Princess maintains the tradition of holding two formal nights per week, with the other nights designated "smart casual" (defined as "an open-neck shirt and slacks for gentlemen and a dress, skirt and blouse, or trouser suit outfit for ladies"). Men, however, should take our advice and pack at least a jacket. Otherwise, you may be down in the gift shop buying one after you realize everyone on the ship except you decided to dress for dinner. We speak from experience on this one.

All of the restaurants offers a **kids' menu,** which includes goodies such as burgers, hot dogs, fish sticks, chicken fingers, and, of course, PB&J sandwiches. This menu is also offered in the Horizon Court buffet during its sit-down Bistro hours, 11pm to 4am nightly.

SPECIALTY   All the Princess ships in Europe this year feature two alternative restaurants. Aboard *Grand, Sea, Pacific,* and *Royal Princess,* the **Sterling Steakhouse** ($15 per person) is a suitably dark and woody space where passengers can choose their favorite cut of beef—rib-eye, New York strip, porterhouse, and filet mignon—and have it cooked to order, with starters such as chili, blooming onion, jalapeño poppers, and fresh Caesar salad, plus the usual sides of baked potato or fries, sautéed mushrooms, creamed spinach, and corn on the cob. Aboard *Emerald* and *Crown Princess,* the **Crown Grill** ($25 per person) serves a steak-and-seafood menu in a similarly woody, clubby atmosphere, but with the addition of an open viewing kitchen facing the bar. All the ships except *Sea Princess* also have **Sabatini's Trattoria** ($20 per person), a traditional Italian restaurant with an airy, Mediterranean decor. Dinners here are eight-course extravaganzas emphasizing seafood, with all dishes brought automatically—you just select your main course. In its place, *Sea Princess* offers **Cafe Corniche,** a sit-down pizzeria that entails no extra charge.

Reservations are recommended for all alternative restaurants, as seating is limited. See the individual ship reviews for more details.

CASUAL   Fleetwide, passengers can choose casual dining at breakfast, lunch, dinner, or any other time in the 24-hour **Horizon Court buffet restaurant.** At breakfast, you'll find the usual: fresh fruit, cold cuts, cereal, steam-table scrambled eggs, cooked-to-order fried eggs, meats, and fish. At lunch, you'll find several salads, fruits, hot and cold dishes, roasts, vegetarian choices, and sometimes sushi. Evenings (until 10pm), the space serves a **casual buffet dinner** that usually has the same dishes as in the main dining room. From 11pm to 4am every night it serves a **late-night menu** of pastas, seafood, poultry, and red meats, along with a chef's special of the day. The food here is as good as you'll find in the main dining rooms, and the atmosphere is strictly casual.

Aboard *Crown* and *Emerald,* one end of the buffet restaurant is given over to **Cafe Caribe,** serving Caribbean specialties such as jerk chicken, grilled Caribbean rock lobster, roast suckling pig, Guiana pepper pots and curries, and paella-style prawns. Musicians play Caribbean music, passengers can order a meal cooked to taste at the cafe's open kitchen, and there's no cover charge.

Romantics sailing aboard any Princess ship can have **dinner under the stars** served by a dedicated waiter on their private balcony, at a table set with a tablecloth, hurricane candle lamp, and champagne. While the waiter is setting everything up, you and your significant other can have a complimentary cocktail in one of the ship's bars. The

Princess Fleet Itineraries

Ship	Sailing Regions	Home Ports
Crown Princess	10-night Northern Europe/Russia	Copenhagen
Emerald Princess	12-night Mediterranean/Greek Isles	Barcelona, Venice, Civitavecchia/Rome
Grand Princess	12-night voyages in the Mediterranean/ Greek Isles, Atlantic Europe, the British Isles, the Norwegian Fjords/North Cape, Iceland/Norway/British Isles, and Egypt/ Aegean	Civitavecchia/Rome, Venice, Southampton/London
Pacific Princess	12- and 16-night voyages in the Mediterranean/Holy Land, and Crimean/ Aegean	Southampton/London, Venice, Piraeus/Athens, Civitavecchia/Rome
Royal Princess	16-night Northern Europe/Atlantic Europe/ Russia	Stockholm, Civitavecchia/Rome
Sea Princess	7- and 14-night voyages in the Mediterranean and Northern Europe	Southampton/London

whole thing costs $50 per person. You can also order breakfast served on the balcony for $28 per couple.

For supercasual lunches, each ship's **poolside grill** serves burgers, hot dogs, and pizza.

SNACKS & EXTRAS   A **patisserie** aboard each ship offers coffee and pastries, and each ship has a **pizzeria** (either on the pool deck or in the buffet) and 24-hour **room service.** *Crown* and *Emerald Princess* also offer two casual snacking venues in the piazza-style atrium: a 24-hour **International Café** serving a rotating menu throughout the day, and a **wine and seafood bar.** *Sea Princess* offers a **wine and caviar bar.** Pricing at these venues is a la carte.

ACTIVITIES

Like the other big mainstream lines, Princess offers onboard activities designed to appeal to a wide range of ages and tastes. For active types, all the ships offer traditional shipboard sports such as Ping-Pong and shuffleboard, more athletic activities such as aerobics classes and water volleyball, and virtual-reality golf simulators or practice cages. *Grand, Crown,* and *Emerald Princess* all offer basketball/volleyball courts and 9-hole **miniature-golf courses.** *Sea Princess* has a basketball/volleyball court and golf simulator.

For something more cerebral, the line's **ScholarShip@Sea** enrichment program offers classes in cooking, computer skills (such as basic Web design, Photoshop, and Excel), finance, photography, scrapbooking, and even ceramics. Large-group seminars are free, while small-group and individual classes carry a charge of around $20 to $25 per person. Charges for paint-your-own ceramics are calculated based on the piece you create.

Sit-down activities include bingo, cards, trivia games, dance lessons, and (aboard *Grand, Crown,* and *Emerald Princess*) **recent-release movies** shown on giant outdoor LCD screens. Activities designed to part you from your cash include art auctions and beauty and spa demonstrations. Others designed to part you from your dignity include belly-flop contests, the perennial Newlywed/Not-So-Newlywed game, and an *American Idol*–style "Princess Pop Star" competition.

All Princess ships offer well-stocked libraries, 24-hour Internet centers, and Wi-Fi hot zones for laptop users (wireless cards are available if you don't have one).

CHILDREN'S PROGRAM

Families planning to sail Princess in Europe should probably stick to *Grand, Sea, Crown,* or *Emerald Princess,* as the smallish *Pacific Princess* and *Royal Princess* have no special facilities for kids (though they often offer kids programs in summers, when 20 or more kids may be aboard on a sailing).

Aboard the larger ships, Princess's Princess Kids program offers activities for three age groups: **Princess Pelicans** (ages 3–7), **Shockwaves** (ages 8–12), and **Remix** (ages 13–17), all supervised by a counseling staff whose size varies depending upon the number of children aboard. Each ship has a spacious indoor/outdoor **children's playroom** with a splash pool, an arts-and-crafts corner, game tables, and computers or game consoles, plus a **teen center** with computers, video games, a dance floor, and a music system. The two-story playroom on *Grand* includes a large fenced-in outside deck dedicated to kids only and featuring a teen section with a hot tub and private sunbathing area. *Crown* and *Emerald* have great fenced-in outdoor play spaces for toddlers.

Traditional kids' activities include arts and crafts, scavenger hunts, game tournaments, spelling bees, movies and videos, coloring contests, pizza and ice cream parties, karaoke, dancing, tours of the galley or behind the scenes at the theater, and teen versions of *The Dating Game.*

Learning activities may include **environmental education programs** developed by the California Science Center that teach about oceans and marine life through printed materials and specially created films. The kids' equivalent of an onboard guest lecturer program is also offered occasionally, allowing children to go stargazing with an astronomer, learn drawing skills from an animator, and so on.

Children must be at least 6 months of age to sail. When kids are registered in the youth program, their parents are given pagers so that they can be contacted if their children need them. Parents may also rent walkie-talkies through the purser's desk if they want two-way communication with their kids. Two **parent "date nights"** let adults have a calm evening while kids dine with counselors in a separate restaurant. Teens have their own group night in one of the main dining rooms, complete with photographs and an after-dinner show. Younger kids can then be taken straight to group babysitting in the children's center (available nightly 10pm–1am for kids 3–12; $5 per hour, per child). Princess does not offer private in-cabin babysitting.

On days in port, Princess offers children's center activities straight through from 8am to 5pm (on sea days the center closes for lunch), allowing parents to explore the port while their kids do their own thing.

ENTERTAINMENT

Princess has some of the best entertainment at sea, with the ships' main stages hosting the usual range of Vegas-style song-and-dance revues and cabaret singers, plus ventriloquists, acrobats, aerialists, stand-up comics, and musical soloists. *Grand, Crown,* and *Emerald* offer three shows nightly, spread among their main theater and two smaller venues; *Sea Princess* offers entertainment in two showrooms; and *Pacific* and *Royal Princess* offer floor shows in their intimate show lounges, which seat between 335 and 345 guests. Pianists, guitarists, string quartets, and jazz bands perform in various venues aboard all the ships. For those who would rather participate, there are regular karaoke nights and a **passenger talent show.** The **casinos** on *Grand, Crown,* and *Emerald* are among the most comfortable at sea, very large and well laid out. Those on *Pacific* and *Royal* are much smaller (as befits the small size of the vessels), but comfortable and classy.

SERVICE

Overall, service is efficient and passengers rarely have to wait in lines, even in the busy Horizon Court buffet restaurants. As is true generally of staff aboard all the mainstream lines, you can expect them to be friendly, efficient, and happy to help, though probably not of the level you'll find aboard the luxe lines or at fine hotels. Cabin steward service is the most consistent, with dining service only slightly behind. Suite guests get extra service goodies, including complimentary Internet access, dry cleaning, laundry, and shoe polishing; complimentary corsage and boutonniere on formal nights; in suite afternoon tea; expedited embarkation and debarkation; and other perks.

Through the line's **Captain's Circle loyalty program,** cruisers who have sailed with Princess before are issued specially colored onboard keycards and cabin-door nameplates (gold after taking 1 to 5 cruises, platinum after 5, and elite after 15) so that staffers will know to be extra helpful. Platinum and Elite Captain's Circle members also get some of the perks offered to suite guests (see above).

Gratuities for all service personnel are automatically added to passengers' shipboard accounts at the rate of $10 per person per day. You can make adjustments up or down by visiting or calling the purser's desk at any time. Passengers who wish to dispense their tips personally can make arrangements for this through the desk.

All of the Princess vessels offer laundry services and also have **self-service laundromats.**

The Grand Class: Grand Princess • Crown Princess • Emerald Princess

The Verdict

These huge, well-accoutered vessels are very easy to navigate, never feel as crowded as you'd expect, and are amazingly intimate for their size.

Grand Princess *(photo: Princess Cruises)*

Specifications

Size (in Tons)		Crew	
Grand	109,000	*Grand*	1,100
Crown/Emerald	113,000	*Crown/Emerald*	1,200
Passengers (Double Occ.)		Passenger/Crew Ratio	
Grand	2,600	*Grand*	2.4 to 1
Crown/Emerald	3,070	*Crown/Emerald*	2.6 to 1
Passenger/Space Ratio		Year Launched	
Grand	42	*Grand*	1998
Crown/Emerald	38	*Crown*	2006
Total Cabins/Veranda Cabins		*Emerald*	2007
Grand	1,300/710	Last Refurbishment/Upgrade	N/A
Crown/Emerald	1,532/880		

Frommer's Ratings (Scale of 1–5)

★★★★ ½

Cabin Comfort & Amenities	5	Dining Options	4
Appearance & Upkeep	4.5	Gym, Spa & Sports Facilities	5
Public Comfort/Space	5	Children's Facilities	4
Decor	4	Enjoyment Factor	4.5

Princess's signature vessels, the Grand-class ships were so ahead of their time when they debuted in 1998 (when *Grand Princess* was briefly the largest passenger ship in the world) that the design of even recent sisters *Crown* and *Emerald Princess* isn't significantly changed. Though the vessels give an impression of immensity from the outside, inside they're extremely well laid out, very easy to navigate, and surprisingly cozy. In fact, their public areas never feel as crowded as you'd think they would with almost 4,000 people aboard, including passengers and crew. The cozy carries over to public rooms like the clubby and dimly lit Explorer's and Wheelhouse lounges, whose traditional accents recall a grander era of sea travel. In the elegant three-story atriums, classical string quartets perform on formal nights and during embarkation.

Crown Princess and *Emerald Princess* are slightly larger versions of the original Grand-class concept, with a similar layout but one extra deck, plus a cafe serving Caribbean dishes, an international cafe, a wine and seafood bar, a steak and seafood house, and a "piazza-style" atrium with a street-cafe vibe.

Cabins & Rates

Cabins	Per Diem From	Sq. Ft.	Fridge	Hair Dryer	Sitting Area	TV
Inside	$124	160	Yes	Yes	No	Yes
Outside	$153	165–232	Yes	Yes	No	Yes
Suite	$272	323–1,314*	Yes	Yes	Yes	Yes

* Including veranda

CABINS   Though Princess sells some different 35 cabin categories on these ships, there are actually fewer than 10 real configurations. For the most part, the category differences reflect location—such as amidships versus aft. Cabins are richly decorated in light hues and earth tones, and all have safes, hair dryers, minifridges, and TVs. Storage is adequate and offers more closet shelves than drawer space. Cabin balconies are tiered so they get more sunlight, but this also means your neighbors above can look down at you. Be discreet.

A standard outside cabin without a balcony, such as categories F and FF, ranges from 165 to 210 square feet, while insides, such as category JJ, measure 160 square feet. Balcony cabins range from 165 to 257 square feet, including the balcony. At 324 square feet (including balcony), the 180 minisuites on each vessel are smaller than the 32 minisuites on the older *Sea Princess,* but are ultracomfortable and offer a roomy sitting area with a full-size pullout couch, two TVs (one facing the bed, the other the sitting area), minifridge, large bathroom with full tub and shower, generous closet and drawer space, and terry robes. When Heidi sailed with her young sons, she had two cribs set up in the living area and there was still plenty of space for playing. Storage was so plentiful that, even with the kids' copious gear, she didn't fill it all.

Two Grand Suites measure 782 square feet and feature all the above amenities plus a bathroom with large whirlpool tub and multidirectional shower, and a separate toilet compartment. There are two 607-square-foot family suites that can sleep up to eight, with two bathrooms. Minibars in the suites are stocked once on a complimentary basis with soda, bottled water, beer, and liquor. Suite guests are also on the receiving end of a slew of perks highlighted in the "Service" section above.

Lifeboats partially or completely obstruct the views from most cabins on Emerald Deck. More than 600 cabins can accommodate a third passenger in an upper berth and each ship has 28 wheelchair-accessible cabins.

PUBLIC AREAS   These are huge ships with a not-so-huge feeling. Because of their smart layout, six dining venues, expansive outdoor deck space, multiple sports facilities, four pools, and nine hot tubs, passengers are dispersed rather than concentrated into one or two main areas. Even sailing with a full load of passengers (as many as 3,100 on *Grand* and almost 3,800 on *Crown* and *Emerald,* if all additional berths in all cabins are filled), you'll wonder where everyone is. Coupled with this smart layout is Princess's pleasing-if-plain contemporary decor. Public areas are done up in tasteful caramel-colored wood tones and color schemes of warm blue, teal, and rust, with some brassy details and touches of marble.

While the decor is soothing, the entertainment is pretty hot. Gamblers will love each ship's sprawling casino. Three main entertainment venues include a well-equipped two-story theater for big Vegas-style musical revues; a second one-level show lounge for smaller-scale entertainment such as hypnotists and singers; and the travel-themed Explorer's Club for bands, comedians, or karaoke nightly. Its decor evokes 19th-century travel, with vaguely Islamic tile motifs, African and Asian art pieces, exotic primitivist paintings, and Tiffany-esque ceiling lights. There's also the clubby, old-world Wheelhouse Lounge, offering laid-back pre- and post-dinner dancing and jazz amid an old ocean-liner atmosphere, as well as a woody sports bar and a wine bar selling small chilled seafood plates or caviar by the ounce, and wine, champagne, and iced vodka by the glass.

Skywalkers multilevel disco/observation lounge, sequestered in the ship's stern like a high-tech tree house, is a unique spot offering floor-to-ceiling windows with two impressive views: forward for a look over the ship itself, or back toward the sea and the giant vessel's very impressive wake. It's well positioned away from any cabins (so the noise won't keep anyone up) and is our favorite disco at sea—particularly on *Grand Princess,* where it sits on stilts about 150 feet above the sea. Check out the view at sunset.

For kids, the indoor/outdoor Fun Zone kids' play area has tons of games, toys, computers, and—the jewel for Heidi's twin boys—an outdoor, fenced-in play area equipped with a fleet of tricycles and a mini basketball setup. Seldom crowded (we're told there are rarely more than 10 children under 3 on any given cruise), it's an awesome place to let your little ones run free while you relax on the sidelines. A kiddie pool is located nearby. A separate teen center has several computers, plus video games, a dance floor, and a sound system, plus an outdoor teens-only sunbathing area with deck chairs and a hot tub. A video game room is located nearby.

Each ship also has a library, a small writing room, a card room, a large Internet center, and an attractive wedding chapel where the captain himself performs about six or seven bona fide, legal marriages every cruise.

DINING OPTIONS   Each ship has three pleasant one-story main dining rooms, with some sections slightly elevated to give a more spacious feel. By way of some strategically placed waist-high dividers, the rooms feel cozy, although the ceilings are a tad on the low side. For a more intimate meal, there are two alternative, reservations-required restaurants. Sabatini's specializes in Italian cuisine, featuring an eight-course menu emphasizing seafood. Service is first rate and the food is decent. The second venue is the Sterling Steakhouse (on *Grand*) or Crown Grill steak and seafood restaurant (on *Crown* and *Emerald*), where you can choose your favorite cut of beef and have it cooked to order.

The 24-hour Horizon Court buffet restaurant is designed to feel much cozier than it actually is. With clusters of buffet stations serving breakfast and lunch items, lines are kept to a minimum and you're hardly aware of the space's enormity. On *Grand Princess,* this restaurant turns into a sit-down bistro from 11pm to 4am, with the same dinner menu each night. On *Crown* and *Emerald Princess,* half the space is devoted to Café Caribe, a themed buffet that's open most of the day, serving Caribbean specialties such as jerk chicken, grilled Caribbean rock lobster, whole roast suckling pig, Guiana pepper pots and curries, and paella-style prawns. Musicians play Caribbean music, and passengers can order their meal cooked to taste at the cafe's open kitchen. There's no cover charge here. *Crown* and *Emerald* also offer food most of the day at the International Cafe: pastries in the morning; tapas, panini, and the like later; and cookies all day long (with some items at extra charge).

POOL, FITNESS, SPA & SPORTS FACILITIES   The Grand-class ships have just under 2 acres of open deck space, so it's not hard to find a quiet place to soak in the sun. On *Grand,* our favorite spot on a hot, humid day is portside aft on the deck overlooking the swimming pool, where the tail fin vent blows cool air. It's like having an outdoor air conditioner. *Crown* and *Emerald* offer a different kind of wonderful at a space called The Sanctuary. Three-quarters canopied and dotted with thickly padded single- and double-width lounge chairs, trees, and private cabanas, it's a perfect onboard chill-out space for adults only, staffed with "serenity stewards" who make sure things stay quiet. Light meals, massages, and beverages are available. Admission carries a $15 fee for half-day use, a measure intended to limit use to those who really want some peace and quiet.

The ships have four great swimming pools: two on the main pool deck; one aft; and, outside the spa, a resistance pool that allows you to swim steadily against a current. Other recreational offerings include a Sports Deck with a jogging track and a 300-square-foot outdoor LED movie screen for watching movies under the stars. You can reserve deck chairs for evening feature films, and, yes, there's popcorn (free) and Raisinettes (for a price). It's great fun, and the sound is awesome.

Spa, gym, and beauty-parlor facilities are located in a large, almost separate part of each ship, surrounding the lap pool and its tiered, amphitheater-style wooden benches. As is the case fleetwide with Princess, the oceanview gym is surprisingly small for ships of this size, although there's an unusually large aerobics floor. The spa is located under the Sports Deck. Hope there's no basketball game going on during your shiatsu appointment.

Royal Princess •
Pacific Princess

The Verdict

Clubby, cozy, midsize vessels that offer some of Princess's most interesting and world-ranging itineraries, in an atmosphere that mimics similarly sized ocean liners of yesteryear.

Pacific Princess *(photo: Princess Cruises)*

Specifications

Size (in Tons)		*Pacific*	334/232
Royal	30,200	Crew	
Pacific	30,277	*Royal*	381
Passengers (Double Occ.)		*Pacific*	373
Royal	710	Passenger/Crew Ratio	1.8 to 1
Pacific	670	Year Launched	
Passenger/Space Ratio		*Royal*	2001
Royal	42.5	*Pacific*	1999
Pacific	45.2	Last Refurbishment/Upgrade	
Total Cabins/Veranda Cabins		*Royal*	2007
Royal	355/257	*Pacific*	2003

Frommer's Ratings (Scale of 1–5)   ★★★★

Cabin Comfort & Amenities	4	Dining Options	4
Appearance & Upkeep	4	Gym, Spa & Sports Facilities	4
Public Comfort/Space	4.5	Children's Facilities	N/A
Decor	4	Enjoyment Factor	4

In the late 1990s and early 2000s, Renaissance Cruises built eight nearly identical midsize vessels, then promptly went belly-up. Princess was one of the beneficiaries: Over the next few years, it purchased three of the lovely little ships, which it renamed *Pacific Princess, Tahitian Princess,* and *Royal Princess.* Like all of the former Renaissance vessels, they're comfortable, traditional, and sedate, with an emphasis on intimate spaces—just like Princess's larger ships, but here it's the real thing. Like European boutique hotels, they're decorated mostly in warm, dark woods and rich fabrics, and offer a small-scale, clubby feel that larger ships can only hope to mimic.

Cabins & Rates

Cabins	Per Diem From	Sq. Ft.	Fridge	Hair Dryer	Sitting Area	TV
Inside	$187	158	Yes	Yes	Yes	Yes
Outside	$200	146–216*	Yes	Yes	Yes	Yes
Suite	$496	322–962*	Yes	Yes	Yes	Yes

* Including veranda

Oceania's *Regatta, Insignia,* and *Nautica,* and Azamara's *Journey* and *Quest* are also ex-Renaissance vessels. All eight ships are nearly identical, save for renovations each line has effected to make the ships their own. *Tahitian Princess* sails predominantly in the South Pacific and Alaska, and also offers a world cruise.

CABINS   Staterooms are straightforward, no-nonsense spaces with a hint of modern European city hotel: plain off-white walls, tasteful wood trim and furniture, and cheery carpeting and bedspreads. The vast majority are oceanview doubles, some with a balcony and some without, and average about 165 square feet—neither tiny nor huge, but perfectly adequate for most people. All come with a sofa or sofa bed, a minifridge, TV, and vanity. Closet space is just about adequate for the typically longer voyages these ships sail, so don't pack too heavily. Storage space in drawers and under the beds helps. Bathrooms in standard cabins verge on cramped, with a fairly small shower stall. Balconies are on the small side, large enough for only a small table and chairs. Five standards in the starboard center of Deck 6 have views obstructed by lifeboats.

On *Pacific Princess,* most cabins on Deck 9 are 322-square-foot minisuites with balconies, adding to the standard cabin amenities a bathtub and a larger seating area with a cocktail table for intimate in-room dining. On both ships, 10 Owner's Suites measure 786 to 962 square feet and are located at the ships' bow and stern, each offering a separate bedroom and sitting room (with dining area and sofa or sofa bed), two bathrooms (one with whirlpool tub/shower), wraparound balcony, two TVs, a minifridge, and substantial closet space. Suite guests get a slew of perks, as highlighted in the "Service" section above.

Three cabins on *Royal* and five on *Pacific* are wheelchair accessible.

PUBLIC AREAS   Like all the former Renaissance vessels, *Pacific Princess* and *Royal Princess* are elegant yet homey ships, with classic styling that includes dark-wood paneling, fluted columns, ornate railings and faux fireplaces, gilt-framed classical paintings, Oriental-style carpets, frilly moldings, marble and brass accents, faux skylights, and deep-hued upholstery. Think Edwardian sitting room, minus the palm trees. Passengers enter into a modest two-story reception Atrium that (intentionally or not—and we suspect the former) mimics the famous Grand Staircase from *Titanic*. In the bow on Deck 10, the spacious observatory lounge has floor-to-ceiling windows and cozy seating areas, and is used for dancing in the evenings and for various activities during the day. Farther astern on the same deck, the cozy library is decorated in a traditional English style, with high-back chairs and deep-cushioned couches, faux mahogany paneling, marble faux fireplace, and a trompe l'oeil garden skylight.

Most of the other public rooms are on Deck 5. Up front, the Cabaret Lounge seats about 350 and offers performances on its floor-level stage. At midships, a smallish but comfortable casino offers gaming tables and slots, while the attached Casino Bar offers musical entertainment in the evenings. A card room and Internet center on Deck 9 round out the public room offerings.

DINING OPTIONS   The main dining room is an elegant single-level space surrounded on three sides by windows. It's spacious and understated, with simple woodveneer wall panels and lighting sconces. Just outside the maître d's station is the cozy, country-club-esque Club Bar, the perfect spot for a pre-dinner drink.

Up on Deck 10, in the stern, are the ships' two alternative restaurants: Sabatini's for Italian cuisine and the Sterling Steakhouse for slabs of beef. Intimately sized (seating only about 90 passengers each), they're decorated to match their cuisine: Mediterranean style for Sabatini's, dark woods for Sterling. The restaurants are open on alternating nights.

In the stern on Deck 9 is a buffet restaurant that incorporates a pizzeria and barbecue. There's also a pool grill out on deck.

POOL, FITNESS, SPA & SPORTS FACILITIES   Each ship has a central pool area with a small pool and two hot tubs, surrounded by wall-to-wall deck chairs. A short jogging track (approximately 11 laps per mile) wraps around the deck above, while one deck above that (Sun Deck) there's additional sunning space, a golf practice cage, and shuffleboard. Just forward of the pool area, the smallish Lotus Spa offers massages, facials, and other treatments, while the next-door beauty salon makes you gorgeous. A decent-size oceanview gym with aerobics floor is attached. Just forward of the spa is a small outdoor lounging area with a hydrotherapy whirlpool overlooking the bow. It's probably the most private sunning spot on the ship, save for your private balcony.

Sea Princess

The Verdict

This relaxed, pretty ship is pleasant and comfortable. It's great for families and for grown-ups who like to enjoy the good life without too much flash.

Sea Princess *(photo: Princess Cruises)*

Specifications

Size (in Tons)	77,000	Crew	900
Passengers (Double Occ.)	1,950	Passenger/Crew Ratio	2.2 to 1
Passenger/Space Ratio	39.5	Year Launched	1998
Total Cabins/Veranda Cabins	975/410	Last Refurbishment/Upgrade	2005

Frommer's Ratings (Scale of 1–5)   ★★★★

Cabin Comfort & Amenities	4	Dining Options	4
Appearance & Upkeep	4	Gym, Spa & Sports Facilities	4
Public Comfort/Space	5	Children's Facilities	4
Decor	5	Enjoyment Factor	4

Here's the scoop on *Sea Princess:* She's just like Princess's newer megaships, only less so. Being among the line's oldest vessels (dating from late 1998), she's a member of the class that led the way toward the design Princess has used ever since: pretty if not exactly daring, with a decor that mixes classic and modern, using materials such as varnished hardwoods, marble, etched glass, granite, and textured fabrics. Light color schemes and buttery wood tones predominate, and the layout is very easy to navigate. By the end of the first day, you'll know where everything is.

Cabins & Rates

Cabins	Per Diem From	Sq. Ft.	Fridge	Hair Dryer	Sitting Area	TV
Inside	$157	135–148	Yes	Yes	No	Yes
Outside	$171	147–160	Yes	Yes	No	Yes
Suite	$352	365–678*	Yes	Yes	Yes	Yes

*Including veranda

CABINS   Though *Sea Princess*'s cabins are divided into some 28 categories, there are actually fewer than 10 configurations—for the most part, the category differences reflect location (amidships versus aft, and so on), and thus price. More than 400 cabins boast private balconies, though they're small, at about 3 × 8½ feet. And that leads to our main point: *Sea Princess*'s staterooms are cramped. Standard outside cabins are 178 square feet *including* their balconies, while Carnival's standards, by comparison, are nearly 186 square feet without balconies. On *Sea Princess,* what little space you gain from having a balcony is deducted from your room.

The ship's six suites sprawl out over 678 square feet of space and include robes to use while aboard and minibars stocked once on a complimentary basis with soda, bottled water, beer, and liquor. Suite guests also get a slew of perks highlighted in the "Service" section above. The 32 minisuites on each ship are really nice, with a separate bedroom area divided from the sitting area by a curtain. Each has a pullout sofa, a chair and desk, a minifridge, two TVs (one facing the bed, the other the sitting area), a walk-in closet, and a whirlpool tub and shower in a separate room from the toilet and sink.

All cabins have minifridges, safes, TVs, and hair dryers, and 300 accommodate third passengers in upper berths. Nineteen cabins are wheelchair accessible.

PUBLIC AREAS   *Sea Princess* has a decidedly unglitzy decor that relies on lavish amounts of wood, glass, and marble. The one-story showrooms offer good lighting and sound, and unobstructed views from every seat, with several spaces in the back reserved for wheelchair users. The smaller Vista Lounge also presents entertainment, with good sightlines and comfortable cabaret-style seating. The elegant, nautical-motif Wheelhouse Bar is done in warm, dark-wood tones and features small bands, sometimes with a vocalist. It's the perfect spot for pre- or post-dinner drinks.

Rounding out the public rooms are a dark and sensuous disco; a bright, spacious casino; a wine bar selling caviar by the ounce and wine, champagne, and iced vodka by the glass; and lots of little lounges.

DINING OPTIONS   *Sea Princess*'s two main dining rooms have an intimate feel, their one-level expanses broken up by dividers topped with frosted glass. There are also two alternative dining venues. The sit-down pizzeria (no extra charge) on Dolphin Deck is open approximately 11am to 2:30pm and 7pm to 1am for casual and quiet dining, with tables seating two, four, and six. Sorry, no takeout or delivery. For casual dining, the 24-hour Horizon Court buffet restaurant offers sit-down bistro-style dinners from 11pm to 4am, as well as a steakhouse option either indoors or out on deck, offered from 6 to 10pm.

POOL, FITNESS, SPA & SPORTS FACILITIES   *Sea Princess*'s pool deck is well laid out, with three adult pools (one of them in the stern), one kids' wading pool, and hot tubs scattered around the Riviera Deck, along with a 300-square-foot LED movie screen for showing feature films, sports events, and other entertainment. Three spacious decks are open for sunbathing.

The ships' gym is appealing, and though it's on the small side for a vessel this size, it's actually roomier than the ones on the much larger Grand-class ships. Aerobics, stretching, and meditation classes are available in the conversely spacious aerobics room, and the nearby spa offers the usual massages, mud treatments, facials, and the like. Men's and women's locker rooms have small steam rooms. The Promenade Deck provides space for joggers, walkers, and shuffleboard players, and a computerized golf center called Princess Links simulates the trickiest holes at some of the world's best golf courses.

10 Royal Caribbean International

1050 Caribbean Way, Miami, FL 33132. ℭ **800/327-6700** or 305/539-6000. Fax 800/722-5329. www.royalcaribbean. com.

THE LINE IN A NUTSHELL   Royal Caribbean's ships are good-looking, activity-packed floating resorts for excitement seekers, and the line is among the most innovative in the cruise biz, always adding something that's never been seen at sea before. Surfing, rock climbing, ice skating, boxing . . . man, what's next?

THE EXPERIENCE   Royal Caribbean prides itself on being ultrainnovative and cutting edge, pushing the envelope with each new class of ship they build. If there's something that's never been done at sea before, Royal Caribbean will figure out how to offer it. The latest ships, *Freedom, Liberty* and *Independence of the Seas,* not only have the rock-climbing walls and ice-skating rink inherited from the Voyager class before them, but also have a surfing simulator, a full-size boxing ring, and the world's first onboard water park. Cruises on these fun, active, and glamorous (but not too over-the-top-glitzy) megaships offer a great experience for a wide range of people, whether your idea of a good time is riding a wave or relaxing in the Solarium pool. There are huge children's centers for the kids and elegant jazz clubs, kick-back sports bars, and flashy entertainment for adults. Decor-wise, these ships are a shade or two toned down from the Carnival brood: Rather than trying to overwhelm the senses, many of their public areas are understated and classy. The Radiance-class vessels are the line's most elegant to date, with a sophistication that's up near the level of Royal Caribbean's sister line, Celebrity Cruises.

Pros

- **Activity central:** With rock-climbing walls, surfing machines, water parks, basketball courts, miniature golf, ice skating, and bungee trampolines among the many diversions, these ships are tops in the adrenaline department.
- **Pretty public areas:** Lounges, restaurants, and outdoor pool decks are well designed, spacious, glamorous, and just plain inviting.
- **Great solariums:** Solariums on the Vision-, Voyager-, Freedom-, and especially the Radiance-class ships are oh-so-relaxing oases designed around a theme (Venice, Africa, and so forth), a pool, and a pair of enormous whirlpool tubs.

Cons

- **Small cabins on the older ships:** At just about 120 to 160 square feet, most cabins aboard the line's pre-1999 vessels are downright tiny.

ROYAL CARIBBEAN: BIG HIP SHIPS

Royal Caribbean was the first company to launch a fleet specializing exclusively in Caribbean ports of call—hence the company name. In the late 1980s, it expanded its horizons beyond the Caribbean (hence the "international") and now offers cruises in every major cruising region. It's the line that launched the megaship trend (with 1988's 73,192-ton *Sovereign of the Seas*), as well as the mega-megaship trend (with 1999's 3,114-passenger *Voyager of the Seas*), the super-duper megaship trend (with the 3,634-passenger *Freedom of the Seas* in 2006), and the you-must-be-joking double-super-duper

Compared with other mainstream lines, here's how RCI rates:

	Poor	Fair	Good	Excellent	Outstanding
Enjoyment Factor					✓
Dining				✓	
Activities					✓
Children's Program				✓	
Entertainment				✓	
Service				✓	
Worth the Money					✓

megaship trend (with the 5,400-passenger "Project Genesis" ship to debut in 2009). But beyond sheer size, its ships have been innovative, challenging any traditional notions of cruise ship activities. *Voyager* launched the idea of ice-skating rinks, interior boulevards, and rock-climbing walls. Now with five Voyager-class vessels and the even larger Free-dom-class ships in the water, these features almost seem standard. Who would have thought?

In 1997, Royal Caribbean acquired the smaller and more high-end Celebrity Cruises, which it continues to operate as a separate brand.

PASSENGER PROFILE

You'll find all walks of life on a Royal Caribbean cruise: passengers in their 20s through 60s and older, mostly couples (including a good number of honeymooners), some singles traveling with friends, and also lots and lots of families during summer-time and holiday periods. Overall, passengers are energetic, social, and looking for a good time, no matter what their age. On Europe cruises, the majority of passengers come from somewhere in North America, but expect more Europeans as well as Asians and Latin Americans than you'd find on the line's Caribbean and Alaska sailings.

Over the past several years, the line has been making a push for younger, hipper, more active passengers via an ad campaign that portrays the ships as a combination of hyperactive urban health club, chic restaurant district, and adventure-travel magic potion—which, of course, is a bit of a stretch. They're active, yes, but don't expect the Shackleton expedition.

DINING

Royal Caribbean's cuisine is tasty, though don't expect anything worthy of a Michelin star. All in all, it's right on par with the other megaship lines. Unlike NCL, Oceania, Princess, and Holland America, which have adopted looser, "walk-in" dining pro-grams, Royal Caribbean sticks to offering early- and late-seating dinners in traditional main dining rooms, with guests assigned a set dinner table. Just like all the other mainstream lines, there are also many casual and specialty dining options that do not adhere to rigid dining times.

TRADITIONAL   Dinner is offered in two seatings in the main dining rooms, with typical entrees including poached Alaskan salmon, oven-roasted crispy duck served with a rhubarb sauce, sirloin steak marinated with Italian herbs and served over a chunky tomato stew, and shrimp scampi. At lunch and dinner, there's always a **light and healthy option,** such as herb-crusted baked cod with steamed red-skinned pota-toes and vegetables; or a pasta tossed with smoked turkey, portobello mushrooms, and red-pepper pesto; as well as a **vegetarian option,** such as vegetable strudel served in a puff pastry with black-bean salsa.

SPECIALTY Unlike lines such as NCL, Royal Caribbean hasn't gone overboard with alternative, extra-charge specialty restaurants. Instead, it's integrated some new dining options into the casual and snacking categories. The Voyager-class ships each have one intimate, reservations-only Italian restaurant called Portofino, while the Radiance- and Freedom-class and *Mariner* and *Navigator of the Seas* have Portofino and the Chops Grill steakhouse. They're all attractive and intimate getaways, and food and service are the best on board, justifying the $20 per-person cover charge. Specialty restaurants are being installed on the line's older ships as they're renovated.

CASUAL Fleetwide, an open-seating casual dinner option is offered every night from 6:30 to 9:30pm in the buffet-style Windjammer Cafe. Meals follow the general theme of dinners in the main restaurants (Italian, Asian, and so on), and the room is made a bit more inviting through dimmed lighting and the addition of tablecloths. Long open hours mean this option rarely gets crowded. You can also eat breakfast and lunch in the Windjammer—and most passengers do. Aboard *Independence* and *Navigator of the Seas,* the buffet area has an Asian specialty buffet called Jade, serving sushi and a variety of traditional and modern dishes.

RCI's Freedom- and Voyager-class ships also have one of the most distinctive casual-dining options at sea: an honest-to-god **Johnny Rockets diner** with red vinyl booths and chrome accents, serving burgers, milkshakes, and other diner staples. There's a nominal $4 per-person service charge, and sodas and shakes are a la carte, but that doesn't stop lines from forming here during prime lunch and dinner times.

SNACKS & EXTRAS Freedom- and Voyager-class ships have an extensive coffee shop on the indoor promenade (serving a variety of pastries, sandwiches, and pizza) plus several self-serve soft ice cream stations, nacho and hot dog type snacks in the sports bars, and a multistation buffet restaurant. The line's other ships have similar options, with decent pizza served afternoons and late night for those suffering from post-partying munchies, and ice cream and toppings available throughout the day from a station in the Windjammer. The Radiance-class ships all have Latte'tudes coffee shops serving gourmet java, cookies, and other baked goods. *Independence* and *Navigator* also have a **Ben & Jerry's** ice cream shop. All ships offer three midnight buffets per week, with "Midnight Treats" hors d'oeuvres served late on the other days.

A fairly extensive **kids' menu** (which is fun in and of itself, with word and picture games and pictures to color in, crayons included) features the usual options: burgers, hot dogs, fries, fish sticks, burritos, oven-fried lemon chicken, spaghetti and meatballs, and pizza, plus lots of desserts.

Room service is available 24 hours a day from a fairly routine, limited menu. During normal lunch and dinner hours, however, a cabin steward can bring many items served in the restaurant to your cabin.

ACTIVITIES

It's safe to say Royal Caribbean's ships offer the greatest variety of activities and sports facilities at sea. Fleetwide, you'll find **rock-climbing walls** (with multiple climbing tracks and training available) plus lots of typical cruise fare: spa and beauty demonstrations, art auctions, wine tastings, salsa and ballroom dance lessons, bingo, oddball crafts/hospitality classes (such as napkin folding), "horse race" gambling, and outrageous poolside games such as the men's sexy legs contest, designed to draw big laughs.

Royal Caribbean Fleet Itineraries

Ship	Sailing Region	Home Ports
Brilliance	10- to 15-night voyages in Atlantic Europe, the Mediterranean/Greek Isles/Egypt (various combinations) and Morocco/Canary Islands	Southampton/London, Barcelona
Independence	4- to 14-night voyages in Ireland, the Canary Islands, and the Mediterranean	Southampton/London
Jewel	3- to 12-night voyages in Northern Europe/Russia	Copenhagen, Amsterdam, Oslo, Hamburg, Harwich/London
Legend	12- and 13-night voyages in the Mediterranean/Greek Isles/Adriatic (various combinations)	Civitavecchia/Rome
Navigator	4- to 12-night Mediterranean	Barcelona, Civitavecchia/Rome
Splendour	6- to 10-night voyages in the Mediterranean/Greek Isles/Adriatic (various combinations)	Lisbon, Venice, Barcelona
Voyager	7-night Mediterranean	Barcelona

Sports facilities vary by ship: There are **ice-skating rinks** and in-line skating tracks on the Freedom- and Voyager-class ships; combo basketball/volleyball courts on the Radiance-, Freedom-, Voyager-, and Vision-class ships; and miniature-golf courses on the Freedom, Radiance, and Voyager classes, as well as *Splendour* and *Legend of the Seas*. Keep in mind that a few thousand of your closest friends may be lining up for the same fun activities, so expect queues and sign-up sheets. If shopping can be considered an activity, Royal Caribbean has an impressive selection of boutiques clustered around each ship's atrium.

For those whose goal is to not gain 5 pounds at the buffet, **gyms** are well equipped fleetwide, with specialized fitness classes such as yoga and cardio-kickboxing available for $10 per person. **Onboard spas** offer the usual range of massages, facials, and other beauty treatments, but here's a piece of advice: If you want a treatment, sign up immediately after boarding, as these are big ships and a lot of people will be competing with you for desirable time slots. If you're flexible, you can often find more openings and special discounts on port days and off times. During one rainy port day, Heidi signed up for a 50-minute combo back massage and mini-facial that was discounted to $89 from $120, not including the tip.

CHILDREN'S PROGRAM

Year-round and fleetwide, Royal Caribbean offers its **Adventure Ocean** supervised kids' programs for children ages 3 to 17, divided into Aquanauts (ages 3–5), Explorers (ages 6–8), Voyagers (ages 9–11), Navigators (ages 12–14), and older teens (ages 15–17). All youth staff have college degrees in education, recreation, or a related field. Each ship has a large children's playroom and facilities for teens, with complimentary supervised activities offered on sea and port days. In general, the scope of the kids' facilities on the Freedom-, Voyager-, and Radiance-class ships far exceeds that of the rest of the fleet, with huge playrooms, and a large, sequestered outdoor deck with ship-shaped play equipment. The *Independence of the Seas* offers an amazing **water park** on a top deck that makes the lawn sprinklers we grew up with seem downright prehistoric. Radiance-class ships and *Voyager* also have a water slide and a kids' pool. Activities fleetwide include movies, talent shows, karaoke, pizza and ice cream parties, bingo, scavenger hunts, game shows, volleyball, face painting, and beach parties. **Internet access** is available to Adventure Ocean kids at half price (25¢ vs. 50¢ per minute for adults).

Three programs mix learning with play. The **Adventure Science** program teaches and entertains kids with fun yet educational (take this with a grain of salt) scientific experiments, while **Adventure Art,** offered in partnership with Crayola, focuses on art projects made with the company's crayons, modeling clay, glitter, glue, markers, and paint. There are also activities geared to the whole family, including Mom and Dad. For younger kids (ages 6 months–3 years), RCI has partnered with Fisher-Price on a program of **supervised play dates** in which babies (6–18 months) and toddlers (18 months–3 years) are invited to daily 45-minute play sessions with their parents. Offered on all but embarkation day, the interactive dates incorporate music, story-telling, and a variety of Fisher-Price toys. In ship cabins, Fisher-Price TV offers programming for kids.

For teens, each ship has a **teen center,** disco, and a video arcade. *Independence* and *Navigator of the Seas* have three teen-only areas, including a dedicated teen sun deck.

Slumber-party-style **group babysitting** for children is available in the kids' play-room nightly between 10pm and 1am. The hourly charge is $5 per child (kids must be at least 3 years old and potty-trained). Private, in-cabin babysitting for kids 1 year and older is available from off-duty crewmembers 8am to 2am, and must be booked at least 24 hours in advance through the purser's desk. The cost: $8 per hour for up to two siblings; $10 per hour for a maximum of three. A few hours of adult time to enjoy dinner, drinks, and entertainment: priceless.

Alternatively, the **Adventure Ocean dinner program** is a kind of "get out of par-enting free" card for adults, inviting kids to dine with the youth staff in the Windjam-mer Cafe, the Solarium, or Johnny Rockets diner (depending on the ship) from 6 to 7pm, then take part in an activities session till 10pm. This is offered on 3 nights of a 7-night cruise and once or twice on shorter cruises. A complete child's menu is offered.

There is no minimum age for kids to sail with Royal Caribbean.

ENTERTAINMENT

RCI doesn't scrimp in the entertainment department, with music and comedy acts, some of the best Vegas-style shows at sea, passenger talent shows, karaoke, sock hops, and occasional **"name" groups and soloists,** such as the Platters, the Drifters, the Coasters, John Davidson, and Marty Allen. Other names may not be as familiar but can be pretty amazing, such as the Knudsen Brothers (a.k.a. Six), a six-member fam-ily a cappella group that mixes great harmonies, human-beat-box rhythms, and a lot of comedy about its male-pattern baldness. The newer the ship, the larger and more sophisticated the stage, sound, and lighting equipment, with some boasting a wall of video monitors to augment live performances.

Aside from its showrooms and huge glitzy casinos, Royal Caribbean is big on sig-nature spaces, with each ship offering the nautical, woodsy **Schooner Bar** as well as the **Viking Crown Lounge,** an observation-cum-nightclub set high on a top deck and boasting panoramic views of the sea and ship in all directions. The Latin-themed **Bolero's bar** (aboard *Independence* and *Navigator*) serves a mean mojito and has Latin music into the night. Atrium bars also feature live music, often from classical trios. On one memorable cruise, two very talented passengers spontaneously began singing opera as the atrium trio played, attracting a huge crowd. Suddenly the 3,000-passenger ship felt like an intimate cabaret lounge.

SERVICE

In general, dining, bar, and cabin service is surprisingly good, considering the sheer volume of passengers with which crewmembers must deal. At meals on a recent cruise, we found that even when staff were rushed, our water glasses were always filled, wine orders were delivered promptly, and our servers always found time for a little friendly chitchat as they skated around their tables. Other times we found ourselves greeted with a smile by a crewman polishing the brass, and had busboys in the buffet restaurant going out of their way to bring coffee and water, even though the room is officially self-service. These folks work long, hard days, though, and on ships this size you'll probably run into some crewmembers who look like they need a vacation.

Laundry and **dry-cleaning services** are available on all the ships, but none have self-service laundromats.

The Freedom Class: Independence

The Verdict

A supersized version of the already supersized Voyager-class ships, *Independence* offers everything those ships do and more, though it comes very close to being too big (and too commercial) for its own good.

Independence of the Seas *(photo: RCCL)*

Specifications

Size (in Tons)	160,000	Crew	1,360
Passengers (Double Occ.)	3,634	Passenger/Crew Ratio	2.7 to 1
Passenger/Space Ratio	44	Year Launched	2008
Total Cabins/Veranda Cabins	1,815/844	Last Refurbishment/Upgrade	N/A

Frommer's Ratings (Scale of 1–5)   ★★★★ ½

Cabin Comfort & Amenities	4	Dining Options	4.5
Appearance & Upkeep	5	Gym, Spa & Sports Facilities	5
Public Comfort/Space	4.5	Children's Facilities	5
Decor	4	Enjoyment Factor	5

Independence of the Seas and sisters *Freedom* and *Liberty* are currently the largest passenger ships in the world, besting Cunard's *Queen Mary 2* by 9,000 gross register tons and 1,000-plus passengers. So are they great? Are they marvelous? Are they everything the biggest passenger ships in the world should be? Well, it kind of depends on what your definition of "great" is and whether you think size really matters. If you love *big*, they're awesome; if not, well, shop around for something smaller. Of course, what really matters is how a ship was designed. Some massive ships feel crowded and uncomfortable, while others are so well designed you wonder where all the people are. For cruise lines, it's all about balance: maximizing the number of cabins (and, thus, revenue) while also making sure passengers don't feel lost in the crowd. For passengers, it's about deciding how many bells and whistles you want in a ship and how many other humans you're willing to travel with. *Independence* pushes the line on that balance.

The ship is, in essence, just a larger version of Royal Caribbean's popular 142,000-ton, 3,114-passenger Voyager-class ships (see review following), which introduced the line's now brandwide "active vacation" image with their rock-climbing walls, ice-skating rinks, and full-size basketball courts. *Independence*, carrying at least 500 more passengers (and more, if all berths are full), offers a nearly identical layout and ambience to the Voyager ships, but stretched out and with a few new eye-catching activities and entertainment features. But those extras come with a price: *Independence*'s Royal Promenade, for instance, is more dominated by shops and corporate co-branding arrangements (a Ben & Jerry's ice cream parlor, a sportswear shop with a dedicated New Balance section, etc.), giving it a feel that's as much mall as theme park. When crowds are low—say, during the early dinner seating or late at night—it can still be a lot of fun to sit at the "sidewalk" cafe or bar and catch a drink, but when things are hopping, you'd be forgiven for thinking your car was parked outside, in lot D.

Overall, *Independence* offers the same big, active, city-vacation feel that's the Voyager ships' stock in trade, and that ain't a bad thing. Additionally, they include an amped-up top-deck experience, with a great kids' water park and a surfing simulator. If you're the type that's already attracted to the Voyagers, there's no real reason to stay away. On the other hand, unless you're a surfing or water park fan, there's little reason to specifically seek out *Independence* instead of the Voyagers, which in a way is good: With six ships to choose from, you can pick your trip based on the destination, which is what you should be doing anyway.

Cabins & Rates

Cabins	Per Diem From	Sq. Ft.	Fridge	Hair Dryer	Sitting Area	TV
Inside	$150	152	Yes	Yes	No	Yes
Outside	$191	161–189	Yes	Yes	Some	Yes
Suite	$345	287–1,406	Yes	Yes	Yes	Yes

CABINS   Standard outside cabins are a livable 161 square feet, though standard insides seem small, at 152 square feet. All cabins come with Internet dataports, minifridges, safes, TVs, pleasant pastel color schemes, and regular hair dryers. Bathrooms are on the cramped side, with little storage space, few amenities (soap and shampoo only), and only a thin sliver of counter. The cylindrical shower stalls, though definitely tight for large-size people, have RCI's standard sliding doors that keep the water and warmth in.

Of the 1,815 cabins, 1,084 have ocean views and 844 have verandas. Suites range from the affordable junior suites (with sitting area and balcony) to a handful of family suites (with two bedrooms, two bathrooms, and a living area with sofa bed) up to the huge Presidential Suite, with its four bedrooms, four baths, and 810-square-foot balcony.

For those who want an "urban" experience, the 168 atrium cabins on the second, third, and fourth levels of the four-story Royal Promenade have windows facing the action below, with curtains and soundproofing to keep most of the light and noise out when you want downtime.

Thirty-two cabins are wheelchair accessible.

PUBLIC AREAS   *Independence* has more than 3 miles of public corridors, and it can feel like a real hike if your cabin's on one end of the ship and you have to get to the other. Running 445 feet down the center of Deck 5 is the bustling, four-story Royal Promenade, designed to resemble Memphis's Beale Street or New Orleans's Bourbon Street. Like those famous thoroughfares, it's lined with shops, bars, and cafes, and features evening musical performances by the ships' various musical groups, including their big bands. Other promenade attractions include a Ben & Jerry's ice cream parlor, a coffee bar, a casual pizza and snacks restaurant, an English-style pub with evening entertainment, a champagne bar, a wine bar that offers tastings (see description in the Voyager-class review), a small bookstore, several shops, and, for our money, the best thing on the whole strip: a men's barber shop offering old-timey professional shaves spiced with a helping of New Age spa frippery. The half-hour Express Shave includes hot towels, deep-cleansing exfoliation, a superclose shave, and did we mention hot towels? Niiiice. Only downside? They use safety razors instead of straight. Wimps.

Down on decks 3 and 4, the two-level disco is entered though a theme-parky "secret passage." There's also a huge multistory theater, a casino with more than 300 slot machines, a Latin-themed bar with live music, and the nautically themed Schooner Bar. One deck down, excellent ice shows as well as game shows and fashion shows are held throughout each cruise at the "Center Ice" ice rink, which has a sliding floor to cover the ice during nonskate events. Other public rooms include a library and Internet center, a sprawling kids' area with a huge oceanview playroom, a living-room-style teen center, a jumbo arcade, a top-deck jazz club and cocktail lounge, a card room, and a wedding chapel.

DINING OPTIONS   *Independence*'s three-level main dining room is, like those on RCI's Voyager-class ships, among the most stunning and classy aboard any of today's megaships, with a design that follows a generally classical theme. Each level—linked by a large open area and grand staircase at its center—is considered a separate restaurant, though service and menus are consistent throughout. A pianist or piano trio entertains from a platform in the aft end of the room, and a huge crystal chandelier hangs overhead, both setting an elegant mood.

Two alternative restaurants occupy spots immediately to port and starboard at the entrance to the buffet restaurant: Portofino, serving Italian meals in a cozy setting, and Chops Grille, a woody room for manly steaks. Both entail an additional $20 per-person charge. Out in the buffet, a section called Jade serves Japanese, Chinese, Indian, and Thai dishes.

Another casual option for lunch, dinner, and late-night snacks is the popular Johnny Rockets, a 1950s-style diner set out on deck and offering burgers, shakes, fries, and the like, with veggie burgers to satisfy non-meat-eaters. There's a nominal $4 per-person service charge, and sodas and shakes are a la carte.

POOL, FITNESS, SPA & SPORTS FACILITIES   Sticking with their active image, Royal Caribbean has outfitted *Independence* with several features sure to entertain both actual athletes and weekend warriors, as well as their active kids. The biggest hoo-ha is the ship's FlowRider surfing simulator—similar to swim-in-place lap pools with their recycling currents, except that this one features a stream that flows up an inclined, wedge-shaped surface 40 feet long and 32 feet wide. At the bottom are powerful jets that pump 30,000 gallons per minute up the slope, creating a wavelike flow on which boarders can ride—at least in theory. Located in the stern of each ship's sports court, spanning decks 12 and 13, the ride is adjoined by bleachers for gawkers and fans, creating a bonding atmosphere where those disinclined to flow can wager on those who are. We had our money on the kid with the puka beads and boarder shorts, who did manage to get to his knees before falling off and being swept up into the padded back bumper—just like everybody else. It's sports as a metaphor for life: Eventually, you fall down and get swept away by the currents, only here you can get back in line and try again. Participants must sign up for free group sessions and go through a quick introduction, after which they and the other members of their group take turns riding the wave, in either traditional stand-up surfing or less-balance-demanding body-boarding. A soft, flexible surface absorbs the impact when you fall. Which you will.

A free-standing "surf shack" bar near the FlowRider offers drinks. Also nearby are Royal Caribbean's signature rock-climbing wall (the biggest one at sea, naturally), a miniature golf course, a golf simulator, a jogging track, and a full-size basketball court.

In the ship's gym, an honest-to-god 20-by-20-foot boxing ring takes the place of the large hot tub that greets guests on the Voyager ships. The ring is part of what the line bills as the largest fitness center at sea, offering an enormous number of aerobics and weight machines, plus workouts that are rare even in shoreside gyms. Options include "Fight Klub" boxing training (one-on-one training sessions using speed bags, jump ropes, heavy bags, and padded punching mitts), personal training with Pilates instructors, onboard yoga, "Boot Camp X-Treme Training," and linked treadmill workouts (all this at an extra cost, of course). Stretch and fitness tips are located at intervals along the onboard running track, and a program of mapped running/jogging routes is available in the ports of call.

On deck, the kid-friendly H20 Zone Water Park takes up almost half the pool deck, with water canons, jets, buckets, and sprays hidden among colorful cartoon statues, some controlled by motion sensors, others by the kids themselves. The area also includes two wading pools (one geared to toddlers) and two hot tubs, a great place for Mom and Dad to soak while the kiddos are having a ball. Farther forward, the main pool area offers two pools (one traditional, one "sports") and two large hot tubs at port and starboard, extending 12 feet over the edge of the ship and some 112 feet above the sea. Extremely popular, they get socially crowded—but, of course, with hot tubs that's the usually the point.

While crowds tend to disperse around the ships' public areas, on sunny days things can get very crowded out on the main pool and sports decks. Guests seeking something more peaceful can sometimes find it in the adjacent, adults-only Solarium, where a second swimming pool is bisected by a little bridge.

The Voyager Class: Voyager • Navigator

The Verdict

Sports club meets Vegas meets theme park meets cruise ship, these enormous vessels are real winners if you like your vacations larger than life. As we overheard one little boy say to his father, "This doesn't look like a ship, Daddy. It looks like a city!"

Voyager of the Seas *(photo: RCCL)*

Specifications

Size (in Tons)	142,000	Passenger/Crew Ratio	2.7 to 1
Passengers (Double Occ.)	3,114	Year Launched	
Passenger/Space Ratio	45.5	*Voyager*	1999
Total Cabins/Veranda Cabins	1,557/757	*Navigator*	2002
Crew	1,176	Last Refurbishment/Upgrade	N/A

Frommer's Ratings (Scale of 1–5)   ★★★★ ½

Cabin Comfort & Amenities	4	Dining Options	4.5
Appearance & Upkeep	4	Gym, Spa & Sports Facilities	5
Public Comfort/Space	5	Children's Facilities	5
Decor	4	Enjoyment Factor	5

Truly groundbreaking when they were first launched, the Voyager-class ships are still among the largest and most activity-rich passenger ships at sea, boasting a full-size ice-skating rink; an outdoor in-line skating track; a 1950s-style diner sitting right out on deck; a 9-hole miniature golf course and golf simulator; regulation-size basketball, paddleball, and volleyball courts; huge two-level gyms and spas; and the rock-climbing walls that have become one of Royal Caribbean's most distinguishing features. And did we mention they also have monumentally gorgeous three-story dining rooms, florist shops, and a "peek-a-boo" bridge on Deck 11 that allows guests to watch the crew steering the ship?

What really sets these ships apart from any other passenger ship, though, are the four-story, boulevard-like Royal Promenades that run more than a football field's length down their center, lined with bars, shops, and entertainment lounges, and anchored at each end by huge twin atria. The promenade is a great place to people-watch, and weirdly enough (think peeping Tom), you can watch from your cabin, if you want to: Three decks of inside cabins have views from bay windows of the "street scene" below.

The strollable feel of these promenades leads to our major conclusion: These vessels are a perfect compromise for couples that can't decide between a tropical cruise and a city vacation. They may, in fact, be the first ships to really live up to the old "city at sea" cliché. There are enough people aboard to warrant the comparison, too: Each ship carries 3,114 guests at double occupancy, but because many staterooms have third and fourth berths, total capacity for each vessel can reach as high as 3,838. Remarkably, though, the ships rarely feel crowded. On our last three sailings, we found many public rooms nearly empty during the day and didn't have to wait in line much at all the entire week, even though more than 3,200 passengers were aboard. As we heard one woman comment to her companion, "I know there are 3,000 people on this ship, but where are they all?" Kudos go to the crew for efficiency and also to Royal Caribbean for a design that features enough appealing public areas to diffuse crowds comfortably, plus a layout that encourages traffic to flow in several different directions. This keeps crowding down and also means you don't tend to find yourself in the same spots day after day—it's entirely possible to be aboard for 6 days, turn a corner, and find yourself in a room you've never seen before. It also means it's nearly impossible to casually bump into a new friend; if you don't set a meeting spot, forget it.

Cabins & Rates

Cabins	Per Diem From	Sq. Ft.	Fridge	Hair Dryer	Sitting Area	TV
Inside	$100	160	Yes	Yes	No	Yes
Outside	$140	161–328	Yes	Yes	Some	Yes
Suite	$340	277–1,325	Yes	Yes	Yes	Yes

CABINS   Though not huge (at 160 sq. ft. for insides and 173 for standard ocean-views, including balcony), Voyager-class cabins are comfortable, offering dataports, minifridges, safes, TVs, pleasant pastel color schemes, and hair dryers. Bathrooms are on the cramped side, with little storage space, few amenities (soap and shampoo only), and only a thin sliver of counter. The cylindrical shower stalls, though definitely tight for large-size people, have good sliding doors that keep the water and warmth in.

Of the 1,557 cabins, 939 have ocean views and 757 have verandas. There's a single huge Penthouse Suite, 10 Owner's Suites, and 4 Royal Family Suites that accommodate a total of eight people with two bedrooms plus a living room with sofa bed and a pair of bathrooms. Smaller and cheaper family cabins sleep six, some on sofa beds. For voyeurs, the 138 atrium cabins on the second, third, and fourth levels of the four-story Royal Promenade have windows facing the action below, with curtains and soundproofing to keep most of the light and noise out when you want downtime.

Twenty-six cabins are wheelchair accessible.

PUBLIC AREAS   Each ship has about 3 miles of public corridors, and it can feel like a real hike if your cabin's on one end of the ship and you have to get to the other. Running down the center of each is the bustling four-story Royal Promenade, designed to resemble Memphis's Beale Street or New Orleans's Bourbon Street. Like those famous thoroughfares, it's lined with shops, bars, and cafes, and features evening musical performances by the ships' various musical groups. Other promenade attractions include an elegant champagne bar; a comfy English/Irish bar with "sidewalk" seating; a self-serve soft ice cream station with lots of toppings; shops; and a bright cafe that serves pizza, cookies, pastries, and coffee 24 hours a day. *Voyager* also has a large sports bar that gets big, raucous crowds when games are broadcast (and puts out free hot dogs and nachos to keep them there) and an arcade stocked with classic 1980s video games. On *Navigator* those were scrapped in favor of Vintages Wine Bar, created in collaboration with the Mondavi, Beringer Blass, and Niebaum-Coppola wineries. Full of wood and leather, with terra-cotta floors, attractive vineyard-themed lithographs, and a 600-bottle "cellar," the bars showcase more than 60 vintages. Prices are reasonable, and guests can taste any variety before ordering. Classes in wine appreciation are held here throughout the week, and passengers can also stage their own tastings by ordering any of 13 special "wine flight" tasting menus, with selections grouped by taste profile, varietal, or region—for example, Merlots, Australian wines, and so on.

In total, there are some 30 places aboard each ship to grab a drink, including the Viking Crown complex on the top deck, with its elegant jazz club and golf-themed 19th Hole bar; the dark, romantic, nautically themed Schooner Bar; and the clubby cigar bar, tucked away behind a dark door and hosting blackjack games on formal evenings. Aboard each ship, the futuristic or Gothic-dungeon-themed disco is entered though a theme-parky "secret passage," while the huge three-story showrooms occupy the opposite end of the kitsch spectrum: beautifully designed, with simple, elegant color schemes and truly lovely stage curtains. Excellent ice shows as well as game shows and fashion shows are held throughout each cruise at the "Studio B" ice rink, which has a sliding floor to cover the ice during nonskate events. Open skating for passengers is scheduled throughout the week.

Each ship has a two-story library-cum-computer-room with about 18 computer stations and Web-cams that allow you to send your picture as an electronic postcard. There are also sprawling kids' areas with huge oceanview playrooms, teen discos, and jumbo arcades.

The best spots for chilling out with a book during days at sea include the sea-view Seven of Hearts card room and Cloud Nine Lounge on Deck 14. Those really wanting to get away from people can retreat up the curving stairway to Deck 15's Skylight Chapel, which gets almost no traffic and is even free of piped-in music (though it also lacks windows).

DINING OPTIONS   The three-level main dining rooms on these ships are among the most stunning and classy aboard any of today's megaships, with designs that follow a general European theme. Each level—linked by a large open area and grand staircase at its center—is considered a separate restaurant, though service and menus are consistent throughout. A pianist or piano trio entertains from a platform in the aft end of the room, and a huge crystal chandelier hangs overhead, both setting an elegant mood.

For a dining alternative, the oceanview Portofino restaurant serves Italian meals in a cozy setting (and at an additional $20 per-person charge), but be sure to reserve a table as soon as you get aboard, as they book up fast.

The pleasant, spacious Island Grill and Windjammer Café restaurants occupy one large space but have separate lines and stations to keep things moving. On *Navigator*, this area also incorporates the Asian-themed Jade buffet. There's no outdoor seating, per se, but the ship's main pool area is on the same deck, just outside the restaurants' entrances.

Another casual option for lunch, dinner, and late-night snacks is the popular Johnny Rockets, a 1950s-style diner set out on deck and offering burgers, shakes, fries, and the like, with veggie burgers to satisfy non-meat-eaters. The international waitstaff is cute enough in their '50s-style soda-jerk clothes, but we could do without the cutesy lip-sync-and-dance routines to songs such as "YMCA" and "Respect." There's a $4 per-person service charge, and sodas and shakes are a la carte.

POOL, FITNESS, SPA & SPORTS FACILITIES   Each ship has a large, well-equipped oceanview gym, though the arrangement of machines and the many pillars throughout can make them feel tight when full. Each has a large indoor whirlpool and a huge aerobics studio (among the biggest on any ship), and their two-level spa complexes are among the largest and best accoutered at sea, with peaceful waiting areas where New Agey tropical-birdsong music induces total relaxation—until you get your bill. (Steiner, the company that manages spas aboard most cruise ships, keeps rates steep in all of 'em.)

While crowds tend to disperse around the ships' public areas, things can get tight out on the main pool decks on sunny days, when deck chairs are squeezed onto every level of the multistoried, amphitheater-like decks. The vibe can be electric (or really loud, depending on your perspective) when the pool band starts playing. Guests seeking something more peaceful can usually find it in the adjacent Solarium, with a second swimming pool and two enormous whirlpool tubs under a sliding roof. Behind the Johnny Rockets diner, *Voyager* has a kids' pool area with a water slide, wading pool, hot tub for adults, and dozens of adorable half-size deck chairs for the kids. On *Navigator* the area is reserved for teens, with deck chairs for sunbathing and an outdoor dance floor with sound and light systems. Deck 13 is the hub of sports action, with the much-touted rock-climbing wall, skating track, miniature-golf course, and basketball court. Appointments must be made to use the more popular options (especially the wall), but this is a good thing, as it cuts down on lines.

The Radiance Class: Brilliance • Jewel

The Verdict

Royal Caribbean's most elegant vessels combine shippy lines and nautical decor with a lot of the fun and games of RCI's Voyager class, including rock climbing and miniature golf.

Brilliance of the Seas (photo: RCCL)

Specifications

Size (in Tons)	90,090	Passenger/Crew Ratio	2.5 to 1
Passengers (Double Occ.)	2,100	Year Launched	
Passenger/Space Ratio	43	*Brilliance*	2002
Total Cabins/Veranda Cabins	1,050/577	*Jewel*	2004
Crew	857	Last Refurbishment/Upgrade	N/A

Frommer's Ratings (Scale of 1–5)   ★★★★ ½

Cabin Comfort & Amenities	4	Dining Options	4.5
Appearance & Upkeep	5	Gym, Spa & Sports Facilities	5
Public Comfort/Space	5	Children's Facilities	4
Decor	5	Enjoyment Factor	5

These ships are just plain handsome, with some of the adventure features of their larger Voyager- and Freedom-class siblings, but a sleeker seagoing profile outside, a more nautical look and feel inside, and acres of windows to bring the two together. When you first board, you'll see one of Royal Caribbean's typical wiry modern art sculptures filling the bright, nine-story atrium, but venture a little farther and you'll see that the ships have a much more traditional interior, with dark-wood paneling, caramel-brown leathers, and deep sea-blue fabrics and carpeting. Some 110,000 square feet of glass cover about half of their sleek exteriors, offering wide-open views from the Viking Crown Lounge, Singapore Sling's piano bar, Crown & Anchor Lounge, Sky Bar, Windjammer Café, Champagne Bar, and even the atrium, which is an uninterrupted wall of glass from decks 5 through 10 portside, and has four banks of glass elevators. All this transparency comes in handy in scenic destinations such as Alaska.

Cabins & Rates

Cabins	Per Diem From	Sq. Ft.	Fridge	Hair Dryer	Sitting Area	TV
Inside	$121	165	Yes	Yes	Yes	Yes
Outside	$150	170	Yes	Yes	Yes	Yes
Suite	$342	293–1,001	Yes	Yes	Yes	Yes

CABINS Cabins are fairly spacious, with the smallest insides measuring 165 square feet and some 75% of outside staterooms measuring at least 180 square feet, some with 40-square-foot verandas. The rest have jumbo-size portholes. Decor is appealing, done in attractive navy blues and copper tones. All cabins have minifridges, hair dryers, interactive televisions (for buying shore excursions, checking your onboard account, and looking up stock quotes), small sitting areas with minicouches, lots of drawer space, roomy closets, bedside reading lights, and TVs. Vanity/desks have pullout trays to accommodate laptops, plus modem jacks to connect them to the Internet. Bathrooms are small, with Royal Caribbean's typical hold-your-breath-and-step-in shower stalls, but they do have lots of storage space.

All but a handful of suites are located on Deck 10. The best, the Royal Suite, measures 1,001 square feet and offers a separate bedroom, living room with baby grand piano, dining table, bar, entertainment center, and 215-square-foot balcony. Six Owner's Suites are about half that size, with 57-square-foot balconies, a separate living room, a bar, and walk-in closet. The 35 Grand Suites are 358 to 384 square feet, with sitting areas and 106-square-foot balconies. Three 586-square-foot Royal Family Suites have 140-square-foot balconies and two bathrooms, and can accommodate six people in two separate bedrooms (one with third and fourth berths) and another two on a pullout couch in the living room. Suite guests are treated to complimentary in-cabin butler service in addition to cabin stewards, and there's also a Concierge Club on Deck 10 where suite guests can request services and grab a newspaper.

One snag on the balcony front: On each ship, cabin decks 7 through 10 are narrower than the rest of the ship, resulting in cabin balconies on Deck 10 (many of them suites) being shaded by the overhang of the deck above. Meanwhile, cabin balconies on the aft and forward ends of Deck 7, being indented, look out onto the top of Deck 6 instead of directly out onto the sea. Balconies on cabins 7652 to 7670 and 7152 to 7170, also aft on Deck 7, are not completely private because the dividers between them don't go all the way to the edge of the space. Keep your clothes on; your neighbors can look right over at you.

Fifteen cabins can accommodate wheelchair users.

PUBLIC AREAS Our favorite space aboard is the cluster of five intimate, wood-and-leather lounges on Deck 6, which recall the decor of classic yachts, university clubs, and cigar lounges. Expect low lighting, inlaid wood flooring, cozy couches, and Oriental-style area rugs. The best of these rooms is the romantic piano bar and lounge that stretches across each ship's stern, with a bank of floor-to-ceiling windows. For amazing views, don't miss having a cocktail here on a moonlit night. Adjacent is a lovely Colonial-style Billiard Club boasting herringbone wood floors, redwood veneer paneling, and a pair of ultra-high-tech gyroscopic pool tables. No excuse for missing shots: The tables compensate for the ship's movements, staying remarkably level.

The main theaters are refreshingly different from most in the cruise biz, with a cool ambience, warm wood tones, and seating in deep sea-blues and greens. Artful handmade curtains, indirect lighting, and fiber optics all come together to create a quiet, ethereal look. But guys, watch those protruding armrests: It's very easy to snag your pants pockets on them.

Other public areas include the attractive Casino Royale, with more than 200 slot machines and dozens of gaming tables; a baseball-themed sports bar with interactive games on the bar top; the nautically themed Schooner Bar; a 24-hour Internet center; a specialty-coffee bar with several Internet stations; a small library; a conference-center complex with a small movie theater; and, high up on Deck 13, Royal Caribbean's signature Viking Crown Lounge, which is divided between a quiet lounge and a large disco with a rotating bar. Even the ships' high-style public bathrooms are impressive, with their marble floors and counters and funky portholelike mirrors.

The huge kids' area on Deck 12 includes a sprawling playroom divided into several areas, with a video arcade and an outdoor pool with water slide. Teens have their own nightclub, with a DJ booth, music videos, and a soda bar.

DINING OPTIONS   The two-story main dining rooms on all four ships are glamorous and elegant, like something out of a 1930s movie set. Four willowy silk-covered columns dominate the vaulted main floor, and a wide double staircase connects the two decks dramatically—all that's missing are Cary Grant and Katharine Hepburn. At the entryway to the *Brilliance*'s Art Nouveau–style dining room, there's a stunning marble floor medallion made from four colors of marble.

The nautically decorated Windjammer Café takes self-serve buffet dining to new levels, with 11 food stations (9 inside and 2 outside) set up as islands to keep the lines down and the crowds diffused. It really works. If you prefer taking your meals while reclining, there's a small strip of cozy tables with oversize rattan chairs and thick cushions between the indoor and outdoor seating areas.

The cozy 90-seat Chops Grille is an oceanview venue with dark woods, rich upholsteries, and high-backed booths that bring home the meat-and-potatoes mood. You can watch your steak being cooked in the open kitchen. Adjacent is the 130-seat Portofino, an oceanview Italian restaurant. Expect more refined and gracious service than in the main dining room, plus a more leisurely pace (and, of course, a $20 per person cover charge). Up on the Sport Deck, the Seaview Cafe is a casual lunch and dinner venue with checkered floors, rattan chairs, and lots of light, serving quick meals such as fish and chips, popcorn shrimp, and burgers.

A counter in the Solarium serves freshly made pizza by the slice, and a coffee shop offers cappuccino and pastries.

POOL, FITNESS, SPA & SPORTS FACILITIES   The Radiance vessels offer tons of recreation outlets and acres of space to flop on a deck chair and sunbathe. At the main pool, passengers pack in like sardines on sunny days at sea, and deck chairs can be scarce during the prime hours before and after lunch—par for the cruise ship course. On *Brilliance*, an east India theme combines pink terra cotta, teak wood, and ceramic tiling; a stone relief of the Taj Mahal palace greets guests in the reception area.

Much more relaxing are the ships' large, lush Solariums, with their exotic Eastern motifs. Tropical foliage and waterfalls impart an Asian-spa mood, and stone reliefs, regional woodcarvings, and statues drive home the atmosphere. The area's adjacent (and popular) pizza counter adds a little pandemonium to the otherwise serene scene (as can kids, if they happen to find the place), but overall this is a great spot to settle in for a lazy afternoon at sea. The padded wooden chaise longues are heavenly. The adjacent spa has 13 treatment rooms and a special steam-room complex with heated tiled lounges and showers that simulate tropical rain and fog.

The Sports Deck has a 9-hole miniature golf course and golf simulators, a jogging track, a rock-climbing wall attached to the funnel, and a combo basketball, volleyball, and paddle-tennis court. The sprawling oceanview gym has a huge aerobics floor and dozens of exercise machines, including sea-facing treadmills and elliptical stair-steppers.

The Vision Class: Legend • Splendour

Splendour of the Seas *(photo: RCCL)*

The Verdict

These ships are glitzy and exciting without going overboard, though they're on the frumpy side compared to the newer, snazzier Radiance, Voyager, and Freedom ships.

Specifications

Size (in Tons)	69,130	Passenger/Crew Ratio	2.5 to 1
Passengers (Double Occ.)	1,804	Year Launched	
Passenger/Space Ratio	38.5	*Legend*	1995
Total Cabins/Veranda Cabins	902/231	*Splendour*	1996
Crew	720	Last Refurbishment/Upgrade	N/A

Frommer's Ratings (Scale of 1–5)   ★★★ ½

Cabin Comfort & Amenities	3	Dining Options	3
Appearance & Upkeep	4	Gym, Spa & Sports Facilities	4
Public Comfort/Space	4	Children's Facilities	4
Decor	3.5	Enjoyment Factor	4

It's a funny thing with cruise ships. One year they're the newest, hottest, biggest thing on water, and just a few cycles around the sun later, you look at them and think, "How quaint. How '90s." They may be just fine and still offer a great cruise experience, but things have changed so fast in the cruise biz that even the best ships from the late 20th century can seem dated. That's sort of the story with RCI's six Vision-class vessels, which offer an open, light-filled feel and many of the same amenities as aboard the line's newer, larger ships. They're just not the new kid on the block anymore.

Cabins & Rates

Cabins	Per Diem From	Sq. Ft.	Fridge	Hair Dryer	Sitting Area	TV
Inside	$107	138–174	No	No	Yes	Yes
Outside	$131	154–237	Some	No	Yes	Yes
Suite	$246	241–1,140	Yes	No	Yes	Yes

CABINS   To be polite, cabins are "compact"—larger than on the line's Sovereign-class ships and *Empress of the Seas,* but smaller than those on the Voyager- and

Radiance-class ships and on many competitors' vessels. For big, check out the 1,140-square-foot Royal Suites, which feature a baby grand piano and huge marble bathroom with double sinks, a big whirlpool bathtub, and a glass-enclosed shower for two. For something in between, try the roomy 190-square-foot category-D1 cabins, with private verandas, minifridges, small sitting areas with pullout couches, and tons of storage space. All told, about a quarter of each ship's cabins have private verandas; about a third can accommodate third and fourth passengers; and all have safes, TVs, and an impressive amount of storage space. Bathrooms are not the largest you'll ever see, with shower stalls that are a tight squeeze for anyone thicker than a supermodel. Expect a decor scheme of pastels and beige with varnished wood trim—not adventurous, but not hideous, either.

Each vessel has between 14 and 17 staterooms equipped for wheelchair users.

PUBLIC AREAS   Throughout each vessel, warm woods and brass, gurgling fountains, green foliage, glass, crystal, and buttery leathers highlight the public areas that have a sort of retro Vegas feel to them. The ambience ranges from classic to glitzy. The bright, wide-open, and easy-to-navigate Promenade and Mariner decks are home to most public rooms, their corridors converging at a seven-story atrium where glass elevators take passengers from Deck 4 all the way up to the stunning, glass-walled Viking Crown Lounge on Deck 11. Full musical revues are staged in glittery, two-story showrooms, where columns obstruct views from some balcony seats. The ships' casinos are Vegas-style flashy, with hundreds of gambling stations so densely packed that it's sometimes difficult to move and always difficult to hear. Other nice spots include the Schooner piano bar (a great place for a pre-dinner drink or late-night unwinding, with a nautical wood-and-rope decor) and the Champagne Terrace at the foot of the atrium, where you can sip a glass of fine wine or bubbly while swaying to the dance band.

In contrast to its showcase spaces, each ship contains many hideaway refuges, including an array of cocktail bars, a library, and card rooms. Hundreds of potted plants and more than 3,000 original artworks aboard each ship add humanity and warmth, though some of that art is a tad crusty or, at best, something that could have been used in a Madonna video 20 years ago.

For kids there's a playroom stocked with toys, books, and games, while the nearby teen center goes the video game route.

DINING OPTIONS   The large dining rooms aboard these vessels span two decks connected with a very grand staircase and flanked with 20-foot walls of glass. The rooms are of their era, with lots of stainless steel, mirrors, dramatic chandeliers, and a bit of a banquet-hall feel. There's also a large indoor/outdoor buffet restaurant serving breakfast, lunch, and dinner.

POOL, FITNESS, SPA & SPORTS FACILITIES   The Steiner-managed spas on these ships offer a wide selection of treatments, as well as the standard steam rooms and saunas. Adjacent Solariums have a pool, lounge chairs, floor-to-ceiling windows, and a retractable glass ceiling for inclement weather. Designed after Roman, Egyptian, or Moorish models, these bright, spacious areas are a peaceful place to lounge before or after a spa treatment, or any time at all. Gyms are surprisingly small and cramped, considering the ships' size.

Each ship has a higher-than-expected amount of open deck space. The outdoor pool on the Sun Deck has the usual blaring rah-rah music during the day, along with silly contests of the belly-flop variety. A rock-climbing wall, a jogging track, shuffleboard, and Ping-Pong round out the on-deck options.

11 Mini-Review: Swan Hellenic Cruises

Swan Hellenic Cruises. 631 Commack Rd, Suite 1A, Commack, NY 11725. (C) **877/219-4239**. www.swanhellenic. com.

THE LINE IN A NUTSHELL   The single-ship, U.K.-based Swan Hellenic is one of those quirky little cruise lines that tend to attract many long-term repeat passengers. Marketing its product as "Discovery Cruising," the line offers long itineraries that mix popular and out-of-the-way ports, all augmented by onboard enrichment lectures.

THE EXPERIENCE   In early 2007, Swan Hellenic had a close call. The beloved little British line was basically dissolved by its parent company, the giant Carnival Corporation, which took away its sole ship and gave it to Princess Cruises for use as *Royal Princess*. Then in stepped a savior in the form of Lord Sterling, aka Baron Sterling of Plaistow, former chairman of P&O Cruises, who bought the Swan brand from Carnival and set out to find a suitable ship. He did, and for longtime Swan passengers it's the perfect one: the 350-passenger *Minerva,* which sailed as Swan's sole vessel from her construction in 1996 until 2003, when she began sailing under charter as *Explorer II* for Abercrombie & Kent and Regent Seven Seas. Returned to her old name, the refurbished vessel was, at press time, set to relaunch the Swan brand in May 2008, offering summer sailings in northern Europe, the Mediterranean, and the Black Sea, then heading south for a series of Antarctica cruises.

Swan's new ownership knows not to gum up a product that was already working just fine, so expect all the good things about the line to stay the same. Its itineraries are beautifully balanced between big and small ports, and between stops that offer nature-oriented appeal and those that are über-historic. Each voyage is planned around a theme connected to the cruise's region, and erudite guest speakers lecture on topics that might include archaeology, history, marine biology, contemporary world affairs, geology, geography, art, or fine wines. A shore excursion is included at nearly every port (though they're typically of the bus-tour variety), and gratuities, air between London and the embarkation port, and airport-to-seaport bus transfers are all bundled into your fare. Optional, extra-cost shore excursions are also available.

Swan Hellenic's passenger base typically skews toward older passengers, most of whom hail from the U.K. and have traveled widely. Unusual in the industry is the fact that Swan Hellenic sets aside a certain percentage of cabins for solo travelers. There are no facilities for children, and the cruise line makes no attempt to market to families.

Swan Hellenic Fleet Itineraries

Ship	Sailing Regions	Home Ports
Minerva	9- to 43-night voyages in the Norwegian Fjords (some with North Cape), Northern Europe, Russia, the British Isles, the Mediterranean, Sicily/Adriatic, Adriatic/ Aegean/Black Sea, Aegean/North Africa	Dover/London, Palermo, Istanbul, Piraeus/Athens, Alexandria (Egypt), Funchal (Madeira), Livorno/Florence, Civitavecchia/Rome

On board, the line's cuisine is excellent, if unsurprising, balanced among traditional British fare, Continental dishes, and dishes from the region in which the ship is sailing. Aside from the daily lectures (typically two per day), there are daytime activities such as art classes, choral singing workshops, and yoga and tai chi classes. Entertainment is also low key, featuring a cocktail pianist, classical concerts, Shakespearean revues, jazz bands, and occasional crew shows.

The 12,500-ton *Minerva* is a homey but tough little ship, carrying only 350 passengers and with an ice-hardened hull that allows her to sail Antarctica itineraries in the polar summer. Inside she's decorated in a classic style and offers an entertainment lounge, one large dining room and a buffet restaurant, two bars, a small cinema, a card room, a beauty shop, a well-stocked library, and a single pool in the stern. Standard cabins are plain and fairly spartan, with en suite shower or bath, TV, vanity table and chair, hair dryer, private safe, bathrobes, binoculars, and books. Standard cabins have windows or portholes only, while suites have private balconies. Per diems run from $158.

7

The Ultraluxury Lines

Do we really have to define luxury? Maybe, since the word gets thrown around so easily these days. Suffice it to say that on these ritzy ships, guests don't line up for frozen yogurt and pepperoni pizza en route to Naples with 3,000 other passengers. Instead they're brought a nice '98 Bordeaux and a *filet de boeuf* in truffle sauce while sailing to St-Tropez. Their waiter knows the art of fine service, and he never, ever twirls a napkin while parading baked Alaska around a dining room.

Ships in the luxury class come in three basic flavors: big (Cunard's big *Queen Mary 2* and *Queen Victoria,* and Crystal's pair of 1,000-passenger vessels), midsize (Regent, Peter Deilmann, and Silversea's vessels, which carry 300–700 guests), and small (the boutique ships of Seabourn and SeaDream, which serve only 110–208 passengers at a time). Whatever their size, they all cater to discerning travelers who don't blink at paying top dollar to be pampered: Though the high-end lines do discount at times, they'll still cost two or three times as much as your typical mainstream cruise. Expect to pay at least $2,800 per person for a week in the Med or northern Europe, and easily more if you opt for a large suite or choose to cruise during the busiest times of the year. The upside? Many extras are often included in the cruise rates, such as wine and liquor, gratuities, and (sometimes) complimentary shore excursions.

Most people attracted to these types of cruises are sophisticated, wealthy, relatively social, and used to the finer things in life. Most are well traveled though not necessarily adventurous, and tend to stick to five-star experiences. These ships are not geared to children, although aboard lines such as Crystal and especially Cunard you might see 100 or more during holidays or school vacation months. Babysitting can often be arranged privately with an off-duty crewmember.

DRESS CODES With the exception of casual SeaDream, these are the most formal cruises out there: For the main dining rooms, you need to bring the tux or a dark suit and the sequined gown or cocktail dress for the 2 or 3 formal nights scheduled each week. Informal nights call for jackets (skip the tie if you want to, as things are getting more casual even on the fancy ships) and smart dresses, skirts, or pantsuits for women. Sports jackets or nice shirts for men, and casual dresses or pantsuits for women are the norm on casual nights. That said, like the rest of the industry, even the high-end lines are relaxing their dress codes, heading closer to SeaDream, which espouses a casual "no jackets required" policy during the entire cruise. All the ultraluxe lines now have casual dining venues, so if you just want to throw on a sundress (or polo shirt and chinos) and be done with it, you'll be fine.

Frommer's Ratings at a Glance: The Ultraluxury Lines

1 = poor   2 = fair   3 = good   4 = excellent   5 = outstanding

Cruise Line	Enjoyment Factor	Dining	Activities	Children's Program	Entertainment	Service	Worth the Money
Crystal	5	5	5	3	4	4	5
Cunard	5	4	5	5	4	4	5
Regent Seven Seas	5	4	3	2	3	5	5
Seabourn	5	5	2	N/A*	2	4	4
SeaDream	5	4	3	N/A*	3	5	5
Silversea	5	5	3	N/A*	2	5	4

Note: Cruise lines have been graded on a curve that compares them only with the other lines in the ultraluxury category. See "How to Read the Ratings," in chapter 5, for a detailed explanation of the ratings methodology.

*Lines with N/A rating for children's programs have no program.

1 Crystal Cruises

2049 Century Park E., Suite 1400, Los Angeles, CA 90067. ℂ 888/799-4625 or 310/785-9300. Fax 310/785-0011. www.crystalcruises.com.

THE LINE IN A NUTSHELL   Stylish and upbeat, Crystal offers top-shelf service and cuisine on ships large enough to offer lots of outdoor deck space, generous fitness facilities, tons of activities, multiple restaurants, and more than half a dozen bars and entertainment venues.

THE EXPERIENCE   Aside from Cunard's *Queen Mary 2*, Crystal has the only truly upscale large ships in the industry. Carrying 940 to 1,080 passengers, they aren't huge, but they're big enough to offer much more than their high-end peers. You won't feel hemmed in and you likely won't be twiddling your thumbs from lack of stimulation. Service is excellent and the line's Asian cuisine is tops. Unlike Seabourn's small ships, which tend to be more calm and staid, Crystal's sociable vibe and large passenger capacity tend to keep things mingly, chatty, and more active. No question, these vessels have a vitality and energy the smaller Seabourn and Silversea ships definitely do not.

Pros

- **Four or five restaurants:** In addition to the formal dining room, there are two or three alternative restaurants (including, on *Serenity*, two with cuisine by famed chef Nobu Matsuhisa), plus a poolside grill, an indoor cafe, and a casual restaurant that puts on great theme luncheon buffets.
- **Best Asian food at sea:** The ships' reservations-only Asian restaurants serve up utterly delicious Japanese food, including sushi. At least once per cruise, an Asian-theme buffet lunch offers an awesome spread.
- **Fitness choices:** There's a nice-size gym, paddle-tennis courts, shuffleboard, Ping-Pong, a jogging circuit, golf driving nets, and a putting green.
- **Enrichment programs:** No other line has as many options, with four or five impressive lecturers, as well as complimentary computer training classes on every

cruise, plus dozens of themed sailings focused on food and wine, art, film, jazz music, wellness, and other subjects.

Cons

- **Least all-inclusive of the luxe lines:** Only nonalcoholic drinks are included in the rates, not tips, booze, and so on.
- **Cabin size:** Accommodations (especially on *Symphony*) are smaller than those aboard Silversea, Seabourn, and Regent.

CRYSTAL: SPARKLING & SPACIOUS

Established in 1990, Crystal Cruises has established its own unique place in the high-stakes, superupscale cruise market. Its ships are the largest true luxury vessels aside from Cunard's *QE2* and *QM2,* and while not quite as generous in the stateroom department (cabins are smaller than those on Regent, Silversea, Seabourn, and Sea-Dream) and the freebies department (Crystal doesn't include complimentary champagne, liquor, and wine in the rates, though cruise fares tend to be less expensive than the lines that do), they provide a truly refined cruise for discerning guests who appreciate really good service and top-notch cuisine. No doubt about it, Crystal is one of our favorite lines.

The line is the North American spin-off of Japan's largest container shipping enterprise, Nippon Yusen Kaisha (NYK). Despite these origins, a passenger aboard Crystal could conceivably spend an entire week at sea and not even be aware that the ship is Japanese owned and funded. More than anything else, Crystal is international, with a strong emphasis on European service. The Japanese exposure is subtler, and you'll feel it in the excellent Asian cuisine and tasty sake served in the alternative restaurants and at the Asian-theme buffets. A Japanese activities director is on board to attend to the handful of Japanese passengers you'll see on many cruises.

In late 2005, the line's oldest ship, the 1990-built *Harmony,* left the Crystal fleet to take up service with parent company NYK's Asian cruise division. In announcing the move, Crystal also hinted at future construction of a replacement vessel, though no details are yet available.

PASSENGER PROFILE

Like other high-end lines, Crystal draws a lot of repeat passengers. On many cruises, more than 50% of the passengers hail from affluent regions of California, and many are Crystal fans who have sailed with the line numerous times. There's commonly a

Compared with the other ultraluxury lines, here's how Crystal rates:

	Poor	Fair	Good	Excellent	Outstanding
Enjoyment Factor					✓
Dining					✓
Activities					✓
Children's Program			✓		
Entertainment				✓	
Service				✓	
Worth the Money					✓

small contingent of passengers (about 15% of the mix) from the United Kingdom, Australia, Japan, Hong Kong, Mexico, Europe, South America, and other places. Most passengers are well-heeled couples over 55. A good number of passengers step up to Crystal from lines such as Princess and Holland America.

Many Crystal passengers place great emphasis on the social scene before, during, and after mealtimes, and many enjoy dressing up (sometimes way up) for dinner. You'll see no shortage of diamonds and gold Rolexes, and it's obvious that women on board have devoted much care and attention to their wardrobes and accessories. The onboard jewelry and clothing boutiques also do a brisk business, and guests forking over $50,000 for a diamond-encrusted watch isn't uncommon. On formal nights—2 or 3 of which occur during every 10- or 11-day cruise—the majority of men wear tuxes and many women wear floor-length gowns, although your classic black cocktail dress is just fine. As on all ships, dress codes are much more relaxed during the day.

Though not a kid-centric line compared to the mainstream lines, in the high-end group, Crystal is the most accommodating for families with kids. Each ship has a dedicated playroom and teen club, and supervised activities for ages 3 and up are offered when demand warrants it. During holidays and the summer holiday months of July and August, 100 or so kids on board is not that unusual.

DINING

Service by the team of ultraprofessional, gracious European waiters is excellent. In the main dining room—and to a somewhat lesser degree in the alternative restaurants—table settings are lavish and include heavy leaded crystal, Frette linens, and Villeroy & Boch as well as Wedgwood china. Even in the Lido restaurant, waiters are on hand to serve you your salad from the buffet line, prepare your coffee, and then carry your tray to wherever it is you want to sit.

TRADITIONAL   Dinner is served in two seatings in the main dining rooms; lunches and breakfasts are open seating. Cuisine selections include dishes such as coq au vin (braised chicken in burgundy red-wine sauce with glazed onions and mushrooms over a bed of linguine), Black Angus beef tenderloin with burgundy wine gravy, oven-baked quail with porcini mushroom and bread stuffing, or seared sea scallops served with a light lobster beurre blanc over a bed of risotto. At lunch and dinner, there's a **light, low-cholesterol selection** such as grilled fresh halibut served with steamed vegetables and herbed potatoes, as well as an entree salad—for example, a mixed salad with grilled herb-marinated chicken breast, lamb, or filet mignon. **Vegetarian selections,** such as spinach and ricotta cannelloni or a brochette of Mediterranean vegetables, are also featured, as are **kosher foods** and **low-carb choices.** Sugar-free, gluten-free, and low-fat options are now part of all menus, too, even at buffets. Virtually any special diet can be accommodated.

In a kind of homage to the California wine industry, Crystal offers one of the most sophisticated inventories of **California wines** on the high seas, as well as a reserve list of two dozen or so rare wines and an extensive selection of French wines. In 2004, the line also created its own proprietary label called **C Wines,** six chardonnays, cabernet sauvignons, and Merlots made in limited production with grapes from the Napa and Sonoma valleys, Arroyo Seco, and the Santa Lucia Highlands. All are available on board by the glass or the bottle.

SPECIALTY   The line's Asian venues are among the best at sea. *Symphony's* Jade Garden showcases the Asian cuisine of Wolfgang Puck's acclaimed Santa Monica restaurant, Chinois on Main. Even better, master chef **Nobuyuki "Nobu" Matsuhisa,** known for his restaurants in New York, Miami, L.A., London, Paris, and other cities, partnered with Crystal to create menus for *Serenity*'s Sushi Bar and its Pan-Asian restaurant Silk Road. Dishes feature Nobu's eclectic blends of Japanese cuisine with Peruvian and European influences. In the Sushi Bar, sample the salmon tartare with sevruga caviar or the yellowtail sashimi with jalapeño; in Silk Road, choices include lobster with truffle yuzu sauce and chicken with teriyaki balsamic. While Nobu himself makes occasional appearances on *Serenity,* chef Toshiaki Tamba, personally trained by Nobu, oversees the restaurants.

Aboard both ships, famed restaurateur Piero Selvaggio showcases the cuisine of his award-winning Santa Monica and Las Vegas Valentino restaurants at the Italian **Valentino at Prego.** Reservations are required for each of the specialty restaurants, and a $7 gratuity is suggested.

CASUAL   Excellent **themed luncheon buffets**—Asian, Mediterranean, Western barbecue, or South American/Cuban, for instance—are generously spread out at lunchtime by the pool; on a recent sailing, the Asian spread offered everything from sushi to satay, Vietnamese spring rolls, sweet and sour pork, and papaya salad. An extraspecial **gala buffet** is put on once per cruise in the lobby/atrium. No expense or effort is spared to produce elaborate food fests, with heaps of jumbo shrimp, homemade sushi, Greek salads, shish kebobs, beef satay, stir-fry dishes, gourmet cheeses, and cakes upon cakes.

While you can have breakfast in the Lido restaurant, the Bistro serves a late continental breakfast from 9:30 to 11:30am and is open between 11:30am and 6pm for complimentary grazing at a buffet-style spread of cheeses, cold cuts, fruit, cookies, and pastries. On a recent cruise, the exquisite Portuguese custard tarts were practically life changing. Nonalcoholic specialty drinks, such as hazelnut latte and fruit shakes, are complimentary here. On a recent *Symphony* cruise, the Bistro was hopping, and a real social hub and people-watching spot for officers and passengers.

For something casual poolside, the Trident Grill serves casual lunches daily between 11:30am and 6pm for those who'd like something simple and easy poolside (beef, chicken, and salmon burgers; wraps and tuna melts; pizza, hot dogs, and fries; fruit; and a special of the day). You can place your order at the counter and either sit down at the adjacent tables or head back to your deck chair and let a waiter bring you your lunch. You don't even have to change out of your bathing suit. It also operates several evenings per cruise between 6 and 9pm, offering an open-air ambience and serving dishes such as grilled shrimp, Cobb salad, and gourmet pizza.

SNACKS & EXTRAS   For **afternoon tea,** it's the chic Palm Court on one of the uppermost decks. A sprawling space with floor-to-ceiling windows and pale-blue and white furniture in leather and rattan, the area gives off a light, ethereal ambience. Predinner and midnight hot and cold canapés in the lounges include the likes of delicious foie gras, caviar, and marinated salmon.

There is, of course, **24-hour room service,** as well as complimentary unlimited nonalcoholic drinks everywhere aboard, from cappuccino to soda and bottled water.

ACTIVITIES

Crystal offers an interesting selection of activities, most of which are part of the ships' Creative Learning Institute. The extensive program features an array of expert speakers, plus alliances with well-known organizations, schools, and brands—Yamaha,

Berlitz, Barnes&Noble.com, The Cleveland Clinic, and the Tai Chi Cultural Center, to name a few—to provide an even greater oomph to the classes. You can count on several **enrichment lectures** throughout each cruise, such as a historian presenting a slide show and speaking about the Panama Canal and how it was built, a former ambassador speaking about regional politics, or a scientist talking about conservation. On a recent cruise, excellent speakers included people such as Bill Toone, a conservation biologist based at the San Diego Zoo and the professorial Dr. Jay Wolf, an author, historian, and commentator for *The History Channel.* Though most speakers are not celebrities, well-known personalities do occasionally show up. Recent guests have included political commentators James Carville and Mary Matalin, songwriter Neil Sedaka, business consultant Ken Blanchard, former press secretary Marlin Fitzwater, medical expert Dr. Art Ulene, biographer Chris Ogden, and publisher Steve Forbes.

In addition to each cruise's guest lecturers, some of Crystal's sailings feature **theme programs** with activities built around them. More than a dozen annual Wine & Food Festival cruises feature a respected wine expert who conducts at least two complimentary tastings, plus guest chefs conducting cooking demonstrations for guests and then presenting the results of those lessons at dinner. There are also music-theme cruises from time to time, featuring big bands, ballroom dance, jazz singers, and film and theater. Other cruises have experts conducting seminars on finance issues, language, and art appreciation, the latter with speakers from the famous auction house Sotheby's.

Guest teachers teach swing, rumba, and merengue dance lessons on some cruises. Group lessons are complimentary, and private lessons can sometimes be arranged with the instructors for about $50 per hour per couple. Other activities include bridge and paddle-tennis competitions, game-show-style contests, trivia games, midafternoon dance music with the resident dance trio or quartet, interesting arts and crafts such as glass etching, and even guest fashion shows. Commonly, a **golf expert** sails on board, too, conducting complimentary group golf lessons by the driving nets several times per cruise (again, private lessons can be arranged; prices start at $50 per hr.). A variety of free aerobics classes is also offered in the fitness center, including Pilates and yoga (private personal trainers are available for a fee).

The line's **Computer University @ Sea** offers some complimentary courses on all cruises, covering topics such as basic computing, understanding the Internet, website design, and creating spreadsheets using Excel. Private lessons are also available for $50 an hour. Internet centers have about 30 workstations apiece, featuring Dell PCs, though oddly enough, you must buy Internet time in 2-hour $50 installments—not convenient if you just need a few minutes to do some emailing toward the end of the cruise. There are now Wi-Fi hot spots for passengers who want to work on their own laptops, and onboard cellphone service via a satellite link, at prices in the same range as your provider's regular roaming charges.

CHILDREN'S PROGRAM

Crystal is a sophisticated cruise line that focuses its attention on adults, but more than any other line in the luxury end of the market, it also does its part to cater to the little people. Each ship has a bright **children's playroom,** primarily used during holiday and summer cruises (mostly in Europe), when some 100 kids may be aboard. Both ships also have another room with PlayStations, computers, and arcade machines for older kids and teens, with counselors on hand to supervise activities such as scavenger hunts, arts and crafts, karaoke, and games that take place during several hours in the morning and in the afternoon, for three age groups between 3 and 17. There are kiddy

Crystal Fleet Itineraries

Ship	Sailing Regions	Home Ports
Crystal Serenity	7- to 12-night voyages in the Mediterranean/ Adriatic/Greek Isles (various combinations), Northern Europe, the Black Sea, and Turkey/ Egypt	Southampton/London, Civitavecchia/Rome, Venice, Piraeus/Athens, Barcelona, Monte Carlo, Lisbon, Istanbul
Crystal Symphony	7- to 14-night voyages in the Mediterranean, Northern Europe/Russia, and the British Isles	Piraeus/Athens, Dover/London, Civitavecchia/Rome, Stockholm, Copenhagen

books and videos in the library for guests to take back to their staterooms, and a children's menu in the main dining room, as well as kid favorites at the poolside Trident Grill.

For children as young as 6 months, **in-cabin babysitting** can be arranged privately through the concierge at an hourly rate of $7.50 for one child, $10 for two kids, and $12.50 for three kids. Cribs, highchairs, and booster seats are available, and if you notify the line ahead of time, they'll special-order jars of baby food for you, at no charge. Or the chef will puree organic food for your baby. Note that children 11 and under pay 50% of the lowest adult fare when accompanied by two full-fare guests.

The minimum age for sailing is 6 months.

ENTERTAINMENT

Onboard entertainment is decent (and plentiful), but it's certainly not the high point of the cruise. Shows in the horseshoe-shaped, rather plain Galaxy Lounge encompass everything from classical concertos by accomplished pianists to comedy, to tired Broadway-style medleys and ventriloquist and magic acts. The bright spot on a recent cruise was an excellent four-man roving a cappella group. From time to time there's a featured celebrity entertainer aboard, such as the Tommy Dorsey Orchestra, Maureen McGovern, Tommy Tune, or Marvin Hamlisch.

After dinner each night, a second large, attractive lounge is the venue for **ballroom-style dancing** to a live band, with a clutch of gentleman hosts aboard each sailing to provide dance (and dinner) partners for single ladies. Both ships have roomy **casinos** and rooms for dancing, in either *Serenity*'s dedicated disco or *Symphony*'s Starlight lounge, where on a recent cruise, karaoke was offered twice and the little space was packed. A pianist in the dark, paneled, and romantic Avenue Saloon—our favorite room on board—plays standards, show tunes, and pop hits before and after dinner. On both ships you can also enjoy cigars (from Monte Cristo to Davidoff) in the Connoisseurs Club, recent-release movies several times a day in the theater (which also serves as a venue for lectures and religious services), and a varied and full menu of movies on the in-cabin TVs.

SERVICE

The hallmark of a high-end cruise such as Crystal is its service, so the line's staff is better trained and more attentive than that aboard most other cruise lines. Dining room and restaurant staffs hail from Italy, Portugal, and other European countries, and have trained in the grand restaurants of Europe and North America, while the stewardess who tidies your stateroom is likely to be from Scandinavia, Hungary, or elsewhere in the E.U. Everyone, from the dining/bar staff to those staffing the information and concierge desks in the lobby, is endlessly good-natured and very helpful. Guests in Penthouse Suites are treated to the services of male butlers. As far as tipping goes, most passengers charge gratuities to their onboard accounts, though you can pay in cash if you wish.

All guests get complimentary unlimited nonalcoholic drinks everywhere aboard, from cappuccino to soda and bottled water.

In addition to laundry and dry-cleaning services, complimentary **self-serve laundry rooms** are available.

Crystal Serenity

The Verdict

Crystal Serenity is Crystal's best ship yet, offering an ultra-elegant cruise with a huge array of onboard choices, from dining to activities and public spaces.

Crystal Serenity *(photo: Crystal Cruises)*

Specifications

Size (in Tons)	68,000	Crew	655
Passengers (Double Occ.)	1,080	Passenger/Crew Ratio	1.6 to 1
Passenger/Space Ratio	63	Year Launched	2003
Total Cabins/Veranda Cabins	540/460	Last Refurbishment/Upgrade	N/A

Frommer's Ratings (Scale of 1–5)   ★★★★ ½

Cabin Comfort & Amenities	4.5	Dining Options	5
Appearance & Upkeep	5	Gym, Spa & Sports Facilities	5
Public Comfort/Space	4.5	Children's Facilities	3.5
Decor	4	Enjoyment Factor	5

The largest truly ultraluxe vessel afloat, *Serenity* is 38% bigger than the older *Symphony* but carries only 15% more guests. It's one of the most spacious ships out there, from the beautifully designed public rooms to an expansive pool deck. There's simply no crowding at any time. In every way, this ship's a star.

Cabins & Rates

Cabins	Per Diem From	Sq. Ft.	Fridge	Hair Dryer	Sitting Area	TV
Outside	$389	226	Yes	Yes	Yes	Yes
Suite	$1020	403–1,345*	Yes	Yes	Yes	Yes

* Including veranda

CABINS   Standard staterooms on this ship are about the same size as those on *Symphony,* though the bathrooms and balconies are larger. The majority of standard cabins (categories A and B) are 226 square feet, not including balconies; cabin size is not Crystal's strong suit when compared to the line's luxury peers. There are 100 suites in three different categories, with the largest running 1,345 square feet.

Most of the standard cabins, called Deluxe Staterooms, have a veranda, while 80 rooms have a large picture window. All feature a seating area, complimentary soft drinks and water, TV and DVD, small refrigerator, computer dataport, Egyptian cotton sheets and feather bed toppers, and a pillow menu. Choose from "regular" king- and standard-size pillows or four specialty options, which include round, foam-filled neck pillows for neck or lumbar support. Besides all of this, Penthouse Staterooms toss in butler service and complimentary beer, while the Penthouse Suites also throw in complimentary liquor and wine setup upon embarkation, a flatscreen TV, a separate bedroom area with a vanity, a Jacuzzi tub, a bidet, and a walk-in closet. If you're going straight to the top, the ship's Crystal Penthouses are incredibly spacious abodes, with a separate living room, a dining area, a CD player, three TVs (one in the bathroom, if that floats your boat!), a cordless phone, a library, a pantry, and, believe it or not, a small gym.

Decor-wise, wood accents and furniture in the staterooms are on the medium to dark side, creating an elegant atmosphere offsetting the more colorful curtains, wall coverings, upholstery, and bedcovers. The feel is soothing. As aboard *Symphony*, the bathrooms are nicely laid out but still on the small side for a ship of such a high quality. You'll find plenty of drawer and closet space for a cruise of up to about 2 weeks.

Only a handful of cabins have a third berth available, and none offers four berths. Eight rooms are designated as wheelchair accessible.

PUBLIC AREAS   Public rooms on the *Serenity* are all so appealing that it's difficult to pick a favorite. The ship has a quiet, elegant atmosphere throughout, so much so that you won't even find glitz in the casino. Color schemes throughout are muted and calming, with lots of blues, greens, reds, golds, and grays. As aboard *Symphony*, one of the most popular lounges is dark and cozy Avenue Saloon, with its wonderful round bar and plenty of table seating. The two show lounges, Galaxy Lounge and Stardust Club, offer great sightlines and comfy seating, both theater- and table-style.

The ship has a good library that's well stocked with books, DVDs, and CDs that can be checked out only when the librarian is on duty. Two large rooms are dedicated to the line's learning programs: one for computer instruction and the other for classes offered in partnership with well-known institutions, such as piano instruction by Yamaha, language immersion by Berlitz, art classes conducted by the Parsons School of Design, and wellness programs run by the Cleveland Clinic and the Tai Chi Cultural Center.

DINING OPTIONS   Fine dining has been a trademark of Crystal's since the line began sailing in 1990, and the *Serenity* carries on the tradition with its two impressive alternative open-seating specialty restaurants, both of which require reservations (and a suggested $7 cover charge). In Prego, the surroundings really make you feel you're in a fine Italian restaurant ashore, with meat, pasta, and fish dishes offered a la carte or through a tasting menu with items selected by Piero Selvaggio, proprietor of the Valentino restaurants in Santa Monica and Las Vegas. On the Asian side of things, famed chef Nobu Matsuhisa oversees the menus in Silk Road, an ultrastylish space designed in a sea of ethereal mints and whites, with seating available at tables or at the sushi bar. Just forward of Silk Road, the Vintage Room is an intimate boardroom-style wine cellar that hosts special wine- and champagne-themed dinners and other events. In the ship's formal restaurant, the Crystal Dining Room, there are two seatings each evening at assigned tables. The lovely decor is a rich blend of dark woods with blue and mauve chairs. The latest dining option on board is Tastes, a casual venue serving breakfast, lunch, and dinner under a retractable roof near the Neptune Pool. It has a completely separate menu from the other dining areas and is a great dinner alternative when you don't feel like dressing up.

Other dining outlets include the Bistro Café, open for a variety of snacks and beverages all day long; the poolside Trident Grill; and the Lido Café, which serves buffet-style breakfast and lunch, with some made-to-order specialties such as omelets and pastas.

The 24-hour room-service menu is quite extensive. During dining hours, guests can also order from the Crystal Dining Room menu for in-cabin delivery.

POOL, FITNESS, SPA & SPORTS FACILITIES   There are two reasonably sized pools, one of which features a sliding glass roof. Indoors, the Crystal Spa was designed according to feng shui principles, putting you right into relaxation mode. The complex includes a quiet room with very comfortable seating and great aft-facing views for those relaxing moments before or after a spa treatment. The changing rooms are stocked with lotions, shampoos, hair dryers, clocks, and bottles of water, while the steam rooms boast large picture windows for great views while you roast. A wide range of treatments includes a handful geared to men, such as a pro-collagen shave, frangipani hair conditioning, and aroma stone therapy massage. There's also a spacious beauty salon and a gym with separate weight room, an aerobics studio, two full-size paddle-tennis courts, table tennis, golf driving nets, and a putting green.

Crystal Symphony

The Verdict

A gracious, floating pleasure palace, small enough to feel intimate and personal, yet large enough for a whole range of entertainment, dining, and fitness diversions.

Crystal Symphony *(photo: Crystal Cruises)*

Specifications

Size (in Tons)	51,044	Crew	545
Passengers (Double Occ.)	940	Passenger/Crew Ratio	1.7 to 1
Passenger/Space Ratio	54.3	Year Launched	1995
Total Cabins/Veranda Cabins	480/276	Last Refurbishment/Upgrade	2006

Frommer's Ratings (Scale of 1–5)   ★★★★ ½

Cabin Comfort & Amenities	4	Dining Options	5
Appearance & Upkeep	4	Gym, Spa & Sports Facilities	5
Public Comfort/Space	4.5	Children's Facilities	3
Decor	4	Enjoyment Factor	5

Plush, streamlined, extravagantly spacious, and pleasingly midsize, *Symphony* competes with the high-end Silversea, Regent, and Seabourn vessels, although she's almost five times as large as Seabourn's, with a broader choice of onboard diversions. In late 2006 she had a major overhaul, to the tune of $23 million, resulting in a more contemporary look—goodbye brass, chrome, and prissy pastels! Cabins and bathrooms were refurbished, along with entertainment lounges, the casino, boutiques, and more.

Cabins & Rates

Cabins	Per Diem From	Sq. Ft.	Fridge	Hair Dryer	Sitting Area	TV
Outside	$502	198–215	Yes	Yes	Yes	Yes
Suite	$1129	287–782	Yes	Yes	Yes	Yes

CABINS Though the majority of *Symphony*'s cabins are smaller than those aboard competing luxe lines Silversea, Regent, and Seabourn, they're still quite comfortable and were completely redone in late 2006. Cabins, which start at 198 square feet (plus 48-sq.-ft. verandas on many), now all feature stylish touches such as Murano glass bedside lamps, Rubelli fabrics, and leather headboards. Each has a 20-inch LCD flatscreen TV, VCR, LED reading lights, sitting area, stocked minibar (snacks and alcoholic beverages consumed are charged to your onboard account except in the Penthouse Suites on Deck 10, where they're complimentary), hair dryer, and safe. Bathrooms, which have both shower and bathtub (a short little one in the lower category cabins), were hugely improved and now have a pair of oval glass sinks atop granite countertops. Egyptian cotton sheets, feather bed toppers, and a pillow menu make sleeping a dream, though when it comes to closets, they're smaller and tighter than you'd expect on ships of this caliber.

Deck 10 holds the ship's spectacular, attractively styled penthouses, the best of which measure more than 750 square feet, plus nearly 200-square-foot balconies, with full-fledged oceanview Jacuzzis in their living rooms, dark-wood furniture, and sofas upholstered in silk and satin, plus Oriental rugs and entertainment centers with 35-inch flatscreen TVs, and DVD and CD players. They also enjoy the services of a doting butler in addition to two stewardesses. The other two categories are about 287 and 396 square feet, plus 72- to 98-square-foot balconies.

Cabins without verandas have large rectangular windows. The category E cabins located amidships on decks 7 and 8 have views obstructed by lifeboats. There are no inside cabins.

Five cabins are wheelchair accessible.

PUBLIC AREAS Throughout the ship you'll find marble, glass, and hardwood paneling mingling with flowers and potted plants. The ship's recent face-lift has given the ship an even more open feel on the main entertainment deck, 6. The three large shops are among the most elegant at sea and really are styled like ritzy Fifth Avenue or Rodeo Drive boutiques. The adjacent Bistro coffee and snack cafe is open to the atrium and is the place to see and be seen; it's the ship's social heart. Have an herbal tea, an ice coffee, or a decaf whatever; there's a lot of choice and the place is hopping. The egg custards at breakfast are to die for.

Aside from the several bar/entertainment lounges, a roaming staff wanders the public areas throughout the day and much of the night, offering to bring drinks to wherever you happen to be sitting. The dark Avenue Saloon, where polished mahogany, well-maintained leather upholstery, and a live pianist draw passengers in, is one of the prime before- and after-dinner cocktail spots and our personal favorite, by far. There are also two large entertainment lounges, including a completely re-created venue called the Starlite Club that's used for lectures by day and dancing by night (though, if there for a lecture, avoid seating in the back of the room, as the noise from passersby looking at mug shots in the adjacent photo gallery is a distraction). The hub has a round bar and walls of sparkling Swarovski crystals. You'll find a large theater for movies and slide lectures, and a hushed library outfitted with comfortably upholstered chairs and a worthy collection of books, periodicals, and videos. The revamped Casino now features a dramatic black and silver color scheme, while next door a new nightclub, called Luxe, attracts attention with its polished aluminum Phillipe Stark bar stools and glass Bizzaza mosaics. The cozy little spot is the venue for karaoke a couple of times per cruise.

If learning is more your speed, there is a 25-seat classroom and an adjacent Internet center, both with brand-new Dell computers. The attractive Connoisseur's Club cigar lounge (Monte Cristo, anyone?) features wood tones and dark leather furniture.

For young kids, *Symphony* has a cute playroom with a tiered movie-viewing nook; for teens there's a teen center/video arcade.

DINING OPTIONS   Designed with curved walls and low, vaulted ceilings, the ship's main dining room is elegant and spacious, with dark wall paneling. Tables are not too close together, and there are well over 20 tables for two, mostly along the side or near the oceanview windows.

The ship's two themed, reservations-only alternative restaurants—the Italian Prego and the Pan-Asian Jade Garden—are right up there with the best at sea, though on a recent cruise Heidi rated Prego better than Jade. The Vintage Room, an intimate boardroom-style wine cellar, was added during the ship's 2004 refit to host special wine and champagne theme dinners and other events.

A casual indoor/outdoor buffet restaurant is open for breakfast and lunch, and the poolside Trident Grill serves ultracasual lunch as well as dinners several evenings per cruise. The newly redecorated Bistro Café is going for an earthy European ambience and it's open from 9:30am to 6pm for continental breakfast, snacks, specialty coffees, and more.

POOL, FITNESS, SPA & SPORTS FACILITIES   *Symphony* offers a lot of outdoor activities and spacious areas in which to do them. There are two outdoor swimming pools separated by a bar, ice cream counter, and sandwich grill, as well as two hot tubs. One of the pools is refreshingly oversize, stretching almost 40 feet across one of the sun decks; the other can be covered with a retractable glass roof. The gym and aerobics area are positioned for ocean views, with space for the line's complimentary yoga, Pilates, and aerobics classes (and personal training sessions too, for a fee). The Steiner-managed spa and beauty salon is accessorized with a quiet ocean-view waiting room to create an atmosphere of peace and relaxation. On deck, there's a pair of golf driving nets, a putting green, a large paddle-tennis court, Ping-Pong tables, and a broad, uninterrupted teak Promenade Deck for walkers and joggers. The ship's gorgeous and generous tiered afterdecks provide quiet places for an afternoon spent dozing in a deck chair.

2 Cunard

24303 Town Center Dr., Suite 200, Valencia, CA 91355-0908. 📞 800/7-CUNARD. www.cunard.com.

THE LINE IN A NUTSHELL   The most venerable line in the cruise industry, Cunard is a classic, offering a link to the golden age of passenger ships.

THE EXPERIENCE   The Cunard of today is not the Cunard of yesterday, but then again, it is. Formed in 1840 by Sir Samuel Cunard, the line provided the first regular steamship service between Europe and North America, and was one of the dominant players during the great years of steamship travel, which lasted roughly from 1905 to the mid-1960s. In 1969, long after it was clear that jet travel had replaced the liners, the company made what some considered a foolhardy move, launching *Queen Elizabeth 2* and setting her on a mixed schedule, half crossing, half cruising. Through sheer persistence, the ship proved the critics wrong, and even today, she is still going strong, even if the company has endured some rough times.

Today *QE2* is about to be retired from the Cunard fleet, having already relinquished her transatlantic routes to the massive *Queen Mary 2*, the first true ocean liner built in more than 30 years. The 148,528-ton *QM2* is as modern as passenger ships get, and was bigger than them all until Royal Caribbean's 160,000-ton *Freedom of the Seas* came along (though *QM2* remains the *longest* passenger ship by 20 ft.). But she's also an homage to all that went before, designed with oversize grandeur, old-world formality, and even a dose of blatant class structure: Some restaurants and outdoor decks are set aside specifically for suite guests only, if you please. Her smaller sibling, the 90,000-ton, 1,990-passenger *Queen Victoria*, debuted in December 2007.

Pros

- **Classic ambience:** Despite a few chintzy touches, both ships really do live up to their billing, with some rooms (especially on *QM2*) that could have come right out of a 1940s liner.
- **S-p-a-c-e:** *QM2* is absolutely enormous, from her hangar-size ballroom to the cavernously high ceilings of many public areas.
- **Pure prestige:** There used to be ships that everyone in the world knew—"Oh, you're sailing on the *Queen Mary*," they'd say. "That's the ship Marlene Dietrich took on her last crossing." *QM2* is the only ship launched in more than a quarter century with that kind of broad public cachet.

Cons

- **Not *quite* luxe:** Despite their grandeur, *QM2* and *QV* carry too many passengers to provide the kind of intimacy and personal feel you get on the other luxe lines— especially smallish ships such as those of Silversea, SeaDream, and Seabourn, but also relatively large vessels such as *Crystal Serenity* and Regent's *Seven Seas Mariner.*
- **Occasional off notes:** On *QM2*, if you're going to design a huge corridor of showy Art Deco wall panels, don't make those panels out of plastic. And what's with the jarring white pillars in the atrium and the virtual market of cheap trinkets set up some afternoons in the main passageway? On *QV,* plain paper towels in the Grill Class public bathrooms are not a fitting substitute for cloth ones.

Compared with the other ultraluxury lines, here's how Cunard rates:

	Poor	Fair	Good	Excellent	Outstanding
Enjoyment Factor					✓
Dining			✓		
Activities					✓
Children's Program					✓
Entertainment				✓	
Service				✓	
Worth the Money					✓

CUNARD: GETTING THERE IS HALF THE FUN

Once upon a time, Cunard ruled the waves. Its ships—first *Mauretania* and *Lusitania,* later *Queen Mary* and *Queen Elizabeth*—were the fastest and most reliable at sea. Then somebody invented the jet airliner and the whole passenger-shipping business went to hell. Numbers dropped. Ships went cruising for their bread. Cunard stuck to its guns, though, keeping *QE2* on the Atlantic until sheer doggedness gave it a certain cachet as the last of the old breed. Fleetmates came and went, including the little *Sea Goddess* yachts (now with SeaDream) and a number of midsize ships acquired from other lines, but *QE2* soldiered on and managed to carry the company, and its reputation, through some rough times.

An almost 3-decade-long period of corporate troubles and shuffling ownership ended in April 1998, when Carnival Corporation acquired Cunard from the Norwegian company Kvaerner Group. To some it seemed a comedown for the venerable line, but Commodore Ronald Warwick and other Cunard employees saw it as an unqualified boon. "To my mind," Warwick told a group of journalists, "Carnival Corporation were the white knights that saved us from demise, and when the planning of the *Queen Mary 2* was announced, I experienced a feeling of pleasure and relief. They'd delivered a message to the world and to those of us on the 'shop floor' that they were determined to build on the maritime heritage for which our company has been famous."

Today Cunard is again very famous indeed after all the media attention that accompanied *QM2*'s launch, but it's hardly the old British brand that its advertising might lead you to believe. In late 2004, for instance, the company was swallowed whole by Carnival Corp. subsidiary Princess Cruises. Its operations and staff were absorbed into Princess's at the latter's suburban Los Angeles headquarters, which meant crew members and officers would be rotated between the two lines—a move considered blasphemous by many hard-core Cunard fans (but frankly, something that the average passenger won't realize or mind if they do). It remains to be seen whether Cunard will maintain an independent identity under the Princess umbrella or, like Celebrity Cruises when it was swallowed by Royal Caribbean in 1997, enter a period of identity crisis and uncertain market image.

With *QE2,* the ship that kept Cunard alive for 3 decades, retiring in November 2008 (off to spend the rest of eternity serving as a hotel, retail, and entertainment destination at the **Palm Jumeirah** resort in Dubai), the fleet will be *QM2* and *QV* until a third new queen—the 2,092-passenger *Queen Elizabeth*—sails her first itineraries in autumn 2010.

PASSENGER PROFILE

In general, Cunard attracts a well-traveled crowd of passengers mostly in their 50s and up, many of them repeaters who appreciate the line's old-timey virtues and are more the 4-o'clock-tea crowd than the hot-tub-and-umbrella-drink set. *QM2* attracts a much wider demographic, especially on summer Atlantic crossings when families travel together and maybe about 50% of passengers might be from the U.S. British passengers make up the next largest percentage, and usually several hundred passengers hail from various other nations, making Cunard one of the few truly international cruises. *Queen Victoria* is also being marketed to a dual audience of North Americans and Brits.

DINING

TRADITIONAL   Cunard is the last bastion of the old steamship tradition of segregating passengers according to class, though for the most part the practice is limited to dining hours. What this means is that passengers are assigned to one of the three reserved-seating restaurants according to the level of cabin accommodation they've booked: Suite and Penthouse passengers dine in the **Queen's Grill** or **Princess Grill;** everyone else dines in the multi-deck **Britannia Restaurant.** The two Grills are always single seating at an assigned table, while the Britannia has early and late seatings for dinner and open seating for breakfast and lunch. On *QM2,* an intimate section of the Britannia Restaurant called the Britannia Club is set aside for passengers who are booked in the deluxe balcony cabins. Those dining here enjoy single-seating dining, more table-side preparation, and enhanced menu options, while avoiding the significantly higher fares that come with Grill accommodations.

Cuisine sticks close to tradition, with nighttime entrees that might include pheasant with southern haggis and port-wine sauce, roasted prime rib, grilled lobster with garden pea risotto, and scallion wild-rice crepes with mushroom filling and red-pepper sauce. The Grill restaurants also offer the option of requesting whatever dish comes into your head—if they have the ingredients aboard, someone in the galley will whip it up for you (caviar is available on request). Otherwise, it's the intimacy and cachet of the Grill restaurants that sets them apart more than the food does, as many of the same dishes are offered in the Britannia as well. At all three restaurants, **special diets** can be accommodated, and vegetarian and health-conscious spa dishes are available as a matter of course.

SPECIALTY Aboard both ships, the **Todd English restaurant** (created by celebrity chef Todd English) serves lunches ($20 per person) and dinners ($30 per person) that range from deceptively simple to extremely rich, followed by some truly amazing desserts. Heidi's Todd English meal was the culinary highlight of her recent *QM2* crossing.

On *QM2,* adjacent to the King's Court, the contemporary **Chef's Galley** serves only two dozen guests (no cover charge), who get to watch the chef prepare their meal via an open galley and several large monitor screens. Just don't expect to be dazzled by the decor—it's minimalist.

CASUAL Almost a third of *QM2*'s Deck 7 is given over to the **King's Court,** a large buffet restaurant that stretches out for nearly half a deck along both sides of the ship. The somewhat overwhelming cluster of food stations, which some passengers find quite frustrating to navigate, runs down the center of the area, with many small, cozy areas along the sides; there is no outdoor seating. At night, the space is partitioned off into three separate casual restaurants: **The Carvery,** serving carved beef, pork, lamb, and poultry, along with gourmet English favorites; **La Piazza,** serving pizza, pasta, and other Italian specialties 24 hours; and **Lotus,** a Pan-Asian restaurant blending Chinese, Japanese, Thai, and Indian influences. All are free, but reservations are recommended at dinner. On *Queen Victoria,* the casual restaurant is more of a traditional buffet set-up, with some items prepared to order. It's open 24-hours, with less-than-usual formality for dinner.

SNACKS & EXTRAS On both ships, the Golden Lion Pub serves English pub grub, while waaaaay up on *QM2*'s Deck 12 you can get standard burgers and dogs at the outdoor Boardwalk Café, weather permitting. Traditional **afternoon tea,** usually accompanied by a string quartet, is served in the Queen's Room, the ship's most classic, traditional space. The selection of some 23 teas includes Darjeeling, Jasmine, and Japanese Green Tea. The elegant room harks back to the dramatic ballrooms of

Cunard Fleet Itineraries

Ship	Sailing Regions	Home Ports
Queen Mary 2	6-night transatlantic and 11- and 12-night Mediterranean	Southampton/London (plus New York for eastbound transatlantics)
Queen Victoria	4- to 14-night voyages in the Mediterranean/ Aegean/Greek Isles (various combinations), Northern Europe/Russia, the Norwegian Fjords/North Cape, the Black Sea, and Egypt/Turkey	Southampton/London, Venice, Civitavecchia/Rome, Piraeus/Athens

yesteryear, with a high arched ceiling and crystal chandeliers. **Room service** is available 24 hours a day.

ACTIVITIES

As you would expect, Cunard offers a more distinguished variety of activities than most other big ships, especially their "Fun Ship" Carnival cousins. Rather than woo-hoo good times, Cunard concentrates on learning experiences and the arts, with a healthy dollop of pampering and some of the cruise staples to keep things light.

Central to the onboard experience is the lecture program, where instructors, celebrities, and other learned authors and superaccomplished authorities present talks on literature, political history, marine science, ocean-liner history, music and culture of the 1960s, modern art, Shakespeare on film, architectural history, cooking, computer applications, languages, and many other topics. On crossings, there are so many worthwhile lectures you may find yourself sitting in the theatre all morning.

Passengers who prefer book learning can take advantage of one of the largest and by the far the most impressive **libraries** at sea, beautifully designed spaces that actually look like libraries, rather than the typical rooms-with-a-few-bookshelves you find on most megaships. On *QM2*, a nearby **bookshop** sells volumes on passenger-ship history, as well as Cunard memorabilia. Other shops on both ships sell everything from high-end Hermès to low-end souvenirs and jewelry.

Spas on both ships are classy spaces with a huge range of treatment options. *QM2* boasts the only spa at sea run by Arizona's Canyon Ranch spa. It's a gorgeous, relaxing space that combines nautical undertones with a modern minimalist motif, and offers a thermal suite, a beauty salon with wonderful ocean views, and more than 20 treatment rooms clustered around a coed thalassotherapy pool and hot tub reserved for spa-goers. *Queen Victoria's* Royal Spa and Fitness Centre offers so many treatments it takes a 40-page guide to list them all. Aside from all these interesting options, you'll find a number of less-cerebral pursuits as well, from wine tasting to art auctions to scarf-tying seminars.

CHILDREN'S PROGRAM

On today's Cunard ships, finger paints and cartoons are just as much a part of the offerings as ballroom dancing and quoits. Both ships accept kids as young as 1, an extraordinarily young minimum age shared only by Disney's ships. (Most ships with kids' programming welcome kids 3 and up, a few ages 2 and up.) Though both ships offer indoor and outdoor kids' facilities, the blue ribbon definitely goes to those aboard *QM2*, which are some of the best aboard any ship today.

At *QM2's* kids' complex, called The Zone, facilities are divided by age. The 1-to-6 set occupies half of a bright, cheery, and roomy area with lots of toys; arts and crafts; a play gym and ball pit; and big-screen TVs (and the staff do change diapers). There's also a separate **nursery** with 10 crib/toddler-bed combos for napping tots (no other line has a separate room for sleepers). Bring a stroller if your kids are young: Remember, this is the longest passenger ship in the world, so getting from one end of a deck to the other is a hike.

Just beyond the oceanview space is a play gym outside on the stern of Deck 6, along with a wading pool, a regular pool, and a water-spray fountain for kids (of all ages) to run through. Officially it's called the "family deck," though anyone who doesn't mind screeching children can lounge there. The other half of the play area is reserved for kids 7 to 17, with the 7-to-12 crowd usually occupying a play area with beanbag chairs, lots of board games, TVs, and a number of Xbox video-game systems. Activities for teens—including ship tours, movies and production shows in the theaters, and pizza parties—are usually held elsewhere.

The best part? Aside from 2 hours at lunchtime and an hour or two in the afternoon, The Zone offers complimentary supervised activities and care from about 9am to midnight, so you can dine with the adults and know that your offspring are being well cared for (on other lines, you must generally pay an hourly fee after 10pm). You can take your kids to eat earlier in the ships' buffet restaurant in a special section of the restaurant that's reserved for a **children's tea** daily from 5 to 6pm (of course, it's not really tea that's served, but the standard kiddy favorites of pasta, chicken fingers, and the like).

Though *QM2's* kids program is awesome, there are rarely more than 250 kids aboard and usually fewer (compared to the 800–1,200 kids and teens typically aboard similar-size ships). This is a plus: Fewer kids means more attention and space for the ones who are there. Keep in mind, though, if a sailing is particularly full, the counselors reserve the right to limit participation and will ask parents to choose either the morning or the afternoon session; everyone can be accommodated in the evenings. In contrast, other major lines have "don't turn away" policies, so you're guaranteed that your child will be accommodated, even if the playrooms are jampacked because of it (as they usually are during the early evening hours).

Cunard's kids' program is staffed by several British nannies, who have completed a 2-year program in the discipline back in England, plus a handful of other activities counselors, many of whom have backgrounds as schoolteachers.

ENTERTAINMENT

Entertainment runs the gamut from plays featuring graduates of Britain's Royal Academy of Dramatic Arts (RADA) to the usual run-of-the-mill song-and-dance revues. Lounges feature a wide variety of live music, from harpists to jazz to disco to high-toned dance music (the latter, on *QM2,* presented in the gorgeous Queen's Ballroom). Both ships offer large casinos as well.

On *Queen Mary 2,* the onboard lecture program is so extensive it requires two theaters. As the secondary theater, Illuminations is smaller than the Royal Court Theater, but is probably the most used room on the ship. It serves triple duty as a lecture hall, a movie theater, and also the world's only oceangoing **planetarium,** showing 3-D films created in conjunction with noted institutions such as the American Museum of Natural History and the Smithsonian's National Air and Space Museum. Up on Deck 12, *QM2's* Boardwalk Café doubles at night as a venue for **outdoor movie screenings** when weather permits. See the ship review below for a discussion of *QM2*'s other theaters and lounges.

Hugely innovative on *Queen Victoria* is the Royal Court Theater with its upper level of seating that includes 16 private boxes. These are sold at a surcharge on nights when there are special performances. On other nights, they're first come, first served.

SERVICE

With their classy uniforms and cordial, gracious efficiency, Cunard's crew exhibits a polished sort of British demeanor—even when they're actually from the Philippines. That said, the sheer size of the vessels and large numbers of passengers mean the staff must do its share of rushing around and keeping up, as aboard all the other huge cruise ships today.

Tipping is handled automatically, with a charge of $13 per person, per day added to the onboard accounts of passengers occupying Grill staterooms and $11 per day added for all other cabin grades.

Queen Victoria

Queen Victoria *(photo: Cunard)*

The Verdict

The newest addition to the Cunard fleet, *Queen Victoria* is far more than a smaller version of the *QM2*. She's got her own style, personality, and decor while maintaining that legendary Cunard heritage.

Specifications

Size (in tons)	90,000	Crew	900
Passengers (double occ.)	1,990	Passenger/Crew Ratio	2.2 to 1
Passenger/Space Ratio	45	Year Launched	2008
Total Cabins/Veranda Cabins	1007/591	Last Major Refurbishment	N/A

Frommer's Ratings (Scale of 1–5)   ★★★★ ½

Cabin Comfort & Amenities	4	Dining Options	4
Ship Cleanliness & Maintenance	5	Gym, Spa & Sports Facilities	4.5
Public Comfort/Space	5	Children's Facilities	3
Décor	5	Enjoyment Factor	4.5

Queen Victoria is a sleek, modern ship that hasn't lost sight of her line's history, with many of Cunard's signature elements in place along with much that's new. Outside, her hull retains the line's traditional black-and-red livery, while inside there's a distinct British flavor along with elements of one of the few residual class structures left at sea today: the Grill restaurants (dedicated to suite passengers only, and with a centralized lounge for suite relaxation) and outside dining and sunning areas for Grill-class guests only.

Public rooms on *QV* are not as over-the-top grand as those aboard *QM2*, making the ship seem more cozy. There are also no marquee features such as *QM2*'s planetarium. Instead, *QV* looks and feels like a very modern, straightforward ocean liner. She's got quiet nooks for quiet moments and plenty of activities, from enrichment lectures to demonstrations, bridge, and bingo, to keep everyone occupied.

Originally planned as a vessel dedicated to the British market, *Queen Victoria* is now targeted to both a British and North American audience, and the U.S. dollar is the official currency on board.

At 90,000 gross tons, she's the second-largest Cunard ship ever.

Cabins & Rates

Cabins	Per Diems From	Sq. Ft.	Fridge	Hair Dryer	Sitting Area	TV
Inside	$199	152–207	yes	yes	yes	yes
Outside	$216	180–249*	yes	yes	yes	yes
Suite	$465	367–2097*	yes	yes	yes	yes

Including veranda.

CABINS   As might be expected on a ship that has a definite class structure about it, *QV* offers quite a range of accommodations: There are 20 different categories of inside and outside cabins alone (not including suites and penthouses) spread out over five decks. All are sleekly contemporary with some traditional touches, and come with a variety of amenities: interactive TV with multi-language films and music channels, refrigerator, safe, hair dryer, bathrobe, slippers, American and British electrical outlets, direct-dial telephone, and dataports, plus a half-bottle of sparkling wine upon embarkation. Outside cabins (with or without balcony) are pleasantly styled with light woods, a small seating area, a makeup/writing desk, ample closet space (though few drawers), and a bathroom with shower. Suites and penthouses come with upgraded linens, bathrobes, toiletries, a pillow menu, concierge service, shoe shine service, separate bath and shower, a larger sitting area, and a full bottle of sparkling wine upon embarkation. Higher up on the accommodations spectrum are the seven categories of Queen's Grill Suites and Penthouses, ranging from 536 to 2,097 square feet. A higher level of amenities includes complimentary canapés, fruit basket, bud vase, butler service, and sugar-iced strawberries to go along with your bottle of champagne upon embarkation. There's also priority embarkation and luggage delivery along with separate Grill check-in.

Twenty wheelchair-accessible cabins are spread out among various cabin categories.

PUBLIC AREAS   Public rooms are located on several decks. The three-deck atrium rises from Deck One, with light mahogany and marble furnishings. Deck Two includes the lower end of the extremely attractive Britannia restaurant (see "Dining"), as well as a series of bars all along one side of the ship: the nautically styled Chart Room, Café Carinthia, the Midships Lounge, the Champagne Bar, and the traditional Golden Lion Pub, which serves pub food during the day and offers piano entertainment nightly. It's located directly opposite the casino. The Queens Room offers a gorgeous 1,000-square-foot inlaid wood floor for dancing to a live orchestra

Deck Three is home to an extensive shopping area, plus the Cunardia Museum, the two-level library (with its two librarians and 6,000-book collection), and the upper entrance to the theater with its 15 private boxes and lounge area. There's a charge for the boxes during special performances, but during regular shows you just have to get to them first. While the sight lines to the stage are fine from all, the boxes more centrally located are by far the best, and make for a nice treat on a special evening.

The upper set of public decks runs from Decks 9 to 12 and includes the Winter Garden (a relaxing space full of rattan furniture, ceiling fans, a central fountain, and movable glass wall and sliding roof), the children's and teens' centers, the very lovely Commodore Club lounge (probably the best place for a relaxing evening drink or quiet time during the day), the cigar lounge, and the 270-degree view Hemispheres disco. Decks 11 and 12 comprise an exclusive area for Grill-Class guests only, with sunning/lounging areas and a Tuscan-themed courtyard. A sign at the stairwell (and the fact that elevator access is restricted) helps keep out . . . us.

DINING OPTIONS   All guests are assigned a table in one of three restaurants, depending on one's room category: the Queens or Princess Grills for Grill-level suite passengers and the gorgeous two-level Britannia Restaurant for all non-Grill guests. Britannia offers two seatings, while the Grills operate on a single-seating basis. Guests in the latter may also have the occasion to dine al fresco in the Tuscan-styled courtyard. The Britannia Restaurant is exceedingly spacious, offering plenty of room for the waitstaff to comfortably maneuver. Visually, there's little difference between the Grill classes (leather instead of fabric seats for the banquets, for instance).

Other dining outlets are available to all guests: the eponymously named and outstanding Todd English Restaurant ($20 per person for lunch, $30 for dinner); the Golden Lion Pub; the Lido Grill for casual pool-side fare; Café Carinthia on Deck 2, which serves coffees and pastries in the morning; and the 24-hour Lido Café, open for dinner and late-night buffets in addition to lunch and breakfast.

POOL, FITNESS, SPA & SPORTS FACILITIES   Pools and whirlpools are located both midships and at the aft end of Deck 9. The forward portion of Deck 9 is dedicated to the Royal Spa and Fitness Centre, a relaxing space that offers so many treatments it takes a 40-page book to describe them all: facials, oxygen treatments, standard massages and scrubs, weird massages (such as the "aromasoul" massage), the regular run of nail and hair services, something described as "Kerastase stylespa" (the Kerastase ambassador is apparently a highly educated scalp and hair professional), and much more. This is indulgence of the highest order, with prices to match. In the gym, there are 15 treadmills and dozens of other weight and aerobics machines, plus plenty of free weights. There's also a lovely room with a hydropool that offers a saunalike feel. In addition, guests can stay fit by walking and jogging on several different decks, playing paddle tennis or quoits (that quintessentially British game), practicing their golf swing, and more.

Queen Mary 2

The Verdict

Faster than a speeding bullet, more powerful than a locomotive, *QM2* is literally in a class by herself: a modern reinterpretation of the golden age luxury liner, bigger than anything that's gone before and built to sail hard seas well into the 21st century.

Queen Mary 2 *(photo: Cunard)*

Specifications

Size (in Tons)	148, 528	Crew	1,253
Passengers (Double Occ.)	2,592	Passenger/Crew Ratio	2.1 to 1
Passenger/Space Ratio	57.8	Year Launched	2003
Total Cabins/Veranda Cabins	1,296/783	Last Major Refurbishment	2005

Frommer's Ratings (Scale of 1–5)   ★★★★★

Cabin Comfort & Amenities	5	Dining Options	4.5
Ship Cleanliness & Maintenance	5	Gym, Spa & Sports Facilities	4.5
Public Comfort/Space	5	Children's Facilities	5
Decor	4.5	Enjoyment Factor	5

Before her launch, we often heard *QM2* referred to by industry types as "Micky's White Elephant"—Micky being Micky Arison, chairman of Carnival Corporation, the criticism referring to the fact that *QM2*'s design and construction sucked up about a billion dollars and 5 years of labor, a record expenditure to match her record-breaking size.

But that was before her launch. That was before the Queen of England did the honors at her naming ceremony. That was before the fireworks and traffic jams that attended her first arrival into every port and, amazingly enough, still continue to this day in many ports. And it was definitely before the media glommed onto her as the first really newsworthy ship to be launched since . . . well, since *QE2*, probably. And when you control about half the cruise industry, as Carnival Corp. does, that kind of publicity is priceless.

When all is said and done, *QM2* deserves all the hype. She's a really remarkable ship: classic yet contemporary, refined yet fun, huge yet homey, and grand, grand, grand. The longest passenger ship at sea (when Royal Caribbean's *Freedom of the Seas* was launched in spring 2006, it snatched the title as biggest in terms of tonnage), she's also the only real ocean liner built since her older sister hit the water in 1969—and that, perhaps, needs some explanation. What is it exactly that makes an ocean liner different?

In a word, "more"—of everything. "We had a working definition that built on the idea of 'enhancement,'" Stephen Payne, *QM2*'s designer, told us just before the ship debuted. "The ship had to have enhanced strength and sea-keeping characteristics to withstand continuous exposure to North Atlantic conditions, enhanced speed to maintain her schedule [because, unlike a cruise ship, a transatlantic liner has no ports that can be skipped to make up time lost to harsh seas], enhanced passenger facilities to keep her passengers happy for 5 days at sea, and enhanced endurance to allow her great range between refueling." All of these mandates created the ship you see today. The need for speed meant her hull had to be more knife prowed than a normal cruise ship's. The need for strength meant her steel plating had to be uncommonly thick and her skeleton unusually dense and super-reinforced. The need to battle high waves meant her superstructure had to be set much farther back on her hull than is common on today's cruise ships. The list goes on and on. In a sense, you could almost say that it was the sea itself that designed *QM2*. They were made for each other.

Inside, *QM2* was laid out in such a way that even after a weeklong crossing, you might still be finding new places to explore on board. And it's very unlikely you'll feel hemmed in or claustrophobic, as Heidi feared before she made her first crossing. She never once felt antsy in the spacious and gracious ship, and, in fact, sort of wished the crossing was a few days longer! Our favorite rooms? The Queen's Room ballroom on formal night; the classic Chart Room for drinks before dinner; the forward-facing Commodore Club with its clubby atmosphere; and the forward observation deck on Deck 11, just below the bridge—probably the best spot aboard when sailing in and out of places such as Monte Carlo. Throughout, artwork functions both as decoration and as mood enhancement, with iconography that recalls the ocean liner's golden age. The most evocative art of all, though, may be a sound: Way up on *QM2*'s funnel, on the starboard side, is one of the original Tyfon steam whistles from the first *Queen Mary*—the same whistle that sounded when the *Mary* made her first crossing in 1936, now on permanent loan from the city of Long Beach, California. Mounted beside an identical replica, it has a low bass "A" note that literally shakes the rafters, and if that doesn't put a smile on your face, nothing will.

Cabins & Rates

Cabins	Per Diem From	Sq. Ft.	Fridge	Hair Dryer	Sitting Area	TV
Inside	$222	162–194	Yes	Yes	No	Yes
Outside	$277	194–269*	Yes	Yes	Yes	Yes
Suite	$545	381–2,249*	Yes	Yes	Yes	Yes

* Including veranda

CABINS   All of *QM2*'s cabins, from the smallest inside (162 sq. ft.) to the largest outside, are decorated in a smooth, contemporary style, with light-blond woods, simple lines, and a clean, uncluttered look. They range from roomy 194-square-foot outside cabins with portholes, mini fridges, and large showers, to the truly over-the-top duplex Grand Suites. Each of the latter is 1,500 to 2,200 square feet and has views of the stern through two-story walls of glass. Heidi is living proof that a family of four can do fine in a standard cabin without a balcony (there are no standard balcony cabins that accommodate families of four), but if you've got a larger budget, the junior suites are ideal. They're almost twice as big as a standard and have a huge bathroom with tub, walk-in closet, sitting area, and oversize balcony. Even standard inside and outside cabins, though by no means huge, have a simple elegance and a nice helping of amenities, including terry robes and slippers, fridge, safe, dataport, and interactive TV with e-mail capability. The vast majority of cabins are outsides with balconies, but in order to ensure they stay dry in even the roughest seas, many of them are recessed back into the hull with steel bulkheads that block ocean views when seated. All suites and junior suites feature Frette linens, flatscreen TVs with Xbox game systems, personalized stationery, pre-dinner canapés, concierge service, a bottle of champagne on embarkation, and use of the Queens Grill Lounge. Queens Grill Suites get fully stocked bars and other niceties, such as use of a large private deck overlooking the stern.

There are 30 wheelchair-accessible cabins total in various cabin grades.

PUBLIC AREAS   Because *QM2* was designed for comfortable sailing in rough seas, most of her public areas are clustered unusually low, down on decks 2 and 3. At midships, the relatively restrained (and a bit too white) Grand Lobby atrium lets onto two central promenades, decorated with huge Art Deco wall panels. Some are stunning and recall decorated glass panels from the opulent liner *Normandie,* while others are a bit chintzy (they look like they're plastic) and miss the mark.

Getting beyond that one flaw, Deck 2's promenade leads down to the elegant Empire Casino and the too-big-to-be-cozy Golden Lion pub. Up one deck, the very attractive Veuve Clicquot Champagne Bar (serving a variety of champagnes, as well as caviar and foie gras) is decorated with slightly abstract images of mid-20th-century movie stars and leads into one of the most beautiful rooms on board, The Chart Room, a high-ceilinged space with green-glass Deco maps on one wall, 1940s-style furnishings, and the feel of a great ocean liner. You expect David Niven to come strolling through any minute. By day, both of these rooms are popular hangouts for book readers, letter writers, and daydreamers. Across, on the ship's port side, Sir Samuel's Wine Bar serves coffee, sandwiches, and cakes in the morning and afternoon. Forward, the Royal Court Theater is a two-deck grand showroom and the principle theatrical venue on board, seconded by the striking Illuminations planetarium farther forward (see "Entertainment," above).

In the stern on Deck 3, the Queen's Room ballroom perfectly captures the essence of Cunard style, running the full width of the ship and boasting a high, arched ceiling; the largest ballroom dance floor at sea; crystal chandeliers; and a truly royal quality. The G32 nightclub, almost hidden behind silver doors at the head of the Queen's Room, is decorated in industrial style to match its name—"G32" was the number by which *QM2*'s hull was known at the shipyard, before Cunard decided what she'd be called.

Other notable spaces include the Winter Garden on Deck 7, a light, airy space designed to provide an outdoor garden feel on long transatlantic crossings that somehow misses the mark; and the Commodore Club bar/observation lounge on Deck 9, with its wonderful white-leather chairs, dramatic bow views, and attached Churchill's cigar room. There's also a card room hidden away on Deck 11, just behind the observation deck, and the remarkable library and bookshop forward on Deck 8 (see "Activities," p. 218).

DINING OPTIONS   Decor-wise, the Queens Grill and Princess Grill restaurants that serve suite passengers exclusively are the very models of restrained good taste, with a series of elegant blown-glass vases as their one bold touch. The Britannia Restaurant, on the other hand, is a large dramatic space, intended to recall *Queen Mary*'s magnificent first-class restaurant and featuring a vaulted, Tiffany-style glass ceiling; a curved balcony that echoes the shape of the *Mary*'s famous bridge; candlelit tables; soaring pillars; and the largest art tapestry at sea, depicting a liner against the New York skyline. Although it's large, the space is exceedingly glamorous and designed to feel grand but not overwhelming. The new Britannia Club area has literally been carved out of a corner of the restaurant but misses out on the full dramatic height of the room. All guests can dine in the cozy and elegant Todd English restaurant for a $30 cover charge. King's Court is the ship's casual buffet option, and it becomes several separate (complimentary) specialty dinner restaurants each evening.

See "Dining," above, for more details on the ship's dining experience.

POOL, FITNESS, SPA & SPORTS FACILITIES   The Canyon Ranch Spa is a two-story complex occupying some 20,000 square feet. At the center of its treatment rooms is a coed 15 × 30-foot aqua-therapy pool whose relaxation gizmos include airbed recliner lounges, neck fountains, a deluge waterfall, an air tub, and body-massage jet benches. There's a hot tub adjacent, and nearby is a thermal suite comprised of aromatic steam rooms and an herbal sauna. A salon occupies the top level of the complex, offering tremendous views from its lofty perch. The gym, one deck down, is sort of drab and chopped up, but is perfectly well equipped to make people sweat, with free weights and the latest digitally enhanced climbers, steppers, runners, and rowers.

A more classic exercise is a walk or jog around the wide outdoor Promenade Deck, which encircles the looooooonggg ship on Deck 7 and offers beautiful sea views; three times around equals 1 mile. For some shoulder work, there's a pair of golf simulators adjacent to the covered pool solarium on Deck 12. Other dips include a splash pool and hot tubs way up on Deck 13, and several in the tiered stern, including a wading pool, family pool, and play fountain on Deck 6, outside of the children's playrooms. Rounding out the sports options are Ping-Pong, basketball, quoits, a paddle-tennis court, and, of course, shuffleboard—this is a transatlantic liner, after all.

3 Mini-Review: Peter Deilmann Cruises

1800 Diagonal Rd., Suite 170, Alexandria, VA. ℭ **800/348-8287.** Fax 703/549-7924. www.deilmann-cruises.com.

THE LINE IN A NUTSHELL　German-owned and -operated, Peter Deilmann Cruises offers high-toned European ocean voyages aboard one of the most beautiful cruise ships in the world.

THE EXPERIENCE　Aboard Deilmann, English-speaking passengers get to immerse themselves in a truly European experience, from the European boutique-hotel interiors to the fine service, onboard classical concerts, and German-speaking fellow passengers. The line was started by its late namesake in 1968 and over the years has operated almost three dozen passenger and container vessels. Today it's run by Deilmann's two daughters and has a fleet of 10 ships, comprising 9 river ships (covered in chapter 10) and the classically styled, 513-passenger, 22,400-ton ocean-goer *Deutschland* (★★★★).

Newly built in 1998, *Deutschland* is an idyllic ship, decorated with an old-world ocean-liner ambience. Cabins would look right at home in a fine European hotel, with their white walls, elegant moldings, rich wooden furniture, and realist European artwork. Cabins run toward the small side (124–154 square feet for standard cabins), but that's consistent with the boutique-hotel aesthetic. Luxury cabins run to 195 square feet, while suites measure between 232 and 382 square feet. Aside from the two owner's suites, all cabins have picture windows rather than balconies—another throwback to the old days. Butler service is provided in suites.

In the bow on decks 6 and 7, the **Kaisersaal** ("Emperor's Ballroom") is a step back in time, with its huge chandelier and frescoed ceiling, looking more like a small European opera hall than a cruise ship theater. Stage shows, concerts, and ballroom dancing are offered here during each voyage. At the deck's opposite end, the **Zum Alten Fritz** (Old Fritz Pub) is a cheerful, classically decorated boozing space with a big wooden bar, brass accents, rich wall paneling, etched mirrors, comfortable leather seating, and windows and doors opening out to a small, enclosed stern-view promenade. German hot dogs with pretzels and mustard are served here in the late afternoon, and hot hors d'oeuvres (such as German meatballs and bread) are set out in the early evening. The **Lili Marleen Salon** is set in the center of the ship on Deck 6 and offers an elegant cocktail atmosphere and unobtrusive piano or small-group music in the evenings.

The main **Berlin Restaurant** is a spacious one-level room decorated in an Art Deco style and topped by a huge backlit, Tiffany-style skylight. Meals are served in two traditional fixed seatings and can run up to seven courses, with specialties from the sailing

Peter Deilmann Fleet Itineraries

Ship	Sailing Regions	Home Ports
Deutschland	5- to 19-night voyages in the Mediterranean, Atlantic Europe, the British Isles, Northern Europe/Russia, the Norwegian Fjords, and the Black Sea	Istanbul, Venice, Civitavecchia/Rome, Bordeaux (France), Hamburg, Kiel and Travemünde (Germany), Monte Carlo

region featured. Vegetarian and "wellness" dishes are also available. As an alternative, the reservations-only (but no extra charge) **Vierjahrezeiten** (Four Seasons) restaurant is an elegant space suffused with golden light. It offers an a la carte menu that changes daily. For supercasual dining, there's a pleasantly homey, light-filled buffet restaurant and an on-deck grill. In the evening, dress is semiformal most nights (jacket and tie for men), formal on 2 nights per weeklong cruise.

Outside, *Deutschland*'s pool deck is one of the very few disappointments on board, lacking much in the way of style. A single small pool dominates the relatively small space, decorated with a few plants and sculptures, and surrounded by wooden deck chairs. Forward of the pool, the lovely **Lido Terrace** is a throwback to ocean liners' palm courts, done up with cushioned wicker furniture, white pillars, and classical statuary. On Deck 8, a small dedicated cinema seats 83 passengers and screens movies daily, while the library offers books in both German and English. On Deck 3, the **Wellness Spa** offers a sauna, solarium, thermo-loungers, and a variety of ayurvedic, thalassotherapy, massage, and cosmetic treatments. A gym on Deck 6 has the usual treadmills, bikes, elliptical trainers, StairMasters, and weights. There are no casino, disco, or children's facilities on board.

On board, the official languages used are German and English, and optional English-speaking shore excursions are offered at all ports of call. The onboard currency is the euro, though U.S. dollars (and, of course, credit cards) are accepted for settling your account. You'll need a currency converter and a two-prong continental-style adapter to use 110-volt electrical appliances in your cabin. Gratuities are given traditionally, in person.

Rates for European itineraries start at about $400 per person. Deilmann offers frequent sailings themed around activities and topics like music, hiking, horseback riding, and gardens.

4 Regent Seven Seas Cruises

1000 Corporate Dr., Suite 500, Fort Lauderdale, FL 33334. (✆ **877/505-5370**. Fax 402/501-5599. www.rssc.com.

THE LINE IN A NUTSHELL   Operating a fleet of stylish and extremely comfortable midsize vessels, Regent (which changed its name from Radisson in 2006) offers a casually elegant and subtle luxury cruise experience. Its service is as good as it gets, and its cuisine is near the top.

THE EXPERIENCE   If you insist on luxury but like to keep it subtle, Regent might be your cruise line of choice. Its ships are spacious and understated, with a relaxed onboard vibe that tends to be less stuffy than Seabourn and Silversea. As aboard all the luxury ships (with the exception of Crystal's larger ships and Cunard's huge *QM2*), entertainment and activities are relatively low key, with passengers left to enjoy their vacations at their own pace. Dress tends toward casual, though tuxedos and gowns aren't uncommon on formal evenings. Service is friendly and absolutely spot-on, and cuisine is some of the best at sea, in both the formal dining rooms and the alternative restaurants. Even if what tickles your fancy isn't on the menu, the chef will prepare it for you. Passengers tend to be unpretentiously wealthy. When we've sailed, our social circles at dinner have included retired executives, a theatrical casting director, an Atlantic City nightclub owner, a graphic artist, and a woman who owned a string of Taco Bell franchises—all of them aboard to enjoy a quiet, relaxed vacation.

Pros

- **Great dining:** Cuisine is superb, and the main dining room and alternative restaurants operate on an open-seating basis, the latter by reservation.
- **Frequent sales:** Regent frequently offers free air and other deals, making its rates attractive to mainstream cruisers looking to move up to the luxe world.
- **Lots of private verandas:** *Seven Seas Navigator* has them in 90% of hers, and *Seven Seas Voyager* has them in every single stateroom.
- **Amazing bathrooms:** Bigger and better than those on Seabourn and Crystal, these ships' cabin bathrooms all have separate shower stalls and full-size bathtubs long enough for normal-size humans.

Cons

- **Not-quite-private balconies:** Walls separating the balconies aboard *Voyager* don't extend to the edge of the ship's rail, making it possible to lean out and see what your neighbors are up to.

REGENT: LOW-KEY ELEGANCE

Originally called Radisson Seven Seas Cruises, this line got its start in the early '90s and has been growing steadily ever since. In 2006, parent company Carlson merged it with its Regent International hotel chain, changing its name to Regent Seven Seas Cruises. Today Regent operates a four-ship fleet, including two ships that are positioned in Europe for 2008, *Seven Seas Navigator* and *Seven Seas Voyager.* The 320-passenger *Paul Gauguin* spends the year doing 7- to 14-night cruises in French Polynesia, while *Voyager*'s sister ship, *Seven Seas Mariner,* is spending the year in the Caribbean, Alaska, South America, and Asia/Pacific.

PASSENGER PROFILE

RSSC appeals primarily to many well-traveled and well-heeled passengers in their 50s and 60s (most from North America, with a smattering of Europeans and Australians in the mix), but younger passengers, honeymooners, and older passengers pepper the mix as well. Many passengers are frequent cruisers who have also sailed on Silversea, Seabourn, and Crystal, or are taking a step up from Holland America, Celebrity, or one of the other mainstream lines. Though they have sophisticated tastes and can do without a lot of inane shipboard activities, they also appreciate the line's less formal ambience. On our recent cruises, casual nights in the formal dining room saw some passengers dressed in polo shirts and jackets, and others in nice T-shirts with khakis and sneakers. You're also likely to find some women in full makeup, coifed hairdos, and coordinated jewelry, shoes, and handbags, and many men sporting Rolexes. A kids' program on summer sailings and some holiday sailings attracts some **families,** but the limited number of third berths in cabins tends to keep those numbers down.

Compared with the other ultraluxury lines, here's how Regent rates:

	Poor	Fair	Good	Excellent	Outstanding
Enjoyment Factor					✓
Dining				✓	
Activities			✓		
Children's Program		✓			
Entertainment			✓		
Service					✓
Worth the Money					✓

DINING

Superb menus are designed for a sophisticated palate, and the overall cuisine is some of the best in the cruise industry. Each ship has an extensive wine list.

TRADITIONAL   In the main restaurants, elaborate and elegant meals are served in open seatings by a staff of mostly Europeans. Caesar salads are tossed to order; appetizers may include baked escargots in garlic-herb butter, beef carpaccio, and an eggplant-tomato-mozzarella roll; and main entrees may include such enticing dishes as grilled venison medallions and mushroom fricassee, Chinese tangerine shrimp, and grilled grouper filet with pink grapefruit. Each dinner menu also offers a **vegetarian option** such as a forest mushroom quiche, and a **light and healthy choice** such as broiled whole Dover sole. When you've had enough of fancy, several standards called **simplicity dishes** are also available daily: pasta with tomato sauce, filet mignon, grilled chicken breast, or salmon filet. **Special diets** (kosher, halal, low fat, low salt, and so on) can be accommodated at all meals, but for very stringent regimes, such as glatt kosher, you must make arrangements before your cruise.

Breakfasts include made-to-order omelets, as well as a typical selection of hot and cold breakfast foods. Lunch entrees include soups, salads, sandwiches, and entrees like pan-seared chicken breast; Indian lamb patties with mint-coriander-lentil chutney; and a fisherman's platter of friend jumbo prawns, scallops, and filets.

SPECIALTY   *Seven Seas Navigator* has only one alternative choice: **Portofino,** an indoor/outdoor Italian restaurant serving dishes such as Genoese minestrone soup, risotto primavera, spaghetti alla Bolognese, and sliced beef steak on wild rice with a balsamic vinegar sauce.

Voyager has three alternate choices. The 110-seat Signatures restaurant is directed by chefs from Paris's famed **Le Cordon Bleu** cooking school, while the Latitudes restaurant serves **Indochine cuisine,** including such dishes as Cambodian wafu salad; steamed fresh halibut in a Matsutake mushroom broth with gingered vegetables; and a spiced rack of lamb with Jasmine rice, wok-seared snow peas, and fresh sprouts in peanut jus. **La Veranda** serves Mediterranean and North African dishes in a casual setting.

All alternative venues are intimate spaces with tables for two or four. Make reservations early in the cruise to guarantee yourself a table. Booked passengers can make specialty-dining reservations online before their cruise.

CASUAL   All three vessels have casual buffet restaurants, plus a poolside sandwich grill staffed by waiters.

Regent Fleet Itineraries

Ship	Sailing Regions	Home Ports
Navigator	7- to 11-night voyages in the Mediterranean/ Adriatic/Greek Isles (various combinations) and Atlantic Europe	Venice, Istanbul, Piraeus/Athens, Monte Carlo, Dover/London, Civitavecchia/Rome
Voyager	7- to 15-night voyages in the Mediterranean/ Adriatic/Greek Isles/Egypt (various combinations), Atlantic Europe, the British Isles, Northern Europe/Russia, and the Norwegian Fjords/ North Cape	Monte Carlo, Venice, Southampton/London, Dover/London, Copenhagen, Istanbul, Piraeus/Athens, Civitavecchia/Rome, Stockholm

SNACKS & EXTRAS   Hot hors d'oeuvres are served in the lounges before dinner, and if you take advantage of the **24-hour room service,** a steward will come in and lay out a white tablecloth along with silverware and china, whether you've ordered a full-course dinner, a personal pizza, or just a plate of fruit. Select wines and spirits, specialty coffees, soft drinks, and mineral water are complimentary at all times, and **high tea** is served each afternoon.

ACTIVITIES

Days not spent exploring the ports are basically unstructured, with a few activities thrown in for those who aren't pursuing their own relaxation. During the day, there may be ballroom dance classes, wine tastings, art auctions, bingo, computer classes, bridge (with instructors sailing on all cruises), and **lectures** by experts in the fields of European art, culture, wine and food, history, and current affairs.

On many cruises, the line's **Circle of Interest** program lets guests book packages of onboard lectures, workshops, and specially created shore excursions, all themed on such topics as art, nature, antiques, photography, performing arts, food and wine, or archaeology. On **Le Cordon Bleu cooking cruises,** for instance, chefs trained in the Le Cordon Bleu cooking method offer three onboard workshops, a special chef's dinner, and a market visit in port to see how the chef chooses the best local ingredients. Participation costs $395 per person. On **Art Experience** cruises, Regent teams with noted museums to offer art-related shore excursions and onboard lectures.

Active passengers can work out in the ships' gyms, run on the tracks, or whack some balls into a golf net, then take a massage at the ships' spas, run by the French company **Carita of Paris.** Staffed by Carita-trained therapists and hairdressers imported from Parisian salons, the spas offer company specialties such as their Rénovateur exfoliating process, as well as cruise spa standards such as hydrotherapy, reflexology, aromatherapy, body wraps, facials, manicure/pedicures, and antistress, therapeutic, and hot-rock massages.

CHILDREN'S PROGRAM

These ships are geared to mature adults, and neither ship has a dedicated children's play space, but summer sailings and select holiday cruises offer a **Club Mariner** kids program in which counselors supervise games, craft projects, and movies for three age groups: 5 to 9, 10 to 13, and 14 to 17. For the youngest set, counselors lead games, crafts projects, movies, and other activities, while teens help the counselor select the activities they prefer. On non-summer/holiday cruises, an ad-hoc kids program is put together if enough kids are aboard to warrant it. Minimum age for children to sail aboard is 1 year, and the line reserves the right to limit the number of children under age 3 on any one sailing. **Babysitting** may be available for $25 an hour if a female crewmember is willing to perform the service outside of her regular duty hours.

ENTERTAINMENT

As on most luxe ships, entertainment is low key and modest, with most passengers content to spend their evenings exploring the cocktail circuit, visiting the casino, singing along in the piano bar, or dancing to the ships' elegant musical groups. Both ships offer **musical revues** in their show lounges, and though they're certainly not a high point of the cruises, they add a nice option to the evenings. Recent shows have included *Thoroughly Modern Broadway,* a mix of musical theater numbers from the 1960s through 1980s; the Beatles tribute *Here, There and Everywhere; Beyond Imagination,* which mixes opera and classical with sea songs, folk tunes, and pseudoclassical modern hits; *On a Classical Note,* with music by Mozart, Verdi, Rossini, Puccini, Gilbert and Sullivan, and Bizet; and *Oh What a Night,* with hits by The Four Seasons, Billy Joel, Simon and Garfunkel, Ray Charles, Neil Diamond, and others.

Occasional sailings offer **themed entertainment**—small-group and big-band jazz, for instance, or performances by a chamber group. Check with the line or your travel agent for a schedule of upcoming theme cruises.

SERVICE

Service by the mostly European and Filipino staff is a major plus. You rarely, if ever, hear the word *no,* and because the crew-to-passenger ratio is quite high, you rarely have to wait for someone else to get served first. Stewardesses care for your cabin ably and unobtrusively, **room service** is speedy and efficient, and restaurant waitstaffs are supremely gracious and professional, with an intimate knowledge of the menu. Bar staff will often remember your drink order after the first day.

The ships have complimentary **self-serve laundries** in addition to standard laundry and dry-cleaning services. **Cellphone service** is available (with passengers charged a roaming fee by their carrier), and **Wi-Fi hot spots** on each ship allow laptop users to connect to the Web without visiting the Internet center.

Gratuities are included in the cruise rates, but many passengers end up leaving more anyway at the end of their trip.

Seven Seas Voyager

The Verdict

Along with sister ship *Mariner,* the 700-passenger, all-suite *Voyager* is Regent's largest ship, boasting balconies on every single stateroom, plus extra helpings of pampering.

Seven Seas Voyager *(photo: Regent)*

Specifications

Size (in Tons)	46,000	Crew	447
Passengers (Double Occ.)	700	Passenger/Crew Ratio	1.6 to 1
Passenger/Space Ratio	65.7	Year Launched	2003
Total Cabins/Veranda Cabins	350/350	Last Refurbishment/Upgrade	2006

Frommer's Ratings (Scale of 1–5)   ★★★★ ½

Cabin Comfort & Amenities	5	Dining Options	4
Appearance & Upkeep	5	Gym, Spa & Sports Facilities	3.5
Public Comfort/Space	5	Children's Facilities	N/A
Decor	4.5	Enjoyment Factor	4.5

Seven Seas Voyager, which entered service in 2003, continues the themes first introduced 2 years before on sister ship *Seven Seas Mariner,* offering exceedingly spacious interiors, all-suite accommodations, and a private balcony on every single stateroom—the latter an industry first. *Voyager* also offers improvements in some areas where we found *Mariner* lacking, particularly public-room warmth and bathroom layout. In addition, *Voyager* was designed with an efficient one-corridor approach, making for extremely smooth traffic flow in the public areas.

Cabins & Rates

Cabins	Per Diem From	Sq. Ft.	Fridge	Hair Dryer	Sitting Area	TV
Suite	$804	306–1,216	Yes	Yes	Yes	Yes

CABINS   Deluxe Suites represent the vast majority of the available accommodations aboard *Voyager,* measuring out at 306 square feet plus a 50-square-foot balcony. All staterooms are designed with blond woods and rich fabrics, and feature king-size beds convertible to twins, cotton bathrobes, hair dryer, flatscreen TV with DVD player (with movies available from the ship's DVD library), stocked refrigerator, safe, and large walk-in closet. In 2006 and 2007, all suites received new upholstery, mattresses, bed linens and duvets, towels, and bathroom amenities, plus slippers and bathrobes for guests to use while aboard. Balconies overall are a little less than private—walls separating them do not extend to the edge of the ship's rail, making it possible to lean out and see what your neighbor is up to. The marble bathrooms that come standard in all suites are absolutely huge, with a separate shower stall, a long tub, and lots of counter space. Along with those on *Seven Seas Navigator* and Silversea's *Silver Whisper,* they're the best bathrooms at sea today.

Top-level accommodations, from Penthouses up to Master Suites, come with butler service and iPods with Bose speakers for use during the trip.

Four suites on *Voyager* are wheelchair friendly.

PUBLIC AREAS   *Voyager* has a beautifully laid-out two-deck theater with terrific sightlines from virtually every seat, plus an Observation Lounge sitting high up on the top deck and featuring a semicircular bar, plush chairs and sofas, and a 180-degree view of the sea. It's a particularly attractive room at night. Lower, there's also a well-stocked library, a cigar lounge, a card and conference room (popular with bridge players), a piano lounge/disco, and a computer center. A very nice feature here is that guests are charged only for transmission time, meaning you can compose a document in Word or another program free of charge, then open your e-mail and paste it in, and incur a cost only while you're in active e-mail mode. Wi-Fi hot spots also let laptop users surf from several public areas.

DINING OPTIONS   *Voyager* has four restaurants. The main dining room, the Compass Rose, serves all three meals in single open seatings. Casual breakfasts and lunches are also available in the indoor/outdoor La Veranda Restaurant, up near the top of the ship on Deck 11.

Two reservations-only (but no-charge) restaurants are open for dinner only. Signatures features world-ranging cuisine prepared in classic French style by chefs trained at Paris's famous Le Cordon Bleu School. Latitudes offers an Indochine menu (see "Dining," above) in a space with an open galley, allowing guests to watch as items are prepared. On a 2006 cruise, one example of the galley's creativity was the different varieties of chicken soup served in the two restaurants: "cappuccino style" in Signatures (with stuffed wild mushroom profiteroles) and Hanoi-style in Latitudes, with Asian noodles. Both used the same base, but the effect was utterly different, and delicious.

In the evening, half of La Veranda is turned into an excellent candlelit, white-tablecloth Mediterranean Bistro with a combination of waiter and self-service dining. Grilled food is available poolside, and room service runs 24 hours—guests can even have the Compass Rose dinner menu served course by course in their suites during dinner hours.

POOL, FITNESS, SPA & SPORTS FACILITIES   *Voyager's* one pool and three hot tubs are located on Deck 11. Deck chairs are set up around the roomy pool area, as well as on the forward half of the deck above, where you'll also find a paddle-tennis court, golf driving nets, shuffleboard courts, and an uninterrupted jogging track. Sunbathing doesn't seem to be the biggest priority for Regent guests, so deck chairs are usually readily available, even on sea days in warm cruising areas.

The ship's Carita spa is located in an attractive but rather small space. A similarly smallish oceanview gym and separate aerobics area are located in the same area, as well as a beauty salon.

Seven Seas Navigator

The Verdict

Warm and appealing, the 490-passenger *Navigator* is an ideal size for an ultraluxe cruise: small enough to be intimate and large enough to offer plenty of elbowroom, more than a few entertainment outlets, and some of the best cabin bathrooms at sea.

Seven Seas Navigator *(photo: Regent)*

Specifications

Size (in Tons)	33,000	Crew	324
Passengers (Double Occ.)	490	Passenger/Crew Ratio	1.5 to 1
Passenger/Space Ratio	67.3	Year Launched	1999
Total Cabins/Veranda Cabins	245/215	Last Refurbishment/Upgrade	2006

Frommer's Ratings (Scale of 1–5)   ★★★★

Cabin Comfort & Amenities	5	Dining Options	4
Appearance & Upkeep	4	Gym, Spa & Sports Facilities	4
Public Comfort/Space	4	Children's Facilities	N/A
Decor	4	Enjoyment Factor	4.5

Navigator has well-laid-out cabins and public rooms, and if you've been on the Silversea ships, you'll notice a similar layout (especially in the Star Lounge and Galileo Lounge), as the interiors were all designed by the same architects and built at the same yard, Italy's Mariotti. While *Navigator*'s interior is very attractive, outside she looks a little bit top-heavy, a consequence of her odd provenance: Her hull was originally built to be a Russian spy ship. When Regent purchased the uncompleted vessel, they redesigned her superstructure with additional decks.

Cabins & Rates

Cabins	Per Diem From	Sq. Ft.	Fridge	Hair Dryer	Sitting Area	TV
Suite	$632	301–1,067	Yes	Yes	Yes	Yes

CABINS   *Navigator* is an all-suite, all-outside-cabin ship, so there's not a bad room in the house. Each elegant suite is done up in shades of deep gold, beige, and burnt orange, with caramel-toned wood furniture and a swath of butterscotch suede just above the beds. Nearly 90% of them have private balconies, with only suites on the two lowest passenger decks having bay windows instead. Of these, the only ones with obstructed views are those on the port side of Deck 6 looking out onto the promenade. The standard suites are a roomy 301 square feet; the 18 top suites range from 448 to 1,067 square feet, plus 47- to 200-square-foot balconies. Every suite has a sitting area with couch, terry robes, pair of chairs, desk, vanity table and stool (with an outlet above for a hair dryer or curling iron), flatscreen TV with DVD player (and movies available from an onboard library), minibar stocked with two complimentary bottles of wine or spirits, private safe, and wide walk-in closet with a tall built-in dresser. The marble bathrooms that come standard in all suites are absolutely huge, with a separate shower stall, a long tub, and lots of counter space. Along with those on *Seven Seas Voyager* and Silversea's *Silver Whisper,* they're the best bathrooms at sea today. In 2006 and 2007, all suites received new upholstery, mattresses, bed linens and duvets, towels, and bathroom amenities, plus slippers and bathrobes for guest use while aboard. Top-level accommodations, from Penthouses up to Master Suites, come with butler service and iPods with Bose speakers.

Four suites are wheelchair accessible.

PUBLIC AREAS   Full of autumn hues and deep blues, *Navigator*'s attractive decor is a marriage of classic and modern design, with contemporary wooden furniture, chairs upholstered in buttery leather, walls covered in suede, and touches of stainless steel, along with silk brocade draperies, dark-wood paneling, burled veneer, and marble. The ship has lots of intimate spaces, so you'll never feel overwhelmed the way you sometimes do on larger ships.

Most of the public rooms are on decks 6 and 7, just aft of the three-story atrium and main elevator bank (whose exposed wiring and mechanics could have been better disguised). The well-stocked library has 10 computers with e-mail and Internet access, while Wi-Fi hot spots let laptop users surf from several public areas. The cozy Navigator Lounge, paneled in mahogany and cherry wood, is a popular place for pre-dinner cocktails, which means it can get tight in there during rush hour. Next door is the Connoisseur Club cigar lounge, a somewhat cold and often underutilized wood-paneled room with umber leather chairs. Down the hall is the roomier Stars Lounge, with a long, curved black-granite bar and clusters of oversize ocean-blue armchairs around a small dance floor. A live music duo croons pop numbers here nightly. The attractive dark-paneled casino with its striking mural is bound to attract your eye, even if you don't gamble.

Galileo's Lounge, surrounded by windows on three sides, is our favorite spot in the evening, when a pianist is on hand and the golden room glows magically under soft light. On warm nights the doors to the outside deck are thrown open and dancers spill out from the small dance floor, creating a truly romantic, dreamy scene. By day, Galileo's is a quiet venue for continental breakfast, high tea, seminars, and meetings, and is also a perfect perch from which to view the seascape.

The stage of the twinkling two-story Seven Seas Lounge is large enough for the kind of sizable Vegas-style song-and-dance revues typical of much larger ships—a rarity in the luxe market. While sightlines are good from the tiered rows of banquettes on the first level, views from the sides of the balcony are severely obstructed.

The cheerful windowed Vista observation lounge is used for meetings and is another great scenery-viewing spot. It opens directly out to a huge patch of forward deck space just over the bridge.

DINING OPTIONS   There are two restaurants, the formal Compass Rose dining room and the more casual Portofino Grill, which serves buffet-style breakfast and lunch, and is transformed every evening into a very cozy, dimly lit, reservations-only restaurant specializing in Tuscan cuisine with southern Italian accents. Many tables for two are available, and wine tastings are done just before dinner. Its menus are inspired by Chef Angelo Elia of Fort Lauderdale's Casa D'Angelo Ristorante, though its overall dinner experience was inherited from the popular Don Vito's restaurant on the line's dear, departed *Radisson Diamond,* with its singing Italian waiters and fun, participatory vibe. The Compass Rose, a pleasant, wide-open room done in warm caramel-colored woods, offers a single open seating at all meals. There's also a casual grill on the pool deck for burgers, grilled-chicken sandwiches, fries, and salads at lunchtime, as well as a Coffee Corner on Deck 6, with complimentary deluxe coffees available (from a machine) 24 hours a day.

POOL, FITNESS, SPA & SPORTS FACILITIES   The oceanview gym is bright and roomy for a ship of this size, and a separate aerobics room offers impressively grueling classes, such as circuit training and step. A pair of golf nets and two Ping-Pong tables are available for guest use, but they're situated high on Deck 12 in an ash-plagued nook just behind the smokestacks, and are accessible only by a hard-to-find set of interior crew stairs. The whole area looks like an afterthought. At the pool area, a wide set of stairs joins a balcony of deck chairs to a large pool and pair of hot tubs on the deck below. Adjacent to the gym is *Navigator's* six-room Carita spa.

5 Seabourn Cruise Line

6100 Blue Lagoon Dr., Suite 400, Miami, FL 33126. ℂ 800/929-9391 or 305/463-3070. www.seabourn.com.

THE LINE IN A NUTSHELL   Genteel and refined, these small megayachts are intimate, quiet, and very comfortable, lavishing guests with plenty of personal attention and very fine cuisine.

THE EXPERIENCE   Strictly upper-crust Seabourn caters to guests who are well mannered and prefer their fellow vacationers to be the same. Generally, they aren't into pool games and deck parties, preferring a good book and cocktail chatter, or a taste of the line's special complimentary goodies, such as free minimassages on deck and soothing Eucalyptus-oil baths drawn in suites upon request.

Due to the ships' small size, guests mingle easily and enjoy mellow pursuits such as trivia games and presentations by guest lecturers. With 165 crewmembers for just 208 guests (a higher ratio than any line but SeaDream, and matching Silversea), service is very personal. Staff members greet you by name from the moment you check in, and your wish is their command.

Pros

- **Top-shelf service:** Staff seems to know what you need before you ask.
- **Totally all-inclusive:** Unlimited wines and spirits are included, as are gratuities.
- **Untouristy ports of call:** These small ships are able to visit smaller, less-touristed ports that bigger ships can't access.
- **One free shore excursion per cruise:** Your exclusive Seabourn outing might be a glass-roofed canal boat ride to the Historical Museum in Amsterdam or a visit to a private villa in Malta—and it's always something not found in most other lines' shore excursion brochures.
- **Excellent dining:** Even the breakfast buffets are exceptional, and having dinner on the outside deck of the Veranda Café is divine, with the ship's wake churning just below you.

Cons

- **Limited activities and nightlife:** There's not a whole lot going on, but most guests like it that way.
- **Aging vessels:** When compared to the newer ships of its competitors, Seabourn's 16- to 20-year-old vessels lack luster and suffer from a poorly configured pool deck.
- **Shallow drafts mean rocky seas:** Because these ships are small, they can get tossed around a lot more (and in less-rough waters) than larger vessels.

SEABOURN: THE CAVIAR OF CRUISE SHIPS

Seabourn was established in 1987 when luxury-cruise patriarch Warren Titus and Norwegian shipping mogul Atle Brynestad commissioned a trio of ultra-upscale 10,000-ton vessels from a north German shipyard. They sold the line to industry giant Carnival Corporation in 1991 and eventually transferred the ships' registries from Oslo to The Bahamas, somewhat diluting the link to the line's Norwegian roots. That said, the ships' captains are still Norwegian; the ships' decor is very Scandinavian, with

---

Compared with the other ultraluxury lines, here's how Seabourn rates:

	Poor	Fair	Good	Excellent	Outstanding
Enjoyment Factor					✓
Dining					✓
Activities		✓			
Children's Program	N/A*				
Entertainment		✓			
Service				✓	
Worth the Money				✓	

Seabourn has no children's program.

its cool, almost icy pastels; and you may still find your suite minibar stocked with bottles of Norwegian Ringnes Pilsener.

Today "The Yachts of Seabourn" (as the line officially calls itself) operates some of the smallest vessels in the luxury market and focuses on the strengths that go along with that: doting, personalized service; fine food and wine; and the ability to venture into exotic harbors where megaships can't go. Over the past few years, it's introduced such niceties as complimentary shore excursions (one per cruise), complimentary minimassages on deck, Molton Brown toiletries in suite bathrooms, and bow-to-stern Wi-Fi Internet access for guests with laptops.

In late 2006, Seabourn announced that it had signed a letter of intent for the construction of **three new ships,** each measuring 32,000 gross register tons and accommodating 450 guests—more than double the size of Seabourn's three current sister ships. They're currently scheduled to enter service in 2009, 2010, and 2011 (see "Preview: *Seabourn Odyssey,*" below, for more details).

PASSENGER PROFILE

On its European voyages, Seabourn's guests are well-traveled, mature adults aged from their 40s to their 70s, and are used to the five-star treatment. Many are lawyers, investment bankers, corporate and real-estate types, and entrepreneurs, and often have net worths in the millions. The majority of passengers are couples, and there's always a handful of singles as well (usually widows or widowers), and even some families with kids on summer Mediterranean voyages. Though most passengers are American, British, German, Swiss, and Australian, other nationalities sometimes spice up the mix. These ships do not cater to kids at all, and Seabourn passengers prefer it that way.

DINING

Seabourn's cuisine is very, very good and remains one of the line's strong points.

TRADITIONAL   Fleetwide, dining is offered in a single open seating in the main dining rooms, allowing guests to dine whenever they choose and with whomever they want, between about 7 and 10pm. Dinner service is high-style, with waiters dramatically lifting silver lids off dishes in unison and almost running at a trot through the elaborate, six-course meals. Service is attentive and unobtrusive, and the waitstaff is programmed to please. Celebrity restaurateur **Charlie Palmer,** of New York's Aureole fame, is behind the ships' menus, and the ships' chefs are trained in Palmer's shoreside restaurants.

Appetizers may include such dishes as citrus-marinated fluke, iced Russian Malossol caviar, sautéed escalope of foie gras, and eggplant relish and hummus. Five entrees change nightly and may include such dishes as pink-roasted rack of veal, rosemary-grilled double-cut lamb chops, roast prime rib, pan-fried sea bass, whole pan-fried Dover sole, scallops wrapped in smoked bacon, and, of course, lobster. **Vegetarian entrees** might include toasted angel-hair pasta with black trumpet mushrooms and barigoule of artichoke with white beans, thyme roasted tomatoes, and saffron potato dice. A number of **classics** are also always on the menu (think baked filet of salmon, grilled New York sirloin, filet mignon, and Caesar salad), as are a number of **lighter-choice** options. If nothing on the menu appeals to you, just ask for something you'd prefer and the galley will do its best to whip it up. Decadent **desserts** include the likes of three-chocolate crème brûlée and hot Grand Marnier soufflé, plus ice creams, sorbets, frozen yogurt, and a selection of international cheeses.

Formal nights (1 per weeklong cruise) are very formal, with virtually every male wearing a tuxedo and ladies dressed in sequined gowns. On other nights, things have relaxed somewhat as Seabourn focuses on attracting a younger crowd (younger as in 40- and 50-somethings), so ties are not required. Regardless, passengers always look very pulled together.

Complimentary wines (about 18 on any given cruise, including champagne) are served not only at lunch and dinner, but basically any time and place you want them. Ditto for spirits and soft drinks. An extensive list of extra-cost vintages is also available, including a collection called **Vintage Seabourn.** For $195, guests can choose three bottles from a list of six premium whites and six premium reds.

SPECIALTY   Every evening per cruise, including formal nights, the Veranda Café (see "Casual") is transformed into a new indoor/outdoor venue called **Restaurant 2,** featuring multicourse tasting menus for up to 72 guests per night (reservations are suggested). A pair of chefs prepares an array of small plates typically served two to a course during the five- to six-course meals. Expect such dishes as artichoke salad, cured and roasted duck breast, lemongrass seafood presse, crisp sea bass, and barbecue-glazed short ribs. Your meal might end with something like a "sweet coffee sandwich" with sea salt caramel ice cream and hazelnut foam. The ambience is more casual here than at The Restaurant, with a "jackets but no ties" rule for men on formal nights.

An outdoor dining alternative is scheduled a couple of nights per cruise, weather permitting, at the **Sky Bar** on Deck 8, with freshly grilled seafood and sizzling steak dinners served to about 40 guests, by reservation only.

Neither of these alternative dining options entails an extra charge.

CASUAL   The indoor/outdoor Veranda Café offers a combination buffet and table-service menu at breakfast and lunch. At breakfast, omelets are made to your specifications, and there's also an impressive fresh-fruit selection along with the usual breakfast spread. At lunch, you'll find salads, sandwich makings, fresh pasta, and maybe jumbo shrimp, smoked salmon, and smoked oysters, plus hot sliced roast beef, duck, and ham on the carving board.

One night on each warm-weather itinerary includes a **festive buffet dinner** served by the pool.

SNACKS & EXTRAS   Daily afternoon **tea service** includes a slew of exotic teas, freshly loose-brewed to order. **Room service** is available 24 hours a day on all ships. During normal lunch or dinner hours, your private multicourse meal can mirror the dining room service, right down to the silver, crystal, and porcelain. Don't expect the same level of service dining you get in the restaurants (courses may arrive together, for instance), but do expect a very cushy, lazy way of "ordering in" one night. Outside of mealtimes, the room-service menu is more limited, though you can order treats such as jumbo shrimp and caviar along with the more humdrum burgers, salads, sandwiches, pizza, pastas, ice cream, and cookies. In-cabin breakfasts are popular, and you can have your eggs prepared any way you like them.

ACTIVITIES

The Seabourn ships are sociable because of their small size, but organized activities are typically limited to such things as trivia contests, galley tours, computer classes, **wine tastings,** bridge tournaments, exercise classes, and makeover demonstrations—all overseen by a cruise director. The lack of in-your-face, rah-rah activities is one of the things

Seabourn Fleet Itineraries

Ship	Sailing Regions	Home Ports
Seabourn Legend	7-night Mediterranean	Lisbon, Barcelona, Monte Carlo, Civitavecchia/Rome, Nice, Malaga
Seabourn Odyssey	7- to 14-night Mediterranean/ Black Sea (2009 only)	Venice, Istanbul, Piraeus/Athens, Malaga
Seabourn Pride	9- to 15-night voyages in the Mediterranean, Atlantic Europe, and Northern Europe/Russia	Lisbon, Venice, Dover/ London, Copenhagen
Seabourn Spirit	7- to 14-night Mediterranean/Black Sea	Alexandria, Piraeus/Athens, Istanbul, Venice, Civitavecchia/Rome

passengers like most about Seabourn. Public announcements are few, and, for the most part, passengers are left alone to enjoy conversation and pursue their personal peace.

Each of the ships has a retractable **watersports marina** that unfolds from its stern (weather and sea conditions permitting), allowing passengers direct access to the sea for water-skiing, windsurfing, sailing, snorkeling, banana-boat riding, kayaking, and swimming. Many cruises feature a **guest lecturer** or two discussing upcoming ports, as well as other random topics. Noted chefs, scientists, historians, authors, or statesmen may be aboard, or maybe a wine connoisseur, composer, anthropologist, TV director, or professor, presenting lectures and mingling with guests.

Each ship has a small business center with computers for e-mail and Internet access. **Wi-Fi** connections are also available everywhere aboard for people who bring their own laptops. **Recent-release movies** are available for viewing in cabins, and movies are sometimes shown out on deck as well, with popcorn. All suites have flatscreen TVs, DVD players, and Bose Wave CD players, and each ship has a library of music and audio books.

CHILDREN'S PROGRAM

These ships are not geared to children, but some summer Mediterranean voyages may see 10 or more kids aboard. Though the line offers no special programs, menus, or playrooms, that's not too much of a concern on these itineraries, which tend to visit a port every, or nearly every, day. In a pinch, you may be able to arrange for an available crewmember to provide babysitting service. Minimum age for sailing is 1 year.

ENTERTAINMENT

Due to the ships' small size, there are no elaborate, splashy production shows such as you sometimes find on the larger luxe ships of Silversea, Regent, and Crystal. Instead, a variety of smaller entertainments is offered each night, with dancing and cabaret in the main lounge (the former accompanied by a six-piece band, the latter often featuring comedians, puppeteers, etc.), dancing to a duo before and after dinner in The Club, and a late-night DJ for dancing. The observation lounge on Deck 8 offers quiet guitar or piano music, while jazz or blues is sometimes performed under the stars at the Sky Bar.

Adjacent to The Club is a small, rather drab casino with a handful of card tables and slots.

Preview: *Seabourn Odyssey*

Seabourn Cruise Line hasn't had a new ship since 1992 (when the 208-passenger *Seabourn Legend* debuted), and no one thought they ever would have one again. For the better part of a decade, executives of Carnival Corporation, Seabourn's parent company, publicly stated that they intended to build no new vessels for the small-ship luxury brand, believing that revenues would not justify the construction costs associated with such relatively small ships.

Then, in October 2006, all that changed when the line announced plans to build three new 32,000-ton, 450-passenger vessels for delivery in 2009, 2010, and 2011. Outside, the new Seabourn vessels will resemble their much smaller cousins, with a long, sleek, yachtlike bow and a bellyband of steel rising from the hull upward and wrapping around the superstructure at the ship's funnels. Their interior layout will also be similar to the older ships, while adding additional facilities and amenities. The ships' passenger space ratio will be one of the highest in the industry, and 13 categories of suites will be available to suit any budget (from just "rich" to "very, very rich," that is), ranging from 277-square-foot oceanview suites to 450-square-foot penthouses and 1,300-square-foot Grand Suites. Like the current Seabourn ships, the new vessels will offer four dining options: an open-seating main restaurant; an intimate specialty restaurant called Restaurant 2; the casual indoor/outdoor Veranda Cafe, serving regional specialties; and a simple pizzeria and grill. Six bars will serve following Seabourn's standard open-bar policy, while other features—some carry-overs from the current fleet, some new—include a fold-out watersports marina; a terraced top-deck enclave furnished with large sun beds; and a large spa with thalassotherapy pool, his-and-hers Finnish saunas, a selection of aromatic steam rooms, and outdoor relaxation decks. Functionally, the ships will be equipped with two bow thrusters to enhance maneuverability, two stabilizers, and advanced wastewater treatment technology to lessen their environmental impact.

The vessels are being built by T. Mariotti S.p.A. of Genoa, Italy. The first, *Seabourn Odyssey,* will become the flagship of the Seabourn fleet when it debuts in mid-June 2009.

SERVICE

Seabourn's staff is one of its most valuable assets, offering service that's friendly, courteous, discreet, eager to please, and highly competent. Most of the staff is European, and most have gained experience at the grand hotels of Europe. The cabin staff is all female. All **gratuities** are included in the rates.

If you don't want to deal with lugging your luggage to the airport (or your car), Seabourn offers a service that will **ship your bags** directly to your vessel and back.

Laundry and **dry cleaning** are available, and there are also complimentary self-service laundry rooms.

Seabourn Pride •
Seabourn Spirit •
Seabourn Legend

The Verdict

These smallish megayachts are in a class by themselves, representing almost a throwback to a more intimate and refined, less frenetic, and definitely less glitzy style of cruising.

Seabourn Legend *(photo: Seabourn Cruise Line)*

Specifications

Size (in Tons)	10,000	Year Launched	
Passengers (Double Occ.)	208	*Pride*	1988
Passenger/Space Ratio	48.1	*Spirit*	1989
Total Cabins/Veranda Cabins	100/6	*Legend*	1992
Crew	165	Last Refurbishment/Upgrade	2008
Passenger/Crew Ratio	1.3 to 1		

Frommer's Ratings (Scale of 1–5)   ★★★★

Cabin Comfort & Amenities	4	Dining Options	3.5
Appearance & Upkeep	4	Gym, Spa & Sports Facilities	3
Public Comfort/Space	5	Children's Facilities	N/A
Decor	3	Enjoyment Factor	4

Want posh and private? Then grab your Louis Vuitton valise and come aboard these sleek, attractive ships for a cruise to some of Europe's poshest ports. The vessels hold just 208 passengers each, so you'll never feel lost in the crowd. In fact, you'll practically feel like you own the place. Choose to be as social or as private as you wish, with no rowdiness or loud music, and no one exhorting you to get involved. While you're aboard, the ship is your floating boutique hotel or your private yacht. You make the call.

Cabins & Rates

Cabins	Per Diem From	Sq. Ft.	Fridge	Hair Dryer	Sitting Area	TV
Suite	$562	277–575	Yes	Yes	Yes	Yes

CABINS Just about everything in Seabourn's standard 277-square-foot suites has the feel of an upscale Scandinavian hotel, offering ocean views, ice-blue or champagne color schemes, lots of bleached oak or birch-wood trim, and mirrors and spot lighting to keep things bright. Only the Owner's Suites have proper balconies, though 36 regular suites on decks 5 and 6 have French balconies with sliding doors and a few inches of decking—not nearly enough to fit a chair, but they do allow sunlight to pour into the cabin and offer a great view up and down the length of the ship. You can sit on the sofa or in a chair and read while sunning yourself out of the wind and out of view. You can also sleep with the doors wide open and the sounds and smells of the ocean pouring in—unless, of course, the officers on the bridge decide to lock the doors: If seas get even a little choppy or the wind picks up, a flick of a switch locks your door automatically and there's not a darn thing you can do about it. (Remember, these ships are small, so you're not that far above the waterline. The line likes to avoid waves and sea spray messing up their lovely decor.)

The best features of the suites are their bathrooms and walk-in closets, with plenty of hanging space for Seabourn's extended cruises. Drawer space, on the other hand, is minimal. White marble bathrooms usually include both a tub and a shower (though 10–14 suites on each ship have showers only), and lots of shelf, counter, and cabinet space. Those on *Seabourn Pride* and *Spirit* have twin sinks; those on *Legend* have single sinks. Molton Brown bath products plus designer soaps by Chanel, Bijan, Hermès, and Bronnley are provided for guests along with a world atlas, terry bathrobes, slippers, and umbrellas to use on board.

The coffee table in the sitting area can be pulled up to become a dining table, and the minibar is stocked upon arrival with two bottles of complimentary liquor or wine of your choice (a request form comes with your cruise documents) and a chilled bottle of champagne. Unlimited bottled water, beer, and soft drinks are restocked throughout the cruise. Ice is replenished twice daily (more often on request), and bar setups are in each room. Each cabin has a desk, hair dryer, safe, radio and CD player (music CDs and audio books are available for borrowing), and flatscreen TVs and DVD players. Fresh fruit and a flower complete the suite scene.

The two Classic Suites measure 400 square feet, and a pair of Owner's Suites on each ship measure 530 and 575 square feet, and have verandas, dining areas, and guest powder rooms. Their dark-wood furnishings make the overall feeling more like a hotel room than a ship's suite, but, as is true of any cabins positioned near the bow of relatively small ships, they can be somewhat uncomfortable during rough seas. Owner's Suites 05 and 06 have obstructed views.

Connecting suites are available. Some are marketed as 554-square-foot Double Suites, and that's exactly what they are: two 277-square-foot suites, with one converted to a lounge. There are four wheelchair-accessible suites.

PUBLIC AREAS   Step onto most ships today, and you'll oooh and ahhh at the decor. Not so here, where the minimalist Scandinavian design aesthetic is in play. For the most part, public rooms are spare and almost ordinary looking. Art and ornamentation are conspicuous by their absence, with the exception of the small lobby area in front of the purser's desk on Deck 5, where attractive murals of ship scenes liven up the curved walls.

The forward-facing observation lounge on Sky Deck is the most attractive public room, a quiet venue for reading or cards, the spot for afternoon tea (during which a pianist provides background music), and a good place for a drink before meals. A chart and compass on the wall outside will help you pinpoint the ship's current position, and a computerized wall map lets you track future cruises.

The Club piano bar in the stern offers great views during daylight hours, is packed before dinner, and sometimes offers after-dinner entertainment such as a Name That Tune game or a cabaret show. Hors d'oeuvres are served here both before and after dinner. A tiny, cramped casino is adjacent, with a couple of blackjack tables, a roulette wheel, and about 10 slots. The downstairs show lounge is a dark, tiered, all-purpose space for lectures, the captain's cocktail party, and featured entertainers such as singers, comedians, and pianists.

One of the best places for a romantic, moonlit moment is the isolated patch of deck far forward in the bow on Deck 5, where a lone hot tub also resides.

DINING OPTIONS   The formal Restaurant, located on the lowest deck, is a large, low-ceilinged room with elegant candlelit tables. It's open for breakfast, lunch, and dinner, and officers, cruise staff, and sometimes guest lecturers host tables at dinnertime. If you're not in the mood for the formal dining room, the Veranda Café serves a combination buffet and full-service breakfast and lunch. Come evening, the cafe becomes the casual specialty Restaurant 2, serving multicourse tasting menus by reservation only.

Along with burgers, chicken, hot dogs, and grilled items, a special of the day—maybe pizza with pineapple topping, or fresh ingredients for tacos—is also available at the pleasant Sky Bar, overlooking the Lido Deck, for those who don't want to change out of their swimsuits. On sunny days, themed lunches are also often set up here, and at night it offers a steak-and-seafood menu by reservation.

POOL, FITNESS, SPA & SPORTS FACILITIES   The outdoor pool, which gets little use, is awkwardly situated in a shadowy location aft of the open Deck 7, between the twin engine uptakes and flanked by lifeboats hanging from both sides. A pair of whirlpools is better located just forward of the pool. A third hot tub is perched far forward on Deck 5. It's wonderfully isolated and a perfect spot (as is the whole patch of deck here) from which to watch a port come into sight or fade away.

A retractable, wood-planked watersports marina opens out from the stern of each ship so that passengers can hop into sea kayaks or go windsurfing, water-skiing, or snorkeling right from the vessel. An attached steel mesh net creates a protected saltwater pool when the marina is in use.

Located forward of the Lido Deck, the gym and Steiner-managed spa are surprisingly roomy for ships this small and were renovated recently with modern equipment. Yoga and Pilates, as well as more traditional aerobics classes, are offered in a lounge or on deck, and you'll also find two saunas, massage rooms, and a beauty salon.

6 SeaDream Yacht Club

2601 S. Bayshore Dr., Penthouse 1B, Coconut Grove, FL 33133. ℂ **800/707-4911** or 305/631-6100. Fax 305/631-6110. www.seadreamyachtclub.com.

THE LINE IN A NUTSHELL   Intimate cruise-ships-turned-yachting-vessels, SeaDream's two small ships deliver an upscale yet casual experience without the regimentation of traditional cruise itineraries and activities.

THE EXPERIENCE   SeaDream was created for independent-minded travelers craving high-end service and food sans formality and rigid schedules. Step aboard one of these 100-passenger yachts, and you're boarding a floating club of mostly like-minded travelers who cringe at the thought of sailing en masse to Livorno. It's an intimate group that wants to feel like it's inhabiting an exclusive and remote seaside hamlet on some hard-to-reach, difficult-to-spell island, where the food is good, the spa well equipped, and the drinks flowing. On a SeaDream cruise, everything is included in the cruise fare and you'll never be pestered to pay for drinks or tip the crew. There also aren't art auctions, roving photographers, or "special" restaurants vying for your money, but instead cool adult toys such as WaveRunners, appealing Adriatic and Aegean ports off the megaship drag, and pampering service that includes complimentary orders of jumbo shrimp served to you in the hot tub (or wherever) whenever the desire strikes. The line's flexible itineraries and fluid daily schedules should appeal to landlubbers used to exclusive resort vacations.

Pros

- **Truly all-inclusive:** Unlimited wines and spirits as well as tips are included in the rates.
- **Cool tech stuff:** These ships were built in the mid-1980s, but they've been outfitted for the 21st century. Every cabin is equipped with a flatscreen TV, Internet access, and CD and DVD players; and jet skis, MP3 players, and Segway Human Transporters are available for passenger use.
- **Late-night departures from key ports:** Instead of leaving port around cocktail hour—just when things begin to get interesting—the ships will stay late or even overnight in places such as St. Tropez or Portofino to allow passengers a night of carousing on terra firma.
- **Flexible itineraries:** Captains have the authority to duck inclement weather by visiting a different port or to extend a stay off an island because of perfect snorkeling conditions.

Cons

- **Rough seas:** While the intimacy of these ships can be a selling point, their size can be a detriment: They bob like buoys in even mildly rough waters, and the diesel engines sometimes produce a shimmying sensation.
- **Limited entertainment:** A piano player and a sidekick are the sum total of the ship's entertainment. Mostly it's socializing with other passengers over cocktails at the Top of Yacht bar (who's complaining?).

SEADREAM: YOUR YACHT AWAITS

In fall 2001, Norwegian entrepreneur Atle Brynestad, who founded Seabourn in 1987 and chaired the company for a decade, bought out Carnival Corporation's stake in Seabourn's *Sea Goddess I* and *Sea Goddess II,* then worked with former Seabourn and Cunard president and CEO Larry Pimentel to form the SeaDream Yacht Club, reintroducing the ships as twin yachts. *SeaDream II* was redesigned and refitted at a Bremerhaven, Germany, shipyard and was unveiled in Miami in February 2002. Her sister ship debuted 2 months later, following her own refurbishment.

Compared with the other ultraluxury lines, here's how SeaDream rates:

	Poor	Fair	Good	Excellent	Outstanding
Enjoyment Factor					✓
Dining					✓
Activities					✓
Children's Program	N/A*				
Entertainment	✓				
Service				✓	
Worth the Money					✓

* *Seabourn has no children's program.*

The mantra from management is that these vessels are not cruise ships. They are yachts and have been painstakingly renovated to invoke the ambience of your best friend's private vessel, on the theory (as president and CEO Pimentel told us recently) that "cruising is about what happens inside the vessel; yachting is about what happens outside." Toward this end, deck space has been expanded and refurbished with such touches as queen-size sun beds. The Main Salon is cozy, with fabrics and art handpicked by Linn Brynestad, the owner's spouse. The dress code steers clear of the traditional tux and sequins dress-up night by favoring "yacht casual" wear. Some men wear jackets, but never ties. Itineraries are designed so that ships stay overnight once or twice a week because, as Pimentel explained, "There's no sense in leaving a port at 5 if it doesn't start really happening till 11." Plus, because SeaDream's ports of call tend to be the less commercialized ones that are generally off the megaship main drag. If the ships are anchoring offshore, their size generally enables them to get close enough so that the tender ride between ship and shore is short. And given how few passengers the ships carry, you'll never have to queue up to be shuttled back and forth—it's practically on demand.

With many crewmembers having migrated to SeaDream from the *Goddess* days, meticulous attention to detail and personalized service are still the ships' greatest assets.

PASSENGER PROFILE

Most passengers are in their 40s and 50s, with the line reporting an average age of 46. About 70% are American (with British, Canadians, and other Europeans making up most of the remainder), and are not veteran cruisers. They're the kind who have refined tastes and want top-notch service and gourmet food, but are secure enough to dispense with a stuffy atmosphere. On a sailing aboard the *SeaDream I,* Heidi met a fun-loving, middle-aged doctor and his wife from Texas; a 30-something couple-next-door from Pennsylvania that ran a successful baking business and liked to swig beer from the bottle; a retired travel executive who was clearly used to the good life; a restaurant owner; and a group of well-dressed, hard-drinking friends celebrating a 40th birthday. Many passengers have chartered their own small yachts for a vacation or actually own one. Passengers were friendly and mingled easily, and by day three, alliances had been made and clusters of new friends were enjoying drinks by the pool and dining together in the open-seating restaurants.

The SeaDream experience is less highbrow and way more playful than Seabourn, whose three small 208-passenger ships attract an older, more sober clientele.

A big chunk of the line's business comes from full charters of the ships, often by large (rich) families. Smaller groups can sometimes take advantage of a deal that offers one free cabin for every four booked, up to a maximum of 25 cabins. Groups of 50 are a significant presence on ships this size, so when booking, inquire whether there will be any large groups aboard, to avoid the "in crowd/out crowd" vibe.

DINING

TRADITIONAL   Dining is a high point of the SeaDream experience; it's roughly on a par with Windstar's cuisine and just under Silversea and Seabourn. Daily five-course dinners in the Dining Salon include five entrees that change nightly, with a **healthy selection** always among them. Expect delicious dishes such as a hot and tangy prawn and fruit salad; sautéed sea scallops with cauliflower crème, herb lettuce, and potato crisps; yellowfin tuna steak on roast zucchini and tomato compote; and a roasted lamb loin with polenta and served on a spinach, forest mushroom, and parsley sauce. You'll also find a **vegetarian option** and a la carte items such as linguine with pesto and rosemary-marinated lamb chops. The kitchen will prepare **special requests,** provided the ingredients are on board. **Local specialties,** such as fresh fish from markets in various ports, are likely to be incorporated into the menu. Open-seating dining is offered from 7:30 to 9:30pm, and table arrangements include everything from the nine-seat captain's table to cozier places for two (though during the evening rush, it's not easy to snag one). Generally, you'll be seated with other guests unless you don't want to, and by the second or third day of the cruise, many passengers prefer to sit at larger tables with new friends.

There are no formal evenings. Jackets are not required; some men wear them, but many just stick to collared shirts. On our recent cruise, passengers' interpretation of the **informal dress code** ranged from a classic navy-blue sport jacket to Bermuda shorts and a T-shirt—the latter frowned upon by the hotel manager, but generally overlooked. It's not easy to tell someone who paid several thousand dollars for his cruise to go back to his cabin to change clothes.

Guests can venture "out" for dinner by requesting a spot in advance at one of several private alcoves on Deck 6, or even on the bridge. These special dining ops may not be advertised heavily on board—you'll have to ask for them.

CASUAL   The partially covered, open-sided Topside Restaurant on Deck 5 serves breakfast and lunch daily, with guests choosing from a buffet or menu.

SNACKS & EXTRAS   Room service is available 24 hours a day for those who don't want to pause their DVD player. You'll also find mini sandwiches, wraps, pastries, and other snacks throughout the day in the Topside Restaurant's buffet area or at the pool. One afternoon on a recent cruise, waiters circulated by the pool at happy hour with trays of Bloody Marys and homemade mini pizzas. For a real treat, you can ask for a generous (and complimentary) order of jumbo shrimp cocktail whenever the mood strikes; on our last cruise, the craving struck while soaking in the hot tub. Caviar is available, though it's no longer complimentary (except on special occasions).

Dining highlights from the old *Sea Goddess* cruises are carried over here, including lavish **beach barbecues,** called the Champagne and Caviar Splash, on deck (see "Activities," below, for more details). A buffet lunch, served on tables with linen and china, includes grilled shrimp and chicken, pork ribs, and plenty of side dishes.

The line's **open-bar policy** means that unlimited alcoholic beverages are served throughout the vessels, though cabin minifridges are stocked only with complimentary beer and soft drinks. If you want wine and spirits for your minifridge, you'll have to pay. Advance requests for favorite libations are encouraged. Each ship's wine cellar includes some 3,500 bottles, of which an excellent selection is complimentary.

ACTIVITIES

If hanging out can be considered an activity, you can do it well on a SeaDream cruise. Who can complain about summoning a waiter from the hot tub for a plate of jumbo shrimp cocktail and a piña colada? As Larry Pimentel, SeaDream's co-owner, chairman, and CEO, is fond of saying, "Yachting is about the outdoors, cruising is about the indoors." The ship's main social hubs are not the indoor entertainment lounge or library, but out on deck at the Top of the Yacht Bar, pool deck, and sunbathing areas, where there are chaise longues, a pair of hammocks, and the line's much-touted ultra-firm **Balinese sun beds** (p. 250). Upon request, you can even sleep on them under the stars with duvets and pillows. There's also a **golf simulator** up top and, below, a **retractable marina for watersports** and swimming that operates a couple of hours a day in ports where the ship anchors, which is at fewer ports in Europe than in the Caribbean. Cabins have DVD players, and you can borrow a portable **MP3 player** from the reception desk (there are about 25, and they're preprogrammed with a wide selection of music).

The ships carry along **mountain bikes** for use in port and even **Segway Human Transporters,** those weird-looking, two-wheeled, upright scooters that can be used when the ship docks (at a cost of $49 for 45 min.).

For those who consider a **massage** a beloved pastime—like we do—the ship's well-equipped spa and gym are very impressive for ships so small. A staff of eight Thai women runs each spa, which feature traditional therapies such as Swedish massage, along with Asian ones. Heidi sampled an excellent Thai massage where the therapist used her arms and legs, as well as hands, to execute a variety of stretching moves. The adjacent ocean-view gym offers up-to-date equipment and daily classes such as tai chi and yoga.

One of the week's highlights is an ultrapopular holdover from the *Sea Goddess* days, the lavish **Champagne and Caviar Splash beach party** thrown on deck in and around the pool while sailing in Europe (in the Caribbean, it's done on a secluded beach, and the hotel manager and his assistants wade into the surf with their uniforms on and serve champagne and caviar from a floating surfboard). Staff get into the pool to serve bubbly and caviar from a floating life ring. Typically, most passengers join them in the water and enjoy a sort of high-end frat party. A nice buffet lunch is served on deck.

CHILDREN'S ACTIVITIES

Though the only actual restriction is that children under age 1 are prohibited, these ships are by no means kid-friendly. There are no babysitting services or child-related activities. Teens, though, may enjoy these cruises' emphasis on watersports and unstructured activities. Keep in mind, the standard Yacht Club staterooms can accommodate only three people; the third person/child sleeps on the couch (which doesn't pull out) and generally pays half of the full per person rate. If you've got a larger family, you'll have to spring for two staterooms.

ENTERTAINMENT

Evening entertainment is mostly of the socializing over drinks variety—and that's how passengers seem to like it. This isn't generally a musical-loving cabaret crowd. On a recent cruise, a **pianist** played after dinner in the Main Salon lounge, while a **guitarist** serenaded diners at the entrance to the restaurant and sometimes afterward up on deck at the Top of the Yacht bar, the liveliest spot to hang out before and after dinner on our most recent sailing. Occasionally, **local performers** are brought on for the

SeaDream Fleet Itineraries

Ship	Sailing Regions	Home Ports
SeaDream I	7- to 14-night voyages in the Mediterranean/ Adriatic/Greek Isles/Black Sea (various combinations) and Atlantic Europe	Seville, Civitavecchia/Rome, Istanbul, Venice, Piraeus/Athens, Monte Carlo, Lisbon
SeaDream II	7- to 11-night voyages in the Mediterranean/ Adriatic/Greek Isles (various combinations) and Atlantic Europe	Nice, Piraeus/Athens, Dubrovnik, Civitavecchia/Rome, Venice, Monte Carlo, Valetta, Lisbon

night—for example, Flamenco dancers in Seville. There's also a **tiny casino** area with two poker tables and a handful of slots. Weather permitting, once per cruise, a large **movie** screen is set up on deck so that passengers can watch a flick under the stars (with popcorn, of course).

SERVICE

Given the small number of guests and large number of crew, everyone is quick to satisfy whims and commit your name to memory. Make sure that your first drink is your favorite; you may find fresh ones reappearing automatically throughout the evening. The dining room waitstaff is courteous and knowledgeable, though a bit harried; even though dining is open seating, most passengers tend to dine about the same time each evening. As aboard the Silversea ships, cabin bathrooms are stocked with Bulgari amenities, and guests all get a complimentary set of frumpy (but comfortable) SeaDream pajamas. **Laundry, dry cleaning,** and **pressing** are available, but there is no self-service laundry.

SeaDream I • SeaDream II

The Verdict

The service, cuisine, and intimacy of the old *Sea Goddess* ships in an even better package, with flexible itineraries and a laid-back atmosphere designed to pry landlubbers from their resorts and out to sea.

SeaDream II *(photo: SeaDream Yacht Club)*

Specifications

Size (in Tons)	4,260	Passenger/Crew Ratio	1.2 to 1
Passengers (Double Occ.)	110	Year Launched	
Passenger/Space Ratio	39	*SeaDream I*	1984
Total Cabins/Veranda Cabins	55/55	*SeaDream II*	1985
Crew	89	Last Refurbishment/Upgrade	2007/2008

Frommer's Ratings (Scale of 1–5)   ★★★★ ½

Cabin Comfort & Amenities	5	Dining Options	3.5
Appearance & Upkeep	4	Gym, Spa & Sports Facilities	4
Public Comfort/Space	4.5	Children's Facilities	N/A
Decor	4	Enjoyment Factor	5

Care for a chronology? The year is 1984, and Sea Goddess Cruises begins offering luxury small-ship cruises for very affluent travelers. Unfortunately, not enough affluent travelers are interested, and within 2 years the line sells out to Cunard, which takes over operation of its two vessels and retains a similar approach, featuring impeccable service and cuisine. In 1998, Carnival Corporation purchases Cunard and transfers the *Sea Goddess* ships to its Seabourn division, which operates similar-size luxury vessels. Then in August 2001, Carnival sells the ships to Atle Brynestad, founder of Seabourn Cruises. Brynestad then brings aboard former Seabourn and Cunard president and

CEO Larry Pimentel as co-owner, chairman, and CEO of the new line, and hires a raft of other ex-Cunard executives to fill the company's top spots.

Man, the business world is complicated. But because this line is geared to affluent travelers, we thought you might be interested. Now let's get to the details.

Cabins & Rates

Cabins	Per Diem From	Sq. Ft.	Fridge	Hair Dryer	Sitting Area	TV
Suite	$638	195–450	Yes	Yes	Yes	Yes

CABINS All of the 54 one-room, 195-square-foot oceanview suites are virtually identical, with the bedroom area positioned alongside the cabin's large window (or portholes, in the case of Deck 2 suites) and the sitting area inside—the exact opposite of most ship cabin layouts. During a May 2007 dry dock, the suites on *SeaDream I* were refreshed with new furniture upholstery, curtains, and bedspreads (*SeaDream II* will get the same treatment in 2008). The standard cabins are about 100 square feet smaller than those of Seabourn, Silversea, and Radisson. None have balconies. Sound-proofing between cabins is good and engine noise minimal, as all cabins are located forward and amidships.

Built in the mid-1980s, these ships have a lot more real wood incorporated into the cabins than you'll see on today's newer ships that sport veneers and synthetics at every turn. Wood cabinetry and moldings are complemented by blue and white fabrics to create an appealing nautical look with a modern twist. Each suite has a small sitting area with a couch (that can accommodate a third adult or a child) and an entertainment center that includes a flatscreen TV with CD/DVD player (and is wired for Internet access). On her last cruise, Heidi was impressed by the amount of storage space (she never used it all) and the stash of large bottles of water. A minifridge is stocked with sodas and beer (though booze from any of the bars and restaurants is included in the rates, oddly enough, if you want liquor for your minibar you'll have to pay for it). Bathrooms are compact, as you would expect on ships of this size, but feature huge marble showers with glass doors and a generous supply of Bulgari toiletries. Each cabin comes with a hair dryer and extrathick bathrobes, and all guests get to take home a set of personalized cotton pajamas with the SeaDream logo. Unlike Silversea and Seabourn, the 24-hour room service menu is limited to salads and sandwiches, and you cannot order from the restaurant menus.

There are 16 staterooms that are connectable to form 8 390-square-foot Commodore Club Staterooms. The gorgeous 450-square-foot Owner's Suite has a bedroom, living room, dining area, main bathroom with bathtub and separate oceanview shower, and guest bathroom.

These ships are not recommended for passengers requiring the use of a wheelchair: Doorways leading to staterooms are not wide enough, many thresholds in public areas are several inches tall, and tenders that shuttle passengers from ship to shore in many ports cannot accommodate wheelchairs. Though there are elevators, they don't reach all decks.

PUBLIC AREAS The SeaDream yachts retain much of *Sea Goddess*'s former sophisticated decor, and a recent face-lift spruced things up even more with new carpeting and other touchups (in spring 2007 for *SeaDream I,* and a year later for *SeaDream II*). Stained wood floors, Oriental carpets, and striking exotic floral arrangements delight the eye. The Main Salon and its small but popular alcove bar is the venue for the weekly captain's cocktail party, plus other group events. One deck above is the Piano Bar, and next door are the ship's small casino, a gift shop, and an attractive library furnished with comfy chairs and stocked with offerings ranging from military history to Oprah's Book Club favorites.

By far, the favorite place to socialize is the Top of the Yacht Bar amidships on Deck 6, which has been designed with teak decking, rattan furniture, and contrasting blue-striped cushions. The bar area is partially covered and offers alcove seating. On this deck you'll also find a flotilla of queen-size sun beds for reading, sunbathing, or napping; they're slightly elevated at the stern of the ship to allow for uninterrupted ocean viewing. For those who might want to sleep on deck one night, management will allow it and will outfit the beds with blankets. There's a large collection of original artwork by exclusively Scandinavian artists, located throughout the ship; they were commissioned or otherwise chosen by Linn Brynestad.

DINING OPTIONS   Dinners are served indoors in the simple but elegant Dining Salon on Deck 2. On 1 or 2 nights during the trip, a festive dinner is served in the open-sided, teak-floored Topside Restaurant on Deck 5, and a festive deck-party lunch is also served up top. (See "Dining," above, for details.)

POOL, FITNESS, SPA & SPORTS FACILITIES   Because yachting is all about being outdoors, there are great open spaces on the SeaDream ships. Stake an early claim to a sun bed because they're prime real estate. Eight of them are aftward on Deck 6, and more are forward, near the golf simulator. Aft on Deck 3 is the attractive pool area, with comfortable lounge chairs and umbrellas, tables, a bar, and, not too far away, a hot tub. It's the place where the social gather when the ship departs a port to enjoy the view. A covered deck above has more chairs.

Toward the bow on Deck 4 are the beauty salon and an impressively well-designed and -equipped spa and gym, with four treadmills with flatscreen TVs, an elliptical machine, two stationary bikes, and free weights (and lowish ceilings, if you're on the tall side). Classes include aerobics, yoga, and tai chi. The uninterrupted ocean views add a calming diversion while you're burning calories. The teak-lined spa, the Asian Spa and Wellness Center, has three treatment rooms and features the usual decadent (and pricey) suspects, including wraps, facials, and massages, plus more exotic options such as hot lava rock massages, a spice and yogurt scrub, and a cucumber and aloe wrap. You can prebook treatments online at **www.seadreamspa.com**.

7 Silversea Cruises

110 E. Broward Blvd., Fort Lauderdale, FL 33301. 📞 **800/722-9955**. Fax 954/522-4499. www.silversea.com.

THE LINE IN A NUTSHELL   It doesn't get better than Silversea if you're looking for a total luxury experience at sea. From exquisite service and cuisine to such niceties as free-flowing Pommery Brut Royal champagne and Acqua di Parma and Bulgari bath products in the marble cabin bathrooms, these handsome ships offer the best of everything.

THE EXPERIENCE   Fine-tuned and genteel, a Silversea cruise caters to guests who are used to the good life, and nothing seems to have been overlooked. The food and service are the best at sea, and the ships' Italian-style decor is warm and inviting. Tables are set with Christofle silver and Schott-Zwiesel crystal. These are dignified vessels for a dignified crowd that likes to dress for dinner, compare travel dossiers, and plan their next big trip. If you want the VIP treatment 24-7, this is your cruise line.

Pros

- **Doting service:** Gracious and ultraprofessional, the Silversea crew knows how to please well-traveled guests with high expectations.
- **Truly all-inclusive:** An impressive selection of wines and spirits is included in the rates, as are gratuities.
- **Excellent cuisine:** Rivaling the best restaurants ashore, cuisine is as exquisite as it gets at sea. Each ship has two alternative venues for dinner, buffets are bountiful, and the room-service menu includes jumbo shrimp and other delish treats.
- **Large staterooms and great bathrooms:** Most of the line's suites are larger than Seabourn's and Crystal's, and the huge marble bathrooms are the best at sea (along with those on Regent's *Seven Seas Navigator* and *Voyager*).

Cons

- **Stuffy crowd:** Of course, not every guest fits that bill, but expect a good portion of the crowd on any cruise to be . . . reserved.

SILVERSEA: THE CROWN JEWELS

Silversea Cruises was conceived in the early 1990s by the Lefebvre family of Italy, former owners of Sitmar Cruises, a legendary Italian line that was merged into P&O/Princess in the late '80s. Created to cater to discerning travelers looking for a superluxurious cruise experience, the line's four ships were built and outfitted at shipyards in Italy, and no expense was spared in their design.

The new line joined Seabourn right at the top of the heap when it introduced the 296-passenger *Silver Cloud* and *Silver Wind* in 1994—and, in fact, features such as stateroom balconies and a two-level show lounge actually gave them the edge. With the introduction of the larger, more impressive *Silver Shadow* and *Silver Whisper* in 2000 and 2001, that bar was raised even higher, with larger staterooms and huge marble bathrooms, dimly lit and romantic cigar lounges, and more entertainment lounges—all in all, the absolute height of style, paired with itineraries that spanned the globe. A concerted effort has been made to play up the line's Italian connections. The specialty Italian restaurants are under the guidance of Marco Betti, owner of Florence's award-winning Antica Posta restaurant; Italian-made bath amenities come from Acqua di Parma and Bulgari; high-end Italian clothes and accessories are in the

Compared with the other ultraluxury lines, here's how Silversea rates:

	Poor	Fair	Good	Excellent	Outstanding
Enjoyment Factor					✓
Dining					✓
Activities			✓		
Children's Program	N/A*				
Entertainment		✓			
Service					✓
Worth the Money			✓		

* Silversea has no children's program.

boutiques; and bronze statues and reliefs from Italian sculptor Francesco Messina are on loan from a private collection.

In early 2007, Silversea announced its intentions to build a new 36,000-ton, 540-passenger ship at Italian shipyard Fincantieri. It's slated to debut in late 2009, and an option for a second ship was also signed.

PASSENGER PROFILE

While Silversea's typical passenger mix is 48-plus, shorter cruise sailings often skew the mix a tad younger, adding at least a handful of 30- and 40-something couples to the pot. Still, the cruise director on a recent *Silver Whisper* cruise told us a 30-something honeymoon couple on the previous sailing had cut out halfway through because the crowd and vibe was older and more sedate than they had expected. Typically, about 70% of passengers are American and they're well traveled, well heeled, well dressed, well accessorized, and well into their 50s, 60s, and 70s. Most guests are couples, though singles and small groups of friends traveling together are usually part of the scene, too. Many have cruised with Silversea before; in fact, every single person Heidi met on a recent cruise had sailed with the line at least once, if not many times.

DINING

Foodies should consider Silversea for the food alone. The cuisine is well prepared and presented, and creative chefs continually come up with a wide variety of dishes. Many ingredients are imported from Italy (the pasta, cheese, and parma ham, for instance), and much of the baked goods—including the excellent foccacia and flatbreads—are made right on board. In Europe, as on all itineraries, at least two local specialties are offered on the menu—for instance, stuffed cabbage with beef or pork loin with horseradish on voyages to Sweden. Each ship has a formal open-seating venue and two more casual options. There are plenty of tables for two in all restaurants, though in the main dining room you may have to wait.

TRADITIONAL   While the cuisine in the elegant main dining room (straightforwardly called The Restaurant) is not quite as impressive as that of the more intimate

Silversea Fleet Itineraries

Ship	Sailing Regions	Home Ports
Silver Cloud	7- to 15-night voyages in the Mediterranean/Greek Isles/Adriatic/Black Sea (various combinations), Atlantic Europe, Northern Europe/Russia, the Norwegian Fjords, the British Isles, and Atlantic Europe	Piraeus/Athens, Istanbul, Barcelona, Monte Carlo, Civitavecchia/Rome, London, Copenhagen, Stockholm, Venice,
Silver Whisper	7- to 12-night voyages in the Mediterranean/Greek Isles/Adriatic (various combinations)	Piraeus/Athens, Civitavecchia/Rome, Barcelona, Monte Carlo, Venice, Lisbon, Istanbul
Silver Wind	7- to 15-night voyages in Northern Europe/Russia, the Norwegian Fjords/North Cape, the British Isles, Atlantic Europe, Iberian Peninsula, the Mediterranean/Greek Isles/Adriatic (various combinations), and the Black Sea	Lisbon, London, Stockholm, Copenhagen, Barcelona, Civitavecchia/Rome, Piraeus/Athens, Monte Carlo, Nice, Venice, Istanbul

and casual La Terrazza, it still offers delicious meals, with entrees such as a duet of king prawn and halibut with wild rice cakes; crispy roasted duck; and a penne pasta with spicy tomato, olive, caper, and anchovy sauce. The wine list is excellent, and a pair of complimentary wines is suggested at each meal from more than 40 choices; if you'd like something other than the featured ones, ask and ye shall find. You can also choose one of the wines not included on the complimentary list—a $745 1990 Château Margaux, anyone?

SPECIALTY   Two specialty restaurants serve dinner on each ship, both by reservation. Open most evenings for dinner, **La Terrazza** is an intimate venue offering Italian cuisine. Start with a plate of antipasto—fresh parmegano, proscuitto, olives, sun-dried tomatoes and marinated eggplant—before moving on to delicious dishes such as a mushroom tartlet or buffalo mozzarella with fresh tomato and basil; gnocchi filled with gorgonzola; and a juicy pork loin. Featured desserts, such as a delicious *millefoglie* (flaky puff pastry layered with cream), are paired with a tray of Italian-made biscotti.

The second alternative venue offers a new twist on cruise dining, offering menus that pair food with wine—and not the other way around. Developed in consultation with master sommeliers trained in the member boutique lodgings and restaurants of Relais & Châteaux–Relais Gourmands, the wine menus reflect regions of the world known for their rich viticultural heritage, including France, Italy, northern California, South Africa, Australia, and New Zealand. Sommeliers describe the origin and craft of each vintage, then offer dishes created especially to bring out the wine's full richness. Guests enjoy a different wine with each course, with the extra charge for dinner varying in accordance with the wines presented. On a recent cruise, it was $150 per person, and frequented mostly by European passengers.

CASUAL   Burgers, sandwiches, and salads are served poolside at lunchtime, in addition to service in The Restaurant and the buffet-style Terrace Cafe (which is transformed into La Terrazza in the evenings). Once per cruise, passengers are also invited into the galley for the traditional **galley brunch,** which features more than 100 delectable dishes, like stone crab claws, pickled herring, Hungarian goulash, rabbit a la Provençal, and German bratwurst. A red carpet is rolled out, literally, through the galley, and the chef is on hand to chat with guests about the feast.

SNACKING & EXTRAS   The line's **24-hour room-service menu** includes such mouthwatering choices as jumbo shrimp cocktail, a snack-sized portion of crabmeat served with lime mayonnaise and guacamole, and delicious thin-crust gourmet pizzas. Plus, if you'd rather dine in one evening, you can order off The Restaurant's menu (during its dinnertime operating hours) and have your meal served course by course on a table set with linens and china in your suite. There's an elegant white-gloved tea service in one of the lounges on most days.

ACTIVITIES

Aside from trivia games, card tournaments, stretch and aerobics classes, and bridge tours, Silversea tries to focus on more cerebral pursuits. **Wine-tasting seminars** are excellent, and the line's enrichment lectures are varied and interesting; at least one guest speaker is featured on every sailing, ranging from explorers and adventurers to authors and journalists. **Culinary theme cruises,** offered in partnership with Relais & Châteaux, are hosted by Relais Gourmands chefs and feature demos and tastings. The line recently launched the Viking Cooking School in a custom-designed demonstration culinary theater on each ship. Ships are outfitted with the latest Viking equipment, and guests can sign up for complimentary cooking seminars that include demos, wine pairing, Q&As with guest chefs, and special lunches.

Other pursuits include language classes, **golf instruction** and driving nets, and computer classes. *Silver Whisper* also offers special golf cruises that feature PGA golf pros, golfing excursions, and the latest video-teaching technology.

Lighter activities include a dip in the pool or two hot tubs, shopping in the boutiques (which include an H.Stern, where you'll find high-end gold, diamond, and gemstone pieces), and Web surfing in the Internet center. Passengers who travel with their laptops can take advantage of Wi-Fi hot spots on board. **Onboard cellphone service** is also now an option. Overall, though, these ships are low key (don't expect any music on the pool deck, for instance) and guests are left to their own devices when it comes to keeping busy—just the way most guests like it. Reading, dozing, or sipping cool drinks seems to keep most happily occupied.

The line recently revamped their spas, now calling them **The Spa at Silversea.** Treatments and packages are centered on specific issues and overall wellness, targeting everything from aging skin to cellulite, arthritis, poor circulation, sore muscles, and other areas. To avoid waiting in line on the first day of the cruise to make your appointments, you can now book your treatments via the line's website up to 48 hours before your cruise. You can also prebook **shore excursions** online up to the week before sailing.

CHILDREN'S PROGRAM

These ships are not geared to children, though every so often one or two are aboard. Babysitting may be arranged with an available crewmember (no guarantee); otherwise, no activities or services are offered specifically for children. The minimum age for sailing is 12 months.

ENTERTAINMENT

For evening entertainment, the ships each have a small casino, a combo entertaining in the nightclub adjacent to the show lounge, a pianist in another lounge, and dozens of in-cabin movies, including oldies and current films. At press time, the small-scale song-and-dance revues that had been offered in the two-level show lounges were being phased out, with the line trying a three-person magic act in its place. On other nights, performers include singers, instrumentalists, and jugglers. Cruise director Steve Lewis told Heidi on a recent cruise that they were trying to experiment with different types of entertainment, as some guests weren't crazy about the glitzy production shows. Popular **theme cruises** from time to time feature classical musicians, guest chefs, and renowned wine experts conducting demonstrations and talks. Occasionally on Europe cruises, local performers are brought on board, such as Flamenco dancers in Barcelona. The pace is calm, and that's the way most Silversea guests like it; most are perfectly content to spend their after-dinner hours with cocktails and conversation. Occasionally, depending on the crowd, the Panorama Lounge (on *Whisper*) or The Bar (on either ship) attracts a contingent of revelers who dance and drink into the wee hours.

SERVICE

Certified by the Guild of Professional English Butlers, the top suites include the services of a butler who will unpack your bags, draw your bath, make spa or dinner reservations, put together an in-suite cocktail party for you and the maharaja, or arrange a private car at the next port—as long as you cough up the bucks to stay in one of the ships' Grand, Royal, Rossellini, or Owner's suites.

Even if you're not in a top suite, though, the gracious staff knows how to please. Staff members are friendly and remember your name, but are never obtrusive or pushy. Waiters and stewards are as discreet as the guests are, and chances are, you'll never hear the word *no*. The room-service menu is extensive, and at dinnertime you can also order from The Restaurant's menu and have it served in your suite course by course. Unlimited wines, champagne, spirits, and soft drinks are included in the rates, as are gratuities. Hot and cold canapés are served in the lounges before dinner, and Godiva chocolates are left on suite pillows on formal evenings. For an extra charge ($100–$150 per person), you can take advantage of flexible embarkation and debarkation, getting into your suite as early as 10:30am on embarkation day and debarking as late as 5pm on the last day.

Laundry and **dry cleaning** are available. There are also **self-service laundry** rooms.

Silver Whisper

The Verdict

This is the most handsome, well-run ship you can find in the ultraluxe market; absolutely as good as it gets for fine cuisine, service, and suites.

Silver Whisper *(photo: Silversea Cruises)*

Specifications

Size (in Tons)	28,258	Crew	295
Passengers (Double Occ.)	382	Passenger/Crew Ratio	1.3 to 1
Passenger/Space Ratio	74	Year Launched	2001
Total Cabins/Veranda Cabins	194/157	Last Refurbishment/Upgrade	2007

Frommer's Ratings (Scale of 1–5)   ★★★★★

Cabin Comfort & Amenities	5	Dining Options	5
Appearance & Upkeep	5	Gym, Spa & Sports Facilities	4
Public Comfort/Space	5	Children's Facilities	N/A
Decor	5	Enjoyment Factor	5

With *Silver Whisper* and her sister ship, *Silver Shadow,* Silversea set the bar very high for the rest of the ultraluxe lines. They're small enough to be intimate, but large enough to offer a classy two-story show lounge, dark and romantic cigar lounge, three dining venues, an impressive spa and gym, and some really great suites, in addition to the fine service and cuisine offered fleetwide.

Cabins & Rates

Cabins	Per Diem From	Sq. Ft.	Fridge	Hair Dryer	Sitting Area	TV
Suite	$710	287–1,435*	Yes	Yes	Yes	Yes

* Including balconies

CABINS   The suites aboard *Silver Whisper* leave nothing to be desired. With a chilled bottle of Pommery Brut Royal at your side, just settle down in the comfy sitting area and bask in the ambient luxury. Private balconies are attached to three-quarters of the plush staterooms, which measure a roomy 287 square feet or more. They're done up in an ultrapleasant color scheme focused on rich blues and soft golds, along with coppery-brown wood tones. Each suite has a walk-in closet, minibar, DVD player, sitting area, lighted dressing table with hair dryer, writing desk, and wonderful marble-covered bathrooms stocked with Acqua di Palma or Bulgari toiletries (the stewardess comes around at the beginning of the cruise to ask your preference). The separate shower stall and long bathtub, along with double sinks, make these among the best loos at sea; only Regent's *Seven Seas Navigator* and *Voyager* have bathrooms this good. All beds have feather-down pillows and duvets, and Egyptian cotton linens. The largest of the four two-bedroom Grand Suites is really something else, measuring 1,435 square feet with three bathrooms, a pair of walk-in closets, an entertainment center, two verandas, and a living room and dining area. All suites now have new flatscreen televisions and plusher mattresses and bedding.

PUBLIC AREAS   The low-key, main lobby area, where the purser's desk resides, branches out into a pair of attractive four-deck-high staircases, with shiplike railings and corridors done in a mix of Wedgwood blue and golden peach fabrics and carpeting, along with warm caramel wood tones. The impressive two-story show lounge has tiered seating and lots of cozy clusters of chairs, while The Bar, just outside the show lounge's first level, can be a social hub, with a long bar, dance floor, and plenty of seating. The Observation Lounge, high on Deck 10 overlooking the bow, is a great place to relax, read, and watch the scenery unfold through floor-to-ceiling windows. You'll find a radar screen, astronomical maps, binoculars, and reference books—and during the day, a self-service coffee, tea, and juice bar. On Deck 8 at the stern, the windowed Panorama Lounge also affords great sea views and lots of comfortable seating. By day, enjoy a continental breakfast or high tea here, while by night the venue becomes an intimate nightspot, with a pianist serenading dancers. The Humidor cigar lounge is a dark, cozy, and plush spot for cocktails—even nonsmokers can't help but be drawn to the ambience, while cigar lovers should enjoy the walk-in humidor. There's also a small casino and attached bar, a card room with felt-topped tables, a boutique, and a pool bar.

DINING OPTIONS   In The Restaurant, the main dining room, a live trio plays romantic oldies on some nights, and guests are invited to take a spin around the small dance floor. There are plenty of tables for two, though during popular times you may have a short wait. Breakfast, lunch, and dinner are served here in high style, while a more casual buffet-style breakfast and lunch are offered in the indoor/outdoor La Terrazza. Service is doting even in the casual venue, with waiters rushing to carry plates to your table, serve drinks, and clear things off just moments after you finish. A special pasta dish is made to order by a chef for guests who do lunch in La Terrazza. Come evenings, it serves a wonderful Italian menu; reservations are required. A third venue offers special wine-pairing menus (see "Dining," above) in an intimate setting on Deck 7 next to the Terrace Cafe.

POOL, FITNESS, SPA & SPORTS FACILITIES   A combination of old-style wooden deck chairs and plastic chaise longues padded with royal blue cushions lines the open decks. Unfortunately, jolting grass-green AstroTurf covers the entirety of decks 9 and 10 (they could have at least chosen a teak-colored synthetic flooring).

There are plenty of places to retire with a good book or an afternoon snooze, either near the pool and hot tubs on Deck 8 (which is teak, by the way), or at the stern on that deck. There's also a golf-driving cage and shuffleboard.

The spa, gym, and hair salon occupy much of Deck 10 and are spacious for a ship of this size. There's a separate workout room with exercise machines, plus a separate aerobics room. The spa features a pleasant subtle Asian decor, but you'll hardly notice once you're under the spell of the masseuse.

Silver Cloud • Silver Wind

The Verdict

Big enough to offer a two-story show lounge and several other entertainment outlets, and cozy enough that you'll feel like you practically have the vessels to yourself, this pair is an absolute dream.

Silver Wind *(photo: Silversea Cruises)*

Specifications

Size (in Tons)	16,800	Year Launched	
Passengers (Double Occ.)	296	*Silver Cloud*	1994
Passenger/Space Ratio	57	*Silver Wind*	1995
Total Cabins/Veranda Cabins	148/110	Last Refurbishment/Update	
Crew	210	*Silver Cloud*	2007
Passenger/Crew Ratio	1.4 to 1	*Silver Wind*	2007

Frommer's Ratings (Scale of 1–5)   ★★★★★

Cabin Comfort & Amenities	4	Dining Options	4
Appearance & Upkeep	4	Gym & Spa Facilities	4
Public Comfort/Space	4	Children's Facilities	N/A
Decor	4	Enjoyment Factor	5

Both superintimate and large enough to have multiple entertainment venues, two restaurants, and lots of outdoor deck space, *Silver Wind* and her sister ship, *Silver Cloud,* were built in the mid-1990s, just in time to get in on must-have ship fashions such as balconies. A few years back, a face-lift to both added an expanded spa, new gym, Internet cafe, wine bar, and lots of new furniture.

Cabins & Rates

Cabins	Per Diem From	Sq. Ft.	Fridge	Hair Dryer	Sitting Area	TV
Suite	$642	240–1,314*	Yes	Yes	Yes	Yes

* Including balconies

CABINS   Like their larger sisters, *Silver Wind* and *Cloud* are all-suite ships, with balconies on more than three-quarters of the staterooms. All 148 suites have sitting areas, roomy walk-in closets, bathtubs, vanities, TVs and DVD players, stocked minibars, and Acqua di Palma or Bulgari toiletries; the top of the lot, the Grand Suites, have two bedrooms, two living rooms, three televisions, two bathrooms, and a full-size Jacuzzi tub. Color schemes revolve around creamy beige fabrics and golden-brown wood. Swirled peachy-gray marble covers bathrooms from head to toe, and though indulgent enough, the bathrooms don't hold a flame to the larger, simply decadent loos on newer fleetmates *Silver Whisper* and *Shadow.* Goose-down pillows ensure a good night's rest.

PUBLIC AREAS   Public areas inside and out are spacious and open. High tea is served by day in the windowed Panorama Lounge, which at night hosts piano entertainment. Magic and other acts are performed in the attractive two-story show lounge, and, on most nights, a dance band plays oldies or a DJ spins in the intimate and dimly lit adjacent bar. There's a small casino, too, plus boutiques where you can spend your winnings, including a fine jewelry shop with the requisite gold and diamond-studded watches. An observation lounge is positioned on the far-forward part of a top deck and is oddly not attached to the ship's interior, so you must go out on deck to enter.

DINING OPTIONS   The formal, open-seating dining venue, called The Restaurant, is delicately decorated in pale pink and gold, and elegant candlelit tables are set with heavy crystal glasses, chunky Christofle silverware, and doily-covered silver show plates. The indoor/outdoor La Terrazza cafe, where buffet-style breakfast and lunch are served, is transformed into a nightly venue for more casual evening dining, featuring a scrumptious Italian menu created under the guidance of chef Marco Betti.

POOL, FITNESS & SPA FACILITIES   There is a pool and two hot tubs. The oceanview gym occupies a roomy space by itself way up on Deck 9, on the far-forward part of the deck (oddly, it's not attached to the ship's interior and you must go out on the deck to enter). The small spa offers a variety of massages and facials.

8

Small Ships, Sailing Ships & Adventure Cruises

Aside from the fact that they both sail in water, mainstream cruise ships and the small ships in this chapter have hardly anything in common. Whereas big ships allow you to see a region while immersed in a resortlike onboard atmosphere, small ships allow you to see it from the waterline, without distraction from anything that's not an inherent part of the locale—no glitzy interiors, no big shows or loud music, no casinos, no spas, and no crowds either, as the majority of these ships carry fewer than 100 passengers. Whether sailing the Baltic, the Norwegian Fjords, the Scottish highlands, or the Greek Isles, you're a part of your destination from the minute you wake up until the minute you fall asleep, and for the most part you're left alone to form your own opinions.

The ships reviewed in this chapter fall under two general headings: **ocean and coastal vessels** (Hurtigruten, Lindblad Expeditions, easyCruise) and **sailing ships** (Sea Cloud, Star Clipper, and Windstar). You won't find the range of public rooms and onboard amenities on these ships that you find on the mainstream or luxury lines, though some are surprisingly comfortable and elegant. All offer a very different experience, both from the mainstream and luxe lines and from each other.

The ships generally visit a port every day, and because they have shallow draughts (the amount of the ship that rides below the waterline), they're able to sail to small, out-of-the-way ports that the big cruise ships would run aground trying to approach. There is generally little time spent at sea on these cruises—the emphasis is on giving everyone the maximum allowable time in each port.

Passengers tend to be well-traveled people who like to learn and explore, and care little about plush amenities (except perhaps on Windstar) or onboard activities of the bingo and horse-racing variety. Don't expect doting service on most of these lines, but do expect very personal attention. Also, because there are so few passengers aboard (generally between 100 and 300), you'll get to know your shipmates more quickly.

The Scoop on Small-Ship Tonnage

When reading the reviews in this chapter, bear in mind that small-ship lines often measure their ships' **gross register tonnage**, or GRTs (a measure of internal space, not actual weight), differently than the large lines. There's not even a definite standard within the small-ship market, so to compare ship sizes, it's best to just look at the number of passengers aboard. Also note that where GRTs measures are nonstandard, **passenger/space measurements** are impossible or meaningless.

Frommer's Ratings at a Glance: The Small-Ship Lines

1 = poor   2 = fair   3 = good   4 = excellent   5 = outstanding

Cruise Line	Enjoyment Factor	Dining	Activities	Children's Program	Entertainment	Service	Worth the Money
Hurtigruten	4	3	N/A	N/A	N/A	3	4
Lindblad Expeditions	5	4	5	N/A	2	4	4
Star Clippers	5	4	4	N/A	3	4	5
Windstar	5	4	2	N/A	2	5	4

Note: Cruise lines have been graded on a curve that compares them only with the other lines in the Small Ships, Sailing Ships & Adventure Cruises category. See chapter 5 for the ratings methodology. Few of the lines and vessels in this chapter offer a children's program. Lines we've covered in mini-reviews have not been rated.

A NOTE ON LINE/SHIP RATINGS   Because the small-ship experience is so completely different from the megaship experience, we've had to adjust our ratings. For instance, because all but a tiny fraction of these ships have just one dining room for all meals, we can't judge them by the same standard we use for ships with 5 or 10 different restaurants. So we've set the default **Dining Options** rating for these ships at 3, or "good," with points deducted if a restaurant is particularly uncomfortable and points added for any options above and beyond. Similarly, we've changed the "Gym & Spa Facilities" rating to **Adventure & Fitness Options** to reflect the fact that, on small ships, the focus is what's outside, not inside. Options covered in this category might include kayaks, trips by inflatable launch, an A-1 ice rating (allowing Arctic sailings), and frequent hiking and/or snorkeling trips.

DRESS CODES   The word is *casual.* Depending on the region sailed, polo shirts, khakis or shorts, and a pullover or light jacket will take care of you all week. Some lines (Windstar, for instance) get a little fancier at mealtimes.

1 Mini-Review: easyCruise

The Rotunda, 42/43 Gloucester Crescent, London NW1 7DL, United Kingdom. ✆ +30-211-211-6211. www. easycruise.com.

THE LINE IN A NUTSHELL   Launched in 2005 by U.K.-based entrepreneur Stelios Haji-Ioannou (the brains behind easyJet, easyHotel, easyCar, and a dozen other "easy" companies), easyCruise occupies a niche all its own—neither mainstream, nor luxury, nor your usual small-ship cruise, either. The idea is actually pretty simple: Throw out everything people expect a cruise to be and start over.

THE EXPERIENCE   Are you used to treating your ship like a home away from home? Not here, where the ship is just a combo transportation device and sleeping compartment. Accustomed to traveling in a bubble, with the cruise line arranging activities, entertainment, and excursions? Not here, where you're completely on your own, with just a concierge to suggest the best restaurants and clubs in port. Accustomed to itineraries that start somewhere, go somewhere, and end up back at the beginning a week or so later? Not here, where passengers have the option of boarding and debarking at almost any of the scheduled ports and sailing as many or few nights

easyCruise Fleet Itineraries

Ship	Sailing Regions	Home Ports
easyCruise Life	7-night voyages in the Greek Isles/Aegean (various combinations)	Piraeus/Athens, Bodrum
easyCruiseOne	4- to 10-night voyages in the Greek Isles/Ionian Sea (various combinations)	Piraeus/Athens

as they want (with the only rule being a minimum 2-night stay). Accustomed to paying a single price for your whole trip, everything included? Not here, where the rates are per day and cover only the cabin charge. Everything else costs extra: meals, daily service by a cabin steward, and niceties such as beach towels. Now the kicker: **easyCruise's rates are fantastically low.** In early 2008, rates for the line's Greek Isles trips were starting at around $60 per person, per day, double occupancy. If you feel like traveling at the last minute, you can book up to 48 hours before sailing as long as cabins are still available.

Essentially, easyCruise is a rail pass for the 25 to 50 set: cheap, flexible, and easy—and they don't hold your hand. "I don't expect a lot of my customers to spend much time in their cabins," says Haji-Ioannou. "This is about making the destination the destination, not the ship."

easyCruiseOne ★★★, the line's first ship, was built in 1990 as *Renaissance II* for now-defunct Renaissance Cruises. As part of its "easy"-fication, the ship's interior walls were all moved to fit more cabins (increasing its passenger load from 114 to 170). Average cabin size is a tiny 100 square feet, with four larger staterooms offering 258 square feet. All cabins have simple platform beds and a private bathroom with shower, but not much else—they're just a place to sleep, not a home away from home. Cabin windows were originally sealed up, but that bizarre decision was mercifully reversed during the ship's 2006 dry dock, and 60 of the ship's 85 cabins now have windows. Once you check in, you won't see a steward showing up to clean or change bedding unless you pay an additional housekeeping charge.

Most passengers dine ashore, but small plates, pizza, pasta, salads, and "big plates" (steak, fish tacos, and so on) are available at the restaurant, FusionOn4. Breakfast is also served there all day, for late risers. All menus are a la carte, with prices listed per item.

Passengers typically find their entertainment in port and return to the ship only to sleep, though there are a few public amenities, including an outdoor cocktail bar and hot tub for socializing, a gym, a sauna, a small spa, and an Internet cafe. The ship's concierge can direct you to the best restaurants, bars, and clubs in each port, and you don't have to be back aboard till midnight or later, giving you plenty of time for nightlife.

At press time, the line had just announced acquisition of its second ship, to be christened *easyCruise Life.* The 12,600-ton vessel, which will carry about 500 passengers, began her pre-easyCruise life as *Lev Tolstoy,* built in 1981 by the Black Sea Shipping Company for cruise ship and ferry use in the Soviet Union. In the intervening years, she also sailed as *Natasha, Palmira,* and *Farah.* EasyCruise will customize the vessels to match its "easy" brand experience.

EasyCruise's vessels are adults-only ships, with a minimum age of 18.

2 Hurtigruten (formerly Norwegian Coastal Voyage)

405 Park Ave., Suite 904, New York, NY 10022. ℭ **800/323-7436** or 212/319-1300. Fax 212/319-1390. www.hurtigruten.us.

THE LINE IN A NUTSHELL   Hurtigruten is unlike any other cruise line in the world, in that it's not really a cruise line at all. Instead, its ships function as a mix of cruise vessel, ferry, and cargo carrier. So what's the attraction? Its route, which takes in the entire gorgeous coast of Norway, calling at 35 villages, towns, and cities along the way.

THE EXPERIENCE   Hurtigruten (Norwegian for "Coastal Voyage," which explains why until recently the line was known as "Norwegian Coastal Voyage" in the U.S.) offers a comfortable, moderately priced way to visit normally expensive Norway and to get to know its people, towns, and incredible scenery. The line's small- and midsize ships operate year-round, offering trips that sail from Bergen in the south to Kirkenes at the very top of Norway, then back again. Along the way, in each direction, they call at 35 coastal ports, sometimes for just a few minutes, but sometimes for a long enough time that you can take a shore excursion inland, if you like. The ships carry cargo and vehicles as well as passengers and are considered a daily lifeline by some coastal and island regions. Passengers are a mix of travelers who are sailing the full 12-night round-trip voyage (which stops at each port twice, at different times of the day), those who are sailing a 6-night one-way trip either north- or southbound, and locals who are making short jaunts between ports. The entertainment on these voyages is the scenery, the port arrivals and departures, and your fellow passengers. There are no evening shows or casinos aboard, and cabins are functional and plain—a place to sleep, not to hang out.

In recent years, Hurtigruten has begun to branch out from its traditional coastal route, sending some ships to Antarctica, building one ship specifically for sailings around **Greenland,** and making expedition voyages to **Spitzbergen** in the Svalbard Archipelago, midway between Norway and the North Pole.

Pros

- **Astounding scenery, up-close and personal.** As these are coastal ships, they stay near land and stop frequently.
- **A thrifty way to see Norway.** Most cabins are moderately priced compared to a land itinerary in this expensive country.
- **Every season has its attractions.** From late spring to early summer, you have 24 hours of daylight (and more, farther north). In the late summer and early fall, you can view the sky's changing colors. In the winter, you can see the Northern Lights.

Cons

- **Little time in port.** A lot of the port calls are for less than an hour—just enough time allowed to unload and load cargo and ferry-service passengers.
- **Ships do not penetrate the deepest fjords.** Unlike big cruise ships that concentrate on the most famous Norwegian fjords, the Hurtigruten fleet mostly hugs the coast and threads a route among the islands, spending little time in the fjords.
- **Rough seas and tough weather.** Many parts of the journey are through rough, open waters, sometimes just for a few minutes, sometimes for hours. Temperatures are typical of a cool maritime climate.

Compared with other European lines, here's how Hurtigruten rates:

	Poor	Fair	Good	Excellent	Outstanding
Enjoyment Factor				✓	
Dining			✓		
Activities	N/A				
Children's Program	N/A				
Entertainment	N/A				
Service			✓		
Worth the Money				✓	

HURTIGRUTEN: HAVE PORTS, WILL TRAVEL

Hurtigruten got its start in 1893, when Captain Richard With sailed the first express steamship from Trondheim to Hammerfest. Six years later, the route was extended from Bergen in the south to Kirkenes in the north—the very same standard route the Hurtigruten vessels sail today. The company's current fleet is divided into five distinct groups: the modern Millennium ships (*Midnatsol, Finnmarken,* and *Trollfjord*), all launched in 2002 and 2003; the so-called Contemporary ships (*Kong Harald, Nordkapp, Nordlys, Nordnorge, Polarlys,* and *Richard With*), dating to between 1993 and 1997; the Mid-Generation ships (*Narvik* and *Vesteralen*), which date about 1982 to 1983 but are not usually marketed to Americans; and the remaining "traditional" ships (*Lofoton* and *Nordstjernen*), built in the early 1960s and today sailing only limited service in fall and winter. The Millennium ships are larger and even more cruise ship–like than the 1990s generation of ships, offering more and more varied cabins (including a few suites with balconies) and 50% more deck space. In 2007, the line introduced *Fram,* the first ship ever built to sail around the coast of Greenland. It also operates the 3,500-ton, 100-passenger icebreaker **Polar Star** on voyages to the Svalbard Archipelago, far north of the Arctic Circle.

Tip: The best time to sail Hurtigruten is just before the middle of May, when you get 24 hours of daylight, fewer crowds, and lower fares.

PASSENGER PROFILE

Hurtigruten passengers making full-length one-way or round-trip passages are generally age 50 and up, and generally pretty sedentary. In summer, there will be some younger passengers. Germans are the most numerous nationality, followed by Brits, Norwegians, and other Scandinavians and Europeans. Some Americans book as part of a tour operator's package. Independent travelers will be aboard in the warmer months.

As the ships provide basic transportation between ports, you'll find Norwegians aboard as deck passengers, on for the day or sleeping overnight in chairs or banquettes, or in an overnight cabin. You'll also see lots of youthful backpackers during the summer holidays. The newer ships have conference facilities, and with oodles of available space in the off season, the Norwegian meetings market is growing.

Announcements are kept to a minimum but are repeated in five or six languages, including English. In high season, there's a courier aboard to handle shore excursions and passenger information, and he or she will likely speak many languages. On shore excursions, English-speaking passengers get an English-speaking guide but may be assigned to a bus with another group, meaning you may have to hear the tour in English and French, or English and Italian.

Smoking is permitted only on outside decks, so hard-core smokers should think twice before booking.

DINING

Dining is low key on Hurtigruten. The food is geared toward Norwegian and European tastes and is prepared and presented in a straightforward manner. Breakfast and lunch are buffets, and dinner is served by the young Norwegian waitstaff. There are two seatings when enough passengers are aboard to warrant them, and tables are assigned at embarkation according to language.

Three full restaurant meals a day are included for full one-way or round-trip passengers. **Breakfast** includes fruit, cereal, cold meats and cheeses, breads, toast, and often boiled or fried eggs with bacon or sausage. **Lunch** is the best meal, with several hot entrees, soup, salad fixings, cold meats, herring served about a half-dozen ways, and cakes and pies. **Dinner** is a set (no menu selection) three-course meal with soup, main course (often fish, chicken, or veal), and dessert. You can head forward to the bar for free coffee service after dinner. If you want a cup of java between meals, you have to buy it at the cafeteria. **Special diets** can be catered to with advance notice. After a week aboard, the food may become somewhat monotonous, though it has improved in recent years.

As this is a domestic service, and taxes on alcohol are high, you can expect to pay a minimum of about $6 for a bottle of beer and $25 for wine. Some passengers bring their own liquor, which they can consume in their cabins or in the lounges, but not in the dining room.

SNACKS & EXTRAS   All the ships have cafes that cater mainly to the short-trip port-to-port passengers, but if you get hungry between meals, you can pay extra for snacks there.

ACTIVITIES

The main activity while underway is viewing the scenery. During their 12-night round-trip voyages, the ships stop in 34 ports heading northbound and 35 heading southbound, sometimes during the day, sometimes at night. Calls may be as short as 15 minutes or as long as a few hours, and passengers may go ashore at each port to explore, go for a short walk, or just step off to buy a newspaper or souvenir before the ship sails again. A package of reasonably priced **shore excursions** provides a worthwhile way to see interior Norway and several fjords by bus. Excursions are booked through the onboard courier or in advance as a package.

There are no activities offered otherwise—you have to be self-motivated enough to play cards or read. Every ship in the fleet has an Internet cafe.

Tips Sailing North—Way North

In addition to the ships profiled here, Hurtigruten also operates the 3,500-ton, 100-passenger icebreaker *Polar Star* (built 1969, renovated 2000) on 11-night voyages that sail around the island of Spitzbergen in the Svalbard Archipelago, midway between Norway and the North Pole. The ship departs from Spitzbergen's main town, Longyearbyen, after passengers have flown in.

Hurtigruten's Classic Fleet: A Retro Coastal Adventure

While most American passengers will book Hurtigruten's newer ships, those seeking something more rustic might be attracted to the line's older vessels, some of which date back more than 40 years.

Built in the early 1960s, the very traditional *Lofoten* and *Nordstjernen* are reminiscent of old steamships. Taking fewer than 200 passengers, they offer the atmosphere of a small, intimate country hotel with traditional wood-paneled walls. Most passengers who book these ships are fans of older vessels and prefer the old seagoing feel. Watching the cargo being lifted aboard by crane is like stepping back into a Humphrey Bogart movie. *Lofoten* and *Nordstjernen* sail October through March only.

The 4,200-ton midgeneration ships *Narvik* and *Vesteralen,* built in 1982 and 1983, carry between 312 and 323 passengers. Each has an attractive dome-style lounge on the top deck, a small forward observation lounge, a dining room and a cafeteria, a small shop, and functional, simply decorated cabins.

CHILDREN'S PROGRAM

Children come aboard with families making short port-to-port hauls, but few families sail the full 6- or 12-night voyages. For those kids who do make it aboard, the Millennium ships offer a small, unstaffed children's playroom and a video arcade. Kids get a 25% discount on shore excursions.

ENTERTAINMENT

Almost none. In the summer season, there may be a band and dancing some evenings, but it's hit or miss. The **Arctic Circle crossing ceremony** is great fun if you enjoy being baptized with ice water, and the 180-degree turn in the tight Trollfjord Basin amidst cascading waterfalls is also diverting.

SERVICE

The crew is all Norwegian (or at least drawn from people living in Norway) and ranges from longtime employees to recent recruits in their early 20s. On the smaller ships, service can be personal and friendly, but on the larger ones, it tends to be efficient but not terribly interactive. Cabin service is limited to bed-making and cleaning. **Gratuities** are included in the cruise fare.

A **laundry room** has coin-operated washers and dryers. Detergent is free.

Hurtigruten Fleet Itineraries

Ship	Sailing Regions	Home Ports
Fram	7- and 15-night Greenland voyages	Kangerlussuaq (Greenland)
Polar Star	11-night Spitzbergen	Longyearbyen
Rest of Fleet	6- ato 12-night Norwegian fjords	Bergen, Kirkenes

Fram

The Verdict

The first (and so far only) ship designed specifically to sail the coast of Greenland, *Fram* is a modern mini cruise ship with a clean Scandinavian design.

Fram *(photo: Hurtigruten)*

Specifications

Size (in Tons)	12,700	Crew	75
Passengers (Double Occ.)	318	Passenger/Crew Ratio	4.2 to 1
Passenger/Space Ratio	39.9	Year Launched	2007
Total Cabins/Veranda Cabins	136/6	Last Major Refurbishment	N/A

Frommer's Ratings (Scale of 1–5)   ★★★★

Cabin Comfort & Amenities	3	Dining Options	4
Appearance & Upkeep	4	Adventure & Fitness Options	4
Public Comfort/Space	4	Children's Facilities	N/A
Decor	4	Enjoyment Factor	4

The United States has Alaska, and Scandinavia has Greenland: a remote, wild place that's technically part of the home turf but still seems completely and utterly *other*. That's the point of *Fram,* a small-to-midsize cruiser that was built specifically to sail the Greenland coast on 7- and 14-night expedition voyages that combine sea and land-based excursions, presentations on Greenland life and culture, and many included and optional activities, such as dog-sledding and hiking tours, helicopter trips, and museum visits. Despite the harsh, remote setting, *Fram* herself is relentlessly modern and comfortable. More so than the rest of the Hurtigruten fleet, she's a thoroughgoing cruise ship.

Fram was named after the polar ship built and sailed by Norwegian explorer Fridtjof Nansen on a 3-year expedition around Greenland in the late 1800s.

Cabins & Rates

Cabins	Per Diem From	Sq. Ft.	Fridge	Hair Dryer	Sitting Area	TV
Inside	$183	118–140	Yes	Yes	No	Yes
Outside	$187	118–248	Yes	Yes	Some	Yes
Suite	$296	269–420	Yes	Yes	Yes	Yes

CABINS   As aboard the rest of the Hurtigruten fleet, standard inside and outside cabins are utilitarian, with two twin beds (one of which converts to a sofa), a small desk and chair, a bathroom with shower, and adequate closet and storage space. Decor is plain-jane, forcing you to look at the scenery out your window or porthole. Mini-suites and balcony suites have queen-size beds and add a seating area with a couch, a TV, and a mini-fridge. Owner's suites have a separate bedroom and living room, a TV and stereo, Internet access, a jacuzzi, and a private balcony.

Two cabins on board are wheelchair-friendly.

PUBLIC AREAS   Hurtigruten incorporated aspects of Greenland arts and culture into *Fram*'s interior design. Several Greenland artists, including Ane Birthe Hove of

Nuuk, are represented on board, and the use of oak, leather, and wool in the ship's interiors lends a Nordic feel.

On the top deck, an observation lounge with floor-to-ceiling glass windows provides a protected space for viewing the Greenland scenery. There are also several outdoor viewing decks, including one in the bow. Other public rooms include a library with books on the Arctic, two bars, a small Internet center, two conference rooms, and a gift shop.

DINING OPTIONS   All meals are served at one comfortable restaurant on Deck 4. There's also a bistro on Deck 4 serving sandwiches, soups, and other light fare.

ADVENTURE & FITNESS OPTIONS   *Fram* has a fitness room, a sauna, and two heated outdoor Jacuzzis. Greenland itineraries include trips ashore by inflatable launch.

The Millennium Class: Finnmarken • Trollfjord • Midnatsol

The Verdict

These modern vessels are more like cruise ships than Hurtigruten's older vessels, with a variety of public rooms and more open deck space. *Finnmarken* even has a swimming pool.

Trollfjord *(photo: Hurtigruten)*

Specifications

Size (in Tons)	15,000	*Midnatsol*	304/5
Passengers (Double Occ.)		Crew	105
Finnmarken	650	Passenger/Crew Ratio	6 to 1
Trollfjord	674	Year Launched	
Midnatsol	674	*Finnmarken*	2002
Passenger/Space Ratio	23	*Trollfjord*	2002
Total Cabins/Veranda Cabins		*Midnatsol*	2003
Finnmarken	294/14	Last Major Refurbishment	N/A
Trollfjord	304/5		

Frommer's Ratings (Scale of 1–5)   ★★★ ½

Cabin Comfort & Amenities	3	Dining Options	3
Appearance & Upkeep	4	Adventure & Fitness Options	4
Public Comfort/Space	4	Children's Facilities	2
Decor	5	Enjoyment Factor	4

Hurtigruten's newest ships for their Norwegian routes, *Finnmarken, Trollfjord,* and *Midnatsol* accommodate 600-plus passengers with significantly more deck space and more passenger cabins than the line's older ships. Plus, they add more suites, a few with balconies and (on *Finnmarken* only) Jacuzzis. The ships are virtual floating art galleries showcasing Norwegian paintings, sculptures, and textiles.

Trollfjord and *Midnatsol* are sister ships. *Finnmarken* is similar, but with slightly fewer cabins and additional public facilities to make up the space.

Cabins & Rates

Cabins	Per Diem From	Sq. Ft.	Fridge	Hair Dryer	Sitting Area	TV
Inside	$183	110	No	Yes	No	Yes
Outside	$187	110	No	Yes	No	Yes
Suite	$296	124	No	Yes	No	Yes

CABINS   The majority of cabins are simply furnished outsides with windows or port-holes, two beds (one of which converts to a couch), a desk and chair, adequate closet and storage space, and a bathroom with shower. Decor is a little better than what you find on the line's older ships, with a greater variety of larger cabins (although space in most is still fairly tight). A lot of the cabins have upper berths for a third passenger. All cabins on *Finnmarken,* as well as suites on *Midnatsol* and *Trollfjord,* come with TVs.

Midnatsol and *Trollfjord* also offer 23 suites and junior suites (5 with small balconies) with queen-size beds. *Finnmarken* has 32 suites, 14 with balconies and Jacuzzis.

Three cabins on *Finnmarken* and four on *Midnatsol* and *Trollfjord* are wheelchair accessible.

PUBLIC AREAS   Norwegian art forms a big part of the decor on these vessels. Works by noted Norwegian artist Kaare Espolin Johnson, which were removed from the old *Harald Jarl* when it was retired from service, adorn *Trollfjord's* small Deck 8 salon. Furnishings are modern Norwegian on *Trollfjord* and *Midnatsol* and Art Nou-veau aboard *Finnmarken,* with lots of windows and even glass elevators to let in the coastal views.

Each ship has a panoramic lounge on the upper decks (a favorite spot for viewing scenery), a children's playroom, shops, a cafe, and a variety of bars and lounges. There are Internet centers and libraries as well, and the *Finnmarken* even has a wine bar and outdoor cafe. Auditorium-like conference facilities on *Trollfjord* and *Midnatsol* are used for groups.

DINING OPTIONS   The main restaurants on all these ships serve all three meals and would not look out of place on an American megaship.

ADVENTURE & FITNESS OPTIONS   All three ships have small fitness rooms and saunas (with windows on *Trollfjord* and *Midnatsol* so you don't miss any views), as well as large sun decks. *Finnmarken* also has a massage area and outdoor swimming pool, as well as a hair salon.

Kong Harald • Richard With • Nordlys • Nordkapp • Polarlys

The Verdict

Attractive, comfortable, and serviceable vessels that provide a moderately priced, casual, low-key cruise up the Norwegian coast.

Nordkapp *(photo: Hurtigruten)*

Specifications

Size (in Tons)		Richard With	23
Kong Harald	11,200	Nordlys	23
Richard With	11,205	Nordkapp	23
Nordlys	11,200	Polarlys	25
Nordkapp	11,386	Total Cabins/Veranda Cabins	230–242/0
Polarlys	12,000	Crew	60
Passengers (Double Occ.)		Passenger/Crew Ratio	7.3 to 1
Kong Harald	490	Year Launched	
Richard With	490	Kong Harald	1993
Nordlys	482	Richard With	1993
Nordkapp	490	Nordlys	1994
Polarlys	482	Nordkapp	1996
Passenger/Space Ratio		Polarlys	1996
Kong Harald	23	Last Major Refurbishment	N/A

Frommer's Ratings (Scale of 1–5)   ★★★

Cabin Comfort & Amenities	3	Dining Options	1
Appearance & Upkeep	4	Adventure & Fitness Options	1
Public Comfort/Space	4	Children's Facilities	3
Decor	4	Enjoyment Factor	3

Hurtigruten's last batch of 20th-century ships are attractive, comfortable, and low key, with cheerful and comfortable public rooms. On the downside, they provide limited outdoor deck space—when you're passing a major sight such as the narrow Trollfjord, it can seem downright crowded as people jockey for views.

Cabins & Rates

Cabins	Per Diem From	Sq. Ft.	Fridge	Hair Dryer	Sitting Area	TV
Inside	$183	100	No	Yes	No	No
Outside	$187	100	No	Yes	No	No
Suite	$296	205	No	Yes	Yes	Yes

CABINS   The majority of cabins are simply furnished outsides with windows or portholes, two beds (one of which converts to a couch), a desk and chair, adequate closet and storage space, and a bathroom with shower. Decor is typical for the line: plain and utilitarian. Many of the cabins have upper berths to accommodate a third passenger. Mini suites and balcony suites add a sitting area, TV, and minifridge, while higher-level suites add a TV and stereo, Internet access, a Jacuzzi, and, in some cases, a separate bedroom and living room and a private balcony.

Three cabins on each ship are wheelchair accessible.

PUBLIC AREAS   The ships feature excellent Norwegian art, with specially commissioned sculpture and paintings depicting maritime scenes such as fishing boats, village life, and older coastal steamers in stormy seas. The furnishings feature bold colors and patterns, and there are lots of shiny surfaces in steel, brass, and glass.

The forward observation lounge is the most popular daytime spot, with comfortable seating and wraparound windows. Getting a seat here in high season can become a blood sport (you are asked not to reserve seats). Aft of this space is a large bar and lounge. Forward on the restaurant deck is an entertainment lounge and bar, a small library, and a conference room. At midships there are shops, a game room for children, and a lounge where you can catch the views from tall windows while sitting in comfortable leather chairs.

DINING OPTIONS The main dining room serves all three meals, with passengers surrounded by wraparound windows. There's also a 24-hour cafeteria where you can purchase meals and snacks.

ADVENTURE & FITNESS OPTIONS Each ship offers a small gym with a few machines (such as treadmills and bikes), a bench press, and a weight machine. There's also a sauna, but no pool. Thanks to the generally cool temperatures, open deck space is limited to a large enclosed area aft on the highest deck, smaller afterdecks, and a wraparound, narrow promenade that's nice for jogging and strolling. Some of the available spaces offer deck chairs.

3 Lindblad Expeditions

96 Morton St., 9th Floor, New York, NY 10014. ℂ **800/EXPEDITION** (800/397-3348) or 212/765-7740. www.expeditions.com.

THE LINE IN A NUTSHELL Lindblad Expeditions is the most adventure- and learning-oriented of all the cruise lines in this book, offering itineraries that stay far away from the big ports, concentrating instead on places of natural beauty and compelling history.

THE EXPERIENCE Operating cruises worldwide for nearly 3 decades, Lindblad has a more international, professional feel than any of its small-ship competitors, its cruises designed for intellectually curious travelers who want a casual, jeans-and-fleece experience that's educational as well as relaxing. Your time is spent learning about places of natural and cultural beauty from high-caliber expedition leaders and guest scientists, many of them aboard as part of Lindblad's alliance with the **National Geographic Society.** Company founder Sven Olof Lindblad, son of expedition travel pioneer Lars Erik Lindblad, is a longtime advocate of environmentally responsible tourism, and Lindblad Expeditions' crew and staff emphasize respect for the local ecosystem in their talks with cruise passengers. Days are spent observing the world around you, either from the ship or on frequent motor-launch, hiking, and kayaking excursions, which are included in the cruise price. Depending on weather and sea conditions, there are usually two or three excursions every day. Camaraderie develops between passengers through participation in excursions and through sharing their experiences at lively recap sessions every evening before dinner.

Pros

- **Great expedition feeling:** Innovative, flexible itineraries, outstanding lecturers/guides, casual dress policy, and a friendly, accommodating staff help make the *Endeavour* one of the top expedition vessels sailing today.
- **Alliance with National Geographic:** Beyond providing top-notch lecturers aboard ship, Lindblad's relationship with the Geographic Society means its ships are actively engaged in scientific research, with passengers right in the thick of things.

- **Built-in shore excursions:** Lindblad programs its shore excursions as an integral part of its cruises, with all excursion costs included in the cruise fare. And they'd better be, because these trips are . . .

Cons

- **Very expensive:** Lindblad's cruise fares are among the highest in the small-ship market.
- **Small cabins.** While most passengers don't seem to mind, cabins are spartan and no-frills. They're places to sleep, not places to recreate.

LINDBLAD: LEARNING CRUISES FOR THE WELL-HEELED

In 1984, Sven-Olof Lindblad, son of adventure-travel pioneer Lars-Eric Lindblad, followed in his father's footsteps by forming Lindblad Expeditions. From the beginning, the line has specialized in providing environmentally sensitive adventure/educational cruises to remote places in the world, with visits to a few large ports thrown in for good measure. In 2004, the company's commitment to true exploration rose to a new level when it formed an alliance with the National Geographic Society, whose scientists, photographers, and film crews now sail aboard Lindblad's ships to provide guests with an enhanced experience and to conduct actual research. The line's most adventure-oriented vessel, the *National Geographic Endeavour,* has been outfitted with advanced research equipment, while NGS explorer-in-residence Sylvia Earle and her advisory group help develop research, conservation, and educational initiatives for the fleet.

In Europe, the line operates the 110-passenger *Endeavour* on itineraries that range from the Greek Isles to Arctic Norway. It also regularly charters several ships for regional, seasonal sailings, including the 54-guest *Lord of the Glens* (sailing the Scottish Highlands) and the 45-passenger sailing yacht *Panorama* (sailing the Greek Isles).

PASSENGER PROFILE

Lindblad tends to attract well-traveled and well-educated professionals who are looking for an active, casual, up-close experience with their destinations. They're the granola crowd with money. Most are in the 55-plus age range, though there are sometimes younger couples and occasionally families. Most tend to share an interest in nature and are intellectually curious about the culture and history of the regions they're visiting. There is often a substantial contingent of British passengers on European itineraries. A Lindblad Expeditions cruise will not appeal to couch potatoes and other sedentary types expecting a big-ship lineup of fun and games.

Compared with other small-ship lines, here's how Lindblad rates:

	Poor	Fair	Good	Excellent	Outstanding
Enjoyment Factor					✓
Dining			✓		
Activities					✓
Children's Program	N/A				
Entertainment		✓			
Service				✓	
Worth the Money				✓	

Smoking is permitted only on outside decks, so hard-core smokers should think twice before booking.

DINING

Hearty buffet breakfasts and lunches and sit-down dinners feature a good choice of both hot and cold dishes with plenty of fresh fruits and vegetables. Many of the fresh ingredients are obtained from ports along the way, and meals may reflect regional tastes. Another plus is the selection of freshly baked breads, pastries, and cakes.

While far from haute cuisine, dinners are well prepared and presented. Varied menus feature primarily Continental cuisine with a choice of fish or meat entrees. **Vegetarian options** are available at every meal, and other special diets (low-fat, low-salt, kosher, and so forth) can be accommodated with advance notice. All meals are served at single open seatings that allow passengers to get to know each other by moving around to different tables. Lecturers and other staff members also dine with passengers.

SNACKS & EXTRAS   Appetizers served in the late afternoon include items such as fruit and cheese platters, and baked brie with pecans and brown sugar.

ACTIVITIES

During the day, most activity takes place off the ship on Zodiac and/or land excursions—which in Europe tends to mean **guided hikes and walks,** visits to castles or other cultural sites, and meals at distinctive venues on shore. While on board, passengers entertain themselves with the usual small-ship activities: wildlife watching, reading, conversation, and maybe a board game (of which the ships carry a good selection on board). Between 3 and 13 or more naturalists, undersea specialists, biologists, and/or geologists sail with each vessel (the most carried by any of the small-ship lines), running the day-to-day aspects of the expedition, presenting lectures and slide shows, and leading guest exploration either from the ship or on kayaking, motor-launch, and hiking excursions, which are included in the cruise price. Depending on weather and sea

---

Expeditions Under Charter

In addition to *National Geographic Endeavour,* Lindblad charters two ships for seasonal sailings in Scotland and Greece.

In Scotland, the 54-passenger *Lord of the Glens* offers 12- to 17-night trips in the Scottish Highlands and the Orkney Islands May through August. While not much to look at from the outside (she resembles a small commuter ferry, truth be told), she's surprisingly nice inside, with two open-air viewing areas, two lounges with large viewing windows, a small library and cozy bar, a comfortable dining room, and rich mahogany wall finishes throughout. Cabins are tastefully appointed, with writing desks and rich wood accents, and each has a picture window or portholes. An onboard naturalist accompanies all sailings. The 12-day sailings are priced from $6,990 per person, double occupancy.

Lindblad's Greek ship is the 177-foot, 41-passenger *Panorama,* a "Lifestyles of the Rich and Famous" type mega-yacht with wide, inviting sun decks and a sternside swimming platform. Inside there's a library area, a lounge, and a single dining room. Cabins all offer windows or portholes. Nine- and 12-night itineraries are available May through September, with 9-night sailings starting from $4,980 per person, double occupancy.

Lindblad Expeditions Fleet Itineraries

Ship	Sailing Region	Home Ports
Lord of the Glens	11- to 13-night Scottish Highlands	Edinburgh, Kyle of Lochalsh, Inverness, Kirkwall (Scotland)
National Geographic Endeavour	13- to 16-night voyages in Northern Europe/Atlantic Europe/Russia (various combinations) and the British Isles	Lisbon, Copenhagen, St. Petersburg, Portsmouth (England), Bergen
Panorama	8- and 11-night Greek Isles/Adriatic	Piraeus/Athens, Dubrovnik

conditions, there are usually two or three excursions every day. Many voyages also feature guest scientists, photographers, and lecturers from the **National Geographic Society.** Internet/e-mail access is available through the purchase of prepaid debit cards on board.

On *Endeavour,* kayaks are available to passengers who wish to explore shoreside locations on their own. On board, the ship's **Undersea Program** lets passengers hear live vocalizations from whales (via a hydrophone) or watch what's going on under the ship via an underwater camera. The program includes a full-time onboard undersea specialist who oversees activities, as well as a video chronicler who captures daily events. Some cruises are designated as **Photo Expeditions** and feature expert assistance and instruction from professional photographers, as well as special photo walks and talks on the creative and technical aspects of photography.

CHILDREN'S PROGRAM
None. This is a very adult product that rarely sees children on board.

ENTERTAINMENT
Each evening the onboard experts lead discussions recapping the day's events, and, after dinner, documentary and feature films are occasionally screened in the main lounge. In some regions, local musicians may come aboard to entertain. Books on the sailing region's nature and culture are available from each ship's small library.

SERVICE
Dining-room staff and room stewards are affable and efficient, and seem to enjoy their work. Recommended tips of $8 to $10 per person per day are pooled and divided among the staff. There's no room service unless you are ill and unable to make it to the dining room, and there's no laundry service, either.

National Geographic Endeavour

The Verdict
A well-run expedition ship with a terrific staff and unique itineraries, *Endeavour* provides one of the richest overall cruise experiences available today.

Endeavour *(photo: Lindblad Expeditions)*

Specifications

Size (in Tons)	3,312	Crew	38
Passengers (Double Occ.)	110	Passenger/Crew Ratio	2.8 to 1
Passenger/Space Ratio	30	Year Launched	1966 (Rebuilt 1983)
Total Cabins/Veranda Cabins	62/0	Last Major Refurbishment	2005

Frommer's Ratings (Scale of 1–5)   ★★★★

Cabin Comfort & Amenities	4	Dining Options	4
Appearance & Upkeep	4	Adventure & Fitness Options	5
Public Comfort/Space	4	Children's Facilities	N/A
Decor	4	Enjoyment Factor	5

The largest ship in the Lindblad Expeditions fleet, *National Geographic Endeavour* (formerly *Caledonian Star*) is a former North Sea fishing vessel that was retooled for expedition cruising in 1983. She's a solid, sturdy, fully stabilized vessel that's ideal for expedition-style cruising, boasting a reinforced hull, a fleet of Zodiac landing boats, and a video-enabled R.O.V. (remote-operated vehicle) that can dive up to 500 feet below the ice to record the goings-on for passengers. After a $3-million renovation in 2005, the ship is more shipshape than ever as she sails itineraries that range from the North Cape of Norway to the British Isles and the Mediterranean, to the fjords of Chile and the white continent of Antarctica. *Endeavour* is also the flagship of Lindblad's partnership with the National Geographic Society and always sails with Geographic experts on board, sometimes to lecture guests and sometimes to conduct research.

Cabins & Rates

Cabins	Per Diem From	Sq. Ft.	Fridge	Hair Dryer	Sitting Area	TV
Outside	$529	135	No	Yes	No	No
Suites	$612	269	Yes	Yes	Yes	Yes

CABINS   All cabins are outsides with windows or portholes, and are simply furnished with two lower beds, a writing desk with chair, a bathroom with shower, just-about-adequate closet space, and either a porthole or windows for natural light. Single cabins have one lower bed each. Decor is simple but pleasant, with light woods and soft colors predominating. The ship's two suites offer separate sitting and sleeping areas and large-view windows.

Fourteen cabins are designated for solo travelers—a pleasant rarity these days. No cabins are wheelchair accessible.

PUBLIC AREAS   The main public room on board is the lounge/bar, a comfortable place with large viewing windows to each side. It's used both for socializing and for onboard lectures. Other facilities include a small library, gift shop, hair salon, laundry, and small medical facility with a full-time doctor. The navigation bridge is open to passengers.

DINING OPTIONS   All meals are served as single, open seatings in *Endeavour*'s spacious dining room. An early-riser's breakfast buffets and pre-dinner hors d'oeuvres are also available in the lounge.

ADVENTURE & FITNESS OPTIONS   Trips by Zodiac landing boat are the main adventure option on *Endeavour*, along with guided hikes and kayaking trips. On board, there's also a tiny swimming pool, a small fitness room, and a mini spa for massages.

4 Mini-Review: Sea Cloud Cruises

32–40 N. Dean St., Englewood, NJ 07631. Ⓒ 888/732-2568 or 201/227-9404. Fax 201/227-9424. www.seacloud.com.

THE LINE IN A NUTSHELL   Germany-based Sea Cloud Cruises caters to a well-traveled clientele looking for a deliciously exotic five-star sailing adventure, and an international one, too: Typical Europe cruises draw American, German, and British passengers. A trip aboard one of the line's sailing ships (the 2,532-ton, 64-passenger *Sea Cloud* ★★★★ or the 3,849-ton, 94-passenger replica *Sea Cloud II* ★★★★) will spoil small-ship lovers forever.

THE EXPERIENCE   In 1931, Wall Street tycoon **E. F. Hutton** commissioned construction of the four-masted sailing ship *Hussar* from the Krupp family shipyard in Kiel, Germany. Outfitting of her interior was left to Hutton's wife, heiress and businesswoman **Marjorie Merriweather Post,** who spent 2 years on the task, eventually drafting a full-scale diagram showing every detail of her design, down to the placement of antiques. After the couple's divorce, Post renamed the vessel *Sea Cloud* and sailed her to Leningrad, where second husband Joseph E. Davies was serving as U.S. ambassador. World War II saw the vessel commissioned to the U.S. Navy, which removed her masts and used her as a floating weather station. After the war, the vessel went though numerous hands: first back to Post, then to Dominican dictator Rafael Leonidas Trujillo Montinas, then to a number of American owners before she was finally purchased by German economist and seaman Hartmut Paschberg. A lover of great ships, Paschberg and a group of Hamburg investors put up the money for an 8-month overhaul that restored *Sea Cloud*'s original grandeur, full of marble, gold, and mahogany detailing. Today the ship offers cabins for 64 passengers, the luckiest (and richest) of whom can stay in Post's own museum-like suite, with its Louis XIV–style bed and nightstands, marble fireplace and bathroom, chandeliers, and intricate moldings. The other original suites are similarly, if less sumptuously, furnished. Standard cabins are comfortable but lack the suites' time-machine quality. Still, everyone aboard gets to enjoy a taste of the past in the main restaurant, with its dark-wood paneling, brass trimmings, and nautical paintings.

The larger, three-masted *Sea Cloud II* is a modern reinterpretation of the classics, built in 2001. Her elegant lounge has rich mahogany woodwork, ornate ceiling

Sea Cloud Fleet Itineraries

Ship	Sailing Regions	Home Ports
Sea Cloud	7-night Mediterranean/Greek Isles/Aegean (various combinations)	Nice, Valletta, Istanbul, Piraeus/Athens, Palma de Majorca, Venice, Civitavecchia/Rome
Sea Cloud II	3- to 12-night voyages in the English Channel, Northern Europe/Russia, Germany, Atlantic Europe, Mediterranean/Adriatic, and the Iberian Peninsula	Barcelona, Honfleur (France), Portsmouth (England), Hamburg, Barcelona, Venice, Malaga, Warnemuende/Berlin, Oslo, Civitavecchia/Rome, Cadiz

moldings, leather club couches, and overstuffed bucket chairs, and she offers several opulent suites, one with burled wood paneling and a canopy bed. On both ships, standard cabins are very comfortable and designed with true yachting elegance. Those on *II* have small sitting areas, and all cabins have TV/VCRs, telephones, safes, hair dryers, bathrobes, and bathrooms with showers and marble sinks.

The dining room on each ship accommodates all guests in a single, open seating, and fine wines and beer are complimentary at lunch and dinner. Breakfast and some lunches are offered buffet style, while the more formal dinners are served on elegant candlelit tables set with white linens, china, and silver. Most men wear jackets nightly, though the 2 formal nights on each cruise are not black-tie affairs—jackets and ties work just fine. Most cruises also feature a barbecue night out on deck.

These being small sailing ships, organized activities are few; it's the ships themselves that entertain, and watching the crew work the riggings, plus visits to less-touristed ports such as St. Tropez; Ponza (Italy); Bonifacio and Ajaccio (Corsica); and Korcula, Sibenik, and Opatija (Croatia). Only 1 day of each cruise is spent at sea. Outside decks of both ships are covered with lines, winches, cleats, brass compasses, wooden deck chairs, and other shippy accouterments, providing a wonderfully nostalgic and nautical setting. Sailing lectures are offered on every cruise, though passengers are not allowed to handle the sails. *Cloud II* also has a library, a small gym, a sauna, and a swimming platform. Evenings may include piano music and mingling over cocktails. Other occasional activities may include talks by resident guest lecturers, local musicians who come aboard for a few hours, and **"open houses,"** where guests enjoy champagne and caviar on the Main Deck before touring each other's cabins (with the residents' permission, of course).

Weeklong *Sea Cloud* cruises in the Mediterranean run from $4,660 to $8,590. Sailings aboard *Sea Cloud II* run from about $4,000 to more than $10,000. Sea Cloud sometimes charters its ships to other entities, notably Lindblad Expeditions, which has used *Sea Cloud II* in both the Caribbean and Europe recently.

At press time, Sea Cloud had just announced its intentions to built a third ship for its fleet. Measuring 445 feet long, flying 27 sails, and carrying 136 passengers, the *Sea Cloud Hussar* is currently set to debut in fall 2009.

5 Star Clippers

4101 Salzedo Ave., Coral Gables, FL 33146. ℂ **800/442-0551** or 305/442-0550. Fax 305/442-1611. www.star clippers.com.

THE LINE IN A NUTSHELL   It's easy to fall in love with the Star Clippers experience—it's simply intoxicating. With the sails and rigging of a classic clipper ship and some of the cushy amenities of modern megas, a cruise on this line's 170 to 227 passenger beauties spells adventure and comfort.

THE EXPERIENCE   The more ships we've sailed on, the more Star Clippers' stock goes up. Few other lines offer the best of two worlds in such an appealing package. On the one hand, the ships offer comfortable, almost cushy public rooms and cabins. On the other, they espouse an unstructured, let-your-hair-down, hands-on ethic—you can climb the masts (with a harness, of course), help raise the sails, crawl into the bow netting, or chat with the captain on the open-air bridge.

On board, ducking under booms, stepping over coils of rope, leaning against railings just feet above the sea, and watching sailors work the winches are constant reminders that you're on a real working ship. Furthermore, listening to the captain's daily talk about the next port of call, the history of sailing, or some other nautical subject, you'll feel like you're exploring some of the Mediterranean's more remote stretches in a ship that really belongs there—an exotic ship for an exotic locale. In a sea of look-alike megaships, *Star Clipper, Star Flyer,* and the newer *Royal Clipper* stand out, recalling a romantic, swashbuckling era of ship travel.

Pros

- **Hands-on experience:** You never have to lift a finger if you don't want to, but if you do, you're free to help out.
- **Comfortable amenities:** Pools, a piano bar and deck bar, a bright and pleasant dining room serving tasty food, and a clubby, wood-paneled library balance out the swashbuckling spirit. *Royal Clipper* also boasts a gym, a small spa, and marble bathrooms.
- **Rich in atmosphere:** On these ships, the ambience is a real treat.
- **Offbeat itineraries:** Itineraries take passengers to more remote places than the megas, such as Croatia, the Italian Riviera, and Portugal.

Cons

- **No fitness equipment on Flyer and Star Clipper.** The newer Royal Clipper has a fitness center, but her two smaller sisters do not.

STAR CLIPPERS: COMFY ADVENTURE

Clipper ships—full-sailed, built for speed, and undeniably romantic—reigned for only a brief time on the high seas before being driven out by steam engines and iron (and then steel) hulls. During their heyday, however, these vessels, including famous names such as *Cutty Sark, Ariel,* and *Flying Cloud,* engendered more romantic myths than any before or since, and helped open the Pacific coast of California during the gold rush of 1849, carrying much-needed supplies around the tip of South America from Boston and New York.

By the early 1990s, despite the nostalgia and sense of reverence that had surrounded every aspect of the clippers' maritime history, nothing that could be technically classified as a clipper ship had been built since *Cutty Sark* in 1869. Enter Mikael Krafft, a Swedish-born industrialist and real-estate developer with a passion for ship design and deep, deep pockets, who invested vast amounts of personal energy and more than $80 million to build *Star Flyer* and *Star Clipper* at a Belgian shipyard in 1991 and 1992.

Compared with the other small-ship lines, here's how Star Clippers rates:

	Poor	Fair	Good	Excellent	Outstanding
Enjoyment Factor					✓
Dining			✓		
Activities			✓		
Children's Program	N/A				
Entertainment		✓			
Service				✓	
Worth the Money					✓

To construct these 170-passenger twins, Krafft procured the original drawings and specifications of Scottish-born Donald McKay, a leading naval architect of 19th-century clipper-ship technology, and employed his own team of naval architects to solve such engineering problems as adapting the square-rigged, four-masted clipper design to modern materials and construction. In mid-2000, Krafft went a step further, launching the 227-passenger *Royal Clipper,* a five-masted, fully rigged sailing ship inspired by the famed *Preussen,* a German clipper built in 1902. The *Royal Clipper* now claims the title of the largest clipper ship in the world, and she's a stunning sight.

Overall, the experience is quite casual, and salty enough to make you feel like a fisherman keeling off the coast of Maine, without the physical hardship of actually being one. As Krafft put it on one sailing, "If you want a typical cruise, you're in the wrong place."

All the Star Clippers vessels are at once traditional and radical. They're the tallest and among the fastest clipper ships ever built and are so beautiful that, even at full stop, they seem to soar. Star Clippers' ships do generally rely on sails alone for about 25% to 35% of the time; the rest of the time, the sails are used with the engines. Each ship performs superlatively—during the *Star Clipper*'s maiden sail in 1992 off the coast of Corsica, she sustained speeds of 19.4 knots, thrilling her owner and designers, who had predicted maximum speeds of 17 knots. The *Royal Clipper* was designed to make up to 20 knots under sail (14 max under engine alone), and on a recent cruise, she easily hit 15 knots one afternoon. During most cruises, however, the crew tries to keep passengers comfortable and decks relatively horizontal, so the vessels are kept to speeds of 9 to 14 knots with a combination of sail and engine power.

At press time, Star Clippers had just announced its intentions to build a new five-masted ship for delivery in 2010. Planned as the most expensive sailing ship ever built, the 7,400-gross-ton, 296-passenger barque is being modeled on *France II,* the world's largest sailing ship when it was launched in 1912, at 5,633 gross tons. The ship will have 37 sails, measure 518 feet long, and have an Ice Class C hull so it can sail anywhere in the world. Though 48% larger than the *Royal Clipper,* it will carry only 30% more passengers. We're very excited!

PASSENGER PROFILE

With no more than 227 passengers aboard the largest ship in the fleet, each Star Clippers cruise seems like a triumph of individuality and intimacy. The line's unusual niche appeals to passengers who might recoil at the lethargy and/or sometimes forced enthusiasm of cruises aboard larger, more typical vessels. Overall, the company reports that a whopping 60% of passengers on average are repeaters back for another Star Clippers cruise.

While you're likely to find a handful of late-20-something honeymoon-type couples and an extended-family group or two, the majority of passengers are well-traveled couples in their 40s to 60s, all active and intellectually curious professionals (such as executives, lawyers, and doctors) who appreciate a casual yet sophisticated ambience and enjoy mixing with fellow passengers. During the day, polo shirts, shorts, and topsiders are standard issue; and for dinner, many passengers simply change into cleaner and better-pressed versions of the same, with perhaps a switch from shorts to slacks for most men. However, men in jackets and women in stylish dresses aren't uncommon on the night of the captain's cocktail party.

With a real mix of North Americans and Europeans (most often from Germany, Austria, Switzerland, France, and the U.K.), the international onboard flavor is as intriguing as the ship itself. Announcements are made in English, German, and French.

DINING

Although the quality can still be inconsistent, Star Clippers' cuisine has evolved and improved over the years as the line has poured more time and effort into it, with an enhanced menu that includes four well-presented entree choices at each evening meal. All meals are open seating, with tables for four, six, and eight in the restaurant; the dress code is always casual (though some guests don jackets on the night of the captain's cocktail party). Breakfast and lunch are served buffet style and are the best meals of the day. The Continental cuisine reflects the line's large European clientele and is dominated at breakfast and lunch by cheeses (such as brie, French goat cheese, and smoked Gouda), as well as marinated fish and meats. Breakfasts also include a hot-and-cold buffet spread and an omelet station, where a staff member will make your eggs the way you like them. Late-afternoon snacks served at the Tropical Bar include such munchies as crudités, cheeses, and chicken wings.

Dinners consist of appetizers, soup, salad, dessert, and a choice of five entrees: seafood (such as lobster and shrimp with rice pilaf), meat (beef curry, for example), vegetarian, a chef's special, and a light dish. Dinner choices such as fusilli in a tomato sauce, grilled Norwegian salmon, and herb-crusted rack of lamb are tasty but tend toward the bland side. Most dinners are sit-down (as opposed to the occasional buffet spread up on deck), and service can feel a bit rushed and frenetic during the dinner rush. Breakfast and lunch don't get as crowded because passengers tend to eat at staggered times. Waiters and bartenders are efficient and friendly and, depending on the cruise director, often dress in costume for several theme nights each week.

A worthwhile selection of wines is available on board, with a heavy emphasis on medium-priced French, German, and California selections.

SNACKS & EXTRAS   Coffee and tea are available from a 24-hour coffee station in the piano bar. On *Star Clipper* and *Flyer,* room service is available only for guests who are sick and can't make it to the dining room; on *Royal Clipper,* passengers staying in the 14 suites and Owner's Suites get 24-hour room service.

ACTIVITIES

If you want action, shopping, and dozens of organized tours, you won't find much of what you're looking for on these ships and itineraries—in fact, their absence is a big part of the line's allure. For the most part, enjoying the experience of being on a sailing ship and socializing with fellow passengers and crewmembers is the main activity, as it is on most any ship this size. Plus, the ships are in port every single day, so boredom is not an issue.

The friendliness starts at the get-go, with smiling waitstaff offering guests complimentary fruit drinks as they board. Throughout the cruise, the captain gives **informal talks** on maritime themes, and, at least once a day, the cruise director speaks about the upcoming ports and shipboard events (though port info may not be as in-depth as you'd expect; on a recent *Royal Clipper* cruise, the cruise director provided only very scant information). Within reason, passengers can lend a hand with deck duties, observe the mechanics of navigation, **climb the masts** (at designated times and with a

Star Clippers Fleet Itineraries

Ship	Sailing Regions	Home Ports
Royal Clipper	10- to 12-night Mediterranean	Civitavecchia/Rome, Venice, Lisbon
Star Clipper	5- to 10-night voyages in the Mediterranean/ Greek Isles/Adriatic (various combinations)	Piraeus/Athens, Venice

safety harness), and have a token try at handling the wheel when circumstances and calm weather permit. Each ship maintains an **open-bridge policy,** allowing passengers to wander up to the humble-looking navigation center at any hour of the day or night (you may have to ask to actually go into the chart room, though).

Other activities may include a brief engine-room tour, morning exercise classes on deck, excursions via tender to photograph the ship under sail, in-cabin movies, and hanging out by the pool (three on *Royal Clipper,* two on *Star Clipper*). Of course, sunbathing is a sport in itself. Best spot for it? In the bowsprit netting, hanging out over the water. It's sunny, it's a thrill in itself, and it's the perfect place from which to spot dolphins in the sea just feet below you, dancing in the bow's wake. Massages are available on all three ships, too, at a reasonable $65 an hour: On *Star Clipper* and *Star Flyer,* they're doled out in a spare cabin or small cabana on deck. *Royal* has a dedicated massage room, divided into two areas by a curtain. *Royal Clipper* also has a small gym.

Port activities are a big part of these cruises. Sailing from one port or island to another and often arriving at the day's port of call sometime after 9am (but usually before 11am, and usually after a brisk early-morning sail), the ships either dock alongside the shore right in town or anchor offshore and shuttle passengers back and forth by tender. On many landings, you'll have to walk a few feet in shallow water between the tender and the beach.

Activities in port revolve around beaches and watersports, and all are complimentary. That's partly because owner Mikael Krafft is an avid scuba diver and partly because itineraries focus on waters that teem with marine life; each ship offers (for an extra charge) the option of PADI-approved **scuba diving.** Certified divers will find all the equipment they'll need on board. Even uncertified/inexperienced divers can pay a fee for scuba lessons that will grant them resort certification and allow them to make a number of relatively simple dives (on every sailing there's a certified diver on the watersports staff). There's also snorkeling (complimentary equipment is distributed at the start of the cruise), water-skiing, windsurfing, sailing, and banana-boat rides offered by the ship's watersports team in all ports. The ships carry along Zodiac motorboats for this purpose, and *Royal Clipper* has a retractable marina at its stern for easy access to the water. Because there are few passengers on board and everything is so laid back, no sign-up sheets are needed for these activities; guests merely hang out by the gangway or on the beach until it's their turn.

Ships tend to depart from their ports early so that they can be under full sail during sunset. Trust us on this one: Position yourself at the ship's rail or dawdle over a drink at the deck bar to watch the sun melt into the horizon behind the silhouetted ships' masts and ropes. It's something you won't forget.

CHILDREN'S PROGRAM

An experience aboard a sailing ship can be a wonderfully educational and adventurous experience, especially for self-reliant children who are at least 10 years old. That said, this is not generally a line for young kids (though the line has no age restrictions, there are no supervised activities and no babysitting unless a well-intentioned crewmember agrees to volunteer his or her off-duty hours).

ENTERTAINMENT

Some sort of featured entertainment takes place each night after dinner by the Tropical Bar, which is the main hub of activity on all three ships. There's a crew talent show one night that's always a big hit with passengers; other nights may offer a trivia contest, dance games, or a performance by local entertainers who come on board for the evening. A keyboard player is on hand to sing pop songs before and after dinner, but the twangy renditions of tunes such as "Chattanooga Choo Choo" and "Day-O" don't really fit in with the ships' otherwise rustic ambience. Most nights, disco music is put on the sound system and a section of the deck serves as an impromptu dance floor, with the action usually quieting down by about 1am.

You can borrow DVDs from the library or watch the movies that are shown each day on cabin TVs in English, German, and French if you feel like vegging. Besides that, it's just you, the sea, and conversation with your fellow passengers.

SERVICE

Service is congenial, low key, unpretentious, cheerful, and reasonably attentive. During busy times, expect efficient but sometimes distracted service in the dining rooms; and during your time on deck, realize that you'll have to fetch your own bar drinks and whatever else you may need. *Royal Clipper* has a second bar on the top deck adjacent to the pools, but even on *Star Clipper* and *Flyer*, you're never more than a 30-second walk from a cool drink.

The crew is international, hailing from Poland, Switzerland, Russia, Germany, Romania, Indonesia, the Philippines, and elsewhere, and their presence creates a wonderful international flavor on board. Crewmembers are friendly and usually good-natured about passengers who want to help with the sails, tie knots, and keep the deck shipshape. Because English is not the mother language of some crewmembers, though, certain details may get lost in the translation.

Officers, the cruise director, and the watersports team may dine with passengers during the week, and if you'd like to have dinner with the captain, just go up to the bridge one day and ask; he may oblige you (it depends on the captain). Unlike a lot of other small-ship lines, Star Clippers has a nurse aboard all sailings. **Laundry service** is available on both ships; Royal Clipper also offers dry cleaning.

Royal Clipper

The Verdict

This stunning, fully rigged, five-masted, square-sail clipper is a sight to behold, and the interior amenities, from marble bathrooms to an Edwardian-style three-level dining room, make it a wonderful way to see the French and Italian Riveras.

Royal Clipper *(photo: Star Clippers)*

Specifications

Size (in Tons)	5,000	Crew	106
Passengers (Double Occ.)	227	Passenger/Crew Ratio	2.2 to 1
Passenger/Space Ratio	22	Year Launched	2000
Total Cabins/Veranda Cabins	114/14	Last Refurbishment/Upgrade	N/A

Frommer's Ratings (Scale of 1–5)   ★★★★

Cabin Comfort & Amenities	4	Dining Options	4.5
Appearance & Upkeep	5	Adventure & Fitness Options	4
Public Comfort/Space	4	Children's Facilities	N/A
Decor	3	Enjoyment Factor	5

Clipper's biggest and poshest ship to date—and, at 439 feet in length, one of the largest sailing ships ever built—the 5,000-ton, 227-passenger *Royal Clipper* boasts more luxurious amenities than the line's older ships, including marble bathrooms, roomier cabins, a small gym and spa, and three pools. With five masts flying 42 sails that together stretch to 56,000 square feet, *Royal Clipper* is powerful, too, able to achieve 20 knots under sail power only, and 14 knots under engine power. (Still, as on *Star Clipper* and *Star Flyer,* the sails are more for show, and typically the engines are also in use 60% to 80% of the time, especially at night.) Engines or not, for true sailors and wannabes, the web of ropes and cables stretched between *Royal Clipper*'s sails, masts, and deck—along with the winches, *Titanic*-style ventilators, brass bells, wooden barrels, and chunky anchor chains cluttering the deck—are constant and beautiful reminders that you're on a real ship. So are the creaking, rolling, and pitching.

The bottom line: This ship is a big winner for those who like the good life, but in a gloriously different way than any mainstream megaship could ever offer.

Cabins & Rates

Cabins	Per Diem From	Sq. Ft.	Fridge	Hair Dryer	Sitting Area	TV
Inside	$260	113	No	Yes	No	Yes
Outside	$278	148	No	Yes	No	Yes
Suite	$640	255–320	Yes	Yes	No	Yes

CABINS   The ship's 114 cabins are gorgeous and roomy, done up in a nautical motif with navy-blue and gold fabrics and dark-wood paneling. All but six are outsides with portholes and measure some 20 to 30 feet larger than cabins aboard *Star Clipper* and *Star Flyer;* they're equivalent in size to the standard cabins on many Royal Caribbean and Norwegian Cruise Line ships, though they're about 40 square feet smaller than Windstar cabins. Bathrooms are marble in all but the six inside cabins, and all have brass and chrome fittings and plenty of elbowroom, as well as brass lighting fixtures, a vanity/desk, a hair dryer, safes, telephones, and TVs with DVD players. One problem: There are no full-length closets in the cabins—but then again, who's bringing an evening gown?

Some 22 cabins on the Main and Clipper decks have a pull-down third berth, but unfortunately, it's only about 2 feet above the beds, so even when folded up, it juts out enough that you can't sit up in bed without bumping your head.

Six tight 113-square-foot inside cabins on the Clipper Deck (category 6) and four outside cabins in the narrow forward section of the bow on the Commodore Deck (category 5) tend to be the best cabin bargains, if you're looking to save a buck. (See chapter 2, "Booking Your Cruise & Getting the Best Price," for more information about cabin categories.)

The 14 Deluxe Suites located forward on the Main Deck are exquisite, with private balconies, sitting areas, minibars, and whirlpool tubs. The Main Deck also has two Owner's Suites measuring 355 square feet; they're connectable, so you could conceivably book them together to create a 710-square-foot suite. Each boasts a pair of double beds, a sitting area, a minibar, and—count 'em—two marble bathrooms. Neither suite has a balcony. Suite guests get 24-hour butler service.

There are no connecting cabins, nor any wheelchair-accessible cabins.

PUBLIC AREAS   *Royal Clipper* is like no other small sailing ship we've ever set foot on, with a three-level atrium and frilly multilevel dining room that are more like what you'd find on a much larger ship. Like the cabins, the decor of the ship's main lounge, library, and corridors follows a strong nautical thread, with navy-blue and gold upholstery and carpeting complementing dark-wood paneling.

The open-air Tropical Bar, with its long marble and wood bar, is the hub of evening entertainment and pre-dinner hors d'oeuvres and drinks, while the more elegant piano lounge just inside hosts the weekly captain's cocktail party. (As on *Star Clipper* and *Star Flyer,* the ceiling of the piano bar is the glass bottom of the main swimming pool, so shave those legs, girls!) A clubby library is adjacent to the Tropical Bar aft on the Main Deck, and far forward on this deck is an observation lounge where you'll find two computers with e-mail and Internet capability (don't expect to see many people here—everyone's out on deck).

On the lowest deck, under the waterline and adjacent to the gym, is a little lounge called Captain Nemos, where an underwater spotlight allows you to see fishy creatures swim past the portholes while at anchor (though we never saw anyone using it when we were on the ship).

DINING OPTIONS   Compared to the dining rooms on *Star Clipper* and *Star Flyer*, the one on *Royal Clipper* is much plusher. It has deep-red velveteen upholstery and dark paneling, and is spread out over three levels. With its brilliant blue sea-scene murals, white moldings and fluted columns, frilly ironwork railings and staircase, and dark-red upholstery, it's vaguely reminiscent of a room on an early-20th-century ocean liner—and somewhat out of place on an otherwise rustic ship. The buffet table is in the center on the lowest level, with seating fanning out and up. Breakfast and lunch are buffet style, and dinner is sit-down. You may notice that the low overhang from the staircase makes maneuvering around the buffet table in the dining room a bit tricky.

ADVENTURE & FITNESS OPTIONS   Considering her size, *Royal Clipper* offers amazing recreation facilities, with three pools, a gym, and a small spa. (In contrast, *Star Clipper* has two pools and no gym or spa.) The spa boils down to one massage room divided by only a curtain into two treatment areas. Leave your American inhibitions behind because not only do you get no modesty towel with these European-style rubs, but the room is so small that you can hear the muffled whispers and massage slaps of the masseuse on the other side of the curtain. Still, the treatments are expertly doled out at a reasonable $65 an hour.

The ship also has a retractable watersports marina at its stern for easy access to kayaking, sailing, and swimming.

Star Clipper

The Verdict

With the sails and rigging of a classic clipper ship and the creature comforts of a modern mega, the 170-passenger *Star Clipper* offers a wonderfully rustic and cozy way to do the Mediterranean.

Star Clipper *(photo: Star Clippers)*

Specifications

Size (in Tons)	2,298	Passenger/Crew Ratio	2.5 to 1
Passengers (Double Occ.)	170	Year Launched	
Passenger/Space Ratio	13.5	*Star Clipper*	1992
Total Cabins/Veranda Cabins	85/0	Last Refurbishment/Upgrade	N/A
Crew	72		

Frommer's Ratings (Scale of 1–5)   ★★★ ½

Cabin Comfort & Amenities	3	Dining Options	3.5
Appearance & Upkeep	4	Adventure & Fitness Options	3
Public Comfort/Space	3	Children's Facilities	N/A
Decor	3	Enjoyment Factor	5

Life aboard this tall ship means hanging out up on deck, and that's where most passengers spend their days. It's a beautiful sight to take in the sea and next port of call through the ship's rigging, a throwback to a simpler age. There's plenty of passenger space, including the many little nooks between the winches, ropes, and other equipment that appealingly clutter the decks of these good-looking working ships. Even with a full load, the ship rarely feels too crowded, except at dinner. Much of the sail-trimming activity occurs amidships and near the bow, so if you're looking to avoid all bustle, take yourself off to the stern.

Cabins & Rates

Cabins	Per Diem From	Sq. Ft.	Fridge	Hair Dryer	Sitting Area	TV
Inside	$260	97	No	Yes	No	No
Outside	$885	118–129	No	Yes	No	Yes

CABINS   Cabins are compact but feel roomy for ships of this size, and were designed with a pleasant nautical motif—blue fabrics and carpeting, portholes, brass-toned lighting fixtures, and a dark-wood trim framing the off-white furniture and walls. The majority of cabins have portholes, two twin beds that can be converted into a double, a small desk/vanity with stool, and an upholstered seat in the corner. Storage space is more than adequate for a 7-night casual cruise in a warm climate, with both a slim floor-to-ceiling closet and a double-width closet of shelves; there's also storage space below the beds, a desk, a nightstand, and a chair. Each cabin has a telephone, hair dryer, and safe, and all but the six smallest windowless inside cabins have a color TV and DVD player.

Standard bathrooms are very small but functional, with marble walls, a nice mirrored storage cabinet that actually stays closed, and a narrow shower divided from the rest of the bathroom by only a curtain; surprisingly, the rest of the bathroom stays dry when the shower's being used. The sink is fitted with water-saving (but annoying) push valves that release water only when they're pressed.

The eight Deluxe Cabins measure about 150 square feet, open right out onto the main deck, and have minibars and whirlpool bathtubs. Because of their location near the Tropical Bar, though, noise can be a problem, especially if there are late-night revelers at the bar. *Take note:* The ship's generator tends to drone on through the night; cabins near the stern on lower decks get most of this noise, though it sometimes filters throughout the lowest deck. Note that four cabins share walls with the dining room, and cabins 311 and 310 actually open right into the dining room itself (so be sure to be dressed before peeking outside to see what's on the menu).

Note that the only difference between the cabins in categories 2 and 3 is a quieter location and a few square feet of space.

None of the units is a suite except for one carefully guarded (and oddly configured) Owner's Suite in the aft of the Clipper Deck that's available to the public only when it's not being set aside for special purposes or occupied by the owner himself (which happens quite often). There are also no connecting cabins, and no cabins designed for wheelchair accessibility. Lacking an elevator, these ships are not recommended for passengers with mobility problems.

PUBLIC AREAS   The handful of public rooms include the dining room; a comfy piano bar; the outside Tropical Bar (sheltered from the sun and rain by a canopy); and a cozy, paneled library with a decorative, nonfunctioning fireplace, a good stock of titles, and a computer with e-mail and Internet access. Receiving messages is free, and debit cards for sending messages can be purchased from the purser.

The roomy yet cozy piano bar has comfy banquette seating and is a romantic place for a drink. That area and the outdoor Tropical Bar are the ship's hubs of activity.

Throughout, the interior decor is pleasant but unmemorable, mostly white with touches of brass and mahogany or teak trim—not as upscale looking as *Royal Clipper,* but cozy, appealing, well designed, and shipshape.

DINING OPTIONS   All meals are served in the single dining room, which has mahogany trim and a series of thin steel columns that pierce the center of many of the dining tables—mildly annoying, but necessary from an engineering standpoint. The booths along the sides, seating six, are awkward when couples who don't know each other are forever getting up and down to let their tablemates in and out. With tables only for six and eight, and no assigned seating, each evening you can dine with a different set of friends, or maybe make some new ones. The *Royal Clipper's* roomier dining-room layout avoids this problem.

ADVENTURE & FITNESS OPTIONS   The ship's two small pools are meant more for dipping than swimming. Both have glass portholes, the one amidships peering from its depths into the piano bar. The pool near the stern tends to be more languid and is thus the favorite of sunbathers, whereas the one amidships is more active, with more noise and splashing, and central to the action. At both, the ship's billowing and moving sails occasionally block the sun's rays, although this happens amidships much more frequently than it does at the stern.

While there's no gym of any sort, aerobics and stretch classes are frequently held on deck between the library and the Tropical Bar. You can sign up for a massage (at $65 an hour) that's doled out in an empty cabin or in a semiprivate area on the top deck.

6 Windstar Cruises

2101 4th Ave., Suite 1150, Seattle, WA 98121. ℭ **800/258-7245** or 206/292-9606. Fax 206/340-0975. www.windstar cruises.com.

THE LINE IN A NUTSHELL   Windstar walks a tightrope between luxury line and sailing-ship line, with an always-casual onboard vibe, beyond-the-norm itineraries, and first-class service and cuisine.

THE EXPERIENCE   You say you want a cruise that visits interesting ports; offers superfriendly yet efficient, on-the-nose service; serves excellent cuisine; offers active options such as watersports from a retractable platform in the stern; has sails for a romantic vibe; and still doesn't cost an arm and a leg? You pretty much have one option: Windstar.

This is no barefoot, rigging-pulling, paper-plates-in-lap, sleep-on-the-deck kind of cruise, but a refined yet down-to-earth, yachtlike experience for a sophisticated, well-traveled crowd that wouldn't be comfortable on a big ship with throngs of tourists. On board, teakwood, brass details, and lots of navy-blue fabrics and carpeting lend a traditional nautical ambience, while the ships' tall masts and white sails cut a traditional profile even though they're controlled by a computer, able to be furled or unfurled at the touch of a button. Despite the ships' relatively large size (*Wind Surf* is one of the world's largest sailing ships, if not the largest), they're able to travel at upward of 12 knots under sail power alone, though more usually the sails are up as a fuel-saving aid to the diesel engines.

Pros

- **Sails:** While you won't get a full-on sailing experience here like you sometimes do with Star Clippers, you do get the ambience, plus the karmic fillip of knowing the sails help save fuel.

- **Service:** Windstar employs mostly Indonesian and Filipino staff, many of whom stay with the line for years. They're extremely professional and friendly as all-get-out.
- **Cuisine:** Few small ships can match Windstar for the quality and ambience of their dining experience, with cuisine served in open-seating restaurants where guests can usually get a table for two.
- **Informal and unregimented days:** Beyond "don't wear shorts in the dining rooms," there's no real dress code here, and most men don't even bother with sport jackets at dinner. Similarly, there are zero rah-rah activities, keeping days loose and languid: Explore ashore (the itineraries visit a port almost every day) or kick back and relax aboard ship without a lot of distraction.

Cons

- **Limited activities and entertainment:** This is intentional, but if you need lots of organized hoopla to keep you happy, you won't find much here.
- **No verandas:** If they're important to you, you're out of luck.

WINDSTAR: CASUAL ELEGANCE UNDER SAIL

Thank goodness there's a company like Windstar in the frequently homogenous cruise industry. It's an individual. It's got personality. Its operations are friendly and almost old-fashioned, small-scale and full of employees who've been with the line for years. Reportedly, many repeat passengers check to make sure their favorite cabin steward, waiter, captain, or host/hostess will be aboard before they'll book a particular sailing.

The line got its start in 1984, founded by a consortium of two ship-owners and Jean Claude Potier, a former U.S. head of the legendary French Line. From the start, it was all about the sails—and, specifically, about a new cruise ship design by the Finnish ship-building company Wartsila. Dubbed the "Windcruiser," the concept combined 19th-century sailing-ship technology with modern engineering to create a kind of vessel never seen before in the cruise ship world: huge by sailing standards, with at least 21,489 square feet of computer-controlled staysails that furl and unfurl at the touch of a button and can work on their own or in concert with a diesel-electric engine. The concept worked then, and it works now: As you see a Windstar ship approaching port, with its long, graceful hull and masts the height of 20-story buildings, you'll forget all about the giant megaships moored nearby and think, "Now that's a ship."

Ownership trivia: In 2007, Ambassadors International, a cruise, marine, travel, and event-management company that also owns Majestic America Line in the U.S., bought Windstar from longtime parent company Holland America Line.

Compared with the other adventure lines, here's how Windstar rates:

	Poor	Fair	Good	Excellent	Outstanding
Enjoyment Factor					✓
Dining				✓	
Activities		✓			
Children's Program	N/A*				
Entertainment		✓			
Service					✓
Worth the Money				✓	

* *Windstar has no children's program.*

Windstar Fleet Itineraries

Ship	Sailing Regions	Home Ports
Wind Spirit	7-night Mediterranean/Greek Isles	Lisbon, Malaga, Barcelona, Civitavecchia/Rome, Piraeus/Athens
Wind Star	7-night Mediterranean/Greek Isles/Adriatic (various combinations)	Lisbon, Barcelona, Civitavecchia/Rome, Athens, Istanbul, Venice, Dubrovnik
Wind Surf	7-night Mediterranean/Greek Isles/Adriatic (various combinations)	Lisbon, Barcelona, Civitavecchia/Rome, Nice, Monte Carlo, Venice, Dubrovnik

PASSENGER PROFILE

People who expect high-caliber service and very high-quality cuisine but dislike the formality of most of the luxe ships (as well as the mass mentality of the megaships) are thrilled with Windstar. Most passengers are couples in their late 30s to early 60s, with the average around 50. Overall, an amazing 60% to 70% of passengers are repeaters, back for their annual or semiannual dose of Windstar. There are also usually a handful of honeymoon couples aboard any given sailing—a good choice on their part, as Windstar ranks high on our list of most romantic cruise lines. The line gets very few families with young kids—rarely more than six or seven on any sailing, and usually only during school holiday periods. Those who do sail are usually in the 10-plus age range.

Overall, Windstar's sophisticated and well-traveled passengers are more down-to-earth than guests on the luxury lines, but not as nature- and learning-focused as guests on most of the other small-ship lines. Most want something different from the regular cruise experience, eschew the "bigger is better" philosophy of conventional cruising, and want their vacation to focus more on the ports than on onboard activities. These cruises are for those seeking a romantic escape and who like to visit ports not often touched by regular cruise ships.

Windstar caters to corporate groups, too, with about 25% of its annual cruises booked as full charters or hosting groups.

DINING

Windstar's cuisine is tops in the small-ship category and is a high point of the cruise, served in two or three always-casual restaurants.

TRADITIONAL   Dinner is served primarily in each ship's spacious, nautically appointed main restaurant, though the vibe here is less formal and regimented than aboard most larger ships. At dinner, the line's **no-jackets-required** policy for men means guests do the "casual elegance" thing—pants or casual dresses for women, and trousers and nice collared shirts for men—and its open-seating policy means you can show up when you want (within a 2-hr. window) and dine with whomever you want. Restaurants aboard all three ships are set up with an unusual number of tables for two, and there's rarely a wait—proof that Windstar is serious about its romantic image.

Overall, Windstar's cuisine tends toward the straightforward, but with surprising twists and regional touches. Appetizers may include golden fried Brie served with cranberry sauce and crispy parsley, or a sweet shrimp and crab salad. Among the main courses, you may see a grilled local fish served with a roast corn salsa and sweet plantains, sautéed jumbo prawns served with garlic spinach and spaghetti, or an herb-and-peppercorn-coated prime rib of beef. Desserts such as an apple tart with raspberry coulis and chocolate crème brûlée are beyond tempting. A selection of exotic fine cheeses (many bought fresh in local markets) is served tableside from a cheese cart, and petits fours are served with coffee after dinner. The restaurant's **wine list** features many boutique labels from California, Australia, New Zealand, Spain, France, and South Africa.

Vegetarian dishes and **healthy "Sail Light" choices** designed by light-cooking expert Jeanne Jones are available for breakfast, lunch, and dinner; fat and calorie content is listed on the menu. The light choices may feature Atlantic salmon with couscous and fresh vegetables, or a Thai country-style chicken with veggies and Asian rice. The vegetarian options may feature a fresh garden stew or a savory polenta with Italian salsa.

ALTERNATIVE   Windstar's largest ship, *Wind Surf,* offers alternative dining at the casual, 128-seat Degrees, an intimate space with an understated fantasy-garden motif and a menu that rotates among steakhouse, Italian, French, and Indonesian dishes. Reservations are required, but there's no additional fee.

CASUAL   Breakfast and lunch are available at the buffet-style Veranda Cafe, which offers a generous spread, as well as a specialty omelet station at breakfast and a grill option at lunch. Waiters will bring the latter to your table, so there's no waiting. You can also opt for a simple continental breakfast at the sternside Compass Rose bar.

The once-a-week evening **barbecues** on the pool decks of the *Star* and *Spirit* are wonderful parties under the stars, with an ample and beautifully designed buffet, tables set with linens, and a band adding ambience. On *Wind Surf,* there's a gala buffet dinner once per cruise in the main lounge, which is transformed into a third dining room for the evening, with a culinary theme matching your cruise region. All three ships also offer weekly barbecue lunches on deck.

Burgers, pizza, hot dogs, and the like are available from a grill in the afternoons.

SNACKS & EXTRAS   Speedy **room service** offers continental breakfast; a menu of about a dozen sandwiches, salads, seafood, and steaks from 11am to 10pm; and a dozen more snack items (from popcorn and chips-and-salsa to a cheese platter or beef consommé) 24 hours a day. During restaurant hours, you can have items from the restaurant's menu served course by course in your cabin, speedy and hot.

ACTIVITIES

Because Windstar's itineraries emphasize days in port over days at sea (in Europe, most cruises hit a port every day or spend just 1 day at sea per week), its ships offer few organized activities, leaving days relaxed and unregimented—the way guests prefer it. The handful of scheduled diversions that are available usually include casino gaming lessons, walk-a-mile and stretch classes on deck, and an occasional vegetable-carving or food-decorating demonstration. A **watersports platform** can be lowered from the stern to allow kayaking, sailing, water-skiing, snorkeling, windsurfing, and ski tubing when the ship anchors offshore, but that doesn't happen very often in Europe. Up top, the pool deck offers a small pool and hot tub, deck chairs, and an open-air bar. Other open areas, especially on the larger *Wind Surf,* offer quiet spots for reading. There's also a scuba diving program for novices and experienced divers.

In port, the company's shore excursions tend to be more creative than usual, and the onboard hosts or hostesses (a.k.a cruise directors, who sometimes double as shore excursions managers and jacks-of-all-trades) are usually very knowledgeable about the ports and are able to point passengers toward good spots for swimming, places of cultural or historical interest, or a nice meal. Brief orientation talks are held before port visits.

The ships all maintain an open-bridge policy, so at most times you're free to walk right in and chat with the captain and officers on duty. There's an extensive DVD and CD collection from which passengers can borrow for use in their cabins. Guests may also check out fully loaded **Apple iPod Nanos** free of charge from the reception desk, using them either with headphones or in conjunction with the Bose SoundDock speakers in each cabin. There are also docking stations and headphones in *Surf*'s Yacht Club Internet cafe lounge. All three ships offer Internet connectivity—*Wind Surf* from eight computers in the Yacht Club, *Star* and *Spirit* via two computers in their libraries. All three vessels are also rigged for **bow-to-stern Wi-Fi service,** and wireless laptops are rentable at the front desk if you don't want to lug your own.

CHILDREN'S PROGRAM

Because children sail infrequently with Windstar, no activities are planned for them. Kids that do sail are generally ages 10 and up, but there are rarely more than six or seven on any sailing, and those only during school breaks. The ships' DVD libraries stock some children's films. The minimum age for children to sail is 2 years.

ENTERTAINMENT

For the most part, passengers entertain themselves, though each ship does carry a number of musicians who provide tunes for evening dancing and background. Most evenings, passengers either retire to their cabins, head for the modest **casino** with its tables games and slots, or go up to the Compass Rose Bar (and also the indoor/outdoor Terrace Bar on the *Surf*) for a nightcap under the stars. Sometimes after 10 or 11pm, disco/pop music is played in the lounge if guests are in a dancing mood, and once per cruise the ship's Indonesian and Filipino crewmembers put on a **crew show** featuring traditional and contemporary music and dance. It's always a crowd pleaser.

SERVICE

Windstar is a class operation, and its level of service is no exception. The staff smiles hello and often learns passengers' names within the first hours of sailing. Dining staff is efficient and first rate as well, but not in that ultraprofessional, five-star-hotel, Seabourn-esque kind of way. That's not what Windstar is all about. As for **tipping,** Windstar automatically adds gratuities of $11 per person, per day to passengers' onboard accounts.

Wind Surf

The Verdict

The big boy. An enlarged version of *Wind Star* and *Wind Spirit,* the 312-passenger *Wind Surf* is a sleek, sexy, supersmooth sailing ship offering a large spa and lots of suites along with an intimate, yachtlike ambience.

Wind Surf *(photo: Windstar Cruises)*

Specifications

Size (in Tons)	14,745	Crew	190
Passengers (Double Occ.)	312	Passenger/Crew Ratio	1.6 to 1
Passenger/Space Ratio	48	Year Launched	1990
Total Cabins/Veranda Cabins	154/0	Last Refurbishment/Upgrade	2006

Frommer's Ratings (Scale of 1–5)   ★★★★

Cabin Comfort & Amenities	4	Dining Options	3.5
Appearance & Upkeep	3.5	Gym, Spa & Sports Facilities	5
Public Comfort/Space	4	Children's Facilities	N/A
Decor	4	Enjoyment Factor	4.5

Wind Surf is the pumped-up big sister of Windstar's smaller original vessels, the *Wind Star* and *Wind Spirit*. Built at French shipyard Societe Nouvelle des Ateliers et Chantiers du Havre, she originally sailed for Club Med Cruises (as *Club Med I*) until purchased by Windstar in 1997.

Despite a passenger capacity more than double that of her sister ships, *Wind Surf* maintains the feel of a private yacht, but also something more: Unlike almost any ship today, she mimics the size and flavor of some older, more intimate ocean liners, with a real seagoing feel that's rare among today's breed of cruise ships. In essence, *Wind Surf* is in a class by herself, offering one of the few cruise experiences that really bridges the gap between casual-luxe and adventure, at prices often as low as $1,650 per week.

In the spirit of keeping up appearances, in late 2006 *Wind Surf* had a multimillion-dollar face-lift that updated her public spaces and staterooms and added a pair of new luxury suites on the Bridge Deck, bringing the ship's capacity to 312 passengers.

Cabins & Rates

Cabins	Per Diem From	Sq. Ft.	Fridge	Hair Dryer	Sitting Area	TV
Outside	$337	188	Yes	Yes	No	Yes
Suite	$621	376	Yes	Yes	Yes	Yes

CABINS   Decor is nearly identical in all cabins and suites, with shippy white walls, varnished wood detailing, patterned upholstery and bedding, and understated carpets. Amenities include flatscreen TVs, DVD/CD players, Bose SoundDocks (usable with preloaded Apple iPod Nanos that you can check out from the reception desk), mini-fridges, terry-cloth bathrobes, large desks with granite tops, and full-length mirrors. At 188 square feet, the standard cabins are as large as some of the largest mainstream megaship cabins, and storage space is adequate, though not overly generous. During a late 2006 dry dock, every single stateroom and suite bathroom was redone. Sporting a more contemporary look, the well-designed bathrooms have updated cabinetry with open glass shelves, granite countertops, white porcelain sinks, new custom shower heads, new shower curtains, and an illuminated magnifying mirror. Fortunately, the lovely teak bathroom floors remain intact.

Thirty suites on Deck 3 (created by combining two regular staterooms) have a single large space divided into a comfortable sitting area and a bedroom, with a thick curtain to separate them as needed. They offer his-and-hers bathrooms (each with shower and toilet) and two flat-panel TVs with DVD players. No cabins or suites have balconies or even picture windows. Instead, chunky portholes add to the ship's nautical ambience. Go with it. We loved 'em.

The 2006 remodeling also created two 500-square-foot plush suites on the Bridge Deck, carved out of the old conference room and Internet cafe. Each has a living and dining area, a separate bedroom, a walk-in closet, and a marble bathroom with a tub and separate shower. Posh perks for these suites include unpacking service, an invitation to dine with the captain, laundry and pressing service, evening appetizers, complimentary bottled water in the suite, chilled champagne upon arrival, and extra L'Occitane bath amenities.

Wind Surf has two elevators (unlike the other Windstar ships, which have none) but no cabins tailored for wheelchairs. The vessel is not recommended for people with serious mobility problems.

PUBLIC AREAS All around, *Wind Surf* is the roomiest of the three Windstar ships, with an airy layout and a passenger-space ratio that matches that of the luxe Seabourn ships.

The vessel's main public room is its nautically decorated main lounge, a bright and airy space with well-spaced tables for four spread around a decent-size dance floor and bandstand. Passengers gather here in the evening for cocktails, music, and port talks, as well as gambling in the adjoining casino. Aft, the Compass Rose bar is the most popular spot aboard, with indoor/outdoor seating, a view over the wake, and music in the evenings. A second small stern lounge, the tiny, adorable Terrace Bar, is decorated with classic wood paneling and thick leather couches and bar stools, and has additional seating and tables just outside, on deck. In the evening, it's the venue for "Cigars Under the Stars" sessions.

Midships on Main Deck, just aft of the Lounge, the former library has been transformed into The Yacht Club, the ship's new social hub and Internet cafe, with an espresso bar, eight computers, and Wi-Fi access for your laptop. A large flatscreen TV anchors a cluster of comfy couches and chairs, and there's a library of books, CDs, and DVDs available for checkout. Nearby are four card tables and the ship's one shop, next to the main reception desk.

DINING OPTIONS *Wind Surf* offers three dining venues: The Restaurant on Main Deck, a casual alternative venue on Star Deck, and the buffet-style Veranda restaurant, also on Star Deck. The Restaurant has 34 tables for two, making it easy for couples to get a romantic dinner alone. Dinners are open seating, served in a 2-hour window between 7:30 and 9:30pm. Dinner in the cozy alternative venue, named Degrees, is by reservation only and features a steakhouse menu 4 nights a week, and rotating menus from northern Italy, France, and Indonesia the other nights.

As on the other Windstar ships, a combo buffet and a la carte breakfast and lunch are served in the glass-enclosed Veranda, which also has outdoor seating. Guests can also get grilled lobster, shrimp, ribs, hamburgers, hot dogs, sausages, veggie burgers, and vegetables from the Grill, right outside the Veranda's doors.

POOL, FITNESS, SPA & SPORT FACILITIES *Wind Surf* has the most elaborate fitness and spa facilities in the Windstar fleet, outclassing most facilities on other similar-size ships. At the spa, therapists dole out a variety of massages and other treatments in rooms that may look suspiciously familiar: They were created out of regular cabins when Windstar expanded the spa. Various spa packages geared to both men and women can be purchased in advance through your travel agent, with appointment times made once you're on board.

The ship's glass-walled gym is located on the top deck and is surprisingly well stocked for a vessel this size, with four treadmills, four bikes, several step machines and elliptical trainers, a full Cybex weight circuit, dumbbells, a ballet bar, and a rowing machine that uses water resistance. Up on deck, you'll find a schedule of yoga, Pilates, "Body Blitz," and self-defense classes for $11 a pop, plus free aerobics, stretching, and abs classes.

There are two pools on board: one on the top deck, beneath the sails, and another in the stern, alongside two hot tubs. Adjacent to the pools are recently installed Balinese sun beds. For joggers, a full-circuit teak promenade wraps around the Bridge Deck. The flying bridge is strung with two-person hammocks, providing a prime relaxation opportunity under the ship's billowing sails.

Wind Spirit • Wind Star

The Verdict

Two of the most romantic, cozy-yet-roomy small ships out there, these vessels look chic and offer just the right combination of creature comforts and first-class cuisine, along with a casual, laid-back, unstructured atmosphere.

Wind Spirit *(photo: Windstar Cruises)*

Specifications

Size (in Tons)	5,350	Passenger/Crew Ratio	1.6 to 1
Passengers (Double Occ.)	148	Year Launched	
Passenger/Space Ratio	36	*Wind Spirit*	1988
Total Cabins/Veranda Cabins	74/0	*Wind Star*	1986
Crew	90	Last Refurbishment/Upgrade	2007

Frommer's Ratings (Scale of 1–5)   ★★★ ½

Cabin Comfort & Amenities	4	Dining Options	3.5
Appearance & Upkeep	3.5	Gym, Spa & Sports Facilities	2
Public Comfort/Space	4	Children's Facilities	N/A
Decor	4	Enjoyment Factor	4.5

These are great ships, combining high-tech design with the lines of a gracious private yacht, from their soaring masts to their needle-sharp bowsprits. They're the kind of lived-in, well-sailed vessels that a certain type of passenger latches on to forever and keeps coming back to year after year. In 2007, both ships received a refurbishment that spruced up their interiors and amenities.

Cabins & Rates

Cabins	Per Diem From	Sq. Ft.	Fridge	Hair Dryer	Sitting Area	TV
Outside	$466	188	Yes	Yes	No	Yes
Suite	$700	220	Yes	Yes	Yes	Yes

CABINS   All cabins are nearly identical, with a burgundy and navy color scheme, a flatscreen TV, a DVD/CD player, Bose SoundDocks (usable with Apple iPod Nanos that you can check out from the reception desk), a minibar, a pair of large round portholes with brass fittings, a compact closet, bathrobes, and fresh fruit. Like the ships' main public rooms, cabins have wood accents and trim, and are attractive and well constructed. Their square footage exceeds that of most small ships and matches the size of the largest standard cabins on the mainstream ships. Teak-decked bathrooms, largish for ships this size, are better laid out than those aboard many luxury vessels, and contain a hair dryer and compact but adequate storage space. Another hair dryer (one with enough power to actually dry hair) is stowed out in the main cabin. Both ships have one Owner's Cabin that offers a little more breathing room, at 220 square feet.

Although all the cabins are comfortable, cabins amidships are more stable in rough seas—a rule of thumb aboard all ships. Note that the ships' engines, when running at full speed, can be a bit noisy.

This line is not recommended for passengers with serious disabilities or those who are wheelchair bound. There are no elevators on board, no wheelchair-accessible cabins, and many raised doorsills.

PUBLIC AREAS   There aren't a lot of public areas on these small ships, but they're more than adequate, as passengers spend most of their time in port. The four main rooms include two restaurants, a library, and a vaguely nautical-looking bar/lounge with cozy, partitioned-off nooks and clusters of comfy caramel-colored leather chairs surrounding a wooden dance floor. This is where passengers congregate for port talks, pre- and post-dinner drinks, dancing, and performances by local musicians and dancers. A second bar is out on the pool deck and also attracts passengers before and after dinner for drinks and sometimes cigar smoking under the stars.

The small wood-paneled library manages to be both nautical and collegiate at the same time. Guests can read, play cards, or check out one of the hundreds of DVDs and CDs for use in their cabins. You can surf the Internet and e-mail in the library; there's also wireless access for laptop users.

DINING OPTIONS   The yachtishly elegant, dimly lit main restaurant is styled with teak trim and paneling, rope-wrapped pillars, navy-blue carpeting and fabrics, and other nautical touches. It's the sole dinner venue and occasionally serves lunch as well. The Veranda breakfast and lunch restaurant is a sunny, window-lined room whose tables extend outdoors onto a covered deck. You have to go outside on deck to enter the restaurant, so if it's raining, you'll get wet.

POOL, FITNESS, SPA & SPORTS FACILITIES   Each ship has a tiny swimming pool and an adjacent hot tub in the stern. Deck chairs around the pool can get filled during sunny days, but there's always space available on the crescent-shaped slice of deck above, outside the Veranda restaurant, and in a nice patch of deck forward of the bridge. The flying bridge is strung with two-person hammocks, providing a prime relaxation opportunity under the ship's billowing sails.

The ships' small gyms offer elliptical trainers, recumbent bikes, a ballet bar, free weights, and a flatscreen TV—not bad for ships this size. Deck 4 offers an unobstructed wraparound deck for walkers. Massages, facials, and a few other treatments are available out of a single massage room next to the hair salon on Deck 1. Don't fault it just on size, though: One of the best massages we've ever had at sea was aboard *Wind Spirit*.

9

River & Canal Cruises

The sea isn't the only water in Europe. Take a look at a good map and you'll see that the continent is crisscrossed by innumerable rivers, canals, and lakes—waterways that are home to hundreds of small river ships and barges offering a leisurely, informal experience that's completely different from what you get aboard the big oceangoing ships. You are, after all, *inland,* and thus able to experience a completely different set of cities, towns, and villages.

RIVER SHIPS

River ships are especially popular with European travelers, although increasing numbers of Americans are discovering their virtues as well. This has led Europe's river-ship companies to add more English-speaking crewmembers, plus amenities such as suites and cabins with balconies.

On these long, low vessels (usually no more than three or four decks), you and between 50 and 220 fellow passengers will enjoy the passing scenery along the Danube, Seine, or Rhine, visiting ports such as Budapest, Prague, and Vienna while immersed in a comfortable atmosphere. The vessels may cruise during the day or at night. Some spend the night in key cities so you can enjoy the local nightlife.

These floating hotels typically offer small though comfortable **cabins,** usually with a window. On the newer ships, the cabins may have TVs and minibars. **Cuisine** is hearty and, in some cases, gourmet, as aboard the Peter Deilmann ships. **Public rooms** are few, as the vessels are small, but they will include a nice lounge and a dining room. Some ships have a separate bar, large viewing decks, small splash pools, spas, and gyms. Light entertainment may be provided by a piano player or singer.

Most passengers on these ships will be adults ages 55 and up. Itineraries generally range from 6 nights to more than 2 weeks, and sail primarily in the Netherlands, Belgium, France, Germany, Austria, Hungary, and the Czech Republic. The season is March to November. Some lines also offer pre- and post-cruise land options. Cruise rates can be under $200 per day, making a river cruise an affordable way to see Europe, especially with the current dollar-euro exchange rate.

BARGES

Barges are the floating equivalent of a B&B—small (many carry fewer than 12 passengers) and sometimes even crewed by the families that own them. Intimate surroundings, gourmet food, and fine wine are what barge cruising is all about.

The barges move very slowly down historic canals that are navigated using a series of locks, and typically sail only between 30 and 100 miles over the course of a week. In port, the barges often arrange private tours, then remain dockside through the night, allowing you additional opportunities to explore.

The passenger mix on board is all-important, as you'll get to know everyone very well during the course of a week: touring together, dining together, and relaxing together.

> ### *Tips* **Piloting Your Own Barge**
>
> Several companies, including the British **Crown Blue Line (www.crownblueline. com)** and **Le Boat (www.leboat.com;** see below) offer self-skippered barges that you can rent for your trip around France, England, Wales, Scotland, Ireland, Germany, Belgium, the Netherlands, or Italy. The easy-to-handle boats allow you the freedom to go where you want, at your own pace, and no previous boating experience is required. The barges accommodate between 2 and 10 passengers, and can be rented for around $1,300 per week (for a four-person boat), varying by boat and sailing date/area.

Meals are a big part of the barge experience and are worth lingering over. Lunch and dinner will include complimentary wine, often from the region you are visiting.

Most barges had an earlier life as supply vessels. Many are antiques and have been rebuilt to accommodate passengers. **Public rooms** typically include a dining room/lounge with a bar area, and there's usually a good amount of deck space to allow for sunning and sightseeing. Some have tiny swimming pools and gyms. **Cabins** tend to be small but comfortable, most with private bathrooms and windows or portholes. On some barges, larger suites are available.

Passengers will mostly be adults, although a few barges specialize in hosting families with kids. A fun option for families is the self-drive barge (see above). **Shore excursions** are usually included in the cruise fare, with the exception of hot-air ballooning.

Barges are most popular in France, but you can also cruise in the Netherlands, Ireland, and elsewhere. The season is spring to fall (with reduced rates in Apr and Oct–Nov), and most itineraries are 6 nights in duration. Cruise rates typically start around $1,700 for a weeklong sailing, though $2,500 to $3,000 is more typical. Some people opt to **rent the entire barge** with family members or friends, which tends to bring the per-person rate down a bit.

BOOKING A RIVER OR CANAL CRUISE

Both river ships and barges are typically represented in the U.S. by **brokers** who market a number of different vessels. Sometimes the same vessel may be booked by several different companies. A few companies operate their own vessels. All rates listed are per person based on double occupancy, and vary by itinerary. You can book through a travel agent or use the listed phone numbers.

Abercrombie & Kent   Upscale tour operator A&K offers barge cruises aboard more than two dozen barges and small river vessels in England, France, Belgium, the Netherlands, Germany, Austria, Hungary, Ireland, Italy, Russia, and Scotland. Barges range in size from 6 to 22 passengers, with most carrying 8 or 12. River ships carry between 32 and 90 passengers. Most cruises last 6 nights, with rates starting around $1,800 per person, double occupancy.

1520 Kensington Rd., Suite 212, Oak Brook, IL 60523. (*) 800/554-7016. www.abercrombiekent.com.

Avalon Waterways   Part of the tour firm Globus, Avalon offers itineraries designed for American tastes, with English-speaking crews. Its fleet consists of six long, modern river ships that carry between 138 and 178 passengers. Cruises are offered April through November on the Rhine, Rhone, Moselle, Main, and Danube rivers, sailing through the Netherlands, Belgium, France, Germany, Austria, Hungary, Croatia, Serbia, Romania, and Bulgaria. Most of the season consists of 10- to 18-night cruises, with prices for 10-nighters ranging upward from $1,750 per person, double occupancy. In November and December, the company offers special 8-night Christmas cruises on the Danube, priced from $1,400.

5301 S. Federal Circle, Littleton, CO 80123. ℂ **877/797-8791**. www.avalonwaterways.com.

The Barge Lady   The Barge Lady represents more than 40 canal and river barges that typically carry between 6 and 12 passengers, with a handful in the 20- to 50-passenger range. Their itineraries sail throughout France (including some departing from Paris), the Netherlands, Germany, England, Scotland, and Ireland between April and November. Prices for 6-night cruises range upward from around $1,800 per person, double occupancy.

101 W. Grand Ave., Suite 200, Chicago, IL 60610. ℂ **800/880-0071**. www.bargelady.com.

French Country Waterways   This firm owns and operates five luxury barges that accommodate between 8 and 18 passengers, sailing routes that take in the Burgundy, Upper Loire Valley, Champagne, and Alsace/Lorraine regions of France. Rates for 6-night cruises start from about $3,400 per person, double occupancy.

P.O. Box 2195, Duxbury, MA 02331. ℂ **800/222-1236**. www.fcwl.com.

Grand Circle Travel   A sister company to Overseas Adventure Travel/Continental Waterways (see below), Grand Circle owns and operates 14 river ships in Europe that carry between 46 and 216 passengers apiece. Cruising destinations include the Netherlands, Belgium, Germany, Austria, France, Switzerland, Hungary, Slovakia, the Czech Republic, Croatia, Serbia, Bulgaria, Romania, the Norwegian fjords, and Russia. Itineraries run from 7 to 32 days, often including pre- and/or post-cruise hotel stays. Longer itineraries are cruisetours that combine a river cruise and a land tour. Prices for 7-night cruises start around $1,400 per person, double occupancy.

347 Congress St., Boston, MA 02210. ℂ **800/959-0405**. www.gct.com.

Le Boat   Le Boat represents more than two dozen barges that sail the rivers and canals of France, the Netherlands, England, Ireland, and Scotland. They range in capacity from 6 to 50 passengers, though most are in the 6- to 12-passenger range. Most barge cruises last 6 nights, and sailings are available from April to October. Prices start at approximately $1,700 per person, double occupancy. The company also represents a number of self-drive barge companies (Crown Blue Line, Connoisseur, Locaboat, and Nicols), with dozens of boats available for sailing in France, England, Wales, Scotland, Ireland, Germany, Belgium, the Netherlands, and Italy. Prices vary depending on the boat and length of itinerary.

980 Awald Rd., Suite 302, Annapolis, MD 21403. ℂ **800/992-0291**. www.leboat.com.

MaupinWaterways   Part of global tour operator Maupintour, this firm offers cruises on barges, river cruisers, and small oceangoing ships in France, England, Ireland, the Netherlands, Italy, Belgium, Germany, Austria, Hungary, the Czech Republic, Croatia, Serbia, Romania, Bulgaria, Turkey, and Russia. Cruises run from 6 to 20 days, with rates for 6-night cruises starting around $2,500 per person, double occupancy.

2688 S. Rainbow Blvd., Suite D, Las Vegas, NV 89146. ℂ **800/572-1709**. www.maupintour.com.

Overseas Adventure Travel/Continental Waterways   Continental Waterways helped pioneer the concept of hotel barges on European waterways, and is now owned and operated by Overseas Adventure Travel, part of Grand Circle Corp. The company offers cruises in Belgium, the Netherlands, and the Alsace-Lorraine, Burgundy, Provence, Camargue, and Bordeaux regions of France, aboard barges that carry between 16 and 24 passengers. Trips are typically 10 to 12 nights and include the cruise and pre- and/or post-cruise hotel stays. Prices start around $3,000 per person, double occupancy, including airfare from several major U.S. cities.

124 Mt. Auburn St., Suite 200 N., Cambridge, MA 02138. (C) 800/248-3737. www.oattravel.com.

Peter Deilmann Cruises   This German firm, which operates the beautiful ocean-going ship *Deutschland* (see p. 226), also owns and operates a fleet of nine deluxe river ships, ranging in size from the 79-passenger *Katharina* and *Frederic Chopin* to the 200-passenger *Mozart*. Cruises operate on the Danube, Rhine, Moselle, Oder, Seine, Rhone, Saone, Havel, Moldau, and Elbe rivers, as well as on the Danube Canal, sailing through Germany, Austria, Hungary, Serbia, Romania, France, the Czech Republic, Poland, the Netherlands, Belgium, and Switzerland. The company markets extensively in the U.S., and about 40% to 50% of its river cruise passengers are American. Itineraries can last from 7 to 14 days, and rates for 7-night cruises start around $1,350 per person, double occupancy.

1800 Diagonal Rd., Suite 170, Alexandria, VA. (C) 800/348-8287. www.deilmann-cruises.com.

Uniworld   This California-based firm operates nine similarly sized river ships, all carrying between 126 and 134 passengers. In Europe, it offers sailings in France, the Netherlands, Hungary, Germany, Austria, Romania, Bulgaria, Serbia, Slovakia, Belgium, Switzerland, Russia, Portugal, and Spain. Itineraries of 7 to 28 days are available, with prices for 7-nighters starting around $1,700 per person, double occupancy. Some cruises are packaged as cruisetours and include a hotel stay.

Uniworld Plaza, 17323 Ventura Blvd., Los Angeles, CA 91316. (C) 800/733-7820. www.uniworld.com.

Viking River Cruises   The world's largest river cruise line, Viking operates 17 hotel-like river ships in Europe, all of them designed with U.S. passengers in mind, all carrying between 124 and 212 passengers. Cruises range from 7 to 15 nights, sailing the river of France, the Netherlands, Belgium, Germany, Switzerland, Austria, Hungary, the Czech Republic, Russia, and Ukraine. Cruise fares for 7-night sailings start around $1,599 per person, double occupancy.

5700 Canogo Ave., Suite 200, Woodland Hills, CA 91367. (C) 877/668-4546. www.vikingrivercruises.com.

WorldWaterways.com   This company books cruises aboard more than 35 canal and river barges and small river ships sailing in France, Germany, the Netherlands, the Czech Republic, Italy, Austria, Bulgaria, Hungary, Romania, Serbia, Slovakia, Belgium, England, Scotland, and Ireland. Cruise lengths are generally 6 nights for barge trips and 7 nights for river ship vacations. Rates for 6-night barge cruises start around $1,800 per person, double occupancy; river ships start around $1,100.

494 8th Ave., 22nd Floor, New York, NY 10001. (C) 800/833-2620. www.worldwaterways.com.

Part 3

Ports of Call

With information and advice on things you can see and do in 34 European ports of call, whether on your own or as part of an organized tour.

10

The Port Experience: An Introduction

On cruises to places such as the Caribbean, Canada, and Mexico, there are lots of people who could care less about where the ship is going; they just want to relax on a deck chair by the pool. On European cruises, it's a different story. Most passengers are there to see something. Well, they've come to the right place. A cruise to Europe is a wonderful opportunity to experience ancient history, spectacular beauty, great food, and stylish people. It's a chance to see some of the world's most famous cities up close, from Rome and Paris to London and Amsterdam.

In the next two chapters, we describe the ports in the Mediterranean and northern Europe on a country-by-country basis. In each we've included what you can walk to from a port and what you can't, tips on when it's best to explore on your own, and information on the best organized tours. For more detailed information on each port, consult the appropriate Frommer's guide, a listing of which appears at the back of this book.

1 Debarkation in Port

Generally, ships on European itineraries stop at a port a day, with typically 1 or 2 days solely at sea thrown into the mix. On cruises longer than 2 weeks, there may be even more sea days, which are wonderful opportunities to relax and recharge after long days of touring.

Coming into port, ships generally arrive right after breakfast, allowing you the morning and afternoon to take a shore excursion or explore on your own. Your ship will either dock right at the pier or tie up slightly offshore, in which case passengers will be transported ashore in a tender (small boat). In either case, there can be as much as 2 hours between the time the ship stops and the time you can actually get off. That's because local authorities have to board and clear the ship, a process that allows you to leave the vessel without going through Customs. Despite the logic, it can be frustrating to see a city laid out in front of you and have to wait to be told when you can step off the ship.

If you're on a large ship, the process may be further delayed because thousands of passengers will want to get off at the same time. In these cases, you will generally be assigned to a specific group, which must wait to leave the ship until it is called. Passengers on shore excursions usually get to disembark first. Ship officials will keep you well informed of the process.

Remember, whether on a shore excursion or touring on your own, to bring your **ship ID card** when you leave the ship, as you won't be able to get back aboard without it. Remember also to bring **money**—after a few days in the cashless atmosphere

Currency Conversion Chart

	US$1	C$1	UK£1	A$1	NZ$1
Euro*	0.72	0.73	1.44	0.64	0.53
Croatia (kuna)	5.08	5.36	10.57	4.66	3.87
Denmark (krone)	5.16	5.43	10.71	4.72	3.92
England (pound)	0.48	0.51	1.00	0.44	0.37
Estonia (kroon)	10.83	11.41	22.51	9.93	8.24
Norway (krone)	5.42	5.72	11.28	4.98	4.12
Russia (ruble)	24.67	26.01	51.29	22.63	18.78
Sweden (krona)	6.42	6.77	13.35	5.89	4.89
Turkey (new lira)	1.17	1.23	2.44	1.07	0.89

*Among the countries covered in this guide, the **euro** is the official currency of Belgium, Finland, France, Germany, Greece, Ireland, Italy, Malta, the Netherlands, Portugal, and Spain.

of a ship, it's remarkably easy to forget. Some ships offer currency exchange services on board. You can also usually find an ATM, bank, or other money exchange within walking distance of the pier. Exchange only what you'll need for that country or you'll end up having to change it back.

We also advise you to wear **comfortable shoes** (cobblestones and uneven surfaces are common in Europe). Bring along **bottled water** (available on the ship), a hat, and sunscreen, especially in the summer months. If you will visit churches or other religious sites, women may be required to cover their arms and legs; it's a great idea to carry a light-weight shawl with you, which you can throw around your shoulders or even use as a skirt, sarong style, if need be.

TAKING THE TRAIN

Intrepid travelers may want to save some big bucks by taking a train to get beyond a port city rather than book the ship's pricier shore excursion or transfer options. We often find it more satisfying to explore solo with a good guidebook in hand, rather than shuffle with 40 others on a group tour. It's a matter of preference and comfort level. Convenient rail service is offered in several ports, including Livorno (to get to Pisa or Florence), Civitavecchia (to get to Rome), and Villefranche (to get to Monte Carlo or Nice); we've indicated where this is an option in the following port chapters. Keep in mind, though, that the train station may not be right near the pier (a cab or bus ride may be required to get there). For train schedules, consult **www.raileurope. com**. Of course, make sure you allow plenty of time for the train ride back to the ship before it sails.

REBOARDING

Whether you do go off to explore on your own or just putter around in a port after your excursion, you'll need to carefully pay attention to your ship's **departure time** and be back at least a half-hour before then. If your shore excursion runs late, the ship will be held, but if you're off on your own and miss the boat, you will be responsible for paying your way to the next port. (If you do miss the boat, immediately contact the ship's representative at the pier.)

Ships usually depart in the early evening, giving you an hour or two to rest up before dinner. Small ships may even stay in port each evening to offer you a chance to sample the local nightlife. Some large ships will overnight in major ports such as Venice, Istanbul, or Monaco.

2 Shore Excursions

The cruise lines offer organized shore excursions (for a fee) to various sites of historical or cultural value, or of natural or artistic beauty, designed to help you make the most of your limited time at each port of call. In general, excursions that take you well beyond the port area are the ones most worth taking—you'll get professional commentary and avoid hassles with local transportation. In ports where attractions are within walking distance of the pier, however, you may be best off touring on your own. In some ports, there could be 10 or 20 (or more) different options, from walking tours to 12-hour bus trips, catamaran coastal cruises, and, increasingly, also fun stuff such as sports car rentals (Recently Heidi and her husband signed up for the convertible sports car excursion in Villefranche and spent a glorious 4 hours exploring the French Riviera at their own pace.)

Typically, though, shore excursions involve buses, with a guide assigned to each bus. Even when you are on a European ship, you will have an English-speaking guide, though some have heavy accents, so be understanding. If there are not enough English-speakers to fill a bus, however, you may have to hear the commentary repeated in another language. On some of the more upscale and educational lines, expert lecturers accompany shore excursions, and tours might be offered via minivans rather than big buses.

Tour prices, which can run as high as $300 or $400 per person (and even more, depending on what you choose; in Europe, $150 per person per tour is about average), include entrance fees to attractions, and some include lunch or local folklore performances, as well as time for shopping either on your own or at a local crafts center (where you may be not-so-subtly encouraged to buy souvenirs). In some cases, you may have the option of lingering in a town and returning to the ship on your own.

Note that tours are usually conducted by local outside contractors and not by the cruise lines themselves. In some countries, including Greece and Turkey, guides are required to be licensed and are very knowledgeable about their subject matter. Elsewhere, we have generally been impressed with the quality of the tours offered, though we have gotten duds from time to time, easily classified as a mumbler, incessant joker, grumpy guy, or the one who just didn't seem to know much. Sometimes groups can be as large as 40 passengers per guide. In this unfortunate case, it may be difficult to hear what's being said unless you make an effort to follow closely behind the guide as he or she trots between attractions. The high-end lines tend to keep their tour groups smaller.

Shore excursion rates were accurate at press time but are subject to change. Some lines, including Princess, Costa, and Royal Caribbean, offer reduced-rate shore excursions for kids. **Tipping** guides after the tour is at your discretion, but we usually tip

Going Nowhere

If you've been there before or just want to chill, you don't have to get off your ship while it's in port. Limited onboard activities are offered, and some of the restaurants remain open. It can be very relaxing to stay on board when just about everyone else is not! (If you do get off the ship, you can come back to eat, although we highly recommend that you try the local European cuisine.)

about $5 per person (more if it's a really good tour). Tipping in U.S. dollars is fine, so bring lots of $5 and $1 bills.

The cruise lines detail their excursions in brochures you'll likely receive in the mail with your cruise documents; these brochures allow you to pre-select excursions that appeal to you. In most cases, you can book your excursions online or by faxing a form before your cruise. In other cases, you must book tours aboard ship (preferably on the first day, as some will sell out). Excursions are sold on a nonrefundable first-come, first-served basis (some have capacity restrictions). Some lines include shore excursions in their cruise fares, but you may still be asked to sign up (to acknowledge you are accepting the offer). If you want to learn more about the tours, the excursions staff will give talks aboard ship to fill you in. Honestly, these are sometimes more like sales pitches (the cruise lines do, after all, make money off the tours), but they do give more background than the one- or two-paragraph summations in the brochures.

3 Touring the Ports on Your Own

Based on personal experience, we highly recommend you consider skipping the ship's organized tours. If you're an independent-minded traveler and don't like to be cooped on a bus for hours, head off on your own. Taking a local train (see above) is often a great option, both cheaper and more comfortable than a motorcoach, and allowing you to leave the cruise ship cocoon environment behind and embrace a bit of spontaneity. If you don't mind buses, consider signing up for your ship's shuttle service to distant cities such as Rome or Florence; you're dropped off and left to your own devices once there. The bus returns to pick you up at a designated time.

Walking is, of course, the most enlightening way to see a port, but when you want to visit a site that's not within walking distance, you'll have to find transportation. In most ports it's both a hassle and expensive to rent a car on your own, so you're better off taking a taxi or public transportation such as buses or subways. In some ports— Naples, for instance—local horse and carriage drivers line up near the port offering city tours. Heidi has done this (after some shrewd bargaining) and found it a wonderful way to get an overview of a city. You can also hire a car and driver—if you get together a small group with whom to share the car, you can divide the cost among yourselves; remember to agree on a price first. Many ships' shore excursion departments these days also offer a private car and driver option for most ports in Europe, but they are very, very pricey—we're talking $1,000 on up per car, in some cases, for an 8-hour day.

Calling Europe from Abroad

The phone numbers listed in our ports chapters are the local numbers, along with their area codes. To call any of these numbers from outside a country, you'll need to dial the international access code for the country you're dialing from, then the country code of the place you're calling, then the local number. For example, to call Italy from the United States, you'd dial 011, then 39, then the local number with its access code (011-39-XXX/XXXXXX). Below, we've listed the international access codes for the major English-speaking countries and the country codes for all countries discussed in this guidebook. For codes of countries not listed here, consult the website **www.countrycallingcodes.com**. Some countries have different rules when calling internally and from abroad. For these, see notes in the individual port profiles in chapters 11 and 12.

International Access Codes

From the U.S.	011	From Ireland	00
From Canada	011	From Australia	0011
From the U.K.	00	From New Zealand	00

Country Codes

Belgium	32	Italy	39
Croatia	385	Malta	356
Denmark	45	The Netherlands	31
England	44	Norway	47
Estonia	372	Portugal	351
Finland	358	Russia	7
France	33	Scotland	44
Germany	49	Spain	34
Gibraltar	350	Sweden	46
Greece	30	Turkey	90
Ireland	353		

11

Mediterranean Ports of Call

No matter how often we cruise the Med, it's as magical as the first time. Just the *idea* of Europe is romantic. It's the history and the beauty of villages with cobblestone streets, temple ruins dating back 2,000 years, and crumbling seaside ramparts once patrolled by Roman warriors. The food alone is reason enough to visit, from the crusty breads and amazing cheeses of Italy and France to those mouthwatering Greek olives and that exquisite grilled fish. And the wine—even the cheap stuff in these parts tastes great. In Europe the senses are in overdrive; it's a thrill just knowing that you're walking in the footsteps of the emperors, kings, and martyrs who laid the foundation for Western civilization, for better or worse. And no less, as influential as Europe's past has been, it's iconic for its modern culture as well. Just look around you to see the world's most stylishly dressed people. No matter what it is you're looking for in a vacation, you'll find it in this diverse region, which stretches from Spain in the west to Turkey and Greece in the east, from the riches of Venice and Rome to the chic Rivieras and gorgeous harbors of Dubrovnik and the Greek Isles.

HOME PORTS FOR THIS REGION
Most Europe cruises sail out of the region's top cities, so definitely plan on staying a few extra days before or after your cruise to check out the local sights. Barcelona (Spain), Lisbon (Portugal), Venice and Civitavecchia/Rome (Italy), Istanbul (Turkey), and Piraeus/Athens (Greece) are the biggies, though smaller ships might also depart from places like Monte Carlo, Nice, or Dubrovnik. Because most flights leave from the U.S. at night, you'll arrive in Europe in the morning, and ships will depart anytime between about 4pm and 10pm. If at all possible, arrive in the embarkation port at least a day early to avoid the possibility of missing your ship due to flight delays, and to have the time to unwind and explore a bit before rushing to the ship.

1 Athens, Greece

Welcome to the cradle of Western civilization, a place that's been a destination for cultured tourists since before a lot of countries were born. The city today is a mix of ancient and modern, with 2,500-year-old monuments coexisting with neoclassical buildings and high-rises, old tavernas and fast-food outlets, craftsmen's shops, and souvenir outlets. By far the country's biggest city, Athens is home to about 5 million Greeks (a full 40% of the country's population), and for decades had a reputation as a crowded, congested, polluted place. Construction associated with the 2004 Olympic Games has left it much better than before, with new Metro (subway) lines and roads helping alleviate some of the traffic, and a series of wonderful pedestrian-only streets linking the city's most venerable sites.

Even though you're probably here to see "the glory that was Greece"—the **Parthenon,** the Ancient Agora (Forum), Hadrian's Arch, the National Archaeological

Museum—don't ignore the rest of the city in the process. Your best moments may be spent sipping a tiny cup of thick Greek coffee at a small cafe, or losing yourself in **the Plaka,** the city's oldest continuously inhabited section, and getting to know its shops, churches, shady courtyards, and monuments. Our advice: Explore the city slowly, and resign yourself to the fact that you won't have time to see everything in your 1 or 2 days here. Climb to the Acropolis, enjoy a leisurely lunch at an outdoor cafe, get caught up in the hustle and bustle of the streets, and then make plans to return, as the Greeks say, *tou chronou* (next year).

COMING ASHORE   Cruise ships dock at the port city of **Piraeus,** about 11km (6¾ miles) southwest of Athens. There's not much to do in Piraeus unless you're a ship nut (this is one of the great ports of the world), so you'll want to head into Athens.

GETTING AROUND   To get from Piraeus into Athens, you can take the **Metro** (www.ametro.gr), grab a **taxi,** or take one of the **buses** most cruise lines offer for a fee. We recommend the Metro, to which you can walk from the pier. Tickets are sold at automatic ticket machines and ticket booths, and cost .80€ ($1.10). Take it to Monastiraki Square, which will put you within sight of the Acropolis, the Ancient Agora, and the Plaka neighborhood.

If you're taking a taxi, bargain with the driver. The fare from Piraeus to Syntagma Square in Athens should be about 10€ ($14), but many drivers will quote a flat rate that can easily be double that. You can pay it or try to find another taxi driver willing to turn on the meter. The trip can take a while, as traffic is often bad. Also be aware that the taxi you flag down may decline to take you if they don't want to go in that direction. They may also stop and pick up additional passengers to fill the cab. If this happens, you're responsible only for your leg of the journey.

LANGUAGE & CURRENCY   **Greek** is the official language, but **English** and **French** are widely spoken. The official currency is the **euro** (€). The exchange rate at press time was $1 = .72€ (1€ = $1.40).

BEST CRUISE LINE SHORE EXCURSIONS

Best of Athens (8 hr.; $124–$139): A full-day tour of the city's major sights, including a walking tour of the Acropolis; a visit to the National Archaeological Museum; about an hour of free time to shop in the Plaka; a brief stop at the Old Olympic Stadium, site of the first modern Olympics in 1896; lunch; and drive-bys of Hadrian's Arch, the Temple of Olympian Zeus, Constitution Square, the Parliament Building (the former Royal Palace), and the National Gardens.

Ancient Athens Walking Tour (7½ hr.; $129–$144): This in-depth, small-group walking tour takes in the Acropolis and a grab-bag of other ancient sites, including the Acropolis Museum; the Ancient Agora, once a sprawling market and public meeting place; the Stoa of Attalus Museum, housing many of the artifacts from the Agora; and the Thission Temple, perched on a hill above the Agora. It also includes a Greek lunch and free time for shopping.

ON YOUR OWN: WITHIN WALKING DISTANCE

There's really nothing to see where your ship docks, in Piraeus. All the sites are in Athens, a subway, bus, or taxi ride away.

ON YOUR OWN: BEYOND THE PORT AREA

In preparation for the 2004 Olympics, Athens created **The Archaeological Park,** a swath of tree-lined walkways that follow the city's ancient street network to connect

Athens

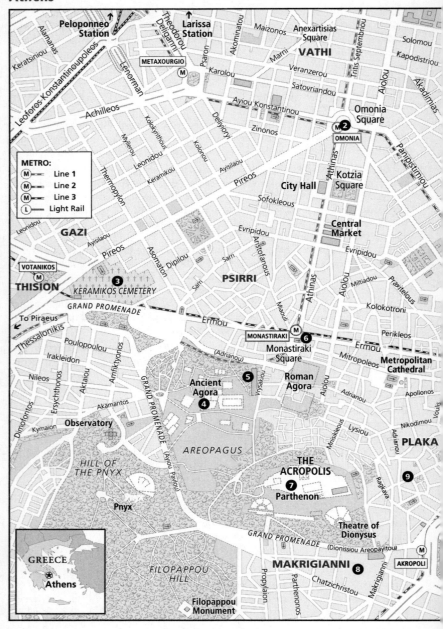

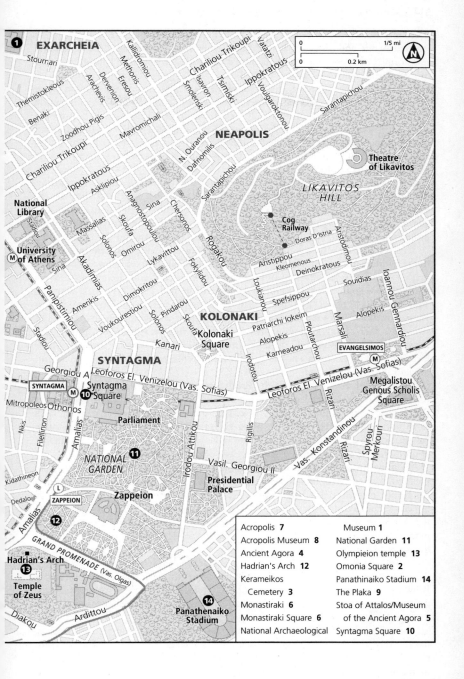

Acropolis **7**
Acropolis Museum **8**
Ancient Agora **4**
Hadrian's Arch **12**
Kerameikos
  Cemetery **3**
Monastiraki **6**
Monastiraki Square **6**
National Archaeological

Museum **1**
National Garden **11**
Olympieion temple **13**
Omonia Square **2**
Panathinaiko Stadium **14**
The Plaka **9**
Stoa of Attalos/Museum
  of the Ancient Agora **5**
Syntagma Square **10**

its most important ancient monuments, from Hadrian's Arch past the Acropolis to the Ancient Agora, and on to the Kerameikos Cemetery. The walkways have completely transformed much of central Athens from a traffic-ridden horror to a delight enjoyed by visitors and Athenians alike.

At the middle of the park is the **Acropolis** (literally, "the top of the city"), a group of structures set at the peak of a wonderfully defensible hill. People began living on the site of the Acropolis as early as 5000 B.C., and by classical times it had become the city's religious center. Today, when you peer over the sides of the Acropolis at the houses in the Plaka district and the remains of the Ancient Agora (once the city's civic and business center) and the theater of Dionysos (part of its cultural center), you're basically looking at the layout of the ancient city.

You'll enter the Acropolis through **Beulé Gate,** built by the Romans and named for the French archaeologist who discovered it in 1852. You'll then pass through the **Propylaia,** the monumental Greek entrance that dates to the 5th century B.C. Just above the Propylaia is the **Temple of Athena Nike** (Athena of Victory), a beautifully proportioned Ionic temple built in 424 B.C. and heavily restored in the 1930s.

The Acropolis's most striking and important structure is the **Parthenon,** a temple to the goddess Athena built in the 5th century B.C. Visitors aren't allowed inside, but that's nothing new: In antiquity, only priests and honored visitors were allowed to see the enormous gold-and-ivory statue of Athena that resided within its central chamber. The necessities of preservation mean that, like those old-timers, you'll have to content yourself with a view of the outside and its 46 columns and wealth of carved art. The structure's roof is long gone, but hasn't been for as long as you might think: It was blown to smithereens in 1687 during fighting between the Venetians and Turks—the former lobbing shells from a nearby hill, the latter hunkered down with all their munitions in the temple. Boom!

To the left of the Parthenon is the **Erechtheion,** which the Athenians honored as the tomb of Erechtheus, a legendary king of Athens. A hole in the ceiling and floor of the northern porch indicates where Poseidon's trident struck to make a spring gush forth during his contest with Athena to have the city named in his or her honor. Athena countered with an olive tree; the olive tree planted beside the Erechtheion reminds visitors of her victory—as, of course, does the city's name.

At this writing, the long-planned **Acropolis Museum,** located 274m (900 ft.) from the Parthenon at the southern base of the Acropolis, was in its final stages, with antiquities being slowly moved in from the old Acropolis Archaeological Museum. The striking contemporary building houses treasures from centuries of archaeological digs on the Acropolis site, including numerous pieces uncovered during excavation of the museum's own foundations. Its design includes a huge glass gallery intended to house the famous Elgin Marbles (aka the **Parthenon Marbles**), which were removed from the site in 1806 by Britain's Lord Elgin and installed at the British Museum. The collection has been a sore spot between Britain and Greece ever since, though public opinion in Britain now strongly favors the return of the pieces. If the marbles are returned, the gallery will display them in their original arrangement, with the Parthenon visible through the gallery's glass walls.

Also below the Acropolis you'll find the **Ancient Agora,** a jumble of buildings, inscriptions, and sculpture fragments that once served as Athens's political and commercial center. Socrates often strolled here with his disciples, including Plato, and drank his cup of hemlock in a prison at the Agora's southwest corner. The rebuilt,

2nd-century **Stoa of Attalos** contains the **Museum of the Ancient Agora** (© **210/ 321-0185**), displaying finds from 5,000 years of Athenian history, including sculpture and pottery, a voting machine, and a child's potty seat, all labeled in English.

Admission to the Acropolis complex costs 12€ ($16.80) for adults, free for kids under 18, and includes admission to the Acropolis Museum, the Ancient Agora and museum, and several other sites. The complex is open daily 8am to 5pm (till 7:30pm in summer). For more information, check the Greek Ministry of Culture's website **www.culture.gr**.

To the east of the Acropolis, the Archaeological Park starts at the **Panathinaiko Stadium,** whose vast marble seating bleachers were built in 329 B.C. After the original structure was excavated, it was refurbished and used for the first modern Olympic games, in 1870. In the 2004 Olympics, it hosted the archery competition and the finish of the marathon. Close by, **Hadrian's Arch** looks like what it is: a Roman arch topped with ornamental Greek columns. It was built around A.D. 131 as a gate between the older section of Athens and a new quarter created by the Roman emperor Hadrian. Hadrian was also responsible for completion of the nearby **Olympieion** temple (aka the Temple of Olympian Zeus), which at 108m long and 43m wide (354 ft./141 ft.) was one of the largest temples in the ancient world. Statues of Zeus and of Hadrian once stood inside. At the western end of the Archaeological Park, the **Kerameikos Cemetery** is Athens's most famous, with tombs dating as far back as the 4th century B.C.

The heart of modern Athens lies north of the ancient city, bounded by **Syntagma (Constitution), Omonia (Harmony),** and **Monastiraki (Little Monastery)** squares. Most Greeks think of Omonia Square, Athens's commercial hub, as the city center. Most visitors, however, take their bearings from Syntagma Square, site of the House of Parliament and next door to the **National Garden,** Athens's largest park. The two squares are connected by parallel streets, Stadiou and Panepistimiou (the latter also known as Eleftheriou Venizelou). West of Syntagma Square, Ermou and Mitropoleos lead slightly downhill to **Monastiraki Square,** home of the city's famous flea market. From Monastiraki Square, **Athinas** leads north back to Omonia past the modern Central Market.

From Omonia, it's only about a 10-minute walk north to the **National Archaeological Museum,** Odos Pattision 44 (© **210/821-7724;** http://odysseus.culture.gr), the largest and most impressive museum in Greece, containing some 20,000 exhibits that stretch across the millennia of Greek civilization, from prehistory to late antiquity. Admission is 7€ ($9.80).

LOCAL FLAVORS

Most Greek meals start off with *mezedes* (appetizers) such as grilled *oktapodi* (octopus), *keftedes* (meatballs), *tzatziki* (yogurt dip with cucumber and garlic), *kalamaraki* (squid), feta (white goat cheese), and *spanakopita* (spinach pies). Typical main dishes are *moussaka* (layers of eggplant, minced meat, and potatoes topped with a cheese sauce and baked), *pastitsio* (macaroni baked with minced meat and béchamel sauce), *gemista* (either tomatoes or green peppers stuffed with minced meat or rice), *dolmades* (cabbage or vine leaves stuffed with minced meat or rice and served with an egg-and-lemon sauce), and *souvlakia* (pieces of meat on small skewers). Baklava, a honey-drenched pastry with nuts, is a popular dessert that is sticky and sweet. Ouzo is a traditional Greek liquor.

Some of the quaintest restaurants in the city can be found in the **Plaka,** but there are also some real tourist traps there. Beware of places with floor shows, or where touts are standing out front, trying to lure you in.

SHOPPING

At the foot of the Acropolis, the **Plaka** is Athens's oldest neighborhood, with many streets named in honor of Greek heroes from either classical antiquity or the Greek War of Independence. Its twisting, labyrinthine streets can challenge even the best navigators, but that's the fun of it: Just get lost. The district isn't all that big, and you can pretty much always navigate by the Acropolis. For the most part, the district has cornered the market on souvenir shops, most selling T-shirts, reproductions of antiquities (including obscene playing cards, drink coasters, bottle openers, and more), fishermen's sweaters (increasingly made in the Far East), and jewelry (often not real gold). But among all that you can still find some places worth a look.

Monastiraki, the area adjacent to the Plaka, has a famous **flea market** that's especially lively on Sunday. Although there's a vast amount of ticky-tacky stuff for sale in its stalls and small shops, you can uncover real finds, including retro clothes and old copper. From the Plaka, head down Adrianou Street to Hadrian's Wall. Go left, then right on Pandrosou Street.

2 Barcelona, Spain

Barcelona, Spain's second-largest city and the capital of the Catalonia region, was developed as a port by the Romans and has long been a Mediterranean center of commerce and passenger shipping, its docks packed daily with the cruise lines' largest megaships. The draws? The city's prime location on the Iberian Peninsula; its wealth of historical, cultural, and artistic offerings; and docks within easy distance of the city center. Pretty much every major cruise line visits here today, and many use the port as a port of embarkation/debarkation.

World renowned for its artists (Picasso, Miró, Dalí, and Tapies), Barcelona is also an architectural showplace, most famous for its modernist buildings by native son Antonio Gaudí, but also boasting contemporary buildings by Santiago Calatrava, Mies van der Rohe, Richard Meier, and Jean Nouvel. All that modernism sits side by side with Roman ruins, buildings from the 13th and 15th centuries, and the narrow streets and medieval architecture of the Gothic Quarter, with its bohemian atmosphere. The city also boasts great museums, friendly people, pleasant cafes, a very active nightlife, and fantastic views from the Montjuïc and Tibidabo mountain parks, both of which are accessible by funicular.

COMING ASHORE   Barcelona's cruise terminal is located on a long peninsula approximately 1.6km (1 mile) from the base of **Las Ramblas,** Barcelona's liveliest and most famous boulevard. Those in decent shape can walk the distance easily, but you can also take one of the **taxis** that congregate outside the terminal or use the free **shuttle** service provided by the cruise line. Taxis will cost you about 8€ ($11.20) to the city center.

GETTING AROUND   Barcelona is a wonderful walking town, with wide boulevards and narrow medieval streets that are a delight to explore. Some sights, though (including La Sagrada Familia and Park Güell), are a little too far for a casual walk. The **Metro** (subway) is your best bet for speedy transportation, as Barcelona's streets are frequently gridlocked with traffic. You can buy individual tickets for 1.25€ ($1.75) apiece or take advantage of several multitrip tickets. The "T10" ticket, which entitles you to 10 trips and can be shared by multiple people, costs 7€ ($9.80) for a single-zone ticket, 13.80€ ($19.30) for a two-zone, and so on. The "T-Dia" ticket

Barcelona

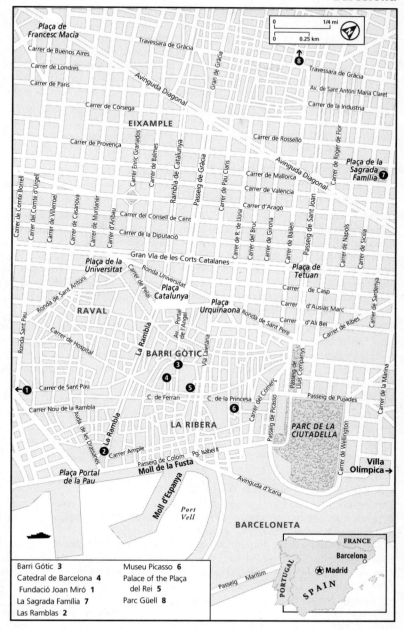

Plaça de Francesc Macià
Carrer de Buenos Aires
Carrer de Londres
Carrer de Paris
Travessara de Gràcia
Gran de Gràcia
Carrer de Còrsega
Avinguda Diagonal
EIXAMPLE
Carrer de Provença
Carrer Enric Granados
Carrer de Balmes
Rambla de Catalunya
Passeig de Gràcia
Carrer de Pau Claris
Carrer de Rosselló
Avinguda Diagonal
Carrer de Mallorca
Carrer de València
Carrer d'Aragó
Carrer de R. de Llúria
Carrer del Bruc
Carrer de Girona
Carrer de Bailèn
Passeig de Sant Joan
Carrer de Roger de Flor
Plaça de la Sagrada Família ⑦

Travessara de Gràcia ⑧
Av. de Sant Antoni Maria Claret
Carrer de la Industria

Carrer de Nàpols
Carrer de Sicília
Carrer de Sardenya

Carrer de Comte Borrell
Carrer del Comte d'Urgell
Carrer de Villarroel
Carrer de Casanova
Carrer de Muntaner
Carrer d'Aribau
Carrer del Consell de Cent
Carrer de la Diputació
Gran Via de les Corts Catalanes
Plaça de la Universitat
Ronda Universitat
Carrer de Pelai
Plaça Catalunya
Plaça Urquinaona
Ronda de Sant Pere
Plaça de Tetuan
Carrer de Casp
Carrer d'Ausias Marc
Carrer d'Ali Bei
Carrer de Ribes

Ronda de Sant Antoni
Ronda Sant Pau
RAVAL
Carrer de Hospital
La Rambla
Av. Portal de l'Àngel
BARRI GÒTIC ③
④
⑤
Via Laietana
Carrer de Sant Pau ①
Carrer Nou de la Rambla
C. de Ferran
C. de la Princesa
⑥
Carrer del Comerç
Passeig de Picasso
LA RIBERA
Passeig de Lluís Companys
Passeig de Pujades
PARC DE LA CIUTADELLA
Carrer de Wellington
Carrer de la Marina

② Carrer Ample
Avda. de les Drassanes
La Rambla
Passeig de Colom
Pg. Isabel II
Moll de la Fusta
Plaça Portal de la Pau
Avinguda d'Icaria
Villa Olímpica →

Moll d'Espanya
Port Vell
BARCELONETA
Passeig Marítim

Barri Gòtic **3**	Museu Picasso **6**
Catedral de Barcelona **4**	Palace of the Plaça
Fundació Joan Miró **1**	del Rei **5**
La Sagrada Família **7**	Parc Güell **8**
Las Ramblas **2**	

FRANCE
Barcelona
Madrid
PORTUGAL
SPAIN

313

allows unlimited rides by one person for a single day and costs 5.25€ ($7.50) for a single-zone ticket, 8.30€ ($11.50) for a two-zone, and so on. Most tourist attractions are within Zone 1. If you prefer to stay above ground, you can ride the **Bus Turístic** (**www.tmb.net/en_US/home.jsp**), whose three routes link 40 of the city's top sights. One-day tickets cost 19€ ($27) and also cover the Tibidabo funicular and the Montjuïc cable car and funicular (both are great for panoramic city views). You can purchase a ticket on the bus, at the transportation booth at Placa de Catalunya, or online.

LANGUAGE & CURRENCY   **Spanish** is the official language, but you'll also hear the local **Catalan** spoken in Barcelona. Many young people also speak **English** or **German.** The official currency is the **euro** (€). The exchange rate at press time was $1 = .72€ (1€ = $1.40).

BEST CRUISE LINE SHORE EXCURSIONS

Though Barcelona is a great walking town, it's also a big town, so a shore excursion may be a good bet if there are several widely scattered sites you want to see in a day.

Antonio Gaudí Tour (4¼ hr.; $40): Antonio Gaudí (1852–1926) was and remains Barcelona's most famous architect, the creator of buildings and environments whose sensuous, idiosyncratic lines seem completely divorced from anything that came before them, and from most of what came after. This tour offers extended visits to his two greatest creations—La Sagrada Familia cathedral and the public Park Güell (see "On Your Own," below)—as well as short drive-by viewings of some of the architect's other Barcelona buildings, including the Casa Batlló and La Pedrera/Casa Milà apartments, both located along the Passeig de Gracia.

Picasso and Barcelona (4 hr.; $40): This tour visits the Picasso Museum (see "On Your Own," below) so you can tour its collection of paintings, drawings, engravings, and ceramics; pays an outside-only visit to La Sagrada Familia and drives by Gaudí's La Pedrera and Casa Batlló; and visits the 13th-century Catedral de Barcelona at the heart of the Gothic Quarter.

Pilgrimage to Montserrat (4½ hr.; $54): This tour heads 58km (36 miles) north of Barcelona to the sacred mountain of Montserrat, whose highest peak reaches 12,216m (40,068 ft.). Approximately halfway up the mountain stands the famous Montserrat Monastery, built by Philip II between 1563 and 1592, and world famous for its shrine of the Virgin Mary, Our Lady of Montserrat, one of Spain's most significant places of pilgrimage.

ON YOUR OWN: WITHIN WALKING DISTANCE

Let's assume for the sake of argument that you're in a walking mood, making the mile-long trek from the docks to the foot of Las Ramblas doable. From there, you're within foot range of several of the city's popular tourist sites.

Las Ramblas itself was dubbed "the most beautiful street in the world" by Victor Hugo, and today its tree-lined length is a perpetual carnival of street performers, flower vendors, cafes, shops, birds singing from cages, and wall-to-wall people. It runs from the docks to Placa de Catalunya, where it meets up with the almost equally enticing **Passeig de Gracia,** a wide, upscale shopping street.

Running north from Las Ramblas (to the right as you're walking inland), the **Barri Gótic** (Gothic Quarter) is a dense warren of narrow streets and buildings from the 13th, 14th, and 15th centuries, when Barcelona experienced a golden age of growth and expansion. Apart from the big attractions such as the **Catedral de Barcelona** on

Plaça de la Seu (begun at the end of the 13th century and completed in the 15th, with a museum of medieval art in its cloister) and the medieval **palace of the Plaça del Rei** (where Columbus was received after returning from the New World), the Barri Gòtic's charm lies in its details—the gargoyles that peer down from ancient towers, small chapels set into the sides of medieval buildings, small squares and fountains, and medieval buildings that were once the headquarters of Barcelona's trade guilds. During the day, half the fun is getting lost and walking the area's cobblestone streets and checking out its vintage stores and cafes. In the evening, the fading Mediterranean light lends the Quarter's stone buildings a warm hue, and musicians jostle for performance spaces around the cathedral.

A few blocks outside the Gothic Quarter's northern boundary (Vía Laietana), **Museu Picasso,** Montcada 15–23 (© **93-256-3000;** www.museupicasso.bcn.es), contains a huge collection of Pablo Picasso's early work, including some 2,500 paintings, engravings, and drawings that Picasso himself donated to the museum in 1970. Born in Málaga, Picasso moved to Barcelona in 1895 after his father was awarded a teaching job at the city's Fine Arts Academy. Although Picasso left Spain at the outbreak of the Civil War—and refused to return while Franco was in power—he maintained a great fondness for Barcelona, where he spent his formative years painting its seedier side and hanging around with the city's bohemians. The collection is housed in five connected medieval mansions and is particularly strong on the artist's Blue and Rose periods. Admission to the museum and temporary exhibits is 8.50€ ($12). Closed Monday.

In Montjuïc Park, about a mile south of cruise docks, the **Fundació Joan Miró,** Placa de Neptú (© **93-443-9470;** www.bcn.fjmiro.cat), contains some 10,000 paintings, graphics, and sculptures donated by Miró himself—so many works that only a portion of the collection can be shown at any one time. Highlights include the magnificent 1979 *Foundation Tapestry,* which Miró executed especially for the space, and the extraordinary *Mercury Fountain* by the American sculptor Alexander Calder. The museum's hilltop setting affords some wonderful views of Barcelona, especially from the rooftop sculpture garden. Admission is 7.50€ ($11). Closed Monday.

ON YOUR OWN: BEYOND THE PORT AREA

Several miles from the cruise docks (though still walkable for those in good shape) lies Antonio Gaudí's masterpiece, **La Sagrada Família** (Church of the Holy Family), Mallorca 401 (© **93-207-3031;** www.sagradafamilia.org), undoubtedly Barcelona's most remarkable structure. The cathedral's history extends back to 1882, when the first stone was laid, and extends forward into the future: It is still far from finished, with completion at least 2 decades off. The basic design follows that of a traditional Gothic church, but its execution is anything but traditional. Reaching toward the heavens, the cathedral's numerous thin spires have a remarkably organic quality, as if they'd been grown rather than built. The **Nativity Facade** on the Carrer Marina was the only part of the facade completed during Gaudí's lifetime. Abundant in detail, upon first glance it seems like a wall of molten wax, its entire expanse crammed with figurines of the Holy Family, flute-bearing angels, ripe fruit, and animals celebrating the birth of Jesus. On the cathedral's opposite side, the more modern **Passion Facade** is adorned with highly stylized, elongated figures acting out Christ's passion and death. Visitors with strong legs and lungs can climb to the top of some of the spires, looking through their glassless window apertures from a dizzying height. There's also an elevator that takes less hearty visitors up about halfway. Admission to the cathedral and its grounds is 8€ ($11).

On a hill northwest of central Barcelona, Gaudí's **Parc Güell,** Carrer del Carmel 28, is one of the architect's most delightful creations and one of the most unique man-made landscapes on the planet. Intended originally as a model community, the site was taken over by the city in 1926 and opened as a public park. At the main entrance in the Carrer Olot, visitors are greeted by two gingerbread-style gatehouses that shimmer with mosaics of broken tile (a signature of the entire park) and are topped with mushroom-shaped chimneys. Within the park, several kilometers of roadways and rustic paths weave amidst Mediterranean vegetation and inspired landscaping. Only two homes were ever built in the park, and neither of them is by Gaudí. One, designed by the architect Ramón Berenguer, became Gaudí's residence in the latter part of his life. It is now the **Casa-Museu Gaudí** (© **93-219-3811;** www.casamuseu gaudi.org) and contains furniture designed by the architect, drawings, and other personal effects. Admission is 4€ ($5.60).

LOCAL FLAVORS
The big meal of the day here is lunch *(almuerzo),* served midafternoon. Fresh seafood is a best bet. You'll find innumerable cafes around the Barri Gòtic and elsewhere serving **tapas,** or Spanish hors d'oeuvres. Be sure to also try the local wines, including **cava,** the Barcelona version of bubbly (the kind marked "brut" is sweeter than the kind marked "brut nature").

SHOPPING
Shop in Barcelona for leather goods, including shoes, jewelry, high fashion, artwork, and straw products. The main shopping area surrounds the **Plaça de Catalunya,** at the northern end of Las Ramblas; upscale shopping can be found on **Passeig de Gracia** from Avinguda Diagonal to Plaça de Catalunya; and Las Ramblas itself is a hive of tourist shops. Dozens of galleries are located in the Barri Gòtic and near the Picasso museum. Some shops close at midday, from about 1:30 to 4pm.

3 Bodrum, Turkey

Bodrum is a vision of whitewashed stucco houses dripping in bougainvillea and clinging to the hillsides, of spectacular vistas and historic splendor, and of a definite "back in time" feeling. **St. Peter's Castle** is the focal point, set on a lofty spot at the middle of the port's twin harbors, where hundreds of the wooden *gulets* offer trips to the nearby islands or for what's known locally as a Blue Cruise. The crumbled yet enduring remains of the **Mausoleum of Halicarnassus,** one of the Seven Ancient Wonders of the World, also reside here. As for modern wonders, there's the fact that Bodrum still remains off the beaten track for most cruise ships, so yours will likely be the only vessel in town.

COMING ASHORE   Most ships anchor just off shore, within a short tender ride of Bodrum's main attraction, St. Peter's Castle.

GETTING AROUND   This is definitely a walking town. The narrow and one-way streets of Bodrum aren't made for cars and buses (though that doesn't stop some drivers from trying).

LANGUAGE & CURRENCY   **Turkish** and **Kurdish** are spoken here, as well as **English, French,** and **German.** The Turkish **new lira** (YTL) is the national currency, and the rate of exchange at press time was $1 = 1.17YTL (1YTL = 85¢).

Calling Bodrum

Dial local calls using the seven-digit phone number; if dialing out of town, you must include a 0 plus the city code. When calling a cellphone (identifiable by the 0531, 0532, 0533, 0534, 0535, 0536, and so on exchanges), you must include the zero. When dialing any number in Turkey from abroad, drop the initial zero.

BEST CRUISE LINE SHORE EXCURSIONS

Aegean Delights (8–9 hr.; $150): This full-day tour includes a visit to St. Peter's Castle, with time spent in its Museum of Underwater Archaeology. The highlight of the day is a ride on a *gulet*, the traditional wooden sailing vessels of the region. You'll sail among the bays and islands of the Bodrum Peninsula, enjoy lunch on board, and have time to swim in secluded bays.

Euromos and Iassos (7 hr.; $119): This full-day tour visits the island city of Iassos, which in its early centuries was ruled by the Spartans, the Persians, and the Romans. Ruins here include a theater with white marble seats embellished with lion's-claw fleet, plus the remains of a medieval fort that guarded the harbor and what's left of the 3,475m (11,400-ft.) city walls. Outside of the city walls are ruins of the aqueducts, a necropolis, a fish market, and a number of mausoleums. Moving on to ancient Euromos, explore ruins of the well-preserved 2nd-century Temple of Zeus. Sixteen of the original columns are still standing with their splendid Corinthian capitals.

ON YOUR OWN: WITHIN WALKING DISTANCE

Bodrum's main attraction is the 600-year-old **St. Peter's Castle** (aka Bodrum Castle), which juts out into the center of Bodrum's two harbors on what was once the island of Zefirya, named after Zephyros, the God of the West Wind. It's the first thing you see as your ship approaches the port. Built by the Knights of St. John, the castle was originally a symbol of the unity of Christian Europe against the Ottoman "infidels." According to the pope, anyone contributing to the construction of the castle would go to heaven; the naming of the castle towers illustrates the involvement of the various European nations, as does the presence of plaques, inscriptions, armor, and other artifacts. Within the inner castle is Bodrum's **Underwater Archaeology Museum** (© 0252-316-2516; www.bodrum-museum.com), where various shipwrecks—one dating back to the 7th century A.D.—have been reassembled for display. Admission is 10YTL ($8.50). While meandering around the extensive castle grounds among peacocks, doves, and geese, be sure to visit the **dungeon,** a kitschy re-creation of an amusement park horror exhibit. The castle's two main courtyards provide respite from the relentless sun. Or you can step into medieval England and sip a glass of white wine in one of the stone alcove booths in the castle's **English Tower.**

On the exterior of the castle's chapel, just beyond the entrance to the main portion of the museum, look for a group of greenish stones. These were once part of the **Mausoleum of Halicarnassus,** built by King Mausolus of Caria and completed in 350 B.C., and long considered one of the wonders of the ancient world. In 1522, after an earthquake caused the Mausoleum to collapse, some of its stones were recycled for the reconstruction of the castle. Today only the excavated foundations of the Mausoleum can be seen, at Turgut Reis Cad, up the hill off Hamam Sokagi (© 0252/316-1219). Admission is 4YTL ($3.40).

ON YOUR OWN: BEYOND THE PORT AREA

Most passengers spend the day strolling historic Bodrum on foot. Those who wish to get farther afield can take the shore excursion to the ancient cities of Iassos and Euromos, located about an hour outside town.

LOCAL FLAVORS

Like its Greek cousin, Turkish food is to die for. For cheap local fare, head to the streets around the post office near **Cevat Sakir Street,** a busy neighborhood with good fast-food options such as *lahmacun* (a delish pizzalike crepe with lamb, chopped onions, and tomatoes) as well as pleasant little *lokantas* (taverns or cafes) with large bins of fresh bread on the table. You might also want to try the legendary **Turkish Delight** (aka *lokum*), a gummy treat made of dried nuts, fruits, syrup, and cornstarch. You may also see *raki* on the menu; it's an alcoholic drink distilled from raisins and then redistilled with aniseed—look out, it's strong. On the other hand, *Ayran* is a refreshing beverage made by diluting yogurt with water. It's salty but very tasty.

SHOPPING

Best buys here include **pottery and ceramics,** especially in the classic coral red and cobalt blue of the Iznik tile, plus **copper** platters and bowls, **leather** products, and gold and silver jewelry. Fun souvenirs to take back home include ivory-colored **meerschaum pipes,** sold in most souvenir shops.

4 Cádiz, Spain

Located on the Atlantic near Spain's southernmost point, Cádiz (pronounced "*Cah-deeth*") is the Western world's oldest continuously inhabited city, founded some 3,000 years ago by Hercules himself, according to legend. Thousands of ships embarked for the New World from this venerable seaport, including those of Christopher Columbus on his second and fourth voyages.

Today the city is geographically divided into two. Lying on the isthmus is the modern city, with its busy commercial area. To the other side are the historic districts of El Populo and Santa Maria, with narrow streets and ancient stone walls. Cádiz also has nice beaches, as well as parks that look out onto the Atlantic.

One of the city's big draws is its proximity to **Seville,** the capital of Spain's Andalusia region, founded more than 2,000 years ago.

COMING ASHORE   It's about a 10-minute walk from the pier to the city center. Taxis are also usually available.

GETTING AROUND   Cádiz can be explored on foot or via taxis.

LANGUAGE & CURRENCY   **Spanish** is the official language, though the Andalusian Spanish dialect is widely spoken and many young people also speak **English** or **German.** The official currency is the **euro** (€). The exchange rate at press time was $1 = .72€ (1€ = $1.40).

BEST CRUISE LINE SHORE EXCURSIONS

A Day in Seville (9 hr.; $135–$165): A full-day excursion from Cádiz takes you to this historic and beautiful city. You'll travel by bus for 2 hours (120km/74 miles) through the countryside until you arrive in Seville, where you'll visit the Cathedral de Sevilla, the world's third-largest cathedral, home to the tombs of King Fernando III and Christopher Columbus. You'll also visit Seville's Alcazar, a 14th-century Mudéjar palace, and the Jewish quarter. You are allowed time to stroll Seville's charming streets. Lunch at a local restaurant or hotel is included.

Cádiz & Puerto de Santa Maria (3½ hr.; $55–$65): This city-highlights tour includes a visit to a local winery. From the bus, you'll see the monument to the Constitution of 1810, the city's ramparts, the historic Castle of San Sebastian, the Cathedral of Cádiz, and other sights. You'll then cross the harbor to Puerto Santa Maria to visit an elegant estate and renowned winery. A flamenco demo may be included.

Cádiz, Jerez & the Royal School of Equestrian Art (7½ hr.; $80–$100): After a brief drive past the highlights of Cádiz, you'll travel for about an hour to the old town of Jerez, where white mansions are guarded by historic walls and towers. Stop at a local cellar for a taste of brandy and sherry. At the equestrian school, you'll see Andalusian horses put through their paces. Lunch is included.

ON YOUR OWN: WITHIN WALKING DISTANCE

Stroll around the narrow streets of Old Cádiz to drink in the region's history and charm, from the Moorish-style Alameda Apodaca gardens to San Francisco Square, with its orange tree grove, and the **Catedral de Cádiz,** Plaza Catedral (✆ **956/28-61-54**). Admission is 9€ ($13). This magnificent 18th-century baroque building has a neoclassical interior and holds the tomb of Cádiz-born musician Manuel de Falla. The cathedral's treasury and museum offers a collection of Spanish silver, embroidery, and paintings. One of Spain's most important Zurbaran collections can be found in the **Museo de Cádiz,** Plaza de Mini (✆ **956/21-22-81**), as can paintings by Rubens and Murillo. The archaeology section displays Roman, Carthaginian, and Phoenician finds. There are also exhibits of pottery, baskets, textiles, and leatherwork. Admission is 1.50€ ($2.10). In 1812, the Cortes (Parliament) met at the **Oratorio de San Felipe Neri,** Santa Ines (✆ **956/21-16-12**), to proclaim its constitution. The history museum displays Murillo's *Immaculate Conception.* Admission is 2.50€ ($3.50).

Popular beaches in Cádiz, in the historic old part of town, include **Playa Victoria** and **Playa de la Caleta,** which forms a half-moon of golden sands.

ON YOUR OWN: BEYOND THE PORT AREA

The most important out-of-town destination is **Seville,** about 121km (75 miles) to the north and reachable via shore excursion (see above). You can also get there by train on your own; the train station is on Avenida del Puerto, Plaza de Sevilla 1, on the southeast border of the main port. There's daily service between Cádiz and Seville, and the 2-hour trip is costs about 9€ ($13) one-way.

LOCAL FLAVORS

Seafood is big here, and sardines are a favorite local treat. Try a nice fish or a bowl of gazpacho (tasty chilled garlic and tomato soup), or sample some tapas (traditional Spanish appetizers) with local wine.

SHOPPING

Best buys are Jerez regional wines, Andalusian handicrafts, leather, and ceramics. The main shopping area in Cádiz is at Columela and San Francisco streets. In Málaga, head for the small shops along Calle Larios; the El Corte Inglés department store doesn't close for siesta and has a decent selection of handicrafts and souvenirs.

5 Corfu, Greece

One of the six Ionian Islands off the western coast of the Greek mainland near Albania, Corfu was originally inhabited by the Phaeacians. Between the 14th and 18th centuries, it was occupied by the Venetians, who introduced the Roman Catholic religion and established Italian as the official language. In the Old Town, you can stroll around the narrow streets and check out the Old Fortress, an impressive 14th-century Venetian structure now used as a popular venue for concerts. You can also rent a motor scooter and spend a leisurely day snaking around the island's gently rolling hills; exploring the lush interior with its villages, farms, and olive trees; or sticking to the coast to unwind on a quiet beach or dropping into a seaside taverna.

Kerkira is the modern Greek name for Corfu. Look for it in many schedules, maps, and so on.

COMING ASHORE   Most ships dock at the New Port, about 2.4km (1½ miles) from the center of Corfu Town. Taxis are usually waiting at the pier; be sure to settle on a price before you get in. A 10- to 15-minute ride should start at about 15€ ($21).

GETTING AROUND   Most everything you'll want to see is within walking distance. If you want to go farther afield, taxis are your best bet. For the more adventurous, there's nothing like seeing Greece from behind the windscreen of a motor scooter—just be careful! **Pegasus,** San Stefanos Avliotes (© **26630-51692**), has rentals starting at 12€ ($17) an hour.

LANGUAGE & CURRENCY   **Greek** is the official language, but **English** is also widely spoken. The official currency is the **euro** (€). The exchange rate at press time was $1 = .72€ (1€ = $1.40).

BEST CRUISE LINE SHORE EXCURSIONS

Achilleion Palace and Old Corfu Town (4 hr.; $75): This half-day tour takes guests to Gastouri village, where the Achilleion Palace stands. At the end of the 19th century, the palace was built by the queen of the Austro-Hungarian Empire, Elizabeth, better known as Sissy. After her assassination, it was bought by Kaiser William II of Germany. Today, after years of neglect, its beautiful gardens—full of exotic flowers and imposing figures of Achilles—offer magnificent views of the Ionian Sea. The tour ends with a walking of town of Corfu's Old Town.

Traditional Tastes of Corfu (4 hr.; $79): After arriving by motorcoach, you'll stroll though the picturesque village of Sikarades with your guide and visit the Historical Folklore Museum. From there you continue on to the village of Kinopiastes, a beautiful whitewashed village and a prime example of traditional Corfiot house architecture. There you will visit the Olive Oil Museum and learn about olive trees and the production of olive oil in the old times, as well as enjoy an olive tasting. Afterward, walk to a local restaurant for lunch (included).

ON YOUR OWN: WITHIN WALKING DISTANCE

Put your walking shoes on, stroll through the narrow streets of the Old Town, and look for the serendipitous discoveries of an old church or monument. To orient yourself, start with the **Esplanade area** bounded by the Old Fort and the sea on one side; the small haven below and to the north of the Old Fort is known as **Mandraki Harbor,** while the shore to the south is home port to the **Corfu Yacht Club.**

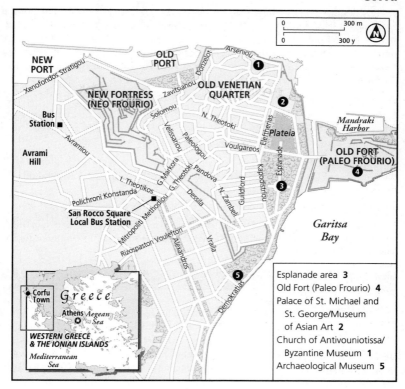

Esplanade area **3**
Old Fort (Paleo Frourio) **4**
Palace of St. Michael and
  St. George/Museum
  of Asian Art **2**
Church of Antivouniotissa/
  Byzantine Museum **1**
Archaeological Museum **5**

Located on the Esplanade, the **Old Fort (Paleo Frourio)** was built on a natural promontory that pokes out into the sea, and at one time the entire population of Corfu lived within its walls. The Venetians dug a deep mote in the 16th century that separated it slightly from the mainland and enabled them to hold off several attempts at conquest by the Turks. Today it's one of the dominant features of the town, providing a look back at the city's medieval days, as well as fine views of the town to the west and Albania to the east. Admission is 4€ ($5.60).

At the far north side of the Esplanade is the **Palace of St. Michael and St. George,** an impressive example of neoclassical architecture built between 1819 and 1824. The palace now houses the **Museum of Asian Art** (© 26610-30-443), whose collection includes some 10,000 objects from China and Japan, with a further 1,000 originating in Korea, Tibet, Nepal, India, Pakistan, Thailand, and Cambodia. Admission is 4€ ($5.60).

Nearby, in the former Church of Antivouniotissa on Arseniou, the **Byzantine Museum** (© 26610-38-313) displays a small but elegant selection of icons from around Corfu. Of particular interest are works by Cretan artists who came to Corfu, some of whom went on to Venice. Admission is 3€ ($4.20). On Monday it's open only in the afternoon.

Head south along the shore road from the Old Fort to reach the **Archaeological Museum,** 1 P. Armeni-Vraila (© **26610-30680**), whose collection includes bronze statues, funeral offerings, and coins from the Archaic, Classical, and Hellenistic eras, plus archaeological finds dating as far back as the 7th century B.C. The highlight is a Gorgon-Medusa pediment from the great temple of Artemis, which dates to 585 B.C. Admission is 4€ ($5.60).

ON YOUR OWN: BEYOND THE PORT AREA

South of Corfu town, the villa known as the **Achilleion** is a feature on some shore excursions. Built between 1890 and 1891 by Empress Elizabeth of Austria, it's filled with many statues and motifs associated with the Greek hero Achilles.

LOCAL FLAVORS

As in the rest of Greece, seafood, olives, and wine are always a great way to sample the local flavors.

SHOPPING

Look for jewelry, leather goods, pottery and olive wood objects, and handmade needlework. If needlework is your thing, head to the shops along Filarmonikis (off N. Teotoki).

6 Dubrovnik, Croatia

Little more than 15 years ago, the 900-year-old city of Dubrovnik was being shelled by Yugoslavian troops during the Croatian War of Independence—a fact you'll find almost impossible to believe today as you stroll the idyllic harbor and old town in the company of thousands of other cruise ship passengers. Strange but true: The beautiful old city (so beautiful it's included on UNESCO's World Heritage List) has bounced back from war to become one of the most popular ports on the Mediterranean/Adriatic run. But who can question why? It has an enviable position on the blue sea, with medieval ramparts surrounding ancient streets and historic architecture and a surrounding countryside that remains redolent of old-world living.

Our two favorite activities are walking the **Placa** (also called Stradun) and the side streets of **Old Town** (which has remained virtually unchanged since the 13th c.), and taking a ride in the country. Shore excursions are offered to pretty Konavle Valley.

COMING ASHORE   Big ships dock in a suburb of Dubrovnik, at Gruz Harbor, about 15 minutes by taxi or bus from the **Old Town.** Smaller ships can anchor right in the beautiful Old Harbor, in the heart of the old city.

GETTING AROUND   Taxis are usually available at the pier. Complimentary shuttle **buses** to Old Town are usually provided by the cruise lines. Public buses that stop at the pier are a third option.

LANGUAGE & CURRENCY   The official language is **Croatian.** The **kuna** (kn) is Croatia's basic currency unit. The exchange rate at press time was $1 = 5.08kn (1kn = 20¢).

BEST CRUISE LINE SHORE EXCURSIONS

Half-Day Historic Dubrovnik (3–4 hr.; $45–$70): This walking tour of Old Town may include a short motor coach ride if your ship is docking outside of town. Visit Sponza Palace, the Dominican church and monastery, the Rector's Palace, Church of

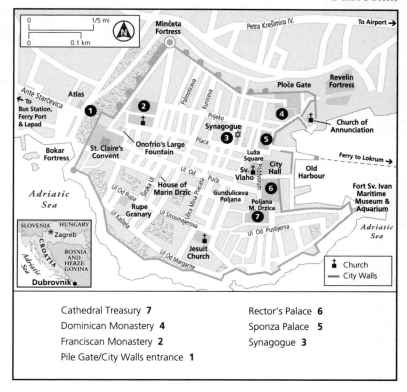

Dubrovnik

Cathedral Treasury **7**

Dominican Monastery **4**

Franciscan Monastery **2**

Pile Gate/City Walls entrance **1**

Rector's Palace **6**

Sponza Palace **5**

Synagogue **3**

St. Blaise, Dubrovnik Cathedral, and the 14th-century Franciscan Monastery. You'll also walk the centuries-old streets of the Placa (Stradun).

Dubrovnik, Konavle Valley & Konavoski Dvori (6–7 hr.; $125–$150): Visit the Konavle region, 30 minutes south of Dubrovnik, to spend time in a natural setting. Enjoy a welcome of brandy and dried figs at the Konavoski Dvori restaurant, situated in an old water mill next to the Ljuta River; then indulge in a lunch of traditional food including grilled roasted lamb, veal, and trout. The excursion includes a tour of historic Dubrovnik.

Dubrovnik, Konavle Valley & Konavle-Style House (4½ hr.; $55–$70): Travel 30 minutes south of Dubrovnik to the Konavle region and the village of Mihanici. Visit the studio of local painter Mijo Sisa Konavljanin, whose theme is daily life in Konavle. Stop at a traditional family home (the family produces and sells brandy, wine, and olive oil) in Poljica. Included is a tour of Dubrovnik's Old Town.

ON YOUR OWN: WITHIN WALKING DISTANCE

Gruz Harbor has money exchangers and souvenir vendors, but for sightseeing, you'll have to take some form of transportation from the port to Old Town.

ON YOUR OWN: BEYOND THE PORT AREA (OLD TOWN)

The **City Walls,** Sv Dominika 3 (© **385/25-942**), run around part of the city for about 1.6km (1 mile). They were built between the 8th and 16th centuries. Walkers can visit five bastions and 15 lookout towers along the way. Entrance is on the west side, via the Pile Gate. Admission is 15kn ($3) adults, 5kn (85¢) children.

The **Cathedral Treasury,** Kneza Damjana Jude 1 (© **385/411-715**), contains such religious treasures as the St. Blaise Reliquary, a reliquary of the Holy Cross from Jerusalem, and an array of paintings and works of art. Admission is 5.71kn ($1).

Construction began on the **Dominican Monastery,** Sveti Dominika 4 (© **385/26-472**), and church complex in 1228, but it wasn't completed till 200 years later. Some of the city's most renowned citizens are buried here, and the treasury is worth a look. Admission is 10kn ($2).

The rector of Dubrovnik once lived in the **Rector's Palace,** Dubrovnik Museum, Pred Dvorom 3 (© **385/26-469**), but the palace, constructed beginning in 1435, was also a seat of government. The rector was not allowed to leave the palace during his short 1-month term unless he was engaged in state business. The architecture combines Gothic and early Renaissance styles, and the palace today houses a museum with furnished rooms, historical exhibits, and baroque paintings. Admission is 15kn ($3).

Dating from the 14th century, the **Franciscan Monastery,** Placa 2 (© **385/26-345**), has an impressive cloister, a rich library with a beautiful reading room, and a pharmacy that dates back to 1317. Admission is 6kn ($1.20).

Sponza Palace, Luza Square, one of the most beautiful buildings in the city, features a mix of late Gothic and early Renaissance styles with impressive stone carvings. Construction started in 1516, and the luxurious building was used as a sort of customhouse. The atrium, with its arched galley, was said to have been the liveliest commercial center and meeting place for businessmen in the city. One wing of the palace housed the state mint. Intellectuals gathered here as "The Academy of the Learned."

The **Synagogue,** Zudioska 5 (© **385/412-219**), is the second-oldest Sephardic synagogue in Europe and home of the Jewish community of Dubrovnik. Admission is free. Closed Saturday and Sunday.

LOCAL FLAVORS

Local favorites include scampi and other seafood dishes, *manistra od bobica* (a bean soup), and *strukle* (rolls made with cottage cheese). Wash your meal down with a local Croatian wine (they're pretty good).

SHOPPING

Shop here for lace (you'll see elderly ladies crocheting everywhere), embroidery, woodcarvings, carpets, ceramics, tapestries, jewelry, and leather and woolen products. Throughout the city are a number of art galleries. Stores generally close for lunch.

7 Florence, Pisa & the Port of Livorno, Italy

Florence and Pisa are among the world's most important centers of culture and history, and two of Italy's most valued treasures. The art of Florence is without compare, and Pisa's famous leaning bell tower is legendary around the world.

The brawny Medici-created port of **Livorno,** the jumping-off spot for trips to Florence and Pisa, is Tuscany's second-largest city but is perhaps unique in the region for its lack of art (beyond some Tuscan "impressionists") and dearth of decorative

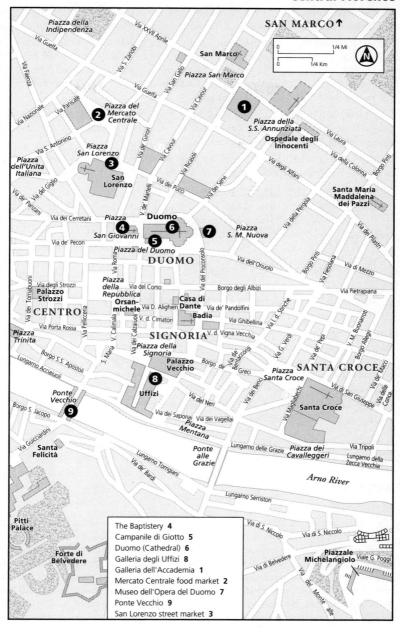

Central Florence

Piazza della Indipendenza

Via Guelfa

Via Faenza

Via XXVII Aprile

Via S. Zanobi

Via S. Gallo

Via Guelfa

San Marco

Piazza San Marco

SAN MARCO↑

Via Nazionale

Via Panicale

Piazza del Mercato Centrale

2

Via de' Ginori

Via Cavour

1

Piazza della S.S. Annunziata

Via Laura

Ospedale degli Innocenti

Via della Colonna

Borgo Pinti

Via S. Antonino

Piazza San Lorenzo

3

San Lorenzo

Via de' Martelli

Via Ricasoli

Via de' Pucci

Via degli Alfani

Via degli Alfani

Santa Maria Maddalena dei Pazzi

Piazza dell'Unità Italiana

Via de' Panzani

Via de' Giglio

Via dei Cerretani

Piazza

San Giovanni

4

Duomo

6

5

Piazza del Duomo

7

Via dei Servi

Via della Pergola

Piazza S. M. Nuova

Via de' Pilastri

Via de' Pecori

DUOMO

Via Roma

Via dell'Oriuolo

Borgo Pinti

Via Fiesolana

Via di Mezzo

Via de' Tornabuoni

Via degli Strozzi

Piazza della Repubblica

Via del Corso

Borgo degli Albizi

Via Pietrapiana

Palazzo Strozzi

CENTRO

Via Pellicceria

Via Calimala

Orsan-michele

Via D. Alighieri

Casa di Dante

Via de' Pandolfini

V. M. Buonarroti

Via Porta Rossa

V. d. Cimatori

Badia

Via Ghibellina

Via G. Verdi

Via de' Pepi

Borgo Allegri

Piazza Trinita

V. Maria

V. d. Cazaiuoli

SIGNORIA

V. d. Vigna Vecchia

Via G. Verdi

Via de' Macci

Borgo S.S. Apostoli

Piazza della Signoria

Borgo de' Greci

Via de' Benci

SANTA CROCE

Lungarno Acciaiuoli

Palazzo Vecchio

8

Piazza Santa Croce

Via di San Giuseppe

Via delle Conce

Ponte Vecchio

Uffizi

Via del Neri

Via Magliabechi

Santa Croce

9

Borgo S. Jacopo

Via dei Saponai

Via dei Vagellai

Via Guicciardini

Santa Felicità

Lungarno Torrigiani

Via de' Bardi

Piazza Mentana

Ponte alle Grazie

Lungarno delle Grazie

Piazza dei Cavalleggeri

Via Tripoli

Lungarno della Zecca Vecchia

Arno River

Lungarno Serristori

Pitti Palace

Forte di Belvedere

Via di S. Niccolo

Via di S. Niccolo

Via di Belvedere

Via del Monte alle

Piazzale Michelangiolo

Viale G. Poggi

The Baptistery **4**
Campanile di Giotto **5**
Duomo (Cathedral) **6**
Galleria degli Uffizi **8**
Galleria dell'Accademia **1**
Mercato Centrale food market **2**
Museo dell'Opera del Duomo **7**
Ponte Vecchio **9**
San Lorenzo street market **3**

0   1/4 Mi
0   1/4 Km

N

churches. The seafood in its restaurants, though, is some of the best in the country, and its back-street canals add a quasi-Venetian romantic touch.

COMING ASHORE   The docks in Livorno's industrial-looking port area are about 1.6km (1 mile) from the center of town. From Livorno, it's about 95km (59 miles) to Florence and about 19km (12 miles) to Pisa. **Taxis** are usually available at the pier. A few ships may also dock farther north at **Le Spezia,** a much more picturesque port, but farther from both Pisa and Florence.

GETTING AROUND   Florence is a 2-hour drive, or about 1¼ hours by train (the train station is about a 15-min. **cab** or **bus** ride from the pier). Pisa is accessible by **train,** with the ride taking about 25 minutes.

LANGUAGE & CURRENCY   The language is **Italian.** The official currency is the **euro** (€). The exchange rate at press time was $1 = .72€ (1€ = $1.40).

BEST CRUISE LINE SHORE EXCURSIONS

Florence City Tour (9–10 hr.; $140–$210): It's a 2-hour drive to the edge of the city center, where buses have to park, with the rest of the tour conducted on foot. Visit the Galleria dell'Accademia, Europe's first drawing school, to view Michelangelo's sculptures, including *David;* the Duomo, the tremendous cathedral (the fourth-largest church in the world); the Campanile, the 15th-century bell tower; Piazza della Signoria, the city's main square; and the 13th-century Church of Santa Croce. Lunch and shopping time are included. Some tours make a photo stop at Pisa. (Ships also offer transfers to Florence for about $80–$100, for those who want to explore on their own but like the security of being under the ship's radar to some extent.)

The Leaning Tower of Pisa (3 hr.; $50–$100): Only 19km (12 miles) from Livorno, Pisa is home of the famous Leaning Tower. Galileo is said to have used the 54m (177-ft.) tower for his gravitational experiments. Be aware, however, that admittance to the tower is not included on most shore excursions. The itinerary includes the Baptistery and Campo Santo, along with time for souvenir shopping.

Cinque Terre (8–10 hr.; $130–$150): If you've been there, done that, and want an alternative to Florence and Pisa, a cruise to Cinque Terre is a great option. After a 1½-hour scenic bus ride to La Spezia, board a modern motorboat for an excursion to Cinque Terre (or Five Islands), a National Park and territory protected by UNESCO. Here, steep slopes and sheer cliffs meet the sea and provide a stunning setting for charming fishing villages and rocky beach coves. Stops may include Riomaggiore, Vernazza, and Monterosso al Mare, with time for lunch and shopping.

FLORENCE

If you're at all interested in art, then you'll find Florence mind-blowing. Known as the Renaissance city, Florence is home to Michelangelo's *David,* Botticelli's *Birth of Venus,* and Raphael's Madonnas. It's where Fra' Angelico painted delicate *Annunciations* in bright primary colors and Giotto depicted monks wailing over the *Death of St. Francis.* The city is so dense in art, history, and culture that even a short visit can wear out the best of us. Certainly try to squeeze in a visit to the Uffizi and have a gander at *David* and the Accademia, but also try to take the time to enjoy the simple pleasures of Florence. Wander the medieval streets in Dante's old neighborhood, sip a cappuccino on Piazza della Signoria and people-watch, haggle for a leather jacket at the street market around San Lorenzo, or immerse yourself in the greenery of the Boboli Gardens.

ON YOUR OWN: WITHIN WALKING DISTANCE

Assuming your bus or taxi drops you off somewhere near the heart of Florence—say, the the Duomo, Campanile, and Baptistery area—you can walk to all of the major highlights. Definitely leave the stilettos and flip-flops at home; you'll need supercomfortable shoes to enjoy the day.

For centuries, people have commented that Florence's **Duomo** (Cathedral of Santa Maria dei Fiori), Piazza del Duomo (© **055-230-2885**), is turned inside out, its exterior boasting Brunelleschi's famous dome, Giotto's bell tower, and a festive cladding of white, green, and pink marble, but its interior left spare, almost barren. By the late 13th century, Florence was feeling peevish: Its archrivals Siena and Pisa sported huge new duomos filled with art while it was saddled with the tiny 5th- or 6th-century Santa Reparata as a cathedral. So in 1296, the city hired Arnolfo di Cambio to design a new duomo. Admission is free. The Duomo's most distinctive feature is its enormous **dome,** which dominates the skyline and is a symbol of Florence itself. You can climb up between the two shells of the cupola for one of the classic panoramas across the city. Admission to the cupola is 6€ ($8.40). At the base of the dome, just above the drum, Baccio d'Agnolo began adding a balcony in 1507. One of the eight sides was finished by 1515, when someone asked Michelangelo—whose artistic opinion was by this time taken as cardinal law—what he thought of it. The master reportedly scoffed, "It looks like a cricket cage." Work was immediately halted, and to this day the other seven sides remain rough brick.

In 1334, the **Campanile di Giotto** (Giotto's Bell Tower), Piazza del Duomo (© **055-230-2885**), was started, clad in the same three colors of marble gracing the Duomo. The **reliefs** and **statues** on the lower levels—by Andrea Pisano, Donatello, and others—are all copies; the weatherworn originals are now housed in the **Museo dell'Opera del Duomo.** You can climb the 414 steps to the top of the tower. What makes the 84m-high (276 ft.) view different from what you get out of the more popular climb up the cathedral dome, besides a cityscape vista, are great views of the Baptistery as you ascend and the best close-up shot in the whole city of Brunelleschi's dome. Admission is 6€ ($8.40).

The **Baptistery,** Piazza San Giovanni (© **055-230-2885**), is one of Florence's oldest, most venerated buildings. Florentines long believed it was originally a Roman temple, but it most likely was raised somewhere between the 4th and 7th centuries on the site of a Roman palace. In choosing a date to mark the beginning of the Renaissance, art historians often seize on 1401, the year Florence's powerful wool merchant's guild held a contest to decide who would receive the commission to design the North Doors of the Baptistery to match the Gothic South Doors cast 65 years earlier by Andrea Pisano. The era's foremost Tuscan sculptors each designed and cast a bas-relief bronze panel depicting their own vision of the biblical story in which God commands Abraham to sacrifice his son, Isaac. Twenty-two-year-old Lorenzo Ghiberti, competing against the likes of Donatello, Jacopo della Quercia, and Filippo Brunelleschi, won hands down. He spent the next 21 years casting 28 bronze panels and building his doors.

Ghiberti was asked in 1425 to do the East Doors, facing the Duomo, this time giving him the artistic freedom to realize his Renaissance ambitions. Twenty-seven years later, just before his death, Ghiberti finished 10 dramatic lifelike Old Testament scenes in gilded bronze, each a masterpiece of Renaissance sculpture and some of the finest low-relief perspective in Italian art. The panels now mounted here are excellent copies; the originals are displayed in the Museo dell'Opera del Duomo. Years later, Michelangelo was standing before these doors and someone asked his opinion. His response sums up Ghiberti's life accomplishment as no art historian ever could: "They are so beautiful that they would grace the entrance to Paradise." They've been called the Gates of Paradise ever since. Admission is 3€ ($4.20).

The **Galleria degli Uffizi,** Piazzale degli Uffizi 6 (off Piazza della Signoria), is one of the world's great museums and the single best introduction to Renaissance painting, with works by Giotto, Masaccio, Paolo Uccello, Sandro Botticelli, Leonardo da Vinci, Perugino, Michelangelo, Raphael Sanzio, Titian, Caravaggio, and the list goes on. Know before you go that the Uffizi regularly shuts down rooms for crowd-control reasons—especially in summer, when the bulk of the annual 1.5 million visitors stampedes the place. Of the more than 3,100 artworks in the museum's archives, only about 1,700 are on exhibit. Since you can't possibly see it all, if you're going to try to spend a few hours at the Uffizi, concentrate on the first dozen or so rooms and pop by the Greatest Hits of the 16th Century. You can bypass the hours-long ticket line at the Uffizi Galleries by reserving a ticket and an entry time in advance by calling Firenze Musei at © **055-294-883** (Mon–Fri 8:30am–6:30pm, Sat until 12:30pm) or heading online to **www.firenzemusei.it**. You can also reserve tickets for the **Academy Gallery** (Galleria dell'Accademia), between Piazza Santissima Annunziata and Via Ricasoli (© **055-238-8609;** www.sbas.firenze.it/accademia), where you can see *David;* as well as for the Galleria Palatina in the Pitti Palace, the Bargello, and several other museums and attractions. Admission is 6.50€ ($9.10).

A hot young sculptor fresh from his success with the *Pietà* in Rome, Michelangelo offered in 1501 to take on a slab of marble that had already been worked on by another sculptor; only 29 years old, in 1504 he finished a Goliath-size *David* that became the most famous sculpture in the world. Originally standing on Piazza della Signoria in front of the Palazzo Vecchio, the sculpture was removed in 1873 to the Accademia to save it from the elements (a copy stands in its place), a plan that didn't keep it entirely safe— in 1991, a man threw himself on the statue and began hammering at the right foot, dislodging several toes. The foot was repaired, and *David*'s Plexiglas shield went up.

The hall leading up to *David* is lined with perhaps Michelangelo's most fascinating works, the four famous *nonfiniti* ("unfinished") *Slaves,* or *Prisoners.* The great master saw a true sculpture as something that was already inherent in the stone, and all it needed was a skilled chisel to free it from the extraneous rock. Whether he intended the statues to look unfinished has been debated by art historians to exhaustion. The *Pietà* at the end of the corridor on the right is by one of Michelangelo's students, not by the master himself, as was once thought.

The oldest and most famous bridge across the Arno, the **Ponte Vecchio,** Via Por Santa Maria/Via Guicciardini, we know today was built in 1345 by Taddeo Gaddi to replace an earlier version. The characteristic overhanging shops have lined the bridge since at least the 12th century. In the 16th century, it was home to butchers until Cosimo I moved into the Palazzo Pitti across the river. He couldn't stand the stench as he crossed the bridge from on high in the Corridorio Vasariano every day, so he evicted the meat cutters and moved in the classier gold- and silversmiths, tradesmen who occupy the bridge to this day. The Ponte Vecchio's fame saved it in 1944 from the Nazis, who had orders to blow up all the bridges before retreating out of Florence as Allied forces advanced. They couldn't bring themselves to reduce this span to rubble, so they blew up the ancient buildings on either end instead to block it off.

LOCAL FLAVORS

Hearty and mouth-watering, Tuscan cuisine includes pasta, seafood, steaks, and veal, all washed down with a glass or two of Chianti. Even a plate of bread, some olives, a serving of pizza, or a cup of gelato will be most satisfying.

SHOPPING

Good bets here include leather jackets, wallets, shoes, and purses; silk scarves; and all those Italian designer labels. Be prepared for some serious temptation. Definitely head for the vast **San Lorenzo street market,** for leather and just about everything you could think of, but do be on guard for pickpockets. It's the same story for the **Mercato Centrale food market;** it's a great place to explore, but watch your wallet.

PISA

The ancient maritime republic of Pisa is one of Italy's grand cities, begun as a seaside settlement around 1000 B.C. and expanded into a naval trading port by the Romans 8 centuries later. By the 11th century, Pisa had grown into one of the peninsula's most powerful maritime republics, along with Venice, Amalfi, and Genoa. Its extensive trading in the Middle East helped import advanced Arabic ideas in the arts and sciences, and its wealth in the late Middle Ages allowed it to create the monumental buildings we see today—including one that's famously off-center. Other than its leaning tower, Pisa's main claim to fame since the end of its naval power has been its university, one of Italy's top schools, established in 1343.

ON YOUR OWN: WITHIN WALKING DISTANCE

Buses, taxis, and the train all drop you off within walking distance of the **Piazza dei Miracoli** (Square of Miracles, aka "Piazza del Duomo"), the home of the Leaning Tower. Admission charges for the group of monuments and museums on the campo, including the Cattedrale, Baptistery, Camposanto, Museo dell'Opera del Duomo, and Museo delle Sinopie, are confusing (some are grouped together and some have individual fees), so figure out what you want to see first. The Cattedrale alone costs 2€ ($2.80). Any other single sight is 5€ ($7). Any two sights are 6€ ($8.40). The Cattedrale plus any two other sights is 8€ ($11). An 8.50€ ($12) ticket gets you into the Baptistery, Camposanto, Museo dell'Opera del Duomo, and Museo delle Sinopie, while an 11€ ($15) version throws in the Cattedrale as well. Children under 10 enter free. Most important, keep in mind that admission to the Leaning Tower itself (15€/$21) is by advance reservation only. For more information, visit the monuments' collective website at **www.opapisa.it** or call ✆ **050-560-547.**

The **Leaning Tower** was, of course, never meant to lean. Its problem is that you can't stack that much heavy marble on top of a shifting subsoil foundation and keep it all on the up and up. Construction began in 1173 by Guglielmo and Bonnano Pisano (who also sculpted the Duomo's original bronze doors), but they hadn't gotten any farther than the third level when they noticed the lean—at that point, only about 3.8cm (1½ inches), but enough to worry them. Everyone was at a loss as to what to do, so work stopped for almost a century and wasn't resumed again until 1275, under the direction of Giovanni di Simone. He tried to correct the tilt by intentionally curving the structure back toward the perpendicular, giving the tower its slight banana shape. In 1284, work stopped yet again just before the belfry. In 1360, Tomasso di Andrea da Pontedera capped it all off at about 51m (167 ft.) with a slightly Gothic belfry that tilts jauntily to the side.

Stabilization projects—some productive, some not—have been going on for years and over the past 2 decades have dictated whether visitors could tour the inside of the tower. In 1990, with the lean at about 4.5m (15 ft.) out of plumb, the mayor's office ordered the tower closed, but a 1997 stabilization effort seems to have corrected some of the problem and visitors can once again enter, albeit under strictly controlled circumstances. The number of visitors is limited, and the only way in is via compulsory 35- to 40-minute guided tours and a hefty 15€ ($21) admission charge. Visit **www.opapisa.it/boxoffice** to book tickets. It's wise to book well ahead; if you show up in Pisa without reservations in the height of the tourist season, you won't be able to get into the tower.

Trivia: In 1590, Galileo dropped some mismatched wooden balls off the tower's leaning side—thus demonstrating his theory of gravity to an incredulous world.

Several other important buildings crowd the Piazza. The **Cattedrale** (aka the *Duomo*) lies at the heart of the Piazza. Begun in 1063 by the architect Brucheto, it was the first building created in what was to become the Pisan Romanesque style. Note the structure's defining style elements: alternating light and dark banding, rounded blind arches with Moorish-inspired lozenges at the top, colored marble inlay designs, and Lombard-style open galleries of tiny mismatched columns stacked to make the facade much higher than the church roof. Brucheto himself is buried in the last blind arch on the left of the facade.

The domed **Baptistry,** Italy's biggest, with its 104m (341-ft.) circumference, was begun in 1153 by Diotisalvi. Most of the exterior statues and decorative elements by Giovanni Pisano are now kept in the city's Museo dell'Opera del Duomo, and only a few have been replaced here with casts. The interior is surprisingly plain but features the first of the great pulpits by Gothic sculptor Nicola Pisano. The baptistery's acoustics are renowned; when a choir sings here, you can hear it for miles.

The **Camposanto** (cemetery) lies at the Piazza's northern edge. Built beginning in 1278, it's formed in the shape of an enormous rectangular cloister, with 43 window-less arches in its outer wall and others that let onto its central courtyard. Once the Camposanto was one of the main reasons visitors came to Pisa—partly to see the Roman sculptures and recycled sarcophagi used to bury Pisa's bigwigs, but mostly to view the gorgeous frescoes that lined its walls. Sadly, the majority of those frescoes were destroyed by Allied incendiary bombs during World War II, but you can still see the few that survived, including the 14th-century *Triumph of Death.* Restoration work on the building and its treasures is ongoing.

LOCAL FLAVORS

Tuscan flavors and ingredients take center stage in Pisa. If you have time for lunch, look for dishes incorporating Monte Pisano olive oil, Pecorino cheese, Parco di Migliarino lamb, Pisan beef, San Miniato truffle, pine nuts, mushrooms, and Pisanello tomatoes. Pisans eat a lot of meat, from the typical Pisan beef to wild boar with olives, lamb fricassee, rabbit, and lots of game. Fish is big, too, from dried cod, which is typically served fried or in a sweet and sour sauce, to mussels, clams, and eels.

SHOPPING

Pisa's main attraction isn't shopping, but as **kitschy souvenirs** go, there's some great stuff here—much of it, of course, "leaning." Running along one side of the Piazza del Duomo, facing the tower, are a fleet of stalls selling everything from mini leaning tower nightlights and lamps to leaning tower sherry glasses, flower vases, and lots

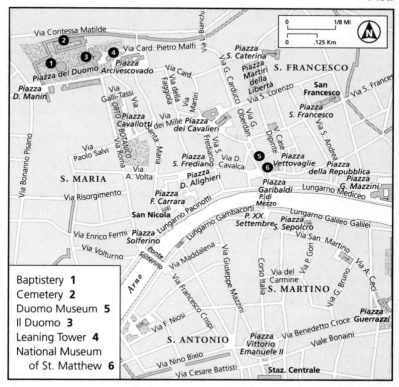

Map legend:

Baptistery **1**
Cemetery **2**
Duomo Museum **5**
Il Duomo **3**
Leaning Tower **4**
National Museum
of St. Matthew **6**

more. Off the beaten track, walk west along Via San Francesco to **Borgo Stretto,** Pisa's arcaded shopping street. Off Borgo Stretto near Piazza Garibaldi is the hidden and arched **Piazza Vettovaglie,** which houses an old-fashioned **food market.**

8 The French Riviera

In any language, the words *French Riviera* (aka the *Côte d'Azur* or "Blue Coast") stand for style, beauty, and access. From P. Diddy and Princess Diana to heads of state and billionaire businessman, you know you've arrived when you count this sinewy sliver of sexy couture among your travel conquests. The yachts, diamonds, expensive cars, and fancy clothes so ubiquitous here are constant reminders that the Riviera is and long has been a playground of the rich and famous, and wannabes alike, and for good reason: The place is even more gorgeous than the people.

Stretching between the sea and the coastal mountains of southern France, it's no wonder artists from Matisse and Cocteau to Picasso, Léger, and Renoir were all drawn to the area's natural beauty. Today numerous museums here are devoted to their work.

Strung along the coast like pearls, the towns of Cannes, Nice, Villefranche, St-Tropez, and Monte Carlo (the latter the capital of the independent principality of Monaco) are all so close together geographically that you're offered nearly the same shore excursions no matter where your ship puts in, although each port has its own special flavor and charms.

All the ports are crowded with tourists in the summer months, particularly in July and August. The scenic drive between the ports is gorgeous but can be slow, depending on the traffic. Keep in mind that though the beaches on the Riviera are fashionable, they're not gorgeous white-sand beaches like you'll find in the Caribbean or the South Pacific; they tend to be pebbly and pretty narrow.

COMING ASHORE   Most ships visiting the Riviera call at **Villefranche,** anchoring offshore and ferrying passengers in via a short tender ride. From here, you can travel to the other towns via shore excursion or taxi. It's about 6km (3¾ miles) to Nice, 38km (24 miles) to Cannes, 118km (73 miles) to St. Tropez, and 9km (5½ miles) to Monte Carlo. Some luxury vessels also dock or anchor directly at Monte Carlo, Cannes, and St. Tropez.

GETTING AROUND   **Taxis** are available at the piers but are expensive (you may want to double up with other passengers if you're planning to go any distance). You can **walk** from all the ports to many local attractions. There is also great **train** service between Nice, Villefranche, and Monte Carlo, and to other locations on the Côte d'Azur.

LANGUAGE & CURRENCY   The language is **French** and the official currency is the **euro** (€). The exchange rate at press time was $1 = .72€ (1€ = $1.40).

BEST CRUISE LINE SHORE EXCURSIONS

The best way to explore the French Riviera ports is on foot. You needn't book a shore excursion unless walking is a problem or you wish to travel to a port other than the one your ship is visiting or an inland destination. If you're looking for something different, try one of the following.

St-Paul-de-Vence (4 hr.; $49–$65): This medieval walled city is the best known of the region's perched villages, a feudal hamlet that blends into a bastion of rock, its ramparts overlooking a peaceful setting of flowers and olive and orange trees. It offers art galleries and shops, cobblestone streets, cafes, and gorgeous country views. The trip may be combined with a visit to Grasse—birthplace of the French perfume industry—and a stop at a perfume factory.

Medieval Eze (3–4 hr.; $45–$75): Eze, literally clinging to the rocks above the sea, is a medieval village worth exploring. This tour includes a guided walk through the narrow streets, with their lovely restored houses and stunning views. Time is allowed for shopping in the town's boutiques and artists' studios. Visits to both St-Paul-de-Vence and Eze may be combined, for a higher fee, with a tour of Nice.

Convertible Sports Car (4 hr.; $295 per couple): If your cruise line offers it, take it! Heidi and her husband did and it was a highlight of their cruise. From Villefranche, they folded themselves into a champagne-colored MG convertible and felt instantly cool and very local. They zipped along the Bas Corniche toward Monte Carlo, with breathtaking views of France's Côte d'Azur's undulating coast and fairy-tale villages framing the drive (because it was morning, the famous Casino hadn't opened yet). Other stops (it's completely up to you where and when you pull over) included Eze and Nice.

LOCAL FLAVORS

Definitely try bouillabaisse, fish stew, and salade niçoise. Another local specialty is pizza served with onions or olives. Of course, the bread, cheese, and wine are to die for; even a simple croissant and a coffee is a great way to sample the local flavors.

SHOPPING

Shop at these ports for high-fashion items, artwork, antiques, and items made of colorful Provençal fabrics. Several of Heidi's favorite wardrobe pieces are from the French Rivera, including two sexy tops and a great pair of chocolate brown espadrilles. It's true that French people are naturally stylish, so anything you buy here is guaranteed to be superfashionable in that "I just threw this on" sort of understated way.

CANNES

The grand hotels made famous during the International Film Festival overlook the seafront boulevards, but it's Coco Chanel, not the festival, who's credited with putting the city on the map after she came, got a suntan, then went back to Paris and started a trend. Cannes' beaches today continue to be more for exhibitionism and voyeurism than for swimming. The top strips of sand (and it is sand here, not pebbles like at Nice) along the fabled promenade, La Croisette, are littered with sun beds and parasols rented at the beach concessions. The beach is actually divided into 32 sections, our favorites being **Plages Gazagnaire, Le Zénith,** and **Waikiki.** Some of the beaches are privately run, but the best public beach is in front of the Palais des Festivals.

The city offers great shopping opportunities, including outlets of major Paris names such as Saint Laurent, Rykiel, and Hermès, which can be found on La Croisette. More reasonably priced shopping can be found a few blocks inland on rue d'Antibes.

The collection at **Musee de la Castre** (© **04/93-38-55-26**), in Château de la Castre, Le Suquet, contains 19th-century paintings, sculptures, decorative arts, and ethnography, including a gallery devoted to relics of ancient Mediterranean civilizations. Admission is 3€ ($4.20) adults, free for students and children.

MONTE CARLO

There really are playboys in tight pants driving Ferraris around Monte Carlo. Plunk yourself near the Casino at one of the cafes, or just lean against a lamppost, and watch for yourself. The adjacent Hotel de Paris is another place to see and be seen; the elegant gilded lobby is tres chic and so is its American Bar.

The 196-hectare (485-acre) principality of **Monaco** became the property of the Grimaldi clan, a Genoese family, in 1297 and has maintained something resembling independence ever since. Its capital, **Monte Carlo,** has for a century symbolized glamour—and the 1956 marriage of Prince Rainier III and the American actress Grace Kelly only enhanced the city's status. Rainier died in April 2005, and his son, Prince Albert II, now rules the country.

Visitors are always surprised by how small Monaco is. The second-smallest independent state in Europe (only Vatican City is smaller), Monaco consists of four tightly packed parts: the Old Town, setting for the royal palace (where a 10-min. changing-of-the-guard ceremony is held daily at 11:55am) and the Monaco Cathedral (where the tombs of Princess Grace and Prince Rainier are located); the residential area of La Condamine; Monte Carlo, where the fancy hotels and famous casino are located; and Fontvieille, the commercial area.

When exploring the city, you can walk up hills or use Monaco's somewhat bizarre system of public elevators that take you, for instance, from the harbor to the casino.

A tram service operates on a circuit between the palace, aquarium, and casino, priced at a reasonable 6€ ($8.40).

The **Monte Carlo Casino,** place du Casino (© **377-92/16-21-21**), was built in 1878 by Charles Garnier, the architect who created the Paris Opera House. It is a very ornate building but not at all glitzy; those used to Las Vegas casinos will be surprised by its small size and lack of fiber-optic lighting. The atrium is surrounded by 28 Ionic columns made of onyx. The gaming rooms, one leading into the next (you pay more for admission the deeper into the casino you go), feature equally elaborate decor, including gilt, frescoes, and bas-reliefs. Games include baccarat, roulette, craps, and blackjack, as well as slot machines (in Salle Américaine). Admission is 10€ ($14), depending on where in the casino you go. No one under 21 is permitted inside. A passport is required to get in, and at night men must wear jackets and ties.

The **Palais du Prince,** place du Palais (© **377-93/25-18-31**), offers a peek into the lifestyle of the ruling Grimaldi family. While the exterior is fortlike, the interior offers an Italianate courtyard and the kind of decorative grand rooms with gold gilt, lush fabrics, and frescoed ceilings that you would expect to find in a royal residence. The tour consists of a recorded commentary, with the tour guide pressing a button at each stop (make sure you get an English-language tour). You can buy a combo ticket that includes the adjacent museum and archives, but it's hardly worth the time or extra money to do the latter unless you are really into Napoleonic-era relics, of which the museum seems to have an abundance. Admission to the palace is 6€ ($8.40) for adults, 3€ ($4.20) for children.

Musée de l'Océanographie, avenue St-Martin (© **377-93/15-36-00**), is one of the best aquariums in Europe, displaying rare and unusual sea creatures. The upper floor offers a history of underwater exploration, complete with early scuba gear and a submarine mock-up from the 1700s. On the main floor is an aquarium with more than 90 tanks containing such endangered species as the fascinating leafy sea dragon. The museum building is an impressive structure in itself. Admission is 11€ ($15) adults, 6€ ($8.40) children 6 to 18, free for children 6 and under.

If you have very big bucks (bank on at least 80€–146€/$112–$204 per person for lunch), you'll want to eat at **Le Louis XV** in the Hôtel de Paris (© **377-92/16-30-01**), next to the Casino, where three-star Michelin chef Alain Ducasse does his six-star magic. Make reservations well in advance.

If you're more the bikini kind, head to the **Monte-Carlo Beach.** Once frequented by Princess Grace, it's actually on French soil. Of all the Riviera's beaches, this is the most fashionable, even though its sands are imported. The property adjoins the ultra-chic **Monte-Carlo Beach Hotel,** 22 av. Princesse-Grace. Keep your eyes peeled for the rich and famous here.

NICE

Nice, once a Victorian playground of the aristocracy, is today a big middle-class city. It's the capital of the Riviera and the largest city between Genoa and Marseille. It's also one of the most ancient cities in the region, founded by the Greeks, who called it Nike, or Victory. Artists and writers have long been attracted to the city, including Dumas, Nietzsche, Flaubert, Hugo, Sand, and Stendahl. Henri Matisse made his home here.

Much of the heart of waterfront Nice is walkable; everything highlighted below can be reached on foot from the Old Town.

Triangulate from **Le Château,** a steep rock promontory right on the coast, topped with a garden of pines and exotic flowers. To the east is the **harbor,** where you can linger over an aperitif at a sidewalk cafe as you watch boats depart for Corsica. To the west, stretching toward Masséna, is the **Vieille Ville,** or Old Town, whose Italianate facades suggest 17th-century Genoese palaces. The Old Town is a maze of narrow streets, some of which (including the rue Masséna, the rue Droite, and the rue Pairolière) are pedestrian only. On these narrow streets, you'll find some of the least expensive restaurants in Nice. Buy *la pissaladière* (an onion pizza) from one of the local vendors. While here, try to visit the **Marché aux Fleurs,** the flower market at cours Saleya. The vendors set up their flamboyant stalls of carnations, violets, jonquils, roses, and birds of paradise Tuesday through Sunday from 8am to 6pm in summer.

Just under a half a kilometer (¼ mile) or so west, Nice's commercial centerpiece is **place Masséna,** with pink buildings in the 17th-century Genoese style and the **Fontaine du Soleil (Fountain of the Sun)** by Janoit, which dates from 1956. Stretching from the main square to the promenade is the **Jardin Albert-1er,** with an openair terrace and a Triton Fountain. With palms and exotic flowers, it's the most relaxing oasis in town.

The **promenade des Anglais,** a wide boulevard on the bay, stretches several miles, offering a lovely walk past cafes, historic buildings, and beaches full of bronzed bodies in teeny-weeny bikinis. The beaches go on for some 7km (4¼ miles), but they're pebbly. If it's beaches you're after, head to St-Tropez or Monte Carlo instead.

If you care to head up **Le Château** for the views, you can walk the 200-plus stairs or take an elevator from the Quai des Etats Unis. At Le Château's north end is the famous old **graveyard** of Nice, visited primarily for its lavishly sculpted monuments. The cemetery is the largest in France and the fourth-largest in Europe. FYI, the château in the area's name refers to the old castle of the ducs de Savoie, which was torn down in 1706. Names die hard.

The city's best museums are inland about 2½ km (1½ miles) or so from place Masséna. Hearty walkers can go on foot; the rest of you should hop a local bus or take a taxi. Located in the once-aristocratic hilltop **Cimiez** neighborhood, is the **Musée National Message Biblique Marc-Chagall,** avenue Du Dr.-Ménard (℅ **04/93-53-87-20;** www.musee-chagall.fr), dedicated to the artist's treatment of biblical themes (which are described in a helpful brochure, available in English). Chagall and his wife donated the works, which include oils, gouaches, drawings, pastels, lithographs, and sculptures, as well as a mosaic and stained-glass windows. Admission is 6.50€ ($9.10) for adults, 4.50€ ($6.30) for students, free for children under 18. Rates may be higher for special exhibitions. The museum is about a 10-minute walk northeast of the Nice-Villa train station or a 30-minute walk or short bus ride—take bus no. 15 or 17—from place Masséna.

Housed in the former residence of Ukrainian Princess Kotchubey, the **Musée des Beaux-Arts,** 33 av. Des Baumettes (℅ **04/92-15-28-28;** www.musee-beaux-arts-nice. org), is devoted to the masters of the Second Empire and the Belle Epoque, with an extensive collection of 19th-century French artists, including Monet, Renoir, and Rodin. Admission is 4€ ($5.60) for adults, 2.50€ ($3.50) for students, and free for children 18 and under. Nearby, the **Musée d'Art moderne et d'Art Contemporain,** Promenade des Arts (℅ **04/93-62-61-62;** www.mamac-nice.org), displays collections of French and American art from the 1960s to the present, including works from the pop art, minimalist, and graffiti art movements. The collection is housed in a striking modern building by architects Yves Bayard and Henri Vidal. Admission is 4€ ($5.60) adults.

Matisse spent the last years of his life in Nice. **Musée Matisse,** 164 av. Des Arénes-de-Cimiez (© **04/93-53-40-53;** www.musee-matisse-nice.org), offers works donated by the artist and his heirs. Included are *Nude in an Armchair with a Green Plant, Nymph in the Forest,* and *Portrait of Madame Matisse,* as well as practice sketches and designs, and items from the artist's own collection and home. Admission is 4€ ($5.60) for adults, 2.50€ ($3.50) seniors, free for children under 18.

Reachable from Nice by taxi, the walled town of **St-Paul-de-Vence** is the most iconic of the region's mountain villages. Most cruise passengers visit by shore excursion, but if you go on your own, drop in to the **Foundation Maeght** (© **04/93-32-81-63;** www.fondation-maeght.com). Located outside the city walls, it's considered by some to be the best art museum on the Riviera. Its contemporary art collection includes works by Calder, Giacometti, Miró, Chagall, Matisse, and more. Admission is 11€ ($15) adults, 9€ ($13) students and ages 10 to 25, free for children under 10.

Some people visit St-Paul-de-Vence solely to dine at **La Colombe d'Or** (© **04/93-32-80-02;** www.la-colombe-dor.com), once the stomping grounds of some of the most important artists of the 20th century. They would trade art for meals and rooms, and the walls and gardens contain works by Picasso, Braque, Miró, Matisse, Léger, Calder, Chagall, and others. Unfortunately, you can't view the collection unless you spring for a meal here. Main courses start around 25€ ($35). Reservations are required.

ST-TROPEZ

Once a quiet fishing village and secluded hideaway for bohemian artist types, the St-Tropez resort was made famous in 1957 when Roger Vadim filmed wife Brigitte Bardot here in *And God Created Woman.* The jet set quickly followed, and fun-in-the-sun is still the word. Though its reputation is for hedonism (and you will see topless and even bottomless sunbathers on the beach) and big names (celebrities are no rarity on the streets, and the harbor is full of fancy yachts), there's also a bit of quaint mixed in. Though the town was destroyed by the Germans in 1944, local residents used old plans and photos to rebuild the village to look exactly as it had before, and today its narrow streets, chic cafes, and pastel-colored buildings are fairy-tale perfect. In addition to its beaches, St-Tropez offers good shopping, including a wealth of antiques dealers and art galleries in Old Town.

The **Musée de L'Annonciade,** place Georges-Grammont (© **04/94-97-04-01**), housed in a former chapel, has one of the best modern-art collections on the Riviera. The collection includes Van Dongen's *Women of the Balustrade,* as well as paintings and sculpture by Bonnard, Matisse, Braque, Utrillo, Seurat, Derain, and Maillol. Admission is 6€ ($8.40) for adults, 3€ ($4.20) for children. Closed in November.

If beaches are more your scene than museums, head for **Plage de Tahiti,** France's most infamous beach, mainly because of all the topless/bottomless action going on. Ever since the days of Brigitte Bardot, this beach has been a favorite of movie stars. It's very cruisy and animated, with a French nonchalance about nudity. If you bother to wear a bikini, it should be only the most daring. The beach is located at the north end of the Baie de Pampelonne, a multimile stretch starting about 10km (6¼ miles) south of St-Tropez.

VILLEFRANCHE-SUR-MER

Located only 6.4km (4 miles) from Nice, Villefranche sits on a big, bowl-shaped blue bay that's large enough to accommodate the largest cruise ships in the world—which explains why it serves as the French Riviera's main port. A great place to just wander on foot, it's a got a seaside strip of outdoor cafes; flower-lined, pedestrian-only cobblestone streets filled with cute shops, private homes, and more cafes; and the **rue Obscure,** a covered street that looks more North African casbah than European resort, with vaulted archways and doors leading to mysterious little houses. (To get there, take rue de l'Eglise from the quais.) The town is also a good starting point for shore excursions to Nice, Eze, St-Paul-de-Vence, and Monaco—the latter just a 15- to 20-minute train ride away. Villefranche's train station is within walking distance of the terminal where tenders drop off passengers from ships anchored offshore.

The artist Jean Cocteau left his mark on the Romanesque **Chapelle St-Pierre,** quai de la Douane/rue des Mariniéres (© **04/93-76-90-70**), in the form of frescoes paying tribute to Gypsies, St. Peter, and the young women of Villefranche. Admission is 3€ ($4.20). If you'd rather do lots of nothing, there's a pebbly beach called **Plage de Villefranche-sur-Mer** within walking distance northeast of the tender terminal.

9 Genoa, Italy

Genoa is no stranger to ships. The city was originally founded as a port by the Ligurian people some 2,500 years ago, then became an important maritime center for the Romans and later a formidable maritime power in its own right. Troubles with Venice in the 1300s led to a decline in the city's fortunes, so much so that when native son Christopher Columbus wanted to mount his voyage of exploration, he had to go to Spain to find financial backing.

Things remained iffy for a long time, and in recent decades Genoa had a reputation as Italy's seediest port city, but things have since changed for the better. In 1992 the city celebrated the 500th anniversary of Columbus's discovery of America, and in 2004 it was the official "European Capital of Culture," a designation that encouraged a huge revitalization effort. The harbor and downtown area have been made more visitor friendly with the refurbishment of many museums, centuries-old homes and palaces, streets, and facades. Today Genoa is a mix of old and new, of sophistication and squalor. It's easy to capture glimpses of the city's glory days in Genoa's portside **Old Town,** whose narrow lanes and alleys are filled with palaces, fine marble churches, and humble houses standing side by side. The other Genoa, the modern city that stretches for miles along the coast and climbs the hills, is a place of international business, peaceful parks, designer shops, and fancy residential neighborhoods.

COMING ASHORE The Genoa cruise docks are located near the foot of the Old Town, though getting from one to the other entails walking through an industrial part of town and crossing a highway. If that sounds unappealing, grab one of the **taxis** that will be lined up at the dock.

Costa ships sail from the port of **Savona,** about 25 miles west of Genoa, near the border with France.

GETTING AROUND You can walk anywhere you need to go in the Old Town and Old Port areas, but metered taxis are also available at taxi stands around the city.

LANGUAGE & CURRENCY The language is **Italian** and the official currency is the **euro** (€). The exchange rate at press time was $1 = .72€ (1€ = $1.40).

BEST CRUISE LINE SHORE EXCURSIONS

Because of the relative compactness of the Old Town, just getting out and walking around with a map is a better option here than an excursion. Unless, that, is, you want to go to . . .

Portofino ($66, 4½ hr.): For quaint fishing villages, you can't beat Portofino, a postcard-perfect place with frescoed houses, lush vegetation, and a lot of luxury yachts in the harbor during summer. Excursions first drive by bus to Rapallo, from which you travel by boat to Portofino. Once there, you can easily explore the tiny town's narrow streets on foot, shopping at the art galleries and jewelry shops or grabbing a cappuccino at one of the waterfront cafes.

ON YOUR OWN: WITHIN WALKING DISTANCE

Though you may choose to take a taxi from the cruise pier, everything here is essentially within walking distance.

Genoa's **Porto Antico (Old Port)** was revitalized for the 1992 Columbus exposition and is now popularly known as the **Expo Area.** Built around a large peninsula, two long wharfs, and the waterfront, it's an all-purpose entertainment area featuring movie theaters, shopping, dining, galleries, ferry docks, and an ice-skating rink in winter. At the center of it all, the **Bigo** is a multiarmed sightseeing lift that takes visitors up in a gondola for great views of the port and the city. Its design was modeled on the freight cranes that are omnipresent in the port, used to hoist cargo onto ships. Tickets are 3€ ($4.20). On the port's northernmost pier, the **Acquario di Genova** (Aquarium of Genoa; ☏ **010/2345678;** www.acquariodigenova.it) is Europe's largest, with 6,000 animals representing 600 species splashing around in 71 exhibition tanks that re-create Caribbean coral reefs, pools in the Central American rainforests, and other marine ecosystems. Admission is 15€ ($21). On the opposite side of the same pier, the **Biosfera** (☏ **010/2345659**) is a little chunk of rainforest growing within a huge glass bubble, brimming with butterflies, chameleons, rubber and mangrove trees, and other tropical flora and fauna. Admission is 5€ ($7).

Just to the north along the waterfront, the **Galata Museo del Mare** (Museum of the Sea; ☏ **010/2345655;** www.galatamuseodelmare.it) offers a multimedia tour of Genoa's relation with the sea, from the development of the port through the age of Columbus and after, with displays of vessels, shipbuilding, armaments, atlases, charts, and navigational instruments. Admission is 10€ ($14).

Inland from the waterfront, **Via Garibaldi** is an Old Town street full of 16th- and 17th-century mansions that now house three of Genoa's best museums, collectively known as the **Strada Nuova Museums.** Admission to all three is 7€ ($9.80), and they're closed Monday. The **Galleria di Palazzo Bianco** (White Palace), Via Garibaldi 11 (☏ **010/5572193;** www.museopalazzobianco.it), is one of Genoa's finest palaces, built of white stone by the powerful Grimaldi family in the 16th century and opened to the public as an art museum in 2004. Its fine collection includes paintings by Van Dyck, Rubens, Veronese, Caravaggio, Jan Steen, and Lucas Cranach the Elder. One room is dedicated to the works of Bernardo Strozzi, whose early-17th-century school made Genoa an important force in the baroque movement. A few doors down, the **Galleria di Palazzo Rosso** (Red Palace), Via Garibaldi 18 (☏ **010/2476351;** www. museopalazzorosso.it), contains a collection primarily assembled by the Brignole-Sale family, which once called the palace home. It includes more Van Dycks and Strozzis, ceiling frescos by Gregorio de Ferrari and Domenico Piola, and works by Dürer, Titian,

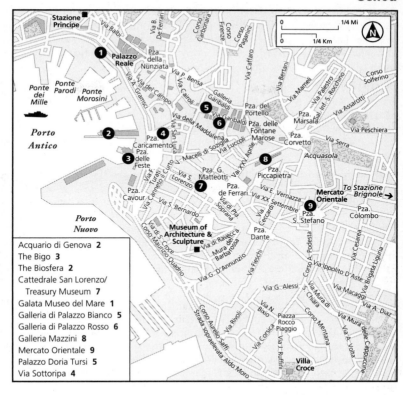

Acquario di Genova **2**
The Bigo **3**
The Biosfera **2**
Cattedrale San Lorenzo/
   Treasury Museum **7**
Galata Museo del Mare **1**
Galleria di Palazzo Bianco **5**
Galleria di Palazzo Rosso **6**
Galleria Mazzini **8**
Mercato Orientale **9**
Palazzo Doria Tursi **5**
Via Sottoripa **4**

and Guercino. The **Palazzo Doria Tursi,** via Garibaldi 9 (© **010/5572193;** www.museo palazzotursi.it), is the most majestic building on the street, dating to 1565. It houses municipal offices but also offers galleries dedicated to tapestries, ceramics, and coins, and another that displays the Guarneri violin once played by Nicolo Paganini, along with scores, documents, letters, and other objects belonging to the great violinist.

About a quarter-mile to the south, the **Cattedrale San Lorenzo** at Piazza San Lorenzo is an austere black-and-white-striped 12th-century structure with a portion of its interior given over to a **Treasury Museum** (© **010/2541250;** www.museo sanlorenzo.it). Objects in its collection include the plate upon which John the Baptist's head was supposedly served to Salome, a bowl allegedly used at the Last Supper, and a bowl thought at one time to be the Holy Grail. Admission to cathedral is free, but a tour of the treasury will cost you 5.50€ ($7.70).

LOCAL FLAVORS

Located just inland from the Aquarium pier, the **Via Sottoripa** dates to 1135 and today maintains an old-world bazaar atmosphere, with quaint shops and restaurants opening off colonnaded walkways, selling everything from Italian fried fish to Chinese wine.

Gourmets should take a walk through the **Mercato Orientale,** a sprawling indoor food market that offers stalls selling olives, herbs, fresh fruit, and other delicacies. It's open Monday through Saturday (closed Wed afternoons) and has entrances on Via XX Settembre and Via Galata, about halfway between Piazza de Ferrari and Stazione Brignole. The streets just north of the market (especially Via San Vincenzo and Via Colombo) are a gourmand's dream, with many bakeries, *pasticcerie* (pastry shops), and stores selling pasta, cheese, wine, olive oil, and other foodstuffs.

SHOPPING

The main shopping corridors of Genoa are the streets that radiate out from Piazza De Ferrari. The best boutiques and fashionable shops are found on **Via XX Settembre** and **Via Roma,** and in the elegant **Galleria Mazzini,** a shopping arcade with a gorgeous glass canopy high above. It connects the Piazza De Ferrari with the central Piazza Corvetto.

10 Gibraltar

The famous rock at the entrance to the Mediterranean is visited by some ships and simply pointed out by others (as in, "We do a daylight passing of the famous Rock of Gibraltar"). If you do set foot on the limestone peninsula, you'll find a small British colony from which you can view Africa on a clear day. In addition to spectacular views, Gibraltar has a small town (also called Gibraltar) with Victorian architecture, natural caves, historical sites, museums, lovely botanical gardens, the famous Barbary apes, and beautiful beaches.

COMING ASHORE   Ships dock about 1.6km (1 mile) from the center of town. **Taxis** and a shuttle service are both available at the pier.

GETTING AROUND   You can walk the majority of this little colony, but to get to the top of the rock, you'll want to take the **cable car** (**www.gibraltarinfo.gi/gibraltar-cable-car.aspx**). Walk down the cruise dock to the Coach Park and either take the No. 4 bus or turn right and walk about 1.6km (1 mile) down Main Street to the cable car station at the Main Street Shopping Centre. One-way tickets cost £6.50 ($13) and round-trips run £8 ($17). A **combo ticket** (£14.50/$30 one-way, £16/$33 round-trip) includes the cable-car ride plus admission to all the sites in the Nature Reserve, including St Michael's Cave, the Great Siege Tunnels, the Moorish castle, and the City Under Siege Exhibition.

LANGUAGE & CURRENCY   The official language is **English** and the currency is the Gibraltar pound, which is equivalent to the British pound sterling. U.S. dollars are, however, readily accepted. The exchange rate at press time was $1 = £ .48 or £1 = $2.07.

BEST CRUISE LINE SHORE EXCURSIONS

Gibraltar Highlights (2 hr.; $50): This overview of the tiny peninsula takes in St. Michael's Cave, a natural grotto with spectacular stalagmites; the Apes' Den, inhabited by semiwild Barbary apes; and the remains of an old Moorish castle. A 3½-hour **walking tour** ($60) visits the same sites and includes a ride by cable car to the top of the rock.

City Under Seige (3½ hr.; $70): This historical tour focuses on the period from 1779 to 1783, when Spain and France attempted to wrest Gibraltar back from the British. It includes a cable car ride to the Top Station, site of a World War II gun emplacement and great views of Africa and Spain; a 45-minute tour of the Great Siege Tunnels, carved by the British for defense; and a visit to the Apes' Den (see above), the Gibraltar Museum, and an exhibit about the siege.

ON YOUR OWN: WITHIN WALKING DISTANCE

Gibraltar covers only about 6 sq. km (2¼ sq. miles), meaning it's all doable on foot, though you'll probably take the **cable car** to the top of the rock and then walk down (see "Getting Around," above). En route to the top, the cable car stops at the **Apes Den,** along Old Queen's Road. Here you can see the famous Barbary apes cavorting on the sides of rocks. Despite their name, they aren't really apes, but cinnamon-colored tailless macaques (monkeys). No one knows for sure where they came from: They may have been brought from Africa by the Moors as pets, they may have been introduced by the British, or (though it's unlikely) they may be the last of a population that long ago disappeared from the rest of southern Europe.

A short walk downhill from the top of the cable car line (you have to walk east along Queen's Road) is the entrance to **St. Michael's Cave.** The caves are a natural grotto whose magnificent stalagmite- and stalactite-filled auditorium is used for concerts and live performances. The final of the big three attractions, the **Great Siege Tunnels,** lies at the western end of the Nature Preserve, in the steep face that looks out toward Spain. The tunnels were dug out by the British during the Great Siege of 1779 to 1783, allowing the small British force to fire on the French and Spanish with little risk. Original gun emplacements, models, and other displays tell the story of the defense of the rock. The cable car fee includes entrance to these attractions.

Directly south of the tunnels lie the ruins of the **Moorish Castle,** constructed by the descendants of Tariq ibn Ziyad, the Berber Muslim general who captured the Rock in 711, putting his name on the map in the process (the name Gibraltar derives from Jabal Tariq, or "mountain of Tariq"). Little remains of the original castle other than parts of its outer walls.

Most day-trippers end their sightseeing at this point. Those who want to make a full day of it return to the Apes Den and take the cable car back down into the center of Gibraltar, where they can explore the city. Some hearty souls walk all the way down the rock, which makes for a good hike. In town, the **Gibraltar Museum,** 18/20 Bomb House Lane (© **74289;** www.gib.gi/museum), is installed in a 14th-century Muslim bathhouse and displays a collection related to the history of the Rock, from prehistoric cave-dwelling days to the present. There is a mass of artifacts, cannon balls, weapons, and military uniforms. Admission is £2 ($4.15). Closed Sunday. Toward the southern end of Main Street, the **Convent** was once a real Franciscan convent, dating to 1531, and became the official residence of Gibraltar's governor in 1728. A ceremonial **changing of the guard** takes place here every Monday at 10:30am, with a full band and the governor and his family on the balcony to accept the salute.

LOCAL FLAVORS

You're technically in Britain here, so stop at one of the pubs on Main Street for fish and chips or steak-and-kidney pie. Buy a pint of ale to wash it all down.

SHOPPING

In town, the **duty-free** shops are a big attraction, selling English china, crystal, woolens, Lladró figurines, electronics, jewelry, watches, cosmetics, and perfume.

11 The Greek Isles: Mykonos, Rhodes & Santorini

Greece is practically tailor-made for cruising; its scenery is drop-dead gorgeous, its seas are relatively calm, and its islands are individual in character. All this, coupled with ancient and medieval historic sites, buckets of ancient and local culture, and excellent food equals one of the world's best travel regions. We can never get enough of the place, and, it seems, neither can anyone else: During the prime tourist months of July and August, expect thousands of other cruise passengers to be enjoying the view along with you. In all of the Greek Isles, you can explore on foot, relax on a beach, or take in a meal and the local color at the nearest taverna; there's really no need to sign up for an organized tour unless you really want to see a specific historical site that isn't close to the port.

LANGUAGE & CURRENCY Greek is the official language, but **English** is also widely spoken. The official currency is the **euro** (€). The exchange rate at press time was $1 = .72€ (1€ = $1.40).

LOCAL FLAVORS

Hearty and full of natural flavor, Greek food is fabulous and varied, featuring goodies like fresh seafood, kalamata olives, lamb and pork, phyllo pastry, tomatoes, eggplant, feta cheese, zucchini, and yogurt.

MYKONOS

The town of Hora itself is the main attraction here, with its quaint whitewashed homes, blue-domed churches, windmills, cobblestone streets, and harbor lined with fishing boats. After you're welcomed by the pelicans that act as Mykonos's unofficial greeters, wander inland from the pier and meander the labyrinth of streets, checking out the art galleries, jewelry stores, and gift shops, or stopping at a cafe or bar. There's a charming, picture-postcard quality here, despite the large numbers of sun seekers, the party-town reputation (especially in July and Aug), and the inevitable souvenir shops.

Mykonos's second town is **Ano Mera,** about 6.4km (4 miles) east of Hora, where you'll find a more traditional ambience and some religious sites. The **Monastery of Panayia Tourliani,** southeast of town, dates to 1580 and has a handsomely carved steeple, as well as a small religious museum inside. Nearby (1km/½ mile away to the southeast) is the 12th-century **Monastery of Paleokastro,** one of the greenest spots on the island.

If you're looking for a beach, you have a choice: **Aghios Stefanos** is the closest beach to Mykonos, located to the north and very popular. The smaller **Agios Ioannis,** on the island's southwest coast, is beautiful and offers a view of the island of Delos. On the island's south coast, **Paradise Beach** and **Super Paradise** are busy party beaches, the former also offering diving (**Mykonos Diving Center,** ⑦/fax **0289/ 24-808;** www.dive.gr), the latter clothing optional. **Platis Gialos** and **Psarou,** also on the south coast, are busy but less raucous. **Buses** go to all the beaches from the central Hora station, located to the left side of the harbor. Depending where you're going, tickets cost about .50€ to 4€ (70¢–$5.60). You can also take a **taxi** from Taxi (Mavro) Square, where you'll find rates posted on a board.

COMING ASHORE Ships tender passengers to the main harbor area along the Esplanade in Hora.

The Greek Isles & Turkey's Aegean Coast

Skýros

SOUTHERN SPORADES

○Paralía Kímis

ÉVVIA

A E G E A N

○Kárystos

Híos

←**Athens**

Ándros

I S L A N D S

Tínos

Sýros

Délos *Mikonos*

Páros *Náxos*

Sérifos

Antíparos

Sífnos

CYCLADES

Mílos

Íos

Folégandros

Santoríni

GREECE

Athens ⊛

Area of detail

Izmir ○

Ephesus

Sámos Kuşadası ○

T U R K E Y

Bodrum ○

Kos

Rhodes○
Town

DODECANESE *Rhodes*

Lindos ○

0 ——————— 50 mi
0 ——————— 50 km

THE BEST CRUISE LINE SHORE EXCURSIONS

Delos Apollo Sanctuary (3–4½ hr.; $55–$65): Unlike other Greek islands visited by cruise ships, Mykonos is not a setting for ancient ruins, so those seeking sacred sights should sign up for this tour. You'll travel by small boat from Mykonos Harbor to Delos for a 2-hour guided walking tour of the tiny island that's known as the birthplace of Apollo. Once the religious and commercial hub of the Aegean, it's now home only to ancient ruins and their caretakers.

RHODES

Rich in history, Rhodes is also dotted with beautiful beaches, mountain villages, and fertile plains. Its most famous inhabitants were the crusading Knights of St. John (aka the Knights Hospitalers), who arrived in 1291 after fleeing Jerusalem. They reigned for more than 2 centuries, and their legacy lives on in the Old Town section of **Rhodes Town,** which also offers charming cafes and plenty of shops. To appreciate its many offerings, walk its maze of streets, sampling from its seafood restaurants and shops. The cobblestone **Street of the Knights** (noted on maps as Ippoton) leads to the **Palace of the Grand Masters** (© 02/41-756-74), a palace and fortress built by the Knights in the 14th century, blown to smithereens in 1856 when its powder magazine exploded, and reconstructed in the 1930s and '40s. Its floors are covered with mosaics from the island of Kos, and a permanent exhibition displays archaeological items from 2,400 years of Rhodes history. Admission to this and the museum below is included in a 10€ ($14) ticket that's good for admission to several other sites as well. The Street of the Knights was where the inns of the various nations of the Knights of St. John were located. The 15th-century **Hospital of the Knights,** on Messaioniki Poli, is now the home of the **Archaeological Museum** (✆ **02410/75-674**), with a collection of sculpture, sarcophagi, mosaics, ceramics, and various funerary pieces (vases, statuettes, jewelry, and more).

Rhodes is also known for its great **beaches,** with some of the best located on the east coast. **Faliaraki,** about 20 minutes south of Rhodes Town, is one of the island's most popular and attracts a rowdy pub crowd. Admission is 4€ ($5.60). You can catch a taxi at the end of the cruise pier and will have to negotiate a fare with the taxi driver. Rental cars and motor scooters are also available near the harbor.

COMING ASHORE   Ships dock at the commercial harbor, which is within walking distance of Rhodes Town's old section.

THE BEST CRUISE LINE SHORE EXCURSIONS
South of Rhodes Town, **Lindos** is the island's top pick for organized excursions. A picturesque village of traditional white-walled homes and cobblestone streets, it's also home to the **Acropolis of Lindos,** which includes the remains of a Doric temple dating back to the 4th century B.C., a Roman temple from the 4th century A.D., and a Greek Orthodox church dating from the 13th or 14th century. The site is spectacular and the sea views from the top are breathtaking, but the crowds can be terrible: The 1.6km (1-mile) pathway to the top of the hill is narrow and often jam-packed with dozens of other tour groups crowding around those ubiquitous little tour flags.

Rhodes & Lindos (4–4½ hr.; $54–$65): Travel by bus for about 72 km (45 miles) through scenic countryside to Lindos for a tour of the Acropolis. The trip may include a walking tour of Old Town Rhodes; a stop at a workshop selling Rhodian ceramics; or a visit to Mount Smith to view the ruins of ancient Rhodes, the Temple of Apollo, and Diagoras Stadium.

Lindos with Lunch by the Beach (8 hr.; $85–$120): Drive to Lindos (see above), then continue on to a secluded beach for some swimming, sunning, and lunch at a beachfront restaurant. Your tour may also include a walk through Rhodes's Old Town.

SANTORINI
Dotted with whitewashed homes, black-pebble beaches, rich vineyards, and ancient ruins, Santorini (aka Thira) is one of the most breathtaking islands in the world, and approaching its beautiful bowl-shaped harbor by ship is a dramatic experience. The bay is actually a caldera, a central crater that was formed when a volcano erupted in 1500 B.C. Ash fell on the remaining land, burying the cosmopolitan city of **Akrotiri,** an event that some believe sparked the legend of the lost continent of Atlantis.

Fira, the capital of Santorini, sits at about 300m (984 ft.) above sea level and lives up to its picture-postcard reputation, with winding streets lined with shops, cafes, and art galleries. From the port, you can get to town on foot or via donkey (see "Coming Ashore," below) for a lazy day of shopping and lunching. For the ultimate meal, try **Selene,** between the Atlantis and Aressana hotels (✆ **22860/22-249;** www.selene.gr), one of the best restaurants in Greece. Reservations are recommended. Main courses cost about 18€ to 25€ ($25–$35). If you're a hiker, you can walk the 10km (6¼-mile)

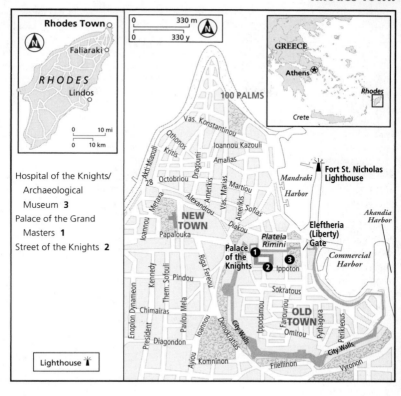

Rhodes Town

Faliaraki

RHODES

Lindos

0   10 mi

0   10 km

Hospital of the Knights/
Archaeological
Museum **3**
Palace of the Grand
Masters **1**
Street of the Knights **2**

Lighthouse

0   330 m

0   330 y

GREECE

Athens

Rhodes

Crete

100 PALMS

Vas. Konstantinou

Othonos

Kritis

Ioannou Kazouli

Amalias

Akti Miaouli

28 Octobriou

Dragoumi

Amerikis

Martiou

Vas. Marias

Amerikis Sofias

Metaxa

Alexandrou

Diakou

NEW TOWN

Ioannou

Papalouka

Riga Fereou

Mandraki Harbor

Fort St. Nicholas
Lighthouse

Akandia Harbor

**Eleftheria
(Liberty)
Gate**

*Plateia
Rimini*

**Palace
of the
Knights** ①

② Ippoton ③

*Commercial
Harbor*

Enoplon Dynameon

Kennedy

Them. Sofouli

Pindou

Pavlou Mela

Ioannou

City Walls

Ippodamou

Sokratous

Fanouriou

Pythagora

**OLD
TOWN**

President

Chimairas

Diagondon

Aviou

Komninon

Denokratias

Omirou

Fiellinon

City Walls

Perikleous

Vyronon

coastal footpath from Fira to **Ia** (also called Oia), an artists' colony located at the northern tip of the island. Along the way, you'll pass several churches, climb two substantial hills, and see some stunning views from the caldera's edge. Ia itself is quite picturesque, with charming homes and galleries showcasing modern and folk art and traditional handicrafts. If you're not up for the hike, you can also take a cab from Fira.

Most significant attractions on Santorini are accessible from the port only by vehicle. On the island's southern coast, excavations at **Akrotiri** (☎ 22860/81-366) have revealed an ancient city preserved under a layer of volcanic ash 3,600 years ago, giving visitors a glimpse of urban life in the Minoan period. Guidebooks are available at the site. Try to visit in the morning, when it's cooler. Admission is 8€ ($11), and a cab ride to the ruins takes about 30 minutes from Fira. Negotiate a rate in advance with your driver, and be sure to make return arrangements. Ditto for reaching **Ancient Thira** (☎ 22860/31-66), atop Mesa Vouna on the island's east coast. From this perch you get incredible views of Santorini and its neighboring islands, and the site's extensive Hellenic, Roman, and Byzantine ruins can be brought to life with the assistance of a good tour guide (for whom you'll have to pay extra; they're usually roaming around). Admission to the ruins is 5€ ($7). Closed Monday. Two popular **beaches,** Kamari and Perissa, lie on either side of the mesa.

Santorini

COMING ASHORE Ships tender passengers to the port of **Skala,** where visitors have three options for reaching town: **donkey, cable car,** or **walking.** The donkey and cable-car rides cost a few euros each way. The walk up the 587 steps to the town of Fira is the same route the donkeys take. *Word to the wise:* Donkeys are fed at the bottom of the hill, so they tend to run down whether they are carrying someone or not. They are also very smelly. Donkey rides take about 20 to 30 minutes, depending on traffic and availability. Cable cars run every 20 minutes. Walking takes about 30 minutes, depending on your legs.

BEST CRUISE LINE SHORE EXCURSIONS

Winery Tour (3–4 hr.; $65): You ride a bus to the village of Mesa Gonia, where you can sample wines at a local winery and enjoy sips on the cliff-hanging balconies.

Volcano Hotel Springs Hike & Swim (3 hr.; $52): Travel by boat to a tiny volcanic island in Santorini's harbor to walk on volcanic sand and lava fragments, and then visit thermal springs and swim in the hot, mineral-rich waters (heavenly!). On the return trip, the drop-off point is in Fira, which you can explore on your own (you take the cable car back to the ship; tickets are provided).

12 Istanbul, Turkey

Istanbul is literally where East meets West, sitting at the point where Europe and Asia touch. It's a place of mosques and minarets, sultans' treasures, crowded bazaars, and holy Christian landmarks—and it's also a chaotic modern city, teeming with energy and looking forward to its country's eventual entry into the European Union. The senses spring to life here, through the smell of the spice market, the taste of traditional Turkish dishes, the feel of a Turkish carpet, and the sound of muezzins chanting the call to prayer. Everywhere you look, museums, palaces, and grand mosques and churches attest to the city's glorious history as the capital of three successive empires—the Roman, Byzantine, and Ottoman.

COMING ASHORE   Most ships dock at either Karakoy or the Sali Pazari Passenger Terminal; both are centrally located but still about a 20- to 30-minute taxi ride from the city's main attractions.

GETTING AROUND   Taxis—yellow, metered, and relatively inexpensive—wait to pick up passengers, and you'll find plenty more of them traveling throughout the city. Always negotiate the fare before hopping in. **Bus** and **tram** services are available, and cruise lines usually provide free shuttle buses to downtown, dropping you off near the expensive rug shops.

The best way to explore the old section of the city is on **foot.** All of the monuments are within walking distance of each other. It's a healthy walk from the pier to the Blue Mosque, and with all the crazy drivers and the generally hectic pace, you're best off taking the shuttle offered by the cruise line, or a cab.

LANGUAGE & CURRENCY   Turkish and **Kurdish** are spoken here, as well as **English, French,** and **German.** The Turkish **new lira** (YTL) is the national currency, and the rate of exchange at press time was $1 = 1.17YTL (1YTL = US85¢).

BEST CRUISE LINE SHORE EXCURSIONS

Highlights of Istanbul (7–9 hr.; $120): Includes the Hippodrome, once the largest chariot race grounds of the Byzantine Empire; Sultan Ahmet Mosque, also known as the Blue Mosque for its 21,000 blue Iznik tiles; the famous St. Sophia, once the largest church in the Christian world; and Topkapi Palace, the official residence of the Ottoman Sultans and home to treasures that include Spoonmaker's Diamond, one of the biggest in the world. You'll also visit the Grand Bazaar, with its 4,000 shops. Some tours bring you back to the ship for lunch, while others include lunch in a first-class restaurant. (Shorter tours that do not include all of the above are available.)

Taste of Istanbul Cooking Class (4–4½ hr.; $149): Visit a Turkish restaurant, meet the chef, and learn how to prepare the regional cuisine. Of course, part of the experience is eating the meal, which is accompanied by Turkish wines.

Calling Istanbul

Dial local calls by using the seven-digit phone number; if dialing out of town, you must include 0 plus the city code. When calling a cellphone (identifiable by the 0531, 0532, 0533, 0534, 0535, 0536, and so on exchanges), you must include the zero. When dialing any number in Turkey from abroad, drop the zero.

ON YOUR OWN: WITHIN WALKING DISTANCE

Built during the 6th century on orders from the Byzantine emperor Justinian, the **Ayasofya** (aka **Hagia Sophia,** or the Church of the Holy Wisdom), on Yerebatan Caddesi (𝐶 **212/522-1750**), was the largest cathedral in the world for more than 1,000 years, famed for its magnificent dome and stunning mosaics and frescoes. In its nearly 1,500-year history, it's served as a patriarchal basilica and a mosque, but today it's a museum of Byzantine art and architecture, of which it's the world's finest example. Admission is 5.50YTL ($4.65). Closed Monday.

The **Blue Mosque** (aka Sultan Ahmet Camii), on Sultanahmet Square, is the other great feature of the Istanbul skyline, with its multiple domes and six thin minarets. Built between 1609 and 1617 by Sultan Ahmet I, it was intended to rival the Ayasofya and was built on a design that relies on successively descending domes to create a large covered interior space. The overall effect is one of great harmony, grace, and power. Admission is free. Guests must leave their shoes at the entrance.

In front of the Blue Mosque, the **Hippodrome** park was once the site of great chariot races and a center of Byzantine civic life. What remains from those times are three tall monuments, including the **Obelisk of Tutmosis III,** a 60-ton granite spike dating to the 13th century B.C. and brought here from the Egypt's Temple of Luxor around A.D. 390.

Diagonally across from the Ayasofya, on Yerebatan Caddesi, the **Yerebatan Cistern** (𝐶 **0212/522-1259**) is a vast underground reservoir built by the emperors Constantine and Justinian in the 6th century A.D., using 336 marble columns recycled from nearby Hellenistic ruins. Abandoned from the mid–15th century until its reopening in 1987, it's a stunning sight, with ancient decorative carvings on the columns; vaulted, shadowing ceilings overhead; and goldfish swimming in the water below. Visitors can walk among the columns via a boardwalk. Admission is 10YTL ($8.50). Closed Tuesday.

Behind Ayasofya, **Topkapi Palace,** at the end of Babuhümayun Caddesi (𝐶 **212/ 512-0480**), served as the residence of sultans and administrative seat of the Ottoman Empire from the 15th century to the mid–19th century. Today the huge complex is a treasure trove of art and history that includes everything from holy relics (a piece of St. John the Baptist's skull) to sexy legend (the harem, which at its peak was home to more than 800 concubines). In summer it's wise to get a ticket to the separate harem tour after arriving at the palace; they're conducted every half-hour. Admission to the palace is 12YTL ($10); the guided harem tour costs 10YTL ($8.50). Closed Tuesday.

ON YOUR OWN: BEYOND THE PORT AREA

The 19th-century **Dolmabahce Palace,** Dolmabahce Caddesi (𝐶 **212/236-9000**), is sometimes referred to as the Ottoman Versailles because of its extravagance, including decorations like a 4-ton Baccarat chandelier that was a gift from Queen Victoria. The palace boasts a mix of architectural styles, including European, Hindu, and Turkish. Admission and a guided tour of the Selâmlik (Sultan's Quarters) cost 12YTL ($10); admission and a guided tour of the Harem Quarters are 8YTL ($6.80). Closed Monday and Thursday.

LOCAL FLAVORS

Turkish food is seriously delicious. Meals generally start with *meze* (hors d'oeuvres), and main courses usually feature fish, beef, and lamb dishes. One of the most popular items here is kebab: lamb or beef, skewered and grilled on a spit. The most common dessert is fresh fruit. The national drink is *raki,* which is flavored with anise. For

Old Istanbul

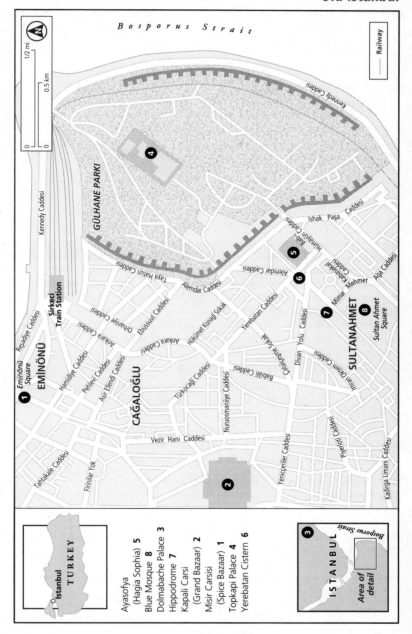

Railway

Bosporus Strait

Kennedy Caddesi

GÜLHANE PARKI

Ishak Paşa Caddesi

Bâb-ı Hümayûn Caddesi

Alemdar Caddesi

Taya Hatun Caddesi

Alemdar Caddesi

Sirkeci Train Station

Eminönü Square

EMINÖNÜ

Reşadiye Caddesi

Kennedy Caddesi

Hamidiye Caddesi

Pehlevi Caddesi

Aşir Efendi Caddesi

Ankara Caddesi

Orhaniye Caddesi

Ebusuud Caddesi

Ankara Caddesi

Hükümet Konağı Sokak

Yerebatan Caddesi

Mimar Mehmet

Kabasakal Caddesi

Ağa Caddesi

SULTANAHMET

Sultan Ahmet Square

Divan Yolu Caddesi

CAĞALOĞLU

Türkocağı Caddesi

Babıâli Caddesi

Nuruosmaniye Caddesi

Çatalçeşme Sokak

İmran Öktem Caddesi

Piyerloti Caddesi

Vezir Hani Caddesi

Yeniçeriler Caddesi

Kadırga Limanı Caddesi

Tahtakale Caddesi

Fırınlar Yok

TURKEY

Istanbul

Ayasofya (Hagia Sophia) **5**
Blue Mosque **8**
Dolmabache Palace **3**
Hippodrome **7**
Kapali Carsi (Grand Bazaar) **2**
Misir Carsisi (Spice Bazaar) **1**
Topkapi Palace **4**
Yerebatan Cistern **6**

ISTANBUL

Bosporus Strait

Area of detail

honest home cooking, try one of the various innocuous *lokantas* (dives with steam tables), particularly along Pierloti Caddesi, between the Hippodrome and Cagaloglu and in the working streets around the Grand Bazaar. The restaurants of Beyoglu and Taksim are more consistent, in that they serve a regular stream of locals and businessmen rather than relying entirely on tourists.

SHOPPING

The **Kapali Çarsi (Grand Bazaar)** is one of the world's largest covered markets, with some 65 vaulted streets holding about 2,600 vendors of carpets, leather goods, jewelry, spices, antique reproductions, and almost anything else you can name. The oldest part of the market, dating back to the mid–15th century, is Cevahir Bedesteni, which specializes in gold and silver works. The **Zeytinburnu tram** (1.35YTL/$1.15) runs from the Sultanahmet district to the Bazaar via Divan Yolu Cadessi. Get off at the Beyazit stop or the Çemberlitas stop to enter the bazaar. If you're worried about finding your way around, maps labeled in English are on sale at newsstands for 5.85YTL ($4.95). Admission to the bazaar is free, but bargains aren't: You'll have to work for them with some serious dickering.

13 Kusadasi & Ephesus, Turkey

Once a sleepy port town, Kusadasi has become a bustling seaside resort and one of the main ports on most eastern Mediterranean cruise routes. The city is used as a starting-off point for excursions to archaeological sites in the area, the most popular and spectacular being Ephesus, one of the best-preserved ancient cities in the world and a major player in the birth and evolution of Christianity.

For a map of the area, see "The Greek Isles & Turkey's Aegean Coast" on p. 343.

COMING ASHORE Ships dock right in downtown. Stores and restaurants are within walking distance of the harbor, and Ephesus is a short drive from town.

GETTING AROUND Minibuses (available from the town center) and **taxis** (yellow and metered) can take you to attractions and the beach. But your real goal should be Ephesus, which is easiest to explore via the ship's organized tours.

LANGUAGE & CURRENCY Turkish and **Kurdish** are spoken here, as well as **English, French,** and **German.** The Turkish **new lira** (YTL) is the national currency, and the rate of exchange at press time was $1 = 1.17YTL (1YTL = US85¢).

BEST CRUISE LINE SHORE EXCURSIONS

Ephesus (3–4 hr.; $50): Visit one of the best-preserved ancient cities in the world. Your guide will take you down the city's marble streets to the baths, the theater, and the incredible library building. Along the way you will pass columns, mosaics, monuments, and ruins. The tour may include a stop for a demonstration on Turkish carpets—with the emphasis on getting you to buy.

Calling Kusadasi

Dial local calls by using the seven-digit phone number; if dialing out of town, you must include 0 plus the city code. When calling a cellphone (identifiable by exchanges like 0531, 0532, 0533, 0534, 0535, 0536, and so on), you must include the zero. When dialing any number in Turkey from abroad, drop the zero.

Ephesus, St. John's Basilica & House of the Virgin Mary (7–8 hr.; $90–$115): This tour combines a visit to Ephesus with the House of the Virgin Mary, a humble chapel located in the valley of Bulbuldagi, on the spot where Jesus' mother is believed to have spent her last days. The site was officially sanctioned for pilgrimage in 1892. Today the house is a church, with the main altar where the kitchen was located. St. John's Basilica is believed to be the site where St. John the Apostle wrote the fourth book of the New Testament. A church at the site, which is now in ruins, was built above a 2nd-century tomb believed to contain John's body. Lunch at a local restaurant is included.

Three Ancient Cities (8 hr.; $80): This tour takes in the ruins that surround the Ephesus region, including Priene, known for its Athena Temple (bankrolled by Alexander the Great); Didyma, known for the Temple of Apollo; and Miletus, which includes a stadium built by the Greeks and expanded by the Romans to hold 15,000 spectators. A light lunch at a restaurant in Didyma is included.

ON YOUR OWN: WITHIN WALKING DISTANCE
The center of town is within easy walking distance of the port area and a fun place to poke around, particularly if you are in the market for carpets.

ON YOUR OWN: BEYOND THE PORT AREA
Located about 20 minutes' drive from Kusadasi, the city of **Ephesus** was built in the 11th century B.C. by the Ionians and is second only to Pompeii as an introduction to ancient Roman civilization. During its heyday, Ephesus served as a center of worship and trade until silt accumulation over the centuries destroyed its harbor. Today what remains (and there's an amazing amount, despite the fact that only 20% of the city has been excavated) lies 4.8km (3 miles) from the sea; the swamp at the end of the Arcadian Way (Harbour Rd.) was once at the water's edge. When touring the site, visitors walk down a street paved in marble to see temples, baths, columns, a 25,000-seat amphitheater, and the two-story facade of the **Library of Celsus,** a 1,900-year-old mausoleum and library that's Ephesus's most striking monument. *Note:* Ephesus is about 21km (13 miles) from Kusadasi, and you are best off visiting on a shore excursion with a professional guide. If you decide to go on your own, hire a guide at the site, shopping around until you're quoted a price that's to your liking. *Tip:* The midday sun here can be almost unbearably hot, so tour in the morning, if possible. Admission is 15YTL ($13).

    St. John's Basilica and the **House of the Virgin Mary** (see "Best Cruise Line Shore Excursions," above) lie about 4km (2.5 miles) east of Kusadasi. Admission to the park and house is 2.90YTL ($2.45).

    About 8km (5 miles) from the port is **Kadinlar Denizi,** Kusadasi's most popular beach, also called Ladies Beach. The small stretch attracts a large crowd. Take a cab.

LOCAL FLAVORS
During the summer, restaurant prices tend to climb. The best place to eat is along the waterfront of Kusadasi, where many establishments offer great views. Seafood dishes are particularly good in this area, as well as fresh fruits such as apricots, cherries, and figs.

SHOPPING
There are plenty of places to shop and haggle both in Kusadasi and immediately outside Ephesus. You will find Turkish carpets, brass, leather goods, copper, jewelry, meerschaum pipes, and onyx. Prices are generally bumped up when cruise ships are in port, so definitely negotiate the price before paying. It is a common practice for shopkeepers

to offer tea or soft drinks to customers, so don't feel obligated to make a purchase if it happens to you.

14 Lisbon, Portugal

Portugal's capital is a cosmopolitan city offering a combination of history, cultural arts, modern life, and great beauty, with some areas bringing to mind Paris and others hilly San Francisco. But mostly Lisbon just looks like Lisbon. It's inimitable.

The city was probably founded by the Phoenicians and was later inhabited by Romans and Moors. In 1755, a great earthquake killed some 40,000 people, destroying much of the city but sparing parts of the **Alfama** (the city's labyrinthine Moorish section), **Belém** (a neighborhood on the banks of the Tagus River, toward the west), and other old sections. The rebuilding of the rest of the city was carefully planned based on a neoclassical grid, and today the old buildings and gorgeous mosaic-tiled sidewalks evince a passionate, melancholy grandeur that matches the country's beautiful *fado* music—the city's most perfect soundtrack.

COMING ASHORE   Cruise ships dock at the **Port of Lisbon,** about 15 minutes by taxi from the city center and approximately equidistant to Belém, in the opposite direction.

GETTING AROUND   Lisbon is a walking city and is easy to get around, although the hills may prove challenging to some. **Taxis** are among the cheapest in Europe and are generally available outside the terminal building. The fare to the central sightseeing and shopping districts is likely to be 12€ to 19€ ($17–$27). Most lines also provide a free **shuttle** to the Praco do Comercio. There's a **funicular** (elevator) connecting the Baixa shopping area with the Bairro Alto, the city's old upper reaches, full of restaurants, bars, antiques shops, and *fado* clubs.

LANGUAGE & CURRENCY   The official language is **Portuguese.** Most young people also speak **English, Spanish,** and/or **German.** The official currency is the **euro** (€). The exchange rate at press time was $1 = .72€ (1€ = $1.40).

BEST CRUISE LINE SHORE EXCURSIONS

Lisbon Walking Tour (3½ hr.; $48): This walking tour takes in the city's old Moorish quarter (including its 12th-century church); takes you down Rua Augusta, the popular pedestrian street, to Rossio Square in Baixa (Lisbon's central shopping district); then ascends the funicular from Rossio Square to the Bairro Alto.

Fatima (6½–7 hr.; $89–$104): Located 161km (100 miles) from Lisbon is the place known to Roman Catholics as the "Lourdes of Portugal." Here, in 1917, three shepherds claimed they saw the Virgin Mary in an oak tree. The town has since become a center of the Christian faith and world pilgrimage. After your guide introduces you to the imposing modern basilica, you'll have approximately 2½ hours of independent time at the site.

Sintra & Estoril (4 hr.; $48): This tour along the famous and scenic Estoril Coast includes such memorable highlights as Sintra, a serene, historic resort nestled in the forested hills of Serra de Sintra. The tour continues inland to Queluz, to visit its magnificent 18th-century palace, built in the style of Versailles.

Lisbon

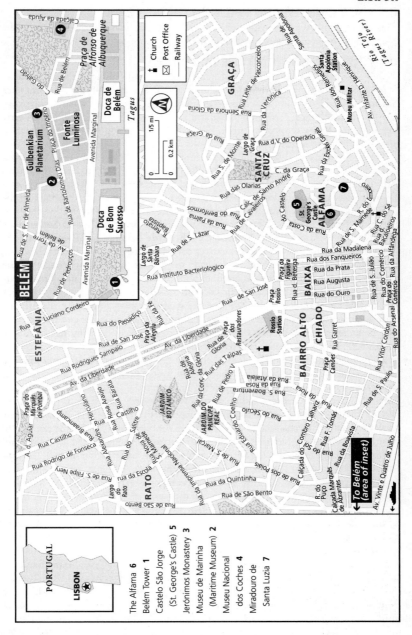

Legend:
- ✠ Church
- ⊠ Post Office
- ----- Railway

0 1/5 mi
0 0.2 km

BELÉM

Doca de Bom Sucesso

Doca de Belém

Fonte Luminosa

Praça de Afonso de Albuquerque

Map labels:
Calçada da Ajuda, Cº do Galvão, Rua de Belém, Praça do Império, Av. da Torre de Belém, Rua de Pedrouços, Avenida Marginal, Rua de S. Fr. de Almeida, Rua de Bartolomeu Dias, *Tagus*

Main map labels:

GRAÇA, SANTA CRUZ, ALFAMA, BAIXA, CHIADO, BAIRRO ALTO, ESTEFÂNIA, RATO

Rio Tejo (Tagus River)

Santa Apolónia Station, Museu Militar

Rua de Santa Apolónia, Av. Infante D. Henrique, Rua dos Remédios, Rua dos Bacalhoeiros, Rua da Alfândega, Rua do Comércio, Praça do Comércio, Rua do Arsenal, Rua Vítor Cordon, Rua do Ouro, Rua Augusta, Rua da Prata, Rua dos Fanqueiros, Rua da Madalena, Rua de S. Julião, Rua de S. Mamede, Rua d. C. do Sé, R. do Limoeiro, Rua de S. Pedro, Rua de S. Estêvão, Rua da Escola Gerais, Rua d.V. do Operário, Rua da Graça, Largo da Graça, C. da Graça, Rua das Olarias, Rua de Santo André, Calç. de Santo André, Rua de Cavaleiros, Rua do Benformoso, Rua da Palma, Rua de S. Lázaro, Rua de S. José, Rua Instituto Bacteriologico, Largo de Santa Bárbara, Renato Baptista, Rua da Escão Graça, Calçada do Castelo, St. George's Castle, Rua de Santa Senhora da Glória, Rua da Verónica, Rua Leite de Vasconcelos, Rua de S. Monte, Largo de Graça

Praça Rossio, Rossio Station, Praça da Figueira, Rua d. Betesga, Praça d. dos Restauradores, Av. da Liberdade, Praça do Marquês de Pombal, Jardim Botânico, Jardim do Príncipe Real, Praça Camões

Luciano Cordeiro, Rua do Passadiço, Rua de San José, Rua da Alegria, Rua da Fé, Rua de San José, Rua Rodrigues Sampaio, Av. da Liberdade, A. d. Aguiar, Rua Rodrigo da Fonseca, Rua Castilho, Rua Braamcamp, Rua Alexandre Herculano, Rua Rosa Araújo, Rua Rosa Barata, Rua Nova de S. Mamede, Rua do Salitre, Rua da Conc. da Glória, Rua Gloria, Rua de Pedro V, Rua das Taipas, Rua da Atalaia, Rua da Rosa, Rua S. Boaventura, Rua do Século, Rua Eduardo Coelho, Rua de S. Marçal, Largo do Rato, rua da Imprensa Nacional, Rua da Escola, Rua da Quintinha, Rua de São Bento, Rua de S. Filipe Nery, Rua de São Bento, Calçada do Combro, Calhariz, Rua do Sol, Calçada do Sol, Rua de São Polais, Rua da Boavista, Rua F. Tomás, Rua de S. Paulo, Rua Garret, Calçada Marquês de Abrantes, R. do Poço, Av. Vinte e Quatro de Julho

To Belém (area of inset)

Inset (top left):
PORTUGAL
LISBON

Point of interest list:
The Alfama **6**
Belém Tower **1**
Castelo São Jorge (St. George's Castle) **5**
Jerónimos Monastery **3**
Museu de Marinha (Maritime Museum) **2**
Museu Nacional dos Coches **4**
Miradouro de Santa Luzia **7**

Gulbenkian Planetarium **2**

ON YOUR OWN: WITHIN WALKING DISTANCE

There is very little within walking distance of the docks. Take a taxi or shuttle to the central sightseeing and shopping districts.

ON YOUR OWN: BEYOND THE PORT AREA

This is a great city to just walk around in and explore while taking in the atmosphere. Start your exploration just off the Tagus at the **Praça do Comércio** (Commerce Square), the gateway to the city. One of the most perfectly planned squares in Europe, it's the site of Portugal's stock exchange and various government ministries. Directly behind is the **Baixa** shopping district, full of buildings dating to the reconstruction after the 1755 earthquake.

For orientation's sake, here's the rundown of everyplace else: If you head west from Baixa, you'll enter this **shopping district,** then do some climbing to reach the **Bairro Alto** (Upper City). East of Baixa is the **Alfama,** whose warren of narrow streets is now home in some parts to stevedores, fishermen, and *varinas* (fishwives). Overlooking the Alfama is **Castelo São Jorge,** or St. George's Castle, a Visigoth fortification that was later used by the Romans. Northwest of Baixa are the beautiful **Rossio Square** (aka Praça de Dom Pedro IV) and **Avenida da Liberdade (Avenue of Liberty),** Lisbon's main drag. This handsomely laid-out street dates from 1880 and is effectively a long park (about 1.5km/1-mile long), with shade trees, gardens, and center walks for the promenading crowds. Flanking it are fine shops, the headquarters of many major airlines, travel agents, coffeehouses with sidewalk tables, and hotels.

To make the most of your limited time, we suggest heading straight for the **Alfama,** once the old, aristocratic Moorish section of Lisbon, and now a kind of casbah, with narrow, sometimes stair-step streets running among evocatively decaying old buildings. From the Praça do Comércio, Rua da Alfândega links lower Baixa to the lower part of the Alfama, just to the east. Highlights here include the **Miradouro de Santa Luzia,** a terrace on the Rua do Limoeiro, by the church of Santa Luzia, from which you can look down over the jumbled district as it seems to tumble into the Tagus, and the **Castelo São Jorge (St. George's Castle),** a hilltop fortress whose history goes back to the Romans, though most of what you see today dates to the 16th century and later, up to its mid–20th century reconstruction. Great views of the Tagus and the Alfama can be had from its esplanades and ramparts, but they may not be worth the 3€ ($4.20) admission.

In the west of the city (to the left of the cruise docks, when facing inland), the suburb of **Belém** contains some of the finest monuments in Portugal, several built during the Age of Discovery. This is where Portuguese explorers such as Magellan launched their voyages. Scenically located on the banks of the Tagus at Praca do Imperio, the 16th-century **Torre de Belém (Belém Tower)** is a monument to Portugal's age of discovery and its famous explorers. One of the finest sights in the city, **Mosteiro dos Jerónimos (Jerónimos Monastery),** Praca do Imperio (✆ 21-362-0034; www.mosteirojeronimos.pt), was built in 1502 to commemorate the discoveries of Portuguese navigators. It's a masterpiece of Manueline architecture, combining flamboyant Gothic and Moorish influences with elements of the nascent Renaissance. Admission is 4.50€ ($6.30). In its west wing, the **Museu de Marinha (Maritime Museum)** is one of the most important of its kind in Europe, containing hundreds of ship models spanning 5 centuries. Not far away, on Praça de Afonso de Albuquerque, the **Museu Nacional dos Coches** (Carriage Museum; ✆ 213-610-850; www.museu doscoches-ipmuseus.pt) is lodged in a former 18th-century riding academy connected to the Belém Royal Palace, and displays ceremonial and promenade carriages from the 17th to the 19th centuries, mostly from the Crown's estate or private property of the Portuguese Royal House. Think opulent. Admission is 3€ ($4.20). Closed Monday.

LOCAL FLAVORS

Fresh seafood is a best bet. Typical dishes include fresh *bacalhau* (codfish), steamed mussels with ham and sausages cooked in white wine, and *acorda de marisco,* a spicy seafood soup. Meat-eaters will want to try the roasted lamb. Complement your meal with a Portuguese wine. The cafes (such as those around Rossio Square) are great places to people-watch.

SHOPPING

Handicrafts, ceramics, and embroidered linens are all good buys. Also look for gold filigree and silver jewelry, knitwear, leather goods, colorful Portuguese wall tiles, and items made out of cork. Many smaller shops close from 12:30 to 3pm.

15 Málaga, Spain

Málaga, the historic capital of Spain's Costa del Sol region, is a bustling commercial and cultural center and the second-most-important port along Spain's Mediterranean coast, after Barcelona. It was the birthplace of Pablo Picasso and one of the last Moorish cities to fall to the Catholics, in the late 15th century. Visually appealing, the city is laid out right along the coast, with Moorish castles, a lovely old town area, and a gorgeous park all within walking distance of the piers. The city is also the port for nearby **Granada,** site of the famed **Alhambra Palace.**

COMING ASHORE   Depending on the size of your ship, you'll either dock immediately alongside the city or at a long pier located right at its base. You can walk or take a taxi.

GETTING AROUND   Taxis are usually available pierside, but the town is easily traversed on foot. You can reach anywhere in about 15 minutes from the entrance to the cruise dock.

LANGUAGE & CURRENCY   Spanish is the official language, but many people also speak **English** and/or **German.** The official currency is the **euro** (€). The exchange rate at press time was $1 = .72€ (1€ = $1.40).

BEST CRUISE LINE SHORE EXCURSIONS

Granada & the Alhambra (9 hr.; $145): This tour highlights historic Granada and includes a number of interesting sights along the 2-hour drive from Málaga, such as the town of Casabermeja, with its notable white houses; and Las Pedrizas, a scenic mountain pass. In Granada, visit the 14th-century Alhambra, a fortress/palace that was once the home of Granada's Muslim kings and is now a spectacular example of Moorish architecture and history. Also visit the nearby Generalife, the royal residence surrounded by water gardens, and El Vino Gate, commissioned by Carlos V in the 16th century. Lunch is included.

Málaga City Tour (4 hr.; $35): On this tour you will see the Alcazaba and the Gibralfaro, an old Muslim castle. You'll also visit the city's Renaissance-style cathedral. You'll drive past the Roman theater, the bullring, and the 19th-century post office and City Hall. This tour is recommended only for people with mobility problems, as Málaga is eminently walkable on your own.

ON YOUR OWN: WITHIN WALKING DISTANCE

Málaga's main destination site for visitors is the **Alcazaba,** Calle Alcazabilla 2 (© **95-212-2020;** www.malagaturismo.com), a Moorish palace whose oldest sections go back to the 9th and 10th centuries. Built on the summit of a hill and following the contours of the land, it's surrounded by defensive walls and offers beautiful views of the city and sea below. Its grounds are lovely, too, offering graceful Moorish architecture, orange trees, purple bougainvillea, and paths that wind among the castle's various sections. An archaeological museum is on-site, and a **Roman theater,** unearthed during excavations in 1951, sits at the foot of the Alcazaba. Built more than 2,000 years ago, it was used until the 3rd century. Admission to the Alcazaba is 2€ ($2.80). You can walk up the zigzagging path from the city center (look for the signs pointing the way up the hill) or take the elevator that runs from Calle Guillén Sotelo, behind Málaga's Town Hall.

Right behind the Alcazaba is **Castillo de Gibralfaro** (© **95-104-1400;** www.malaga turismo.com), another Moorish structure whose fortifications were built in the 14th century to defend the Alcazaba. In 1487, it was the site of a 3-month siege by the Spanish Catholic monarchs Ferdinand and Isabella, which ended when hunger forced the Moors' capitulation. Ferdinand and Isabella took up residence in the Alcazaba thereafter. The Gibralfaro isn't as well preserved as the Alcazaba (only its stone ramparts remain, rising among the trees and vegetation), but it's definitely worth a look. Admission is 2€ ($2.80).

The long park you can see right below from the Alcazaba and Gibralfaro is the **Paseo del Parque,** a beautiful pedestrian promenade filled with tropical flowering trees and shrubs, fountains, lawns, statues, and duck ponds. Take some time to walk around, for a taste of how the locals spend their free time. It begins near the center of town at Plaza de la Marina and runs to the east, ending at the **Plaza de Toros la Malagueta,** the city's bullring.

Málaga's **old town,** which fans out from the western end of the Paseo del Parque, is full of charming squares, narrow streets, baroque buildings, and cafes. **Málaga Cathedral,** right in the city's heart at Calle Molina Lario 9 (© **95-221-5917**), is a vast and impressive 16th-century Renaissance cathedral. Its most notable interior features are the richly ornamented choir stalls. There's a cathedral museum inside, with an admission price of 3.50€ ($4.90).

Just a few blocks away, the **Museo Picasso Málaga,** San Agustín 8 (© **95-212-7600;** www.museopicassomalaga.org), celebrates the work of Málaga's most famous son, who was born just a few blocks to the north, at Plaza de la Merced, in 1881. Many of the works are Picasso family heirlooms, including paintings depicting one of the artist's wives (*Olga Kokhlova with Mantilla*) and one of his lovers (*Jacqueline Seated*). The collection comprises some 200 paintings, drawings, sculpture, ceramics, and graphics in all. A combo ticket to the permanent collection and temporary exhibitions is 8€ ($11). Closed Monday.

LOCAL FLAVORS

The old town area is full of tapas bars where you can fill up with small plates and wet your whistle after clambering around the Alcazaba.

SHOPPING

Shop here for the region's rustic pottery, leather goods, silver and gold jewelry, and local wines. Many shops close for a break in the afternoon. Small mall shops and boutiques can be found along Calle Larios.

16 Marseille, France

With more than a million inhabitants (a full quarter of them from North Africa), Marseille is the second-largest city in France, and its port is France's busiest. It's an ancient city, founded by Greeks in the 6th century B.C., and like most big old cities, it mixes areas of high style with others that are dirty and slumlike, and others that are just plain industrial. The **Vieux Port,** the old harbor, is especially colorful, full of churches, galleries, museums, and restaurants. To some extent, it compensates for the dreary industrial dockland nearby.

The city's main draw for cruise passengers is its proximity to the idyllic small towns, historic treasures, and vineyard-dotted countryside of **Provence,** which are easily accessible through a variety of shore excursions.

COMING ASHORE   Ships dock in an industrial section of town north of the Vieux Port, a shuttle or taxi ride away. Small ships may dock closer to the main part of town.

GETTING AROUND   **Taxis** meet arriving ships, and the price for a ride into town is approximately 10€ to 15€ ($14–$21). Once you're in the Vieux Port, you can walk to the major sites, though some are up steep hills.

LANGUAGE & CURRENCY   The language is **French** and the official currency is the **euro** (€). The exchange rate at press time was $1 = .72€ (1€ = $1.40).

BEST CRUISE LINE SHORE EXCURSIONS

Avignon & Marseille City Highlights (8 hr.; $140): This tour takes you into Provence to explore the walled city of Avignon and the former Palace of the Popes, dating from the period (1309–77) when the papal court resided here instead of in Rome. Nine popes occupied this Holy See during the Avignon exile, ultimately leaving behind this huge, fortified palace with its now-deserted galleries, chambers, and chapels. The tour includes time to explore Avignon's beautiful cobblestone streets and shop its plethora of small crafts stores and modern boutiques.

Le Pont Du Gard & Avignon (8 hr.; $85): This tour combines a visit to Avignon (see above) with a viewing stop at Le Pont du Gard, a bridge that forms one part of a Roman aqueduct that once carried water 48km (30 miles) from Uzès to Nimes. Built in A.D. 40, the bridge reaches a height of 49m (161 ft.) and has an upper level spanning 274m (899 ft.), and has resisted the floods of the River Gardon for nearly 2,000 years.

Arles & Les Baux De Provence (8 hr.; $155): Arles was founded in 46 B.C. and has long been an inspiration for artists—including Vincent van Gogh, who lived here from 1888 to 1889, painting some 250 canvases. Participants in this tour take a guided walking tour of the city and visit the Roman amphitheater (which once seated 20,000); Republic Square and its Roman obelisk; and the 5th-century St. Trophime Church, with its graceful 12th-century cloisters. The tour also visits the hilltop town of Les Baux de Provence, whose old cobbled lanes are lined with artisan workshops and craft stores.

Aix-En-Provence Walking Tour (4 hr.; $55): The cultural and political capital of Provence is a city of wide boulevards, majestic trees, gracious squares, and centuries-old buildings, and was the birthplace of painter Paul Cezanne. This guided walking tour explores the old town of Aix and includes some browsing and shopping time.

Marseille

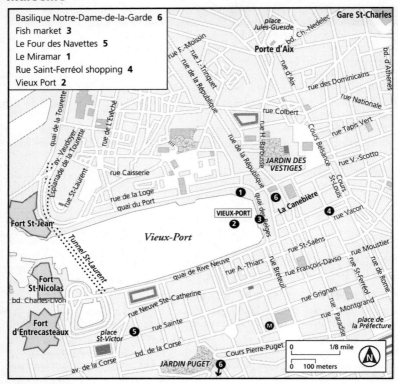

Basilique Notre-Dame-de-la-Garde **6**
Fish market **3**
Le Four des Navettes **5**
Le Miramar **1**
Rue Saint-Ferréol shopping **4**
Vieux Port **2**

ON YOUR OWN: WITHIN WALKING DISTANCE

All sites in town are beyond the industrial port area and require transportation to reach.

ON YOUR OWN: BEYOND THE PORT AREA

The **Vieux Port** area, the city's colorful old harbor, is dominated by two massive forts: St-Jean on the north side of the port (dating from the Middle Ages) and St-Nicholas on the south (built around 1680). In between, the harbor is filled with fishing craft and yachts, and seafood restaurants and cafes dot the quays. On the port's Quai des Belges, the daily **fish market** is one of the most characteristic sights in Marseille, with fishermen selling the day's catch almost right from their boats. Marseille's wide main street, **La Canebière** (known as "can of beer" to American GIs in World War II), runs east from Quai des Belges and is lined with shops, hotels, restaurants, and some beautiful, ornate 19th-century buildings.

Crowning a limestone bluff overlooking the southern flank of the Vieux Port is the **Basilique Notre-Dame-de-la-Garde,** rue Fort-du-Sanctuaire (✆ **04-91-13-40-80;** www.notredamedelagarde.com). Built in 1864 in the Romanesque-Byzantine style, and capped with a 9m (30-ft.) gilded statue of the Virgin Mary, it sits atop the foundations of a fortress that was commissioned during the Renaissance by French monarch François I. Although the architecture shows France's Gilded Age at its most evocative, visitors come here not so much for the church as for the view from its terrace, which takes in the city, the islands, and the sea. Admission is free.

LOCAL FLAVORS

For the most characteristic Marseille dining experience, stop into one of the many seafood restaurants clustered around the Vieux Port and order **bouillabaisse,** the traditional fish stew of the Provence region, which originated here in Marseille as a simple fisherman's dish. **Le Miramar,** 12 Quai du Port (℃ **04-91-91-10-40;** www.bouillabaisse.com), serves a pricey, labor-intensive version of the dish that'll cost you about 50€ ($70) per person. Closed Sunday and Monday.

For something just as "Marseille" but not as dear, seek out *les navettes,* the small, boat-shaped cookies that commemorate the legend of *Les Trois Maries,* three saints named Mary who Christianized ancient Provence. You can find *les navettes* all around the city, including at **Le Four des Navettes,** 136 rue Sainte (℃ **04-91-33-32-12;** www.fourdesnavettes.com), which has been serving them since 1781. A dozen will cost you about 7€ or 8€ ($9.80–11).

SHOPPING

The Vieux Port and its surrounding streets are full of shops selling folk crafts and souvenirs. The pedestrian-only **Rue Saint-Ferréol,** running south of La Canebière near the Vieux Port (see "On Your Own," above), is full of boutiques and shops selling handicrafts, including the pastel-colored bars of **savon de Marseille,** the city's famous soap, known for its moisturizing qualities.

17 Naples, Italy

Though this city doesn't get the accolades Rome, Venice, Florence, and other more glamorous Italian cities do, it's a great port, both as a jumping-off port for **Pompeii** and the **Amalfi Coast,** and for its own historic treasures within close walking distance of the cruise terminal. Founded in the 6th century B.C. by the Greeks and named Neapolis, or New City, the metropolis came to be dominated by many groups, including the Romans, Goths, Byzantines, Lombards, Normans, Spaniards, and French. Today traces of those cultures remain, along with a revitalized cultural scene, a certain urban grittiness, and a city center that holds a place on the UNESCO World Heritage list.

COMING ASHORE   Ships dock right in the center of town at the Maritime Station, near the 13th-century Castle Nuovo. It's about a 10- to 15-minute walk through the terminal and right into the heart of Naples.

GETTING AROUND   You can explore quite a bit on foot or spend an hour clip-clopping around the city in a horse-drawn carriage; they're usually waiting near the docks (negotiate the price before hopping in; recently we paid 36€/$50 for an hour's tour for two adults and two kids). Taxis are also waiting at the pier; settle on a price before getting in.

LANGUAGE & CURRENCY   The language is **Italian.** The official currency is the **euro** (€). The exchange rate at press time was $1 = .72€ (1€ = $1.40).

BEST CRUISE LINE SHORE EXCURSIONS

Pompeii (4 hr.; $60): After a 30-minute bus drive, you reach the excavated town of Pompeii, which thrived as a prosperous provincial capital until A.D. 79, when an eruption of nearby Mt. Vesuvius caught the city and its 20,000 people by surprise, literally burying them under 20 feet of ash and pumice stone. Buried for centuries, the city was rediscovered in 1748 and eventually excavated. Today it's Italy's top attraction and a World Heritage Site. While touring the ruins, your guide will show you the mansions of the city's wealthy inhabitants, many of whom moved here from Rome to escape the capital's turmoil and filled their new homes with splendid mosaics, frescoes, and marble decorations. Tours also include visits to the city's Forum, theaters, and Stabian Baths, as well as opportunities to view numerous paintings and everyday inscriptions, including notices about wine sales, apartment vacancies, upcoming events, political announcements, and even love notes. Some tours of Pompeii are a few hours longer and include a hike to the rim of the Vesuvius crater walls for awesome views of the bay of Naples.

Sorrento, Positano, and Amalfi Drive (9–10 hr.; $130): Travel by bus on one of the world's most beautiful drives, heading along the snaking cliff-top roadway of the Amalfi coast. Take in spectacular views of mountain peaks rising on one side of the road and steep cliffs plunging down to the sea on the other. The tour visits the beautiful resort town of Sorrento, set high atop the Mediterranean cliffs, and also neighboring Positano, a posh outpost for the yachting set, full of designer shops and art galleries. White Moorish-style houses cling dramatically to slopes around a small sheltered bay. Some tours offer different combos, such as Pompeii and the Amalfi Coast drive ($125-plus); or Pompeii, Sorrento, and Capri ($200-plus).

Day on Capri (8–9 hr.; $130): Travel by hydrofoil across the Gulf of Naples to the Island of Capri, often called the "Island of Dreams," where dramatic cliffs and brightly colored villas create a picture-perfect setting. Roman emperors Augustus and Tiberius loved coming here, as do modern-day celebrities and just about everybody else— though in the months of July and August, thousands of others will be admiring the scenery along with you. Once on the island, you'll hop on a bus for a picturesque ride to the village of Anacapri. Take the chairlift to Monte Solaro, the island's highest point; stroll past the many shops; or walk to the Augustus Gardens, where there are great views of the Faraglioni rocks, three enormous rocks that protrude from the blue waters of the Tyrrhenian Sea.

Flavors of Sorrento (3–5 hr.; $75–$200): Sample local specialties in a restaurant, at a local citrus or olive farm, or at a vineyard. Watch how mozzarella cheese is made and then see how oil is extracted from olives. Enjoy a wine tasting and sample limoncello, the Sorrentine liqueur made from locally grown lemons.

ON YOUR OWN: WITHIN WALKING DISTANCE

Most cruise ship passengers flee Naples for Pompeii and the region's other major attractions, but there are some lesser sights located right in town. From the terminal, walk to Piazza del Municipio and the 13th-century **Castel Nuovo** (© **081-7955877**), a grim fortress that was built beginning in 1279 by order of Charles I, king of Naples, as a royal residence for the House of Anjou. The castle is distinguished by a trio of imposing round battle towers at its front, and by a magnificent triumphal entrance arch designed by Francesco Laurana. Inside you can visit a chapel and see frescoes and sculptures from the 14th and 15th centuries, along with Naples-themed paintings. Admission is 5€ ($7).

Near the Castel Nuovo, **Piazza Plebiscito** is one of Naples's most architecturally interesting squares, with a long colonnade; the **church of San Francesco di Paola,** built in the style of the Roman Pantheon; and the 17th-century **Royal Palace,** once home to the Bourbon kings of Naples.

Naples

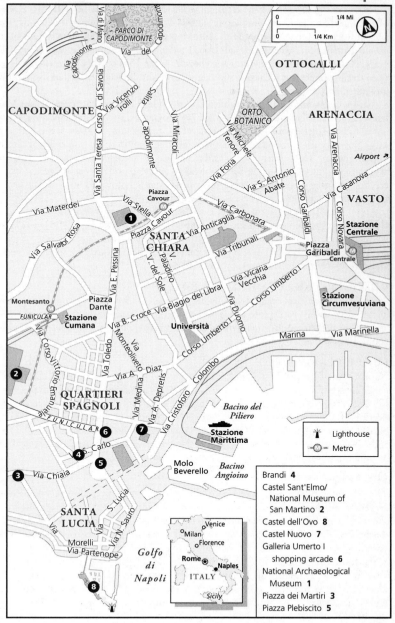

PARCO DI CAPODIMONTE

Via di Miano

Via del Capodimonte

OTTOCALLI

CAPODIMONTE

Via Capodimonte

Corso A. di Savoia

Via Santa Teresa

Via Vicenzo Irolli

Salita Capodimonte

Via Miracoli

ORTO BOTANICO

Via Michele Tenore

ARENACCIA

Via Arenaccia

Airport ↗

Via Materdei

Via Stella

Via Foria

Via S. Antonio Abate

Corso Garibaldi

Via Casanova

VASTO

Piazza Cavour

Piazza Cavour

Via Carbonara

①

Via Salvator Rosa

SANTA CHIARA

Via Anticaglia

V. Paladino

V. del Sole

Via Tribunali

Via Vicaria Vecchia

Corso Novara

Stazione Centrale

Piazza Garibaldi

Centrale

Via E. Pessina

Montesanto

Piazza Dante

Via B. Croce

Via Biagio dei Librai

Università

Corso Umberto I

Via Duomo

Corso Umberto I

Stazione Circumvesuviana

FUNICULAR

Stazione Cumana

Via Montesanto

Via Toledo

Corso Vittorio Emanuele

Via A. Diaz

Marina

Via Marinella

②

QUARTIERI SPAGNOLI

Via Medina

Via A. Depretis

Via Cristoforo Colombo

Bacino del Piliero

FUNICULAR

⑥

⑦

S. Carlo

④

⑤

Stazione Marittima

③

Via Chiaia

Molo Beverello

Bacino Angioino

☀ Lighthouse

◉ Metro

SANTA LUCIA

S. Lucia

Via N. Sauro

Morelli

Via Partenope

Golfo di Napoli

ITALY

Venice

Milan

Florence

Rome ✹ ● Naples

Sicily

⑧

Brandi **4**
Castel Sant'Elmo/
  National Museum of
  San Martino **2**
Castel dell'Ovo **8**
Castel Nuovo **7**
Galleria Umerto I
  shopping arcade **6**
National Archaeological
  Museum **1**
Piazza dei Martiri **3**
Piazza Plebiscito **5**

0   1/4 Mi
0   1/4 Km

Less than a mile south of the terminal is the lovely seaside **Castel dell'Ovo (Castle of the Egg)**, on Piazza del Municipio (© **081-2464334**). The site gets its name from a legend that says that Virgil built the fort atop a magic egg buried on the floor of the ocean. True or not, this is an ancient place, its site used for defense for well over 2,500 years, though the current castle mostly dates from the 15th century. The interior is not open to the public, but the site is superpanoramic and there are cafes and shops set up just outside its walls.

Naples is also home to two notable museums. The **National Museum of San Martino,** Largo San Martino 5 (© **081-5781769**), magnificently situated on the grounds of the hilltop **Castel Sant'Elmo,** was built as a Carthusian monastery in the 14th century. Now a museum, it displays notable religious paintings in the original church building, along with stately carriages, historic documents, ships' replicas, china and porcelain, military costumes and armor, and a vast collection of Neapolitan Christmas crèches spanning 4 centuries. A balcony opens onto a panoramic view of Naples and the bay, as well as Vesuvius and Capri. Admission is 6€ ($8.40).

About 1km (½-mile) to the north, the **Museo Archeologico Nazionale di Napoli (National Archaeological Museum of Naples),** Piazza Museo 19 (© **081-4422149;** www.archeona.arti.beniculturali.it/sanc_it/mann/home.html), contains one of Italy's great archaeological collections, including mosaics and sculpture excavated at Pompeii and Herculaneum. Admission is 6.50€ ($9.10).

ON YOUR OWN: BEYOND THE PORT AREA

All the important sites outside the downtown area are covered in "Shore Excursions," above. If you want to explore **Pompeii** on your own, you can get there in a taxi for about 90€ ($126) round-trip (with a 2-hour wait while you tour). The drive takes about 30 minutes.

LOCAL FLAVORS

Naples is the birthplace of pizza. Need we say more? Even the casual sidewalk cafes generally serve up tasty Neapolitan fare, but **Brandi,** Salita Santa Anna di Palazzo 2 (© **081-416-928**), is the most historic pizzeria in Italy. In 1889, to celebrate the unification of the country, owner Raffaele Esposito, prepared a pizza made with tomato, basil, olive oil, and mozzarella (red green, and white: the colors of the new Italian flag) and served it to Margherita di Savoia, the country's queen. And thus was Pizza Margherita born. A pizza starts at about 7€ ($9.80).

SHOPPING

The shopping in Naples can't compare to that in Milan, Venice, Florence, and Rome. Nevertheless, there are some good buys for those willing to seek them out. The finest shopping area lies around **Piazza dei Martiri** and along such streets as **Via Roma, Via dei Mille, Via Calabritto** and **Via Chiaia.** Naples is known for cameos and other **coral** jewelry, though much of the coral today is imported from Thailand.

For one-stop shopping in a beautiful setting, head for the **Galleria Umberto I,** on Via San Carlo. Modeled on Milan's galleria, it was built as part of Naples's urban renewal scheme following an 1884 cholera epidemic. The massive glass- and iron-frame barrel vaults of its four wings and central dome soar some 60m (197 ft.) above the inlaid marble flooring.

18 Palermo, Sicily

Sicily is the largest island in the Mediterranean, a place of beauty, ancient culture, and world-class monuments left by the Romans, Greeks, Moors, Spanish, Phoenicians, and pretty much every other old-world power you can name. **Palermo,** the island's biggest city, was first established by the Phoenicians in the 8th century B.C. and has changed hands from invader to invader and king to king ever since, including during World War II, when it was bombed to smithereens by the Allies. Today it's home to some 700,000 Sicilians and mixes panache and beauty with poverty, noise, pollution, and traffic—just like all the best cities. Its Arabo-Norman buildings have no equal, and the entire city is a treasure trove of museums and baroque oratories. Its outdoor markets evoke North Africa and are still dominated by the influence of the Arabs who departed centuries ago.

COMING ASHORE   Palermo's cruise docks are within walking distance of downtown.

GETTING AROUND   Palermo is a city designed for walking, especially to the museums, monuments, and palaces in the medieval core. Alternatively, you can find **taxis** at the pier and at stands around town, but traffic is often terrible and cabbies tend to overcharge.

LANGUAGE & CURRENCY   Standard **Italian** is the most common language here, though you may also hear the native **Sicilian;** many people speak **English.** The official currency is the **euro** (€). The exchange rate at press time was $1 = .72€ (1€ = $1.40).

BEST CRUISE LINE SHORE EXCURSIONS

Cefalu Sightseeing (4 hr.; $40): About an hour's drive east of Palermo is the charming town of Cefalù, whose history dates to at least 396 B.C. This excursion takes you on a guided tour of the town, noting the Roman, Arab, and Norman influences in its layout and architecture; exploring its narrow streets; and taking in its massive Norman cathedral, built between A.D. 1131 and 1240, and with remarkable abstract stained-glass windows added in 1990 by the Sicilian artist Michele Canzoneri. The tour includes time for shopping in Cefalù's shops and boutiques.

Palermo Sightseeing (4½ hr.; $54): On this bus and walking tour of Palermo, you'll visit the Martorana, a Norman church built in 1143; the huge 12th-century cathedral dedicated to the Virgin Mary; and the small hilltop town of Monreale, whose cathedral is considered one the finest examples of Norman architecture in Sicily. Free time for shopping and browsing is included.

ON YOUR OWN: WITHIN WALKING DISTANCE

Palermo's treasures are concentrated in the old section of the city, located within walking distance of the cruise docks. Measuring about 2.6 sq. km (1 sq. mile), the district contains more than 500 palaces, churches, monasteries, and convents.

The closest major attraction to the cruise docks is the **Museo Archeologico Regionale,** Piazza Olivella 24 (© **091/6116805**), one of Italy's grandest archaeological museums. Spread over several buildings (the oldest from the 13th c.), the museum's collection includes major Sicilian finds from prehistoric times through the Phoenician, Punic, Greek, Roman, and Saracen periods, along with several noteworthy treasures from Egypt. Admission is 6€ ($8.40).

Palermo

Catacombe dei Cappuccini **3**

Museo Archeologico Regionale **2**

Palazzo Abatellis/Galleria
Regionale della Sicilia **5**

Palazzo dei Normanni **4**

Piazza della Kalsa **6**

Santa Teresa alla Kalsa **6**

Via della Libertà shopping **1**

Via Principe di Belmonte shopping **1**

In the southeastern part of the old city, **La Kalsa** is the medieval core of old Palermo and its most intriguing neighborhood. Established by Sicily's Arab rulers in the 9th century (its name comes from the Arabic *al khalisa*, meaning "pure" or "true"), it was heavily bombed by the Allies in World War II, and for years in the postwar era little was done by way of repair. Today the bombed area has been turned into a green park, but the neighborhood still has plenty of narrow alleys and streets that are evocative of its Arabic past. A good place in the heart of the quarter to begin your rambling is the fancifully baroque church of **Santa Teresa alla Kalsa** (✆ **091/6171658**), which opens onto the area's primary square, **Piazza della Kalsa.** The church was constructed between 1686 and 1706, and has a luminous interior graced with impressive stuccoes. Admission is free. From Piazza della Kalsa, walk north along Via Torremuzza until you come to **Via Alloro,** La Kalsa's main street in the Middle Ages. Head west along this street for a close encounter with the decaying district. Most of its old elegant palaces are long gone, but the late-15th-century **Palazzo Abatellis**, at 4 Via Alloro, has survived and now houses the **Galleria Regionale della Sicilia** (✆ **091/6230011**), Sicily's greatest gallery of regional art, with works dating from the 13th to the 18th centuries. Admission is 6€ ($8.40). La Kalsa is bounded by the port of La Cala on one side and Via Garibaldi and Via Paternostro to the east and west, and by Corso Vittorio

Emanuele and Via Lincoln to the north and south. To reach Piazza della Kalsa, enter near La Cala through Porta dei Greci, right off busy Foro Italico.

At the western edge of the old city center, the **Palazzo dei Normanni** (Palace of the Normans), Piazza del Parlamento (© **091/7051111**), is Palermo's greatest attraction and Sicily's finest treasure trove. Built by the Arabs in the 9th century atop an older Roman and Punic fortress, it was restored by the Normans and later by the Spanish viceroys, who turned it into a royal residence in the 16th century. Today it's the seat of Sicily's regional government and is filled with extraordinary Byzantine mosaics, mammoth frescoes, stunning architectural details, and the private residence of King Roger II (1095–1154). Admission is 6€ ($8.40).

Farther west, below the Capuchins Monastery, the **Catacombe dei Cappuccini** (Catacombs of the Capuchins), Piazza Cappuccini 1 (© **091/212117**), contains the mummified remains of some 8,000 Sicilians, some dating back as far as the late 16th century, some as recently as 1920. Visitors can wander through the catacombs' dank corridors among the bodies, some of which are remarkably preserved, others not so much. Admission is 2€ ($2.80).

LOCAL FLAVORS

Most of the cuisine you'll find here is typically Sicilian, although there's more diversity in Palermo than anywhere else in Sicily. For seafood, try the *pasta con le sarde* (pasta mixed with fresh sardines) or spaghetti with clams or mussels. If you're a street-food fanatic, Palermo is your kind of town. As you walk along any section of the city, you'll encounter peddlers touting the local specialties—such delights as *panelle* (fritters made with chickpea flour) and *calzoni* (deep-fried meat- or cheese-filled dough pockets). Desserts are also sold on the street. Some of the best concoctions are holdovers from the days of Arab occupation, including sweetened ricotta with cinnamon, pistachios, candied fruit, and cloves. Some of the best restaurants are hidden in the medieval Kalsa neighborhood.

SHOPPING

Palermo is like a grand shopping bazaar, with specialties that include coral jewelry, embroidered fabrics, and ceramics. For the best shopping, head for **Via della Libertà,** north of the city's medieval core within a 19th-century residential neighborhood of town houses and mid-20th-century apartment buildings. In this same neighborhood, **Via Principe di Belmonte** is an all-pedestrian thoroughfare with many hip and elegant shops, as well as fashionable cafes.

19 Palma de Majorca, Spain

Known as "The Island of Tranquility," Majorca (also spelled Mallorca) is the largest of Spain's 16 Balearic Islands, a group that also includes Ibiza and Minorca. Lying about 97km (60 miles) from the Spanish mainland, Majorca offers a lush and rugged landscape in which picturesque villages mix it up with big high-rise hotels. Millions of tourists come here each year, and the resort area is particularly popular with northern Europeans.

Palma, the capital, is a cosmopolitan city of 300,000 nestled on the southern tip of Majorca, its bay crowded with yachts and its streets filled with an international cast of vacationers. The city's Gothic Quarter offers a maze of narrow alleys and cobblestone streets, as well as historical sites left by the island's Byzantine, Arab, and Spanish rulers. Outside the city are mountains, lush valleys, fine beaches, little fishing villages, and some terrifically winding roads connecting them all. It's not surprising that writers, painters, and musicians have all found inspiration here.

COMING ASHORE   Ships dock about 15 minutes by taxi or bus from the center of town. **Taxis** are generally available at the pier. The walk into town is about 6½ km (4 miles), along the rim of the harbor.

GETTING AROUND   You can walk easily around Palma's central section, but you'll need a taxi, bus, rental car, or excursion to get elsewhere on the island. **Taxis** are on the pricey side, so they are good only for getting to and around the city.

The electric **Sóller Train** (© **90-236-4711;** www.sollernet.com/trendesoller) runs from Palma to the popular coastal village of Sóller, along the same 27km (17 miles) of narrow-gauge track it's operated on since 1912. En route, the antique locomotive passes through beautiful mountain scenery and the 13 tunnels of the Serra de Tramuntana, taking about an hour to reach its destination. Round-trip tickets are 11€ ($15). The train departs from the station in central Palma, just next to the Plaza de España, at Eusebio Estada 1. The central bus station is just down the street.

LANGUAGE & CURRENCY   **Spanish** is the official language, but you'll also hear people speaking **Catalan** in Palma. Many people also speak **English** or **German.** The official currency is the **euro** (€). The exchange rate at press time was $1 = .72€ (1€ = $1.40).

BEST CRUISE LINE SHORE EXCURSIONS

A Taste of Palma: Costa Nord & Wine Tasting (5 hr.; $81): This excursion travels to Majorca's gorgeous North Coast, a 64km (40-mile) mass of limestone that has formed a wall against winds and invasions for centuries. The tour starts with a visit to the Costa Nord Foundation in Valldemosa, established to promote the culture and landscape of the Tramuntana mountain range. It then continues on to the Bodega Santa-Catarina winery for a tasting and some insight into Majorca's winemaking business.

Valldemossa & Chopin (4 hr.; $58): This tour explores the west side of the island. Drive 45 minutes to the quaint village of Valldemossa, located at the foot of the Northern Mountain Range. Its history dates back to the 14th century. Visit Cartuja, a former royal residence turned monastery in the Middle Ages. In 1838, both George Sand and Frederic Chopin came to live at the monastery, a visit that inspired Sand's book *A Winter in Majorca,* Chopin's composition "Raindrop Prelude," and other works. The tour includes a short piano recital.

Palma's Contemporary Art (4½ hr.; $79): A tour of the recently opened Es Baluard museum of modern and contemporary art (displaying more than 300 works by Picasso, Miró, Tàpies, Barceló, and others), along with visits to several art galleries and cultural centers.

Caves of Drach (5 hr.; $65): These mysterious caves hide the world's largest underground lake. It's a sight to behold. Your bus will probably stop at a furniture factory where olive wood is inlaid with pearl.

ON YOUR OWN: WITHIN WALKING DISTANCE

Because the port is several kilometers from the city center, we're considering all sites here beyond walking distance.

ON YOUR OWN: BEYOND THE PORT AREA

The old section of Palma, full of narrow alleys and cobblestone streets, centers on the magnificent **La Seu,** Placa Almoina S/N (© **971/72-31-30;** www.catedraldemallorca. org), a Catalonian Gothic cathedral whose construction began during the reign of Jaume II (1276–1311) and was completed in 1610. Of note is the scallop-edged, wrought-iron canopy by Gaudí over the main altar. The treasury contains pieces of the True Cross (they say) and relics of St. Sebastián. Admission to the cathedral is free; museum and treasury admission is 3.50€ ($4.90).

Nearby, the **Palau de l'Almudaina Fortress,** Carrer Palau Reial (© **971/21-41-34**), is a reminder that the island was once ruled by Muslims. A palace was built here soon after the Arab conquest, and during the short-lived reign of the kings of Majorca, it was converted into a royal residence. Today it's the king of Spain's official residence when he's visiting Majorca and houses a museum displaying antiques, artwork, suits of armor, and Gobelin tapestries. Panoramic views of Palma's harbor can be seen from here. Admission is 3.20€ ($4.50). A few blocks in the other direction from La Seu, the **Banys Arabs** (Arab Baths), Carrer Serra 7 (© **97-172-15-49**), date from the 10th century and are among the few Islamic buildings remaining in Palma, displaying characteristic architectural elements. Admission is 1.5€ ($2.10).

A little to the north, the **Art Espanyol Contemporani,** Carrer Sant Miquel 11 (© **971/71-35-15;** www.march.es/arte/palma), features 70 works by Picasso, Miró, Dalí, Juan Gris, and other 20th-century Spanish artists, along with a rotating series of temporary exhibits. Admission is free. Closed Sunday. Closer to the cruise terminal, the **Fundació Pilar i Joan Miró a Mallorca,** Carrer Joan de Saridakis 29 (© **97-170-14-20;** http://miro.palmademallorca.es), preserves the four workshops in which the great artist worked from 1956 until his death in 1983. Rotating exhibitions devoted to Miró's life and work are presented along with a permanent collection of his art and sculptures. Admission is 5€ ($7). Closed Monday.

LOCAL FLAVORS

Meat-eaters will want to try Majorcan specialties such as pork loin *(lomo)* or sausage *(sabrasada).* Another favorite is fish pie. Finish your meal with a *café carajillo* (coffee with cognac).

SHOPPING

Shop here for Majorca pearls, inlaid wood products, needlework, pottery, hand-blown glass, olive-wood carvings, and leather goods (including shoes). The upscale shops are located along **Avenida Jaume III** and **Paseo del Borne,** while specialty shops are clustered on the pedestrian streets around the **Placa Major,** located north of the cathedral area. Other good shopping opportunities can be found on San Miguel, Carrer Sindicato, Jaume II, Carrer Platería, and Via Roman. Many shops close between 1:30 and 4:30pm, as well as on Sunday.

20 Rome, Italy

Heidi's been to Rome six or seven times and still gets goose bumps when another visit is in the works. Iconic places such as the Coliseum, the Vatican, and the Trevi Fountain are of spectacular historical importance, while the city's famous designer stores represent the most modern ideals. Italy's capital and most populous city, Rome is a magical place that has been immortalized not only in history books, but by 20th-century cinema as well. From *Roman Holiday* and *Ben Hur* to *Gladiator* and *A Funny*

Thing Happened on the Way to the Forum, movies have helped bring Rome into our collective consciousness and into our hearts.

As legend would have it, Rome was founded by the twins Romulus and Remus in 753 B.C., but it seems more likely that Rome evolved from farmland into a city in the 8th century B.C. in the area where the Roman Forum would eventually be built. The city developed into the capital of the Roman Kingdom, then the Roman Republic, and by 27 B.C., the Roman Empire. For almost a thousand years, Rome was the most politically important, richest, and largest city in the Western world. Over the next thousand years, its political power may have waned, but its mythic stature has not. As one of the few major European cities to escape World War II relatively unscathed, its essential Renaissance and baroque character remains intact. Hidden piazzas, palaces, and ruins of antiquity have all been absorbed into the bustling, frenetic fabric of modern Rome. If ever there was a place to just wander about and discover, it's Rome.

COMING ASHORE   Though the cruise lines don't like harping on this one little detail very much, Rome is not along the coast and ships actually dock in the port of Civitavecchia, about a 90-minute drive from the city. Civitavecchia has served as Rome's port since Emperor Trajan declared it such in A.D. 108. The town is pleasant enough, but there's really not much to see, with the exception of a few landmarks, including the Vanvitelli Fountain, the Roman dock of Lazaretto, and the ancient city walls. Definitely make the schlep into Rome.

GETTING AROUND   From the Civitavecchia pier, it's about a 15-minute walk to town; most ships have free shuttle buses running passengers back and forth. The drive to Rome takes about 90 minutes. A much better bet is to use the frequent **train** service from Civitavecchia's train station (a 10-min. walk from the shuttle's drop-off point; follow the signs—it's 2 blocks north of Viale Giuseppe Garibaldi) to Rome's Stazione Termini. The train ride takes about an hour and costs about 9€ ($13) round-trip—substantially less than the cruise lines' shore excursions, though, of course, you don't get a guide. Depending on the time of day, rail service into Rome runs hourly or twice hourly.

LANGUAGE & CURRENCY   The language is **Italian,** but many people know some English as well. The official currency is the **euro** (€). The exchange rate at press time was $1 = .72€ (1€ = $1.40).

BEST CRUISE LINE SHORE EXCURSIONS

In addition to the excursion below, most ships offer a **bus transfer** to Rome so you can explore on your own; the cost is $75 to $100. Some lines offer the option of a half-day on your own and a half-day of group touring for $92 to $139.

Rome City Tour (9–11 hr.; $100–$350): Most ships have a variety of Rome tours. Some try to hit several major sites, including the Colosseum, Trevi Fountain, Spanish Steps, the Vatican, Piazza San Pietro, St. Peter's Basilica, and the Vatican Museums. Others do drive-bys of landmarks such as the remains of the Roman Forum, Trajan's Column, the Arch of Constantine, and the Circus Maximus. Some tours focus on just one or two marquee sites (a better idea), such as the Vatican City attractions.

ON YOUR OWN: WITHIN WALKING DISTANCE

There's not really much to see in Civitavecchia, where the ships dock, so take the train or bus transfer to Rome to see the sights.

Rome

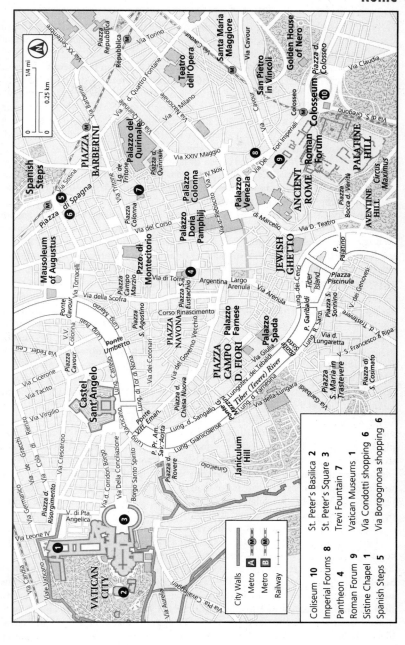

Map labels:

Piazza Repubblica
Via Torino
Via XX settembre
Via Cavour
Santa Maria Maggiore
Golden House of Nero
Piazza d. Colosseo
Via Claudia
Teatro dell'Opera
Via Milano
Via Nazionale
Via d. Quattro Fontane
Via Barberini
San Pietro in Vincoli
Colosseo
Colosseum 10
Via di S. Gregorio
PIAZZA BARBERINI
Palazzo del Quirinale
Via del Quirinale
Via XXIV Maggio
Fori Imperiali
Roman Forum
PALATINE HILL
Spanish Steps
Via Sistina
Lg. de Tritone
Via Tritone
Piazza d. Quirinale
Via IV Nov.
ANCIENT ROME
Via dei
Piazza di Spagna
Piazza S. Pietro
Palazzo Colonna
Palazzo Venezia
Via S. Teatro
Bocca d. Verità
AVENTINE HILL
Circus Maximus
Piazza Colonna
Via del Corso
Palazzo Doria Pamphilj
Via d. Plebiscito
di Marcello
Via D. Teatro
JEWISH GHETTO
Mausoleum of Augustus
Via Tomacelli
Pzzo. di Montecitorio
Via di Torre
Piazza Campo Marzio
Piazza S. Eustachio
Argentina
Largo Arenula
Lung. dei Cenci
Tiber Island
P. Palatino
Piazza Piscinula
Via della Scrofa
Piazza S. Agostino
Corso Rinascimento
Via Arenula
Lung. R. Sanzio
Piazza S. Sonnino
Ponte Cavour
Via d. Corenari
PIAZZA NAVONA
Palazzo Farnese
Lung. Garibaldi
Via d. Lungaretta
V.V. Colonna
Ponte Umberto
Piazza d. Chiesa Nuova
Via del Governo Vecchio
PIAZZA CAMPO D. FIORI
Palazzo Spada
Via d. Sisto
Lung.
Piazza S. Maria in Trastevere
Piazza di S. Cosimato
Via Feder. Cesi
Via Fed. Cavour
Via Cicerone
Via Tacito
Via Virgilio
Castel Sant'Angelo
Lung. Castello
Via di Tor di Nona
Ponte Vittorio Eman.
Lungotev. dei Fiorentini
Lungotev. dei Tebaldi
Tiber (Tevere) River
Via Giulia
Lung. d. Farnesina
Via della Lungara
Via Garibaldi
Via de' Gracchi
Via de Cola di Rienzo
Via Crescenzio
Piazza d. Risorgimento
Via d. Corridori Borgo
Borgo Santo Spirito
Via d. Conciliazione
P. Pr. Am. Sav. Aosta
Lung. d. Vaticano
Lung. Gianicolense
Janiculum Hill
Gianicolo
Via Germanico
Via Vaticano
Via Leone IV
V. di Pta. Angelica
VATICAN CITY
Via Candia
Viale Vaticano
Via Aurelia
Via Pta. Cavalleggeri
Piazza d. Rovere

Legend:

City Walls
Metro A
Metro B
Railway

Coliseum 10	St. Peter's Basilica 2
Imperial Forums 8	St. Peter's Square 3
Pantheon 4	Trevi Fountain 7
Roman Forum 9	Vatican Museums 1
Sistine Chapel 1	Via Condotti shopping 6
Spanish Steps 5	Via Borgognona shopping 6

N
1/4 mi
0.25 km
0

ON YOUR OWN: BEYOND THE PORT AREA

For visitors with only a day or two to sightsee, Rome means three things: the Roman Empire, Roman Catholicism, and *la gente di Roma*—all those modern-day Romans you see around you, livin' la vita dolce.

For Romans of the ancient variety, head first to the **Colosseo (Coliseum),** Piazzale del Colosseo, Via dei Fori Imperiali (© **06-39967600**), probably the most recognizable site in the city. Built by order of the emperor Vespasian between A.D. 72 and 80, it's an incredible architectural achievement, standing 48m (157 ft.) high, taking up an area of over 2.4 hectares (6 acres), and able to seat more than 50,000 patrons. It was in active use for nearly 500 years and saw the whole panoply of Roman "sport": gladiatorial contests, fights between men and animals, dramas, executions, and even naval battles staged by flooding the arena's floor with water. Once it fell into disuse, the Coliseum was used as a quarry, its marble and stones used to build palaces and churches. Imagine that: The huge, majestic facade we see today is just what's left after centuries of plunder. Admission is 11.50€ ($16).

Just northwest of the Coliseum, on the Via de Fori Imperiali, the **Roman Forum** was the center of Roman life in the days of the Republic, full of temples, triumphal arches, and other public edifices. Today there's only fragments and ruins, an arch or two, and lots of boulders, but all you have to do is reach out your hand to one of those fragments and know that you've now touched a piece of "the glory that was Rome." Just to the north, the **Imperial Forums** were begun by Julius Caesar to replace the older, smaller forums, and at the time of their construction conveyed the unquestioned authority of the emperors at the height of their power. The best-known remaining monument on the site is **Trajan's Column,** a 30m (98-ft.) pillar with a spiral bar-relief carving depicting the Emperor Trajan's victories in the region of modern-day Romania.

Continue less than 1km (½ mile) to the northwest to see the **Pantheon,** at Piazza della Rontonda (© **06-68300230**). Built as a temple to the seven gods of Rome around A.D. 125, it features a massive dome punctured by a circular 5.4m (18 ft.) opening at its very peak. The best preserved of all Roman buildings, it's been in continuous use for nearly 2,000 years, first as a temple and (since A.D. 609) as a Roman Catholic church.

Back eastward and a little to the north, the **Trevi Fountain,** at Piazza di Trevi, is one of the most photographed sights in Rome. Designed by Nicolo Salvi and completed in 1762, it features Neptune standing on a shell chariot, drawn by winged steeds. A bit farther north, the wide **Spanish Steps** are another stop on the sightseeing hit parade. Named for their proximity to the Spanish Embassy (which stood nearby in the 19th century), this azalea-flanked triumph of landscape design was built between 1723 and 1725, rising from the boat-shape Barcaccia fountain to the Trinità dei Monti church, 136 steps above.

And then there's **Vatican City** (www.vatican.va), the earthly locus of the Roman Catholic Church, a 44-hectare (109-acre) walled enclave that exists as its own separate country—the world's smallest—completely surrounded by the neighborhoods of Rome. The only entrance for visitors is through **Piazza San Pietro (St. Peter's Square),** designed by Gianlorenzo Bernini between 1656 and 1667, and enclosed by two semicircular, Doric-pillared colonnades surmounted by statues of 140 saints. Beyond lies the **Basilica di San Pietro (St. Peter's Basilica),** a massive church built in the 16th century on the alleged site of St. Peter's grave. Predominantly High Renaissance and baroque in style, it's a massive testament to the church's wealth and power, measuring the length of two football fields, topped by a 120m (394 ft.) central dome, and filled with works by some of Italy's greatest artists. Michelangelo's famed *Pietà,* depicting Mary holding the body of Jesus, is located in the first chapel on the right.

Other "must-do" sights in Vatican City include the **Vatican Museums** (home to one of the world's greatest art collections) and the **Sistine Chapel** (on whose ceiling Michelangelo painted what's probably the most recognized image of God in the Christian world). However, they are difficult to visit on your own on a 1-day visit since (a) huge crowds line up early (before you can get to Rome from Civitavecchia), and (b) you need several hours to really explore. If a view of Michelangelo's ceiling is on your life-list, book a shore excursion and get in with a group; many ships offer VIP tours that can get you in shorter lines, though you pay a higher price for the privilege.

LOCAL FLAVORS

Rome remains one of the world's great capitals for dining, with a tradition of borrowing from (and sometimes improving on) the cuisine of Italy's other regions. For a quick bite, stop at one of the city's many bars (which sell alcohol but function mostly as cafes, serving *panini* and other varieties of sandwiches) or a *pizza a taglio* or *pizza rustica,* where you can order pizza by the slice. *Enoteca* wine bars are also growing in popularity, letting you order from a menu of local and regional wines by the glass while snacking on finger foods. A full-fledged restaurant will go by the name *osteria, trattoria,* or *ristorante,* all of which mean basically the same thing: a sit-down meal. And then there's the many, many places serving *gelato,* Italy's distinctive and delicious take on ice cream. What's the difference? There actually doesn't seem to *be* any, but somehow it just tastes so Italian. Go figure.

SHOPPING

Name three top designers off the top of your head, and chances are, they're all Italian: Gucci, Prada, Armani, Versace, Zegna, Roberto Cavalli . . . and the list goes on. They've all got slick stores in Rome, and the city also harbors a zillion other less prestigious boutiques. Fashionistas should head to shopping strips like the **Via Condotti** (which begins at the base of the Spanish Steps and is Rome's poshest and most prominent shopping street) and the nearby **Via Borgognona,** another mecca for wealthy, well-dressed internationalists.

If you don't plan on venturing past Civitavecchia, there are souvenir shops and some shoe and leather goods stores along the main road, but nothing overly impressive.

21 Sorrento, Italy

Known as the City of Sirens (those lovely mermaids who lured sailors to their deaths with their pretty songs), Sorrento has for centuries been a favorite resort of wealthy Romans. Dramatically located atop a cliff overlooking the sea, the charming town has great shops and quaint streets, although it can get very crowded and snarled with traffic in the summer high season.

As is the case with the busier port of Naples, most ships stop here for easy access to the ancient city of **Pompeii,** the scenic **Amalfi Coast,** and the nearby romantic **isle of Capri.** However, Sorrento itself makes for a pleasant stroll and is a good place to shop for inlaid wood and other local crafts.

COMING ASHORE   Ships tender passengers to the pier, where you'll usually find **taxis.**

Sorrento

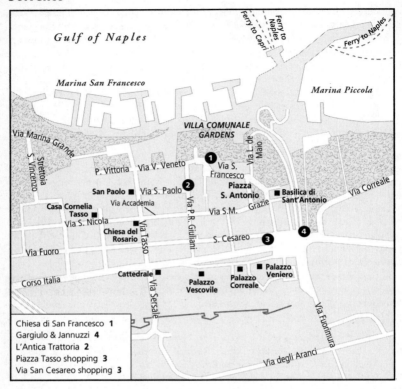

GETTING AROUND   The center of Sorrento is about a 15-minute uphill walk from the pier. **Minibuses** operated by the city make the uphill climb.

LANGUAGE & CURRENCY   The language is **Italian.** The official currency is the **euro (€).** The exchange rate at press time was $1 = .72€ (1€ = $1.40).

BEST CRUISE LINE SHORE EXCURSIONS
Sorrento offers the same basic selection of shore excursions as Naples (see p. 359), though travel times will vary slightly.

ON YOUR OWN: WITHIN WALKING DISTANCE
Though few people come here to look at churches, **Chiesa di San Francesco (Cloister of St. Francis),** Via San Francesco, is worth a peek. It dates from the 14th century and offers pretty archways and a lovely garden. The convent is also an art school that regularly offers exhibits. Admission is free.

ON YOUR OWN: BEYOND WALKING DISTANCE
You can catch a boat to **Capri** (three to four hydrofoils or ferries leave every hour); make sure you can get back to your ship on time. If you're looking for exercise, the green hills above Sorrento offer decent hiking. Many trails are marked, and the local tourist office (Via Luigi De Maio, 35) can offer specifics. Driving the **Amalfi Coast**

on your own is a nerve-racking experience (unless you like steep cliffs, twists, and turns). Taking a bus is white-knuckle, too, but at least you're not the one at the wheel (a blue SITA bus [**www.sitabus.it**] runs between Sorrento and Amalfi several times an hour; the trip takes about 1½ hours).

LOCAL FLAVORS

Pasta with seafood and fish cooked in salt crust are popular selections here. One of the best places to sample the local cuisine is the venerated **L'Antica Trattoria,** Via P. R. Giuliani 33 (© **081-8071082;** www.lanticatrattoria.com). The restaurant, open for lunch and dinner, specializes in antipasti. Reservations are recommended. Main courses run 18€ to 35€ ($25–$49).

SHOPPING

The best areas for strolling and window-shopping are Piazza Tasso and Via San Cesareo. Locally made wooden inlaid items make great souvenirs, although prices are steep. The region's best-known maker of inlaid furniture is **Gargiulo & Jannuzzi,** Piazza Tasso (© **081-8781041;** www.gargiulo-jannuzzi.it), which opened in 1863. Employees demonstrate the inlay technique to tourists in the shop's basement. Embroidery and lace are two of Sorrento's best bargains, and coral jewelry and *limoncello* (a local lemon liqueur) are also popular.

22 Valletta, Malta

Located at a strategic crossroads about 97km (60 miles) from Sicily and 290km (180 miles) from North Africa at the southernmost tip of Europe, the island nation of Malta has been a coveted prize for thousands of years and at one time or another was ruled by the Phoenicians, Romans, Arabs, Normans, Castilians, Knights of St. John (aka the Knights of Malta, who ruled from 1530 to 1798), French, and British. Malta gained independence from Britain in 1964 and became a republic in 1974, and today its golden capital city offers a wealth of history (cathedrals, palazzos, and fortifications, mostly from the period of the knights' rule), as well as museums, restaurants, and shopping opportunities. Its Grand Harbour also offers one of the cruise world's best "coming into port" experiences, with massive honey-colored stone fortresses rising up like ornate sand castles. Other parts of the island offer quaint towns, ancient sites (including the oldest known free-standing prehistoric temple structures in the world), and historic churches.

COMING ASHORE   Ships dock about a 15-minute walk or a 5-minute taxi ride from the center of town and its central Republic Street.

GETTING AROUND   Valletta is quite compact and easy to explore on foot, and **taxis** are available at the pier to get you to other parts of the island. Though they do except cash (settle on a price first), they also operate on a prepaid voucher system: Tell the taxi dispatcher where you want to go and he'll tell you the price.

LANGUAGE & CURRENCY   People here speak **Maltese** and **English.** The official currency, newly adopted in 2008, is the **euro** (€). The exchange rate at press time was $1 = .72€ (1€ = $1.40).

BEST CRUISE LINE SHORE EXCURSIONS

Valletta and Mdina (4–4½ hr.; $42–$50): This bus-and-walking tour of Valletta (stopping at City Gate) visits St. John's Co-Cathedral and the Palace of the Grand

Valletta

Marsamxett Harbour

St. Michael's Bastion

Spencer's Bastion

S. Salvatore Bastion — German Curtain — S. Sebastion Curtain

✝ Church

Hastings Gardens

St. John's Cavalier

Marsamxett St.
Mattia Preti Square
St. Patrick Street

St. Paul's Cathedral

Carmelite Church ✝

West Street

English Curtain

St. Gregory's Bastion

French Curtain

War Museum

Old Street — Mint Street — Street — **1**

Old Bakery Street — St. Lucia Street — Old Theatre Street

Main Guard — Strait Street — Republic Street — St. Dominic Street — Fountain Street

Strait Street

Freedom Square

Auberge Vittoria of Italy

Republic Street — St. Barbara — Zachary St. — **2**

Law Courts

Republic Square — **4**

National Library — Armoury

St. Elmo Place

St. James Cavalier ✝

3

St. John Street

P.O.
Auberge of Castille

Castille Place

Melta Street

St. Paul Market

St. Paul's Street

Merchant's Street

University

Archbishop Street

St. Christopher Street

St. Dominic Street

St. Nicholas Street

Old Hospital Street

North Street

5

St. Lazarus Bastion

St. Lazarus Curtain

Victoria Gate

St. Ursula Street

East Street

Castille Curtain

Mediterranean Street

Ta' Liesse

St. Barbara Bastion

Barriera Wharf

Lower Barracca

Lascaris Bastion

Grand Harbour

Fish Market

The Malta Experience/
Mediterranean Conference Center **5**
Manoel Theatre **1**
Palace of the Grand Master **4**
Republic Street shopping **3**
St. John's Co-Cathedral **2**

Masters. You are then driven by bus to the walled city of Mdina, Malta's medieval capital, where you'll find quaint winding streets and beautiful homes, as well as a cathedral dedicated to St. Peter and St. Paul.

Tour of the Temples (4 hr.; $60–$85): This bus tour includes some of the world's most impressive prehistoric temples. In the Cottonera region, you'll visit the Malta Maritime Museum, which houses relics of Malta's history. You'll then visit the temple of Hagar Qim, with its decorated pillar and two altars, constructed in the Late Megalithic period on a slope facing the tiny island of Filfla. Your final visit is to Tarxien Temples, where the archaeological remains date back to 2,500 B.C.

Malta Trekking (4 hr.; $55): This 10km (6¼-mile) trek is a great way to get off the beaten path, visiting dramatic and undeveloped western parts of the island that are accessible only by foot. Views include striking sea cliffs over the ocean. Some of the trekking is on uneven terrain and over boulders, so participants should be physically fit.

The Blue Grotto (4 hr.; $50–$65): Drive by bus for about 30 minutes to the south side of the island, where you'll find the Blue Grotto and the stunning rock formations of Wied iz Zurrieq valley. Hop in a local Maltese fishing boat to get close-up views of the caves, colorful coral formations, and beautiful clear waters. There may be time for swimming here or for browsing in the shops of Marsaxlokk, a nearby village.

ON YOUR OWN: WITHIN WALKING DISTANCE

Stroll Republic Street to meet the island's friendly populace. One of the oldest theaters in Europe still in operation, **Manoel Theatre** (© **356/22-26-18**), Old Theatre Street, was built by the Portuguese Grand Master Antonio Manoel de Vilhena in 1731. Admission is about 2€ ($2.80). The **Palace of the Grand Master** (© **56/22-12-21**), Republic Street, is a grand 500-year-old residence completed in 1574. Today the palace is the seat of the president and Parliament of the Republic of Malta. Inside are portraits of European monarchs and the Grand Masters of the Order of St. John; a furniture collection; Gobelin tapestries; and frescoes, friezes, and other artworks. Admission is 2€ ($2.80). The outside of **St. John's Co-Cathedral,** St. John's Square (© **21/220-536;** www.stjohnscocathedral.com), built between 1573 and 1577, is rather austere, but the interior is gorgeous and holds art treasures such as Caravaggio's *The Beheading of St. John,* as well as a collection of Flemish tapestries, silver objects, and church vestments. Admission is 6€ ($8.40).

A must-see in Valletta for those interested in the island's history is **The Malta Experience** audiovisual presentation, Mediterranean Conference Center, Old Hospital Street (© **21/243-776;** www.themaltaexperience.com). The 45-minute presentation is offered on the hour Monday to Friday 11am to 4pm, Saturday to Sunday 11am and noon. Admission is about 7€ ($9.80).

ON YOUR OWN: BEYOND WALKING DISTANCE

Outside Valletta, you can explore the town of Mdina or the Blue Grotto (see the shore excursions) on your own, via taxi. Both are about a 30-minute drive from Valletta, and the ride should cost you about 20€ ($28) one-way.

LOCAL FLAVORS

The food here is rustic and hearty, with fresh fish, local vegetables, and cheese worked into many dishes. Pastry-covered pies filled with everything from spinach and anchovies to fish, goat cheese, and egg are also popular.

SHOPPING

Local, traditional crafts include hand-blown glass and lace, ceramics, silver and gold jewelry, metalwork, pottery, and tiles. Shops can be found on Republic Street and on the small streets near Palace Square.

23 Venice, Italy

Is Venice the most beautiful city in the world? You wouldn't get much argument from us if you said so. Everywhere you look here, you're stunned by the sheer beauty of the city's architecture and its absurd wealth of art; by the seemingly organic nature of the place, as if it had grown rather than been built; and by the inventive ways Venetians have found both to adapt their city to the modern world and to ensure that it doesn't simply sink into the lagoon. That eternal tenuousness—of an ancient city that just keeps managing to stay afloat, no matter what nature and man throw at it—gives Venice a gauzy, fairy-tale quality. It shouldn't exist, but it does.

The settlement that would become *La Serenissima,* the Serene Republic of Venice, was founded in the middle of the 5th century by refugees seeking shelter from barbarian invasions of the islands of the Venice Lagoon. In 727, the Venetians elected a duke (*doge,* in the local dialect) to lead them, thus beginning a system of government that was to last almost 1,100 years, making Venice the world's longest-lived republic. Over the centuries, the republic's power grew as its trading empire expanded, while the treacherous waters of the lagoon proved a mighty defense against invading armies. From 1203 to 1204, the Venetian Doge Enrico Dandolo engineered the sacking of Constantinople (then the world's richest city) by the forces of the fourth crusade, resulting in much of its wealth and art treasures, and many of its lands in and around the Adriatic Sea being transferred to Venetian control. Today you can still see some of the riches from that period, along with a treasure trove of other paintings and statues, ornate churches and palaces, and other wonders assembled over the centuries of Venice's power.

COMING ASHORE   Ships generally dock west of the central tourist areas, near the train station and the western end of the serpentine Grand Canal. It's about 15 to 20 minutes by boat to St. Mark's Square.

GETTING AROUND   One of Venice's wonders is that it's a major city that does completely without cars. All travel here is either on foot or on the water, the latter via **water taxi** (which will be pricey) or *vaporetti* water bus (which is much cheaper). Prices for vaporetti trips are about 6€ ($8.40). If you'll be making more than three trips, consider buying a discount-fare **Venice Card** (**www.venicecard.com**). A card that's good for unlimited travel within a 12-hour window (and also gets you discounts to some museums, churches, restaurants, and more) costs 19€ ($26).

Some ships provide free **water transfers** to a spot near St. Mark's Square.

LANGUAGE & CURRENCY   The language is **Italian.** The official currency is the **euro** (€). The exchange rate at press time was $1 = .72€ (1€ = $1.40).

BEST CRUISE LINE SHORE EXCURSIONS

If this is your first visit to Venice, you probably don't need to take an excursion. Instead, do some advance reading, arm yourself with a good map, and just start walking. This isn't a city to rush through on a tour; its joys are in the details.

That said, here are a few good excursion options.

Hidden Venice Walking Tour (4 hr.; $75): A short transfer by motor launch takes you to Piazzale Roma, where your walking tour begins. Along Venice's narrow streets, you'll see the 14th-century Santa Maria Gloriosa Dei Frari church; the Campo San Polo, one of Venice's oldest squares and now site of the Venice Film Festival; the Riva del Vin, a rare spot where pedestrians can get down next to the Grand Canal; the Rialto Bridge (see below); the Fondaco dei Tedeschi post office; and the monumental Campo San Giovanni e Paolo square. The tour ends near San Marco, where you can either return to the ship or keep exploring on your own.

Grand Canal & Waterways by Water Taxi (2½ hr.; $115): Seeing Venice from the water is a must, whether you do so via vaporetto (see above) or on a tour like this one. Here, a 12- to 20-person water taxi takes you out on a portion of the Grand Canal and other of the city's most historic and picturesque canals, slipping under bridges and passing baroque and Renaissance palaces.

Murano Glass Factory & Burano Island (5 hr.; $52): Central Venice isn't the only island in the Venetian Lagoon. On this tour, you'll travel by motor launch to the island of Murano, visiting one of its famous glass factories, then move on to the island of Burano, where you'll view a demonstration of traditional lace-making before having some free time to wander the village streets. On the boat ride to and from the

Venice

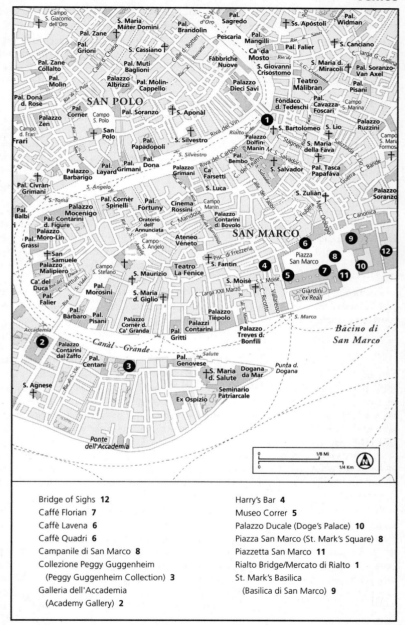

Bridge of Sighs **12**
Caffé Florian **7**
Caffè Lavena **6**
Caffè Quadri **6**
Campanile di San Marco **8**
Collezione Peggy Guggenheim
   (Peggy Guggenheim Collection) **3**
Galleria dell'Accademia
   (Academy Gallery) **2**

Harry's Bar **4**
Museo Correr **5**
Palazzo Ducale (Doge's Palace) **10**
Piazza San Marco (St. Mark's Square) **8**
Piazzetta San Marco **11**
Rialto Bridge/Mercato di Rialto **1**
St. Mark's Basilica
   (Basilica di San Marco) **9**

islands, you'll pass the Arsenale (Venice's old shipyard) and the Island of St. Elena, enjoying views of another famous island, the Lido, in the distance.

Evening Gondola Ride with Serenade (2 hr.; $115): It may sound hokey, but there is something magical about exploring the canals of this romantic city on these black pointed vessels, with a gondolier singing in Italian. The trip takes you onto narrow canals, past historic homes, and under old stone bridges.

ON YOUR OWN: WITHIN WALKING DISTANCE

Venice lies 4km (2½ miles) from terra firma, connected to the mainland town of Mestre by a long motor and rail causeway. At the end of the causeway, train passengers debark and motorists park, and everyone steps into an alternate reality where the wheel no longer holds dominion. Here the **Canal Grande (Grand Canal)** is the main highway, snaking in a great S-shape for 3.2km (2 miles) past ornate bridges and palaces, and plied by everything from commuter and pleasure boats to ambulance boats and delivery barges.

Central Venice refers to the built-up block of islands in the lagoon's center. Greater Venice includes all the inhabited islands of the lagoon: central Venice plus Murano, Burano, Torcello, and the Lido. The city itself is divided into six *sestieri* ("sixths," or districts or wards), including **San Marco (St. Mark's)**, the city's commercial, religious, and political heart, anchored by the magnificent Piazza San Marco and St. Mark's Basilica to the south, and by the Rialto Bridge to the north.

Piazza San Marco (St. Mark's Square) is the cultural hub of the city, a place where you can spend hours sitting at a cafe, people-watching, feeding the pigeons (hundreds of which gather around anyone who buys a bag of feed), visiting the Basilica and the Doge's Palace, shopping, and just marveling at the sheer beauty of the place. It's a trapezoid that stretches some 175m (574 ft.) from the Ala Napoleonica at the narrow end to the Basilica at the wide end, right next to the Doge's Palace and the **Piazzetta San Marco** (a much smaller side square that opens onto the Grand Canal), and fronted by the **Campanile di San Marco,** a bell tower that, at 97m (318 ft.), is the highest spot in the city and offers spectacular views (tickets 6€/$8.40). An elevator takes visitors to the top. San Marco is a zoo most days, packed with tourists from around the world, but you just have to see it anyway. It's one of the world's most beautiful civic spaces.

The **Palazzo Ducale (Doge's Palace; ©️ 041-2715911;** www.museicivici veneziani.it), a Venetian Gothic palazzo, is Italy's grandest civic structure. And it literally gleams. While it dates back to 1309, most was destroyed by a fire and rebuilt in the 16th century. Many of the greatest Venetian painters of that century helped with the restoration. After climbing the Sansovino stairway of gold, proceed to the Anti-Collegio salon to view Veronese's *Rape of Europe* and Tintoretto's *Three Graces* and *Bacchus and Ariadne*. Downstairs you can visit the apartments of the Doges and the grand Maggior Consiglio, with its allegorical *Triumph of Venice* by Veronese on the ceiling. Tintoretto's *Paradise* over the Grand Council chamber is said to be the largest oil painting in the world. Follow the arrows to the **Bridge of Sighs,** which links the Doge's Palace with the prisons of the Palazzo delle Prigioni. The sighs allegedly refer to the laments of those getting their last view of Venice before descending to their cells, but full credit for that goes to Lord Byron, who made up the story in the 19th century. Admission is 13€ ($18) and also includes entrance to the **Museo Correr** (a museum of art and artifacts at the narrow west end of the Piazza) and several other sites.

Next door, **St. Mark's Basilica (Basilica di San Marco),** Piazza San Marco (© 041-5225205; www.basilicasanmarco.it), the "Church of Gold," is one of the greatest and most elaborate churches in the world, and once served as the doges' private chapel. Predominantly Byzantine in style, its facade is adorned with replicas of the four famous horse sculptures looted from Constantinople by the crusaders in 1204 (the originals are inside, in a museum). The interior is stunning, with marbles, alabaster, pillars, and an ocean of mosaics. The treasury contains skulls and bones of ecclesiastical authorities, as well as goblets, chalices, and Gothic candelabra. In the presbytery rests the alleged sarcophagus of St. Mark, whose body was smuggled out of Alexandria in 828, hidden in a pork barrel. In addition to the *Quadriga,* the four bronze horses that have been attributed to the 4th-century Greek sculptor Lysippos, the museum contains liturgical vestments, illuminated manuscripts, Persian carpets, and fragments of ancient mosaics removed during the restoration in the 19th century. From the museum, which also contains mosaics and tapestries, you can walk out onto the loggia for a view of Piazza San Marco. *Note:* Men and women are barred from wearing shorts or exposing bare arms and shoulders, and women may not wear skirts above the knee in the Basilica. Silence is required, and you may not take photos. Admission to the Basilica is free, but there's a 3€ ($4.20) fee for the museum.

Away from St. Mark's are several must-dos. To the north, the **Rialto Bridge** was once the only bridge across the Grand Canal and served as the hub of the city's powerful banking industry during the medieval period. The current bridge dates to 1592, and today its graceful arch is lined with overpriced boutiques and an unending stream of tourists. You can still get a dose of history at the **Mercato di Rialto,** in the streets beneath the bridge's southern end, where barges full of fish, produce, and baked goods have been arriving since 1097 to fill Venice's tables. Many of the retailers close up shop at midday, so arrive early.

West of St. Mark's, on the opposite side of the Grand Canal, the **Galleria dell'Accademia (Academy Gallery),** Dorsoduro, at the foot of Accademia Bridge (© 041-5222247; www.gallerieaccademia.org), houses the definitive collection of Venetian paintings, exhibited chronologically from the 13th through the 18th centuries and containing works by all the great Venetian masters, including Bellini, Giorgione, Tintoretto, Veronese, Titian, and Tiepolo. Admission is 6.50€ ($9.10).

To the east, on the same bank of the Grand Canal, the **Collezione Peggy Guggenheim (Peggy Guggenheim Collection),** Dorsoduro 701 (© 041-2405411; www.guggenheim-venice.it), is a major museum of early-20th-century European and American art. Housed in the former home of its art patron namesake, the museum displays works by such greats as Pollock, Rothko, Calder, Giacometti, Kandinsky, Picasso, Duchamp, and Mondrian. Admission is 10€ ($14). Closed Tuesday.

ON YOUR OWN: BEYOND THE PORT AREA

Once you get to St. Mark's Square (see above), pretty much everything is within walking distance, though you can take a vaporetto (water bus) or water taxi to some of the more distant spots if you don't feel like hoofing it.

LOCAL FLAVORS

Venice has a distinguished culinary history, much of it based on its geographical position on the sea and, to a lesser degree, its historical ties with the Orient. For first courses, both pasta and risotto are commonly prepared with fish or shellfish. *Bigoli,* homemade pasta of whole wheat, is not commonly found elsewhere, while creamy polenta, often served with *gamberetti* (small shrimp) or tiny shrimp called *schie,* is a staple.

Several dining and drinking establishments in town are legendary. Ernest Hemingway liked **Harry's Bar,** Calle Vallaresso, San Marco (© **041-528-5777;** www.cipriani. com/cipriani/Locs/ven.htm), but its fame has made the prices here downright shocking, with dinners running into the hundreds. Still, you might stop in and order a bellini at the bar. They were, they say, invented here.

Piazza San Marco is the home of three legendary cafes with both indoor and outdoor seating. On the southern side of the Piazza, near the Campanile, **Caffè Florian** (© **041-5205641;** www.caffeflorian.com) has been in business since December 29, 1720, and boasts a gloriously ornate interior full of frescoes, mirrors, and ornate moldings. Everyone from Casanova to Woody Allen has dined here. On the opposite side of the square are the almost equally old-world **Caffè Lavena** (© **041-5224070;** www. lavena.it) and **Caffè Quadri** (© **041-5222105;** www.quadrivenice.com), the latter of which has an upstairs restaurant with great piazza views. At all three places, a cappuccino, tea, or Coca-Cola at a table will set you back at least 5€ ($7). But no one will rush you, and if the sun is warm and the orchestras are playing, there's no more beautiful public open-air salon in the world. In winter, Quadri is closed Monday, Lavena is closed Tuesday, and Florian is closed Wednesday.

SHOPPING

Venice is uniquely famous for local crafts that have been produced here for centuries: **glassware** from the island of Murano, **delicate lace** from Burano, and papier-mâché **Carnevale masks.** You'll find an endless number of shops selling them all on all the blocks of San Marco, though be warned: If it's cheap, it's not real. There are so few traditional lace-makers left on Burano that the real stuff goes for stratospheric prices; anything else is probably made by machine in Hong Kong. Ditto for the truly high-quality Murano glass, though the Murano-ish trinkets can be fun and cheap. A discerning eye can cut through the junk to find some lovely mementos.

Shops in tourist areas stay open long hours (many close for lunch, however), and some are open on Sunday.

12

Ports of Call in Northern Europe & the British Isles

Cruises in northern Europe are often called "northern capitals" or some variation thereof because most of the ports here are also the capitals of their countries—from coastal capitals such as Amsterdam, Stockholm, and St. Petersburg (the latter a former capital, but who's counting?) to landlocked capitals such as Paris and Berlin, the latter accessible via shore excursions from the nearest ports. All these cities offer history, museums, and great shopping and dining opportunities. If it's scenery you're after, you'll find it in abundance, especially on cruises that thread their way up the Norwegian Fjords.

HOMEPORTS FOR THIS REGION   **Copenhagen** and **Stockholm** are the most common embarkation ports for cruises in the Baltic, though some also depart from Amsterdam and other ports. **Amsterdam** is a hub for cruises of the Norwegian Fjords. **Southampton,** England, is a homeport for ships sailing the British Isles, Europe's Atlantic coast, and elsewhere.

1 Amsterdam, Netherlands

Amsterdam is a human-scale city, full of low buildings, cozy neighborhoods, and a populace that keeps busy by zipping around on bicycles, skating through parks, enjoying their city's multicultural dining and arts scenes, and just watching the parade of street life go by. The city's historic center still reflects its Golden Age, when it was the hub of a vast trading network and colonial empire, and its wealthy merchants constructed their gabled residences along neatly laid canals. The city will quickly capture you with its atmosphere. At night, many of the more than 1,200 bridges spanning 160 canals are lined with tiny lights, giving them a fairy-tale appearance. Some mornings, the cityscape emerges from a slowly dispersing mist to reveal its enchanting form.

The quirkier side of the Amsterdam coin is that the city long ago decided to control what it can't effectively outlaw. Thus, prostitution is legal in the city's famed **Red Light District** (as much a tourist attraction as any of the major museums here), and hashish and marijuana are sold and consumed in euphemistically designated "coffee shops." Live and let live, baby.

COMING ASHORE   Most cruise ships dock at the Passenger Terminal Amsterdam close to Centraal Station (the central railroad station) near Dam Square, from which you can easily walk to the city center.

GETTING AROUND   Amsterdam is easy to explore on **foot,** by **boat,** or (the Dutch way) by **bicycle.** You can rent bikes from **Mac Bike** (© **020/620-0985;** www.macbike.nl), which has several locations around the city. The one at Centraal Station,

Amsterdam

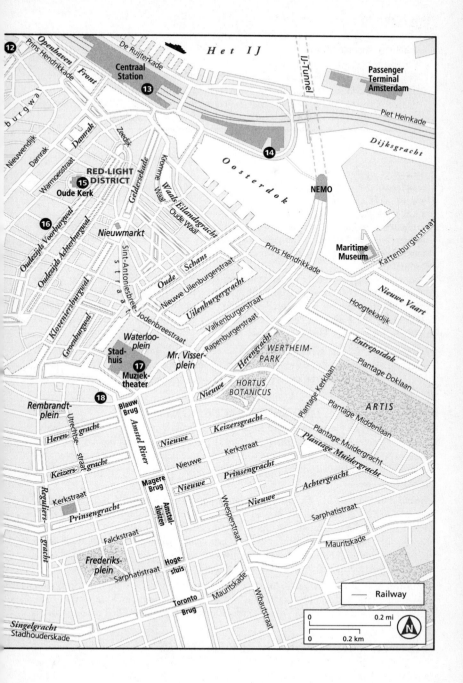

Calling Amsterdam

When making local telephone calls within Amsterdam, drop the "020" at the beginning of the numbers listed in this chapter. When calling from elsewhere in the Netherlands, use the "020." When calling from outside the Netherlands, drop the zero in the area code (dial the country code, then "1," then the local number).

---

near the cruise docks, is the most convenient. Rental rates start at 8.50€ ($12) per day and go up for fancier bikes.

Taxis are available at the pier or can be hailed on the street. The meter starts at a base price of around 5€ ($7) and adds about 2€ ($2.80) per kilometer thereafter. Prices are slightly higher if you're a party of four or more.

The city also has an extensive and easy-to-use **bus** and **tram** network, as well as two **subway** lines. A 24-hour ticket good for the entire network costs 6.30€ ($8.80) and is available at GVB info stands (including at Centraal Station) and from drivers and conductors.

To travel easily on the city's canal system, you can buy a ticket for the **Canal Bus** (© 020/626-5574; www.canal.nl), which offers a hop-on/hop-off service along three routes that together offer 14 stops near major museums and other sites. All-day tickets are 18€ ($25) and can be purchased at Canal Company shops near Centraal Station, the Anne Frank House, and other outlets.

LANGUAGE & CURRENCY   **Dutch** is the official language, but pretty much everyone also speaks **English**—better than we and a lot of our friends do, in fact. The official currency is the **euro** (€). The exchange rate at press time was $1 = .72€ (1€ = $1.40).

THE BEST CRUISE LINE SHORE EXCURSIONS

Walking Tour & Canal Cruise (3 hr.; $48): The walking portion of this tour passes through Amsterdam's oldest district, visiting the flower market and the Art Gallery of the Amsterdam Historical Museum. Your canal cruise departs from the boat pier near Centraal Station, passing historic sites and the old houses of Amsterdam's wealthy merchant class.

Grand Holland (8 hr.; $115): This tour visits Holland's Royal City, The Hague, where you'll be driven past the Royal Palace, Houses of Parliament, and Peace Palace. You'll also visit Delft, one of the oldest cities in Holland and home of the Delft pottery factory, famous for its blue-and-white porcelain. Lunch is included. Some tours include a stop at Aalsmeer to view the flower auction, or a stop at Madurodam, a miniature reproduction of Holland's greatest landmarks.

Traditional Fishing Villages (4 hr.; $52): This bus-and-walking tour visits the quaint towns of Marken, Monnikendam, and Volendam. Highlights include views of the lush countryside, cobblestone streets with colorful homes, boat-filled harbors, and a visit to a cheese factory.

ON YOUR OWN: WITHIN WALKING DISTANCE

Much of Amsterdam's pleasure arises from just being in it, so we suggest wandering almost aimlessly—keeping some idea of the city's highlights in mind, sure, but not to the extent it distracts you from the vibrant street life going on all around you.

Let's triangulate from **Centraal Station,** near the cruise docks. When you step out the station's main entrance, you're facing south toward the City Center, which is laid out around you along four concentric semicircles of canals: Singel, Herengracht, Keizersgracht, and Prinsengracht. Along these canals, 16th- and 17th-century merchants lived in elegant homes, most of which are still standing. Connecting these canals are many smaller canals and streets radiating outward and effectively dividing the city into an archipelago of tiny islands linked by bridges. Farther out, the **Singelgracht** canal marks the boundary of the Old City—an area so compact that a fit person should be able to walk across it in about 30 minutes.

The heavily touristed **Damrak** street leads from Centraal Station to the main central square, called the **Dam.** This is the center of the city's oldest section, encompassing the main downtown attractions and shopping areas, as well as the city's famed **Red Light District,** the warren of streets around Oudezijds Achterburgwal and Oudezijds Voorburgwal. The easiest way in is on Damstraat, beside the Krasnapolsky Hotel on the Dam. Once you're in, you'll know it: There really are red lights, the ladies beckon from their parlor windows, peep-shows and theaters advertise just what you'd expect, and shops sell every kind of device, apparel, and video you can imagine. It's kind of like a sex-themed Disney World, where tourists mingle happily with folks who really are there to sample the pleasures. The main streets are perfectly safe, though keep a hand on your wallet.

Okay, back to the other sites. On the Dam, the 17th-century **Koninklijk Paleis** (Royal Palace; ✆ **020/620-4060;** www.koninklijkhuis.nl) was originally the city hall and was converted into a royal residence by Napoleon in 1808, when he came to Amsterdam. Decorated in the Empire Style, it is still used for receptions and official ceremonies by the Queen. When not in such use, it's open to the public and hosts exhibitions highlighting one of its historical or artistic features. Admission is 5€ ($7).

Not far to the west is one of Amsterdam's most edifying sights, the **Anne Frankhuis (Anne Frank House),** Prinsengracht 263 (✆ **020/556-7105;** www.annefrank.nl). The young Jewish girl Anne Frank wrote her diary here while hiding from the Nazis between 1942 and 1944. There's a small exhibit on the Holocaust, and you can view the famous attic where Anne and her family lived. The house is so small that groups are not allowed, so you can visit only on your own (and not on shore excursions). Admission is 7.50€ ($11).

South of the Dam, the **Amsterdams Historisch Museum (Amsterdam Historical Museum),** Nieuwezijds Voorburgwal 357 (✆ **020/523-1822;** www.ahm.nl), will put everything you're seeing in Amsterdam in context. Gallery by gallery, century by century, you learn how a small fishing village founded around A.D. 1200 became a major sea power and trading center. The focus is on the city's 17th-century Golden Age, when Amsterdam was the world's wealthiest city, and some of the most interesting exhibits explore the trades that made it rich. Admission is 7€ ($9.80).

Continuing south, you'll find the city's famous **Bloemenmarkt (Flower Market),** on the Singel canal at Muntplein, where awnings stretch across a row of permanently moored barges full of brightly colored blossoms, bulbs, and potted plants. It's the city's largest and most colorful plant assortment, and one of its most heart-lifting experiences. If you want to buy bulbs, be certain they bear the obligatory certificate clearing them for entry into the United States.

Farther out, beyond the Singelgracht at the end of Nieuwe Spiegelstraat, the wide green **Museumplein** is home to the city's three most famous museums: the

Rotterdam, Netherlands

A few cruise lines—notably Holland America, whose roots are here and whose flagship is named for the city—make stops in the bustling Dutch port of Rotterdam, located about 30 minutes from The Hague and an hour from Amsterdam. Bombed to bits during World War II, the city re-created itself afterward as a totally modern urban center full of contemporary architecture and home to the busiest commercial seaport in the world. Only two parts of the city—Delfshaven (Delft Harbor) and Oude Haven (Old Harbor)—retain their prewar look. **Delfshaven** was where the Pilgrims said their last prayers before setting off for the New World aboard the *Speedwell,* a ship that proved so unseaworthy that the Pilgrims traded up to the *Mayflower* once they reached England. Today Delftshaven is full of art dealers, antiques and gift shops, and museums. **Oude Haven** is where Rotterdam's huge port got its start. Today it's a busy entertainment district full of restaurants, bars, and clubs, along with some historic vessels.

Shore excursions out of Rotterdam are generally offered to Amsterdam, the Hague, Delft, and other locations described in "The Best Cruise Line Shore Excursions" in the Amsterdam section.

Rijksmuseum, the Van Gogh, and the Stedelijk. The **Rijksmuseum,** Jan Luijkenstraat 1 (© **020/670-7047;** www.rijksmuseum.nl), houses the largest art collection in the Netherlands, encompassing the period from the 15th century to the 19th. The collection includes 22 Rembrandts (*Night Watch* is the most famous), plus works by Vermeer, Frans Hals, Alvert Cuyp, Jan Steen, and many others. Admission is 10€ ($14). The nearby **Van Gogh Museum,** Paulus Potterstraat 7 (© **020/570-5200;** www3.vangoghmuseum.nl), houses more than 200 paintings by Vincent van Gogh, along with nearly every sketch, print, etching, and piece of correspondence the artist ever produced. There's also a collection of van Gogh's 19th-century friends and contemporaries. Admission is 10€ ($14). The **Stedelijk** modern art museum, the third of the Museumplein's showcases, is closed until December 2009. Their temporary home, on the second and third floors of the Post CS-building, Oosterdokskade 5 (© **020/5732911;** www.stedelijk.nl), displays temporary exhibits but none of the museum's extensive permanent collection. Admission is 9€ ($13).

LOCAL FLAVORS

Distinctive Dutch dishes include **white asparagus** (in season in May), **raw herring** (in May or early June), and **Zeeland oysters and mussels** (in Sept). The city's restaurant choices span the international spectrum. The Indonesian **rijsttafel** (a sampling of various dishes) has been Holland's favorite feast ever since the United East India Company sea captains introduced it to Amsterdam's wealthy burghers in the 17th century. A good place to try this dining experience is **Kantjil & de Tijger,** Spuistraat 291–293 (© **020/620-0994;** www.kantjil.nl), where a rijsttafel for two will cost you 42€ to 50€ ($59–70), dinner only.

For the ultimate street food, stop in at one of the many, many places you'll see in the shopping areas selling **french fries** (aka *patates frites*). What makes them distinctive is the mind-boggling array of toppings, which includes mayonnaise, curry, and Indonesian saté.

And if you care to sip a little tea (wink, wink), try **The Rookies,** Korte Leidsedwarsstraat 145–147 (*©* **020/694-2353;** www.rookies.nl); **Borderline,** Amstelstraat 37 (*©* **020/622-0540**); and the **Bulldog** chain (www.bulldog.nl), which has branches around the city. The **Bulldog Rockshop** is close to Centraal Station and the cruise docks, at Singel 12 (*©* **020/627-8900**). The **Bulldog Mack** is at Oudezijds Voorburgwal 132 (*©* **020/627-0295**). Each coffee shop has a menu listing different types of hashish and marijuana, and the THC content of each.

SHOPPING

The city's busiest pedestrian-only shopping stretch is **Kalverstraat,** one end of which is at the Dam and the other end of which is the Muntplein traffic hub. In between, Kalverstraat is a hodgepodge of shopping possibilities, from punky boutiques to athletic-shoe emporiums, bookstores, fur salons, and record stores, interspersed with everything in the way of fast food. Parallel to Kalverstraat (and also running from the Dam to Muntplein) is **Rokin,** where you'll find art galleries, antiques stores, and elegant fashion boutiques.

Next to the Rijksmuseum, 4 blocks of **Nieuwe Spiegelstraat and Spiegelgracht** make up one of Europe's finest antiques-hunting grounds.

For Amsterdam's most colorful shopping experience, head for the **Waterlooplein Flea Market,** on Waterlooplein (Waterloo Square), less than 1km (½ mile) east of the Flower Market. It's a real flea market, selling every kind of junk, from old CDs to clothes, antiques, nuts and bolts, and whatever the sellers could round up that week. Closed Sunday.

2 Berlin & the Ports of Hamburg, Rostock & Warnemünde, Germany

With its field of new skyscrapers, hip clubs, and fashion boutiques, postmillennium Berlin has recast itself as Europe's capital of cool, reconciling itself to its notorious history and moving with confidence into its future. The city dates back to at least the 13th century, and in later years it served as the capital of Prussia, the German Empire, the Weimar Republic, and Hitler's Third Reich, during whose collapse it was almost bombed out of existence. Today structures of steel and glass tower over streets where before only piles of rubble lay, and parks and gardens are again lush. Nonetheless, even in the daily whirl of working, shopping, and dining along the Ku'damm, Berliners encounter reminders of less happy days: At the end of the street stands the Kaiser Wilhelm Memorial Church, with only the shell of the old neo-Romanesque bell tower remaining.

Before the war, the section of the city that became East Berlin was the cultural and political heart of Germany, where the best museums, finest churches, and most important boulevards lay. In the postwar rebuilding, East Berliners turned to restoring their museums, theaters, and landmarks (especially in the Berlin-Mitte section), while walled-in West Berliners built entirely new museums and cultural centers. This contrast between the two parts of city is still evident, though east and west are coming together more and more within the immense, fascinating whole that is Berlin.

Because the city is landlocked, most ships dock in the port cities of **Hamburg, Warnemünde,** and **Rostock,** and offer shore excursions to Berlin, which lies about 3 hours away by train.

LANGUAGE & CURRENCY   German is the country's official language, but **English** is commonly spoken, particularly by young people. The official currency is the **euro** (€). The exchange rate at press time was $1 = .72€ (1€ = $1.40).

THE BEST CRUISE LINE SHORE EXCURSIONS

Berlin City Tour (12–13 hr.; $249–$325): The itinerary includes the fascinating Checkpoint Charlie Museum, which provides an overview of how the Berlin Wall divided East and West Berlin for more than 40 years. The display here includes descriptions of how people tried to escape from East Berlin (many didn't make it). Other highlights are a visit to the impressive 19th-century Berlin Cathedral; a photo stop at famous Brandenburg Gate; and a tour of lavish Charlottenburg Palace, built as a summer palace in 1695 for the first Prussian king (it was heavily damaged during World War II but rebuilt in the 1950s). The tour includes lunch and shopping time.

Berlin Jewish Heritage Tour (12 hr.; $285–$315): This excursion combines a Berlin city tour with a drive through the former East Berlin to visit the New Synagogue/Centrum Judaicum, which offers a look at historic and modern Jewish life in the city. The tour passes the Jewish school and the Jewish cemetery, a reminder of Nazi violence in Berlin. Also visited are several memorials and a train station used by the Nazis for deportations.

Berlin's Allied Life (12 hr.; $275–$310): This tour emphasizes the 45 years of Allied presence in Berlin. Included is Glienicker Bridge, where American and Russian spies were exchanged; the former American residential areas of Berlin; and a stop at the new Allied Museum, where displays show the city from the Allied point of view. Lunch is served at Schoneberg Town Hall, where John F. Kennedy made his famous Berlin speech.

LOCAL FLAVORS

Germany isn't the first country that comes to mind when thinking about great food, but at least you know the beer will be good. Some specialties you might want to try in that regard are ***Berliner weisse,*** a wheat beer made with a dash of raspberry or woodruff syrup, and the extra-dark ***doppelbock.*** You might also try typical Berlin desserts like *Kugelhupf,* a marvelous coffeecake, and *Käsekuchen* cheesecake.

HAMBURG

Located on the River Elbe, Hamburg is known as both "the Venice of the North" for its numerous bridges (2,100 of them) and "Sin City" for its famous Red Light district, **St. Pauli.** Though the 1,200-year-old city was nearly destroyed during World War II, some buildings that date back to medieval times survived in the Old Hamburg area, while a new city of parks and impressive buildings grew out of the rubble all around. The Port of Hamburg is the world's fifth largest, a center of trade on the Continent since 1189.

Hamburg's baroque **Hauptkirche St. Michaelis (St. Michael's Church),** Krayenkamp 4C, Michaeliskirchplatz (© **040/3767-8100**), is Hamburg's favorite landmark. Take the elevator or climb the 449 steps to the top of the hammered-copper tower for a sweeping view. The crypt, one of the largest in Europe, contains the tombs of famous citizens, including noted composer Carl Philipp Emanuel Bach, son of Johann Sebastian Bach. Entrance to the church is free, but use of the stairs or elevator costs 2.50€ ($3.50).

Berlin

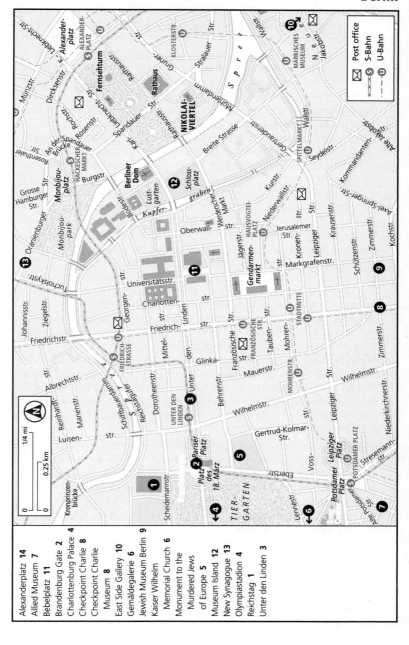

A (Very) Quick Guide to the Landmarks of Berlin

Because almost everyone going to Berlin from Hamburg, Warnemünde, or Rostock is doing so via shore excursion and will thus get a narration of the top sights, we haven't gone into depth on them here. Here's a very quick overview, though, just to put things into perspective.

Checkpoint Charlie: The most famous Cold War crossing point between East and West Berlin stood at the intersection of Friedrichstrasse with Zimmerstrasse and Mauerstrasse. Today a re-creation of the official booth stands on the spot. Nearby is the **Checkpoint Charlie Museum** (www.mauermuseum.de), whose displays tell the history of the Berlin Wall and those who tried to cross from east to west.

The Brandenburg Gate: Erected between 1788 and 1791 on a design that mimics the entrance to the Acropolis in Athens, this enormous ceremonial gateway is the symbol of Berlin. During the Cold War it was part of the Berlin Wall, but today it's restored and constitutes the grand western end of the . . .

Unter den Linden: Eastern Berlin's most celebrated street was the cultural heart of Berlin before World War II and is named for the Linden trees that grow in two long rows along its length. Today it's lined with restored buildings and has a lovely pedestrian path down its center. Off the south side of the street, the beautiful **Bebelplatz** square was the location of the Nazis' infamous 1933 book-burning ceremony. Today an underground room lined with empty bookcases commemorates the event. It's viewable through a glass plate set into the square's paving stones.

The Reichstag: On February 17, 1933, a fire broke out in the German Parliament building. Though it was almost certainly set by the Nazis, Hitler blamed the communists and used the event as an excuse to begin mass arrests, leading to the death of German democracy. Today the neo-Renaissance building is once again home to Germany's Parliament. It's located just north of the Brandenburg Gate.

Museum Island (www.museen-berlin.de): Located at the eastern end of the Unter den Linden, Museum Island is home to five museums, including the **Pergamon Museum,** displaying classical, near-Eastern, and Islamic antiquities and art, and the **Alte Nationalgalerie,** known for its collection of 19th-century German and French Impressionists.

The East Side Gallery (www.eastsidegallery.com): One of the few large, surviving sections of the Berlin Wall stands along the banks of the Spree River

If you're looking for the opposite of a church, head to **St. Pauli,** Hamburg's old Red Light district and now the nightlife center of the city. The district is split by its most famous street, the **Reeperbahn,** neon lit and dazzling, offering all sorts of pleasures: cafes, sex shows, bars, discos, and music halls. The area is located west of the cruise dock.

near the city's east railway station. About 1.3km (.75 mile) long, it's covered with more than 100 paintings by international artists, celebrating the end of Cold War separation.

Kaiser Wilhelm Memorial Church: Dedicated in 1895, this once grand red-sandstone church was mostly destroyed by British bombing in 1945, and the ruins of its belfry have stood ever since as a reminder of the horrors of war.

The New Synagogue (www.cjudaicum.de): Once the largest synagogue in Germany, this 1866 temple was vandalized in 1938 during *Kristallnacht* and blasted by Allied bombs in 1945, but has been partially rebuilt in recent years.

Jewish Museum Berlin (www.juedisches-museum-berlin.de): Built on a design by architect Daniel Liebeskind, this museum covers the whole of German-Jewish history, from its achievements through the horrors of the Nazi years.

Monument to the Murdered Jews of Europe: Just south of the Brandenburg Gate, Berlin's Holocaust memorial takes the form of 2,711 gravestonelike concrete columns arranged in rows across a sloping 1.9 hectare (4.7-acre) site. Below ground is an exhibit documenting Nazi crimes against humanity.

Allied Museum (www.alliiertenmuseum.de): This museum documents the Western powers' presence in Berlin from 1945 to 1994, with exhibits that include the original guardhouse from Checkpoint Charlie.

The Gemäldegalerie (Picture Gallery; www.smb.spk-berlin.de): One of Germany's greatest art museums, featuring German and other European masters, including Dürer, Raphael, Titian, Botticelli, van Eyck, Bosch, Brueghel, and Rembrandt.

Olympiastadion (www.olympiastadion-berlin.de): Built for Hitler's 1936 Olympics, this was the site where African American Jesse Owens showed *der fuhrer* who was boss. It's still used for sporting and cultural events.

Charlottenburg Palace: One of the finest examples of baroque architecture in Germany, this massive palace was commissioned by Sophie Charlotte, wife of King Friedrich I of Prussia, and later named for her memory.

Alexanderplatz: Named for Russian Czar Alexander I, this square was the center of activity in the old East Berlin. Neon lights and bright murals now coexist alongside the dull and fading GDR-era structures, and street musicians and small markets have given the area new life.

COMING ASHORE   Though the cruise port is only about 1km (½ mile) from the city center, it's in an area that's undergoing tremendous construction, so most people take a **taxi** or cruise line **shuttle bus** into town, which is busy but walkable. Metered fares for taxis begin at about 2.50€ ($3.50).

ROSTOCK & WARNEMÜNDE

Set on a wide and navigable estuary of the Warnow River, **Rostock** was founded in 1218 and spent the Cold War serving as East Germany's largest and busiest seaport, built on a scale to rival Hamburg. The town still bustles with maritime activity, though its importance has declined since German reunification. **Warnemünde** is a seaport town located about 8km (5 miles) north of Rostock.

During World War II, Rostock was blasted by British bombers, but some historic buildings were restored at great expense, often from little more than piles of rubble. The city's most photographed street, **Kröpeliner-Strasse** is a pleasant, pedestrian-only promenade lined with shops and restored old buildings constructed between 1500 and 1850. It runs parallel to the more much less charming Lange Strasse, Rostock's principal thoroughfare. The **St-Marien-Kirche (St. Mary's Church),** Am Ziegenmarkt (© **0381/4923396**), set on a narrow side street off Lange Strasse, is another of the buildings that survived war damage. It's one of the finest (and largest) ecclesiastical structures of the Baltic world. Inside are an enormous organ dating from 1770 and an astronomical clock originally built in the late 1400s and reconfigured in 1643. You can also climb the church's tower for a panoramic city view. Admission is 1.50€ ($2.10). Those into nautical history will want to swing by the **Schiffahrtsmuseum,** August-Bebel-Strasse 1 (© **0381/4-44-37-41**), which houses exhibits related to the town's nautical history, from the Vikings on up to the early 20th century. Admission is 5€ ($7).

There's not much to do in small Warnemünde besides sit at the long white beach and cute old port area. Taxis and a train with frequent service provide transportation to Rostock. The train station is located very close to the cruise port, and a round-trip ticket costs only a few euros.

3 Copenhagen, Denmark

The royal city of **Copenhagen** was founded in 1167 and is the capital of the oldest kingdom in the world. It's also the largest city in Scandinavia, with a population of more than 1.5 million. Here visitors enjoy a blend of history and culture, lots of green city parks, and much charm. This is a lively city where people like to have fun, especially at **Tivoli Gardens,** an extraordinary amusement park that's a must-visit attraction. In the summer, Copenhageners come outdoors (the winters are long), and that means lots of **outdoor cafes,** as well as people sunbathing in the city's parks. The city's most famous resident was fairy-tale author Hans Christian Andersen, whose memory is embodied at the famous *Little Mermaid* statue.

The name Copenhagen comes from the word *københavn,* meaning "merchants' harbor." Much of the city is located on the water, be it the sea or canals. The entrance to the city through The Sound (the Øresund) that separates Denmark and Sweden is worth being out on deck for.

LANGUAGE & CURRENCY   The official language is **Danish,** but **English** is commonly spoken and widely understood, especially by young people. The **Danish krone** (kroner in its plural form) is the official currency, and the rate of exchange at press time was $1 = 5.16DKK (1DKK = 19¢).

COMING ASHORE   It's about a 20-minute walk from the pier to the Royal Theater area; add another 15 to 20 minutes to get to Tivoli.

GETTING AROUND   You can easily cover Old Copenhagen, with its narrow cobbled streets and old houses, on foot. Especially pedestrian friendly is the Strøget,

Europe's longest and oldest walking street. If you want a **taxi,** they're available at the pier. Be sure to get one with a meter and be aware that rates are not cheap, though tips are included in the meter price. The flag drops at 19DKK ($3.60). The city also has an excellent **bus** system that runs on a zone pricing scheme (for information, call *C* **36/13-14-00).** There are also places to **rent bikes** throughout the city. A rental arrangement allows you to pick up a bike from a rack and return it to the same place for a refundable deposit of 20DKK ($3.80); see **www.bycyklen.dk** for more info.

THE BEST CRUISE LINE SHORE EXCURSIONS

City Tour (3 hr.; $44–$59): Visit Christiansborg, the seat of Denmark's government since 1918, and Christiansborg Palace. Drive past the Stock Exchange, with its stunning spire of entwining dragons' tails, built by King Christian IV; the Danish Royal Theater, home of the Royal Ballet Troupe, built in 1824; and Nyhavn, the one-time sailor's district. Stop briefly outside Amalienborg Palace to photograph the Queen's guards. Then check out the *Little Mermaid* statue. You'll also pass Tivoli Gardens; the Glyptotek Art Museum; the Round Tower; Copenhagen Cathedral; and the Gammeltorv, a marketplace and the oldest part of the city.

Copenhagen's Royal Palaces (4 hr.; $72): This tour includes Rosenborg Castle, home of the Danish crown jewels; and Christiansborg Palace, a massive 12th-century fortress surrounded by canals on three sides.

North Zealand & Helsingør (7 hr.; $145): After a brief city tour of Copenhagen, travel by bus through the Danish countryside to Frederiksborg Castle in Hillerod. This magnificent Renaissance castle is now home to the National Museum of History. In the small chapel, you will find the oldest organ in the world, still in use today. Next stop is Fredensborg Palace, summer residence of the Royal Family. Continue north to the town of Helsingør (Elsinore), where you'll explore the courtyard and ramparts of Kronborg Castle, which dates back to the 16th century. The castle is better known as Hamlet's Castle, immortalized when Shakespeare chose it as the setting for his play. Return to Copenhagen along the coastline known as the Danish Riviera.

Copenhagen by Bike (3 hr.; $87): Cycle with a guide past the city's harborfront and yacht marina. Stop to pay your respects to the *Little Mermaid* before viewing Amalienborg Palace. Continue to Nyhaven Canal, and then view the exterior of the Royal Theatre and Rosenborg Castle, the latter featuring verdant park grounds. You'll pass by Nyboder, a historic neighborhood of yellow row houses built for members of the Royal Navy in the 1630s; it's still occupied by military families. The ride covers about 7.3km (4½ miles).

ON YOUR OWN: WITHIN WALKING DISTANCE

Located no more than a 10-minute walk from the cruise ship docks, on rocks along the shore, the *Little Mermaid* **(Den Lille Havfrue)** is a life-size bronze statue of the character from Hans Christian Andersen's fairy tale of the same name. Unveiled in 1913, it has been attacked several times over the years, losing an arm in one misadventure and getting beheaded in another, but since the original mold exists, missing body parts can be recast.

Amalienborg Palace, Christian VIII's Palace (*C* **33/12-21-86;** www.ses.dk), is within easy walking distance of the ship's pier. The palace's four 18th-century French-style rococo mansions open onto a gorgeous square, guarded by the Royal Guard in black bearskin hats. Look for the flag indicating whether the Danish Royal Family is in residence. If you're lucky, you'll see the guards suddenly snap to attention when a large door opens and one of the princes drives out in a Land Rover. A few of the official and private rooms are open to the public. Admission is 75DKK ($14).

Keep walking a few more blocks and you'll come to **Nyhavn,** once the city's Red Light District and now a popular cafe spot and scenic attraction, with colorful historic canalfront buildings. From here you can take a **barge ride along Nyhavn Canal.** The comfortable little crafts leave from the heart of town and pass much of historic Copenhagen in less than 2 hours. Fares start at 45DKK ($8.55) adults, 20DKK ($3.80) kids.

ON YOUR OWN: BEYOND THE PORT AREA

Tivoli Gardens, Vesterbrogade 3 (© **33/15-10-01;** www.tivoli.dk), always surprises first-time visitors, as it really is as much garden as amusement park. The gardens offer thousands of flowers, and the fun includes a merry-go-round of tiny Viking ships, pinball arcades, slot machines, shooting galleries, bumper cars, and a Ferris wheel of hot-air balloons. There are more than two dozen restaurants located in an Arabian-style fantasy palace, plus a lake with ducks, swans, and boats. Entertainment includes parades, regimental band concerts, and pantomime. Admission is 79DKK ($15); multiride ticket 170DKK ($32).

Art lovers will want to check out the **Ny Carlsberg Glyptotek,** Dantes Plads 7 (© **33/41-81-41;** www.glyptoteket.dk), located near Tivoli Gardens and founded in the 19th century by Carl Jacobsen, who also started the Carlsberg Brewing Company. It is one of Scandinavia's most important museums, with a collection that highlights French and Danish art, mostly from the 19th century. Sculptures by Rodin can be found on the ground floor, and works of the Impressionists, including van Gogh's *Landscape from St. Rémy,* are located on the upper floors. Admission is 50DKK ($9.50).

Those who are into all things royal will find no shortage of palaces in Copenhagen. **Christiansborg Palace,** Christiansborg Slotsplads (© **33/92-64-92;** www.ses.dk), housing the Parliament House and the Supreme Court, is where the queen officially receives guests in the Royal Reception Chamber. The baroque structure is impressive, even by European standards, and you can tour such richly decorated rooms as the Throne Room, Queen's Library, and banqueting hall. Under the palace, you can visit the well-preserved ruins of the 1167 castle of Bishop Absalon, the founder of Copenhagen. Admission is 35DKK ($6.65). The redbrick **Rosenborg Castle,** Øster Voldgade 4A (© **33/15-32-86;** www.rosenborgslot.dk), was built in 1607 by King Christian IV as a summer residence and was converted into a museum in the 19th century. It houses the Danish crown jewels, costumes, and other impressive royal memorabilia. Admission is 70DKK ($13).

For a little something different, visit the **Museum Erotica,** within walking distance of Tivoli at Købmagergade 24 (© **33/12-03-11;** www.museum-erotica.dk). The collection surveys erotica through the ages and includes Etruscan drawings, Greek vases, and Indian miniatures depicting sexual activity, plus information about the sex lives of luminaries like Freud, Nietzsche, and Duke Ellington. Admission is 70DKK ($13).

LOCAL FLAVORS

Copenhagen's favorite dish at lunch is *smørrebrød,* open-faced sandwiches that are practically a national institution. Our favorite is piled with tiny Danish shrimp, but other popular versions include sliced pork loin, roast beef, and liver paste. Wash the sandwiches down with a local Carlsberg or Tuborg beer.

Copenhagen

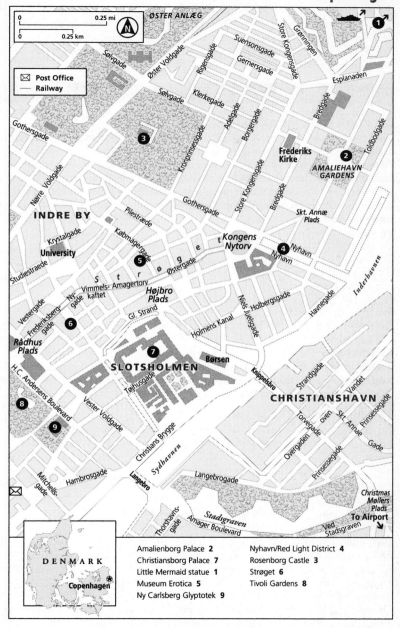

ØSTER ANLÆG

0   0.25 mi
0   0.25 km

⊠ Post Office
---- Railway

Søvgade
Øster Voldgade
Suensonsgade
Store Kongensgade
Grønningen
Rigensgade
Gernersgade
Esplanaden

Sølvgade
Klerkegade
Adelgade
Borgergade
Bredgade
Toldbodgade

Gothersgade
Kronprinsessegade

3

Frederiks
Kirke

2
AMALIEHAVN
GARDENS

Nørre Voldgade
Gothersgade
Store Kongensgade
Bredgade
Skt. Annæ
Plads

INDRE BY
Pilestræde
Krystalgade
Købmagergade
University
Kongens
Nytorv

4 Nyhavn
Nyhavn

Studiestræde
S t r ø g e t
Østergade

Inderhavnen

Vimmels- Amagertorv
Nyr. gade kaftet
Højbro
Plads

Niels Holbergsgade

Vestergade
Frederiksberg gade
6
Gl. Strand
Holmens Kanal
Havnegade

**Rådhus
Plads**

H.C. Andersens Boulevard
7
SLOTSHOLMEN
Tøjhusgade
Børsen

Knippelsbro
Strandgade
Vandet

8
Vester Voldgade

CHRISTIANSHAVN

9

Tonegade
oven
Skt. Annæ
Prinsessegade
Gade

Christians Brygge
Sydhavnen

Overgaden
Prinsessegade

Mitchells-
gade
Hambrosgade
Langebro
Langebrogade

Christmas
Møllers
Plads
To Airport

Stadsgraven
Amager Boulevard
Thorshavns-
gade
Ved
Stadsgraven

DENMARK

Copenhagen

Amalienborg Palace **2**   Nyhavn/Red Light District **4**
Christiansborg Palace **7**   Rosenborg Castle **3**
Little Mermaid statue **1**   Strøget **6**
Museum Erotica **5**   Tivoli Gardens **8**
Ny Carlsberg Glyptotek **9**

SHOPPING

Much of the shopping action in Copenhagen takes place on **Strøget,** the pedestrian street in the heart of the capital, lined with shops and restaurants. Strøget begins as Frederiksberggade, north of Rådhuspladsen, and winds to Østergade, which opens onto Kongens Nytorv.

4 Helsinki, Finland

Founded by Swedes in 1550, Helsinki became Finland's capital in 1812 and continued in the role while the country was an autonomous Grand Duchy of Russia and after it gained independence in 1917. In addition to being a business and industrial center, Helsinki today is a sophisticated, intellectual town with a major university and many cultural institutions. It offers tourists a clean environment with great museums, nice harbor views, and lots of shopping. Surrounded by water on three sides and including in its territory a number of islands, the city is notable for its parks and squares and for its neoclassical city buildings, dating from the 19th century and planned out by German-born architect Carl Ludvig Engel.

COMING ASHORE   Cruise ships dock at the city's commercial port, about a 15-minute taxi or shuttle ride from the heart of Helsinki. Most ships have free buses going back and forth, generally dropping passengers off at Kauppatori Market Square (at the harbor end of the Esplanade) or the Swedish Theatre (at the upper end of the Esplanade). There is not much to see or do near the pier.

GETTING AROUND   Once you're downtown, the main attractions are easy to get to on foot. Helsinki also has an efficient transportation network that includes buses, hop-on/hop-off tour buses, trams, subway (metro), and ferries. **Taxis** are available at the pier, with fares starting at 5€ ($7).

LANGUAGE & CURRENCY   Finnish, the country's official language, is one tough nut to crack. Luckily, English is commonly spoken, too. Finland uses the **euro** (€) as its currency. The exchange rate at press time was $1 = .72€ (1€ = $1.40).

THE BEST CRUISE LINE SHORE EXCURSIONS

Art & Architecture (4 hr.; $59–$85): This tour combines a city tour with a visit to the charming Finnish countryside, including the coastal road, woodlands, and lake country. Visit Hvittrask, once the home of the famous Finnish architects Eliel Saarinen, Armas Lindgren, and Herman Gesellius, and now an exhibition center for Finnish art and handicrafts. Continue on to Tarvaspaa, the former home and studio of Finland's national painter, Akseli Gallen-Kallela, in a parklike setting right on the sea. Gallen-Kallela's works and the story of his colorful life are on display here, as are exhibits by other famous artists depicting Finnish life.

City Tour (3 hr.; $47–$55): Pass the famous Uspenski Orthodox Cathedral, with its brilliant gold onion domes, en route to the Senate Square, site of several important buildings attributed to the neoclassic architect Carl Ludwig Engel. On Mannerheim Street, view the Parliament House, National Museum, and Finlandia Hall, designed by the famous architect Alvar Aalto. Continue through lovely residential districts to Olympic Stadium, site of the 1952 Olympic Games. You'll pass the Opera House, completed in 1993; stop at Temppeliaukio Rock Church, a unique house of worship blasted into solid rock and topped by a copper dome; and make a photo stop at

Central Helsinki

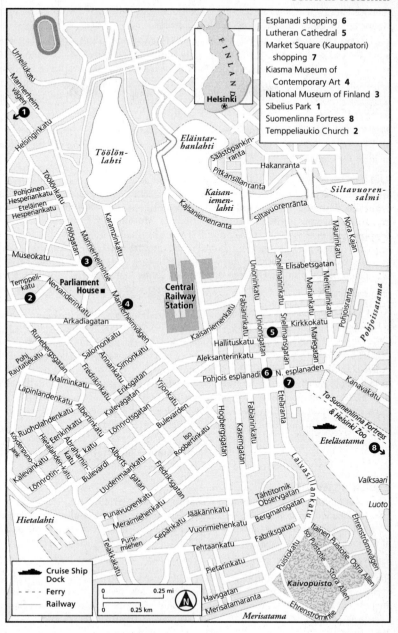

Esplanadi shopping **6**
Lutheran Cathedral **5**
Market Square (Kauppatori) shopping **7**
Kiasma Museum of Contemporary Art **4**
National Museum of Finland **3**
Sibelius Park **1**
Suomenlinna Fortress **8**
Temppeliaukio Church **2**

Helsinki

Urheilukatu
Mannerheim-vägen

Helsinginkatu

Töölönkatu
Pohjoinen Hesperiankatu
Eteläinen Hesperiankatu

Museokatu

Temppeli-katu
Nervanderinkatu
Parliament House ■
Arkadiagatan

Runebergsgatan
Pohj Rautatiekatu
Malminkatu
Lapinlandenkatu
Ruoholahdenkatu
Köydenpuno- Kalevankatu Lönnrotin- Hietalahden- P. Eerikinkatu Abrahamin- puisto katu katu

Salomonkatu
Annankatu
Fredrikinkatu
Eriksgatan
Kalevagatan
Albertinkatu
Alberts
Bulevardi
Uudenmaankatu

Hietalahti

Simonkatu
Yrjönkatu
Lönnrotsgatan
Bulevarden
Iso Roobertinkatu
Fredriksgatan
Punavuorenkatu
Meraimiehenkatu
Pursi-miehen
Telakkakatu

Mannerheimintie
Mannerheimvägen

Töölön-lahti
Karamzinkatu

Eläintar-hanlahti

Kaisan-iemen-lahti
Kaisaniemenranta

Central Railway Station

Kaisaniemenkatu
Fabianinkatu
Hallituskatu
Aleksanterinkatu
Pohjois esplanadi **6** N. esplanaden **7**

Hööbergsgatan
Kaserngatan
Fabianinkatu
Eteläranta

Jääkärinkatu
Sepänkatu
Vuorimiehenkatu
Tehtaankatu
Pietarinkatu

Havsgatan
Merisatamaranta

Säästöpankin-ranta
Hakanranta
Pitkänsillanranta
Siltavuorenränta

Siltavuoren-salmi
Nora Kajan
Maurinkatu

Unioninkatu
Snellmaninkatu
Elisabetsgatan
Mariankatu
Merituliinkatu

Fabianinkatu
Unionsgatan
Snellmansgatan
Kirkkokatu
Mariegatan

Pohjoisranta
Pohjoissatama

To Suomenlinna Fortress & Helsinki Zoo
Kanavakatu
Eteläsatama

Valksaari
Luoto

Laivasillankatu
Tähtitornik Observgatan
Bergmansgatan
Fabriksgatan

Itäinen Puistotie Ostra Allén
Iso Puistotie Stora Allén
Puistokatu
Kaivopuisto
Ehrenströmsvägen
Itäinen Puistotie Ostra Allén
Ehrenströminte

Merisatama

Cruise Ship Dock
Ferry
Railway

0   0.25 mi
0   0.25 km
N

Sibelius Park, where you can photograph a monument constructed of 527 steel pipes honoring the great Finnish composer Jean Sibelius.

Porvoo & Highlights (7 hr.; $155): Drive 45 minutes along the picturesque, shipyard-lined coastal road to Porvoo, a popular artistic center that's the second-oldest town in Finland, dating back to 1346. Here you will visit the majestic 1418 medieval cathedral and walk along the cobblestone streets of the Old Quarter, with its ancient, multicolored wooden houses. The tour also does a brief tour of Helsinki and stops at Haikko Manor, one of the country's leading spas.

ON YOUR OWN: WITHIN WALKING DISTANCE

Unless you are on a ship that docks downtown, you will want to take the ship's shuttle into the city. The service is typically free.

ON YOUR OWN: BEYOND THE PORT AREA

Museum buffs who want to know more about Finland's history should head for the **National Museum of Finland,** Mannerheimintie 34 (𝄐 **09/4050-9544;** www. nba.fi). Admission is 6€ ($8.40). The **Kiasma Museum of Contemporary Art,** Mannerheiminaukio 2 (𝄐 **09/1733-6501;** www.kiasma.fi), is also worth a look-see, with its collection of post-1960 Finnish and international art. Admission is 6€ ($8.40). Classical music aficionados will definitely want to swing by **Sibelius Park** on Mechelininkatu (a long walk from downtown), home to an unusual monument featuring hundreds of steel pipes that pays homage to Jean Sibelius (1865–1957), Finland's most famous composer. Admission is free.

The Russian-designed Senate Square's prime attraction is historic **Lutheran Cathedral,** Unioninkatu 2–9, erected between 1830 and 1852. Another religious-oriented place worth visiting is the funky **Temppeliaukio Church,** Lutherinkatu 3, nicknamed "the Rock Church" because it is carved out of solid rock. Admission to the churches is free.

Accessible in 15 minutes by ferry, **Suomenlinna Fortress,** Suomenlinna (𝄐 **09/ 684-1880;** www.suomenlinna.fi), is known as the Gibraltar of the North. It dates back to 1748, when Finland was part of Sweden, and occupies five interconnected islands that guard maritime approaches to Helsinki. The main attractions include a well-preserved bastioned fort on the island of Kustaanmiekka, and another, larger fortress on Susisaari, where you will also find a number of parks, squares, and gardens. Admission to the fortress museum is 5€ ($7).

LOCAL FLAVORS

Typical ingredients of a Finnish *smörgåsbord* included herring, lightly salted fish and roe, smoked and cold fish dishes, reindeer meat, and desserts, including fresh berries. Crayfish are in season late July to September (you'll need a bib when you eat them). If a picnic is your fancy, get the fixings at Market Square.

SHOPPING

The city's **waterfront** is bustling, not only with boats and ferries, but with markets as well—some vendors even sell their wares from boats. Other good places to shop include the **Esplanadi,** for more upscale Finnish design offerings; and **Market Square (Kauppatori),** an open-air market where locals and tourists alike shop for flowers, fresh fruit, fish (herring is a local delicacy), crafts, and souvenirs.

5 London, England

London is America's favorite foreign city, a place that's both comfortingly familiar and appealingly "other." We speak the same language, but there's no question we're from very different worlds.

Though there's a certain eternal quality to the idea of London—biggest city in Europe, capital of the British Empire, Houses of Parliament, Big Ben, the Beefeaters, Churchill, *God Save the Queen*—the city has by no means sat still for the past half-century. Today techno music's pouring out of Victorian pubs, experimental theater is popping up on stages built for Shakespeare, chefs are putting a creative spin on traditionally bland Brit-food, and an international feel brought by big business and immigration is changing the very nature of Britishness. It's becoming easier to find a café au lait and a croissant than a scone and a cup of tea, and for every bowler hat you're as apt to find two baseball caps and a turban.

If this sea change gives you more worries than thrills, rest assured that traditional London still exists, basically intact under the veneer of hip. From high tea almost anywhere to the Changing of the Guard at Buckingham Palace, the city still abounds with the culture and charm of days gone by.

Exploring London fully can be a bit of a challenge on limited cruise time. Even in the 18th century, Daniel Defoe found London "stretched out in buildings, straggling, confused, out of all shape, uncompact and unequal; neither long nor broad, round nor square." The actual City of London proper is 2.6 sq. km (1 sq. mile) of very expensive real estate around the Bank of England. All of the gargantuan rest of the city is made up of separate villages, boroughs, and corporations, each with its own mayor and administration. Together, however, they add up to a mammoth metropolis.

Luckily, whether you're looking for Big Ben or Harrods department store, only the heart of London's huge territory need concern you—and it's one of the most fascinating places on earth. Just get yourself to the Trafalgar Square/Westminster area and walk in any direction. Buckingham Palace, Hyde Park, and Kensington Gardens lie to the west; the British Museum and Piccadilly Circus (the city's famously crowded, neon-lit crossroads) are to the north; and Big Ben, the Houses of Parliament, and Westminster Abbey are due south. With every step, you'll feel the tremendous influence this city exerted over global culture at the height of its power, and the influence it once again wields via finance, fashion, film, music, and just about everything else. London once again stands at the cutting edge, just as it did in the swinging '60s.

COMING ASHORE   Some small ships (such as those operated by Seabourn, Regent Seven Seas, and Silversea) actually sail up the Thames and dock adjacent to Tower Bridge, opposite the Tower of London. Other ships dock at farther-out port towns, including **Southampton, Dover, Portsmouth,** and **Harwich,** all a longish bus ride from London.

GETTING AROUND   Once you're in London, getting around is not difficult at all. The **Underground** or **Tube** (subway) runs on a zone system, with the average price for a single trip in Central London around £4 ($8.30). You save significantly by picking up a 1-day, 2-zone pass, which costs £6.60 ($14) and also covers London's famous red **double-decker buses.** A single bus trip costs £2 ($4.15). Tube and bus maps are available at all Tube stations, or you can download them at **www.londontransport. co.uk.** You can also call the 24-hour **travel hot line** (© 020/7222-1234) for

London

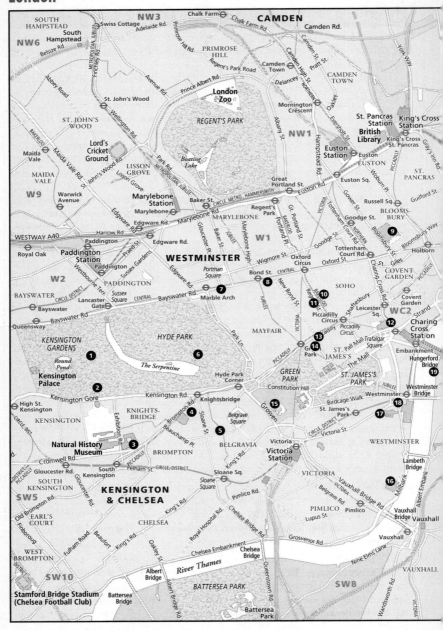

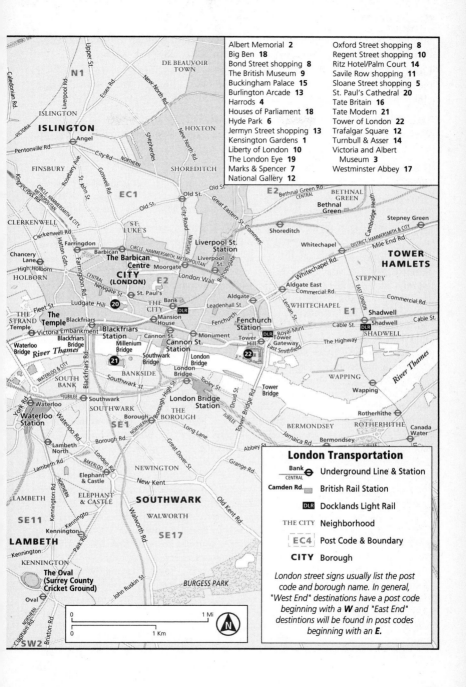

information on how to get from one point to another. In addition to public transport, there are **taxis** everywhere, though these can be a very expensive option.

LANGUAGE & CURRENCY   English (of the Queen's variety) is the language of the land. The British unit of currency is the **pound sterling** (£), which is divided into 100 pence. The exchange rate at press time was $1 = 48 pence (£1 = $2.07).

THE BEST CRUISE LINE SHORE EXCURSIONS

We recommend that you take the transfer to London offered by the cruise line (typically $75–$80) and then go it on your own.

ON YOUR OWN: WITHIN WALKING DISTANCE

If you are on a small ship, you may be able to walk to the Tower of London from the cruise pier, and if you're a good walker, you might also make it to the Tate Modern. If you arrive on a big ship, you'll be bused from your port to a central location in the city.

ON YOUR OWN: BEYOND THE PORT AREA

The greatest concentration of London's attractions is to be found in **The West End,** an area unofficially delineated by the River Thames to the south, Farringdon Road/ Street to the east, Marylebone Road/Euston Road to the north, and Hyde Park and Victoria Station to the west. You'll probably spend most of your time here, whether at Buckingham Palace, the British Museum, or the shops and theaters of Soho. To the east, **The City** (aka the financial district) is the original square mile that the Romans called *Londinium,* where London as we know it began. Rich in historical, architectural, and social interest (if a bit devoid of life after business hours), the City is one of the world's great financial areas and is jeweled with historic sights such as the Tower of London and St. Paul's Cathedral.

Running along the Thames east of St. James's Park, **Westminster** has been the seat of the British government since the days of Edward the Confessor (1042–66). At the area's northern end, next to Westminster Bridge, **The Houses of Parliament** (© **0870/906-3773** for tour information; www.parliament.uk) are the ultimate symbols of London and the strongholds of Britain's democracy. Both the House of Commons and the House of Lords are in the former royal Palace of Westminster, which was the king's residence until Henry VIII moved to Whitehall. The current Gothic Revival buildings date from 1840 and contain more than 1,000 rooms and 3km (1¾ miles) of corridors. Outside, the **Big Ben** clock tower is the world's most famous timepiece. (*Trivia:* Big Ben isn't the name of the tower itself, but of the largest bell in the chime, which weighs close to 14 tons.) You may observe debates for free from the "Strangers' Galleries" in both houses, where sessions usually begin in mid-October and run to the end of July. You can also book a guided tour in summer, generally from late July to late September. Admission to the Houses and Strangers' Galleries is free. Tours cost £7 ($15).

Just behind the Houses of Parliament, the early-English Gothic **Westminster Abbey** (© **020/7654-4832** for tours; www.westminster-abbey.org) was founded in 1065 by the Saxon king Edward the Confessor. Today it's one of the greatest examples of ecclesiastical architecture on earth and the shrine of the British nation, the place where most of its rulers were crowned and where many of its great citizens are buried—including writers Geoffrey Chaucer, Charles Dickens, and Rudyard Kipling; scientists Isaac Newton and Charles Darwin; and prime ministers William Pitt and William Gladstone. Admission is £10 ($21) and tours cost an additional £5 ($10). On Sunday and religious holidays, the Abbey is open for worship only.

A little to the south, along the Thames, the **Tate Britain,** Millbank (*C* 020/7887-8888; www.tate.org.uk/britain), is the most prestigious gallery in Britain, housing the national collections that cover British art from the 16th century to the present day, as well as an array of international works. Admission is free, though there is a charge for special exhibitions.

Across the Thames, the giant sphere you can see from Westminster is the **London Eye,** Millennium Jubilee Gardens (*C* 0870/5000-600; www.ba-londoneye.com), the world's largest Ferris wheel. Opened for the Millennium celebrations in 2000, it's the fourth-tallest structure in London and offers views that extend 40km (25 miles) if the weather's clear. Standard 30-minute "flights" are £15 ($31), though fancier options (including one with champagne) are also available.

Back in Westminster, across from St. James's Park, **Buckingham Palace** (*C* 020/7766-7300; www.royalresidences.com) is the massive yet graceful official London residence of the Queen. If Her Majesty is at home, the Royal Standard flag will be flying outside. In the summer, when she's away, visitors are allowed to tour parts of the palace, including the State Apartments, Throne Room, Royal Mews, and picture galleries. The **Changing of the Guard,** the world's most famous military ritual, takes place daily in the palace's forecourt at 11:30am May through July and on alternate days for the rest of the year, weather permitting. Admission to all the publicly accessible areas of the palace is £27 ($56). Viewing of the guard change is free.

At the northern extreme of Westminster, **Trafalgar Square** is one of the city's major landmarks, named to mark England's victory over Napoleon in 1805. The impressive neoclassical building on the northern edge of the square is the **National Gallery** (*C* 020/7747-2885; www.nationalgallery.org.uk), home to a comprehensive collection of Western paintings representing all the major schools from the 13th to the early 20th century. Very famous works in the museum's collection include Leonardo's *Virgin of the Rocks,* Titian's *Bacchus and Ariadne,* van Eyck's *Arnolfini Marriage,* and El Greco's *Agony in the Garden.* Admission is free.

Head a little farther to the north and you'll find **The British Museum,** Great Russell Street (*C* 020/7323-8299; www.thebritishmuseum.ac.uk), home to one of the most comprehensive assemblages of art and artifacts on the planet. The overall collections are split into the national collections of antiquities; prints and drawings; coins, medals, and banknotes; and ethnography. Even on a cursory first visit, be sure to see the Asian collections, the Chinese porcelain, the Indian sculpture, and the prehistoric and Romano-British collections. Special treasures you might want to seek out on your first visit include the Egyptian Room's Rosetta Stone, whose discovery led to the deciphering of hieroglyphics, and the Elgin Marbles, a series of carvings taken from the Parthenon in Athens—unless, that is, they've been returned to Greece by then (see "Athens" on p. 306 for more on that saga). Admission is free.

West of Westminster lies vast **Hyde Park** (**www.royalparks.org.uk/parks/hyde_park**), London's largest. Once a favorite deer-hunting ground of Henry VIII, it offers urban Londoners a taste of velvety lawns, ponds, flowerbeds, and trees. Running through its width is the lake known as the **Serpentine,** where you can row, sail model boats, or swim. Blending with Hyde Park and bordering the grounds of Kensington Palace, well-manicured **Kensington Gardens** (**www.royalparks.org.uk/parks/kensington_gardens**) is planted with acres of ornamental flowerbeds and magnificent trees, and contains a famous statue of Peter Pan, with bronze rabbits that toddlers are always trying to kidnap. The park is also home to a Victorian extravaganza called the

Albert Memorial, erected by a bereft Queen Victoria in honor of her beloved husband. Just outside the park boundaries, the memorial **Victoria and Albert Museum,** Cromwell Road (② 020/7942-2000; www.vam.ac.uk), is one of the world's great museums of decorative arts. The collections include Islamic carpets, cartoons by Raphael, the greatest collection of Indian art outside India, the largest collection of Renaissance sculpture outside of Italy, and more, more, more. Admission is free, though some special exhibitions charge extra.

Over in "The City," **St. Paul's Cathedral,** St. Paul's Churchyard (② 020/7236-4128; www.stpauls.co.uk), was designed by Sir Christopher Wren after the Great Fire of 1666 and still makes quite an impression with its massive classical dome. Inside are many monuments, including a memorial chapel to American servicemen and women killed during World War II. Wren lies in the crypt, as do the Duke of Wellington and Lord Nelson. Admission to the cathedral and galleries is £9.50 ($20). The Cathedral is dedicated to worship only on Sunday.

At the ancient fortress known as the **Tower of London,** Tower Hill (② 0844/482-7777; www.hrp.org.uk/toweroflondon), exhibits include armories that date back to the time of Henry VIII (check out his suit of armor!); a display of torture devices that recall some of the tower's more gruesome moments; and the Jewel House, where the British Crown Jewels are kept. Go early, as the Tower is extremely popular with Brits and tourists alike, and you're likely to encounter long lines. Admission is £16 ($33). One-hour guided tours (included in the price of admission) given by the Beefeaters are given every half-hour, starting at 9:30am, from the Middle Tower near the main entrance. The last guided walk starts about 3:30pm in summer.

Across the Thames from The City, the **Tate Modern,** 25 Sumner St. (② 020/7887 8888; www.tate.org.uk/modern), is the U.K.'s finest museum of international 20th- and 21st-century art. Its collection includes representative works from all the major art movements, from Fauvism onward, with works by Matisse, Picasso, Miró, Pollock, Rothko, Flavin, Giacometti, and countless others. Admission is free. To reach the museum, cross the pedestrian-only Millennium Bridge from the steps of St. Paul's over the Thames.

LOCAL FLAVORS

You can find all the international favorites here—Indian food is cheap and favored by locals—along with British specialties such as **fish and chips** and steak-and-kidney pie. Food is also served in pubs, where you can wash down your meal with a pint of good British ale.

If you want to experience **high tea,** head to a teahouse or one of the better hotels. A traditional tea includes a choice of sandwiches, cakes, and scones with clotted cream. The most fashionable place in London to order afternoon tea is the Ritz hotel's **Palm Court,** Piccadilly, W1 (② 020/7493-8181; www.theritzlondon.com/tea). Dress up and make reservations well in advance. Tea and sandwiches will cost you £36 ($75) per person.

SHOPPING

Good news for shoppers on a strict cruise line schedule: In London, many of the best retail stores are concentrated on a few key streets and neighborhoods, mostly in the same areas as the city's big attractions.

The West End is home to the core of London's big-name shopping. Most of the department stores, designer shops, and chain stores have their flagships here. The key streets are **Oxford Street** (in either direction) for affordable shopping (start at Marble Arch Tube station if you're ambitious, or Bond St. station if you care to see only some of it), and **Regent Street,** which intersects Oxford Street at Oxford Circus. The Oxford Street flagship of private-label department store **Marks & Spencer,** 458 Oxford St., at Marble Arch (© 020/7935-7954; www.marksandspencer.com), is worth visiting for quality goods. Regent Street, which leads all the way to Piccadilly, has more upscale department stores, including the famed **Liberty of London,** 214–220 Regent St. (© 020/7734-1234; www.liberty.co.uk).

Parallel to Regent Street, **Bond Street** (Tube: Bond St.) connects Piccadilly with Oxford Street and is synonymous with the luxury trade. Divided into New and Old, it has experienced a recent revival and is the hot address for international designers. **Burlington Arcade** (www.burlington-arcade.co.uk), the famous glass-roofed, Regency-style passage leading off Piccadilly, looks like a period exhibition and is lined with intriguing shops and boutiques. Lit by wrought-iron lamps and decorated with clusters of ferns and flowers, its small, smart stores specialize in fashion, jewelry, Irish linen, cashmere, and more.

Jermyn Street, on the far side of Piccadilly, is a tiny 2-block stretch devoted to high-end men's haberdashers and toiletries shops, many of them in business for centuries. Several hold royal warrants, including **Turnbull & Asser,** 71–72 Jermyn St. (© 020/7808-3000; www.turnbullandasser.com), where HRH Prince Charles has his pj's made. A bit to the northwest, **Savile Row** (between Regent St. and New Bond St.) is synonymous with the finest in men's tailoring.

Just below Hyde Park, in Knightsbridge, **Harrods,** 87–135 Brompton Rd., Knightsbridge (© 020/7730-1234; www.harrods.com), is London's most famous store and lives up to its motto, OMNIA OMNIBUS UBIQUE ("Everything for Everyone"). Goods are spread across 300 departments, and the range, variety, and quality will dazzle you. Make sure to check out the Food Halls in Harrods's lower levels. Knightsbridge (just below Hyde Park) offers lots of other shopping opportunities as well, including designer shops on **Sloane Street.**

6 The Norwegian Fjords

If you ever needed proof that Norway is one of the world's most seafaring places, you need look no further than the country's name, which derives from *Norvegr,* a 1,000-year-old Viking term meaning "the way north"—in other words, the shipping route along the Norwegian coast. Today that long, 1,500-mile coast—so ruggedly indented with fjords and dotted with islands that its actual length would be about 19,200km (11,904 miles)—is one of the most gorgeous cruising regions in the world.

Whereas the Baltic is all about historic cities and grand art and architecture, and the Mediterranean is all about that *plus* gorgeous resort towns, the fjords are all about natural beauty and small, isolated towns and villages, some of which are almost inaccessible any other way but by ship. Cruises run anywhere from 7 to 21 days, departing from Amsterdam, Copenhagen, or one of the U.K. ports and sailing up the Norwegian coast with its never-ending string of fjords, wildflower-painted fields, medieval cathedrals, and tiny fishing villages. Some ships sail above the Arctic Circle into the land of the midnight sun. **Hurtigruten,** a Norwegian company with a 115-year history in these waters, offers trips aboard its combo cruise, ferry, and cargo vessels, taking in the entire gorgeous coast and calling at 35 towns, cities, and villages along the way. (See p. 262.)

COMING ASHORE Some of the stops on a typical Norwegian coastal cruise are at towns and cities, while others are in areas of natural beauty where the ship simply cruises around. Docking information is provided in the individual write-ups below.

LANGUAGE & CURRENCY **Norwegian** is the official language, but **English** is widely spoken and understood. The Norwegian currency is the **krone** (plural kroner). The exchange rate at press time was $1 = 5.42NOK (1NOK = 18¢).

BERGEN

Squeezed between mountain ranges and the North Sea, Bergen is Norway's second-largest city and the capital of its fjord district. The city was founded nearly 1,000 years ago and until the 14th century was the seat of the medieval kingdom of Norway. Today it's a commercial capital, but it's also a town with important traditions, especially with regard to shipping. Besides being a starting point for exploration, Bergen has its own sightseeing attractions, including the historic medieval district of **Bryggen** (www.stiftelsenbryggen.no), which is on the UNESCO World Heritage List. Located on the east side of Bergen's central harbor, within walking distance of the pier, this row of timbered Hanseatic-era commercial buildings represents all that remains of medieval Bergen, following several disastrous fires. Skillfully blended with modern Bergen, the red, white, and mustard-colored buildings now house shops, restaurants, and craftspeople's workshops and galleries. At the area's western end, the **Bryggen Museum** (✆ 55-58-80-10) displays artifacts unearthed during archaeological excavations of Bryggen from 1955 to 1972, and illustrates the daily and cultural life of Bergen in the Middle Ages. Admission is 40NOK ($7.20). At its eastern end, one of the area's best-preserved buildings houses, **Det Hanseatiske Museum (The Hanseatic Museum)**, Finnegårdsgaten 1A, Bryggen (✆ 55/54-46-90; www3.bergen.kommune.no/hanseatisk_/ekstern/museum), is furnished with artifacts that illustrate what life was like for the German merchants, representatives of the Hanseatic League of trade guilds, who did business here in the early 18th century. Admission is 50NOK ($9). Near the museum, the **Fløibanen Funicular,** Vetrlidsallmenning 21 (✆ 55/33-68-00; www.floibanen.com), offers a steep ride up Fløien, the most famous of Bergen's seven hills, from which you can view the city, the neighboring hills, and the harbor. The ride takes about 5 to 6 minutes in each direction. Round-trip fare is 70NOK ($13).

Located at the tip of the peninsula across the harbor from Bryggen, the **Akvariet Bergen (Bergen Aquarium),** Nornesbakken 4 (✆ 55/55-71-71; www.akvariet.no), is one of the largest and nicest aquariums in Scandinavia, featuring seals, penguins, and piranha. Most popular are the penguin feedings, scheduled at noon, 3pm, and (summer only) 6pm. Admission is 150NOK ($27). Southeast of the harbor, the **Bergen Kunstmuseum (Bergen Art Museum),** Rasmus Meyers Allé 3–7 (✆ 55/56-80-00; www.bergenartmuseum.no), displays works by both Norwegian and international artists, including some of Edvard Munch's most important works, and paintings by Picasso, Braque, Miró, Kandinsky, and Paul Klee. Admission is 50NOK ($9).

COMING ASHORE Ships dock at Bergen Harbor, within walking distance of Bryggen and the city center. **Taxis** are also available at the pier.

THE BEST CRUISE LINE SHORE EXCURSIONS

Bergen City Highlights & Troldhaugen (3–4 hr.; $50–$75): Drive past historic row houses and other city sights, then visit Troldhaugen, a Victorian house in the countryside outside of Bergen that was the home of Norway's famous composer Edvard Grieg. The house contains Grieg's furniture, paintings, and other mementos. It was here that

he composed many of his famous works. The tour may include a piano recital at the nearby turf-roofed Concert Hall.

Hiking Mount Fløien (4½ hr.; $49): Stroll with a guide along Bergen's historic waterfront and wharfs to Fløibanen Funicular (see below). Take the 8-minute ride to the top, then walk along gravel paths above the city. The route travels through hilly woods to Lake Skomakerdiket and continues uphill to view the fjord and its many islands. Weather permitting, you'll ascend to the city's highest point at 540m (1,771 ft.). The hike covers about 4.8km (3 miles) total, and you climb about 240m (787 ft.) on foot (being physically fit is a good idea).

FLÅM

About 160km (100 miles) east of Bergen (p. 406), the picturesque village of Flåm (pronounced "Flawm") is surrounded on three sides by the **Aurlandsfjord,** a branch of the **Sognefjord.** It's the terminus of the **Flåm Railway,** which climbs 869m (2,850ft) in just 19km (12 miles). The town is pretty but small. Most passengers sign up for excursions here, which take them out amid the gorgeous scenery.

COMING ASHORE   Ships dock right at the foot of town, within walking distance of everything.

THE BEST CRUISE LINE SHORE EXCURSIONS

Flåm Railroad (3½ hr.; $85): Board the Flåm Railway and head basically straight up, passing the Kjosfoss Waterfall and Rjoande Waterfall (the latter with a sheer drop of 137m/449 ft.), seeing towering Vibmesnosi mountain, and crossing the long Naali tunnel. At Vatnahalsen, the penultimate station on the line, you'll debark for refreshment before getting back aboard and returning to Flåm.

Flåm Valley Train & Hike to Berekvam (4½ hr.; $100): Same train trip as above, except in Vatnahalsen you'll debark to begin a 9.6km (6-mile) hike along a road built during the railroad's construction. After negotiating its 21 hairpin switchbacks, you'll reach Berekvam and rejoin the train for the journey back to Flåm.

Kayaking the Huarlandfjord (3 hr.; $80): Get out on the calm waters of the Huaurlandfjord, paddling past mountain farms that seem to climb the hillside.

Flåm by Land & Sea (4 hr.; $105): Travel by boat through the gorgeous scenery of the Aurlandsfjord and the Nareoyfjord, surrounded by steep mountainsides, waterfalls, and narrow passages. After a 2-hour cruise, you'll board a bus in tiny Gudvangen and continue up the Naeroey Valley, climbing the steepest road in Norway before returning back to Flåm via two tunnels, the larger measuring more than 9.6km (6 miles) long.

GEIRANGER & GEIRANGERFJORD

Some 413km (256 miles) northeast of Bergen, Geirangerfjord is probably the most majestic fjord in Norway, stretching 16km (10 miles) long, measuring nearly 305m (1,000ft) deep, and hemmed by mountain walls rising to a height of 1,600m (5,248 ft.). Waterfalls, such as the celebrated Seven Sisters (Syr Søstre), the Wooer, and the Bridal Veil, send their shimmering waves cascading down the rock face, while small farmsteads stand perched on rocky ledges high above. The tiny village of **Geiranger** is set at the very head of the narrow fjord, giving it one of the most scenic locations in the country.

COMING ASHORE   Ships anchor in Geirangerfjord and ferry passengers into Geiranger by tender. Everything is within walking distance of the tender pier, though, as at the other small towns along the coast, there's little to see. Most people take shore excursions to see the natural sights.

THE BEST CRUISE LINE SHORE EXCURSIONS

Mt. Dalsnibba Scenic Drive (3¼ hr.; $98): This scenic drive climbs the steep slopes of Mount Dalsnibba to its 1,450m (4,756 ft.) summit for panoramic views of Geirangerfjord and the Flydal Valley.

Hiking Westeras (3½ hr.; $68): Hike a zigzagging path up the mountainside through former summer pastures to the Storseterfossen, a waterfall whose curtain curves away from the mountainside, letting you stand underneath. The hike itself is about 1 hour.

Kayaking the Geirangerfjord (3 hr.; $88): Do Geirangerfjord by paddle, gliding along-side the steep mountain walls and past landmarks such as the Preacher's Pulpit and the Seven Sisters Waterfall. The time spent kayaking is approximately 2 to 2½ hours.

HAMMERFEST

In 1891, Hammerfest bought a generator from Thomas Edison and became the first European town with electric streetlights—a testament to just how eager its residents were to find relief from the area's long, dark winters. This is, after all, the most northerly large town in the world, located some 480km (298 miles) north of the Arctic Circle and with a population of about 9,200. A major port with a year-round ice-free harbor, it was occupied by the Nazis during World War II and subsequently destroyed when they were in retreat. Today it's a modern town with good shops catering to tourists on their way to the North Cape.

Several sights in town are worth exploring. Close to Quay no. 1, the **Royal and Ancient Polar Bear Society,** Havnegata 3 (© 78-41-31-00; www.isbjornklubben.no), offers a small museum devoted to Hammerfest's hunting heyday, when first the English and then the Germans came to nab eagles, arctic foxes, and polar bears. Mostly, though, the society exists so you can become a member: For 160NOK ($29), you get the official Polar Bear Society pin to show your friends. Membership fees go to conservation programs that help protect endangered Arctic animals. If you just want to see the place, the entrance fee is 40NOK ($7.20).

About a 5-minute walk from the harbor, **Hammerfest Kirke (Church),** Kirkegate 33 (© 78-42-74-70), was consecrated in 1961 and is known for its modernist architecture, designed by Hans Magnus using primarily triangular motifs. The minimalist interior includes a large stained-glass window by artist Jardar Lunde. Admission is free.

Opened in 1998, the **Gjenreisningsmuseet (Reconstruction Museum),** Kirkegata 21 (© 78-40-29-30; www.gjenreisningsmuseet.no), commemorates the years after World War II, when local residents rebuilt the region after the Nazis' scorched-earth withdrawal. Admission is 50NOK ($9).

COMING ASHORE   Ships dock in town, within walking distance of all attractions.

THE BEST CRUISE LINE SHORE EXCURSIONS

Sami Experience (1½ hr.; $59): The Sami people (aka Lapps or Laplanders) are northern Europe's indigenous people, with ancestral lands that extended through parts of Norway, Sweden, Finland, and Russia. On this tour, visitors learn about Sami life and culture, visiting a traditional turf hut, sampling Sami delicacies such as reindeer meat and cloudberries, hearing Sami *joik* singing and traditional stories, and viewing Sami crafts.

Voyages to Spitsbergen & the Lofoten Islands

Some ships, notably those of the Norwegian line **Hurtigruten,** make special voyages to the northerly Lofoten Islands and the even more northerly Spitzbergen. The **Lofotens** are a group of islands located some 197km (122 miles) north of the Arctic Circle but with a mild climate due to the Gulf Stream and the North Atlantic Drift Current. One of Norway's most beautiful regions, the Lofotens are home to small villages, towering mountains, and amazing fishing. Farther north, **Spitsbergen** is one of four islands that make up the Svalbard Archipelago, an Arctic wilderness located halfway between mainland Norway and the North Pole. Some 60 percent of the archipelago is covered in glacial ice, and the remainder is rugged mountains and tundra. Polar bears can be seen in summer, as can reindeer, walrus, and Arctic fox. Europe's gateway to the High Arctic, Spitzbergen is sparsely populated and without a road system, so ships are the only way to get around.

HONNINGSVAG & THE NORTH CAPE

The modern fishing port of Honningsvag lies 77km (48 miles) north of Hammerfest (though its small size allows its southerly neighbor to claim the "most northerly large town in the world" prize) and serves as a gateway to the North Cape, which almost all passengers visit via shore excursion (see below). The town itself was leveled by the Nazis in 1944: Only the chapel survived. Attractions in town are pretty much limited to the **Nordkappmuseet (North Cape Museum),** located right at the harbor in the Nordkapphuset, Fergeveien 4 (© **78-47-72-00;** www.nordkappmuseet.no). It offers exhibits relating to the cultural history of the North Cape, which lies 21 miles away. Admission is 30NOK ($5.40).

COMING ASHORE   Ships dock close to the center of town.

THE BEST CRUISE LINE SHORE EXCURSIONS

The North Cape (3½ hr.; $120): Drive about 45 minutes to the Nordkapp, the northernmost point in Europe. Here the Nordkapphallen visitor center offers a video presentation and museum exhibits on the history of the North Cape, including displays covering the visit by King Oscar (king of Norway and Sweden) in 1873 and the arrival of King Chulalongkorn of Siam (now Thailand) in 1907. Stop by the post office for a Nordkapp postmark. And if it's not foggy, check out the incredible sea views from the top of Europe.

STAVANGER

Sitting at the spot where the Ryfyllkefjord meets the North Sea, Stavanger is the southernmost Norwegian city on most fjords cruises. It's Norway's fourth-largest population center and one of its busiest seaports, and offers a mix of medieval and modern architecture. Most of the city's attractions lie within an easy walk of the historic harbor, with the old **Gamle Stavanger** section offering small wooden houses and cobbled streets. More than 170 beautifully preserved buildings date from the late 18th and early 19th centuries. Once a working-class district, the area is now gentrified and beautifully dolled up. In the evening, lampposts from the 1890s light your way through the fog. Nearby, at the head of the historic harbor, the 12th-century

Domkirke (Cathedral) is one of Norway's most beautiful medieval buildings, while the nearby fish and vegetable marketplace has been in business since the 9th century.

COMING ASHORE   Ships dock in the center of town, next to the Gamle Stavanger and about 10 minutes' walk to the city center and marketplace. Taxis are also available.

THE BEST CRUISE LINE SHORE EXCURSIONS

A Sightseeing Cruise along the Lysefjord (3½ hr.; $95): A tour boat takes you through the beautiful Lysefjord, which runs some 56km (35 miles) into the countryside and offers views of forested mountains, dramatic cliffs, and graceful waterfalls.

A Taste of Everyday Life (2 hr.; $80): This small-group tour takes you to a typical Stavanger home for a talk with your hosts, a tour of their house, and Norwegian waffles washed down with coffee or tea.

TROMSØ

The capital of northern Norway, the island city of Tromsø is located 402km (249 miles) north of the Arctic Circle, midway between the Lofoten Islands and the North Cape, and has long served as a starting point for expeditions to the North Pole. It's home to about 63,000 souls and has a history of sophistication going back to the 19th century, when it was somewhat reachingly dubbed "The Paris of the North." Today it's a regional cultural and financial center, and home to the world's northernmost university, the Universitetet Tromsø.

Sights of interest include the A-frame **Arctic Cathedral,** Hans Nilsens vei 41 (© 77-75-34-50; www.ishavskatedralen.no), one of the city's most distinctive symbols. Inside, light filters in through a huge Arctic blue stained-glass window and a gridwork of thin glass strips, producing a mystical effect. **Polaria,** Hjalmar Johansengst 12 (© 77-75-01-00; www.polaria.no/en), is a seaside adventure center themed on the Polar and Barents Sea region. Its building is shaped like ice floes piling up onto the land—or like dominos tumbling over, depending on your perspective. Inside there's an Arctic aquarium, a panoramic cinema, and exhibits about snowstorms, polar bears, the tundra, and the Northern Lights. Admission is 95NOK ($17). The polar opposite (yuk, yuk) of this modern museum is **Polarmuseet (The Polar Museum),** Søndre Tollbodgt 11 (© 77-68-43-73; www.polarmuseum.no/en), which tells the story of the 19th- and 20th-century fishermen, hunters, trappers, and explorers who made the Arctic their home, with displays highlighting the difficulties of survival. The museum is housed in an old Customs warehouse at the Skansen pier, dating from 1830. Admission is 45NOK ($8.10). To get an overview of town, ride the small **Fjellheisen** cable car (© 77-63-00-00; www.fjellheisen.no) from a spot near the Arctic Cathedral to the small Fjellstua Restaurant perched 420m (1,378 ft.) up Mt. Storsteinen. At the top there's an outdoor terrace and a network of hiking trails. The ride up costs 85NOK ($15)

COMING ASHORE   Ships dock in downtown Tromsø, putting all the major sights within walking distance.

THE BEST CRUISE LINE SHORE EXCURSIONS

Most of the excursions available here combine visits to the sites mentioned above.

Polar Museum & Husky Wilderness Camp (3½ hr.; $92): This excursion stops at the Polar Museum (see above) before visiting a camp on mountainous Kvaloya Island, where sled dogs are raised and trained.

Sommaroy Fishing Village (4½ hr.; $54): Take a short driving tour of Tromsø before heading out to Sommaroy Island, site of the area's biggest fishing village. Your guided tour includes details of day-to-day life, stunning views, and waffles at a local restaurant.

TRONDHEIM

Founded by the Viking king Olaf I Tryggvason in the 10th century, Trondheim served as Norway's capital until the early 1200s and is today the country's third-largest population center, a modern city with some 161,700 citizens. A scenic, active university town carved by the curving swath of the Nidelva River, Trondheim offers a nice mix of modern city and historical repository. Its Gothic-style **Nidaros Cathedral,** Bispegaten 5, in the city center (© **73-92-44-70;** www.nidarosdomen.no), dates from the 11th century and was the coronation site and burial place for Norway's medieval kings. Its high altar stands on the spot where King Olaf Haraldson was buried after the battle of Stiklestad. When Olaf was declared a saint 1 year later, a small wooden chapel was built on the site. The cathedral that eventually took its place became a pilgrimage site and remains one to this day. The church's west facade is particularly impressive, with its carved figures of royalty and saints. Its interior is a maze of mammoth pillars and columns with beautifully carved arches and gorgeous stained-glass windows. Next door, the 12th-century **Archbishop's Palace** has become a museum complex, featuring original sculptures from the cathedral, an archaeological exhibition, the historic archbishop's great hall and quarters, and a museum devoted to Norwegian military history and the resistance during World War II. A separate display exhibits the crown jewels of Norway. Combined admission to the cathedral and all the museums is 100NOK ($18).

The city also has several other museums. The **Nordenfjeldske Kunstindustrimuseum (National Museum of Decorative Arts),** Munkegaten 3–7 (© **73-80-89-50;** www.nkim.museum.no), houses a collection of furniture, silver, glass, textiles, and handicrafts from the 16th century through the modern period. Admission is 60NOK ($11). About 10 minutes by car outside Trondheim, the **Ringve Museum,** Lade Allé 60 (© **73-87-02-80;** www.ringve.com), is Norway's national museum of music, displaying instruments from all over the world, along with sheet music, photographs, and a sound archive. Guided tours include musical demonstrations on some of the historic instruments. Admission is 75NOK ($14). Located 5km (3 miles) west of the city center, the **Sverresborg Trøndelag Folk Museum,** Sverresborg Allé 13 (© **73-89-01-10;** www.sverresborg.no), is one of Norway's major folk-culture museums, its open-air exhibition filled with more than 60 farmhouses, cottages, churches, and town buildings, representing aspects of everyday life in the region over the past 3 centuries. Admission is 80NOK ($14).

COMING ASHORE   Ships dock in town, only about 1km (about ½ mile) from the city center.

THE BEST CRUISE LINE SHORE EXCURSIONS

City Tour & Folk Museum (3 hr.; $60): This tour combines a short driving tour of Trondheim with visits to Nidaros Cathedral and Trøndelag Folk Museum (see above).

7 Oslo, Norway

Founded in 1048 by the Viking king Harald, Oslo was named Norway's capital around 1300 and today is the seat of both the Royal Family and the Norwegian

Aker Brygge **2**	Kon Tiki Museum **1**
Akershus Castle **3**	Nobel Peace Center **4**
Edvard Munch Museum **10**	Rådhuset (City Hall) **5**
Grand Café **8**	Stortovet **9**
Henie-Onstad Art Center **6**	Vigeland Sculpture Park **6**
Karl Johans Gate shopping **7**	Viking Ship Museum **1**

Parliament. Though it's never been on the mainstream tourism circuit, Oslo is a growing city permeated by a kind of Nordic joie de vivre and offers a wealth of sights and activities plus new restaurants, cafes, and shopping areas. One of the world's largest capital cities (encompassing 453 sq. km/177 sq. miles), Oslo is also one of Europe's least densely populated capitals, since its urban area covers only about a tenth of its full acreage. The rest is a vast outdoor playground.

COMING ASHORE   There are enough cruise ship piers to handle four or five ships at one time. All are close to downtown, with the main cruise terminal being a 5-minute walk from City Hall and Akershus Castle. The secondary dock is a 20-minute walk away.

GETTING AROUND   You might not always be able to find a **taxi** to flag on the street, though you can always call **Oslo Taxi** (© **22/38-80-90**) for one. The city has an efficient system of **buses, subways** and **trams/streetcars** (for the latter, single adult tickets are 20NOK/$3.60 if you pre-purchase them or 30NOK/$5.40 if you buy from the driver). You can also borrow one of the **city bikes** offered at bike stations all over the city. The cost is 70NOK ($13) for 1 day, and you'll have to purchase a smartcard at City Hall, in the Rådhusplassen just steps from the main cruise dock.

LANGUAGE & CURRENCY   **Norwegian** is the official language, but **English** is widely spoken and understood. The Norwegian currency is the **krone** (plural kroner), and the exchange rate at press time was $1 = 5.42NOK (1NOK = 18¢).

THE BEST CRUISE LINE SHORE EXCURSIONS

Oslo Highlights (3 hr.; $45–$49): Drive through the capital, passing Akershus Castle; the Parliament building; the National Theater; the university; the Royal Castle; and Karl Johan Street, Oslo's main thoroughfare. Continue on through beautiful residential areas to the Holmenkollen Ski Jump, used for the 1952 Olympics. Visit Vigeland Sculpture Park for a walking tour, then head to Bygdøy Peninsula, a former royal preserve that's now the site of important museums, including the Viking Ship Museum.

Maritime Oslo (5 hr.; $59): This city tour makes stops at the Fram Museum, featuring a polar ship; the Maritime Museum, offering a video presentation with spectacular views of Norway's coastline and a depiction of life on the high seas; and the Viking Ship Museum. The tour may include a visit to Vigeland Sculpture Park.

Hiking the Nordmarka Forest (4½ hr.; $52): Walk to the subway station (about 10 min.) for a 25-minute ride with a guide to the Hollmenkollen area, popular with locals (who love nature). Hike about 2.4km (1½ miles) uphill to the Tryvann Observation Tower. Ride an elevator to the top deck for views of vast Nordmarka Forest. Hike about 10km (2¼ miles) downhill to Tryvann Lake and back to the subway.

ON YOUR OWN: WITHIN WALKING DISTANCE

If Oslo has one must-see attraction, it's the **Nobel Peace Center,** Radhusplassen (© 47/48-30-10-00; www.nobelpeacecenter.org), on the waterfront right near Oslo City Hall. In this former train station, originally built in 1872, the various Peace Prize Laureates are profiled, along with the father of the institution, Alfred Nobel. The Center offers multimedia presentations of art, photography, and film that you can experience on your own or on a guided tour. The small gift shop sells items with peace symbols. The museum's lovely cafe has both indoor and outdoor seating. Admission is 80NOK ($14). More Nobel history is on tap at the **Rådhuset (City Hall),** Rådhusplassen (© 23/46-16-30), where the Peace Prize ceremonies are held annually. The City Hall also has a fantastic series of murals depicting everything from Norwegian daily life to the Resistance during World War II, when Norway was occupied by German forces for 5 years. Tours are 40NOK ($7.20). Close to the ship piers, the Medieval Quarter is home to interesting historic relics, including **Akershus Castle,** Akershus Festning (© 23/09-56-70), a fortress whose current Renaissance structure dates back to the 17th century. The castle is infamous for having served as a prison during the Nazi regime, but today it's home to state and royal events. See the changing of the guard at 1:30pm each afternoon. The site has gorgeous gardens, and its hilltop locale offers great views of Oslo and the fjords. Admission is free.

About 2km (1¼ miles) west of the Nobel Center, the **Vigeland Sculpture Park,** Frogner Park, Nobelsgate 32 (© 22/54-25-30; www.vigeland.museum.no), is a 30-hectare (74-acre) park that displays 211 stone, bronze, and iron sculptures of humans and animals by Gustav Vigeland, Norway's greatest sculptor. The nearby museum is the sculptor's former studio and contains more of his works, sketches, and woodcuts. Admission to the park is free; museum admission is 45NOK ($8.10).

About a mile in the other direction, the **Edvard Munch Museum,** Tøyengate 53 (© 23/49-35-00; www.munch.museum.no), is devoted exclusively to the works of Edvard Munch (1863–1944), Scandinavia's leading painter and creator of *The Scream.*

The artist's gift to the city, the collection contains some 1,100 paintings, 4,500 drawings, and 18,000 prints, plus graphic plates, sculptures, and documentary material. Two of Munch's masterpieces, *The Scream* and *Madonna,* were stolen from the museum in 2004 and recovered in 2006, and at press time were about to be exhibited again on a limited basis, though they were still undergoing restoration. Admission is 65NOK ($12).

ON YOUR OWN: BEYOND THE PORT AREA

On the Oslofjord, about 11km (6¾ miles) west of Oslo, **Henie-Onstad Kunstsenter (Henie-Onstad Art Center),** Høkvikodden, Baerum (© **67/80-49-00;** www.hok.no), displays the art collection of skating champion Sonja Henie and her husband, Niels Onstad, a shipping tycoon. There are some 1,800 works by Munch, Picasso, Matisse, Léger, Bonnard, and Miró. Also on display are Ms. Henie's three Olympic gold medals and other trophies. On the premises is a top-notch, partly self-service grill restaurant, The Piruetten. Admission is 80NOK ($14) adults, 30NOK ($5.40) kids 7 to 16, free for kids under 7.

Several miles west of the city center, on the Bygdøy peninsula, the *Kon Tiki* **Museum,** Bygdoynesveien 36 (© **23/08-67-67;** www.kon-tiki.no), houses original boats and exhibits from explorer Thor Heyerdahl's journeys. The namesake *Kon Tiki* was the flimsy balsa raft on which Heyerdahl and five companions sailed 6,923km (4,292 miles) across open seas from Peru to Polynesia, to prove that it might have been done centuries ago. Admission is 50NOK ($9). Also on the peninsula is the **Viking-skiphuset (Viking Ship Museum),** Huk Aveny 25 (© **22/13-52-80**), which displays three Viking burial vessels that were found preserved in clay on the shores of the Oslofjord. The most spectacular is the 9th-century dragon ship, which features a wealth of ornaments and was the burial chamber of a Viking queen and her slave. Admission is 50NOK ($9).

LOCAL FLAVORS

At the harbor, in front of the Rådhuset, you can buy a bag of freshly caught and cooked **shrimp** from a fisherman and shell your meal as you check out the harbor scenery. Those looking for smart restaurants serving Norwegian and foreign food (especially American) should also head to the waterfront, in particular to **Aker Brygge,** the former shipbuilding yard, now a restaurant and shopping complex. The famous **Grand Café** in the Grand Hotel, Karl Johans Gate 31 (© **23/21-20-00;** www.grand.no), serves traditional Norwegian country cuisine and is where Edvard Munch and Henrik Ibsen used to hang out. Reservations are recommended. Lunch courses are 88NOK to 225NOK ($16–$41).

SHOPPING

Though Oslo is one of the most expensive cities in Europe, it offers many pedestrian streets for shoppers. A good place to start is **Stortovet,** the main square of town. Another large cluster of stores can be found along **Karl Johans Gate.**

8 Paris & the Port of Le Havre, France

But wait, you say, isn't Paris about 160km (99 miles) from the ocean? How do ocean-going ships stop there? *Answer:* They don't, and they never have. Instead, Paris-bound ships have been calling instead at the port of **Le Havre ("The Harbor")** since at least 1066, when the Normans conquered England. Located at the mouth of the Seine, Le Havre today remains the leading port on France's west coast and offers visitors access not only to Paris, but also to the nearby D-Day beaches and the rest of Normandy. The city itself is extremely modern (almost everything old was destroyed during World War II), but unless you're a particular fan of postwar architecture, it's probably not worth your time to stick around. The best option here is to sign on to one of the excursions described below.

COMING ASHORE   The port is about 1.6km (1 mile) from the center of Le Havre. Some ships also dock at the port of Honfleur, France, for access to Paris.

GETTING AROUND   Almost everyone takes an excursion here, right from the dock, but cruise lines often provide shuttles into Le Havre city center as well.

LANGUAGE & CURRENCY   The language is **French** and the currency is the **euro** (€). The exchange rate at press time was $1 = .72€ (1€ = $1.40).

THE BEST CRUISE LINE SHORE EXCURSIONS

When reading the options below, keep in mind that Paris is about 3 hours from Le Havre by bus or car. See our "A (Very) Quick Guide to the Landmarks of Paris" sidebar for a short explanation of the sights.

Paris Highlights (10½ hr.; $169): This quick tour of Paris's highlights includes a visit to Notre-Dame Cathedral, perhaps the world's supreme example of Gothic architecture; photo stops at the Eiffel Tower and the Place de la Concorde; a drive along the elegant Champs-Elysees and past the Arc de Triomphe; and lunch in a Parisian restaurant.

Paris & Seine River Cruise (10½ hr.; $199): After arriving in Paris via motorcoach, you'll get a narrated drive around the city, with a photo stop at the Eiffel Tower, a drive along the Champs-Elysees, and views of the Arc de Triomphe, the Opera House, the Tuileries Gardens, the Louvre, Pont-Neuf, and the Champ de Mars. You'll then board a sightseeing boat for a leisurely cruise through the heart of Paris, with lunch served on board. The tour includes a shopping stop at the Galeries Lafayette, the famous 1890s department store with its glass and steel dome, and Art Nouveau staircase.

Montmartre Walking Tour (10½ hr.; $125): This walking tour of Paris's famed bohemian district visits such legendary sights as the Moulin Rouge cabaret, the Lapin Agile cafe, Clos de Montmartre (Paris's last vineyard), the Sacre-Coeur Basilica (which offers stunning views), and the Bateau Lavoir studios, once the workplace of Pablo Picasso, Georges Braque, Juan Gris, and Amadeo Modigliani. Time is built in for you to grab lunch at one of the area's restaurants or cafes.

The Louvre Museum & Eiffel Tower (10½ hr.; $199): This tour introduces you to the Louvre, which is a definite contender for the title of "greatest art museum in the world." Your guide walks you through the museum's highlights, including the *Mona Lisa,* the *Venus de Milo, Winged Victory,* and other masterpieces. The tour includes lunch at Altitude 95, a restaurant perched on the first level of the Eiffel Tower offering wonderful views.

Paris on Your Own (10½ hr.; $119): Familiar with Paris, or just feel confident doing it on your own? This excursion is for you because it's no excursion at all: It's just a bus ride to and from the Place de la Concorde, with 4 hours in between for you to fill as you please.

Versailles Palace & Gardens (10 hr.; $195): A visit to the world's most opulent palace, Louis XIV's dream house. The tour visits the king's and queen's apartments; the Hercules Drawing room with its elaborate painted ceiling; the Hall of Mirrors,

Paris

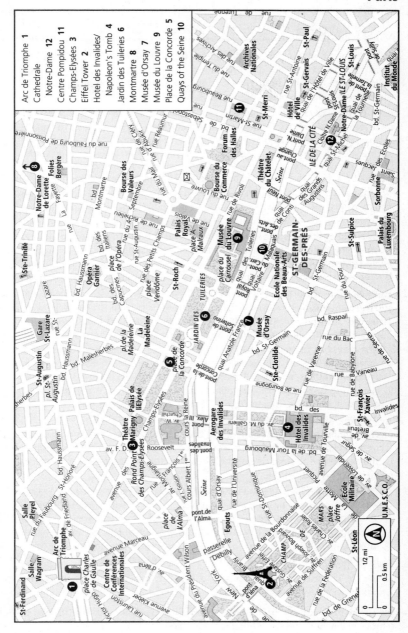

Arc de Triomphe **1**
Cathedrale
Notre-Dame **12**
Centre Pompidou **11**
Champs-Elysées **3**
Eiffel Tower **2**
Hotel des Invalides/
Napoleon's Tomb **4**
Jardin des Tuileries **6**
Montmartre **8**
Musée d'Orsay **7**
Musée du Louvre **9**
Place de la Concorde **5**
Quays of the Seine **10**

417

A (Very) Quick Guide to the Landmarks of Paris

Because almost everyone going to Paris from Le Havre is doing so via shore excursion and will thus get a narration of the top sights, we haven't gone into depth on them here. Here's a very quick overview, though, just to put things into perspective.

The Eiffel Tower (www.tour-eiffel.fr): Built as the centerpiece of the 1889 World Exposition, this 317m (1,040-ft.) tower was never intended to be permanent, but was saved from demolition by the advent of radio—as the world's tallest building, it made a perfect perch for a radio antenna. Somewhere along the line, it became the very symbol of Paris. If the afternoon is clear, you can see for about 65km (40 miles) from its observation deck.

Musée du Louvre (www.louvre.fr): Arguably the world's greatest art museum, with some 30,000 works on display—more to see than you could absorb in a week, much less an afternoon. Still, you can hit the highlights (the *Mona Lisa,* the sexy *Venus de Milo,* and the headless *Winged Victory*) and then pick a wing to gnaw on with the rest of your time.

Cathedrale Notre-Dame (www.notredamedeparis.fr): Founded in the 12th century, Notre-Dame is one of the supreme masterpieces of Gothic art, its three sculpted portals (dedicated to the Virgin Mary, the Last Judgment, and St. Anne) and flying buttresses fairly defining the word *cathedral* (and, of course, the *word sanctuary*—this is, after all, the setting for Victor Hugo's novel *The Hunchback of Notre-Dame*).

The Quays of the Seine: The River Seine is Paris, and its tree-shaded banks offer the city's most splendid vistas, plus old men with fishing rods, second-hand booksellers, and (très Paris!) young lovers walking hand in hand. Fourteen bridges span the river, including the Pont Neuf, which is both the oldest and most evocative, dating from 1578 and looking much as it did then. The river views from the bridge are perhaps the most memorable in Paris.

Place de la Concorde: This octagonal traffic hub, built in 1757, is dominated by an Egyptian obelisk from Luxor, and during the French Revolution was the site where thousands lost their heads to the guillotine. For a spectacular view, look down the . . .

Champs-Elysées: A boulevard designed for promenading, the Champs-Elysées was laid out in 1667 by Louis XIV and today stretches 1.8km (1 mile) from Place de la Concorde to the Arc de Triomphe. This is where Hitler's armies paraded after they conquered the city in 1940, but the stench of that day is long gone. Instead, you'll find thousands of Parisians and visitors strolling its wide, tree-lined sidewalks and popping into the many cafes, cinemas, and shops.

scene of lavish court receptions; and the Versailles Gardens, with their formal paths, statues, ornamental ponds, and sculpted fountains.

Landing Beaches of Normandy (10½ hr.; $179): On June 6, 1944, the 50th British Division towed a massive prefabricated port across the English Channel as part of the

Arc de Triomphe: The largest triumphal arch in the world, the 49m (161-ft.) Arc was erected in 1806 to commemorate the victories of Napoleon's Grand Armée. Sculptures depicting the uprising of 1792 are embedded in the arch, and an observation deck at the top gives a fantastic view.

Musée d'Orsay (www.musee-orsay.fr/en): This splendid museum holds the world's greatest collection of Impressionist paintings, including works by Manet, Monet, and van Gogh. Lodged in a former railway station, the museum also holds vast collections of sculpture, decorative arts, architectural items, photographs, and film.

Hotel des Invalides/Napoleon's Tomb (www.invalides.org): Built in the 1670s as a hospital and home for aged and infirm soldiers, Invalides became the final resting place for the Emperor Napoleon I in 1861, nearly 40 years after his death. You can see his elaborate tomb, as well as a death mask by Antommarchi and a number of his possessions. Elsewhere in the building, the Musée de l'Armée is a celebration of French military history.

Centre Pompidou (www.centrepompidou.fr): Looking like a building turned inside out—with exoskeletal supports and brightly painted pipes and ducts crisscrossing its transparent facade (green for water, red for heat, blue for air, yellow for electricity)—the Centre Pompidou is one of the world's greatest modern art museums, home to works by all the world's modern masters as well as lesser-known (so far) contemporary artists.

Montmartre: Hilltop Montmartre used to be a village of artists, glorified by masters such as Utrillo and painted, sketched, sculpted, and photographed by 10,000 lesser lights. Today it's overrun by tourists and nightclubs, but the villagelike charm of this place lingers, with its cobbled streets, back alleys, and crooked little streets.

Jardin des Tuileries: As much a part of Paris as the Seine, these formal, sculpture-studded gardens were laid out by Le Nôtre, Louis XIV's gardener and planner of the Versailles grounds. In orderly French manner, the trees are arranged according to designs, and the paths are arrow-straight, the overall orderliness broken only by bubbling fountains.

Château de Versailles (www.chateauversailles.fr): Located 21km (13 miles) southwest of Paris, this is what God (or at least Louis XIV) meant when he wrote the dictionary definition of *palace*. For centuries, it was the most dazzling royal residence in Europe and a pleasure dome for France's aristocracy. Today it's a symbol of what happens when a country doesn't make its leader stick to a budget.

D-Day invasion and installed it at the small fishing port of Arromanches-les-Baines, enabling supplies to be brought in for the Allied forces. The wreckage of this artificial harbor lies just off Arromanches Beach, which you'll visit on this tour, along with the Museum of the Landing, also in town. Included are visits to Omaha Beach and the

American Cemetery (cemetery of Colleville–Saint Laurent); Point du Hoc, site of a memorial to the three companies of the 2nd Ranger Battalion who climbed the hundred-foot cliffs on D-Day to capture the strategic position; and a drive past Sword, Juno, and Gold beaches.

A Day with Claude Monet (10 hr.; $165): Travel about 2½ hours by bus through rural France to Giverny, the artist's famous home and garden. See the famous water lilies and other inspirations for Monet's genius. Lunch at a local restaurant and then stop in historic Rouen, the capital of Normandy. (The famous cathedral in Rouen was painted by Monet more than 30 times.)

ON YOUR OWN: WITHIN WALKING DISTANCE

Either take a shore excursion or transfer to Paris, or see below.

ON YOUR OWN: BEYOND THE PORT AREA

Le Havre's city center has the distinction of being a UNESCO World Heritage Site honored for, among other things, urban planning and "the innovative exploitation of the potential of concrete"—a fact that's given the city both its usual reviews ("dull, angular, dreary, gray") and its more rarified plaudits ("classical, symmetrical, harmonious"). Chalk it up either way to the architect, **Auguste Perret,** who in 1945 was tasked with rebuilding a city smashed by World War II and responded by creating a thoroughly modern center full of low, reinforced-concrete buildings, and uniform prefabricated housing—all laid out in a grid of wide streets interspersed with green squares. The question is, do you appreciate that kind of thing? At the least, try to take a quick walk around after your excursion, if time permits, and keep an open mind.

The **Eglise St-Joseph (Church of St. Joseph),** on Boulevard François 1 at Rue Louis Brindeau, is the city's most recognizable landmark and its most beautiful. Outside, its blocky base and octagonal 110m (361-ft.) tower have a stark, futurist character, but all that changes when you get inside. There, massive concrete pillars soar up to support what proves to be the completely hollow central tower, and the entire space is suffused with a mystical light from nearly 13,000 pieces of stained glass. It's essentially a spiritual lighthouse, which can be seen far out to sea. It was built on Perret's design between 1951 and 1957, but the architect didn't live to see its completion. Admission is free.

About half a kilometer (⅓ mile) to the south, the **Musée Malraux,** 2 Boulevard Clemenceau (✆ **02-35-19-62-62**), was the first new French museum to open after the war and displays a major collection of Fauvist and Impressionist works by Degas, Manet, Renoir, Seurat, Raoul Dufy, and others. Admission is 3.80€ ($5.30). Closed Tuesday.

LOCAL FLAVORS

Regional specialties in Normandy include cider, Calvados brandy, and Camembert cheese. You can track down a meal or a gourmet item along the **Halles Centrales,** a pedestrian mall that runs east from St-Joseph for several blocks, full of restaurants, cafes, and food shops, as well as other shopping.

SHOPPING

Shop here for ceramic ware, antiques (especially in Rouen), Calvados, and Camembert. The Halles Centrales (see above) is Le Havre's most characteristic shopping destination.

Paris is, of course, Paris: You can find everything and anything there.

9 St. Petersburg, Russia

Founded in 1703 by Tsar Peter the Great, St. Petersburg was once the glittering capital of Imperial Russia, but its course through the 20th century was marked by trauma and bloodshed. The 1917 Russian Revolution ushered in the Soviet era and saw the city renamed Leningrad in honor of Vladimir Lenin. In the early 1940s, Nazi troops lay siege to Leningrad for 900 days, leaving approximately a million dead and the city badly battered. The city finally returned to its original name in 1991 after the fall of the Soviet Union. Today Russia's second-largest city is both a cultural and an industrial center, with more than five million citizens and the country's largest port.

St. Petersburg is a coherent and carefully planned city, and the value of its individual buildings is best appreciated when you take a step back and view the ensemble as a whole. Some 360 bridges cross the Neva River and the city's many winding canals, each lined with baroque and neoclassical palaces, cathedrals, and monuments. The city's restoration project requires that all existing facades in the downtown area be retained. Top sights include the **Hermitage Museum,** which has one of the richest art collections in the world; the **Peter and Paul Fortress,** the burial place of the Romanov dynasty; and **St. Isaac's Cathedral,** the fourth-largest cathedral in the world. Outside the city, you can visit the lavish **summer homes of the tsars.**

Now for the legal disclaimer: Because of Russian **visa regulations** (not to mention the fact that most street signs are in the Cyrillic alphabet), it's very difficult to see the city on your own. Only visa holders are allowed off the ship for independent exploration of the city, but cruise passengers booked on organized tours are allowed to participate without a visa. For this reason, the overwhelming majority of cruise passengers stopping here see the city via organized excursions. Many ships spend more than 1 day in St. Petersburg to allow a fuller exploration of the city's sights, including its evening arts.

COMING ASHORE   The main cruise terminal is about a 20-minute drive from the city center. Small ships come up the Neva River right into town.

GETTING AROUND   As an alternative to group shore excursions, you can hire a car, limo, or van with a private guide through your ship's shore excursion desk (see shore excursions, below). This is the only way to get around more or less on your own without getting a Russian visa ahead of time.

LANGUAGE & CURRENCY   **Russian** is the language of the land, and signs are in the Cyrillic alphabet. The official currency is the **ruble** (RUB), and the rate of exchange at press time was $1 = 25RUB (1RUB = 4¢). Street vendors accept U.S. dollars.

THE BEST CRUISE LINE SHORE EXCURSIONS

St. Petersburg Grand Tour (19 hr., spread 2 two days; $350): This all-encompassing tour takes in all the major St. Petersburg sights. The **Peterhof Palace,** sitting atop a hill overlooking the Gulf of Finland, was designed by Peter the Great to rival Versailles, with 120 hectares (300 acres) of fountain-dotted gardens. The palace tour visits the Throne Room, the Portrait Room, the White Dining Room, and many other impressive interiors. The **Peter and Paul Fortress** was originally built to protect the city from Swedish attack but soon became a place for holding political prisoners captive. The **Peter and Paul Cathedral** houses the tombs of many tsars and tsarinas, including Peter the Great and Catherine the Great. **St. Isaac's Cathedral,** commissioned by Alexander I in 1818, took more than 3 decades to complete. It's topped by one of the world's largest domes, covered with 100kg (220 lb.) of pure gold and dominating the

Tips   Important Visa Information

Passengers who participate in St. Petersburg shore excursions or arrange for private transportation through the ship's shore excursions desk (see "Getting Around" and "Best Cruise Line Shore Excursions") do not need to obtain a Russian visa.

Those of you who wish to go ashore on your own, however, do have to obtain a tourist visa prior to departure. To apply, you must have a passport that remains valid at least 30 days past the last day of your cruise. The visa-processing fee is $100 for a processing time of 6 to 10 business days. Faster processing entails higher fees.

Information and visa applications forms are available through the website of the **Embassy of the Russian Federation in the United States;** go online to **www.russianembassy.org** or call ✆ 202/298-5700.

city skyline. The **Hermitage** houses one of the world's premier art collections, spread among the tsars' former Winter Palace and four other buildings. Its collection includes more than three million artworks, including paintings by Da Vinci, Rafael, Monet, Rembrandt, and Renoir. The **Yusupov Palace,** built in 1760, is most famous as the site where several noblemen assassinated the monk Rasputin, whom they feared was giving bad advice to Tsar Nicholas II. The tour here includes the cellar room where Rasputin was poisoned and then shot. The **Church of the Savior on Spilled Blood** was built on the site of the March 1, 1881, assassination of Tsar Alexander II. The tour also includes a 60-minute cruise that sails on the Neva, Fontanka, and Moika rivers and the Kryukov Canal, passing under many of the city's picturesque bridges and past historic buildings. Lunch is included both days, accompanied by champagne, vodka, red caviar, and entertainment one day.

St. Petersburg City Highlights & Hermitage (8½ hr.; $185): This is a shorter version of the tour above, visiting the Hermitage and the Peter and Paul Fortress, and stopping for photo ops at the Church of the Savior on Spilled Blood, St. Isaac's Cathedral, the Nevsky Prospekt (St. Petersburg's most famous street), and the cruiser *Aurora,* a naval ship that fired its guns to signal the beginning of the Bolshevik Revolution. Lunch with entertainment, drinks, and caviar is included. Another version of this tour combines the city highlights with a visit to the **Catherine Palace** (8½ hr.; $175): Yet another excursion drops the city tour and concentrates exclusively on the **Hermitage.** Two versions of the latter tour are available: the 1-day, 3½-hour tour ($85), and the two-day version, which spends 3½ hours at the museum each day ($140).

Catherine & Peterhof Palaces (9 hr.; $185): This tour concentrates on two country palaces located outside the city. The Catherine Palace at Tsarskoye Selo ("Village of the Tsars") lies 25km (16 miles) south of St. Petersburg and is the world's longest palace. The palace's masterpiece is the famous **Amber Room,** originally decorated with engraved amber wall panels gifted to Peter the Great from the king of Prussia in 1716. The Nazis who occupied the palace during the siege of Leningrad stole them when they fled. One of the mosaics, *Smell and Touch,* was recovered from Bremen, Germany, in 1997, but most of the panels and the amber-inlaid furniture you see now are copies

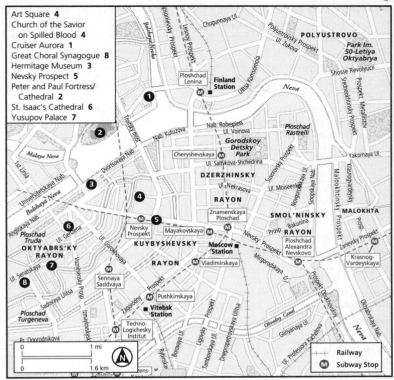

Art Square **4**
Church of the Savior
  on Spilled Blood **4**
Cruiser Aurora **1**
Great Choral Synagogue **8**
Hermitage Museum **3**
Nevsky Prospect **5**
Peter and Paul Fortress/
  Cathedral **2**
St. Isaac's Cathedral **6**
Yusupov Palace **7**

created based on photos of the originals. See St. Petersburg Grand Tour above for a description of the Peterhof Palace, located 30km (19 miles) west of St. Petersburg.

Great Choral Synagogue & Jewish Community (4 hr.; $115): This Jewish heritage tour of St. Petersburg visits the second-largest synagogue in Europe, built in 1893, where you'll have a chance to interact with members of the city's Jewish community. The tour includes a performance by cantor Gregory Yakerson and daily worship at the attached Little Synagogue.

Hidden Scenes Walking Tour (4 hr.; $55): This unusual tour heads down into the St. Petersburg Metro (subway), which was completed in 1955 based on the model of Paris's system and offers beautiful tilework and lighting. After a ride with the locals, you'll explore the Kuznechny Food Market; browse a craft market near the Church of the Savior on the Spilled Blood; and do a walking tour in the city center, taking in the Nevsky Prospekt, Ostrovsky Square and its monument to Catherine the Great, and Art Square, home to the Russian Museum, Philharmonic Hall, and a statue of poet Alexander Pushkin.

Evening at the Russian Ballet (3 hr.; $85): Visit the historic Conservatoire Theater for an evening performance featuring principal dancers from the St. Petersburg Ballet in a full-length ballet or a selection of scenes. Champagne is served during the intermission.

Musical Evening at the Hermitage (3½ hr.; $200): This evening visit to the Hermitage begins with a guided tour through its buildings, from the Winter Palace to the Old Hermitage. From there, participants proceed to a small champagne party and a concert of classical music performed by the State Hermitage Orchestra.

Private-vehicle tours: Vehicles with an English-speaking guide are offered on a half-day (4 hr.; morning or afternoon) or full-day (8 hr.) basis, and allow you to choose from any of several preset tour routes. Prices are charged on a per-vehicle basis, and participating passengers are responsible for divvying up the cost among themselves. Car tours (max. three passengers) cost $399 half-day, $725 full day. Van tours (max. eight passengers) cost $829 half-day, $1,399 full day.

Journey to Moscow (15½ hr.; $679): Take the 1-hour flight from St. Petersburg to Moscow, where you and your English-speaking guide will tour Red Square; ride the Moscow metro to see the stations' mosaics, crystal chandeliers, and marble columns; take a walking tour of the Kremlin (including the Armory Chamber, which houses a collection of royal crowns, jewelry, and Faberge eggs); then take a driving tour of the city, ending with dinner at a restaurant housed in one of Moscow's old mansions.

ON YOUR OWN

It's best to see St. Petersburg's attractions via a shore excursion or hired car tour.

LOCAL FLAVORS

Many tours include stops at various city restaurants for a typical Russian meal with champagne, vodka, and entertainment.

SHOPPING

Many tours include stops at souvenir and crafts markets located near the major sights, particularly around St. Isaac's Square and the Church of the Savior on Spilled Blood. Some of the usual suspects are nesting *matryoshka* dolls, hand-painted lacquer boxes, caviar, fur hats, vodka, and amber jewelry. The Hermitage has an excellent gift shop.

10 Stockholm, Sweden

Mixing Renaissance splendor with modern skyscrapers, Stockholm is built on 14 bridge-connected islands in Lake Mälaren—the first in a string of 24,000 islands, skerries, and islets stretching all the way to the Baltic Sea. Plan to be on deck as your ship cruises through the archipelago.

While the medieval walls of Stockholm's Old Town are no more, the 13th-century cobblestone streets are well preserved and a real treat to visit. Here, within walking distance of the cruise ship pier, you'll find the Royal Palace, ancient churches, historic merchant houses, and dozens of restaurants and shops (including art galleries and antiques stores). Another must is Djurgården (Deer Park), site of many of the city's popular attractions, including the open-air museums of Skansen and the *Vasa* man-of-war. You can get there easily by ferry. If you want to explore the archipelago further or are looking for some quiet time, boats leave frequently in the summer from the harbor for the bathing resort of **Vaxholm** and other scenic islands.

COMING ASHORE   You will dock either literally right in town or, depending on how busy the port is on the day of your arrival, at the commercial port about 15 minutes away (longer if there's traffic). Most ships will have shuttles to take passengers into town if docked at the farther pier.

Stockholm

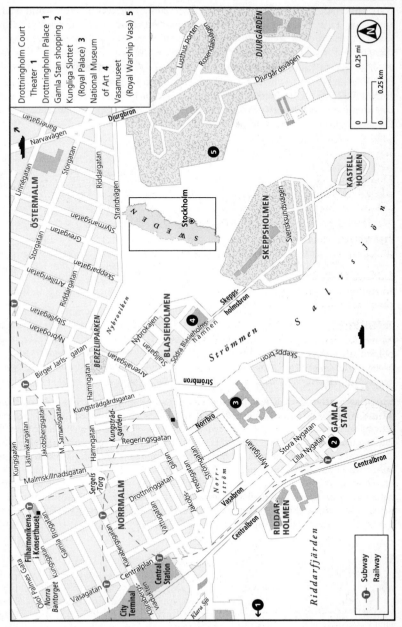

Drottningholm Court Theater **1**
Drottningholm Palace **1**
Gamla Stan shopping **2**
Kungliga Slottet (Royal Palace) **3**
National Museum of Art **4**
Vasamuseet (Royal Warship Vasa) **5**

Subway
Railway

GETTING AROUND   You can get around by **bus, subway** (T-bana), and **tram** (streetcar). Once inside town, consider a 1-day **Stockholm Card;** it costs 290SEK ($46) and is valid for 24 hours of unlimited travel by T-bana, bus, and commuter trains within Stockholm, plus free entry to 75 museums and many sites. **Taxis** are available at the pier, and you'll rarely pay more than 200SEK ($32) to reach anywhere with the city limits.

LANGUAGE & CURRENCY   The official language is **Swedish,** but English is also commonly spoken. Sweden's basic unit of currency is the **krona** (plural kronor), and the exchange rate at press time was $1 = 6.42SEK (1SEK = 16¢).

THE BEST CRUISE LINE SHORE EXCURSIONS

City Tour (3 hr.; $55–$72): This comprehensive city tour begins with a short drive up to Fjällgatan for a panoramic view of the city, then heads through Gamla Stan, the medieval Old Town, and passes the Royal Palace. The itinerary proceeds past the Royal Dramatic Theater along Strandvägen to the island of Djurgården for a tour that includes the *Vasa* Museum. You continue through to Østermalm, a fashionable residential neighborhood, then on to Hamngatan and Sergel's Torg, the focal point of modern Stockholm. From there you proceed south past the Parliament Building, past the House of Nobility, and via the narrow canal at Slussen to Södermalm, the large island on Stockholm's south side. In place of the *Vasa* Museum, an alternative tour substitutes a visit to Stadshuset, Stockholm's imposing, redbrick city hall (where the Nobel Prize Banquet is held).

Historic Stockholm & Sigtuna (6–7 hr.; $110–$140): This tour offers a driving tour of the city, a walk through Old Town, a stop at the *Vasa* Museum, and a drive through the scenic countryside to visit Sigtuna on Lake Mälaren. The religious village was founded some 1,000 years ago by the first Christian king of Sweden, and even today is a bastion of religion and education. The tour includes both lunch and shopping time.

ON YOUR OWN: WITHIN WALKING DISTANCE

Kungliga Slottet (The Royal Palace), Kungliga Husgerådskammaren (© **08/402-61-30;** www.royalcourt.se), is a 608-room Italian baroque showcase, one of the few official residences of a European monarch open to the public (though the king and queen prefer to live and bring up their children at Drottningholm—see below). A changing-of-the-guard ceremony is offered here Monday to Saturday at noon and on Sunday at 1pm. You can also tour the State Apartments. The Treasury exhibits a celebrated collection of crown jewels, while the Royal Armory displays weapons, armor, gilded coaches, and coronation costumes from the 16th century. Admission to the Royal Apartments, Armory, Museum of Antiquities, and Treasury is 90SEK ($14). A combo ticket to all parts of the palace is 130SEK ($21).

ON YOUR OWN: BEYOND THE PORT AREA

The actual home of Sweden's royal family, **Drottningholm Palace,** Drottningholm (© **08/402-62-80;** www.royalcourt.se), was built on an island about 11km (6¾ miles) from Stockholm and modeled on Versailles. Inside are courtly art, royal furnishings, and Gobelin tapestries; outside are fountains and parks. Admission to the palace is 70SEK ($11), and the best way to get there is by boat from Stadshuskajen (the City Hall Quay); the ride takes about 50 minutes one-way. Nearby is the **Drottningholm Court Theater** (© **08/759-04-06**), the best-preserved 18th-century theater in the world. Admission is 60SEK ($9.60). One of the oldest museums in the world,

Nationalmuseum (National Museum of Art), Södra Blasieholmshamnen, just across the Strommen River from the Royal Palace (© **08/519-54-300;** www.national museum.se), was established in 1792 and is home to a collection of decorative art, rare paintings, and sculpture. Artists represented range from Rembrandt and Rubens to Bellini and van Gogh. Admission is 80SEK ($13). On the island of Djurgården, a royal park near the center of Stockholm is the **Vasamuseet (Royal Warship *Vasa*),** Galärvarvet, Djurgården (© **08/519-54-800;** www.vasamuseet.se), a must-do for history buffs. This 17th-century man-of-war is the world's oldest identified and complete ship—and the biggest tourist attraction in Stockholm. It capsized and sank on its maiden voyage in 1628. Salvaged in 1961, the ship has been carefully restored. Admission is 80SEK ($13). Referred to as "Old Sweden in a nutshell," **Skansen,** Djurgården (© **08/442-80-00;** www.skansen.se), is an open-air museum featuring more than 150 dwellings from Lapland to Skaøne, most from the 18th and 19th centuries. They have been reassembled on about 30 hectares (74 acres) of parkland within walking distance of the Vasamuseet. Exhibits range from a windmill to a complete town quarter; there's also a decent zoo. Programs include folk dancing and open-air concerts. Admission is 60SEK to 90SEK ($9.60–$14), depending on week and time of day.

LOCAL FLAVORS
In recent years Stockholm has emerged as a citadel of fine dining, partly because of the legendary freshness of Swedish produce and game, and partly to the worldwide success of its new chefs. There are an estimated 1,500 restaurants and bars (self-service cafeterias) in Stockholm alone, so you'll have plenty of choices. For good value, try ordering the *dagens ratt* (daily special; aka *dagens* lunch or *dagens* menu), if one is available.

SHOPPING
It seems that anything of Swedish design is gorgeous, including housewares, handblown glass, wood items, and handicrafts, but they can all be pricey. Items to watch for include kids' clothes, silver jewelry, reindeer gloves, Swedish clogs, hand-woven items, and woolens. The favorite shopping area is the network of cobblestone streets in **Gamla Stan,** near the Royal Palace, especially along **Västerlånggatan.**

11 Tallinn, Estonia
Located on the Baltic Sea, about 60km (37 miles) across the Gulf of Finland from Helsinki, Estonia spent 2 centuries as one of Russia's Baltic Provinces before becoming an independent republic in 1918. Little more than 2 decades later, it fell back under Russian control when Soviet troops rolled in and incorporated the country into the Soviet Union. It became independent once again in 1991. Separated from the West for 50 years, the capital city of **Tallinn** is now a popular tourist spot, visited by many cruise ships as well as folks arriving by ferry from Helsinki and Stockholm.

Tallinn was founded in the 12th century and is today one of northern Europe's best-preserved medieval towns—a fact that's earned it a place on UNESCO's World Heritage List. It makes a beautiful impression from the sea, with its ancient city walls, church spires, and tile-roofed homes. At the Old Town, you pass beneath the arches of Tallinn's ancient stone walls to enter a world of cobblestones, narrow alleys, and medieval buildings. The place is fun to explore on foot.

While under German occupation in 1944, the city was bombed and about 11% of the Old Town was destroyed, later to be replaced by bleak Soviet structures. Today the city is growing rapidly, with modern buildings joining the old.

Tallinn

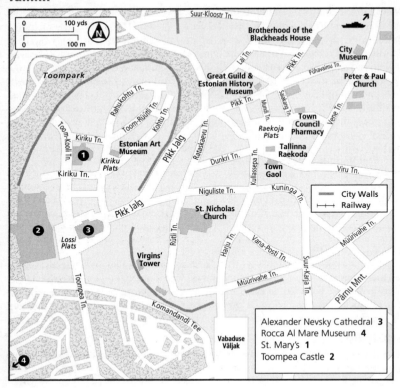

COMING ASHORE   The Old City Harbor is about 1km (½ mile) from Tallinn's Old City, an easy walk.

GETTING AROUND   Taxis queue up at the pier, and the fare to the city center is about 60EEK ($5.40). In Old Town, everything's within walking distance, and streets are even pedestrian-only. Just remember to wear comfortable shoes: Streets are mainly cobbled and uneven, and there are lots of steep hills.

LANGUAGE & CURRENCY   The language of the land is **Estonian.** Most shopkeepers (though not all) speak some **English** too. The national currency is the **kroon,** abbreviated EEK. The rate of exchange at press time was $1 = 10.83EEK (1EEK = 9¢).

THE BEST CRUISE LINE SHORE EXCURSIONS

Historic Walking Tour (4 hr.; $55): Visit Old Town, including Toompea Castle, the Alexander Nevsky Cathedral, the Holy Ghost Church, the Gothic Town Hall, and the partly ruined historic Dominican Monastery, where you'll hear a concert of medieval music before a final walk. Time is allowed for shopping.

Biking the Estonian Countryside (4½ hr.; $85): Bus from the pier to Rocca al Mare Open-Air Museum, where you will collect bikes and head off on a guided tour of the Estonian countryside. Total distance cycled is 4km (2½ miles). En route, you'll have a chance to watch local performers do a folkloric show. Afterward, you'll head to Old Town for a 1.6km (1-mile) walking tour.

Rocca Al Mare Open-Air Museum & Panoramic Tallinn (4½ hr.; $55): About 15 minutes from Tallinn's city center, the Open Air Museum at Rocca-al-Mare preserves 2 centuries of Estonian rural architecture—a 1699 church, several mills, an inn, a fire station, a schoolhouse, 12 exhibit farmsteads, and dozens of others, all transported here and rebuilt on nearly 81 forested hectares (200 acres) fringing Kopli Bay. Original furniture and farm implements keep things real, while living history programs give a time-warp taste of old-time village life. The tour also includes a tour of Old Town, including Toompea Hill (aka the "Upper Town") and Alexander Nevsky Cathedral.

ON YOUR OWN: WITHIN WALKING DISTANCE

Walk the winding, cobblestone streets, past towers and the old city wall, and you'll feel like you're taking a step back into history. Among the main draws here is **Toompea Castle,** 1 Lossi Plats, on Toompea Hill (© **63/16-537**). Built in the 13th and 14th centuries, the castle is situated on the steep limestone coast, 50m (164 ft.) above sea level, and has been used by several of the powers that have ruled Estonia over the centuries. The castle is fronted by a pink Parliament House, built in 1773 and today home to the Estonian parliament. Admission is free.

Alexander Nevsky Cathedral, 10 Lossi Plats (© **64/43-484**), is a 19th-century Russian Orthodox church built in the 17th-century style that dominates Upper Town's skyline. Inside are numerous golden icons and mosaics. Another church, the Gothic **St. Mary's,** Toom-Kooli 6 (© **64/44-140**), houses more than 100 medieval coats of arms. Admission is free.

ON YOUR OWN: BEYOND THE PORT AREA

The Rocca Al Mare museum is about 15 minutes outside town but is usually visited via shore excursion.

LOCAL FLAVORS

Estonian food is pretty plain. Local favorites include **trout** (smoked, pickled, or salted). The city is also home to a surprising array of international cuisine, even Mexican and Asian food.

SHOPPING

Shop in the town center for handicrafts, hand-knit woolen sweaters, ceramics, leather goods, amber jewelry, and artwork.

Index

There's a parking lot where my ocean view should be.

 À la place de la vue sur l'océan, me voilà avec une vue sur un parking.

 Anstatt Meerblick habe ich Sicht auf einen Parkplatz.

 Al posto della vista sull'oceano c'è un parcheggio.

 No tengo vista al mar porque hay un parque de estacionamiento.

 Há um parque de estacionamento onde deveria estar a minha vista do oceano.

 Ett parkeringsområde har byggts på den plats där min utsikt över oceanen borde vara.

 Er ligt een parkeerterrein waar mijn zee-uitzicht zou moeten zijn.

 هنالك موقف للسيارات مكان ما وجب ان يكون المنظر الخلاب المطل على المحيط .

 眼前に広がる紺碧の海・・・じゃない。窓の外は駐車場！

 停车场的位置应该是我的海景所在。

I'm fluent in pig latin.

Hotel mishaps aren't bound by geography.
Neither is our Guarantee. It covers your entire travel experience, including the price. So if you don't get the ocean view you booked, we'll work with our travel partners to make it right, right away. See www.travelocity.com/guarantee for details.

You'll never roam alone.